COMPUTER APPLICATIONS IN MUSIC

THE COMPUTER MUSIC and DIGITAL AUDIO SERIES

John Strawn, Series Editor

DIGITAL AUDIO SIGNAL PROCESSING: AN ANTHOLOGY
Edited by John Strawn

COMPOSERS AND THE COMPUTER
Edited by Curtis Roads

DIGITAL AUDIO ENGINEERING: AN ANTHOLOGY
Edited by John Strawn

COMPUTER APPLICATIONS IN MUSIC: A BIBLIOGRAPHY
COMPUTER APPLICATIONS IN MUSIC: A BIBLIOGRAPHY, Supplement 1
Deta S. Davis

THE COMPACT DISC HANDBOOK, 2nd Edition
Ken C. Pohlmann

COMPUTERS AND MUSICAL STYLE
David Cope

MIDI: A COMPREHENSIVE INTRODUCTION
Joseph Rothstein

SYNTHESIZER PERFORMANCE AND REAL-TIME TECHNIQUES
Jeff Pressing

THE COMPUTER MUSIC and DIGITAL AUDIO SERIES
Volume 10

COMPUTER APPLICATIONS IN MUSIC
A Bibliography

Supplement 1

DETA S. DAVIS

A-R Editions, Inc.

Madison, Wisconsin

Library of Congress Cataloging-in-Publication Data

Davis, Deta S.
   Computer applications in music: a bibliography, supplement 1 /

Deta S. Davis.
      p. cm. — (The Computer music and digital audio series ; v.
   10)
      Includes index.
      ISBN 0-89579-267-2 (cloth)
      1. Computer music—History and criticism—Bibliography.
I. Title.   II. Series
ML128.C62D4   1988 Suppl.
016.78'0285—dc20   92–13289
                                                           CIP
                                                           MN

A-R Editions, Inc.
801 Deming Way
Madison, Wisconsin 53717
(608) 836-9000

© 1992 by A-R Editions, Inc.
All rights reserved
Printed in the United States of America

10   9   8   7   6   5   4   3   2   1

CONTENTS

PREFACE

Purpose and Arrangement

This bibliography is a continuation of my earlier work, *Computer Applications in Music: A Bibliography,* published in 1988. It includes citations that were not contained in the earlier work as well as more recent citations through 1989. The arrangement of the earlier volume has been largely retained, although efforts have been made to enhance the organization of material. The chapter on microcomputers has been subdivided into chapters for each major microcomputer, and chapters on performance practices and trade shows have been added. Each of the thirty-five chapters on a specific subject area is arranged alphabetically by author. In addition, the chapter subjects were chosen to place citations that would be of interest to the reader working in any given area of computer music together. As before, the decision to place an article or book in one chapter rather than another has been based on the primary content of the item and my assessment of potential user needs. Information from users of the previous volume suggests that the organization of material has been highly effective.

This bibliography does not include specific software packages that contain discs and similar supporting material with musical applications. It does include reviews of such software packages, and these can be found under the software names in the subject index.

The growth in the field of computer applications in music over the past few years has been phenomenal. The previous bibliography contained over 4,500 citations and covered a time period of approximately twenty-five to thirty years. This volume covers approximately three years and is virtually the same size. The task of compiling a comprehensive bibliography in this field has become daunting, if not overwhelming. Effective future information management in this field will be possible only with automation.

Content

Each citation lists all authors, the full title, and a complete bibliographic description. Numbers, symbols, and wording on title pages of books and journals have been transcribed exactly so that material can be located easily in library catalogs and computer data bases. The format of the citations generally follows *The Chicago Manual of Style*. When guidelines have been lacking for unusual citations, I have incorporated parts of the International Standard Book Description (ISBD) for bibliographic description. Any title that is not in English, French, or German has an English translation in brackets following the original title. Translations are not included for French and German because these languages are fairly commonly known and it is not standard practice to translate them. Citations that do not convey the content of the work in the title are accompanied by a short, descriptive annotation. This volume also includes an extensive subject index with substantial cross-referencing. It includes terms for concepts taken from the titles and content of the indexed items. Also included are titles of reviewed software and the names of persons or musical groups interviewed or profiled. Commercial hardware is usually indexed under the manufacturer's name, followed by the model name of number. There are a few items of commercial hardware with a generally recognized name that differs from the name of the manufacturer. In these cases the index contains cross-references to both names. Software packages are indexed under their trade titles.

A brief description of each chapter follows. "Aesthetics" is about aesthetic and philosophical concerns related to the computer and its relationship to or effect on music. "Composition" concerns the use of the computer in the art of music composition. Here, one finds stochastic algorithms for the creation of a piece of music, the use of the computer as an aid for determining tone rows, and other forms of computer-aided composition. "Compositions" is about specific pieces that were created using the computer. Concert reviews and descriptions of pieces by composers can be found here as well. "Computers in Music Education" includes references on how to use the computer in the teaching of music and reports of specific applications. "Conferences" contains reports and reviews of conferences on the computer in music and conference proceedings.

"Digital Audio" includes items about the sampling theorem, analog-digital conversion theory, storing and editing sound on disk, the compact disk, and related fields. "Digital Signal Processing" covers the use of the computer to modify signals or sounds for many purposes, including record restoration. "Electronic and Pipe Organs" includes the ways the computer has been used to modify or control the performance of electronic and pipe organs. "Microcomputers" contains articles about microcomputers that are either general or describe more than one major microcomputer. Seven related chapters are on specific uses of the Amiga, Atari, Commodore, IBM and compatibles, Macintosh, and Tandy. The chapter "Microcomputers—Other" is about specific microcomputers that did not have enough citations to create a chapter for each one of them. In most cases of microcomputers being used in a specific application covered in another chapter in the bibliography, the citation has remained in the specific microcomputer chapter and indexing for the application has been added.

"MIDI" (Musical Instrument Digital Interface) is about the protocol, its history, and applications that have arisen from its establishment. "Music Industry" covers the many areas in which the computer has been used in the industry. "Music Printing and Transcription" includes articles on the use of the computer to print music, for score and part creation, as well as for transcriptions. "Musical Instruments" contains items on the use of the computer to analyze and create specific instrument sounds and the modification of acoustic instruments to be played by the computer. "Musicological and Analytic Applications" includes items on musical analysis with the use of the computer, and musicological and ethnomusicological studies. "Programming Languages and Software Systems" has articles and books on specific software languages and software descriptions for use in music (but not sound synthesis software, which is placed under "Sound Generation for Music—Software). "Psychology and Psychoacoustics" covers psychological applications of the computer in music as well as how sound is heard and how specific sound synthesis techniques relate to human auditory perception. "Reference, Research, and Music Library Applications" contains books and articles on how the computer has been used in music research or as a reference tool. On-line searching and library applications such as music cataloging are covered.

Four chapters concern different aspects of music sound generation. "Sound Generation for Music—Hardware" has citations on hardware and computer systems for the generation of music. I considered subdividing this chapter into specific types of equipment such as keyboards, drum machines, and samplers. However, there were too many instances of hybrid components containing more than one musical function to be able to do this without creating confusion. "Sound Generation for Music—Performance Practices" contains citations of sources that describe how to make optimal use of instruments and various performance techniques. "Sound Generation for Music—Software" includes software applications specific to the generation of sound.

"Sound Generation for Music—Synthesis Techniques" contains information on various techniques for the synthesis of sound. "Sound Generation with Real-Time Applications" covers the use of the computer for real-time sound generation or the live performance of computer music. "Spatial Simulation and Room Acoustics" includes research on the use of the computer to model acoustics in actual or hypothetical spaces. "Speech" covers the use of speech in musical applications only. It does not include items that only address the production of speech by computers. "Studios" includes descriptions and reports of various studios or computer music facilities. "Trade Shows" is a new chapter that includes citations of reports from the various trade shows, such as NAMM and Frankfurt. These shows are the arena for the initial presentation of digitized components.

"General" is the catch-all for citations that either do not fit into any of the other chapters, or cover so many aspects of the field that they could not be placed in any one chapter. In particular, citations of the "How does the computer make music?" genre are here.

Research Methodology

In preparing this continuation, I became more skeptical of secondary sources and self-citations than I had been previously. I reached this position because of the increasing number of bad citations I encountered. In these citations, I found many incorrect statements of authors, titles, books, publishers, serials, volume numbering, dates, and pages. This misinformation was not restricted to references found in composers' written works, but also appeared in other published bibliographies in the field. One such book did not have even one correctly cited journal article. Fortunately, in most cases I was able to construct enough data to find correct citations. As a result, this bibliography consists almost exclusively of citations that were verified by myself, Michael Toman, Denise Ondisko, or Garrett Bowles, In a very few instances I found impeccable citations that I was unable to verify but did include. The number of other citations that I was unable to verify was substantial and, if I had included them, this continuation would have been even larger than the original volume.

In addition to utilizing the resources at the Library of Congress, which does not include everything published in the United States in its collection, I visited the University of Maryland Libraries and the Peabody Music Library. Denise Ondisko searched the resources at the Sibley Music Library, Michael Toman contained information on material at the CCRMA Library and Stanford University Library, and

Garrett Bowles added citations from issues of *Music, Computers, and Software.*

This bibliography was compiled using ProCite software on an IBM compatible computer. I used the ProCite software to generate both the author/title and subject indexes. The ProCite data was converted to a WordPerfect file for the final product.

Acknowledgments

I would like to thank my husband, Michael A.Toman, who kept house and home together while I worked on this project and for the work he did at Stanford for me. I would also like to thank Denise Ondisko for the research she did for me at the Sibley Music Library and for her suggestion of creating the chapter on performance practices. My thanks to Garrett Bowles for the citations from *Music, Computers, and Software* and his assistance on editing the volume. For title translations, I thank Sean Roach, Louis Borea, Jurij Dobczansky, Theresa Ellenwood, and Phyllis Rasmussen. I also thank Ed Bartlett of Computer Data Solutions for his technical support for getting my computer and software up and running. I greatly appreciate the support of my publisher, A-R Editions, particularly Cynthia Horton, for her continued interest in my work, and John Strawn, who smoothed the way when the going got bumpy. Finally, I thank Julia Toman, who doesn't seem to mind getting books as siblings, and John Toman for keeping so quiet in all the libraries we visited in the first year of his life.

LIST OF
ABBREVIATIONS

ACM	Association for Computing Machinery
AEDS	Association for Education Data Systems
AES	Audio Engineering Society
AFCET	Association Français pour la Cybernetique Economique et Technique
AFIPS	American Federation for Information Processing
AICA	Associazione Italiana per il Calcolo Automatico
AICP	Artificially Intelligent Computer Performer
AIM	Artificial Intelligence and Music
AIMI	Associazione di Informatica Musicale Italiana
ALMA	Alphanumeric Language for Musical Analysis
AMPLE	Advanced Music Programming Language and Environment
ASCAP	American Society of Composers, Authors, and Publishers
ASP	Automated Sound Program
ASP	Automated Synthesis Procedures
BARZREX	Bartok ARchives Z-symbol Rhythm EXtraction
BASIC	Beginner's All-purpose Symbolic Instruction Code
CAI	Computer Assisted Instruction
CAMP	Computer Assisted Music Project
CARL	Computer Audio Research Laboratory (University of California, San Diego
CASS	Computer Assisted Synthesizer System
CCRMA	Computer Center for Research in Music and Acoustics (Stanford University)
CEMAMu	Centre d'Etudes de Mathematique et d'Automatique Musicales

CHORDAL	Crane Heuristic ORgan DAta Language
CIRPA	Canadian Independent Record Producers Association
CLOS	Common Lisp Object System
CME	Center for Music Experiment (University of California, San Diego)
CNMAT	Center for New Music and Audio Technologies (University of California, Berkeley)
CNRS	Centre National de la Recherche Scientifique
CNUCE	Centro Nazionale Universitario di Calcolo Elettronico
CONHAN	CONtextual Harmonic ANalysis
COMMPUTE	Computer-Oriented Music Materials Processed for User Transformation of Exchange
CPEMC	Columbia-Princeton Electronic Music Center
CPU	Central Processing Unit
CRT	Cathode Ray Tube
CSC	Centro di Sonologia Computazionale (University of Padova)
CSRG	Computer Systems Research Group (University of Toronto)
DARMS	Digital Alternative Representation of Music Scores
DCMP	Digital Computer Music System
DECUS	Digital Equipment Computer Users Society
DIEM	Danish Institute of Electroacoustic Music
DOS	Disk Operating System
DUPACK	Darms Utility PACKage
ELMOL	ELectronic Music Oriented Language
EMAMu	Equipe de Mathematique et Automatique Musicale
EMS	ElektronMusikStudion (Stockholm)
ERATTO	Equipe de Recherche sur l'Analyse et la Transcription des Textes par Ordinatuer
FATNA	Foundation pour l'Application des Technologies Nouvelles aux Arts
FOF	Fonction d'Onde Formantique
GAIV	Groups d'Art et d'Informatique de Vicennes
GAM	Groupe d'Acoustique Musicale
GEM	Gesellschaft für Elektroakoustiche Musik
GMEB	Groupe de Musique Experimentale de Bourges
GRIPHOS	General Retrieval and Information Processor for Humanities-Oriented Studies

GRM	Groupe de Recherches Musicale
HMSL	Hierarchical Music Specification Language
IASM	Instituto per l'Assistenza allo Sviluppo del Mezzogiorno
ICA	Institute of Contemporary Arts
ICASSP	IEEE International Conference of Acoustics, Speech, and Signal Processing
ICMA	International Computer Music Association
ICMC	International Computer Music Conference
ICRH	Institute for Computer Research in the Humanities
IDEAMA	International Digital ElectroAcoustic Music Archive
IEEE	Institute of Electronic and Electrical Engineers
IERIV	Institut d'Etude et de Recherche en Information Visuelle
IETE	Institution of Electronics and Telecommunication Engineers (India)
IMA	International MIDI Association
IML	Intermediary Musical Language
IMS	Interactive Music System (University of Illinois)
INA-GRM	Institut National de l'Audiovisual Groupe de Recherches Musicales
I/O	Input/Output
IRCAM	Institute de Receherche et de Coordination Acoustique/Musique
IRE	Institute of Radio Engineers
IRMA	Information Retrieval for Multiple Musicological Applications
IRMA	Interactive, Real-Time Assembler
ISMUS	Iowa State computer MUsic System
K	Kilobyte(s) (1,024 bytes)
KCS	Keyboard Controlled Sequencer
LENA	Laboratoire d'Electroacoustique Numerique-Analogique (University of Montreal)
LFO	Low Frequency Oscillator
LIM	Laboratorio di Informatica Musicale (Milan)
LIMB	Laborattorio par l'Informatica Musicale (Biennale di Venezia)
LIME	Lippold's Interactive Music Editor
LMI	Linear Music Transcription
LSI	Large Scale Integration
MASC	Meta-language for Adaptive Synthesis and Control

MCAM	MIDI-Controlled Audio Mixers
MDI	Music Description Instruction
MEG	Music Editing and Graphics system
MESA	Music Editor Scorere and Arranger
MIDI	Music Instrument Digital Interface
MIDIM	MInimum Description of Music
MIR	Music Information Retrieval
MIT	Massachusetts Institute of Technology
MMA	MIDI Manufacturers Association
MTC	MIDI Time Code
MUSCOR	MUsic SCORing system
MUSICOL	MUsic Simulator-Interpreter for COMpositional Procedures
MUSTRAN	MUSic TRANslator
NAMM	National Association of Music Merchandisers
NARM	National Association of Recording Merchandisers
PBS-er	Performance, Score, and Braille music system in Waseda University for education and research
PROM	Programmable Read Only Memory
RAM	Random Access Memory
RMS	Root Mean Square
ROM	Read Only Meory
SAM	System for Analysis of Music
SEAMUS	Society for Electro-Acoustic Music in the United States
SID	Sound Interface Device (Commodore-64)
SIM	Società per l'Informatica Musicale (Rome)
SMDL	Standard Music Description Language
SMUT	System for MUsic Transcription
SMPTE	Society of Motion Picture and Television Engineers
SPL	Sound Pressure Level
SSSP	Structured Sound Synthesis Project (University of Toronto)
STREAM	Studio per la Ricerca ElettroAcustica Musicale
TEMPO	Transformational Electronic Music Process Organizer
TRAILS	Tempo Reale-Audiomatica Interactive Location System
VLMI	Very Large Musical Interval
VLSI	Very Large Scale Integration
WMN-code	White Mensural Notation code

AESTHETICS

4586. Anderton, Craig. "Making Musical Instruments Magical." *Electronic Musician* 4 (Feb. 1988): 45–51.

Excerpt of a lecture given at Musicom in 1986 and printed in French in *Les Cahiers de l'Acme* 61 (Oct. 1987).

4587. Appleton, Jon H. "Aesthetic Direction in Electronic Music." *Western Humanities Review* 18 (1964): 345–50.
Previously **3.**
Reprinted in *On the Wires of Our Nerves,* ed. Robin Julian Heifetz. Lewisburg, Pa.: Bucknell University Press, 1989: 69–75.

4588. ——, and Lars-Gunnar Bodin. "Guest Editorial: What's Wrong with Electronic Music." *Keyboard* 12 (June 1986): 8, 170.

4589. Becker, Frank. "Bleibt der Mensch als Musiker auf der Strecke? Diskussionsbeitrag über den Einsatz von Computern in der U-Musik." *Neue Musikzeitung* 36 (Oct.–Nov. 1987): 12.

4590. Bernardini, Nicola. "Estetica e tecnica: appunti imbarazzati." [Aesthetics and Technology: Random Thoughts] In *I profili del suono: scritti sulla musica electroacustica e la computer music,* ed. Serena Tamburini and Mauro Bagella. Salerno: Musica Verticale-Galzerano, 1987: 109–18.

4591. Boulez, Pierre. "Technology and the Composer." In *The Language of Electroacoustic Music,* ed. Simon Emmerson. New York, N.Y.: Harwood Academic Publishers, 1986: 5–14.
Originally published: *Times Literary Supplement* (May 6, 1977).

4592. Bourne, Anne. "Keyboards: What's a Real Piano?" *Canadian Musician* 11 (Apr. 1989): 23–25.

4593. Brün, Herbert. "Composer's Input Outputs Music." In *On the Wires of Our Nerves,* ed. Robin Julian Heifetz. Lewisburg, Pa.: Bucknell University Press, 1989: 133–47.

4594. ——. "Guest Editorial: Volume, the Tyranny of the Beat, Mating Video with Audio & Improvisation vs. Originality." *Keyboard* 11 (Dec. 1985): 11, 132.

4595. Butler, Chris. "KCS Speculations." *Keyboards, Computers & Software* 1 (Aug. 1986): 8, 74.

The author suggests that computer-controlled music is changing from being a new technology to a total transformation of music.

4596. Carl, Robert. "The Distant Shore Seen from Two Sides." *College Music Symposium* 24 (Spring 1984): 148–57.

A comparison of French and American contemporary music.

4597. Darreg, Ivor. "The Digital-Analog Question." *Interval* 5 (Fall–Winter 1985–86): 10–13.

The author makes the point that digital instruments, such as the organ, have been around a long time before the computer.

4598. Donato, Peter. "The Song Is Still the Thing." *Canadian Composer* n233 (Sept. 1988): 20–23.

French version: Un mordu de l'électronique qui déchante . . .

4599. Ehle, Robert C. "Music and Change: The Music of the New Millennium." *Music Review* 45 (1984): 287–92.

4600. Emmerson, Simon, ed. *The Language of Electroacoustic Music.* New York, N.Y.: Harwood Academic Publishers; London: Macmillan Press, 1986. 231 p.

Contains items: 4591, 4601, 4606, 4613, 4617, 4621, 4629, 4634, 4639, 4646.

Review by Ernest Lee Hammer in *Computer Music Journal* 11,4 (Winter 1987): 49–50.

Review by Jonty Harrison in *Music and Letters* 69 (1988): 296–98.

Review by Alistair MacDonald in *Musical Times* 129 (June 1988): 303.

4601. ———."The Relation of Language to Materials." In *The Language of Electroacoustic Music,* ed. Simon Emmerson. New York, N.Y.: Harwood Academic Publishers, 1986: 17–39.

4602. Freff. "Creative Options: Let Us Now Praise Famous Samples." *Keyboard* 12 (July 1986): 26–27.

A fresh perspective on sampling.

4603. Gaburo, Kenneth. "Murmur." In *On the Wires of Our Nerves,* ed. Robin Julian Heifetz. Lewisburg, Pa.: Bucknell University Press, 1989: 37–42.

Poem on the aesthetics of electronic and computer music.

4604. Gann, Kyle. "Music: Yearning for Ismism." *Village Voice* 32 (Aug. 4, 1987): 76.

The author describes how he is waiting for composers to come up with new ideas.

4605. Harvey, Jonathan. "Electronics in Music: A New Aesthetic?" *Journal of the Royal Society of Arts* 133 (Apr. 1985): 313–19.
Originally given as a paper to the Royal Society of Arts, 28 November 1984.
Reprinted in *Composer* n85 (Summer 1985): 8–15.

4606. ———. "The Mirror of Ambiguity." In *The Language of Electroacoustic Music,* ed. Simon Emmerson. New York, N.Y.: Harwood Academic Publishers, 1986: 175–90.

4607. Heifetz, Robin Julian. "Computer Music Warmware: The Human Perspective." *Music Review* 45 (1984): 283–86.
Also in *On the Wires of Our Nerves,* ed. Robin Julian Heifetz. Lewisburg, Pa.: Bucknell University Press, 1989: 85–89.

4608. ———, ed. *On the Wires of Our Nerves: The Art of Electroacoustic Music.* Lewisburg, Pa.: Bucknell University Press, 1989. 204 p.
Contains items: 4587, 4593, 4603, 4607, 4610, 4612, 4614, 4615, 4616, 4620, 4622, 4625, 4632, 4633, 4788, 4808, 8328.

4609. Henricksen, Clifford A. "Guest Editorial: No Sweat, No Music—A Player Laments the Spread of Computer Dependency." *Keyboard* 11 (Aug. 1985): 10.

4610. Janzen, Thomas E. "Aesthetic Appeal in Computer Music." *Computer Music Journal* 10,3 (Fall 1986): 83–88.
Reprinted in *On the Wires of Our Nerves,* ed. Robin Julian Heifetz. Lewisburg, Pa.: Bucknell University Press, 1989: 111–20.

4611. Junglieb, Stanley. "Guest Editorial: Beyond User Friendliness." *Keyboard* 12 (Apr. 1986): 10, 138.

A call for the use of creativity with technologically sophisticated instruments.

4612. Kasdan, Leonard, and Jon H. Appleton. "Tradition and Change: The Case of Music." *Comparative Studies in Society and History* 12 (Jan. 1970): 50–58.
Also in *On the Wires of Our Nerves,* ed. Robin Julian Heifetz. Lewisburg, Pa.: Bucknell University Press, 1989: 17–27.

4613. Keane, David. "At the Threshold of an Aesthetic." In *The Language of Electroacoustic Music,* ed. Simon Emmerson. New York, N.Y.: Harwood Academic Publishers, 1986: 97–118.

4614. ———. "The Quest for 'Musically Interesting' Structures in Computer Music." In *On the Wires of Our Nerves,* ed. Robin Julian Heifetz. Lewisburg, Pa.: Bucknell University Press, 1989: 97–110.

4615. ———. "Some Practical Aesthetic Problems of Electronic Music Composition." *Interface* 8 (1979): 193–205.

Reprinted in *On the Wires of Our Nerves,* ed. Robin Julian Heifetz. Lewisburg, Pa.: Bucknell University Press, 1989: 43–56.

4616. Luening, Otto. "Electronic Music." In *On the Wires of Our Nerves,* ed. Robin Julian Heifetz. Lewisburg, Pa.: Bucknell University Press, 1989: 28–31.

Aesthetic considerations in electronic and computer music.

4617. Machover, Tod. "A Stubborn Search for Artistic Unity." In *The Language of Electroacoustic Music,* ed. Simon Emmerson. New York, N.Y.: Harwood Academic Publishers, 1986: 191–215.

4618. Mansfield, Richard. "Now-Silent Beethovens." *Compute!* 7 (Jan. 1985): 51.

The author comments on the possible decline in musicians' skills because of the computer.

4619. McLean, Barton. "Symbolic Extension and Its Corruption of Music." *Perspectives of New Music* 20 (Fall–Winter 1981/Spring–Summer 1982): 331–56.

4620. McLean, Priscilla. "Fire and Ice: A Query." *Perspectives of New Music* 16 (Fall–Winter 1977): 205–11.
Also in *On the Wires of Our Nerves,* ed. Robin Julian Heifetz. Lewisburg, Pa.: Bucknell University Press, 1989: 148–54.

4621. McNabb, Michael. "Computer Music: Some Aesthetic Considerations." In *The Language of Electroacoustic Music,* ed. Simon Emmerson. New York, N.Y.: Harwood Academic Publishers, 1986: 141–53.

4622. Melby, John. "*Computer* Music or Computer *Music.*" In *On the Wires of Our Nerves,* ed. Robin Julian Heifetz. Lewisburg, Pa.: Bucknell University Press, 1989: 90–96.

4623. Minsky, Marvin. "Music, Mind, and Meaning." *Computer Music Journal* 5,3 (Fall 1981): 28–44.
Previously **35.**
Reprinted in *The Music Machine,* ed. Curtis Roads. Cambridge, Mass.: MIT Press, 1989: 639–55.

4624. Moog, Bob. "Guest Editorial: Where's the Knobs?" *Keyboard* 13 (Dec. 1987): 12.

A request for the addition of expressiveness to musical sounds.

4625. Morthenson, Jan W. "Aesthetic Dilemmas in Electronic Music." *Dansk Musiktidskrift* 2 (1981/1982): 47–61.
Reprinted in *On the Wires of Our Nerves,* ed. Robin Julian Heifetz. Lewisburg, Pa.: Bucknell University Press, 1989: 57–68.

AESTHETICS 5

4626. Motte-Haber, Helga de la. "Historische und aesthetische Positionen der Computermusik." *Musica* 41 (1987): 128–34.

4627. ———. "Maschinenmusik—Musikmaschinen: Vom Singenden Automaten zum Playcard-gesteuerten Computer." *Österreichische Musikzeitschrift* 39 (1984): 435–41.

4628. Nobre, Marlos. "The Composer's New World." *ISME Yearbook* 13 (1986): 78–82.
The effect of technology on composers' choices of instruments and media, and on audience listening.

4629. Pennycook, Bruce W. "Language and Resources: A New Paradox." In *The Language of Electroacoustic Music,* ed. Simon Emmerson. New York, N.Y.: Harwood Academic Publishers, 1986: 119–37.

4630. Razzi, Fausto. "Musica di plastica?" [Plastic Music?] In *I profili del suono: scritti sulla musica electroacustica e la computer music,* ed. Serena Tamburini and Mauro Bagella. Salerno: Musica Verticale-Galzerano, 1987: 21–24.

4631. Richter, Peter H. "Fraktale-Chaos—auf der Suche nach Ordnung zwischen Unvorhersagbarkeit und gebrochenen Dimensionen." *Österreische Musikzeitschrift* 44 (June 1989): 276–79.

4632. Schrader, Barry. "The Development of Personal Compositional Style." In *On the Wires of Our Nerves,* ed. Robin Julian Heifetz. Lewisburg, Pa.: Bucknell University Press, 1989: 76–82.

4633. Semegen, Daria. "Electronic Music: Art Beyond Technology." In *On the Wires of Our Nerves,* ed. Robin Julian Heifetz. Lewisburg, Pa.: Bucknell University Press, 1989: 32–36.

4634. Smalley, Denis. "Spectro-morphology and Structuring Processes." In *The Language of Electroacoustic Music,* ed. Simon Emmerson. New York, N.Y.: Harwood Academic Publishers, 1986: 61–93.
Revision of a paper originally presented at a conference organized by EMS (Elektronmusikstudion), Stockholm, 1981.

4635. Stewart, Michael. "The Feel Factor: Music with Soul." *Electronic Musician* 3 (Oct. 1987): 56–65.
How to make computer music feel more human.

4636. Strange, Allen. "Guest Editorial: Creativity vs. Mechanics." *Keyboard* 13 (July 1987): 19, 169.
A call for bringing technology to music and not vice versa.

4637. Thomas, Jean-Christophe. "Parolier des musiques." *Revue musicale* n394–97 (1986): 19–20.

4638.   Tomatz, David. "Technology: Technology in Music: Cultural, Artistic, and Ethical Implications." *Proceedings of the National Association of Schools of Music* n77 (1989): 67–69.

4639.   Truax, Barry. "Computer Music Language Design and the Composing Process." In *The Language of Electroacoustic Music,* ed. Simon Emmerson. New York, N.Y.: Harwood Academic Publishers, 1986: 155–73.

4640.   Vogt, Matthias Theodor. "Grenzen der Akousmatik: Kleine Reflexion zur Musik vom Computer." *NZ, Neue Zeitschrift für Musik* 146 (Apr. 1985): 35–37.

4641.   Vorhees, Jerry L. "Music in a New Age: The Challenge of Electronics." *Music Educators Journal* 73 (Oct. 1986): 32–36.

4642.   Weiss, Peter. "Computer können nicht singen." In *Die Musikerziehung in Zeitalter der Elektronik: 20. DACH-Tagung, Golling, Salzburg, April–Mai 1988: Tagungsbericht,* ed. Brigitte Peschl. Vienna: VWGÖ, 1989: 89–97.

4643.   Wheeler, Tom. "The New Guitar Revolution." *Guitar Player* 20 (June 1986): 12–15.

The effects of the computer on guitar players and other musicians.

4644.   Whitney, John. "Letters: More Reflections upon Future Olympic Arts Festivals." *Computer Music Journal* 10,2 (Summer 1986): 7–9.

4645.   Wishart, Trevor. "Beyond Notation." *British Journal of Music Education* 2 (Nov. 1985): 311–26.

A condensation of the author's thoughts from *On Sonic Art.*

4646.   ———. "Sound Symbols and Landscapes." In *The Language of Electroacoustic Music,* ed. Simon Emmerson. New York, N.Y.: Harwood Academic Publishers, 1986: 41–60.

Based on the author's *On Sonic Art.*

COMPOSITION

4647. Ames, Charles. "Automated Composition in Retrospect: 1956–1986." *Leonardo* 20,2 (1987): 169–85.

4648. ——. "The Markov Process as a Compositional Model: A Survey and Tutorial." *Leonardo* 22,2 (1989): 175–87.

4649. ——. "Music, AI in." In *Encyclopedia of Artificial Intelligence,* ed. Stuart C. Shapiro. New York, N.Y.: J. Wiley, 1987: 638–42.

4650. ——. "Tutorial on Automated Composition." In *Proceedings of the 1987 International Computer Music Conference: University of Illinois at Urbana-Champaign, Urbana, Illinois, USA, August 23–26, 1987,* comp. James Beauchamp. San Francisco, Calif.: Computer Music Association, 1987: 1–8.

4651. Amiot, E.; Gerard Assayag; C. Malherbe; and André Riotte. "Duration Structure Generation and Recognition in Musical Writing." In *Proceedings of the International Computer Music Conference 1986, Royal Conservatory, The Hague, Netherlands, October 20–24, 1986,* ed. Paul Berg. San Francisco, Calif.: Computer Music Association, 1986: 75–81.

4652. Arcela, Aluizio. "Time-Trees: The Inner Organization of Intervals." In *Proceedings of the International Computer Music Conference 1986, Royal Conservatory, The Hague, Netherlands, October 20–24, 1986,* ed. Paul Berg. San Francisco, Calif.: Computer Music Association, 1986: 87–89.

4653. Arveiller, Jacques. "Comments on University Instruction in Computer Music Composition." *Computer Music Journal* 6,2 (Summer 1982): 72–78.
Previously **82.**
Reprinted in *The Music Machine,* ed. Curtis Roads. Cambridge, Mass.: MIT Press, 1989: 169–75.

4654. Austin, Larry, and Eugene DeLisa. "Modeling Processes of Musical Invention." In *Proceedings of the 1987 International Computer Music Conference: University of Illinois at Urbana-Champaign, Urbana,*

Illinois, USA, August 23–26, 1987, comp. James Beauchamp. San Francisco, Calif.: Computer Music Association, 1987: 206–11.

4655. Bain, Reginald. "A Musico-linguistic Composition Environment." In *Proceedings of the 14th International Computer Music Conference, Cologne, September 20–25, 1988,* ed. Christoph Lischka and Johannes Fritsch. Cologne: Feedback-Studio-Verlag; San Francisco, Calif.: Dist. by Computer Music Association, 1988: 101–7. (Feedback Papers; 33)

4656. Baker, Robert A. *MUSICOMP: MUsic-Simulator-Interpreter for COMpositional Procedures for the IBM 7090.* Urbana, Ill.: University of Illinois Experimental Music Studio, 1963. 44 p. (Technical Report; no. 9)

An early account of computer-assisted composition.

4657. Barrière, Jean-Baptiste. "Computer Music as Cognitive Approach: Simulation, Timbre, and Formal Processes." *Contemporary Music Review* 4 (1989): 117–30.

4658. Basinée, Pierre-François; Jean-Baptiste Barrière; Marc-André Dalbavie; Jacques Duthen; Magnus Lindberg; Yves Potard; and Kaija Saariaho. "Esquisse: A Compositional Environment." In *Proceedings of the 14th International Computer Music Conference, Cologne, September 20–25, 1988,* ed. Christoph Lischka and Johannes Fritsch. Cologne: Feedback-Studio-Verlag; San Francisco, Calif.: Dist. by Computer Music Association, 1988: 108–18. (Feedback Papers; 33)

4659. Batel, Günther. "Musique concrète, elektronische Musik und Computerkomposition." In *Radiophonische Musik.* Celle: Moeck, 1985: 61–81.

4660. Belkin, Alan. "Orchestration, Perception, and Musical Time: A Composer's View." *Computer Music Journal* 12,2 (Summer 1988): 47–53.

4661. Bellini, S. "Un sistema per l'analisi/sintesi di testi musicali." [A System for the Analysis/Synthesis of Musical Texts] Tesi di Laurea in Fisica, A.A., Università degli Studi, Milano, 1986.

4662. Bernardini, Nicola. "Riproducibilità, semiotica e composizione per elaboratore." [Reproducibility, Semiotics, and Composition by Computer] In *Musica e tecnologia: industria e cultura per lo sviluppo del mezzogiorno: VI Colloquio di Informatica Musicale, Napoli 16–19 ottobre 1985,* ed. Carlo Acreman; Immacolata Ortosecco; and Fausto Razzi. Milan: Edizioni Unicopli, 1987: 384–410.

4663. Beyls, Peter. "The Musical Universe of Cellular Automata." In *Proceedings, 1989 International Computer Music Conference, November 2–5, the Ohio State University, Columbus, Ohio.* San Francisco, Calif.: Computer Music Association, 1989: 34–41.

4664. Bianchini, Riccardo. "Composizione automatica di strutture musicali." [Automatic composition of musical structures] In *I profili del suono: scritti sulla musica electroacustica e la computer music,* ed. Serena Tamburini and Mauro Bagella. Salerno: Musica Verticale-Galzerano, 1987: 35–39.

4665. Boulez, Pierre, and Andrew Gerzso. "Computers in Music." *Scientific American* 258 (Apr. 1988): 44–50.

A lengthy description of the use of the computer as a compositional tool with Boulez' *Repons* detailed as an example.

4666. Bowcott, Peter. "Cellular Automation as a Means of High Level Compositional Control of Granular Synthesis." In *Proceedings, 1989 International Computer Music Conference, November 2–5, the Ohio State University, Columbus, Ohio.* San Francisco, Calif.: Computer Music Association, 1989: 55–57.

4667. Brown, Frank. *La musique par ordinateur.* Paris: Presses universitaires de France, 1982. 127 p.

An examination of the computer's role in musical composition.

4668. Burbat, Wolf. "Jazz arrangieren und komponieren am Computer." *Musik und Bildung* 21 (Juni 1989): 323–27.

4669. Butler, Chris. "The Computer as Collaborator: Random Minds." *Keyboards, Computers & Software* 1 (Apr. 1986): 13–14.

Ed Tomney, a New York composer, uses the computer as a collaborator in music composition.

4670. Buxton, William; Sanand Patel; William Reeves; and Ronald Baecker. "Scope in Interactive Score Editors." *Computer Music Journal* 5,3 (Fall 1981): 50–56.
Previously **128.**
Reprinted in *The Music Machine,* ed. Curtis Roads. Cambridge, Mass.: MIT Press, 1989: 255–61.

4671. Camurri, Antonio; M. Giacomini; S. Ponassi; and Renato Zaccaria. "Key—Music: An Expert System Environment for Music Composition." In *Proceedings of the 14th International Computer Music Conference, Cologne, September 20–25, 1988,* ed. Christoph Lischka and Johannes Fritsch. Cologne: Feedback-Studio-Verlag; San Francisco, Calif.: Dist. by Computer Music Association, 1988: 119–26. (Feedback Papers; 33)

4672. Cappuccio, Sergio. "Studi intermedi per l'ideazione e strutturazione di un sistema personalizzato di progettazione e composizione musicale assistiti da elaboratore." [Intermediate Studies for the Ideation and Structuring of a Personalized System of Projections and Musical Compositions Assisted by the Computer] In *Musica e tecnologia: industria e cultura per lo sviluppo del mezzogiorno: VI Colloquio di*

Informatica Musicale, Napoli 16–19 ottobre 1985, ed. Carlo Acreman; Immacolata Ortosecco; and Fausto Razzi. Milan: Edizioni Unicopli, 1987: 435–47.

4673. Carlos, Wendy. "Wendy Carlos on Algorithmic Composition." *Active Sensing* 1 (Summer 1989): 3.

4674. Chadabe, Joel. "Interactive Composing: An Overview." *Computer Music Journal* 8,1 (Spring 1984): 22–27.
Previously **133.**
Reprinted in *The Music Machine,* ed. Curtis Roads. Cambridge, Mass.: MIT Press, 1989: 143–48.

4675. Chang, Debra. "Programming the Blues." *Jazz Educators Journal* 16 (Feb./Mar. 1984): 18–20.
A BASIC program for generating blues melodies.

4676. Cobham, Wayne. "Song Construction." *Music, Computers & Software* 3 (Aug. 1988): 70–71.
A discussion of song writing with the aid of MIDI sequencers.

4677. Colombo, W. "Definizione di algoritmi e di strutture di dati per l'inferenza di modelli formali di testi musicali." [Definition of an Algorithm and of Data Structures for the Inference of Formal Models of Musical Texts] Tesi di Laurea in Matematica, A.A., Università degli Studi, Milano, 1985.

4678. "The Computer's Nod to Bach." *Ovation* 9 (Jan. 1989): 7.
A short description of Kemal Ebcioğlu's CHORAL program, which produces harmonizations.

4679. Cope, David. "Experiments in Music Intelligence (EMI)." In *Proceedings of the 1987 International Computer Music Conference: University of Illinois at Urbana-Champaign, Urbana, Illinois, USA, August 23–26, 1987,* comp. James Beauchamp. San Francisco, Calif.: Computer Music Association, 1987: 174–81.

4680. ———. "Experiments in Musical Intelligence (EMI): Non-linear Linguistic-based Composition." *Interface* 18 (1989): 117–39.

4681. ———. "An Expert System for Computer-assisted Composition." *Computer Music Journal* 11,4 (Winter 1987): 30–46.

4682. ———. "Music & LISP." *AI Expert* 3 (Mar. 1988): 26–34.
Describes a linguistic approach to music composition.

4683. Decker, Shawn L.; Gary S. Kendall; Brian L. Schmidt; M. Derek Ludwig; and Daniel J. Freed. "A Modular Environment for Sound Synthesis and Composition." *Computer Music Journal* 10,4 (Winter 1986): 28–41.
Outlines the development of the eled (Event List EDitor) program.

4684. Degazio, Bruno. "Musical Aspects of Fractal Geometry." In *Proceedings of the International Computer Music Conference 1986, Royal Conservatory, The Hague, Netherlands, October 20–24, 1986,* ed. Paul Berg. San Francisco, Calif.: Computer Music Association, 1986: 435–42.

4685. Doati, Roberto. "Symmetry, Regularity, Direction, Velocity." *Perspectives of New Music* 22 (Fall–Winter 1983/Spring–Summer 1984): 61–86.

4686. Dodge, Charles, and Curtis R. Bahn. "Musical Fractals." *Byte* 11 (June 1986): 185–96.
Discusses some basic techniques of computer-aided composition. Includes BASIC programs for generating musical fractals.

4687. Donato, Peter. "Writers Turn Computer into Modern Age Muse; Composers Say Computers Can Up Creativity Once Mastered." *Canadian Composer* n218 (Feb.–Mar. 1987): 10–15.
French version: Des machines à connaître et à apprivoiser: l'expérience électronique de certains compositeurs.

4688. Dreier, Ruth. "Computers for Composers: New Adventures in Music." *ASCAP in Action* (Spring 1986): 44–45, 48.
How various composers use the computer.

4689. Dydo, J. Stephen. "Surface Relations between Music and Language as Compositional Aids." *Interface* 12 (1983): 541–56.
A description of the LIMID program. Based on a paper given at ICMC, Venice, 1982, item *162.*

4690. Ebcioğlu, Kemal. "An Expert System for Harmonization of Chorales in the Style of J. S. Bach." Ph.D. diss., State University of New York at Buffalo, 1986. 297 p.
Technical report no. 86–09.

4691. ———. "An Expert System for Harmonizing Four-part Chorales." In *Proceedings of the International Computer Music Conference 1986, Royal Conservatory, The Hague, Netherlands, October 20–24, 1986,* ed. Paul Berg. San Francisco, Calif.: Computer Music Association, 1986: 447–49.

4692. ———. "An Expert System for Harmonizing Four-part Chorales." *Computer Music Journal* 12,3 (Fall 1988): 43–51.

4693. ———. *Report on the CHORAL Project: An Expert System for Harmonizing Four-part Chorales.* Yorktown Heights, N.Y.: IBM Research Division, 1987.

4694. ——. "Strict Counterpoint: A Case Study in Musical Composition by Computers." M.S. diss., Middle East Technical University, Ankara, 1979.

4695. Eigenfeldt, Arne. "Modeling Compositional Gestures after Selected World Music Strategies in Point, Counterpoint." M.A. thesis, Simon Fraser University, 1988.

4696. Englert, Giuseppe G. "Automated Composition and Composed Automation." *Computer Music Journal* 5,4 (Winter 1981): 30–35.
Previously **167.**
Reprinted in *The Music Machine,* ed. Curtis Roads. Cambridge, Mass.: MIT Press, 1989: 131–36.

4697. Evans, Brian. "Integration of Music and Graphics through Algorithmic Congruence." In *Proceedings of the 1987 International Computer Music Conference: University of Illinois at Urbana-Champaign, Urbana, Illinois, USA, August 23–26, 1987,* comp. James Beauchamp. San Francisco, Calif.: Computer Music Association, 1987: 17–24.

4698. Fagarazzi, Bruno. "Metodo compositivo basato sull'algoritmo del volo di Lévy per la generazione di composizioni autosimili." [A Composition Method Based on Lévy's Algorithm of Flight for the Self-Similar Generation of Compositions] In *Musica e tecnologia: industria e cultura per lo sviluppo del mezzogiorno: VI Colloquio di Informatica Musicale, Napoli 16–19 ottobre 1985,* ed. Carlo Acreman; Immacolata Ortosecco; and Fausto Razzi. Milan: Edizioni Unicopli, 1987: 417–25.

4699. ——. "Self-similar Hierarchical Processes for Formal and Timbral Control in Composition." *Interface* 17 (1988): 45–61.

4700. Foss, Richard J. "A Computer Music System for the Modern Composer." M.S.C. diss., University of South Africa, 1986. 129 p.

4701. Fraser, Jill. "MCS Scoring." *Music, Computers & Software* (June 1987): 76–77.
A discussion of scoring music for the television series "Cagney and Lacey."

4702. Free, John, and Paul Vytas. "The CAMP Music Configuration Database: Approaching the Vanilla Synthesizer." In *Proceedings of the 14th International Computer Music Conference, Cologne, September 20–25, 1988,* ed. Christoph Lischka and Johannes Fritsch. Cologne: Feedback-Studio-Verlag; San Francisco, Calif.: Dist. by Computer Music Association, 1988: 127–41. (Feedback Papers; 33)

4703. Friberg, Anders, and Johan Sundberg. "A Lisp Environment for Creating and Applying Rules for Musical Performance." In *Proceedings of the International Computer Music Conference 1986, Royal*

Conservatory, The Hague, Netherlands, October 20–24, 1986, ed. Paul Berg. San Francisco, Calif.: Computer Music Association, 1986: 1–3.

4704. Fry, Christopher. "Flavors Band: A Language for Specifying Musical Style." *Computer Music Journal* 4,3 (Fall 1980): 48–58.
Previously **180.**
Reprinted in *The Music Machine,* ed. Curtis Roads. Cambridge, Mass.: MIT Press, 1989: 295–309.

4705. Garton, Brad. "The Elthar Program." *Perspectives of New Music* 27 (Winter 1989): 6–41.

A large signal-processing expert system to interpret natural language requests.

4706. ———. "Elthar—A Signal Processing Expert that Learns." In *Proceedings of the 1987 International Computer Music Conference: University of Illinois at Urbana-Champaign, Urbana, Illinois, USA, August 23–26, 1987,* comp. James Beauchamp. San Francisco, Calif.: Computer Music Association, 1987: 96–103.

4707. Giomi, Francesco, and Marco Ligabue. "An Interactive System for Musical Improvisation." In *Proceedings of the 14th International Computer Music Conference, Cologne, September 20–25, 1988,* ed. Christoph Lischka and Johannes Fritsch. Cologne: Feedback-Studio-Verlag; San Francisco, Calif.: Dist. by Computer Music Association, 1988: 412–19. (Feedback Papers; 33)

A report on the development of a composition software package for jazz improvisation.

4708. Greenberg, Gary. "Procedural Composition." In *Proceedings of the 1987 International Computer Music Conference: University of Illinois at Urbana-Champaign, Urbana, Illinois, USA, August 23–26, 1987,* comp. James Beauchamp. San Francisco, Calif.: Computer Music Association, 1987: 25–32.

4709. Greenhough, Michael. "The Philosophy and Design of a Real-Time Music-Structure Generating System." *Interface* 17 (1988): 25–44.

A description of a computerized music-structure generating system.

4710. ———. "A Real-Time Music-Structure Generating System for Microcomputer." *Contemporary Music Review* 3 (1989): 161–75.

4711. Greenwald, Ted. "Beyond Sequencers: Machines that Improvise." *Keyboard* 13 (June 1987): 112, 125.

4712. Grossman, Gary. "Instruments, Cybernetics, and Computer Music." In *Proceedings of the 1987 International Computer Music Conference: University of Illinois at Urbana-Champaign, Urbana, Illinois, USA,*

August 23–26, 1987, comp. James Beauchamp. San Francisco, Calif.: Computer Music Association, 1987: 212–19.

4713.   Hamel, Keith A.; Bruce W. Pennycook; Bill Ripley; and Eli Blevis. "Composition Design System: A Functional Approach to Composition." In *Proceedings of the 1987 International Computer Music Conference: University of Illinois at Urbana-Champaign, Urbana, Illinois, USA, August 23–26, 1987,* comp. James Beauchamp. San Francisco, Calif.: Computer Music Association, 1987: 33–39.

4714.   Harrison, Malcolm C.; Suzanne Haig; and Gershon Horowitz. "The Shortest-Path Algorithm for Musical Harmony." In *Proceedings, 1989 International Computer Music Conference, November 2–5, the Ohio State University, Columbus, Ohio.* San Francisco, Calif.: Computer Music Association, 1989: 119–22.

4715.   Holland, Simon. "New Cognitive Theories of Harmony Applied to Direct Manipulation Tools for Novices." In *Proceedings of the 1987 International Computer Music Conference: University of Illinois at Urbana-Champaign, Urbana, Illinois, USA, August 23–26, 1987,* comp. James Beauchamp. San Francisco, Calif.: Computer Music Association, 1987: 182–89.

4716.   Hospers, Al. "The Transcontinental MIDI Songwriting Shuffle." *Electronic Musician* 4 (Dec. 1988): 36–48.

Suggestions on how to do long distance, computerized, MIDI songwriting collaborations based on the author's experience.

4717.   "Island U.K. Computer Arm Bows; Music Composing Package Offered." *Billboard* 96 (Oct. 6, 1984): 9.

4718.   Johnson, Jim. "KCS Applications." *Keyboards, Computers & Software* 2 (Feb. 1987): 8, 76–77.

A description of algorithmic composition, available software, and books on the subject.

4719.   Jones, Kevin. "Compositional Applications of Stochastic Processes." *Computer Music Journal* 5,2 (Summer 1981): 45–61.
Previously **246.**
Reprinted in *The Music Machine,* ed. Curtis Roads. Cambridge, Mass.: MIT Press, 1989: 381–97.

4720.   ——. "Generative Models in Computer-assisted Musical Composition." *Contemporary Music Review* 3 (1989): 177–96.

4721.   Kirck, George T. "Computer Realization of Extended Just Intonation Compositions." *Computer Music Journal* 11,1 (Spring 1987): 69–75.

4722.   Koenig, Gottfried Michael. "Aesthetic Integration of Computer-composed Scores." *Computer Music Journal* 7,4 (Winter 1983): 27–33.

Previously **256.**
Reprinted in *The Music Machine,* ed. Curtis Roads. Cambridge, Mass.: MIT Press, 1989: 399–404.

4723. ——. "Genesis of Form in Technically Conditioned Environments." *Interface* 16 (1987): 165–75.

4724. Langston, Peter S. *Six Techniques for Algorithmic Composition.* Morristown, N.J.: Bellcore, 1988. (Bellcore Technical Memorandum)

4725. ——. "Six Techniques for Algorithmic Music Composition (Extended Abstract)." In *Proceedings, 1989 International Computer Music Conference, November 2–5, the Ohio State University, Columbus, Ohio.* San Francisco, Calif.: Computer Music Association, 1989: 164–67.

4726. Lansky, Paul. "Compositional Applications of Linear Predictive Coding." In *Current Directions in Computer Music,* ed. Max V. Mathews and John R. Pierce. Cambridge, Mass.: MIT Press, 1989: 5–8.

4727. Laske, Otto E. "Composition Theory in Koenig's *Project One* and *Project Two.*" *Computer Music Journal* 5,4 (Winter 1981): 54–65.
Previously **282.**
Reprinted in *The Music Machine,* ed. Curtis Roads. Cambridge, Mass.: MIT Press, 1989: 119–30.

4728. ——. "Composition Theory: An Enrichment of Music Theory." *Interface* 18 (1989): 45–59.

4729. Leppig, Manfred. "Wie Computer komponieren: ein Arbeitsmodell." *Musik und Bildung* 17 (Feb. 1985): 91–95.

4730. Lewis, J. P. "Algorithms for Music Composition by Neural Nets: Improved CBR Paradigms." In *Proceedings, 1989 International Computer Music Conference, November 2–5, the Ohio State University, Columbus, Ohio.* San Francisco, Calif.: Computer Music Association, 1989: 180–83.

4731. Ligabue, Marco. "A System of Rules for Computer Improvisation." In *Proceedings of the International Computer Music Conference 1986, Royal Conservatory, The Hague, Netherlands, October 20–24, 1986,* ed. Paul Berg. San Francisco, Calif.: Computer Music Association, 1986: 345–48.
Italian version: "Un sistema di regole per l'improvisazione col computer." In *Musica e tecnologia: industria e cultura per lo sviluppo del mezzogiorno: VI Colloquio di Informatica Musicale, Napoli 16–19 ottobre 1985,* ed. Carlo Acreman; Immacolata Ortosecco; and Fausto Razzi. Milan: Edizioni Unicopli, 1987: 426–34.

4732. Lisella, Julia. "Computer Music Moves into the Fractal Void." *Village Voice* 31 (Nov. 25, 1986): FF17–FF20.

How various composers are using fractals in composition.

4733.   Lohner, Henning. "The UPIC System: A User's Report." *Computer Music Journal* 10,4 (Winter 1986): 42–49.

4734.   Lorrain, Denis. "A Panoply of Stochastic 'Cannons'." *Computer Music Journal* 4,1 (Spring 1980): 53–81.
Previously **297.**
Reprinted in *The Music Machine,* ed. Curtis Roads. Cambridge, Mass.: MIT Press, 1989: 351–79.

4735.   Loy, D. Gareth. "Composing with Computers: A Survey of Some Compositional Formalisms and Music Programming Languages." In *Current Directions in Computer Music,* ed. Max V. Mathews and John R. Pierce. Cambridge, Mass.: MIT Press, 1989: 291–396.

4736.   Mahin, Bruce P. "Digital Composition." *Instrumentalist* 41 (Dec. 1986): 15–18.
A general overview of music produced by computers.

4737.   Mathews, Max V., and John R. Pierce. "The Bohlen-Pierce Scale." In *Current Directions in Computer Music,* ed. Max V. Mathews and John R. Pierce. Cambridge, Mass.: MIT Press, 1989: 165–73.

4738.   Mechtler, Peter. "Ist Komponieren formalisierbar?" *Österreichische Musikzeitschrift* 39 (1984): 447–51.

4739.   Merrill, Sally. "Composing Computers." *Science Digest* 90 (Jan. 1982): 79.

4740.   Mollia, Michela. "Modelli generativi e compositivi nella computer music." [Generative Models and Composites in Computer Music] In *Musica e tecnologia: industria e cultura per lo sviluppo del mezzogiorno: VI Colloquio di Informatica Musicale, Napoli 16–19 ottobre 1985,* ed. Carlo Acreman; Immacolata Ortosecco; and Fausto Razzi. Milan: Edizioni Unicopli, 1987: 411–16.

4741.   Müller, Werner. "Entwurf eines Systems zur digitalen Musikverarbeitung." M.A. diss., Üchnische Univ., Wien, 1982. 49 p.

4742.   Nelson, Gary Lee. "Algorithmic Approaches to Interactive Composition." In *Proceedings, 1989 International Computer Music Conference, November 2–5, the Ohio State University, Columbus, Ohio.* San Francisco, Calif.: Computer Music Association, 1989: 219–22.

4743.   Nieberle, Rupert C.; Paul Modler; and Marcus Verwiebe. "The CAMP System: An Approach for Integration of Realtime, Distributed and Interactive Features in a Multiparadigm Environment." In *Proceedings of the 14th International Computer Music Conference, Cologne, September 20–25, 1988,* ed. Christoph Lischka and Johannes

Fritsch. Cologne: Feedback-Studio-Verlag; San Francisco, Calif.: Dist. by Computer Music Association, 1988: 250–57. (Feedback Papers; 33)

A description of the requirements and design goals for a universal computer music system suitable for both algorithmic composition and interactive performance using a connected network of Atari ST computers.

4744. Oppenheim, Daniel V. "Dmix: An Environment for Composition." In *Proceedings, 1989 International Computer Music Conference, November 2–5, the Ohio State University, Columbus, Ohio.* San Francisco, Calif.: Computer Music Association, 1989: 226–33.
Also issued as: Technical Report STAN-M-60. Stanford, Calif.: Center for Computer Research in Music and Acoustics, Department of Music, Stanford University, 1989. 8 p.

4745. ———. "The Need for Essential Improvements in the Machine-Composer Interface Used for the Composition of Electroacoustic Computer Music." In *Proceedings of the International Computer Music Conference 1986, Royal Conservatory, The Hague, Netherlands, October 20–24, 1986,* ed. Paul Berg. San Francisco, Calif.: Computer Music Association, 1986: 443–45.

4746. ———. "The P-G-G Environment for Music Composition: A Proposal." In *Proceedings of the 1987 International Computer Music Conference: University of Illinois at Urbana-Champaign, Urbana, Illinois, USA, August 23–26, 1987,* comp. James Beauchamp. San Francisco, Calif.: Computer Music Association, 1987: 40–48.

4747. Oppenheimer, Larry. "The Arrival of Intelligent Instruments." *Electronic Musician* 3 (Aug. 1987): 36–52.

An overview of algorithmic composition, with comments from Joel Chadabe and Laurie Spiegel, and reviews of some programs.

4748. Pagni, C. "Generazione automatica di strutture musicali ritmiche e melodiche per l'elaboratore CX5M." [The Automatic Generation of Rhythmic and Melodic Musical Structures with the CX5M Computer] Tesi di Laurea in Scienze dell'Informazione, A.A., Università degli Studi, Milano, 1987.

4749. Pope, Stephen T. "Modeling Musical Structures as EventGenerators." In *Proceedings, 1989 International Computer Music Conference, November 2–5, the Ohio State University, Columbus, Ohio.* San Francisco, Calif.: Computer Music Association, 1989: 249–52.

4750. Pope, Stephen T. "Music Notations and the Representation of Musical Structure and Knowledge." *Perspectives of New Music* 24 (Spring–Summer 1986): 156–89.

4751.   Pressing, Jeff. "Nonlinear Maps as Generators of Musical Design."
         Computer Music Journal 12,2 (Summer 1988): 35–46.

4752.   Roads, Curtis. "Esperienze di composizione assistita dal calcolatore."
         [Experiences of Computer Assisted Composition] In *I profili del*
         suono: scritti sulla musica electroacustica e la computer music, ed.
         Serena Tamburini and Mauro Bagella. Salerno: Musica Verticale-
         Galzerano, 1987: 173–96.

4753.   Rona, Jeff. "Applications: Taming the Wild Algorithm." *Electronic*
         Musician 5 (Feb. 1989): 86–90.
         A description of how Jam Factory can be utilized in algorithmic
         composition.

4754.   Ruschkowski, André. "Computer in der Musikproduktion." *Musik*
         und Gesellschaft 37 (June 1987): 306–9.
         An historical look at the use of the computer for composition.

4755.   Scaletti, Carla. "Composing Sound Objects in Kyma." *Perspectives of*
         New Music 27 (Winter 1989): 42–69.

4756.   ———. "Kyma: An Object-oriented Language for Music Composi-
         tion." In *Proceedings of the 1987 International Computer Music*
         Conference: University of Illinois at Urbana-Champaign, Urbana,
         Illinois, USA, August 23–26, 1987, comp. James Beauchamp. San
         Francisco, Calif.: Computer Music Association, 1987: 49–56.

4757.   Scheidt, Daniel J. "A Prototype Implementation of a Generative
         Mechanism for Music Composition." M.S. diss., Queen's University,
         1985.

4758.   Schottstaedt, Bill. "Automatic Counterpoint." In *Current Directions in*
         Computer Music, ed. Max V. Mathews and John R. Pierce. Cam-
         bridge, Mass.: MIT Press, 1989: 199–214.

4759.   ———. "A Computer Music Language." In *Current Directions in*
         Computer Music, ed. Max V. Mathews and John R. Pierce. Cam-
         bridge, Mass.: MIT Press, 1989: 215–24.
         A description of the PLA language for composition.

4760.   Schroeder-Limmer, Walter. "Die Orgelklänge kommen aus dem Com-
         puter: Wie 'kreative' Rechner Choräle und Fugen generieren können.
         Teil I." *Neue Musikzeitung* 35 (Juni–Juli 1986): 38.

4761.   ———. "Die Orgelklänge kommen aus dem Computer: Wie 'kreative'
         Rechner Choräle und Fugen generieren können. Teil II." *Neue*
         Musikzeitung 35 (Aug.–Sept. 1986): 38.

4762.   Schulz, Claus-Dieter. "Algorithmen, Computer und Komposition: ein
         Beispiel." *Musica* 41 (1987): 151–52.

4763. Schweizer, Alfred. "Elektronik und Kompositorisches Schaffen." In *Die Musikerziehung in Zeitalter der Elektronik: 20. DACH-Tagung, Golling, Salzburg, April–Mai 1988: Tagungsbericht,* ed. Brigitte Peschl. Vienna: VWGÖ, 1989: 79–81.

4764. Spangler, Clark. "Song Construction." *Music, Computers & Software* 3 (Oct. 1988): 80–82.

A discussion of song writing with the aid of MIDI sequencers.

4765. Steels, Luc. "Learning the Craft of Musical Composition." In *Proceedings of the International Computer Music Conference 1986, Royal Conservatory, The Hague, Netherlands, October 20–24, 1986,* ed. Paul Berg. San Francisco, Calif.: Computer Music Association, 1986: A-27–A-31.

4766. Stiglitz, Alberto. "Un sistema per l'elaborazione automatica di strutture musicali mediante operatori geometrici." [A System for the Automatic Computation of Musical Structures by Means of Geometric Operations] Tesi di Laurea in Fisica, A.A., Università degli Studi, Milano, 1988.

4767. Strawn, John. "Computer und Musik in den USA, ein kurzer historischer Überblick." *Österreichische Musikzeitschrift* 39 (1984): 459–62.

A history of the use of the computer in composition.

4768. Streitberg, Bernd, and Klaus Balzer. "The Sound of Mathematics." In *Proceedings of the 14th International Computer Music Conference, Cologne, September 20–25, 1988,* ed. Christoph Lischka and Johannes Fritsch. Cologne: Feedback-Studio-Verlag; San Francisco, Calif.: Dist. by Computer Music Association, 1988: 158–65. (Feedback Papers; 33)

4769. Sundberg, Johan; Anders Askenfelt; and Lars Frydén. "Musical Performance: A Synthesis-by-Rule Approach." *Computer Music Journal* 7,1 (Spring 1983): 37–43.
Reprinted in *The Music Machine,* ed. Curtis Roads. Cambridge, Mass.: MIT Press, 1989: 693–99.

4770. Taube, Heinrich. "Common Music: A Compositional Language in Common Lisp and CLOS." In *Proceedings, 1989 International Computer Music Conference, November 2–5, the Ohio State University, Columbus, Ohio.* San Francisco, Calif.: Computer Music Association, 1989: 316–19.

4771. Thomas, Marilyn Taft; Siddhartha Chatterjee; and Mark W. Maimone. "CANTABILE: A Rule-based System for Composing Melody." In *Proceedings, 1989 International Computer Music Conference, November 2–5, the Ohio State University, Columbus, Ohio.* San Francisco, Calif.: Computer Music Association, 1989: 320–23.

4772.   Tipei, Sever. "The Computer: A Composer's Collaborator." *Leonardo* 22,2 (1989): 189–95.

Includes a description of the author's composition software, MP1.

4773.   ———. "Manifold Compositions: A (Super)Computer-assisted Composition Experiment in Progress." In *Proceedings, 1989 International Computer Music Conference, November 2–5, the Ohio State University, Columbus, Ohio.* San Francisco, Calif.: Computer Music Association, 1989: 324–27.

4774.   Todd, Peter M. "A Connectionist Approach to Algorithmic Composition." *Computer Music Journal* 13,4 (Winter 1989): 27–43.

4775.   Vandenheede, Jan. "Musical Experiments with Prolog II." In *Proceedings of the International Computer Music Conference 1986, Royal Conservatory, The Hague, Netherlands, October 20–24, 1986*, ed. Paul Berg. San Francisco, Calif.: Computer Music Association, 1986: 5–10.

4776.   Waschka, Rodney, and Alexandra Kurepa. "Using Fractals in Timbre Construction: An Exploratory Study." In *Proceedings, 1989 International Computer Music Conference, November 2–5, the Ohio State University, Columbus, Ohio.* San Francisco, Calif.: Computer Music Association, 1989: 332–35.

4777.   Wehinger, Rainer. "Musik und Computer: Anregung zu Kompositorischen Experimenten." In *Die Musikerziehung in Zeitalter der Elektronik: 20. DACH-Tagung, Golling, Salzburg, April–Mai 1988: Tagungsbericht*, ed. Brigitte Peschl. Vienna: VWGÖ, 1989: 63–78.

4778.   Winsor, Phil. *Computer Assisted Music Composition: A Primer in BASIC.* Princeton, N.J.: Petrocelli Books, 1987. 339 p.

4779.   ———. *Computer Composer's Toolbox.* Blue Ridge Summit, Pa.: Windcrest, 1989. 246 p.

4780.   Yavelow, Christopher. "Composition or Improvisation? Only the Computer Knows." In *The Proceedings of the AES 5th International Conference: Music and Digital Technology*, ed. John Strawn. New York, N.Y.: Audio Engineering Society, 1987: 83–99.

4781.   ———. "The Impact of MIDI upon Compositional Methodology." In *Proceedings of the International Computer Music Conference 1986, Royal Conservatory, The Hague, Netherlands, October 20–24, 1986*, ed. Paul Berg. San Francisco, Calif.: Computer Music Association, 1986: 21–27.

4782.   Yocum, Neal W. "Using a Digital Soundfile Mixing Program as a Compositional Tool; *Extensions* for Concert Band and Tape." D.M.A. diss., Ohio State University, 1988. 156 p.

4783. Zahler, Noel. "Isomorphism, Computers, and the Multi-Media Work." In *Proceedings of the 1987 International Computer Music Conference: University of Illinois at Urbana-Champaign, Urbana, Illinois, USA, August 23–26, 1987,* comp. James Beauchamp. San Francisco, Calif.: Computer Music Association, 1987: 228–29.

4784. "Zwölftonmusik auf dem Computer." *Musik und Bildung* 18 (Juni 1986): 598–99.

COMPOSITIONS

4785.   Ames, Charles. *"Concurrence."* *Interface* 17 (1988): 3–24.

A description of the automated techniques used by the author to create the piece *Concurrence* for solo violin.

4786.   ———. "Stylistic Automata in *Gradient."* *Computer Music Journal* 7,4 (Winter 1983): 45–56.
Reprinted in *The Music Machine,* ed. Curtis Roads. Cambridge, Mass.: MIT Press, 1989: 157–68.

4787.   ———. "Two Pieces for Amplified Guitar." *Interface* 15 (1986): 35–58.

The article addresses the problems encountered by the author while programming a computer to compose his *Excursion* and *Artifacts* for solo amplified guitar.

4788.   Appleton, Jon H. "Otahiti: The Evolution of A Personal Style." In *On the Wires of Our Nerves,* ed. Robin Julian Heifetz. Lewisburg, Pa.: Bucknell University Press, 1989: 155–62.

4789.   Bachmann, Claus-Henning. "Inventionen '84 in West-Berlin; eine Zwischenbilanz elektroakustischer Musik." *Österreichische Musikzeitschrift* 39 (1984): 260–61.

Concert review.

4790.   Beggio, Bernardino. "Performance strumentale e supporto magnetico: alcune esperienze di esecuzione." [Instrumental Performance and Magnetic Stand: Some Experiences of Execution] In *I profili del suono: scritti sulla musica electroacustica e la computer music,* ed. Serena Tamburini and Mauro Bagella. Salerno: Musica Verticale-Galzerano, 1987: 165–71.

4791.   Boulanger, Richard. "Interview with Roger Reynolds, Joji Yuasa, and Charles Wuorinen." *Computer Music Journal* 8,4 (Winter 1984): 45–54.
Previously **484.**
Reprinted in *The Music Machine,* ed. Curtis Roads. Cambridge, Mass.: MIT Press, 1989: 51–60.

4792.   Briner, Andres. "Eine Zürcher Konzertreihe mit Computer-Musik." *Österreichische Musikzeitschrift* 44 (Feb. 1989): 94.

Concert review.

4793.   Butler, Allen P. "*Dispeace,* A Hexachordal Composition Using a Computational Model of Common-Tone Design." D.M.A. diss., University of Wisconsin, Madison, 1987. 131 p.

4794.   Campbell, Philip. "Commentary: The Music of Digital Computers." *Nature* 324 (Dec. 11–17, 1986): 523–28.

Descriptions of Jonathan Harvey's *Mortuos Plango, Vivos Voco* and Pierre Boulez' *Répons,* both realized at IRCAM, as representative works of music created by using the computer.

4795.   Chapman, Davis H. "*Three Ideas,* A Collection of Three One-Act (Musical) Plays for Mixed Ensemble." M.M. diss., University of North Texas, 1986. 120 p.

Original musical plays using intermedia, computer music, and performance art.

4796.   Clark, Thomas. "Duality of Process and Drama in Larry Austin's *Sonata Concertante.*" *Perspectives of New Music* 23 (Fall–Winter 1984): 112–25.

4797.   Corner, Philip, and Larry Polansky. "*Delicate Computations.*" *Perspectives of New Music* 25 (Winter 1987/Summer 1987): 473–89.

Score.

4798.   Dashow, James. "Looking into *Sequence Symbols.*" *Perspectives of New Music* 25 (Winter 1987/Summer 1987): 108–37.

4799.   Dodge, Charles. "On *Speech Songs.*" In *Current Directions in Computer Music,* ed. Max V. Mathews and John R. Pierce. Cambridge, Mass.: MIT Press, 1989: 9–17.

4800.   ———. "*Profile:* A Musical Fractal." *Computer Music Journal* 12,3 (Fall 1988): 10–14.

4801.   Gann, Kyle. "Music: Machine Aged." *Village Voice* 33 (Jan. 12, 1988): 80.

Review of a Composer's Forum concert, curated by Neil B. Rolnick.

4802.   Graboca, Marta. "Creazione dell'opera *Krios: il segno dell'ariete* di Laszlo Tihanyi e la Scuola de l'Itineraire." [Creation of the work *Krios: The Sign of Aries* by Laszlo Tihanyi and the Scuola de l'Itineraire] In *I profili del suono: scritti sulla musica electroacustica e la* *computer music,* ed. Serena Tamburini and Mauro Bagella. Salerno: Musica Verticale-Galzerano, 1987: 87–92.

4803.   Grigsby, Beverly P. *"The Mask of Eleanor:* A Chamber Opera in the Form of a Tenso; Music, Libretto, and Staging." D.M.A. diss., University of Southern California, 1986.

4804.   Hall, Jeffrey J. *"Talisman:* The Essay and the Computer Codes." D.M.A. diss., Columbia University, 1987. 162 p.

4805.   Harvey, Jonathan. *"Mortuos Plango, Vivos Voco:* A Realization at IRCAM." *Computer Music Journal* 5,4 (Winter 1981): 22–24.
Previously **508.**
Reprinted in *The Music Machine,* ed. Curtis Roads. Cambridge, Mass.: MIT Press, 1989: 91–99.

4806.   Hendricks, John. "How's Reality: A Study of Art Rock: An Examination of Pop Commercialism, and a Full Length Rock Album." Senior Honors Project, Stanford University, 1989. 69 p. + cassette tape
Discusses the role of computer-generated sounds in art rock; cassette produced using MIDI.

4807.   Hiller, Lejaren A. "Composing with Computers: A Progress Report." *Computer Music Journal* 5,4 (Winter 1981): 7–21.
Previously **516.**
Reprinted in *The Music Machine,* ed. Curtis Roads. Cambridge, Mass.: MIT Press, 1989: 75–89.

4808.   ——. *"Electronic Sonata."* In *On the Wires of Our Nerves,* ed. Robin Julian Heifetz. Lewisburg, Pa.: Bucknell University Press, 1989: 123–32.
A discussion of work realized in 1976 with above title.

4809.   ——. "Sulla programmazione del *Gioco musicale dei dadi* di Mozart." [On the Programming of the *Musical Dice Game* of Mozart] In *I profili del suono: scritti sulla musica electroacustica e la computer music,* ed. Serena Tamburini and Mauro Bagella. Salerno: Musica Verticale-Galzerano, 1987: 137–57.

4810.   ——, and Charles Ames. "Automated Composition: An Installation at the 1985 International Exposition in Tsukuba, Japan." *Perspectives of New Music* 23 (Spring–Summer 1985): 196–215.

4811.   Husarik, Stephen. "John Cage and Lejaren Hiller: *HPSCHD,* 1969." *American Music* 1 (Summer 1983): 1–21.
A discussion of the creation of *HPSCHD.*

4812.   Johnson, David C. "Concert Series with Computer Music, Zurich, Switzerland, 9–12 December 1988." *Computer Music Journal* 13,4 (Winter 1989): 82–85.
Concert review.

4813. Kaske, Stephan. "A Conversation with Clarence Barlow." *Computer Music Journal* 9,1 (Spring 1985): 19–28.
Previously **533.**
Reprinted in *The Music Machine,* ed. Curtis Roads. Cambridge, Mass.: MIT Press, 1989: 25–34.

4814. Keane, David. "Computer Music and Human Engineering: The Making of *Labyrinth.*" In *Proceedings of the 1987 International Computer Music Conference: University of Illinois at Urbana-Champaign, Urbana, Illinois, USA, August 23–26, 1987,* comp. James Beauchamp. San Francisco, Calif.: Computer Music Association, 1987: 364–71.

4815. ———. "*Labyrinth:* i percorsi intricati della progressione e perceziona musicale." [*Labyrinth:* The Intricate Roots of Progression and Musical Perception] In *I profili del suono: scritti sulla musica electroacustica e la computer music,* ed. Serena Tamburini and Mauro Bagella. Salerno: Musica Verticale-Galzerano, 1987: 59–73.

4816. Krupowicz, Stanislaw. "*Only Beatrice* for Amplified String Quartet and Tape." D.M.A. diss., Stanford University, 1989. 32 p.

4817. Langston, Peter S. "(201) 644–2332: Eedie & Eddie on the Wire: An Experiment in Music Generation." In *USENIX Association Summer Conference Proceedings, Atlanta, 1986.* El Cerrito, Calif.: USENIX Association, 1986: 12–27.
Describes the hardware and software of a short automated music concert available over telephone lines.

4818. Lorrain, Denis. ". . . *Black It Stood as Night,* for Magnetic Tape. Duration 1'15". Work Realized at IRCAM, in 1985. Performed in the Final Concert, Saturday, October 19th, 21 h." In *Musica e tecnologia: industria e cultura per lo sviluppo del mezzogiorno: VI Colloquio di Informatica Musicale, Napoli 16–19 ottobre 1985,* ed. Carlo Acreman; Immacolata Ortosecco; and Fausto Razzi. Milan: Edizioni Unicopli, 1987: 461–62.

4819. Mann, Marjorie. "Music: The Arts." *Omni* 9 (Dec. 1986): 38.
Loran Carrier, professor of composition and electronic music at Virginia Commonwealth University, has sampled the sounds made by his hogs and used these sounds in a work called *Swine Lake.*

4820. McNabb, Michael. "*Dreamsong:* The Composition." *Computer Music Journal* 5,4 (Winter 1981): 36–53.
Previously **552.**
Reprinted in *The Music Machine,* ed. Curtis Roads. Cambridge, Mass.: MIT Press, 1989: 101–18.

4821. "MIDI Turns Skyscraper into Synthesizer!" *Music Trades* 134 (Feb. 1986): 52–54.

Review of *OxyLights,* a light and music presentation at the Occidental Chemical Corp. headquarters in Niagara Falls, N.Y.

4822. Momo, Sahlan. "*Euterpe e le sue sorello* o dell'opera multimediale." [*Euterpe and Her Sisters*; or, On Multimedia Opera] In *I profili del suono: scritti sulla musica electroacustica e la computer music,* ed. Serena Tamburini and Mauro Bagella. Salerno: Musica Verticale-Galzerano, 1987: 45–49.

4823. Muggler, Fritz. "Digitale und konkrete Klänge live und ab Band: Computermusik-Tagung in Zürich." *NZ, Neue Zeitschrift für Musik* 150 (Mär. 1989): 44–45.

Concert review.

4824. Négyesy, János, and Lee Ray. "Zivatar: A Performance System." In *Current Directions in Computer Music,* ed. Max V. Mathews and John R. Pierce. Cambridge, Mass.: MIT Press, 1989: 283–89.

4825. Nogueira, Ilza Maria Costa. "*Transforms* for Saxophone Quartet and Computer Generated Magnetic Tape." Ph.D. diss., State University of New York, Buffalo, 1985. 103 p.

4826. Oliveira, Jamary. "*Pseudopodes II.*" D.M.A. diss., University of Texas, Austin, 1986. 101 p.

An orchestral composition written with use of the computer.

4827. "*Oxylights* at Niagara Falls." *Computer Music Journal* 10,2 (Summer 1986): 4.

A musical suite by Thomas Rhea presented at the Fifth Annual Festival of Lights at Niagara Falls.

4828. Pennycook, Bruce W. "*Speeches for Dr. Frankenstein:* An Orchestral Approach to Music Synthesis." *Canadian University Music Review* 4 (1983): 196–203.

4829. Phillips, Gordon. "Electronic Music." *Musical Opinion* 109 (July 1986): 238.

Review of a concert sponsored by the Electro-Acoustic Music Association of Great Britain.

4830. Roads, Curtis. "Sound Structure in *Message.*" In *Proceedings of the 14th International Computer Music Conference, Cologne, September 20–25, 1988,* ed. Christoph Lischka and Johannes Fritsch. Cologne: Feedback-Studio-Verlag; San Francisco, Calif.: Dist. by Computer Music Association, 1988: 392–97. (Feedback Papers; 33)

4831.   Rockwell, John. "Stage: *Hungers,* Computer Opera in Los Angeles." *New York Times* 137 (Sept. 28, 1987): C14.

Concert review of the work by Morton Subotnick and Ed Emshwiller.

4832.   Sapir, Sylviane, and Alvise Vidolin. "Interazioni fra tempo e gesto: note tecniche sulla realizzazione Informatica di *Prometeo.*" [Interactions between Time and Gesture: Technical Notes on the Real-Time Realization of *Prometeo*] In *Musica e tecnologia: industria e cultura per lo sviluppo del mezzogiorno: VI Colloquio di Informatica Musicale, Napoli 16–19 ottobre 1985,* ed. Carlo Acreman; Immacolata Ortosecco; and Fausto Razzi. Milan: Edizioni Unicopli, 1987: 249–74.

4833.   Sbacco, Franco. "Processi di strutturazione in *Variazioni I* e *Riflessioni.*" [The Processes of Structuring in *Variazioni I* and *Riflessioni*] In *I profili del suono: scritti sulla musica electroacustica e la computer music,* ed. Serena Tamburini and Mauro Bagella. Salerno: Musica Verticale-Galzerano, 1987: 75–85.

4834.   Spagnoletti, Luca, and Antonella Talamonti. "*Life Fragments:* per soprano e dispositivo elettroacustico." [*Life Fragments:* For Soprano and Electroacoustic Device] In *I profili del suono: scritti sulla musica electroacustica e la computer music,* ed. Serena Tamburini and Mauro Bagella. Salerno: Musica Verticale-Galzerano, 1987: 95–105.

Text, illustrations, and code for the work *Life Fragments.*

4835.   Terry, Peter R. "*Into Light:* Concerto #1 for Saxophone, Chamber Ensemble, and Computer-generated Tape." D.M.A. diss., University of Texas, Austin, 1986. 104 p.

4836.   Thorington, Helen. "Harris Skibell's *Exchange:* Barter and Bow." *Ear* 14 (June 1989): 16–17.

Describes how Harris Skibell is using the computer to utilize the sounds of the New York Stock Exchange and the violin into a composition.

4837.   Tipei, Sever. "*Maiden Voyages:* A Score Produced with MP1." *Computer Music Journal* 11,2 (Summer 1987): 49–58.

4838.   Torres-Santos, Raymond J. "A Comparative Study of the Formal Structure in Music for an Ensemble and Tape; *Areytos:* A Symphonic Picture for Orchestra and Computer-generated Sound." Ph.D. diss., University of California, Los Angeles, 1986. 141 p.

An analysis of two pieces—Herbert Bielawa's *Spectrum* and Jean-Claude Risset's *Dialogues*—and an original composition.

4839.   Truax, Barry. "*Sequence of Earlier Heaven:* una registrazione di musica elettroacustica." [*Sequence of Earlier Heaven:* A Recording of

Electroacoustic Music] In *I profili del suono: scritti sulla musica electroacustica e la computer music,* ed. Serena Tamburini and Mauro Bagella. Salerno: Musica Verticale-Galzerano, 1987: 25–33.

4840. ———. "Timbral Construction in *Arras* as a Stochastic Process." *Computer Music Journal* 6,3 (Fall 1982): 72–77.
Previously **587.**
Reprinted in *The Music Machine,* ed. Curtis Roads. Cambridge, Mass.: MIT Press, 1989: 137–42.

4841. Vaggione, Horacio. "The Making of *Octuor." Computer Music Journal* 8,2 (Summer 1984): 48–54.
Previously **588.**
Reprinted in *The Music Machine,* ed. Curtis Roads. Cambridge, Mass.: MIT Press, 1989: 149–55.

4842. Waschka, Rodney. "*Missa Salve Regina.*" M.Mus. diss., University of Oregon, 1985. 205 p.
An original composition for chorus and computer.

4843. Wilson, Peter Niklas. "Instrument—Klang—Objekt: Kasseler Musiktage und 'documenta.'" *NZ, Neue Zeitschrift für Musik* 148 (Nov. 1987): 36–37.
Concert review.

4844. Wishart, Trevor. "The Composition of *Vox-5.*" *Computer Music Journal* 12,4 (Winter 1988): 21–27.
Soundsheet in *Computer Music Journal* 13,1 (Spring 1989).

4845. ———. "The Function of Text in the *VOX* Cycle." *Contemporary Music Review* 5 (1989): 189–97.

4846. Wolman, Amnon Y. "*M* for Orchestra and Computer-processed Tape." D.M.A. diss., Stanford University, 1987. 37 p.

COMPUTERS IN MUSIC
EDUCATION

4847.   Albin, Oskar. "Der Computer, ein Weg zur Musik?" In *Die Musik-erziehung in Zeitalter der Elektronik: 20. DACH-Tagung, Golling, Salzburg, April–Mai 1988: Tagungsbericht,* ed. Brigitte Peschl. Vienna: VWGÖ, 1989: 39–50.

4848.   ———. "Der Computer, ein Weg zur Musik?" *Musikerziehung* 42 (Feb. 1989): 99–105.

4849.   Allvin, Raynold. *Basic Musicianship: An Introduction to Music Fundamentals with Computer Assistance.* Belmont, Calif.: Wadsworth Pub. Co., 1985. 180 p. + diskette

For the Apple II series.

4850.   Anshell, Pearl. "Music and Micros—Software Reviews." *Instrumentalist* 39 (Nov. 1984): 90–92.

Review of Practical Music Theory; for the Apple or Commodore.

4851.   Ashley, Richard D. "A Computer System for Learning Analytic Listening." In *Proceedings, 1989 International Computer Music Conference, November 2–5, the Ohio State University, Columbus, Ohio.* San Francisco, Calif.: Computer Music Association, 1989: 5–8.

4852.   ———. "Computer-based Learning: Models and Lessons for Computer Music Systems." In *Proceedings, 1989 International Computer Music Conference, November 2–5, the Ohio State University, Columbus, Ohio.* San Francisco, Calif.: Computer Music Association, 1989: 9–12.

4853.   ———. "Toward a Theory of Instruction in Aural Skills." D.M.A. diss., University of Illinois, Urbana-Champaign, 1982. 170 p.

4854.   Bales, W. Kenton. "Computer-based Instruction and Music Technology in Education." *Journal of Computer-based Instruction* 13 (Winter 1986): 2–5.

4855.   ———, and Roger E. Foltz. "A Comparison of Synthesized and Acoustic Sound Sources in Lower-Division Theory Courses." *Journal of Music Theory Pedagogy* 1 (Spring 1987): 91–103.

4856.   Ball, Matthew P. "Computers in the Band Room." *Woodwind, Brass & Percussion* 24 (Feb. 1985): 21.

4857.   Bartle, Barton K. *Computer Software in Music and Music Education: A Guide.* Metuchen, N.J.: Scarecrow Press, 1987. 252 p.
Review by John Swackhamer and Ann P. Basart in *Cum Notis Variorum* n118 (Dec. 1987): 13.
Review by R.L. Blevins in *Computer Music Journal* 12,2 (Summer 1988): 58.
Review by Marcus L. Neiman in *Instrumentalist* 42 (Apr. 1988): 6.
Review by Peter Manning in *Music and Letters* 70 (1989): 137–39.
Review by Kate Covington in *Computers in Music Research* 1 (Fall 1989): 117–22.

4858.   Baugh, Ivan W. "Using LOGO to Teach the Elements of Music." *Music Educators Journal* 73 (Dec. 1986): 37–39.

4859.   Bieler, Helmut. "Keine Überraschung durch den Synthesizer: Musikelektronik in der Lehrerbildung am Beispiel der Universität Bayreuth." *Neue Musikzeitung* 35 (Feb.–Mär. 1986): 12.

4860.   Biermann, David. "Microtechnology and Music Education." *Music Teacher* 64 (Sept. 1985): 20.

Uses of the computer for music education in Britain.

4861.   ———. "The Yamaha Conquest." *Music Teacher* 62 (Nov. 1983): 18.

How Yamaha instruments were utilized in a British school.

4862.   Blackman, Jaimie M. "The MIDI Potential." *Music Educators Journal* 73 (Dec. 1986): 29.

Discusses the potential uses of MIDI in music education.

4863.   Bleckmann, Heiner, and Niels Knolle. "MIDI-Recording und Musikunterricht: Schülerinnen und Schüler einer Sonderschule produzieren einen Blues auf dem Computer." *Musik und Bildung* 21 (Juni 1989): 334–37.

4864.   Blombach, Ann K. "Tools for Macintosh Music Courseware Development: Hewlett's Representation System and Structured Programming." *Journal of Computer-based Instruction* 16 (Spring 1989): 50–58.

A discussion of computer-assisted music instruction at the Ohio State University.

4865.   Boody, Charles G. "Floppy Discography: Magic Piano." *Music Educators Journal* 74 (Feb. 1988): 104–7.

Software review; for the Apple II.

4866.   Bowen, Sandra. "Electrify Your Students!" *Electronic Music Educator* 1 (Mar. 1989): 1–4.

4867. ———. "Summer Synthesizer Projects." *Clavier* 28 (July/Aug. 1989): 40–41.

The author uses an Apple IIe computer and Kawai and Yamaha synthesizers to attract summer students in a change from the usual piano lessons.

4868. Bowman, Judith A. "Bridging the Gap: Preparing Students for College Music Theory." *Music Educators Journal* 73 (Apr. 1987): 49–52.

4869. ———. "An Investigation of Two Methods of Preparation for College Level Music Theory." Ph.D. diss., Eastman School of Music, University of Rochester, 1984. 160 p.

4870. Brawer, Jennifer. "A+ Teachers' Toolbox." *A+* 6 (June 1988): 90–93.

Describes the San Jose High Academy Music Lab which uses Apple IIe computers as MIDI workstations.

4871. Bray Roger. "The Microcomputer and the Music Teacher." *Music Teacher* 64 (Oct. 1985): 14–15.

4872. Breen, Christopher. "Music for Minors." *MacUser* 4 (Dec. 1988): 40.

Review of KidsNotes, a music education program aimed at young children; for the Macintosh.

4873. Bresler, Liora. "The Role of the Computer in a Music Theory Classroom: Integration, Barriers, and Learning." Ph.D. diss., Stanford University, 1987. 234 p.

4874. Brown, Daphne. "Advantage to Music Teachers!" *Music Teacher* 64 (Nov. 1985): 9.

4875. Bruhn, Gothard. "Mit der Technik sinnvoll umgehen lernen: Zur Verwendung elektronischer Musikinstrumente im Musikunterricht." *Neue Musikzeitung* 34 (Feb.–Mär. 1985): 26.

4876. Burch, Fern. "Bach by Computer: Making Music on the Atari 800." *Classroom Computer Learning* 4 (Apr.–May 1984): 62–63.

The author uses computer music as an incentive to teach students programming in PILOT and BASIC.

4877. "CAI in Music—Minnesota Style: An Inservice and Evaluation Project." *Council for Research in Music Education Bulletin* n87 (Spring 1986): 92.

A project conducted by the Minnesota Department of Education.

4878. Calhoun, Kathryn Scott. "Computerized Drill—Is It Really Helpful?" *Instrumentalist* 40 (June 1986): 24–26.

On the use of computer programs for charting marching band drills.

4879.   Callahan, Gary L. "The Measurement of Finger Dexterity in Wood-wind and Brass Instrumentalists: A Developmental Study." Ph.D. diss., Ohio State University, 1986. 281 p.

4880.   Carey, Doris, and Ray Morse. "Readers Comment: Select Software Carefully." *Music Educators Journal* 71 (Nov. 1984): 7, 11, 14.

4881.   Carlsen, James C., and David Brian Williams. *A Computer Annotated Bibliography: Music Research in Programmed Instruction, 1952–1972.* Reston, Va.: Music Educators National Conference, 1978. 71 p.

4882.   Carpenter, Robert. "MIDI Goes to (Public) School." *Music, Computers & Software* 3 (Nov. 1988): 47, 50.
        A brief overview of the use of MIDI systems in music education.

4883.   Chertok, Nancy M. "The Significance of Computer-assisted Instruction in Teaching Music Fundamentals in the Elementary School." M.M.Ed. diss., University of Louisville, 1986. 102 p.

4884.   Chopp, Joseph M. "The Computer: Integrating Technology with Education." *Music Educators Journal* 73 (Dec. 1986): 22–25.

4885.   Clancy, Glen. "Bank Street MusicWriter." *Computing Teacher* 12 (May 1985): 40–42.
        Review with emphasis on educational applications; for the Commodore 64 or Atari.

4886.   Coale, Kristi. "Scale Models." *MacUser* 4 (Dec. 1988): 42.
        Describes the educational software Guitar Wizard.

4887.   Codding, Peggy A. "The Effect of Differential Feedback on Beginning Guitar Students' Intonational Performance in Tuning Strings." Ph.D. diss., Florida State University, 1985. 206 p.

4888.   Codeluppi, G., and E. Iannuccelli. "Computer and Music Software in an Educative-Formative Role in Italy." In *Proceedings of the International Computer Music Conference 1986, Royal Conservatory, The Hague, Netherlands, October 20–24, 1986,* ed. Paul Berg. San Francisco, Calif.: Computer Music Association, 1986: 341–43.

4889.   Coffman, Don D., and Duane Smallwood. "Some Software Cures for the Rhythm Blues." *Music Educators Journal* 73 (Dec. 1986): 40–43.
        Review of fourteen CAI programs to teach rhythm.

4890.   Cohen, Danny. "Music Shapes: Music Systems for Learning Education Software for the Apple IIe, II+, IIGS, Casio CZ Synthesizer, and

Passport-compatible MIDI Card." *Music, Computers & Software* 2 (Dec. 1987): 64.

Review.

4891. "Companies and Consultants: Products and Services for Electronic Music Educators." *Electronic Music Educator* 1 (Sept. 1988): 16–17.

4892. Conant, Barbara H. "A Study of Cognitive Processes of Children Creating Music in a Computer Learning Environment." Ed.D. diss., University of Massachusetts, 1988. 131 p.

4893. Courtney, James M. "Computerized Drill Writing: A Comparison of Traditional Marching Band Drill Writing Techniques with a Computerized Marching Band Drill Writing Package." D.M.A. diss., Memphis State University, 1987. 279 p.

4894. Crimlisk, Tony. "Music in Action: Music and the Micro." *Music Teacher* 63 (May 1984): 18–20.

A look at the effect the microcomputer has had in music, with a focus on music education.

4895. Dames, Jean, and Douglas Susu-Mago. "Magic Piano." *Computing Teacher* 13 (Nov. 1985): 16–18.

Review; for the Apple II series.

4896. ——, and Douglas Susu-Mago. "Music and Micros—Software Reviews." *Instrumentalist* 39 (June 1985): 44.

Review of Songwriter; for the Apple, Atari, Commodore, or IBM.

4897. ——, and Douglas Susu-Mago. "Music and Micros: Software Reviews: Music Readiness." *Instrumentalist* 39 (July 1985): 59.

For the Apple II series.

4898. ——, and Douglas Susu-Mago. "On Line." *Clavier* 23 (Dec. 1984): 33.

Review of the software program, Songwriter.

4899. ——, and Douglas Susu-Mago. "On Line." *Clavier* 24 (Jan. 1985): 27.

Review of the software program, Music Readiness.

4900. ——, and Douglas Susu-Mago. "On Line." *Clavier* 26 (Sept. 1987): 28–30.

Review of instructional software for the Apple IIGS.

4901. ——, and Douglas Susu-Mago. "On Line." *Clavier* 26 (Nov. 1987): 38.

Describes the A.T.M.I. (Association for Technology in Music Instruction) Courseware Directory.

4902. ——, and Douglas Susu-Mago. "On Line: Alfred's Basic Piano Theory Software." *Clavier* 26 (Mar. 1987): 42.

Software review.

4903. ——, and Douglas Susu-Mago. "On Line: Concertmaster." *Clavier* 24 (Oct. 1985): 30–31.

Software review.

4904. ——, and Douglas Susu-Mago. "On Line: Croakoff Note Recognition." *Clavier* 25 (Jan. 1986): 40–41.

Software review.

4905. ——, and Douglas Susu-Mago. "On Line: Crossword Magic, Music FUNdamentals." *Clavier* 25 (Oct. 1986): 34–35.

Software review.

4906. ——, and Douglas Susu-Mago. "On Line: DiscCovering Rudiments." *Clavier* 26 (Feb. 1987): 30–31.

Software review.

4907. ——, and Douglas Susu-Mago. "On Line: Maestro Scope." *Clavier* 25 (Feb. 1986): 34–35.

Review of Maestroscope Music Theory I, a music theory tutorial; for the Apple II.

4908. ——, and Douglas Susu-Mago. "On Line: Maestroscope Music Theory Level II." *Clavier* 26 (May–June 1987): 28.

Software review.

4909. ——, and Douglas Susu-Mago. "On Line: Mr. Metro Gnome/ Rhythm I." *Clavier* 25 (Nov. 1986): 34–35.

Review of the teaching software Mr. Metro Gnome and Rhythm I; for the Apple or Commodore 64.

4910. ——, and Douglas Susu-Mago. "On Line: Music FUNdamentals." *Clavier* 25 (Oct. 1986): 35.

Review; for the Apple or Atari.

4911. ——, and Douglas Susu-Mago. "On Line: Music Made Easy." *Clavier* 24 (May–June 1985): 30–31.

Software review.

4912. ——, and Douglas Susu-Mago. "On Line: Music Software Reviews." *Clavier* 23 (Nov. 1984): 46–47.

Review of Music Games.

4913.   ——, and Douglas Susu-Mago. "On Line: Practical Music Theory." *Clavier* 24 (Apr. 1985): 24–25.

Software review.

4914.   ——, and Douglas Susu-Mago. "On Line: Rhythmmaster." *Clavier* 24 (Dec. 1985): 25.

Software review.

4915.   ——, and Douglas Susu-Mago. "On Line: So You're a Novice." *Clavier* 24 (July–Aug. 1985): 27.

A review of past articles.

4916.   ——, and Douglas Susu-Mago. "On Line: Teaching Assistant, Study Guide." *Clavier* 24 (Sept. 1985): 28.

Software review.

4917.   ——, and Douglas Susu-Mago. "On Line: Waterloo Software: 'Bare Facts' Series." *Clavier* 25 (Apr. 1986): 24–25.

Software review.

4918.   Dangelo, Eugene M. "The Use of Computer Based Instruction in the Teaching of Music Fundamentals." Ph.D. diss., University of Pittsburgh, 1985. 85 p.

4919.   Davies, Rick. "Resonate's Listen! 2.0: Ear Training Software for the Apple Mac." *Music Technology* 2 (Mar. 1988): 66–67.

Review.

4920.   De Genaro, Mary Jane. "Piano Teachers in a New Age." *Electronic Music Educator* 1 (Dec. 1988): 1–4.

4921.   Deal, John J. "Computer-assisted Instruction in Pitch and Rhythm Error Detection." *Journal of Research in Music Education* 33 (1985): 159–66.

4922.   DeLaine, Thomas H. "The Status of Music Education in the Public Schools of Maryland, 1983–84." D.M.A. diss., Catholic University, 1986. 249 p.

4923.   Dell, Chris. "Off the Peg: Equipment Review." *Classical Guitar* 5 (Nov. 1986): 46.

Review of Guitar Studio 1, educational software; for the Commodore 64.

4924.   DeLoughry, Thomas J. "Computers Are Giving Music Educators New Sounds and New Ways to Teach: Although Many Universities Have High-Tech Studios, Some Professors Are Less Than Enthusiastic." *Chronicle of Higher Education* 34 (Oct. 21, 1987): A14–A16.

4925.   Dennis, Pamela R. "A Manual for the Use of the Computer as an Instructional Tool in the Private Piano Studio." M.C.M. diss., Southern Baptist Theological Seminary, 1986. 137 p.

4926.   Deutsch, Herbert A. "Music Education: Pondering the Future." *Music, Computers & Software* 3 (Nov. 1988): 40–44.

A brief overview of the use of synthesizers in music education.

4927.   Dods, Stuart C. "Preventing Dis-Chord: Learn the Positions of Keyboard Chords." *Rainbow* 7 (June 1988): 140–43.

Program listing of Chord Producer, software to teach piano fingering positions in chords; for the Tandy.

4928.   Dolson, Mark; Abe Singer; and David Rivas. "Personal-Computer Microworlds for Learning about Signals and Sound." In *Proceedings of the 1987 International Computer Music Conference: University of Illinois at Urbana-Champaign, Urbana, Illinois, USA, August 23–26, 1987,* comp. James Beauchamp. San Francisco, Calif.: Computer Music Association, 1987: 341–48.

4929.   Dworak, Paul D. "A Real-Time Pitch Detector for Instructional and Research Applications." *Proceedings of the Research Symposium on the Psychology and Acoustics of Music* (1985): 84–93.

4930.   "An Educator's Guide to Music Software for Kids." *Electronic Music Educator* 1 (Dec. 1988): 17–19.

4931.   Ehle, Robert C. "Some Applications of Computers in Music Theory and Composition." *American Music Teacher* 35 (June–July 1986): 21, 43.

4932.   Eisele, Mark J. "Development and Validation of a Computer-assisted Instructional Lesson for Teaching Intonation Discrimination Skills to Violin and Viola Students." D.Mus.Ed. diss., Indiana University, 1985. 113 p.

4933.   Embry, Dinah. "Music Computer-assisted Instruction." *American Music Teacher* 34 (June–July 1985): 27.

4934.   Enders, Bernd. ". . . Es gibt viel zu tun, warten wir's ab! Anmerkungen zum Vortrag von W. Gruhn." In *Schulmusiklehrer und Laienmusik: Musiklehrerausbildung vor neuen Aufgaben?,* ed. Hans Günther Bastian. Essen: Die Blaue Eule, 1988: 245–48.

4935.   Enders, Bernd, and Ansgar Jerrentrup. "Die Bedeutung der neuen Musiktechnologien für die Musikkultur und die Musikpädagogik." In *Schulmusiklehrer und Laienmusik: Musiklehrerausbildung vor neuen Aufgaben?,* ed. Hans Günther Bastian. Essen: Die Blaue Eule, 1988: 233–39.

4936. Feldstein, Sandy. "An Ear to the Past, an Eye to the Future." *Music Educators Journal* 76 (Nov. 1989): 38–40.

Suggestions for music teachers to take advantage of technology rather than competing with it.

4937. ———. *Music Made Easy: Machine-readable Data File.* Sherman Oaks, Calif.: Alfred Pub., 1984. 48 p. + program disk

Review by Donald Beattie in *American Music Teacher* 36 (June/July 1987): 44–45.

4938. ———. "Technology for Teaching." *Music Educators Journal* 74 (Mar. 1988): 35–37.

4939. Fibich, Friedrich J. "Mikrocomputer in der Musiktheorie: Anwendungen in der Pädagogik." *Zeitschrift für Musikpädagogik* 20 (Nov. 1982): 37–39.

4940. Fisher, Dennis. "Mannheim's Electronic Musicians." *Electronic Music Educator* 1 (Dec. 1988): 6–8.

4941. Flagg, Helen S. "A Computer Concert that Showcases Student Compositions." *Music Educators Journal* 73 (Dec. 1986): 30–32.

4942. "Floppy Discography." *Music Educators Journal* 72 (Sept. 1985): 54–57.

Review of Clef Notes; for the Apple II, Commodore, IBM PC, and Tandy.

4943. Frick, Theodore. "Micros, Minis & Mainframes: What Computer Is Best for You?" *Jazz Educators Journal* 18 (Feb./Mar. 1986): 42–47.

4944. Fritsch, Rolf. "Die zeitgenössische Musik im Tonstudio: Aufgaben und Möglichkeiten der Selbstdarstellung für Musikschulen." *Neue Musikzeitung* 35 (Aug.–Sept. 1986): 23.

4945. Garton, Janet C. "The Efficacy of Computer-based and Tape-recorded Assistance in Second-Semester Freshman Ear-Training Instruction." Ph.D. diss., Louisiana State University and Agricultural and Mechanical College, 1981. 129 p.

4946. Gies, Stefan. "Perspektiven der Computeranwendung in der Musikpädagogik." *Musik und Bildung* 21 (Juni 1989): 328–30.

4947. Gilkes, Lolita Walker. "Magic Piano." *Educational Technology* 25 (Apr. 1985): 49–50.

Review; for the Apple II series.

4948. Gill, Michael J. "Zyklus: A Performer's Analysis; A Video Taped Timpani Method Utilizing Computer Assisted Instruction for Ear Training." Ph.D. diss., University of Southern Mississippi, 1988. 162 p.

4949. Glass, Jacqualine S. "The Effects of a Microcomputer-assisted Tuning Program on Junior High School Students' Pitch Discrimination and Pitch-matching Abilities." Ph.D. diss., University of Miami, 1986. 102 p.

4950. Goldberg, Joe. "Making Music by the Byte: The Computer Offers Musicians and Students a Creative Tool, But Some Say It Can Lead to Passive Users." *New York Times* 137 (Aug. 7, 1988): EDUC56–EDUC60.

4951. Green, Gussie L. "Instructional Use of Microcomputers in Indiana Public High Schools." Ed.D. diss., Ball State University, 1983. 255 p.

4952. Greenberg, Gary. "Computers and Music Education: A Compositional Approach." In *Proceedings of the International Computer Music Conference 1986, Royal Conservatory, The Hague, Netherlands, October 20–24, 1986,* ed. Paul Berg. San Francisco, Calif.: Computer Music Association, 1986: 349–51.

Use of LOGO.

4953. ———. "Music Learning—Compositional Thinking." In *Proceedings of the 14th International Computer Music Conference, Cologne, September 20–25, 1988,* ed. Christoph Lischka and Johannes Fritsch. Cologne: Feedback-Studio-Verlag; San Francisco, Calif.: Dist. by Computer Music Association, 1988: 150–57. (Feedback Papers; 33)

A discussion of Deluxe Music Construction Set.

4954. Greenfield, Dianne G., and Peggy A. Codding. "Competency-based vs. Linear Computer Instruction of Music Fundamentals." *Journal of Computer-based Instruction* 12 (Autumn 1985): 108–10.

4955. Gregory, Dianne. "Applications of Computers in Music Therapy Education." In *Perspectives in Music Therapy Education,* ed. Cheryl D. Maranto and Kenneth E. Bruscia. Philadelphia, Pa.: Temple University, 1987: 71–78. (Temple University Studies on Music Therapy Education; v. 1)

4956. Griffey, Terry, and Dick Grove. "Music and Computers." *Jazz Educators Journal* 18 (Dec./Jan. 1986): 24–25.

4957. Grijalva, Francisco J. "Factors Influencing Computer Use by Music Educators in California Independent Elementary and Secondary Schools." Ed.D. diss., University of San Francisco, 1986. 190 p.

4958. Grove, Dick, and Terry Griffey. "Music and Computers." *Jazz Educators Journal* 18 (Dec./Jan. 1986): 24–25.

A discussion of the IBM PC and Macintosh.

4959. Gruhn, Wilfried. "Musiklernen mit dem Computer? Skill Training versus ästhetische Erfahrung." In *Schulmusiklehrer und Laienmusik:*

Musiklehrerausbildung vor neuen Aufgaben?, ed. Hans Günther Bastian. Essen: Die Blaue Eule, 1988: 204–19.

4960. Grushcow, Bea. "Computers in the Private Studio." *Music Educators Journal* 71 (Jan. 1985): 25–29.

4961. Guérin, François. "Music Pedagogy and the Chip." *Musicanada* n57 (June 1986): 6.
French version: Pédagogie musicale et micro-ordinateur.

4962. Hahn, Christopher. "Musikschulen: Syntone, die erste Synthesizerschule." *Musik International* 42 (Jan.–Feb. 1988): 102.

4963. "Hal Leonard & Syntauri Issue Computer Music Education Program." *Music Trades* 132 (Jan. 1984): 50.
Medley Way music course; for the Syntauri's Simply Music system and an Apple II.

4964. Hansen, Finn E. "Music Education and Technology." *ISME Yearbook* 11 (1984): 60–67.
The effect of technology on musical style and distribution.

4965. Hermanson, Christine. "The MTNA Symposium on Computer-assisted Music Instruction: A Review of the 1988 Symposium and a Preview of the 1989 Sessions." *American Music Teacher* 38 (Feb./Mar. 1989): 26–28.

4966. Hesser, Lois A. "Effectiveness of Computer-assisted Instruction in Developing Music Reading Skills at the Elementary Level." Ed.D. diss., State University of New York at Albany, 1988. 117 p.

4967. Hewig, Dirk. "Musikerziehung im Elektronik-Zeitalter." *Musikerziehung* 41 (Juni 1988): 219–22.

4968. ———. "Musikerziehung im Elektronikzeitalter." In *Die Musikerziehung in Zeitalter der Elektronik: 20. DACH-Tagung, Golling, Salzburg, April–Mai 1988: Tagungsbericht*, ed. Brigitte Peschl. Vienna: VWGÖ, 1989: 7–16.

4969. Hofstetter, Fred T. "Computers in the Curriculum: Art and Music." *Electronic Learning* 4 (May–June 1985): 45–47.

4970. ———. "Evaluation of a Competency-based Approach to Teaching Aural Interval Identification." *Journal of Research in Music Education* 27 (Winter 1979): 201–13.
An evaluation of GUIDO.

4971. ———. "PODIUM: Presentation Overlay Display for Interactive Uses of Media." *Academic Computing* 4 (Nov. 1989): 48–50.

4972. Holland, Marianne. "The Effect of Computer Instruction on the Vertical/Horizontal Music Reading Skills of the Grand Staff for Students Enrolled in Senior High School Beginning Keyboard Classes." Ph.D. diss., University of South Carolina, 1987. 93 p.

4973. Holsinger, Erik. "The Musical Tutor." *Macworld* 4 (Dec. 1987): 148–49.

> Review of Listen 2.0, ear training software; for the Macintosh.

4974. Horan, Catherine. "On Line: Elements of Music." *Clavier* 24 (Mar. 1985): 24, 33.

4975. Hudson, Julie. "The Influence of Computers on Music Educators." *Jazz Educators Journal* 16 (Feb./Mar. 1984): 21.

4976. Hunkins, Arthur B. "Guitar Wizard." *Compute!* 10 (Feb. 1988): 52–53.

> Software review; for the Commodore, Atari, Apple, or Macintosh.

4977. "Idea Bank: Computers in the Classroom." *Music Educators Journal* 73 (Dec. 1986): 44–54.

4978. Ingber, Phil. "The Apple District: The Apple as Musician: New Software Packages Are Music to the Ear." *Electronic Learning* 6 (Nov.–Dec. 1986): 42–43.

> An evaluation of Hear Today . . . Play Tomorrow and Music Printer.

4979. Isaak, Troy J.; Fritz J. Erickson; and John A. Vonk. *Micros and Music: Lesson Plans, a Directory of Software for Achieving Educational Objectives and Procedures for Evaluating Software.* Holmes Beach, Fla.: Learning Publications, 1986. 145 p.

4980. Jackson, Hanley. "CAI in Jazz Education: Converting the Basic Program. Part II." *Jazz Educators Journal* 17 (Feb./Mar. 1985): 51–53.

4981. Jacobs, Richard M. "Technology for Teaching: Computer-controlled Videodiscs: Interactive Lessons." *Music Educators Journal* 76 (Dec. 1989): 64–65.

4982. Jacobsen, Jeffrey R. "Effectiveness of a Computer-assisted Instruction Program in Music Fundamentals Applied to Instruction for Elementary Education Majors." D.M.E. diss., University of Northern Colorado, 1986. 141 p.

4983. Jerrentrup, Ansgar. "Die Angst des Musiklehrers vor Bomben und anderen Überraschungen beim Einsatz des Computers in Unterricht." *Musik und Bildung* 21 (Juni 1989): 331–33.

4984. ———. "Gedanken zu Wilfried Gruhns Beitrag: Musiklernen mit dem Computer?" In *Schulmusiklehrer und Laienmusik: Musiklehrerausbildung vor neuen Aufgaben?*, ed. Hans Günther Bastian. Essen: Die Blaue Eule, 1988: 240–44.

4985. ———, and Jürgen Terhag. "Vom Schüleralltag zur Schülerfreizeit: Möglichkeiten der praktischen Auseinandersetzung mit den neuen kulturellen und musiktechnologischen Entwicklungen. 1. Teil." *Musik und Bildung* 19 (Feb. 1987): 108–15.

4986. ———, and Jürgen Terhag. "Vom Schüleralltag zur Schülerfreizeit: Möglichkeiten der praktischen Auseinandersetzung mit den neuen kulturellen und musiktechnologischen Entwicklungen. 2. Teil." *Musik und Bildung* 19 (Mär. 1987): 204–8.

4987. Jessop, Scott G. "An Application of Sage Analysis in Determining Weaknesses in a Program for Training Secondary Music Teachers." Ph.D. diss., Brigham Young University, 1980. 536 p.

4988. Jordahl, Gregory. "Teaching Music in the Age of MIDI." *Classroom Computer Learning* 9 (Oct. 1988): 78–82.

4989. Jordan-Anders, Lee. "Create Your Own Computer Quiz." *Clavier* 24 (Jan. 1985): 44–45.

4990. Jumpeter, Joseph. "Personalized System of Instruction Versus the Lecture-Demonstration Method in a Specific Area of a College Music Appreciation Course." *Journal of Research in Music Education* 33 (1985): 113–22.

4991. Karpinski, Gary S. "Music and Data Structures: The Application of Music Theory in Programming Computer Assisted Instruction." In *Proceedings, 5th Symposium on Small Computers in the Arts, October 5–8, 1985, Philadelphia, Pennsylvania.* Los Angeles, Calif.: IEEE Computer Society, 1985: 69–72.

4992. Kassner, Kirk. "Rx for Technophobia." *Music Educators Journal* 75 (Nov. 1988): 18–21.

Discusses the new flood of technologically sophisticated electronic instruments, recording and listening devices, and computer music programs, and ways for music teachers to cope.

4993. Kerr, Charles W. "Ear Trainer for the Commodore 128." *Commodore Magazine* 9 (Mar. 1988): 97–99.

Ear training software.

4994. Kevorkian, Kyle. "Teaching & Learning Music." *Keyboard* 14 (June 1988): 58–64.

4995. Killam, Rosemary N. "An Effective Computer-assisted Learning Environment for Aural Skill Development." *Music Theory Spectrum* 6 (1984): 52–62.

4996. King, Richard V. "The Effects of Computer-assisted Music Instruction on Achievement of Seventh-Grade Students." Ph.D. diss., University of Illinois, Urbana-Champaign, 1988. 199 p.

4997. Kirshbaum, Thomas M. "Using a Touch Tablet as an Effective, Low-Cost Input Device in a Melodic Dictation CAI Game." *Journal of Computer-based Instruction* 13 (Winter 1986): 14–16.

4998. Knolle, Niels. "Neue Technologien in der Amateur-Musikszene und Jungendarbeit: Eine Herausforderung für Musiklehrer und Musiklehrerausbildung." In *Schulmusiklehrer und Laienmusik: Musiklehrerausbildung vor neuen Aufgaben?,* ed. Hans Günther Bastian. Essen: Die Blaue Eule, 1988: 220–32.

4999. Kolb, Randall M. "A Real-Time Microcomputer-assisted System for Translating Aural, Monophonic Tones into Music Notation as an Aid in Sightsinging." Ph.D. diss., Louisiana State University and Agricultural and Mechanical College, 1984. 364 p.
Review by William R. Higgins in *Bulletin of the Council for Research in Music Education* n93 (Summer 1987): 49–52.

5000. Kolosick, J. Timothy. "Creative Applications of Technology." *ISME Yearbook* 13 (1986): 59–65.
Describes the MIDI laser videodisk, Postscript (laser printer programming language).

5001. ——. "A Machine-Independent Data Structure for the Representation of Musical Pitch Relationships: Computer-generated Musical Examples for CBI." *Journal of Computer-based Instruction* 13 (Winter 1986): 9–13.

5002. Konecky, Lawrence W. "A Comparison of Two Sequences of Aural Interval Identification Drill Administered to College Students through Computer-assisted Instruction." Mus.Ed.D. diss., University of Southern Mississippi, 1986. 176 p.

5003. Kozerski, Russell A. "Personal Computer Microworlds for Music Composition and Education." Ph.D. diss., University of California, San Diego, 1988. 181 p.

5004. Krout, Robert E. "Microcomputer Use in College Music Therapy Programs." *Journal of Music Therapy* 26 (Summer 1989): 88–94.

5005. ——. "Software Review: MusicShapes." *Journal of Music Therapy* 25 (Winter 1988): 226–29.

5006. Kufrin, Richard. "PRECOMP/GT—A Graphic Tool for Learning Topics in Computer-assisted Composition." In *Proceedings of the 1987 International Computer Music Conference: University of Illinois at Urbana-Champaign, Urbana, Illinois, USA, August 23–26, 1987,* comp. James Beauchamp. San Francisco, Calif.: Computer Music Association, 1987: 349–55.

5007. Kunitz, Jim. "Business of Teaching: Does Your Studio Need a Computer?" *Clavier* 24 (Sept. 1985): 42–44.

5008. ———. "On Line." *Clavier* 27 (Jan. 1988): 30–31.

Guidelines on evaluating instructional software packages.

5009. Kunitz, Sharon Lohse. "I Like My Computer Because." *Clavier* 23 (Dec. 1984): 42–43.

Discusses various possible uses of the computer.

5010. Kuzmich, John. "Computers for Music Teachers: Consider the Software." *Instrumentalist* 38 (Apr. 1984): 10–14.

5011. ———. "Four Distinctive Marching Band Programs: Product Summaries." *School Musician* 56 (June–July 1985): 6–12.

Covers MEI Marching Band Show Design, Charting Aid System, Show Writer, and MEI Precision Drill.

5012. ———. "Four Distinctive Marching Band Programs: What to Look for in Show Designer Software." *School Musician* 56 (May 1985): 10–13.

Describes MEI Marching Band Show Design, Charting Aid System, Show Writer, and MEI Precision Drill.

5013. ———. "Instrumental Music Technique Software—Check It Out." *School Musician* 57 (Mar. 1986): 10–13.

5014. ———. "Marching Band Computer Show Designs: Getting Involved—Step-by-Step." *School Musician* 57 (June–July 1986): 8–11.

5015. ———. "New Styles, New Technologies, New Possibilities in Jazz." *Music Educators Journal* 76 (Nov. 1989): 41–46.

5016. ———. "Tuning Software: Applied Ear Training." *School Musician* 58 (Nov. 1986): 4–7.

5017. Lamb, Martin. "Sympathetic Computerised Ear Training." *ISME Yearbook* 11 (1984): 159–62.

Uses the organ keyboard and computer for ear training.

5018. Lancaster, E. L. "A Computer for Every Studio." *Clavier* 23 (Sept. 1984): 44–46.

5019.   ——. "On Line: Music Software Reviews." *Clavier* 23 (Oct. 1984): 46–47.

An overview of nine music software programs.

5020.   LaRose, Paul. "Synthesizers and Smiles in Broward County Schools." *Electronic Music Educator* 1 (Sept. 1988): 1–4.

5021.   Lawn, Rick. "Computer Assisted Instruction in Jazz Education: Sequencers and Software: A Descriptive Guide for Music Educators." *Jazz Educators Journal* 20 (Feb./Mar. 1988): 27–31, 56–58.

Includes recommendations for sequencer software for Macintosh and IBM computers.

5022.   Littlefield, Patti. "Basic Guitar 1, Tutorial-Software Package for Apple." *InfoWorld* 5 (Jan. 24, 1983): 46–48.

Review.

5023.   Lowe, Donald R. "Floppy Discography: Orchestral String Teacher's Assistant." *Music Educators Journal* 74 (Jan. 1988): 65–67.

Software review; for the Apple II, Commodore, and IBM PC.

5024.   Mahin, Bruce P.; E. L. Lancaster; and Ken Renfrow. "On Line." *Clavier* 28 (Sept. 1989): 36–37.

Reviews of Perceive, a computer-assisted ear training program for the Macintosh, and Theory Readiness, a program to introduce music fundamentals to young students for the Apple.

5025.   Makas, George. "On Line: Sebastian II." *Instrumentalist* 40 (May 1986): 76–79.

Software review; for the Apple II.

5026.   Margolis, Jerome N. "A School Music Synthesizer Program Comes of Age." *Music Educators Journal* 74 (Dec. 1987): 32–36.

5027.   Mash, David S. "Future Class: Digital Music Workstations as Creative Classroom Tools." *Jazz Educators Journal* 21 (Winter 1989): 19–21, 39.

5028.   McCarthy, James F. "Computer Assisted Instruction in Music: What Managers Should Know." *Proceedings of the National Association of Schools of Music* n72 (1984): 52–55.

5029.   McDowell, Linwood. "The Laptop Music Teacher." *PCM: The Personal Computer Magazine for Tandy Computer Users* 4 (June 1987): 12–17.

Includes a BASIC program that assists in the teaching of music notation.

5030. McGreer, Dennis M. "The Research Literature in Computer-assisted Instruction." *Update: Applications of Research in Music Education* 3 (Fall 1984): 12–15.

5031. McPherson, Gary. "Computer Programs." *International Journal of Music Education* n11 (1988): 74.

    Review of Practica Musica; for the Macintosh.

5032. Mechtler, Peter. "Computermusik an Österreichs Hochschulen: Eine topograhische Zusammenfassung." *Österreichische Musikzeitschrift* 39 (1984): 463–64.

5033. Meckley, William A. "The Development of Individualized Music Learning Sequences for Non-Handicapped, Handicapped, and Gifted Learners Using the LOGO Music Version Computer Language." Ph.D. diss., Eastman School of Music, University of Rochester, 1985. 190 p.

5034. Medsker, Larry. "A Course in Computers and Music." *Collegiate Microcomputer* 1 (May 1983): 133–40.

5035. Mee, Robert Arthur. "The Integration and Evaluation of *Musicland* in a Music Listening Course and Acoustics Course for Tenth Grade Students." Ph.D. diss., Eastman School of Music, University of Rochester, 1988. 309 p.

5036. Messina, Tony. "Building a MIDI Studio." *Down Beat* 56 (June 1989): 56–57.

    A checklist for assembling a MIDI studio in a school.

5037. ——. "Guest Editorial: Educators Get with It!" *Keyboard* 14 (May 1988): 14–16.

5038. Milak, Melba S. "A Study Comparing Computer Pitch Drills with Piano Pitch Drills." *Missouri Journal of Research in Music Education* 5,1 (1982–83): 80–107.

5039. Miller, Anne W. "Feasibility of Instruction in Instrumental Music Education with an Interactive Videodisc Adapted from Existing Media." Ph.D. diss., University of Illinois, Urbana-Champaign, 1987. 143 p.
Review by Steven K. Hedden in *Council for Research in Music Education Bulletin* n100 (Spring 1989): 27–33.

5040. Miller, Michael. "Sounds Useful: A Primary Music Project with the BBC Micro." *British Journal of Music Education* 3 (Nov. 1986): 259–66.

    Sounds Useful is a collection of music programs designed for elementary school use; for the BBC micro.

5041.   Moore, Brian R. "Music and Computers in the Middle School." *Dialogue in Instrumental Music Education* 11 (Fall 1987): 86–94.

5042.   Moore, Herb, and Holly Brady. "Kids Can Write Music!" *Classroom Computer Learning* 6 (May 1986): 12–15.
A short overview of the following programs: Bank Street MusicWriter, Magic Piano, Music Construction Set, Music Shop, Music Studio, and Rock 'n' Rhythm.

5043.   Moorhead, Jan Paul. "Software: Computers and Your Brain: Musical Aerobics." *Electronic Musician* 3 (Oct. 1987): 26–36.
A listing of music-instruction programs.

5044.   ——. "Take Note, Ear-Training Software." *Electronic Musician* 5 (Sept. 1989): 82–83.

5045.   Moran, Karen M. "Music Logo." *Classroom Computer Learning* 7 (Mar. 1987): 16.
Review; for the Apple II series.

5046.   Morgenstern, Steve. "The Notable Phantom." *Family Computing* 4 (Apr. 1986): 83.
Review of software to teach the names, sounds, and position of the notes on the staff; for the Apple, Commodore 64/128, and IBM PC and PCjr.

5047.   Mulhern, Tom. "Software: Chro-Magic: Guitaristics for the Atari ST." *Guitar Player* 23 (Feb. 1989): 159.
Review of software to teach scales and chords on the guitar.

5048.   "Musiklernen mit dem Computer." *Instrumentenbau-Musik International* 43 (Juli–Aug. 1989): 36–39.
Interview with Bernd Enders.

5049.   Myers, Mike. "Teachers' Forum: MIDI and the Percussion Teacher." *Modern Drummer* 12 (July 1988): 50–52.

5050.   Neiman, Marcus L. "On Line." *Instrumentalist* 41 (Aug. 1986): 49–50.
Software review of Tuner Intonation Drill, Interval Drillmaster, and Double Reed Fingering; for the Apple II series.

5051.   ——. "On Line." *Instrumentalist* 41 (Dec. 1986): 92–93.
Software review of Clef Notes, Elements of Music, Music Flash Cards; for the Apple, Commodore, Victor, and IBM.

5052.   ——. "On Line." *Instrumentalist* 41 (Jan. 1987): 77.
Software review of CAMUS (Computer-assisted Music Units in Solfege); for the Apple or IBM.

5053. ———. "On Line." *Instrumentalist* 41 (Feb. 1987): 12.
Software review of Early Music Skills; for the Apple, IBM, or Commodore.

5054. ———. "On Line: Aural Skills." *Instrumentalist* 41 (May 1987): 88.
Software review; for the Apple, Commodore, or IBM.

5055. ———. "On Line: Music Education Series." *Instrumentalist* 42 (Nov. 1987): 8–10.
Software review; for the Apple and Commodore.

5056. ———. "On Line: Swan Software." *Instrumentalist* 41 (Nov. 1986): 93.
Software review; for the Apple and Commodore.

5057. ———. "On Line: The Percussion Rudiment Tester." *Instrumentalist* 42 (Jan. 1988): 74.
Software review; for the Apple.

5058. ———. "On Line: The Rhythm Machine." *Instrumentalist* 41 (Sept. 1986): 95.
Software review; for the Apple.

5059. Nelson, Beth Johanna P. "The Development of a Middle School General Music Curriculum: A Synthesis of Computer-assisted Instruction and Music Learning Theory." D.M.A. diss., Eastman School of Music, University of Rochester, 1988. 306 p.

5060. Nelson, Judy Ruppel. "Music Software for Kids." *Electronic Music Educator* 1 (Dec. 1988): 16–17.

5061. Nelson, Robert, and Carl J. Christensen. *Foundations of Music: A Computer-assisted Introduction.* Belmont, Calif.: Wadsworth Pub. Co., 1987. 221 p. + floppy disc
For Apple II series.

5062. Newcomb, Steven R. "Computer-based Arts Instruction: How Are We Doing?" *Design for Arts in Education* 89 (May–June 1988): 46–49.

5063. Pembrook, Randall G. "Some Implications of Students' Attitudes toward a Computer-based Melodic Dictation Program." *Journal of Research in Music Education* 34 (1986): 121–33.

5064. Perelman, Charles R. "Education: B$ Sharp." *80 Micro* n38 (Mar. 1983): 236–43.
A BASIC program for the TRS-80 to teach note recognition to children.

5065.   Peters, G. David. "The Fourth Revolution in Education and Music." In *Symposium in Music Education: A Festschrift for Charles Leonhard,* ed. Richard Colwell. Urbana: University of Illinois, Urbana-Champaign, 1982: 299–316.

5066.   ——, and David Atwater. "MIDI-Tutor Laboratory: Keyboard Instruction with Computers." *Jazz Educators Journal* 19 (Oct./Nov. 1986): 29–30, 76–77.

5067.   Phillips, Chris. "This Guitar Tutor Doesn't Fret." *Rainbow* 3 (June 1984): 162–73.

A BASIC program that teaches major, minor, seventh, minor seventh, augmented, and diminished chords in all 12 keys; for the TRS-80.

5068.   "Piano Teachers Are Joining the Computer Age." *Changing Times* 39 (June 1985): 70–71, 73.

5069.   Pierce, Susan; William D. Davis; and Dwight D. Satterwhite. "Viewpoint: The Pros and Cons of Computer Applications to Music Education." *Georgia Music News* 47 (Fall 1986): 44–45.

5070.   Placek, Robert W. "Floppy Discography." *Music Educators Journal* 72 (Oct. 1985): 20–23.

Review of Micro-trumpet; for the Apple II.

5071.   ——. "Floppy Discography." *Music Educators Journal* 72 (Nov. 1985): 14–17.

Review of Basic Musicianship; for the Apple II.

5072.   ——. "Floppy Discography." *Music Educators Journal* 72 (Dec. 1985): 8–11.

Review of Practical Music Theory; for the Apple II and Commodore.

5073.   ——. "Floppy Discography." *Music Educators Journal* 72 (Jan. 1986): 17–19.

Review of Mr. Metro Gnome and Rhythm II; for the Apple II and Commodore.

5074.   ——. "Floppy Discography." *Music Educators Journal* 72 (Feb. 1986): 18–21.

Review of Tuner Intonation Drill; for the Apple II.

5075.   ——. "Floppy Discography." *Music Educators Journal* 72 (May 1986): 67–70.

Software review of Music FUNdamentals—Beginning Music III: Extending Rhythm and Melody Skills; for the Apple II and Atari.

5076.   ——. "Floppy Discography: AtariMusic I—Notes and Steps." *Music Educators Journal* 72 (Apr. 1986): 21–22.

Software review; for the Atari.

5077.   ——. "Floppy Discography: Foundations of Music: A Computer-assisted Introduction." *Music Educators Journal* 73 (Mar. 1987): 56–58.

Software review; for the Apple II.

5078.   ——. "Floppy Discography: GUIDO Music Learning System: Ear Training Lessons." *Music Educators Journal* 74 (Oct. 1987): 76–79.

Software review; for the IBM.

5079.   ——. "Floppy Discography: Guitar Wizard." *Music Educators Journal* 73 (Sept. 1986): 57–59.

Software review; for the Apple II.

5080.   ——. "Floppy Discography: Keyboard Fingerings." *Music Educators Journal* 72 (Mar. 1986): 18–20.

Software review; for the Apple II and Commodore.

5081.   ——. "Floppy Discography: Keyboard Jazz Harmonies." *Music Educators Journal* 74 (Dec. 1987): 68–71.

Software review; for the Apple II, IBM PC, Tandy, and Commodore.

5082.   ——. "Floppy Discography: Listen." *Music Educators Journal* 73 (Jan. 1987): 18–21.

Software review; for the Macintosh.

5083.   ——. "Floppy Discography: Music: Scales and Chords." *Music Educators Journal* 73 (Nov. 1986): 60–61.

Software review; for the Commodore, Atari, and Acorn.

5084.   ——. "Floppy Discography: MusicShapes." *Music Educators Journal* 74 (Apr. 1988): 57–60.

Software review; for the Apple II.

5085.   ——. "Floppy Discography: Piano Theory Software." *Music Educators Journal* 74 (Sept. 1987): 73–76.

Software review; for the Apple II or IBM PC.

5086.   ——. "Floppy Discography: Rhythmaticity." *Music Educators Journal* 73 (Oct. 1986): 72–75.

Software review; for the Commodore.

5087.   ——. "Floppy Discography: Trumpet Fingerings." *Music Educators Journal* 73 (Apr. 1987): 58–61.

Software review; for the Commodore and Apple.

5088. ——. "Floppy Discography: University of Delaware Videodisc Music Series." *Music Educators Journal* 73 (May 1987): 22–24.
Review.

5089. ——, and David L. Jones. "Getting Started: Designing and Programming a CAI Music Lesson." *Music Educators Journal* 73 (Dec. 1986): 33–36.

5090. Pogue, David. "Reviews: Practica Musica 2.0." *Macworld* 5 (Dec. 1988): 164–66.
Ear training software; for the Macintosh.

5091. Prevel, Martin, and Fred Sallis. "Real Time Generation of Harmonic Progressions in the Context of Microcomputer-based Ear Training." *Journal of Computer-based Instruction* 13 (Winter 1986): 6–8.

5092. "Publishing Pioneer Re-defines Sheet Music with Computer Venture." *Music Trades* 132 (July 1984): 96.
Describes Computer Sheet Music, a program that provides beginning keyboard students an interactive way to play music and learn; for the Apple II and Commodore 64.

5093. Rae, Richard. "AmigaNotes." *Amazing Computing* 2,9 (1987): 43–45.
Reviews of Music Student I and Quiz Master; for the Amiga.

5094. Rees, F. J. "A PLATO-based Videodisc Self-Instructional Program for Directing the Development of String Vibrato Technique." *Journal of Educational Technology Systems* 14,4 (1985–86): 283–96.
Previously presented as a paper at the NCCBMI interest group session of the Twenty-seventh Annual ADCIS Conference, Philadelphia, March 1985.

5095. Reimer, Bennett. "Music Education as Aesthetic Education: Toward the Future." *Music Educators Journal* 75 (Mar. 1989): 26–32.

5096. Riggs, Robert L. "Computers: A Music Teacher's Asset." *Instrumentalist* 40 (Oct. 1985): 40–42.
A short look at uses of a computer for music teachers.

5097. Righter, Dennis, and Rebecca Mercuri. "The Yamaha DX-7 Synthesizer: A New Tool for Teachers." In *Proceedings, 5th Symposium on Small Computers in the Arts, October 5–8, 1985, Philadelphia, Pennsylvania.* Los Angeles, Calif.: IEEE Computer Society, 1985: 73–75.

5098. Roach, Donald W. "Automated Aural-Visual Music Theory Instruction for Elementary Education Majors." *Journal of Research in Music Education* 22 (1974): 313–18.

5099. Robinson, Phillip. "The Music Class: Software." *A +* 6 (Feb. 1988): 70–77.

Review.

5100. "Roland Advances Computer Music Education." *Music Trades* 133 (Nov. 1985): 32.

Roland donates CMU-800 Compu-Music Systems to schools.

5101. Rose, Richard F. "Computer-assisted Swing!" *Jazz Educators Journal* 17 (Feb./Mar. 1985): 14–15.

5102. Ross, Gary S., and Jeremy Bernstein. "Breakdancing with the Turtle." *Classroom Computer Learning* 6 (May 1986): 65.

A short description of a student project to choreograph music and dance in Logo.

5103. Rumery, Kenneth R. "Computer Applications in Music Education." *T.H.E. Journal* 14 (Sept. 1986): 97–99.

The results of a survey show that significant numbers of postsecondary schools use computers for music instruction.

5104. Saif, Yasin Ramadan. "Development of Computer-assisted Instruction for Use in Teaching Arabic Music Theory." Ph.D. diss., University of Southern California, 1988.

5105. Salbert, Dieter. "Eine ungeheuere Menge von Möglichkeiten: Computergestützte Keyboards in der Anwendung im Hochschulbereich." *Neue Musikzeitung* 35 (Apr.–Mai 1986): 38.

5106. Schaffer, John W. "Developing an Intelligent Music Tutorial: An Investigation of Expert Systems and Their Potential for Microcomputer-based Instruction in Music Theory." Ph.D. diss., Indiana University, 1988. 269 p.

5107. Schechter, Jeffrey. "TechnoTeens: Kids Confront Computer Music Making at Summer Camp." *High Fidelity/Musical America* 34 (Apr. 1984): 50.

A report on the Appel Farm Arts and Music Center in Elmer, N.J.

5108. Schmitt, Rainer. "Es herrscht eine trügerische Ruhe im Land: Gedanken zur Notwendigkeit einer Neuorientierung in der Musikdidaktik." *Neue Musikzeitung* 37 (Juni–Juli 1988): 26–27.

5109. Schmitt, Werner. "Das Elektronische Instrumentarium an der Musikschule: Allgemeine Betrachtungen aus der Sicht eines Musikschulleiters." In *Die Musikerziehung in Zeitalter der Elektronik: 20. DACH-Tagung, Golling, Salzburg, April–Mai 1988: Tagungsbericht*, ed. Brigitte Peschl. Vienna: VWGÖ, 1989: 99–106.

5110. Schooley, John H. "Learning & Teaching through Technology at Home and in School: Computers Open the Door to New Ways of Mastering Music." *High Fidelity/Musical America* 34 (Feb. 1984): MA14–MA17.

5111. Schultz, Russ. "Bibliography: An Annotated List of Available Computer Programs." *Proceedings of the National Association of Schools of Music* n71 (1983): 121–27.

5112. Shannon, Don W. "Aural-Visual Interval Recognition in Music Instruction: A Comparison of a Computer-assisted Approach and a Traditional In-Class Approach." D.M.A. diss., University of Southern California, 1982.

5113. Skelton, Dennis L. "The Implementation of a Model Program of Computer-assisted Instruction for Children's Choirs in a Church Setting." D.M.A. diss., Southern Baptist Theological Seminary, 1988. 270 p.

5114. Smith, Dorothy. "Technology that Teaches." *Gallaudet Today* 18,4 (1988): 3–13.

The use of technology to teach the hearing-impaired subjects such as music.

5115. "Software: Side by Side." *Electronic Learning* 4 (May–June 1985): 48–49.

A comparison of eight music-software packages.

5116. Solomon, Edward S. "The P.C. and the P.I." *Instrumentalist* 43 (Apr. 1989): 52.

Uses of the computer by the private instructor.

5117. Sorisio, Linda. "Design of an Intelligent Tutoring System in Harmony." In *Proceedings of the 1987 International Computer Music Conference: University of Illinois at Urbana-Champaign, Urbana, Illinois, USA, August 23–26, 1987,* comp. James Beauchamp. San Francisco, Calif.: Computer Music Association, 1987: 356–63.

Describes THEory of MUSic Expert Systems (THE MUSES), a tutoring system in harmony.

5118. Steinhaus, Kurt A. "Putting the Music Composition Tool to Work." *Computing Teacher* 14 (Dec.–Jan. 1986/87): 16–18.

How to use music composition packages in the classroom.

5119. ——. "Software That's Music to Your Ears." *Computing Teacher* 14 (Feb. 1987): 23–26.

Includes descriptions of seven software packages for the Apple II.

5120. Steinke, Greg A. "Performance and Composition in the Future: Towards a New Interdisciplinarity." *Proceedings of the National Association of Schools of Music* n77 (1989): 11–24.

5121. Sternberg, Kristen. "Software Reviews: Making Music on Micros." *Electronic Learning* 5 (Feb. 1986): 52.

Review of software issued by Random House; for the IBM PC or Apple II series.

5122. Strudler, Neal. "Exploring Music with Logo." *Computing Teacher* 12 (Mar. 1985): 16–18.

Use of Logo programming to create monophonic music on the Apple II.

5123. Swan, Paul D. "Running a Computer in the Bandroom." *Instrumentalist* 41 (Aug. 1986): 46–48.

5124. "Taking Computers into the Classroom: Two New Software Packages." *Musical Opinion* 110 (May 1987): 143.

A description of Mupados and Music Master for the BBC Micro.

5125. Taylor, Jack A. "Computers in Music and Music Instruction: The Joys of Hardware and the Woes of Software." *Design for Arts in Education* 89 (May–June 1988): 50–55.

5126. Thornburg, David D. "Computers and Society: Creativity with Constraints." *Compute!* 10 (Apr. 1988): 46–47.

Discusses the use of programs such as Jam Session and Dancin' Feats to develop basic music skills.

5127. ——. "Learning Curve: Computers in Space and Music." *A + 7* (Apr. 1989): 85–86.

5128. Turner, Tony. "Sorting the Sheep from the Goats." *Music Teacher* 68 (Apr. 1989): 21–22.

How to make choices about educational music computer programs.

5129. Tutaj, Duane. "Music and Micros—Software Reviews." *Instrumentalist* 39 (Feb. 1985): 95–97.

Review of M.E.C.C. Music Theory; for the Apple.

5130. ——. "On Line: Wenger's Akron Series Music Software." *Instrumentalist* 40 (Mar. 1986): 63, 81.

Software review.

5131. ——. "On Line: Wenger's Akron Series Music Software." *Instrumentalist* 40 (Apr. 1986): 94.

Continuation of review.

5132. Vail, Mark. "MIDI with Class: Leading College Educators on Their Electronic Music Programs." *Keyboard* 14 (Sept. 1988): 74–88.

5133.   Wagner, Michael J. "Technology: A Musical Explosion." *Music Educators Journal* 75 (Oct. 1988): 30–33.

A reminder to teachers to come up-to-date with music technology to be on the same level as students.

5134.   Walnum, Clayton. "Review: Guitar Wizard." *Analog Computing* n59 (Apr. 1988): 76–77.

For the Atari and Commodore.

5135.   Walsh, Kevin. "Imaja: Listen: Ear Training Software for the Macintosh." *Music, Computers & Software* 2 (Aug. 1987): 76.

Review.

5136.   ———. "Practica Musica, an Ear Training Program by Jeffrey Evans." *Music, Computers & Software* 3 (Apr. 1988): 69, 76.

Review.

5137.   ———. "Reading, 'Riting, and Algorithmatic: An Overview of Music Education Software." *Music, Computers & Software* 2 (Oct. 1987): 45–48.

5138.   Waltzer, Neil. "Basics: Educating the New Musician." *Electronic Musician* 2 (Oct. 1986): 28–29.

5139.   Warrick, James. "Starting a High School Synthesizer Ensemble. Part I." *Jazz Educators Journal* 19 (Dec./Jan. 1987): 30–33, 81–83.

5140.   Wasjack, Brigitte, and Stephan Knaf. "Microcomputer und Musiklernen—ein Anachronismus?" *Musik und Bildung* 18 (Okt. 1986): 895–97.

5141.   Watt, Dan. "Musical Microworlds: New Software Could Lead to a Breakthrough in Music Learning and Creativity." *Popular Computing* 3 (Aug. 1984): 91–94.

Educational uses of MusiCalc I, Music Construction Set, Music Designer II, Musicland, and Songwriter.

5142.   Weeks, Douglas G. "The Effectiveness of Using Computer-assisted Instruction with Beginning Trumpet Students." Ed.D. diss., Boston University, 1987. 94 p.

Review by Joseph D. Secrest in *Bulletin of the Council for Research in Music Education* n102 (Fall 1989): 89–94.

5143.   Weinberg, Norman. "Focus on Performance: Electronic Percussion—The Educational Side of Electronic Drums. Part 1." *Percussive Notes* 26 (Fall 1987): 51–54.

How job-related skills can be gained by learning to work with the various components of an electronic percussion studio.

5144. ――. "Focus on Performance: Electronic Percussion—The Educational Side of Electronic Drums. Part 2." *Percussive Notes* 26 (Winter 1988): 43–47.

How drum machines can be used to improve a player's technique and control of time, tempo, and rhythmic accuracy.

5145. Weiss, Lane. "Rock 'n' Rhythm." *Computing Teacher* 12 (May 1985): 37–38.

Review; for the Commodore 64 or Atari.

5146. Weissman, Ronald F. E. "Workstations in Higher Education." *Academic Computing* 3 (Oct. 1988): 10–65.

5147. Wesley, Michael D. "Playing It by Ear." *MacUser* 3 (July 1987): 55–56.

Review of Practica Musica, ear training software; for the Macintosh.

5148. "What's New in the Electronics Industry?" *Electronic Music Educator* 1 (Mar. 1989): 9–14.

5149. Whiston, Sandra K. "The Development of Melodic Concepts in Elementary School Age Children Using Computer-assisted Instruction as a Supplemental Tool." Ph.D. diss., Ohio State University, 1986. 264 p.

5150. Wilbers, Jan. "Hoe staat het met de computergestuurde gehoortraining?" [How Is the Situation with Computerized Ear Training] *Mens en Melodie* 40 (Jan. 1985): 14–22.

5151. Willett, Barbara E., and Anton J. Netusil. "Music Computer Drill and Learning Styles at the Fourth-Grade Level." *Journal of Research in Music Education* 37 (Fall 1989): 219–29.

5152. Williams, David Brian, and Dennis R. Bowers. *Designing Computer-based Instruction for Music and the Arts.* Bellevue, Wash.: Temporal Acuity Products, 1986. 210 p.

For the Apple II series.

5153. Wittlich, Gary E. "Computers and Music: Marching Band Show Design Computer Software." *School Musician* 56 (Jan. 1985): 22–23.

Review.

5154. ――. "Computers and Music: Software Reviews. Part 1, Maestroscope: Music Theory, Level I and II." *School Musician* 56 (Mar. 1985): 28–29.

5155. ――. "Computers and Music: Software Reviews. Part 2." *School Musician* 56 (May 1985): 24–25, 27.

Review of Clef Notes, Spell and Define, Early Music Skills, and Music Flash Cards.

5156. ———. "The State of Research in Music Theory—Computer Applications: Pedagogy." *Music Theory Spectrum* 11 (Spring 1989): 60–65.

5157. Wolfe, George. "CAI in Jazz Education." *Jazz Educators Journal* 16 (Feb./Mar. 1984): 12–14.
Includes reviews of five software packages.

5158. ———. "CAI in Jazz Education: Considerations for Designing Jazz Software." *Jazz Educators Journal* 18 (Oct./Nov 1985): 43–45.

5159. ———. "CAI in Jazz Education: What to Look for in Educational Software. Part II." *Jazz Educators Journal* 16 (Apr./May 1984): 23–24, 82.

5160. ———. "Computer Systems for Disabled Musicians." *Jazz Educators Journal* 19 (Dec./Jan. 1987): 70–74.
Describes an alternative keyboard interface.

5161. ———, and John Kuzmich. "CAI in Jazz Education." *Jazz Educators Journal* 17 (Oct./Nov. 1984): 27–28.

5162. Wood, Robert W., and Peter J. Clements. "Systematic Evaluation Strategies for Computer-based Music Instruction Systems." *Journal of Computer-based Instruction* 13 (Winter 1986): 17–24.

5163. Wuellner, Guy. "Word Processing and Piano Lessons." *American Music Teacher* 38 (Jan. 1989): 28–29.

5164. Yelton, Geary. "Review: Listen: Ear Training for the Mac." *Electronic Musician* 3 (May 1987): 86–87.

5165. Zientara, Marguerite. "Hitting the High Notes: Software for Teaching Music Gives Students New Enthusiasm." *InfoWorld* 6 (Apr. 30, 1984): 22–23.
A general description of educational software for microcomputers.

CONFERENCES

5166. Acreman, Carlo; Immacolata Ortosecco; and Fausto Razzi, eds. *Musica e tecnologia: industria e cultura per lo sviluppo del mezzogiorno: VI Colloquio di Informatica Musicale, Napoli 16–19 ottobre 1985.* [Music and Technology: Industry and Culture for the Development of the South: Sixth Colloquium of Musical Informatics, Naples, 16–19 October 1985] Milan: Edizioni Unicopli, 1987. 515 p. (Quaderni di Musica/Realtà; 14)
Contains items: 4662, 4672, 4698, 4740, 4818, 4832, 5210, 5245, 5860, 6780, 6784, 7729, 8065, 8093, 8107, 8128, 8136, 8152, 8221, 8244, 8250, 8256, 8276, 8279, 8342, 8365, 8395, 8396, 8562, 8571, 8601, 8620, 8725, 8743, 8751, 8789, 8817, 8820, 8850.

5167. Anderton, Craig. "Commentary: AES: The Changing of the Guard: Music and MIDI Make Inroads." *Electronic Musician* 4 (Jan. 1988): 25–26.

Comments on new trends in the AES conventions.

5168. ———. "High-Tech Update: Signal Processing, Recording, and Synthesis." *Guitar Player* 19 (Feb. 1985): 42–47.

A review of the AES Convention, New York, 8–11 October 1984.

5169. ———. "The Man Behind Musicom: Felix Visser." *Polyphony* 10 (Apr. 1985): 18–20.

Interview by Craig Anderton.

5170. Austin, Larry. "Report from Vancouver: 1985 International Computer Music Conference." *Perspectives of New Music* 23 (Spring–Summer 1985): 252–65.

5171. Austin, Robert. "Digicon 85." *Perspectives of New Music* 23 (Spring–Summer 1985): 266–72.

5172. Batel, Günther. "Zeitgenössische Computermusik: Bemerkungen zum 4. Synthesizer-Musik-Festival Braunschweig." *Musik und Bildung* 17 (Sept. 1985): 623–24.

5173.   Beauchamp, James, comp. *Proceedings of the 1987 International Computer Music Conference: University of Illinois at Urbana-Champaign, Urbana, Illinois, USA, August 23–26, 1987.* San Francisco, Calif.: Computer Music Association, 1987. 373 p.
Contains items: 4650, 4654, 4679, 4697, 4706, 4708, 4712, 4713, 4715, 4746, 4756, 4783, 4814, 4928, 5006, 5117, 5246, 5261, 5271, 5283, 5692, 5955, 6361, 6524, 6676, 6689, 6695, 6700, 6703, 6709, 6719, 6738, 6744, 6893, 6911, 6914, 6959, 6966, 6975, 7296, 8270, 8287, 8307, 8312, 8322, 8334, 8338, 8341, 8360, 8379, 8385, 8614.

5174.   Beckman, Jesper. "Længe leve mangfoldigheden: Systemes Personnels et Informatique Musicale Ircam d. 11–13/10 1986, International Computer Music Conference 1986, Royal Conservatory, The Hague 20–24/10 1986." *Dansk Musiktidsskrift* 61 (1986–87): 211–12.
In Danish.

5175.   Benneth, Gerald. "Enkelhed og kompleksitet i elektro-akustisk musik: et indlæg ved ICEM konferencen 26/9 1985 i Stockholm." [Singularity and Complexity in Electroacoustic Music: A Contribution at the ICEM Conference, Sept. 26, 1985, in Stockholm] *Dansk Musiktidsskrift* 60,2 (1985–86): 79–81.
In Danish.

5176.   Berg, Paul, ed. *Proceedings of the International Computer Music Conference 1986, Royal Conservatory, The Hague, Netherlands, October 20–24, 1986.* San Francisco, Calif.: Computer Music Association, 1986. 463, 36 p.
Contains items: 4651, 4652, 4684, 4691, 4703, 4731, 4745, 4765, 4775, 4781, 4888, 4952, 5234, 5279, 5635, 5952, 6097, 6677, 6681, 6693, 6713, 6740, 6748, 6758, 6759, 6765, 6781, 6782, 6797, 6821, 6862, 6863, 6865, 6866, 6877, 6887, 6889, 6894, 6899, 6903, 6904, 6912, 6919, 6943, 6960, 6998, 7164, 7223, 7224, 7412, 7555, 7628, 7700, 7728, 7761, 7767, 7907, 7924, 8077, 8092, 8121, 8138, 8204, 8293, 8295, 8297, 8299, 8300, 8303, 8311, 8314, 8318, 8319, 8323, 8324, 8330, 8332, 8333, 8337, 8339, 8340, 8347, 8349, 8351, 8352, 8362, 8364, 8367, 8369, 8375, 8383, 8392, 8406, 8510, 8675, 8773, 8821.

5177.   Blum, Thomas L. "Concerts at the 1988 International Computer Music Conference, Cologne, September 1988." *Computer Music Journal* 13,2 (Summer 1989): 86–89.

5178.   Camurri, Antonio, and Roberto Pischiutta. "Report from the Sixth Colloquium on Musical Informatics." *Interface* 15 (1986): 59–68.
Conference held in the Villa Pignatelli, Naples, Italy, 17–19 October 1985.

5179.   Desain, Peter, and Henkjan Honing. "Report on the First AIM Conference, Sankt Augustin, Germany, September 1988." *Perspectives of New Music* 27 (Summer 1989): 282–89.

5180.   Dupler, Steven. "Biggest Ever AES Sees Future in Digital Light." *Billboard* 99 (Oct. 31, 1987): 1, 98.

5181. Elder, Molly. "Confab: On the Future of Computer Music; Experts Gather at Univ. of Illinois." *Billboard* 99 (Sept. 26, 1987): 51.

A report on the 1987 ICMC.

5182. Essl, Karlheinz. "12. Internationale Computermusik-Konferenz in Den Haag." *Österreichische Musikzeitschrift* 41 (1986): 652–53.

5183. Fischer, Martin. "14. Internationale Computermusik Konferenz (ICMC) in Köln." *Österreichische Musikzeitschrift* 44 (1989): 54–55.

5184. Foster, Peter. "Numero e suono." *Bulletin, the Dolmetsch Foundation* n42 (Sept. 1984): 14.

A report on the 1982 ICMC.

5185. Frederick, Dave. "Art in the Computer Age: A View from Silicon Valley." *Keyboard* 12 (May 1986): 18.

A report on the Silicon Valley Festival of Electronic Arts.

5186. Gabrielsson, Alf, ed. *Action and Perception in Rhythm and Music: Papers Given at a Symposium in the Third International Conference on Event Perception and Action.* Stockholm, Sweden: Royal Swedish Academy of Music, 1987. 237 p. (Publications Issued by the Royal Swedish Academy of Music; no. 55)
Contains items: 6937, 6945, 6946, 6986, 6997.
Review by Robert Rowe in *Computer Music Journal* 13,3 (Fall 1989): 90–92.

5187. Gann, Kyle. "Music: Big Machine, Little Issues: 1987 International Computer Music Conference." *Village Voice* 32 (Sept. 29, 1987): 88.

A report on the 1987 ICMC, Urbana, Illinois.

5188. Goldstein, Dan, and Paul Wiffen. "AES Convention Report." *Music Technology* 1 (Jan. 1987): 44–51.

A review of the AES Convention, Los Angeles, California, November 1986.

5189. Hanemann, Dorothee. "Bach Database-Symposion in Kassel." *Musikforschung* 39 (1986): 348–49.

5190. Harris, Brian. "Keyboards: A Look into the Future—Digicon '83." *Canadian Musician* 5 (Dec. 1983): 61.

A report on Digicon '83, Vancouver, B.C.

5191. Harris, Craig R.; Vaughn D'Alia; Paul Berg; Nicola Bernardini; Thomas L. Blum; Michael Century; Roger B. Dannenberg; Denis L'Espérance; John Free; JoAnn Kuchera-Morin; Paul Lansky; Ira Mowitz; Curtis Roads; Allan Schindler; and John Strawn. "Report on the 1985 International Computer Music Conference." *Computer Music Journal* 10,2 (Summer 1986): 10–32.

5192.   Howe, Hubert S. "1984 International Computer Music Conference 19–23 October, Paris, France." *Perspectives of New Music* 23 (Spring–Summer 1985): 236–50.

5193.   Jacoby, Jan. "Elektronmusikfestivalen i Stockholm." [Electronic Music Festival in Stockholm] *Dansk Musiktidsskrift* 58 (1983–84): 200–202.
         In Danish.

5194.   Jenkins, Mark. "Keyboards: Facing the Music: Yamaha DX Convention." *Melody Maker* 61 (Jan. 25, 1986): 34.
         A review of the Yamaha X Series Convention held in London, December 1985.

5195.   Keane, David. "The 1985 Bourges Festival: A Report." *Computer Music Journal* 10,2 (Summer 1986): 56–68.

5196.   Kendall, Gary S.; Richard D. Ashley; Jean-Baptiste Barrière; Roger B. Dannenberg; F. Richard Moore; Jean-Claude Risset, Denis Smalley; and Barry Truax. "Essays on the 1986 International Computer Music Conference." *Computer Music Journal* 11,2 (Summer 1987): 35–48.

5197.   Kuchera-Morin, JoAnn, and Robert Morris. "The 1987 International Computer Music Conference: A Review." *Perspectives of New Music* 26 (Winter 1988): 288–304.

5198.   LaBarbara, Joan. "Electronics: Alive in Brussels." *High Fidelity/Musical America* 32 (Mar. 1982): MA16, MA30–MA31.
         A report on the Second Annual International Festival of Electronic Music, Video and Computer Art, Brussels, October 28–November 10, 1981.

5199.   Laske, Otto E. "Comments on the First Workshop on A.I. and Music: 1988 AAAI Conference, St. Paul, Minnesota." *Perspectives of New Music* 27 (Summer 1989): 290–98.

5200.   Lehrman, Paul D. "State of the Arts." *High Fidelity/Musical America* 34 (Jan. 1984): 60–61.
         A report on Digicon '83.

5201.   Lischka, Christoph, and Johannes Fritsch, eds. *Proceedings of the 14th International Computer Music Conference, Cologne, September 20–25, 1988*. Cologne: Feedback-Studio-Verlag; San Francisco, Calif.: Dist. by Computer Music Association, 1988. 436 p. (Feedback Papers; 33) Contains items: 4655, 4658, 4671, 4702, 4707, 4743, 4768, 4830, 4953, 5233, 5235, 5699, 5784, 5880, 5956, 6046, 6110, 6156, 6214, 6718, 6721, 6864, 6869, 6886, 6892, 6977, 6991, 6996, 7653, 7730, 8142, 8223, 8252, 8298, 8301, 8304, 8305, 8308, 8310, 8313, 8335, 8504, 8545, 8603, 8749, 8770, 8799.

5202. Logemann, George W. "Report on the Last STEIM Symposium on Interactive Composing in Live Electronic Music." *Computer Music Journal* 11,3 (Fall 1987): 44–47.

5203. Lunell, Hans. "Rapporter: ICMC 86 i Haag-Några Intryck." [Reports: ICMC 86 in the Hague: Some Impressions] *Nutida Musik* 30,3 (1986–87): 52.
In Danish.

5204. ——. "Rapporter: ICMC—Konferense i Köln." [Reports: ICMC Conference in Cologne] *Nutida Musik* 32,3 (1988–89): 52–53.
In Danish.

5205. Martin, Gottfried. "Acustica 86—Symposium für elektroakustische Musik." *Österreichische Musikzeitschrift* 41 (1986): 402–3.
Symposium held May 12–16, 1986, sponsored by GEM, the Hochschule für Musik, and Darstellende Kunst Wien.

5206. McConkey, Jim, and Ruth Dreier. "Report on the Fifth Annual Symposium on Small Computers in the Arts." *Computer Music Journal* 10,2 (Summer 1986): 69–74.
Held in Philadelphia, Pennsylvania, 6–8 October 1985.

5207. Moog, Bob. "International Computer Music Conference: Platypus, Granules, Kyma, Daton & the DSP56001 in Your Future." *Keyboard* 13 (Dec. 1987): 24–25.

5208. Page, Stephen. "Conference." *Musical Times* 127 (Oct. 1986): 576.
A description of the Oxford University Programming Research Group, 9–10 July 1986.

5209. Peschl, Brigitte, ed. *Die Musikerziehung in Zeitalter der Elektronik: 20. DACH-Tagung, Golling, Salzburg, April–Mai 1988: Tagungsbericht.* Vienna: VWGÖ, 1989. 123 p. (AGMÖ-Publikationsreihe; Bd. 16)
Contains items: 4642, 4763, 4777, 4847, 4968, 5109, 5866, 6928.

5210. Piccialli, Aldo. "Obiettivi ed articolazione del VI Colloquio di Informatica Musicale." [Objectives and Articulations of the VI Colloquio di Informatica Musicale] In *Musica e tecnologia: industria e cultura per lo sviluppo del mezzogiorno: VI Colloquio di Informatica Musicale, Napoli 16–19 ottobre 1985,* ed. Carlo Acreman; Immacolata Ortosecco; and Fausto Razzi. Milan: Edizioni Unicopli, 1987: 60–61.

5211. Pope, Stephen T., and Elizabeth Gibson. "ACM SIGCHI 1989 Conference on Computer Human Interaction, Austin, Texas, 30 April–5 May 1989." *Computer Music Journal* 13,4 (Winter 1989): 78–82.

5212. *Proceedings, 1989 International Computer Music Conference, November 2–5, the Ohio State University, Columbus, Ohio.* San Francisco, Calif.: Computer Music Association, 1989. 339 p.

Contains items: 4663, 4666, 4714, 4725, 4730, 4742, 4744, 4749, 4770, 4771, 4773, 4776, 4851, 4852, 5251, 5254, 5269, 5272, 5275, 5282, 5285, 6176, 6290, 6541, 6692, 6694, 6754, 6790, 6791, 6805, 6830, 6895, 6897, 6898, 6905, 6979, 7166, 7177, 7485, 7508, 8066, 8110, 8127, 8129, 8130, 8144, 8257, 8266, 8267, 8294, 8296, 8302, 8315, 8317, 8321, 8327, 8329, 8331, 8344, 8355, 8361, 8363, 8366, 8371, 8386, 8390, 8391, 8399, 8400, 8403, 8599, 8646, 8647, 8676, 8691, 8718, 8762, 8771, 8793, 8805, 8810.

5213.   Rahn, John. "ICMC88: Crossroads at Cologne." *Perspectives of New Music* 27 (Winter 1989): 264–71.

5214.   Ranada, David. "Bits & Pieces: Digital News from the AES." *High Fidelity/Musical America* 36 (Jan. 1986): 21.

5215.   Rimmer, John. "Composing for the Computer." *Canzona* 1 (Mar. 1980): 33–34.

The author relates his experiences at the Experimental Music Studio at MIT in 1979.

5216.   Roads, Curtis. "International Workshop on Models of the Singing Voice and Musical Sounds, Sorrento, Italy, 28–30 October 1988." *Computer Music Journal* 13,2 (Summer 1989): 90–92.

5217.   ———. "The Second STEIM Symposium on Interactive Composition in Live Electronic Music." *Computer Music Journal* 10,2 (Summer 1986): 44–50.

5218.   ———; Nicola Bernardini; and Fausto Razzi. "Musica e Tecnologia: Report on the Sixth Italian Computer Conference." *Computer Music Journal* 10,2 (Summer 1986): 33–38.

5219.   Ruschkowski, André. "1. Werkstatt-Tage elektroakustischen Musik." *Musik und Gesellschaft* 38 (Aug. 1988): 436–37.

5220.   Sani, Nicola, and Nicola Bernardini. "1986 International Computer Music Conference, Den Haag: Review in Two Parts." *Perspectives of New Music* 25 (Winter 1987/Summer 1987): 618–37.

5221.   Schloss, W. Andrew. "Report on the Second International Conference of Electroacoustic Music, Varadero, Cuba." *Computer Music Journal* 10,4 (Winter 1986): 89–90.

5222.   Schweiger, Walter. "Acustica 85: Internationales Symposium für elektroakustische Musik." *Österreichische Musikzeitschrift* 40 (1985): 494–95.

A review of a symposium held at the Institut für Elektroakustik und Experimentalmusik, Wien, 25 May–5 June 1985

5223.   Siegel, Wayne. "Rapport fra International Computer Conference, Köln 19.–25. Sep. 1988." *Dansk Musiktidsskrift* 63,3 (1988–89): 110–12.
In Danish.

5224. Stiglitz, Alberto, and Dante Tanzi. "Report on the VIIth Colloquium on Musical Informatics." *Interface* 17 (1988): 127–31.

5225. Strawn, John. "AES 5th International Conference, Music and Digital Technology, 1987 May 1–3, Biltmore Hotel, Los Angeles, Calif., USA." *Journal of the Audio Engineering Society* 35 (Mar. 1987): 154–58.

An introduction to the conference and preliminary program.

5226. ——, ed. *The Proceedings of the AES 5th International Conference: Music and Digital Technology.* New York, N.Y.: Audio Engineering Society, 1987. 248 p.

Contains items: 4780, 6098, 6250, 6366, 6379, 6382, 6495, 6517, 6716, 6909, 7585, 7627, 7629, 7685, 7719, 8099, 8156, 8213, 8541, 8740.

Review by Jim Aikin in *Keyboard* 14 (Feb. 1988): 20.

Review by John Duesenberry in *Computer Music Journal* 12,3 (Fall 1988): 64–68.

5227. Strom, David. "Hollywood's Software Symphony Hums 'Play It Again, Mac' at Festival." *PC Week* 4 (Dec. 15, 1987): 19.

A conference for Macintosh-based musicians, MacMusicFest 1.0, held in Hollywood, December 1987.

5228. Vetter, Hans-Joachim. "Musikerziehung in Zeitalter der Elektronik: 20. D-A-CH-Tagung vom 28. April bis 1. Mai 1988 in Golling bei Salzburg." *Neue Musikzeitung* 37 (Juni–Juli 1988): 44.

5229. Villon, Julie. "Conferences: Report on the Audio Engineering Society Conference on Music and Digital Technology." *Computer Music Journal* 11,4 (Winter 1987): 47–48.

5230. Weiss, Peter. "Computer können nun einmal nicht singen: Ein vortrag bei der D-A-CH-Tagung Ende April in Österreich." *Neue Musikzeitung* 37 (Juni–Juli 1988): 25.

5231. ——. "Computer können nun einmal nicht singen: Ein Vortrag bei der D-A-CH-Tagung Ende April in Österreich. Teil 2." *Neue Musikzeitung* 37 (Aug.–Sept. 1988): 25.

DIGITAL AUDIO

5232.   Barnes, Vince. "Audio-Frequency Analyzer: Build IBM PC Accessories to Analyze Your Stereo." *Byte* 10 (Jan. 1985): 223–50.

5233.   Castine, Peter. "A Survey of Users' Experience with Digital Audio Synthesis." In *Proceedings of the 14th International Computer Music Conference, Cologne, September 20–25, 1988,* ed. Christoph Lischka and Johannes Fritsch. Cologne: Feedback-Studio-Verlag; San Francisco, Calif.: Dist. by Computer Music Association, 1988: 277–96. (Feedback Papers; 33)

5234.   Cogan, Robert. "Imaging Sonic Structure." In *Proceedings of the International Computer Music Conference 1986, Royal Conservatory, The Hague, Netherlands, October 20–24, 1986,* ed. Paul Berg. San Francisco, Calif.: Computer Music Association, 1986: 407–12.

5235.   Garnett, Guy E., and Bernard Mont-Reynaud. "Hierarchical Waveguide Networks." In *Proceedings of the 14th International Computer Music Conference, Cologne, September 20–25, 1988,* ed. Christoph Lischka and Johannes Fritsch. Cologne: Feedback-Studio-Verlag; San Francisco, Calif.: Dist. by Computer Music Association, 1988: 297–312. (Feedback Papers; 33)

   Presentation of a view of waveguide networks that permits them to be decomposed and recomposed modularly or hierarchically.

5236.   Greenspun, Philip. "Audio Analysis V: Time- and Frequency-Domain Distortions in Digital Signal Processing Systems." *Computer Music Journal* 10,4 (Winter 1986): 79–88.

5237.   Grossmann, A.; M. Holschneider; Richard Kronland-Martinet; and J. Morlet. "Detection of Abrupt Changes in Sound Signals with the Help of Wavelet Transforms." In *Inverse Problems: An Interdisciplinary Study,* ed. P. C. Sabatier. London; Orlando, Fla.: Academic Press, 1987: 289–306. (Advances in Electronic and Electron Physics; suppl. 19)

5238.   Pierce, John R. *The Science of Musical Sound.* New York, N.Y.: Scientific American Library, 1983. 242 p. + 2 sound discs

5239. Pohlman, Ken C. *Principles of Digital Audio.* Indianapolis, Ind.: H. W. Sams, 1985. 285 p.
Review by John Strawn in *Computer Music Journal* 10,3 (Fall 1986): 89.
Review by David Doty in *Electronic Musician* 3 (Sept. 1987): 94–95.

5240. ———. *Principles of Digital Audio.* 2d ed. Indianapolis, Ind.: H. W. Sams, 1989. 474 p.

5241. Radauer, Irmfried. "Bereicherung oder Verarmung." In *Österreich zum Beispiel: Literatur, Bildende Kunst, Film und Musik seit 1968,* ed. Otto Breicha and Reinhard Urbach. Salzburg: Residenz, 1982: 385–87.

Describes a computer program that reproduces sound curves in digital form.

5242. Yates, Keith. "Hi-Fi Floppy." *PC World* 3 (Apr. 1985): 190–96.

Review of CompuSonics' DSP-1000, a prototype digital recording and playback stereo component.

DIGITAL SIGNAL
PROCESSING

5243. Anderton, Craig. "Sonic Tonic: 49 Hot Signal Processing Tips." *Electronic Musician* 5 (Mar. 1989): 28–40, 100–101.

5244. "Applications of Digital Signal Processing in Computer Music." *Woodwind, Brass & Percussion* 23 (Mar. 1984): 24–25.

5245. Balena, F., and Giovanni De Poli. "Un modello semplificato del clarinetto mediante oscillatore non lineare." [A Simplified Model of the Clarinet by Means of a Non-linear Oscillator] In *Musica e tecnologia: industria e cultura per lo sviluppo del mezzogiorno: VI Colloquio di Informatica Musicale, Napoli 16–19 ottobre 1985,* ed. Carlo Acreman; Immacolata Ortosecco; and Fausto Razzi. Milan: Edizioni Unicopli, 1987: 111–38.

5246. Brown, Judith C., and Miller Puckette. "Musical Information from a Narrowed Autocorrelation Function." In *Proceedings of the 1987 International Computer Music Conference: University of Illinois at Urbana-Champaign, Urbana, Illinois, USA, August 23–26, 1987,* comp. James Beauchamp. San Francisco, Calif.: Computer Music Association, 1987: 84–88.

5247. Chafe, Chris, and David A. Jaffe. "Source Separation and Note Identification in Polyphonic Music." In *ICASSP 86 Proceedings: April 7, 8, 9, 10, 11, 1986, Keio Plaza Inter-continental Hotel, Tokyo, Japan.* Piscataway, N.J.: IEEE, 1986: 1289–92.
Also issued as: Technical Report STAN-M-34. Stanford, Calif.: Center for Computer Research in Music and Acoustics, Department of Music, Stanford University, 1986. 4 p.

  Discusses acoustic analysis issued in accurately transcribing polyphonic input.

5248. Chaffin, Jan. "Digital Signal Processing: How It Works, Where It Came from, How It's Being Used." *Keyboard* 15 (Aug. 1989): 32–41, 126.

5249. Chowning, John M., and Bernard Mont-Reynaud. *Intelligent Analysis of Composite Acoustic Signals.* Stanford, Calif.: Dept. of Music, Stanford University, 1986. 29 p. (Department of Music Technical Report STAN-M-36)

5250. Combs, Jim. "A Room with a Vu." *Music, Computers & Software* 3 (Apr. 1988): 39–42.

A discussion of the use of digital signal processing systems.

5251. Desain, Peter. "A Connectionist Quantizer." In *Proceedings, 1989 International Computer Music Conference, November 2–5, the Ohio State University, Columbus, Ohio.* San Francisco, Calif.: Computer Music Association, 1989: 80–85.

5252. "DOD Develops New Custom VLSI Chip." *Music Trades* 136 (Jan. 1988): 30–32.

Describes a new digital signal processing chip.

5253. Dolson, Mark. "The Phase Vocoder: A Tutorial." *Computer Music Journal* 10,4 (Winter 1986): 14–27.

5254. Dutilleux, Pierre. "Spinning the Sounds in Real-Time." In *Proceedings, 1989 International Computer Music Conference, November 2–5, the Ohio State University, Columbus, Ohio.* San Francisco, Calif.: Computer Music Association, 1989: 94–97.

5255. Fryer, Terry. "Digital Sampling: The Roots of Keyboard Sampling." *Keyboard* 12 (Jan. 1986): 114.

A history of current digital sampling techniques.

5256. Gibilaro, W. "Un sistema per l'acquisizione, l'elaborazione e la sintesi di segnali audio digitali." [A System for the Acquisition, Computation, and Synthesis of Digital Audio Signals] Tesi di Laurea in Scienze dell'Informazione, A.A., Università degli Studi, Milano, 1987.

5257. Gotcher, Peter. "Applications: Making Waves. Part 2, Digital Signal Processing." *Electronic Musician* 2 (Aug. 1986): 36–38.

5258. ——. "Digital Sampling: Real-World Uses for Digital Formats." *Keyboard* 14 (Oct. 1988): 125.

Expresses the need to allow digital devices to share audio data directly.

5259. Hebel, Kurt J. "An Environment for the Development of Software for Digital Signal Processing." Ph.D. diss., University of Illinois, Urbana-Champaign, 1989.

5260. ——. "Javelina: An Environment for Digital Signal Processing Software Development." *Computer Music Journal* 13,2 (Summer 1989): 39–47.

5261. ———. "Javelina: An Environment for the Development of Software for Digital Signal Processing." In *Proceedings of the 1987 International Computer Music Conference: University of Illinois at Urbana-Champaign, Urbana, Illinois, USA, August 23–26, 1987,* comp. James Beauchamp. San Francisco, Calif.: Computer Music Association, 1987: 104–7.

5262. Jaffe, David A. "Spectrum Analysis Tutorial. Part 1: The Discrete Fourier Transform." *Computer Music Journal* 11,2 (Summer 1987): 9–24.
Also issued as: Technical Report STAN-M-33. Stanford, Calif.: Center for Computer Research in Music and Acoustics, Department of Music, Stanford University, 1987 (with part 2).

5263. ———. "Spectrum Analysis Tutorial. Part 2: Properties and Applications of the Discrete Fourier Transform." *Computer Music Journal* 11,3 (Fall 1987): 17–35.
Also issued as: Technical Report STAN-M-33. Stanford, Calif.: Center for Computer Research in Music and Acoustics, Department of Music, Stanford University, 1987 (with part 1).

5264. Knapp, R. Benjamin, and Hugh S. Lusted. "A Real-Time Digital Signal Processing System for Bioelectric Control of Music." In *ICASSP 88: 1988 International Conference on Acoustics, Speech, and Signal Processing.* Piscataway, N.J.: IEEE, 1988: 2556–58.

Describes how music is created by placing electrodes on the skin. Signals are then digitally processed using MIDI.

5265. Kovach, Mark A. "MCS Recording." *Music, Computers & Software* 2 (June 1987): 78, 86.

A discussion of noise reduction systems.

5266. ———. "MCS Recording." *Music, Computers & Software* 2 (Aug. 1987): 84–85.

A discussion of equalization in recording.

5267. Kronland-Martinet, Richard. "The Wavelet Transform for Analysis, Synthesis, and Processing of Speech and Music Sounds." *Computer Music Journal* 12,4 (Winter 1988): 11–20.
Soundsheet in *Computer Music Journal* 13,1 (Spring 1989).

5268. Laroche, Jean. "A New Analysis/Synthesis System of Musical Signals Using Prony's Method: Application to Heavily Damped Percussive Sounds." In *ICASSP 89: 1989 International Conference on Acoustics, Speech, and Signal Processing: 23–26 May 1989, Scottish Exhibition & Conference Centre, Glasgow, Scotland.* Piscataway, N.J.: IEEE, 1989: 2053–56.

5269. ———, and Xavier Rodet. "The Use of Prony's Method for the Analysis of Musical Sounds: Application to Percussive Sounds." In

Proceedings, 1989 International Computer Music Conference, November 2–5, the Ohio State University, Columbus, Ohio. San Francisco, Calif.: Computer Music Association, 1989: 168–71.

5270.   Linacher, Joseph James. "A Spectral Analysis of Eight Clarinet Tones." Honors thesis, Stanford University, 1979. 123 p.

5271.   Loy, D. Gareth. "On the Scheduling of Multiple Parallel Processors Executing Synchronously." In *Proceedings of the International Computer Music Conference: University of Illinois at Urbana-Champaign, Urbana, Illinois, USA, August 23–26, 1987,* James Beauchamp. San Francisco, Calif.: Computer Music Association, 1987: 117–24.

5272.   McGee, W. F. "Real-Time Acoustic Analysis of Polyphonic Music." In *Proceedings, 1989 International Computer Music Conference, November 2–5, the Ohio State University, Columbus, Ohio.* San Francisco, Calif.: Computer Music Association, 1989: 199–202.

5273.   Mellinger, David K.; Guy E. Garnett; and Bernard Mont-Reynaud. "Virtual Digital Signal Processing in an Object-oriented System." *Computer Music Journal* 13,2 (Summer 1989): 71–76.

5274.   Miura, Jun; Yasuhiko Yahata; and Kiminori Yamaguchi. "A Study on Annoyance of Musical Signal Using Laeq Measurement and Digital Signal Processing." In *ICASSP 86 Proceedings: April 7, 8, 9, 10, 11, 1986, Keio Plaza Inter-continental Hotel, Tokyo, Japan.* Piscataway, N.J.: IEEE, 1986: 1281–84.

5275.   Naranjo, Michel, and Irène Duc. "Musical Paste and Geometric Image Modelling." In *Proceedings, 1989 International Computer Music Conference, November 2–5, the Ohio State University, Columbus, Ohio.* San Francisco, Calif.: Computer Music Association, 1989: 215–18.

5276.   O'Neill, John C. "Computer Analysis and Synthesis of a Sung Vowel." D.M.A. diss., University of Illinois, Urbana-Champaign, 1984. 131 p.

5277.   Pickover, Clifford A. "Representation of Melody Patterns Using Topographic Spectral Distribution Functions." *Computer Music Journal* 10,3 (Fall 1986): 72–78.

5278.   Pollard, H. F., and Erik V. Jansson. "Analysis and Assessment of Musical Starting Transients." *Acustica* 51 (1982): 249–62.
Summaries in English, French, and German.

    Describes a measuring system for transient musical sounds.

5279.   Potard, Yves; Pierre-François Basinée; and Jean-Baptiste Barrière. "Experimenting with Models of Resonance Produced by a New Technique for the Analysis of Impulsive Sounds." In *Proceedings of the International Computer Music Conference 1986, Royal Conservatory, The Hague, Netherlands, October 20–24, 1986,* ed. Paul Berg. San Francisco, Calif.: Computer Music Association, 1986: 269–74.

5280.   Schumacher, Robert T., and Chris Chafe. *Characterization of Aperi-odicity in Nearly Period Signals.* Stanford, Calif.: Stanford University, Dept. of Music, 1989. 7 p. (Department of Music Technical Report STAN-M-62)

5281.   Smith, Julius O. "Fundamentals of Digital Filter Theory." *Computer Music Journal* 9,3 (Fall 1985): 13–23.
Previously **1166.**
Reprinted in *The Music Machine,* ed. Curtis Roads. Cambridge, Mass.: MIT Press, 1989: 509–19.

5282.   ———. "Unit-Generator Implementation on the NeXT DSP Chip." In *Proceedings, 1989 International Computer Music Conference, November 2–5, the Ohio State University, Columbus, Ohio.* San Francisco, Calif.: Computer Music Association, 1989: 303–6.

5283.   ———. "Waveguide Filter Tutorial." In *Proceedings of the 1987 International Computer Music Conference: University of Illinois at Urbana-Champaign, Urbana, Illinois, USA, August 23–26, 1987,* comp. James Beauchamp. San Francisco, Calif.: Computer Music Association, 1987: 9–16.

5284.   Smoot, Richard J. "The Synthesis and Manipulation of Fused Ensemble Timbres and Sound Masses by Means of Digital Signal Processing." D.M.A. diss., Ohio State University, 1986. 197 p.

5285.   Tarabella, Leonello. "A Digital Signal Processing System and a Graphic Editor for Synthesis Algorithms." In *Proceedings, 1989 International Computer Music Conference, November 2–5, the Ohio State University, Columbus, Ohio.* San Francisco, Calif.: Computer Music Association, 1989: 312–15.

5286.   Wheeler, Douglas B. "An Analytical Study of Bass Drum Sounds." D.A. diss., University of Northern Colorado, 1982. 173 p.
The computer is used to study the variations in spectra of a bass drum.

5287.   Zimmerman, Mark. "A Beginner's Guide to Spectral Analysis. Part 2." *Byte* (Mar. 1981): 166–98.
Part 1 is item **1198.**

RECORD RESTORATION

5288.   Fisher, Lawrence M. "Remove That Static from Old Recordings." *New York Times* 138 (Dec. 21, 1988): D7.

5289.   Uiuagov, A. V. "Vosstanovlenie starykh zvukozapiseĭ s pomoshch'iu évm." [Restoration of Old Sound Recordings with ADP] In *Koli-chestvennye metody v· muzykal'noĭ fol'kloristike i muzykoznanii:*

sbornik stateĭ, ed. É. E. Alekseev; E. D. Andreeva; M. G. Boroda; and A. S. Tangīan. Moscow: Sov. kompozitor, 1988: 218–34.

5290. Vaseghi, Saeed V. "Algorithms for Restoration of Archived Gramophone Recordings." Ph.D. diss., Cambridge University, 1988.

5291. Vaseghi, Saeed V., and Peter J. W. Rayner. "A New Application of Adaptive Filters for Restoration of Archived Gramophone Recordings." In *ICASSP 88: 1988 International Conference on Acoustics, Speech, and Signal Processing.* Piscataway, N.J.: IEEE, 1988: 2548–51.

ELECTRONIC AND PIPE ORGANS

5292. Anderson, Richard C. "Church Organ MIDI Revolution." *Pastoral Music* 12 (June–July 1988): 53.

How church organs can be equipped with MIDI to control other instruments.

5293. Phelps, Lawrence. "The Digital Computer and the Organ." *Pastoral Music* 11 (June–July 1987): 22–26.

MICROCOMPUTERS

5294. Aikin, Jim. "Keyboard Report: Leaping Lizards, MIDI Utilities for the Ensoniq Mirage." *Keyboard* 14 (Jan. 1988): 139.

Review of Iguana, librarian program; Diagnos, diagnostic program; LLDU-1, utility programs; and Mirage Monitor, to program the Mirage's operating system.

5295. Anderton, Craig. "Computers: Making Your Micro Musical." *Electronic Musician* 2 (Aug. 1986): 18–19.

5296. ———. "Computers: Making Your Micro Musical. Part 2, The Software." *Electronic Musician* 2 (Sept. 1986): 41–43.

5297. ———. "MIDIMouse Atari ST Matrix 12/Xpander Librarian with 100 Sounds; Opcode Patch Librarians (with Patch Factory) for the MAC; MIDI Station Xpandit #1 Patch Disk with 100 Sounds." *Electronic Musician* 3 (Dec. 1987): 79–80.

Reviews of patch librarians.

5298. ———. "The Musical Computer: Introduction." *Electronic Musician* 4 (Apr. 1988): 33.

A brief introduction to the "Big Four" computers for music applications: Apple Macintosh, IBM PC and compatibles, Atari ST, and Commodore Amiga.

5299. ———. "New Computers for Electronic Musicians: Bold Challengers Will Test Commodore's Dominance." *Record* 4 (June 1985): 43.

5300. ———. "Snap Software GM70 Companion." *Electronic Musician* 4 (June 1988): 100–101.

A program to assist with system exclusive data to and from the GM70; for the Roland GM70 and Macintosh or IBM

5301. ———. "Software: Ten Software Tips." *Electronic Musician* 3 (Feb. 1987): 36–37.

5302. Arnell, Billy. "MCS Applications." *Music, Computers & Software* 2 (June 1987): 8, 75.

Discusses the use of SMPTE coding with personal computers.

5303. Baker, Gary W. "Personal Computers: To Buy or Not to Buy." *Instrumentalist* 38 (Mar. 1984): 10–11.
Aspects to consider when buying a personal computer.

5304. Bassett, Rick. "Other MIDI Music Makers: Alternatives to PC Sequencing." *PC Magazine* 7 (Nov. 29, 1988): 230–31.
Descriptions of MIDI applications on the Macintosh, Atari, and Commodore.

5305. Bateman, Selby. "The New Music." *Compute!* 9 (May 1987): 18–20.
A general discussion of making music with computers and MIDI.

5306. Beecher, Mike. "Control Zone: Review Computers—Things to Come." *Melody Maker* 59 (Feb. 4, 1984): 38.
Uses of various microcomputers by home hobbyists to make music.

5307. Bigelow, Steven. *Making Music with Personal Computers.* La Jolla, Calif.: Park Row Press, 1987. 118 p.
Review by Bruce P. Mahin in *Instrumentalist* 42 (June 1988): 66–67.
Review by Tom Mulhern in *Guitar Player* 22 (July 1988): 168, 170.

5308. Blech, Volker. "Eine neue Hausmusik? Möglichkeiten und Tendenzen der Heimcomputerpraxis." *Musik und Gesellschaft* 39 (Apr. 1989): 182–86.

5309. Bonner, Paul. "The Sound of Software: New Programs Help You Understand Music and Turn Your Computer into an Instrument." *Personal Computing* 8 (June 1984): 94–107.
A general overview of commercial music software. Includes a listing of publishers.

5310. Boody, Charles G. "Floppy Discography: Deluxe Music Construction Set and Concertware Plus." *Music Educators Journal* 74 (May 1988): 55–57.
Software review; Deluxe Music Construction Set is for the Macintosh and Amiga, ConcertWare + is for the Macintosh.

5311. Bradfield, David. "Zero One Research's Roland D-50 Editor and D-50 Librarian." *Electronic Musician* 5 (Jan. 1989): 99–101.
For the Macintosh and IBM PC.

5312. Bubenik, Anton. "Sättigungsgrenzen, Innovationen, Fossilien: Ein- und Ausblicke auf Vielfalt und Einfallt unserer Medienlandschaft. Teil II." *Neue Musikzeitung* 38 (Apr.–Mai 1989): 39.

5313. Bumgarner, Marlene Anne. "Education/Fun Learning: Bank Street Music Writer." *Family Computing* 3 (May 1985): 80–81.
Review; for the Commodore 64 or Atari.

5314. Burgess, Jim. "The Computer Music Revolution." *Canadian Musician* 8 (June 1986): 56–71.

A broad overview of microcomputers and supporting software, and how they are used by professional musicians.

5315. "Can Your Computer Make Music?" *Changing Times* 39 (June 1985): 72.

A list of software for learning or creating music.

5316. Chaley, Chris. "MIDI: Choosing Your Music Computer." *Canadian Musician* 9 (Oct. 1987): 28.

5317. Chandler, James C. "Applications: Additive Programming: The Secret Life of the Kawai K5." *Electronic Musician* 5 (Feb. 1989): 24–35.

Program listing that converts Mirage samples into a K5 waveform; for a Macintosh or Commodore.

5318. "Coda Music Software Announces Industry-First in Music Transcription." *Canadian Musician* 10 (Oct. 1988): 76.

Introduction to Finale; for Macintosh and IBM computers.

5319. *CODA—The New Music Software Catalog.* Owatonna, Minn.: Wenger Corp, 1986. 160 p.

A listing of software for the Apple II, Commodore, Macintosh, IBM, Atari, and Amiga computers.

5320. Cooper, Jim. "Modifications & Maintenance: Computers: Love 'em or Leave 'em Alone." *Keyboard* 11 (July 1985): 80–81.

Describes the IBM, Apple IIe, Commodore 64, and Macintosh.

5321. Cummings, Steve. "Computer Software for Musicians." *Pastoral Music* 11 (June–July 1987): 16–21.

An overview of Professional Composer for the Macintosh, Personal Composer for the IBM PC, and Polywriter and MIDI/8 Plus; for the Apple II.

5322. ——. "Computers: Brain Power of an Intelligent System: The Top Computers for Music." *Keyboard* 12 (Jan. 1986): 40–42.

5323. ——. "Keyboard Report: Notation/Sequencing Software for IBM PC, Apple IIe & Macintosh Computers." *Keyboard* 11 (Aug. 1985): 82–88.

Review of Professional Composer, Personal Composer, and Passport Designs software.

5324. ——. "Keyboard Report: Voice Editors, Librarians, and System-Exclusive Miscellany." *Keyboard* 12 (Oct. 1986): 126–36.

Review of FM Drawing Board for the Apple or IBM PC, Voice Manager for the IBM PC, CZ Rider for the Commodore or

Apple, CZ Patch Librarian for the Commodore, Apple or Atari, Super Jupiter Secretary for the Apple, Prolib for the IBM PC, and Modzilla for the Apple.

5325.   "Current Events: Computers and Software." *Electronic Musician* 2 (Jan. 1986): 10.

Various new products for microcomputers.

5326.   De Furia, Steve. "Software for Musicians: Programmable MIDI Interfaces." *Keyboard* 12 (Oct. 1986): 114.

An overview of programmable MIDI interfaces; for the Apple, Atari, Commodore, and IBM PC.

5327.   Ehle, Robert C. "Musicians and Computers." *American Music Teacher* 35 (Apr./May 1986): 30–31, 45.

Covers use of microcomputers for music printing, composition, and music instruction.

5328.   Eltgroth, Marlene Bumgarner. "The Music Studio." *Family Computing* 4 (Oct. 1986): 96.

Review of music composition software; for the Amiga, Atari, Commodore, IBM PCjr, and Tandy 1000.

5329.   Emmett, Arielle. "The New Sound of Computerized Music: Digital Synthesis and Personal Computers Put Composers in Tune with a New Kind of Music." *Personal Computing* 7 (July 1983): 72–77, 166–67.

5330.   Fast, Larry. "Attack of the Microprocessors." *Electronic Musician* 2 (Mar. 1986): 26–27.

5331.   Favaro, Peter; Sarah Kortum; and Steven C. M. Chen. "A Musical Departure: Turn Your Computer into a Piano; Then Discover the Secret." *Family Computing* 3 (Feb. 1985): 72–84.

Program listing for a musical puzzle; for the Adam, Apple, Atari, Commodore 64, IBM PC and PCjr, TI-99/4A, TRS-80, and VIC-20.

5332.   Frederick, Dave. "Keyboard Report: Dump Your Sound Storage Problems on System-Exclusive Software." *Keyboard* 12 (Mar. 1986): 98–100.

System-exclusive data storage and transmission software for the Apple, Commodore, and IBM: Key Clique Sys/Ex, MusicData SoundFiler, and J.L. Cooper MidiDisk.

5333.   Freff. "Microprocessors for the Masses. Pt. 2, Further Revelations on the Mysteries of the Digital Future." *Musician* n65 (Mar. 1984): 84, 91–94.

Potential problems of microprocessors, MIDI, and predictions on future trends.

5334. ———. "The Well-Tempered Computer Family: How the Hell Did All These Computers Get in My Studio?" *Musician* n82 (Aug. 1985): 78–83, 94.

The author describes his Apple II, Commodore, VIC-20, Apple Macintosh, and IBM PC.

5335. Gann, Kyle. "Music: A Mouse that Roars." *Village Voice* 34 (July 4, 1989): 90.

A description of Music Mouse and its author, Laurie Spiegel; for the Macintosh, Atari ST, or Amiga.

5336. Gies, Stefan. "Computer und Musik: Zum Stand der gegenwärtigen Entwicklung: Gedanken nach der Lektüre der folgenden Beiträge." *Musik und Bildung* 21 (Juni 1989): 307–8.

5337. Goldsmith, Larry. "From the Home Office: Getting Organized." *Piano Technicians Journal* 31 (Feb. 1988): 8.

Using a home computer as an organizational tool.

5338. Gotcher, Peter. "Computers for Keyboardists: Choosing a Computer for Music. Part II." *Keyboard* 13 (July 1987): 131, 168.

5339. ———. "Computers for Keyboardists: Choosing a Computer for Musical Applications." *Keyboard* 13 (May 1987): 103.

5340. Gray, David Julian, and James Stockford. "No More Violins: Jamming on Home Computers." *Whole Earth Review* no. 49 (Winter 1985): 110.

A short discussion on how personal computers are used to produce music.

5341. Haerle, Dan. "Computer for Jazzers: An Overview of Applications." *Jazz Educators Journal* 16 (Feb./Mar. 1984): 6–8.

An overview of types of software that can be used with microcomputers.

5342. Hagerty, Roger. "Random Music." *Compute!* 6 (Mar. 1984): 176–78.

A program that plays random combinations of pitch, duration, and volume; for the VIC, Commodore 64, or Atari.

5343. Halfhill, Tom R. "Sound Synthesis." *Compute!* 5 (Jan. 1983): 26–34.

A history of synthesized music including the use of personal computers and the SID chip.

5344. Herman, David. "The Computer and the Church Musician. II: A Computer System." *American Organist* 18 (Nov. 1984): 31.

5345. ———. "The Computer and the Church Musician. III: Selecting a Computer." *American Organist* 18 (Dec. 1984): 31.

5346. ———. "The Computer and the Church Musician. V: Additional Uses." *American Organist* 20 (Jan. 1986): 77.

Statistics, hymn settings, journal articles, combined libraries, recordkeeping.

5347. ———. "The Computer and the Church Musician: Introduction." *American Organist* 18 (Oct. 1984): 29–30.

Use of the computer for cataloging music and word processing.

5348. Hofstetter, Fred T. *Making Music on Micros: A Musical Approach to Computer Programming.* New York: Random House, 1985. 189 p. + 5″ diskette.

Review by William R. Higgins in *Council for Research in Music Education Bulletin* n87 (Spring 1986): 83.

For Apple or IBM.

5349. Hopper, Dale. "On Line: Multi-Dimensional (Corps Style) Show Design Software." *Instrumentalist* 40 (July 1986): 46.

Review of a program for marching band drill; for Radio Shack, IBM, and Apple computers.

5350. "Intelligent Music Adds Six Software Programs." *Music Trades* 136 (Aug. 1988): 95–96.

A short description of new software programs.

5351. Jackson, Hanley. "Computers for Piano Teachers." *American Music Teacher* 33 (Feb./Mar. 1984): 32–33.

Describes various applications of a microcomputer, from computer-assisted instruction to cataloging music.

5352. Jenkins, Mark. "Control Zone: Computer News." *Melody Maker* 59 (Oct. 13, 1984): 36–37.

Covers MIDI interfaces and music packages for home computers.

5353. Johnson, Jim. "Computing." *Music, Computers & Software* 3 (June 1988): 18–21.

A tutorial on video graphics on personal computers.

5354. Jones, Henry L. "Economic Affairs: Are You Tired of Playing Games?" *Piano Technicians Journal* 31 (Jan. 1988): 12–13.

A suggestion to use a home computer in managing the piano tuning and repair business.

5355. Jones, Kevin. *Exploring Music with the BBC Micro and Electron.* London: Pitman, 1984. 284 p.

5356. Kahn, Robert A. "Bank Street MusicWriter." *Classroom Computer Learning* 6 (Jan. 1986): 24–25.

Review of composition software; for the Atari or Commodore 64.

5357. Kolosick, J. Timothy. "Technology Notebook." *Piano Quarterly* 33,n129 (Spring 1985): 44–47.

A general introduction to microcomputers and answers to commonly asked questions.

5358. Kozak, Donald P. *A Guide to Computer Music: An Introductory Resource.* Peabody, Mass.: Sound Management, 1988. 88 p.

Covers Apple II, GS, Macintosh, and MIDI products.

5359. Krout, Robert E. "Information Sharing: The Microcomputing Music Therapist: A Primer." *Music Therapy Perspectives* 4 (1987): 64–67.

5360. ——. "Microcomputer Applications in Music Therapy." E.D.D. diss., Columbia University Teachers College, 1988. 202 p.

5361. Krutz, Jamie. "The Competition Heats Up." *MacWeek* 2 (Aug. 16, 1988): 40.

Describes the development of the IBM PC and clones, Atari ST, and Amiga in the use of MIDI.

5362. Kusek, David. "Computers: Choosing a Computer for Musical Applications." *Electronic Musician* 2 (Jan. 1986): 21–26.

5363. Lambrecht, Homer. "Christmas Mouse: New Music Software Stirs through the House." *Ear* 14 (Dec.–Jan. 1989–90): 20–21.

Suggestions of software for microcomputers costing between $50 and $250.

5364. Lancaster, Don. "Don Lancaster's Micro Cookbook." Indianapolis, Ind.: H. W. Sams, 1982–83. 2 v.
Review by David B. Doty in *Electronic Musician* 2 (Jan. 1986): 56.
Contents: vol. 1. Fundamentals — vol. 2. Machine Language Programming.

5365. Languepin, Olivier. "Les Micro-ordinateurs." *Diapason-Harmonie* n346 (Fev. 1989): 58.

Describes the three computers used to test eight score writing software programs.

5366. Latimer, Joey. "1986 Buyer's Guide to Music Hardware and Software: Regardless of Musical Talent, Your Family Can Make Beautiful Music." *Family Computing* 4 (Aug. 1986): 36–40.

Covers the Apple, Macintosh, Atari, Coleco Adam, Commodore, IBM, and Tandy.

5367. ——. "Buyer's Guide to Music Hardware and Software." *Family Computing* 3 (Aug. 1985): 33–38.

5368. ——. "Compose a Tune or a Symphony." *Family Computing* 3 (July 1985): 31.

Brief summaries of seven educational or entertaining music programs.

5369. ——. "Making Music." *Family Computing* 5 (July 1987): 35–39.

How people who are not musically literate can make music on microcomputers.

5370. ——. "Microtones." *Family Computing* 3 (Apr. 1985): 78–79.

Program listing of "Hacksville Hoedown"; for the Atari, Commodore, TI-99/4A, and VIC-20.

5371. ——. "Microtones." *Family Computing* 3 (May 1985): 70–71.

Program listing of "Fat Keyboard"; for the Atari, Commodore 64, and TI-99/4A.

5372. ——. "Microtones." *Family Computing* 3 (June 1985): 70–71.

Program listing of "Ultimate Pitch Pipe"; for the Apple, Commodore, IBM PC and PCjr, and TI-99/4A.

5373. ——. "Microtones." *Family Computing* 3 (July 1985): 62–64.

Program listing of "The Curly Calypso"; for the Atari, Commodore 64, and VIC-20.

5374. ——. "Microtones." *Family Computing* 3 (Aug. 1985): 70–71.

Program listing of "Take Me out to the Ball Game"; for the Atari, Commodore 64, IBM PCjr, and TI-99/4A.

5375. ——. "Microtones." *Family Computing* 3 (Sept. 1985): 86–87.

Program listing of "Arcade Alley"; for the Atari, Commodore, TI-99/4A, and VIC-20.

5376. ——. "Microtones." *Family Computing* 3 (Oct. 1985): 78–79.

Program listing of "Hacker's Rap"; for the Apple, Atari, Commodore, and IBM PCjr.

5377. ——. "Microtones." *Family Computing* 3 (Nov. 1985): 86.
Program listing of "Dance of the Sugar-Plum Fairy"; for the Apple II, Atari, and Commodore.

5378. ——. "Microtones." *Family Computing* 3 (Dec. 1985): 84–86.

Program listing of "Rudolph, the Red-nosed Reggae"; for the Atari, Commodore, IBM PC, and Macintosh.

5379. ——. "Microtones." *Family Computing* 4 (Jan. 1986): 84–86.

Program listing of "Old-Time Rock 'n' Roll"; for the Atari, Commodore, IBM PCjr, and Tandy Color Computer.

5380. ——. "Microtones." *Family Computing* 4 (Mar. 1986): 76–77.
Program listing of "Armchair Arranger"; for the Atari, Commodore, and IBM PCjr.

5381. ——. "Microtones." *Family Computing* 4 (Apr. 1986): 73–74.
Program listing of "Turkey in the Straw"; for the Adam, Apple II, Atari, Commodore, IBM PC, and Tandy Color Computer.

5382. ——. "Microtones." *Family Computing* 4 (May 1986): 74.
Program listing of "Fanfare"; for the Apple II, Commodore, IBM PC, and Tandy Color Computer.

5383. ——. "Microtones." *Family Computing* 4 (June 1986): 80.
Program listing of "Boogie Bass"; for the Apple II, Atari, Commodore, IBM PC, Tandy Color Computer, and VIC-20.

5384. ——. "Microtones." *Family Computing* 4 (July 1986): 56–58.
Program listing of "Spy Music"; for the Atari, Commodore, IBM PCjr, and VIC-20.

5385. ——. "Microtones." *Family Computing* 4 (Sept. 1986): 81–82.
Program listing of "School Days"; for the Apple II, IBM PCjr, Macintosh, Tandy Color Computer, and TI-99/4A.

5386. ——. "Microtones." *Family Computing* 4 (Nov. 1986): 112–14.
Program listing of "A Musical Round (Hey, Ho, Nobody Home)"; for the Atari, Commodore, IBM PCjr, and Macintosh.

5387. ——. "Microtones." *Family Computing* 5 (Jan. 1987): 89–90.
Program listing of "Computer Shake"; for the Atari, Commodore, and IBM PCjr.

5388. ——. "Microtones." *Family Computing* 5 (May 1987): 59–60.
Program listing of "On Top of Spaghetti"; for the Adam, Apple II, Atari, Commodore, IBM PC, Tandy Color Computer, and TI-99/4A.

5389. ——. "Microtones: A Christmas Medley." *Family & Home-Office Computing* 5 (Dec. 1987): 114–18.
For the Apple II, Atari, Commodore, IBM PC & PCjr, and Macintosh.

5390. ——. "Microtones: Bourrée." *Family & Home-Office Computing* 6 (May 1988): 89–90.
Program listing; for the Apple II, Commodore, IBM PC & PCjr, and Macintosh.

5391.   ———. "Microtones: Cradle Song." *Family & Home-Office Computing* 5 (Nov. 1987): 119–20.

> Brahms' Lullaby; for the Apple II, Atari, Commodore, IBM PC & PCjr, Macintosh, and Tandy Color Computer.

5392.   ———. "Microtones: Flight of the Bumble Bee." *Family & Home-Office Computing* 6 (Mar. 1988): 90–91.

> Program listing; for the Apple II, Commodore, IBM PC, Macintosh, and Tandy Color Computer.

5393.   ———. "Microtones: Grand Old Flag." *Family & Home-Office Computing* 6 (July 1988): 74–75.

> Program listing; for the Apple II, Commodore, IBM PC, and Tandy 1000.

5394.   ———. "Microtones: Music Programs." *Family Computing* 3 (Jan. 1985): 106–7.

> Program listing of Tune Generator, a program that randomly selects chords and notes; for the Adam, Atari, Commodore 64, TI-99/4A, and VIC-20 computers.

5395.   ———. "Microtones: Music Programs." *Family Computing* 3 (Feb. 1985): 90–91.

> Four music programs that use multivoice sound and white noise; for the Atari, Commodore 64, VIC-20, and TI-99/4A.

5396.   ———. "Microtones: Music Programs." *Family Computing* 3 (Mar. 1985): 70–71.

> Program listing of "Techno-Rock Fugue"; for the Atari, Commodore 64, and VIC-20.

5397.   ———. "Microtones: Music Programs." *Family Computing* 3 (Apr. 1985): 78–79.

> Program listing of "Hacksville Hoedown"; for the Atari, Commodore 64, TI-99/4A, and VIC-20.

5398.   ———. "Microtones: Raz-Ma-Jazz." *Family Computing* 5 (Sept. 1987): 89–91.

> Program listing; for the Atari, Commodore, IBM PCjr, Macintosh, and TI-99/4A.

5399.   ———. "Microtones: Riffraff." *Family & Home-Office Computing* 6 (Apr. 1988): 92.

> Program listing; for the Apple II, Commodore, IBM PC, and Macintosh.

5400.   ———. "Microtones: The Duelin' Computer." *Family & Home-Office Computing* 5 (Oct. 1987): 100–102.

> A program that is a take-off on "Dueling Banjos"; for the Atari, Commodore, IBM PCjr, Macintosh, and TI-99/4A.

5401. ———. "Microtones: Three-voice Sound Effect." *Family Computing* 5 (Aug. 1987): 75.

Program listing; for the Atari, Commodore, IBM PCjr, Macintosh, and TI-99/4A.

5402. ———. "Music by the Numbers." *Compute!* 10 (Dec. 1988): 40–46.

A discussion of hardware and software for creating a music system with a variety of microcomputers.

5403. ———. "The Twelve Days of Christmas." *Family Computing* 4 (Dec. 1986): 92–105.

Program listing; for the Apple II, Atari, Commodore, IBM PC, Tandy Color Computer, TI-99/4A, and VIC-20.

5404. Lawn, Rick. "Scoring with Computers." *Jazz Educators Journal* 21 (Fall 1988): 22–23, 50.

Background on composition/arranging software.

5405. ———, and Gary Powell. "Scoring with Computers. Part 2." *Jazz Educators Journal* 21,2 (1989): 33–37, 78–79.

A discussion of Music Publisher for the Macintosh, Deluxe Music Construction Set for the Macintosh, and MusicPrinter Plus for the IBM PC.

5406. Leemon, Sheldon. "Commodore's Port: More on Amiga: Software, BASIC, and IBM Compatibility." *Creative Computing* 11 (Nov. 1985): 92–95.

Includes a short description of MusicCraft.

5407. Lehrman, Paul D. "PC Chart Busters." *PC Computing* 2 (Feb. 1989): 174–85.

Reviews of the IBM Music Feature, Cakewalk, Dr. T's patch editors for Roland D-110 and MT-32 synthesizers, SampleVision, M, Music Mouse, and Finale.

5408. Leonard, Steve. "Computers for Keyboardists: Choosing a Computer, MIDI Interface Card & Software Sequencer & Librarian." *Keyboard* 11 (Aug. 1985): 74–75.

5409. ———. "Computers for Keyboardists: Some Computer Basics: Bits, Bytes, Buses & Turning Little Numbers into Big Ones." *Keyboard* 11 (Sept. 1985): 78, 91.

5410. Lewis, Bill. "Computer Synthesis: Flexibility and Expandibility Make the Computer an Attractive 'Instrument.'" *Keyboards, Computers & Software* 1 (Apr. 1986): 41–44.

How a microcomputer can make music without a synthesizer.

5411.   ——. "Hardware: System Expansion: Bigger, Better, Stronger, Faster." *Keyboards, Computers & Software* 2 (Feb. 1987): 50–52.

Discusses the advantages and options in upgrading RAM on IBM PCs, Apple II, Commodore 128, Amiga, Atari 800, Atari ST, and Apple Macintosh.

5412.   ——, and Steve Friedman. "Musicians & Computers . . . the Creative Interface." *Keyboards, Computers & Software* 1 (Feb. 1986): 32–36.

Advice for finding the right computer for one's musical needs.

5413.   ——, and Bob Styles. "Software: A Complete Guide to Music Programs." *Keyboards, Computers & Software* 1 (Feb. 1986): 37–41, 44, 49.

Includes charts of software for the Apple, Atari, Commodore, Macintosh, Amiga, and IBM PC that list the application, whether or not MIDI compatible, the market, price, and manufacturer.

5414.   Lipson, Stefan B. "The Music Studio for Amiga and Atari ST." *Compute!* 8 (Nov. 1986): 70.

Review of composition software.

5415.   Litterst, George F. "An Introduction to Computer Technology for the Classical Pianist." *Piano Quarterly* 36,n140 (Winter 1987–88): 28–31.

5416.   Livingston, Dennis. "Microprocessors Change the Sound of Music." *EDN* 33,n22A (Oct. 27, 1988): 86–90.

A historical look at how microprocessors have changed music recording.

5417.   Mace, Scott. "Electronic Arts' Music Program Scores a Hit." *Info-World* 5 (Oct. 10, 1983): 1, 4–5.

Announcement of Music Construction Set, music composition and notation software for the Apple II, Atari, and Commodore 64.

5418.   Mahin, Bruce P. "Choosing a Computer." *Instrumentalist* 41 (June 1987): 23–31.

5419.   ——. "Choosing Music Notation Software." *Instrumentalist* 43 (June 1989): 20–29.
Also in *Clavier* 28 (July/Aug. 1989): 17–23.

Review of music notation programs for the Macintosh, Atari, and IBM.

5420.   ——. "An Educator's Guide to Music Notation Software. Pt. 1." *Electronic Music Educator* 1 (Mar. 1989): 6–8.

5421.   ——. "Software Review." *Instrumentalist* 43 (Oct. 1988): 70.

Review of Master Tracks Pro, Version 2.0, a 64-track MIDI sequencer for the Macintosh, IBM, and Atari.

5422. Mansfield, Richard. "Dr. T's Sequencer for 64 and Apple." *Compute!* 8 (Jan. 1986): 86–87.

Review.

5423. Many, Chris. "Dr. T Copyist: Software for IBM PC and Atari ST." *Music Technology* 1 (June 1987): 60–62.

Review of music transcription software.

5424. ——. "MegaMix MR16/IPC: Software for IBM PC and Apple Mac." *Music Technology* 1 (Mar. 1987): 42–43.

Review of a program that uses a personal computer to assist in automated mixdown.

5425. ——. "Texture Version 2.5: Software for IBM PC and Commodore Amiga." *Music Technology* 1 (May 1987): 56–58.

Review of a MIDI sequencer.

5426. Marans, Michael. "Keyboard Report: Graphic Sample Editing Software for Macintosh, IBM, Atari & Amiga." *Keyboard* 15 (Dec. 1989): 126–42.

Review of Alchemy, Avalon, Genwave, MIDI Sample Wrench, SampleVision, and Sound Designer II SK.

5427. Massey, Howard. *The Complete Guide to MIDI Software.* New York: Amsco Publications, 1987. 252 p.
Review by Jim Aikin in *Keyboard* 13 (June 1987): 28.
Review by Craig Anderton in *Electronic Musician* 3 (July 1987): 20.

Covers a variety of software programs and their features for Apple II, Atari ST, Commodore 64 and 128, IBM PC, Macintosh, and TI-99/4a computers.

5428. McClain, Larry. "A Crescendo of Products: Apple II MIDI Software." *A + 4* (Feb. 1986): 44–48.

An overview of hardware and software for the Apple II and Macintosh.

5429. Means, Ben, and Jean Means. "Desktop Music Video: From Music to Visuals—A Users Guide." *Music, Computers & Software* 3 (Feb. 1988): 55–59.

Discusses the use of personal computers in the production of music videos.

5430. Milak, John J. "Programming Music for the Non-Programmer." *Jazz Educators Journal* 16 (Feb./Mar. 1984): 9–11, 67–68.

Advice on selecting a microcomputer and software.

5431. Miller, Jim. "Personal Composer." *Computer Music Journal* 9,4 (Winter 1985): 27–37.

Previously **1519**.
Reprinted in *The Music Machine,* ed. Curtis Roads. Cambridge, Mass.: MIT Press, 1989: 243–53.

5432. Minor, David. "Music: A Buyer's Guide to Software." *Popular Computing* 4 (Dec. 1984): 244.

Short overviews of Synthy-64, Music Construction Set, Musicalc, Advanced MusicSystem, Songwriter, Orchestra 90, the Mockingboard, ALF MC1 and MC16, Mountain Computer music plug-in board, and Decillionix DX-1.

5433. Mocsny, Daniel. "The Tapeless Home Studio: Turning Your PC into a Digital Audio Workstation." *Music, Computers & Software* 3 (Feb. 1988): 38–44.

A tutorial and brief product overview of digital recording systems for personal computers.

5434. ———; Chuck Fisher; Bill Lewis; Billy Arnell; and Constantine Peters. "MIDI Users: Software Reviews from MC&S." *Pastoral Music* 13 (June–July 1989): 51–52.

Reviews of PC Desk Top Studio, Amiga Soundscape, Apple Alchemy, Atari MIDISoft Studio, and Music Printer Plus. Reprinted from articles in *Music, Computers & Software.*

5435. "Music Programs for Home Computers." *American Recorder* 29 (Nov. 1988): 157–61.

Reviews of the music printing programs: Deluxe Music Construction Set by Electronic Arts, Professional Composer by Mark of the Unicorn, Score Desktop Music Publishing System by Passport Designs, and Music Printer by Temporal Acuity Products.

5436. Neiman, Marcus L. "On Line: Dr. T's The Copyist." *Instrumentalist* 42 (Feb. 1988): 12.

Software review; for the IBM or Atari.

5437. Newquist, Harvey P. "Multitasking." *Music Technology* 2 (May 1988): 72–76.

A discussion of multitasking on the Amiga, IBM, and Macintosh.

5438. ———. "Sing a Song of Software, a PC Full of RAM." *Computerworld* 20 (Dec. 15, 1986): 17.

How the Roland Corp. supports software for both IBM and Apple computers, and positive comments on Roland's customer support.

5439. O'Brien, Walter. "KCS Telecom." *Keyboards, Computers & Software* 1 (Dec. 1986): 12, 18, 70.

Telecommunications software; for the Commodore, Apple, and IBM.

5440. Ogasapian, John. "A Computer Primer for the Minister of Music." *Journal of Church Music* 29 (May 1987): 8–11.

An article for musicians who know nothing about microcomputers.

5441. Petersen, George. "Portable Power: Computers for the Road." *Electronic Musician* 4 (July 1988): 123–26.

A discussion of computers that can be used by musicians on the road for performance and other tasks.

5442. Pierson-Perry, Jim, and Jim Aikin. "Keyboard Clinic #19: Dr. T's Keyboard Controlled Sequencer." *Keyboard* 15 (June 1989): 58–73.

For use on the Atari ST, Macintosh, and Amiga.

5443. Pitta, Julie. "An Irresistible Oppor-tune-ity: MIT Researcher Conducts Computerized Symphony via Networks, Workstations." *Computerworld* 23 (Apr. 17, 1989): 37.

Michael Hawley, MIT researcher, has combined workstations using a Sun, Apple, and IBM, and two grand pianos.

5444. Placek, Robert W., and Leonard V. Ball. "Floppy Discography: Texture II." *Music Educators Journal* 75 (Jan. 1989): 59–62.

Software review; for the IBM and Amiga.

5445. Pollack, Andrew. "New Alliances Seen in Computers: Apple-Digital Deal Said to Be Close." *New York Times* 137 (Jan. 14, 1988): D1, D22.

Apple is expected to introduce a MIDI interface for the Macintosh and Apple IIgs.

5446. Powell, Roger, and Richard Grehan. "Four MIDI Interfaces: MIDI Interfaces for the Commodore 64, IBM PC, Macintosh, and Apple II Family." *Byte* 11 (June 1986): 265–72.

A comparison and review of TDS-AP (Syntech), MPU-401 (Roland), and MIDIMac (Opcode).

5447. Regena, C. "The Beginner's Page: Making Music with BASIC." *Compute!* 10 (Mar. 1988): 55–56.

An overview of BASIC sound commands for the Amiga, Atari, Commodore-128, and IBM.

5448. Rimmer, Steve. "Computer Music Software." *Canadian Musician* 7 (May 1985): 40–47.

Reviews of software for various microcomputers.

5449. Rudolph, Thomas E. "Technology for Teaching: Selecting a Personal Computer: General Considerations." *Music Educators Journal* 76 (Sept. 1989): 63–66.

5450.   ——. "Technology for Teaching: Selecting a Personal Computer: Manufacturers and Models." *Music Educators Journal* 76 (Oct. 1989): 68–70.

5451.   Scholz, Carter. "MIDI Resources: Programming Languages for Do-It-Yourself Software." *Keyboard* 14 (Nov. 1988): 74–88.

A survey of languages for all major microcomputers.

5452.   Scott, Jordan. "MIDI Applications." *Music, Computers & Software* 3 (Aug. 1988): 24–25.

A discussion on the uses of Digidesign's "Softsynth" program for the Macintosh and the Atari ST.

5453.   Selman, Tom, and David Lourik. "Computers On-Line: Mac II & MIDI, IBM Emulation, & Developments." *Keyboard* 13 (Dec. 1987): 131.

A miscellany on micros.

5454.   ——, and David Lourik. "Computers On-Line: Mega Ataris, Apple Meets MIDI, PS/2 Noise & Vapor Trails." *Keyboard* 14 (Apr. 1988): 128–30.

5455.   ——, and David Lourik. "Computers On-line: Multitasking & Other News from the Front Lines." *Keyboard* 13 (Nov. 1987): 122.

5456.   ——, and David Lourik. "Computers On-Line: News from the Front." *Keyboard* 14 (Aug. 1988): 120.

Introduction to several new ideas in microcomputers.

5457.   Serafine, Frank, and Rick Schwartz. "Review: Passport's MIDI/8 Plus." *Electronic Musician* 2 (Jan. 1986): 66–69.

A MIDI sequencer; for the Commodore and Apple.

5458.   Sillery, Bob. "The Computer Composer." *Personal Computing* 9 (June 1985): 189–90.

Review of Bank Street MusicWriter (Atari, Commodore 64) and The Music Shop (Commodore 64).

5459.   Sirota, Warren. "Electronic Guitarist: Music Programs for Computers, 1." *Guitar Player* 21 (June 1987): 126, 129.

Advice to select a computer based on availability of desired supporting software.

5460.   Skinner, Robert. "Music Software." *Notes* 46 (Sept. 1989): 104–13.

Review of the University of Delaware Videodisc Music Series and Bachdisc, as well as a list of available music software for microcomputers and publishers addresses.

5461.   Slepian, Don. "What Can Be Done with a Music Mouse?" *Electronic Musician* 3 (Aug. 1987): 52–54.

Review of Music Mouse, an algorithmic composition program; for the Macintosh and Amiga.

5462.   Stephen, Greg. "Computers & Music: The CX5M Revisited." *Canadian Musician* 8 (Apr. 1986): 73–74.

New developments in the Yamaha CX5M computer.

5463.   ———. "Computers & Music: Yamaha CX5M." *Canadian Musician* 7 (Aug. 1985): 71.

Discusses the capabilities of the Yamaha CX5M and its supporting software.

5464.   Stockford, James. "Data/7 and Performance/7." *Whole Earth Review* no. 49 (Winter 1985): 111.

Very brief review; for the Yamaha DX7, and the Apple II series, Commodore 64/128, or IBM PC.

5465.   Strange, Allen. "Building Blocks for Computer-generated Music: Do-It-Yourself C-64 & Apple II Software." *Keyboard* 13 (June 1987): 106–21.

5466.   Summers, Tan A. "Rock 'n' Rhythm." *Family Computing* 3 (Apr. 1985): 89.

Review; for the Commodore 64 and Atari.

5467.   "Syntech Introduces New Computer Programs." *Music Trades* 133 (Dec. 1985): 112–13.

DX-TX Master for the Commodore 64, and DX-TX editing and storage program for the IBM PC.

5468.   The', Lee. "The Music Connection: Even if You Can't Read or Write Music, Your Computer Can. Music Software and Hardware Working in Harmony Can Turn You into a Virtuoso." *Personal Computing* 10 (Jan. 1986): 89–95.

An overview of various possible music systems for personal computers with a widely varying price range.

5469.   Thomas, Tony. "Review: Yamaha RX-Editor." *Electronic Musician* 2 (July 1986): 76–77.

Drum machine software.

5470.   Tommasini, Anthony. "A Computer Program That Really Knows the Score." *Boston Globe* (Aug. 28, 1988): A3.

Describes Finale.

5471.   ———. "A Computer Program that Really Knows the Score." *Boston Globe* (Aug. 28, 1988): A3.

Describes the software; Finale.

5472. Tully, Tim. "Interactivity in Action: Understanding 'M.'" *Electronic Musician* 5 (Apr. 1989): 28–32.

An algorithmic composition program; for the Macintosh, Atari ST, Amiga, and IBM PC.

5473. Vail, Mark. "Keyboard Report: Editor/Librarians for the Roland D-110." *Keyboard* 15 (Apr. 1989): 118–19, 128.

Caged Artist D-110 Editor, MIDImouse D-10/110/20 Capture!, and Beaverton D-110 Editor/Librarian.

5474. Van Gelder, Lindsy. "Enjoying the Brave New World of Computer Music." *Ms* 16 (Oct. 1987): 42–47.

A general discussion of the uses of microcomputers in music with mention of several commercial software packages.

5475. Visco, Christopher. "Guitar Tuner." *Compute!* 7 (Jan. 1985): 99–101.

A BASIC program to help tune a six- or twelve-string guitar; for the TI, Commodore, Atari, or IBM.

5476. Williams, Linda. "Mixing Music and Micros." *Family Computing* 3 (Apr. 1985): 74.

Short descriptions of Computer Sheet Music, MacMusic, Music Video Kit, and the Music Shop.

5477. Wright, Jim. "The Computer-Software Connection." *Keyboards, Computers & Software* 1 (Apr. 1986): 37–40.

A general overview of types of software and specific programs for the major microcomputers.

5478. Yavelow, Christopher. "Personal Computers and Music: The State of the Art." *Journal of the Audio Engineering Society* 35 (Mar. 1987): 160–88.

An extensive overview.

5479. Zuckerman, Faye. "Composers Know How to Make Computers Hum." *Billboard* 96 (Jan. 21, 1984): 31.

Music for computer software packages; music played with a joy stick; Songwriter used for composition.

MICROCOMPUTERS—
AMIGA

5480.   Aikin, Jim. "Keyboard Report: Sound Lab from Blank Software for the Ensoniq Mirage." *Keyboard* 12 (Jan. 1986): 126–30.

A sound waveform and voice parameter editing program for the Ensoniq Mirage.

5481.   "Amiga Audio Products." *Amazing Computing* 3,4 (1988): 70–71.

A list of software and hardware for the Amiga.

5482.   Baird, Jock. "Software City: The Amiga Heats up." *Musician* n118 (Aug. 1988): 60–64.

Review of software for the Amiga.

5483.   Bassen, Howard. "Upgrade Your A 1000 to 500/2000 Audio Power." *Amazing Computing* 3,4 (1988): 58–69.

An upgrade for the Amiga 1000 to improve musical applications.

5484.   Battle, Ron. "Amazing Reviews: The Perfect Sound Digitizer." *Amazing Computing* 2,5 (1987): 17–18.

5485.   Blank, David N. "Playing Dynamic Drums on the Amiga." *Amazing Computing* 2,12 (1987): 47–49.

Review.

5486.   Block, Warren. "Amazing Reviews: The FutureSound Sound Digitizer." *Amazing Computing* 2,5 (1987): 19–20.

5487.   Braunstein, Mark D. "Amiga 1000 MIDI Interface." *Electronic Musician* 4 (Feb. 1988): 90–94.

How to build a MIDI interface for the Amiga 1000.

5488.   Brown, Michael, and Gary A. Ludwick. "Music Mouse." *Amiga World* 4 (Mar. 1988): 74–78.

Review of interactive sound software.

5489.   Burger, Jeff. "Review: Mimetics' SoundScape Pro MIDI Studio." *Electronic Musician* 3 (Feb. 1987): 100–108.

5490.   Burgess, Jim. "Very Vivid Mandala: Video-MIDI Instrument." *Music Technology* 1 (Feb. 1987): 76–78.

Review of Mandala, a video-based real-time performance instrument that uses an Amiga.

5491.   Dupler, Steven. "Amiga Program Offers Desktop Video Production." *Billboard* 98 (July 26, 1986): 51.

5492.   Ellis, Robert. "Digital Signal Processing in AmigaBASIC." *Amazing Computing* 3 (Oct. 1988): 65–73.

5493.   Fay, Todor. "Programming with MIDI, the Amiga, and SoundScape: Writing a SoundScape Module in C." *Amazing Computing* 2,5 (1987): 27–39.

Describes MIDI and SoundScape and two sample programs for manipulating music in the SoundScape environment.

5494.   ———. "Programming with SoundScape: Manipulating Samples in the Sampler Module." *Amazing Computing* 2,9 (1987): 81–87.

5495.   ———. "Writing a SoundScape Patch Librarian: Working within the System Exclusive." *Amazing Computing* 3,4 (1988): 38–48.

A patch librarian module that can load and save patch information from Yamaha synthesizers using system exclusive dumps.

5496.   Fisher, Chuck. "Amiga Music: MIDISynergy I by Geodesic Publications." *Music, Computers & Software* 3 (Oct. 1988): 66–67.

Review of the MIDI sequencer.

5497.   ———. "Amiga Music: Soundscape in a Multi-Tasking Environment . . . A Current Look." *Music, Computers & Software* 3 (Nov. 1988): 56–57.

Review of the MIDI control program; for the Commodore Amiga.

5498.   ———. "Amiga Music: Very Vivid 'Mandala.'" *Music, Computers & Software* 3 (June 1988): 58–59.

Review of Mandala, an audio/video/MIDI sequencer; for the Commodore Amiga.

5499.   ———. "Commodore Amiga: The Avant-garde in Home Computer Animation Becomes the Musician's Choice through Splitting Screens, Multitasking and Stretching the Imagination." *Keyboards, Computers & Software* 2 (Feb. 1987): 44–47, 62.

A product overview of the Commodore Amiga, with emphasis on sampling and MIDI.

5500.   ———. "Deluxe Music Construction Set for the Amiga from Electronic Arts." *Music, Computers & Software* 3 (Feb. 1988): 76.

Review.

5501. Fisher, Steve. "Aegis Sonix for the Commodore Amiga." *Music, Computers & Software* 2 (June 1987): 68.

Review of the MIDI sequencing software; for the Commodore Amiga.

5502. Freff. "Sound Oasis, Mirage Sample Disk Reader for the Amiga." *Keyboard* 14 (Nov. 1988): 155–56.

5503. Friedman, Dean. "The Musical Computer: Music on the Amiga." *Electronic Musician* 4 (Apr. 1988): 34–45.

A general overview of the use of the Amiga 500 for musical applications.

5504. ———. "Review: DXII Master Editor/Librarian." *Electronic Musician* 4 (Mar. 1988): 102–6.

5505. Grantham, Tim. "Very Vivid!" *Amazing Computing* 2,7 (1987): 9–11.

Describes the Mandala system, which combines performers, dancers, and musicians.

5506. Greenwald, Ted. "Keyboard Report: SoundScape, Sequencer/Sampler & MIDI Operating System." *Keyboard* 14 (Jan. 1988): 126–35, 150–53.

5507. Herrington, Peggy. "Amiga Jamboree: A Buyer's Guide to Music Products." *Amiga World* 4 (June 1988): 44–54.

5508. ———. "Music-X." *Amiga Resource* 1 (Dec. 1989): 58–63.

Review of MIDI sequencing software.

5509. ———. "Musical Accessories: What Do a Box of Chocolates and the Amiga Have in Common?" *Amiga World* 3 (July–Aug. 1987): 74–76.

A comparison of six disks with sound samples with an assortment of chocolates.

5510. ———. "Software: Amiga: The Software Behind the Hardware." *Electronic Musician* 2 (Apr. 1986): 44–46.

5511. Jones, Tim. "An Exclusive Preview: Music Mouse." *Commodore Magazine* 8 (Sept. 1987): 54–57, 113, 127.

An overview of software that utilizes a mouse to create music.

5512. Karr, David. "Computers: Amiga!" *Electronic Musician* 2 (Apr. 1986): 38–43.

5513. King, Steve. "MIDI Sequencers for the Amiga." *Commodore Magazine* 10 (Mar. 1989): 50–53, 96–99.

5514. Kottler, John J. "AudioMaster." *Commodore Magazine* 9 (Apr. 1988): 46–47.
Review of sampling software.

5515. ——. "Software Reviews: Sonix." *Commodore Magazine* 8 (Sept. 1987): 32, 114–15.
Music composition software.

5516. Larson, Brendan. "Amazing Review: AudioMaster." *Amazing Computing* 3,4 (1988): 27–28.
Review of a sampling program.

5517. Lindstrom, Bob. "D-50 Parameter Editor, Caged Artists's D-50 Editor/Librarian, the D-50 Master Editor/Librarian." *Amiga World* 4 (Sept. 1988): 66–70.
Reviews; for use with the Roland D-50 FM synthesizer.

5518. ——. "MIDI Magic: Saw Measures in Half and Make Notes Disappear." *Amiga World* 5 (Mar. 1989): 14–16.
Review of the MIDI sequencer.

5519. Lipson, Stefan B. "Commodore Amiga: The Alternative Micro." *Music Technology* 2 (Nov. 1987): 64–65.
A short overview of the Amiga.

5520. ——. "In Brief: Music Mouse." *Music Technology* 2 (Dec. 1987): 28.
Review of a mouse-controlled, music-generating program.

5521. ——. "Sound Quest DXII Master Editor/Librarian: Voice Editing Software for the Yamaha DX7II and the Amiga." *Music Technology* 2 (Mar. 1988): 67.
Review.

5522. ——. "Synthia: Digital Synthesis Software for the Amiga." *Music Technology* 2 (Feb. 1988): 66–67.
Review.

5523. Loffink, John. "Reviews: Synthia: A Digital Synthesizer for the Amiga." *Electronic Musician* 4 (Dec. 1988): 120–23, 137.

5524. Lowengard, J. Henry. "Amazing Review: Music Mouse." *Amazing Computing* 3,4 (1988): 29–30.
Review of a high-level software-based musical instrument.

5525. Mahin, Bruce P. "Software Review." *Instrumentalist* 44 (Nov. 1989): 68.
Review of Music-X, a MIDI sequencer; for the Amiga.

5526. Massoni, Barry. "Barry Massoni's MIDI Interface Adapter for the Amiga 500 and 2000." *Amazing Computing* 2,12 (1987): 109–10.

5527.   McConkey, Jim. "Program Your Amiga for Music." *Electronic Musician* 4 (Dec. 1988): 61–73.

5528.   Meadows, Jim. "Real Stereo Sound Effects: Using FutureSound with AmigaBASIC." *Amazing Computing* 2,5 (1987): 21–26.

5529.   Means, Ben, and Jean Means. "76 Trombones, 110 Cornets, a Thousand Reeds . . ." *Amiga World* 4 (June 1988): 30–42.
         How to equip a MIDI music system with an Amiga.

5530.   ——, and Jean Means. "Amiga Music: Dr. T's 'KCS 1.6.' " *Music, Computers & Software* 3 (Aug. 1988): 52–53.
         Review of the MIDI sequencer.

5531.   ——, and Jean Means. "MCScope System." *Music, Computers & Software* 3 (Feb. 1988): 62–71.
         An overview of the Amiga computer and music-related software.

5532.   ——, and Jean Means. "A Musical Environment: The SoundScape Pro MIDI Studio." *Amiga World* 3 (July–Aug. 1987): 35–40.
         Review.

5533.   ——, and Jean Means. "Sonix: Once Upon a Time There Was Musicraft." *Amiga World* 3 (July–Aug. 1987): 54–58.
         Review of the sequencer and scoring software.

5534.   ——, and Jean Means. "Texture." *Amiga World* 3 (July–Aug. 1987): 68–70.
         Review of the MIDI sequencer.

5535.   "MIDI: Ear Training Software Introduced." *Canadian Musician* 9 (Oct. 1987): 28.
         Review of Master Librarian and Ear Master by Music Visions Inc.; for the Commodore Amiga.

5536.   Milano, Dominic. "Keyboard Report: Commodore Amiga Computer." *Keyboard* 12 (Feb. 1986): 112–15.

5537.   Mohansingh, Tim. "Amazing Audio Reviews: MIDI Recording Studio." *Amazing Computing* 4 (May 1989): 41–42.
         Review of the MIDI sequencing software.

5538.   ——. "Amazing Reviews: E.C.T. SampleWare: Incredible Multisampled Sounds in SoundScape and IFF Formats." *Amazing Computing* 3 (Dec. 1988): 38–39.

5539.   Pattison, David. "Product Evaluation: The TAB Player: Tab Playing Software for the Amiga 1000, by Jeff deRienzo." *Banjo Newsletter* 15 (Mar. 1988): 16.

5540.   Peck, Rob. "Reaching the Notes: Easy Access to Amiga Audio: Simple and Straight Forward C Routines for Getting at the Power of the Amiga's Audio Device." *Amiga World* 3 (July–Aug. 1987): 18–22, 90–94.

5541. Pietrowicz, Stephen. "Amazing Reviews: Instant Music, from a Non-musician's Point of View." *Amazing Computing* 1,9 (1986): 45.

5542. Proffitt, K. K. "Amiga Music: The Quest I Texture." *Music, Computers & Software* 3 (Dec. 1988): 52–53.
Review of the Amiga version of the MIDI sequencer program.

5543. Quinzi, Stephen. "AudioMaster." *Amiga World* 4 (Feb. 1988): 67–68.
Review of the sampling and sound-editing software.

5544. ———. "Sound Lab." *Amiga World* 4 (Mar. 1988): 68–72.
Review of interface software; for the Ensoniq Mirage.

5545. Rae, Richard. "AmigaNotes." *Amazing Computing* 1 (June 1986): 11–14.
Inaugural article; discusses the fundamentals of digital audio.

5546. ———. "AmigaNotes." *Amazing Computing* 3 (June 1988): 39–45.
An overview of DX-Heaven from Dr. T.

5547. ———. "AmigaNotes: A Look at 8SVX IFF Data Files." *Amazing Computing* 3 (Sept. 1988): 23–26.
A dissection of IFF sample storage.

5548. ———. "AmigaNotes: A Look at Some MIDI Interfaces." *Amazing Computing* 2,1 (1987): 57–59.

5549. ———. "AmigaNotes: Applied Visions' FutureSound." *Amazing Computing* 2,6 (1987): 51–54.
Review of an audio digitizer.

5550. ———. "AmigaNotes: Digital Music Generation." *Amazing Computing* 3,1 (1988): 51–53.

5551. ———. "AmigaNotes: Hum Busters; No Stereo? Y Not?; Speaking of Schematics . . ." *Amazing Computing* 2,3 (1987): 73–75.

5552. ———. "AmigaNotes: MIDI and the Amiga . . . an Excellent Combination." *Amazing Computing* 1,8 (1986): 37–40.

5553. ———. "AmigaNotes: Mimetics SoundScape Sound Sampler." *Amazing Computing* 2,5 (1987): 51–56.
Review of the SoundScape Digitizer, a sampling program.

5554. ———. "AmigaNotes: Music on the New Amigas." *Amazing Computing* 2,12 (1987): 85–87.
A overview of the audio changes in the Amiga 500 and 2000.

5555. ———. "AmigaNotes: Rick Takes a Look at Synthia." *Amazing Computing* 3 (July 1988): 83–87.

Review.

5556. ———. "AmigaNotes: Sonix from Aegis Development (Formerly Musi-Craft)." *Amazing Computing* 2,8 (1987): 61–65.

Review.

5557. ———. "AmigaNotes: The Amazing MIDI Interface." *Amazing Computing* 2,2 (1987): 57–62.

5558. ———. "AmigaNotes: The Amiga Sound Situation Is Looking . . . er . . . Sounding . . . Better by the Moment." *Amazing Computing* 1,9 (1986): 83–86.

Review of Electronic Arts' Instant Music.

5559. ———. "More AmigaNotes: SunRize Industries Perfect Sound Audio Digitizer." *Amazing Computing* 2,5 (1987): 57–60.

Review.

5560. Randall, Neil. "Instant Music for the Amiga." *Compute!* 9 (Apr. 1987): 67–68.

Review of music composition software.

5561. Raudonis, Chuck. "Amazing Music Reviews: Dynamic Studio." *Amazing Computing* 4 (May 1989): 31–34.

Review of the drum machine and sequencing software.

5562. Ritter, Lynn, and Gary Rentz. "Amiga 1000 Serial Port and MIDI Compatibility for Your Amiga 2000." *Amazing Computing* 3,3 (1988): 68–69.

5563. Saunders, Phil. "Amazing Audio Reviews: AudioMasterII." *Amazing Computing* 4 (May 1989): 24–29.

Review of the sampling and editing software.

5564. ———. "Converting Patch Librarian Files, or, How to Get Your Sounds from There to Here." *Amazing Computing* 3 (Dec. 1988): 74–76.

5565. Shields, James. "Waveform Workshop in AmigaBASIC." *Amazing Computing* 2,5 (1987): 41–50.

A utility program for using the sound facilities of the Amiga.

5566. Souvignier, Todd. "Reviews: MicroIllusions' Music-X for the Amiga." *Electronic Musician* 5 (Nov. 1989): 92–99.

MIDI sequencing software.

5567. Sullivan, Jeffrey. "Amazing Reviews: SoundScape Pro MIDI Studio: A Powerful Music Editor/Player." *Amazing Computing* 2,5 (1987): 11–16.

Review.

5568. Summers, Tan A. "Instant Music." *Family Computing* 5 (Apr. 1987): 78–79.
Review of music composition software; for the Amiga.

5569. Theberge, Andre. "Amazing Hardware Projects: Building the Amazing Stereo Audio Digitizer." *Amazing Computing* 4 (May 1989): 35–40.

5570. Theil, David D. "Sound and the Amiga." *Byte* 11 (Oct. 1986): 139–42.

5571. Tully, Tim. "Dr. T's 4-Op Deluxe Editor/Librarian for the Amiga and Yamaha TX81Z, FB-01, DX100/27/21." *Electronic Musician* 4 (Nov. 1988): 92–93.
Review.

5572. ——. "Dynamic Studio." *Amiga World* 5 (Jan. 1989): 20–22.
Review of sequencer and drum machine software.

5573. ——. "M: Do, Re, M . . ." *Amiga World* 5 (Apr. 1989): 12–13.
Review of M, algorithmic composition software.

5574. ——. "The Sound of Music." *Amiga World* 5 (May 1989): 16–26.
Describes the workings of the Amiga sound system and how MIDI enhances these music making abilities.

5575. Wallace, John. "The Amiga is Amazin', but Where's the Software?" *Village Voice* 30 (Nov. 26, 1985): 77–79.

5576. Webster, Bruce. "Season's Greetings." *Byte* 11 (Dec. 1986): 305–16.
Includes a review of Instant Music, music composition software.

5577. Wetzler, Peter. "Techno: Strum the LYR; Computer Program with Strings Attached." *Ear* 12 (Apr. 1987): 7.
The author explains that he chose to buy an Amiga so he could run a program called LYR.

5578. White, Len A. "Amazing Audio Programming: Digitized Sound Playback in Modula-2." *Amazing Computing* 4 (May 1989): 45–47.

5579. Winslow, Br Seraphim. "Amazing Hardware Projects: MIDI out Interface." *Amazing Computing* 4 (May 1989): 43–44.

5580. ——. "The MIDI Must Go Thru." *Amazing Computing* 4 (Dec. 1989): 12–14.
The author describes how he established a MIDI studio using his Amiga.

MICROCOMPUTERS— APPLE

5581. Adams, Christopher. "Sound Table: Fast Sound Effects from Basic." *Creative Computing* 9 (July 1983): 188–92.

A sound table in machine language that produces 256 waveforms.

5582. "Apple Computer Pledges Commitment to Music Market: Unveils MIDI Interface, But Will Not Sell to Music Dealers." *Music Trades* 136 (Feb. 1988): 92–93.

5583. "Apple Introduces the Apple MIDI Interface." *Canadian Musician* 10 (June 1988): 27.

5584. Boudreaux, Paul J. "Getting into Integer BASIC." *Microcomputing* 8 (July 1984): 102–5.

Includes a short description of Music, a machine language program, accessible from Integer Basic on the Apple II+.

5585. Brewin, Bob. "The Monitor: Joe Ely's 'Hi-Res' Rock." *Village Voice* 29 (May 15, 1984): 26–27.

Joe Ely, a country-western-rock musician, describes how he uses an Apple II to produce his music.

5586. Burger, Jeff. "Review: Syntech's Studio II." *Electronic Musician* 2 (Oct. 1986): 82–87.

MIDI sequencer for the Apple II+ or IIe.

5587. "Buyers' Guide to Apple II Music Software." *A+* 4 (Feb. 1986): 50–51.

5588. Campbell, Alan Gary. "Computers: The Musical Apple II." *Electronic Musician* 2 (Oct. 1986): 50–56.

5589. Chien, Phil. "The Synthetic Sound of Music." *Apple II Review* (Spring/Summer 1987): 54–58.

Use of the Apple IIGS for music applications.

5590.   Chin, Kathy. "AlphaSyntauri Music System: A Series of Three Programs for Creating Music." *InfoWorld* 6 (Apr. 30, 1984): 57–58.

  Review; for the Apple II series.

5591.   Coker, Frank. "Random Music: Generate Music with a Special Twist—Just Type These Four Little Listings." *InCider* 2 (Dec. 1984): 93–96.

  BASIC program listings.

5592.   Cowart, Robert, and Steve Cummings. "A New Musical Revolution: What Is MIDI and How Does Your Apple II Fit in?" *A+* 4 (Feb. 1986): 26–32.

5593.   Cummings, Steve. "Keyboard Report: Synthestra, MIDI Performance Software for the Apple II+/e." *Keyboard* 12 (Aug. 1986): 124–25, 140.

  Review of a MIDI sequencer and master control keyboard system program.

5594.   Dames, Jean, and Douglas Susu-Mago. "On Line: Polywriter." *Clavier* 25 (July–Aug. 1986): 34–35.

  Software review.

5595.   ——, and Douglas Susu-Mago. "On Line: The Apple IIGS and KidsTime II." *Instrumentalist* 42 (Sept. 1987): 86–89.

  Hardware and software review.

5596.   Doherty, W. Charles. "Music Construction Set." *InCider* 2 (Dec. 1984): 138–39.

  Review of music composition software.

5597.   Dupler, Steven. "Digital Sampling Unit for Apple Due." *Billboard* 98 (July 19, 1986): 64.

  DS:4 by Greengate, a digital sampling system; for Apple IIe.

5598.   "Ensoniq Chip Incorporated in New Apple Computer." *Music Trades* 134 (Nov. 1986): 70.

5599.   Fischer, Michael. "Telecommunications: Modems, Music, and Your Apple II." *A+* 6 (June 1988): 81–83.

  An overview of musical files and information available on online services.

5600.   Fisher, Chuck. "Apple Music: The Music Studio 2.0 for the Apple IIGS from Activision Software." *Music, Computers & Software* 3 (Dec. 1988): 54–55.

  Review of the MIDI sequencer and synthesis program.

5601. Freff. "Breaking the Sound Barrier: Extending Your Apple: The AlphaSyntauri Digital Sound Synthesizer Can Expand Your Musical Horizons." *A +* 2 (Feb. 1984): 62–64.

5602. ——. "MIDI Gear Galore: An Endless Array of Instruments and Accessories Awaits You." *A +* 4 (Feb. 1986): 34–41.

5603. Fudge, Don. "Fudge It!: Tuning up Your Apple: Add Melody and a Little Charm to Your Programs with Apple Music." *InCider* 3 (June 1985): 53–60.

Programs in BASIC.

5604. Gotcher, Peter. "Computers for Keyboardists: Preview of the Apple IIGS." *Keyboard* 13 (Jan. 1987): 112–17.

5605. Greenwald, Ted. "Keyboard Report: Master Tracks for Apple II from Passport." *Keyboard* 12 (May 1986): 112–17.

MIDI sequencing software.

5606. Gustafsson, Roland. "Ensoniq Sounds." *A +* 5 (Jan. 1987): 52.

A BASIC sound demo program for the Apple IIGS.

5607. ——. "IIGS Sound: Sound Sampler: A Program That Lets You Play with Pitch Changes." *A +* 5 (Apr. 1987): 93.

5608. ——. "IIGS Update: IIGS Sound Oscilloscope: A Wealth of Waveforms Awaits You with This BASIC Program." *A +* 5 (Sept. 1987): 83–84.

5609. Jainschigg, John. "Apple Harmony." *Family Computing* 4 (Aug. 1986): 62–64.

Machine code subroutine for the Apple II to simulate three-part harmony.

5610. Jones, David L. "Floppy Discography: Uniform Manager Program." *Music Educators Journal* 74 (Nov. 1987): 67–71.

Software review; for the Apple II.

5611. Kovach, Mark A. "Drumfile by Blank Software." *Music, Computers & Software* 2 (June 1987): 68–69.

Review of the patch librarian; for the E-mu SP-12 and the Apple Macintosh.

5612. Krutz, Jamie. "Apple Sounds Serious at Summer NAMM Expo." *MacWeek* 2 (July 5, 1988): 10.

Describes the Apple products at the NAMM expo.

5613. Latimer, Joey. "Apple MIDI Interface." *Family & Home-Office Computing* 6 (June 1988): 58.

Review.

5614. ———. "The Music Studio 2.0." *Compute!* 10 (Oct. 1988): 80–82. Review.

5615. Lehrman, Paul D. "Sample and Hold: Digital Sound Recording, Real-Time and Sequencer Playback Functions in an Add-on Package for the Apple II Computer." *High Fidelity/Musical America* 34 (Oct. 1984): 56–57.

5616. Leonard, Steve. "Computers for Keyboardists: Getting MIDI Bytes out of Your Computer." *Keyboard* 12 (Apr. 1986): 104–5.

5617. Levinger, Lowell. "Review: Passport's Master Tracks." *Electronic Musician* 2 (Oct. 1986): 76–80.

5618. Lindstrom, Bob. "The Dream Machine: Music." *A+* 6 (July 1988): 42–44.

Descriptions of variously priced computer music systems based on the Apple II.

5619. ———. "Product Spotlight: A Synthesizer, Sound Generator, Sampler, and Speakers, Plus a Book for MIDI Musicians." *A+* 6 (June 1988): 48–49.

Short descriptions of music products for the Apple II and a review of *MIDI for Musicians* by Craig Anderton.

5620. ———. "Software: Maximum MIDI: Serious Music-making Comes to the IIGS." *A+* 7 (Feb. 1989): 56–60.

Review of Diversi-Tune and Master Tracks Jr., a MIDI sequencer; for the Apple IIGS.

5621. Little, Gary B. "Editor's Page: The Music Machine." *A+* 6 (June 1988): 9–10.

Music developments of the Apple II.

5622. Longeneker, Patrick, and Chuck Fisher. "The Apple IIgs." *Keyboards, Computers & Software* 1 (Dec. 1986): 33–35, 40, 70.

Product overview of the updated Apple II, with emphasis on the Ensoniq digital oscillator chip designed into the unit.

5623. Mann, Steve. "S Is for Sound: Apple IIGS: A Sonic Preview for Apple's Newest Computer." *A+* 5 (Jan. 1987): 49–50.

A preview of the sound generation capabilities of the Apple IIGS.

5624. McClain, Larry. "A+ All-Stars: Music, the Best Tuneful Software for the Apple II." *A+* 5 (Dec. 1987): 82–92.

Short descriptions of Music Studio, Instant Music, Kids Time II, Music Construction Set, The Music Class, MIDI Music Tutor, Guitar Wizard, Stickybear Music, Peter & the Wolf Music, and Foundations of Music.

5625. ———. "Making Music: Serious Software for Music Mavens." *A* + 6 (June 1988): 36–45.

A basic overview of available music software for the Apple II.

5626. Meizel, Janet. "Notewriter." *InCider* 1 (Oct. 1983): 224–25.

Review of music transcription software; for use with the Soundchaser music system.

5627. ———. "Polywriter." *InCider* 3 (Mar. 1985): 85–86.

Review of music transcription and printing software.

5628. ———. "Songwriter." *InCider* 2 (Nov. 1984): 122–23.

Review of music composition software.

5629. "Mirage Visual Editing System Available from Ensoniq." *Music Trades* 133 (Dec. 1985): 102.

5630. Moore, Billy. "Piano Plinkin." *InCider* 1 (Jan. 1983): 148–49.

A program that turns an Apple II keyboard into a one octave piano keyboard.

5631. "Music Sequencer Released for the Amiga." *Computer Shopper* 9 (Jan. 1989): 112.

Product announcement of MIDI Magic, a MIDI sequencer.

5632. Newell, Andrew. "Software: Apple II Memory Dump Program." *Electronic Musician* 2 (Oct. 1986): 57–64.

5633. O'Brien, Bill. "Cricket." *InCider* 2 (Dec. 1984): 154–56.

Review of a speech synthesizer, music generator, and clock.

5634. O'Donnell, Bob. "Sound, Song & Vision, Pitch Recognition Software: A Pitch-to-MIDI Conversion Program for the Apple II+ or Apple IIe." *Music Technology* 2 (May 1988): 71.

Review.

5635. Orlarey, Yann. "MLOGO: A MIDI Composing Environment for the Apple IIe." In *Proceedings of the International Computer Music Conference 1986, Royal Conservatory, The Hague, Netherlands, October 20–24, 1986,* ed. Paul Berg. San Francisco, Calif.: Computer Music Association, 1986: 211–13.

5636. Parfitt, Rick. "Making IIGS Music." *Compute!'s Apple Applications* 5 (Dec. 1987): 12–18.

Describes the music-making capabilities of the Apple IIGS.

5637. "Passport Adds Software for Roland MIDI Interface." *Music Trades* 133 (Dec. 1985): 107.

5638.   Petersen, Marty. "AlphaSyntauri Computer Music System for Apple."
               InfoWorld 5 (Oct. 10, 1983): 78–81.
               Review.

5639.   ———. "Soundchaser Digital, Music Synthesizer for Apple." *Info-*
               World 5 (Jan. 3–19, 1983): 58–60, 64.
               Review.

5640.   ———. "Turbo-Traks, a 16-Channel Music Synthesizer." *InfoWorld* 5
               (Sept. 12, 1983): 61–63.
               Review.

5641.   Rudolph, Thomas E. *Music and the Apple II: Applications for Music*
               Education, Composition, and Performance. Drexel Hill, Pa.: Unsinn,
               1984. 175 p.
               Review by Jim Aikin in *Keyboard* 11 (July 1985): 27–28.

5642.   ———. *Music and the Apple II: Applications for Music Education,*
               Composition, and Performance. 2nd ed. Drexel Hill, Pa.: Unsinn,
               1988. 175 p.

5643.   Slepian, Don. "Video Focus: Apple Graphics for Music Video."
               Electronic Musician 1 (Sept. 1985): 14–15, 44.

5644.   Stackpole, Bob. "Computer Music: What's in It for Banjoists?" *Banjo*
               Newsletter 16 (Nov. 1988): 6–7.
               Review of Music Studio software.

5645.   Steere, Leslie. "One-Man Band." *A+* 6 (Dec. 1988): 37.
               Conductor Jeff Whitmill turned to an Apple IIe and other
               equipment for his theater orchestra when unable to find musi-
               cians.

5646.   ———; Mary Bohannon; and Shannon Cullen. "Product Roundup:
               Have a Blast." *A+* 7 (Mar. 1989): 101.
               A short description of Sonic Blaster, a stereo digitizer.

5647.   ———; Mary Bohannon; and Shannon Cullen. "Sound, Song &
               Vision." *A+* 6 (Nov. 1988): 122.
               Very brief overview of the pitch recognition software.

5648.   Stockford, James. "DX-Heaven." *Whole Earth Review* n49 (Winter
               1985): 111.
               Very brief review of a patch editor/librarian for the Yamaha DX7.

5649.   ———, and Joe West. "MIDI Interface, MIDI/8 Plus, Leadsheeter."
               Whole Earth Review n49 (Winter 1985): 110–11.
               Very brief reviews of MIDI/8 Plus and Leadsheeter.

5650.   Swigart, Rob. "Making Music: MIDI Makes Music." *A +* 6 (June 1988): 32–35.

Describes MIDI interfaces; for the Apple.

5651.   ——, and Steve Mann. "IIGS Update: Super Sounds." *A +* 5 (July 1987): 60–68.

Reviews of SuperSonic Cards, Music Construction Set, and Music Studio.

5652.   Thornburg, David D. "Learning Curve: A Homebrew Music Connection: Connecting Your Apple II to a CD Player." *A +* 6 (June 1988): 85–88.

5653.   Tully, Tim. "Review: Roland's Muse." *Electronic Musician* 2 (Oct. 1986): 72–75.

An eight-track sequencer for the Apple IIe.

5654.   Tutaj, Duane. "On Line: Music Printer." *Instrumentalist* 41 (Oct. 1986): 70–71.

Software review; for the Apple.

5655.   Walker, Russ. "FM Drawing Board, a Comprehensive DX-7 Editor-Librarian for the Apple II." *Canadian Musician* 8 (Oct. 1986): 32.

5656.   West, Joe, and James Stockford. "Breathe in Sound, Breathe out Music . . . The Decillionix DX-1/The Interpolator." *Whole Earth Review* n45 (Mar. 1985): 99.

Very brief reviews.

5657.   Wittlich, Gary E. "Computers and Music: Product Review: Drum-Key, a Real-Time Percussion Instrument for the Apple II, II +, or IIe." *School Musician* 56 (Aug.–Sept. 1984): 38–39.

MICROCOMPUTERS— ATARI

5658. Abramowitz, David, and Ralph Talbott. "Atari 1040 ST." *Keyboards, Computers & Software* 1 (June 1986): 44–49.

Ideas on the use of the Atari in the studio with software programs and additional equipment.

5659. Aikin, Jim. "Keyboard Report: C-Lab Creator, Sequencer Software for the Atari ST." *Keyboard* 14 (Apr. 1988): 142–52.

5660. ——. "Keyboard Report: C-Lab Notator, Sequencing/Notation for Atari ST." *Keyboard* 15 (Feb. 1989): 132–40.

5661. ——. "Keyboard Report: CZ-Droid, Editing and Librarian Software for the Atari ST." *Keyboard* 12 (Nov. 1986): 136–38.

Editor/librarian software; for Casio CZ synthesizers.

5662. ——. "Keyboard Report: Fingers & Tunesmith, Interactive MIDI Music Generators for the Atari ST." *Keyboard* 14 (Oct. 1988): 144–47.

Interactive MIDI music generators.

5663. ——. "Keyboard Report: KCS & Midisoft Studio, Sequencer Software for the Atari ST." *Keyboard* 13 (Feb. 1987): 130–36, 176.

5664. ——. "Keyboard Report: *Ludwig,* Algorithmic Composition for the Atari ST." *Keyboard* 15 (Mar. 1989): 123–36.

5665. ——. "Keyboard Report: Miditrack ST Hybrid Arts Sequencer Software." *Keyboard* 13 (Aug. 1987): 136–43.

MIDI sequencer software.

5666. ——. "Keyboard Report: MT-32 Capture! & SynthWorks MT-32, Editor/Librarians for the Atari ST." *Keyboard* 14 (Sept. 1988): 141–43.

5667. ——. "Keyboard Report: Sonus SST Sequencer Software for the Atari ST." *Keyboard* 14 (Feb. 1988): 152–54, 169.

5668. ——. "Keyboard Report: Soundfiler ST, S900 Sample Editor." *Keyboard* 14 (May 1988): 136, 142.

For the Atari ST and the Akai S900 sampler.

5669. ——. "Keyboard Report: Steinberg Cubase, Sequencer Software for Atari ST." *Keyboard* 15 (Oct. 1989): 116–22.

5670. ——. "Keyboard Report: Steinberg Pro-24 Sequencer for the Atari ST." *Keyboard* 12 (Dec. 1986): 122–28.

5671. ——. "Keyboard Report: Steinberg SynthWorks D-50 Editor/Librarian for the Atari ST." *Keyboard* 15 (Jan. 1989): 135–36.

5672. ——. "Keyboard Report: Steinberg SynthWorks DX/TX 2.0, Editor/Librarian." *Keyboard* 14 (Apr. 1988): 155–57.

5673. ——. "Keyboard Report: Steinberg SynthWorks M1, Editor/Librarian for Atari ST." *Keyboard* 15 (Sept. 1989): 127–28, 136.

5674. ——. "Keyboard Report: Sys-ex Potpourri—Editor/Librarians & Miscellany for the Atari ST." *Keyboard* 13 (May 1987): 126–28.

DX-Heaven, 4-Op Deluxe, Perfect Patch, CZ-Patch, and Data Dumpstor ST.

5675. ——. "Keyboard Report: Updates—E-mu SP-1200 & Dr. T's KCS-ST 1.5." *Keyboard* 13 (Oct. 1987): 158.

5676. ——. "Short Takes: K1 Ed-Lib, for the Atari ST." *Keyboard* 14 (Nov. 1988): 155.

For the Kawai K1 synthesizer and the Atari ST.

5677. Alberts, Randy. "Compu-Mates Korg DW-8000 Synthdroid + Programming Software." *Electronic Musician* 3 (Dec. 1987): 85.

Review of voice editor, random patch generator, and librarian software; for the Korg DW-8000 and Atari ST.

5678. Allgeier, Jeffrey H. "It's Immaterial." *Music, Computers & Software* 3 (Apr. 1988): 32.

Profile/interview with members of the rock band, who discuss their use of MIDI and the Atari ST.

5679. Anderson, John J. "Sound Advice: The State of the Art in Audio Digitization." *Atari Explorer* 8 (May–June 1988): 39–42.

Describes ST Sound Digitizer, Parrott II, and ST Replay, three digitizers.

5680. ——, and Robert Swirsky. "Outpost: Atari: The State of Atari and a Musical Instrument to Make." *Creative Computing* 11 (Mar. 1985): 152–53.

How to create a computerized Theremin with an Atari.

5681. Anderton, Craig. "Dr. T. Atari ST K3 Editor; Compu-Mates K3PO+ Atari ST K3 Editor." *Electronic Musician* 3 (July 1987): 21–22.
Reviews of editor/librarian software; for the Kawai K3M synthesizer.

5682. ———. "Review: Hybrid Arts DX Droid." *Electronic Musician* 2 (June 1986): 72–75.
An editor-librarian; for the Atari ST and Yamaha DX7.

5683. ———. "Reviews: Interval Music Systems GenWave." *Electronic Musician* 5 (Nov. 1989): 108–13.
Sample editing software; for the Atari.

5684. Arnell, Billy. "Atari Music: Drumware 'Soundfiler ST.'" *Music, Computers & Software* 3 (Aug. 1988): 56–57.
Review of the sample editor; for the Akai S-900 and the Atari ST.

5685. ———. "Atari Music: MIDISoft Studio Advanced Edition." *Music, Computers & Software* 3 (Nov. 1988): 60–61.
Review of the MIDI control program.

5686. ———. "Atari Music: Sonic Flight from MIDIMouse Music." *Music, Computers & Software* 3 (Dec. 1988): 56–57.
Review of the series of patch editor/librarians for synthesizers from Roland, Ensoniq, and Casio, and for the Atari ST.

5687. ———. "Atari Music: Steinberg 'Synth Works DX/TX.'" *Music, Computers & Software* 3 (June 1988): 68–69.
Review of the patch editor/librarian; for the Yamaha DX7II and TX802 and the Atari ST.

5688. ———. "MCScope System." *Music, Computers & Software* 3 (Apr. 1988): 58–63.
The commercial arranger discusses his use of an Atari ST as the main controller in his MIDI system.

5689. ———. "Savant Audio's Edit 8000 Librarian and Editor for the Korg DW800 and EX800 and the Atari ST." *Music, Computers & Software* 3 (Feb. 1988): 77.
Review.

5690. "The Atari ST: Putting It All Together." *Music, Computers & Software* 2 (Aug. 1987): 42–50.
An overview of the Atari ST computers, emphasizing their musical uses. Also includes a brief guide to music software for the ST.

5691. "Atari to Sell Computers through Music Stores." *Music Trades* 135 (July 1987): 92–94.

5692. Atkins, Martin; Andrew Bentley; Thomas Endrich; Rajmil Fischman; David Malham; Richard Orton; and Trevor Wishart. "The Composers' Desktop Project." In *Proceedings of the 1987 International Computer Music Conference: University of Illinois at Urbana-Champaign, Urbana, Illinois, USA, August 23–26, 1987,* comp. James Beauchamp. San Francisco, Calif.: Computer Music Association, 1987: 146–50.

5693. Barbour, Eric. "Software: Why Buy a MIDI Sequencer When You Could Get an Atari ST Instead?" *Electronic Musician* 2 (June 1986): 42–43.

5694. "BASIC Sound on the Atari ST." *Compute!* 8 (Mar. 1986): 110–12.

An excerpt from *Compute!*'s *ST Programmers Guide.*

5695. Belian, Barry. "The Atari Musician." *Compute!* 5 (May 1983): 214–16.

Two programs that compute pitch values for scales and chords.

5696. Beutel, Thomas. "Software: A Practical MIDI Application for the Atari ST." *Electronic Musician* 3 (Feb. 1987): 28–30.

5697. Brilliant, Lee S. "Bits 'n' Pieces: Pops." *Analog Computing* n66 (Nov. 1988): 54–60.

A hardware project for adding four-channel stereo sound to an Atari.

5698. Cecil, Malcolm. "Computers: Atari 520ST: The MIDI PC." *Electronic Musician* 2 (June 1986): 37–40.

5699. Collinge, Douglas J., and Daniel J. Scheidt. "Moxie for the Atari ST." In *Proceedings of the 14th International Computer Music Conference, Cologne, September 20–25, 1988,* ed. Christoph Lischka and Johannes Fritsch. Cologne: Feedback-Studio-Verlag; San Francisco, Calif.: Dist. by Computer Music Association, 1988: 231–38. (Feedback Papers; 33)

Describes Moxie, an event scheduler; for the Atari ST.

5700. "Compu-Mates Software—Expanding a New Market." *Music Trades* 136 (Jan. 1988): 118.

5701. Cowart, Robert. "Keyboard Report: Atari 520ST Computer." *Keyboard* 12 (Feb. 1986): 116–19.

5702. Daniel, Walter K. "MIDI: MIDIPrint for the Atari ST." *Electronic Musician* 3 (June 1987): 74–75.

How to modify the software MIDIPrint, originally for the Commodore 64, so it will run on an Atari.

5703. Davies, Rick. "ADAP Soundrack." *Music Technology* 1 (Sept. 1986): 86–87.

Review of sampling software.

5704.   ———. "Dr T Keyboard Controlled Sequencer for Atari ST Computer." *Music Technology* 1 (Feb. 1987): 92–94.
Review.

5705.   ———. "In Brief: Hybrid Arts DX-Droid." *Music Technology* 1,1 (1986): 30.
Review of DX sound-editing package.

5706.   Di Perna, Alan. "ST Heresy and the Cult of Computer Worship." *Musician* n105 (July 1987): 54–63.
Music software; for the Atari ST.

5707.   Dimond, Stuart Dudley, III. "Sound Chip: Reviews of Guitar Wizard and Dr. T's MIDI Recording Studio and a Look at Things to Come." *Atari Explorer* 8 (Jan.–Feb. 1988): 26.

5708.   Dorfman, Len, and Dennis Young. *Atari ST Introduction to MIDI Programming.* Grand Rapids, Mich.: Abacus Software, 1986. 256 p.

5709.   Duberman, David. "Review: Softsynth." *ST-Log: The Atari ST Monthly Magazine* n22 (Aug. 1988): 84–85.

5710.   Ebling, Tim. "Do-It-Yourself: The Slick MIDI Slider for the Atari ST." *Electronic Musician* 5 (July 1989): 76–83.
A structured BASIC program that lets an Atari ST change synth parameters.

5711.   ———. "Percussion: Random Rhythms." *Electronic Musician* 3 (Apr. 1987): 36–44.
A program in BASIC that generates random rhythms and melodies; for the Atari 800.

5712.   "Electronic Music Swings on the Air Waves." *Personal Computing* 7 (May 1983): 53.
A short description of how songwriter Bob Federer uses an Atari 400 to write music.

5713.   Enders, Bernd, and Wolfgang Klemme. *MIDI and Sound Book for the Atari ST.* Translated ed. Redwood City, Calif.: M&T Pub., 1989: 293 p.
English version of *MIDI- und Sound-Buch zum Atari ST.*

5714.   Frederick, Dave. "Keyboard Report: DX-Droid Voicing & Librarian Software for the Atari ST." *Keyboard* 12 (July 1986): 140–42.

5715.   Gershin, Scott. "Akai S900 Sample Editors: Steinberg Sound Works; Drumware Soundfiler." *Music Technology* 2 (Feb. 1988): 73–77.
Review of two visual editing programs.

5716. ———. "Compu-Mates R100 DrumDroid." *Music Technology* 2 (Feb. 1988): 63.

Review of drum machine software; for an Atari ST and a Kawai R100.

5717. ———. "Hybrid Arts ADAP Soundrack." *Music Technology* 2 (Oct. 1987): 37–41.

Review of the 16-bit stereo sampling sound processor.

5718. ———. "In Brief: Aegix Perfect Patch Editor/Librarian." *Music Technology* 2 (Sept. 1987): 38.

Review of software; for the Yamaha DX7.

5719. ———. "In Brief: Savant Audio Edit8000." *Music Technology* 2 (Dec. 1987): 52.

Review of editor/librarian software.

5720. Giwer, Matt. "Adding Sound Effects to Atari." *Compute!* 7 (Feb. 1985): 109–11.

Five BASIC programs to create notes, chords, and harmonics.

5721. ———. "Atari Sound Experimenter." *Compute!* 5 (July 1983): 200–203.

A BASIC program that allows control over all sound registers.

5722. Gotcher, Peter. "Computers for Keyboardists: Choosing a Computer: A Closer Look at the Atari ST." *Keyboard* 13 (Aug. 1987): 102.

5723. Hague, James. "Atari Sound Commander." *Compute!* 8 (Nov. 1986): 61–63.

Sound programs using machine language subroutines and BASIC to create sound effects and music.

5724. Hallas, Aaron. "Hybrid Arts EZ-Score Plus." *Music Technology* 2 (Mar. 1988): 71–73.

Review of scoring software.

5725. Hatchard, Mike. "Playing the Synthesizer: Sequencing." *Crescendo International* 25 (Mar. 1988): 32.

Describes Creator software from C-Labs on the Atari ST.

5726. ———. "The World of Electronics: C-Labs Notator Update." *Crescendo International* 26 (Feb. 1989): 36–37.

5727. ———. "The World of Electronics: Composing on the Atari ST: One Man's Method." *Crescendo International* 25 (Nov.–Dec. 1988): 36–37.

Use of C-Labs Notator software.

5728. ———. "The World of Electronics: Score-Writing Software." *Crescendo International* 25 (May 1988): 31.

Describes C-Labs Notator software.

5729.   Havey, Paul N. "Musical Atari Keyboard." *Compute!* 5 (Aug. 1983): 204–7.

Description and listing of a BASIC program to generate the sound of bells, piano, or organ via the computer keyboard.

5730.   Herzberg, Larry. "MIDIMON." *ST-Log: The Atari ST Monthly Magazine* n22 (Aug. 1988): 22–25.

A program that provides a detailed analysis of MIDI data output from most standard controllers.

5731.   Jablonski, Dennis. "Applications: Dr. T's KCS Made Easy." *Electronic Musician* 4 (Sept. 1988): 32–35.

5732.   Johnson, Bruce A. "First Take: Capsule Comments: Dr. T's KEYS! for the Atari ST." *Electronic Musician* 5 (Aug. 1989): 70–72.

5733.   ———. "Megatouch Atari ST Keyboard Modification." *Electronic Musician* 5 (June 1989): 89.

A bag of springs to install on an Atari keyboard.

5734.   Johnson, Jim. "Applications: In the Public Eye: Free Atari Software." *Electronic Musician* 5 (Oct. 1989): 28–35.

5735.   ———. "Applications: Using Dr. T's Programmable Variations Generator." *Electronic Musician* 5 (Aug. 1989): 28–31.

5736.   ———. "The Atari ST Power User. Pt. I, The Hardware." *Electronic Musician* 4 (Nov. 1988): 29–34.

5737.   ———. "Atari ST Public Domain Patch Editors and Librarians." *Electronic Musician* 4 (Feb. 1988): 113–14.

Review of CZLIB, DXLIB, FB-Patch, and DX7-Patch.

5738.   ———. "Caged Artist's ESQ-apade: Editor/Librarian Program for the Ensoniq ESQ Synthesizers and the Atari ST." *Music, Computers & Software* 2 (Oct. 1987): 72–73.

Review.

5739.   ———. "Chord: An Algorithmic Composing Program in Atari ST BASIC." *Electronic Musician* 4 (Apr. 1988): 22–30.

5740.   ———. "Dr. T's Keyboard Controlled Sequencer for the Atari ST." *Music, Computers & Software* 2 (June 1987): 70–72.

Review of the MIDI sequencer program for the Atari ST.

5741.   ———. "Music Service Software's Data Dumpstor ST." *Music, Computers & Software* 2 (May 1987): 63.

A universal MIDI system exclusive data storage program; for the Atari ST.

5742. ———. "The ST Power User. Pt. II, The Software." *Electronic Musician* 4 (Dec. 1988): 22–27.

5743. Knolle, Niels. "Anhang: Informationen zum MIDI-Recording mit einem einfachen schulgeeigneten Computer-Synthesizer-Set für DM5000." *Musik und Bildung* 21 (Juni 1989): 337–39.

5744. Krutz, Jamie. "Dr. T's Atari ST 'The Copyist,' Version 1.4." *Electronic Musician* 3 (Dec. 1987): 78–79.
Review.

5745. ———. "First Take: Savant Audio Atari ST Edit-8000; Synergy Resources Atari ST SynthView." *Electronic Musician* 4 (Mar. 1988): 90–91.
Review of sequencer, editor, and librarian programs.

5746. ———. "Hybrid Arts ST 'GenPatch.'" *Electronic Musician* 3 (Dec. 1987): 80–81.
Review of a generic patch librarian.

5747. ———. "HyperTek/Silicon Springs Atari ST OmniRes Monitor Emulator." *Electronic Musician* 4 (Mar. 1988): 91, 101.
Review.

5748. ———. "MIDIMouse Music Atari ST Fast Tracks ST 1.0." *Electronic Musician* 4 (Mar. 1988): 101.
Review of sequencing software.

5749. ———. "The Musical Computer: The Atari Arrives." *Electronic Musician* 4 (Apr. 1988): 64–71.
A general overview of the use of the Atari ST for musical applications.

5750. ———. "Reviews: RealTime 1.1 for the Atari ST." *Electronic Musician* 5 (Aug. 1989): 92–97.
Sequencing software.

5751. Many, Chris. "Command Development D50 Command: A Patch Editor, Librarian, and Creator for the Atari ST." *Music Technology* 2 (May 1988): 70–71.
Review of patch editor/librarian/sound design software for the Atari ST and Roland D50.

5752. ———. "Hybrid Arts' MIDITrack ST." *Music Technology* 1 (June 1987): 68–70.
Review of sequencing software.

5753. Meyer, Chris. "Fair Results." *Music Technology* 1 (Dec. 1986): 44–46.
Review of the Northern California Atari Expo, San Jose, Sept. 1986.

5754. Moorhead, Jan Paul. "First Take: Capsule Comments: D-50 Command for the Atari ST." *Electronic Musician* 4 (Dec. 1988): 94–96.

5755. ———. "Reviews: Notator and Creator: New Levels of Sequencing for the Atari ST." *Electronic Musician* 5 (Jan. 1989): 108–13.

5756. O'Donnell, Bob. "Dr. T's MT32 Editor/Librarian." *Music Technology* 2 (Feb. 1988): 66.

Review of voice editing software; for the Roland MT32 and Atari ST.

5757. ———. "Intelligent Music's M: Interactive Music Composition Package for the Atari ST." *Music Technology* 2 (Mar. 1988): 66.

Review.

5758. ———. "Transform XSyn: Sound Editing Programs." *Music Technology* 2 (Nov. 1987): 36–39.

Review of Transform Modular Music System, software for sequencing, scoring, editing, and printing.

5759. Pierson-Perry, Jim. "Reviews: Dr. T's TIGER Graphic Sequence Editing for the Atari ST." *Electronic Musician* 5 (Dec. 1989): 116–19.

5760. ———. "Reviews: Hybrid Arts EZ-Score Plus V. 1.1." *Electronic Musician* 5 (June 1989): 94–97.

Scoring software for the Atari ST.

5761. ———. "Reviews: Steinberg/Jones Avalon." *Electronic Musician* 5 (Dec. 1989): 126–31.

Sample editing software.

5762. Proper, Darcy. "Microcomputers for Musicians: Strike up the Band." *Active Sensing* 1 (Summer 1989): 8–9.

A description of how the Atari is used by musicians.

5763. Reed, Tony. "Control Zone: Greate ST." *Melody Maker* 64 (Feb. 20, 1988): 42–43.

An overview of what an Atari ST can do musically and a chart of available software.

5764. Rodriguez, Toni. *Fare musica con Atari.* [Make Music with the Atari] Padua, Italy: F. Muzzio, 1987. 234 p. (Gli strumenti della musica; 23)

5765. Russell, Benjamin. "Dr. T Sequencer for Atari ST." *Canadian Musician* 10 (Feb. 1988): 32.

Describes some features and the product release history.

5766. Ryder, Michael. "Atari Sound Development System." *Compute!* 8 (July 1986): 69–75.

A BASIC program to design sounds on screen with a joystick and keyboard.

5767. Ryle, Geoffrey. "Applications: Secrets of the Steinberg/Jones Pro-24 III Sequencer." *Electronic Musician* 5 (June 1989): 74–79.

An in-depth discussion of using the Pro-24 sequencer with the Atari ST.

5768. Scarborough, John. "Atari's Sound System." *Compute!* 5 (Jan. 1983): 48–50.

How to bypass the SOUND command to improve the Atari's sound and music.

5769. Sharp, Daniel, and Joe West. "MIDIMate and MIDITrack II." *Whole Earth Review* no. 49 (Winter 1985): 111.

Very brief reviews of a MIDI interface and a sequencer.

5770. Snow, David. "Beat-it: A Drum Sensor Interface for the Atari ST." *Electronic Musician* 4 (Dec. 1988): 87–93.

5771. ———. "Do-It-Yourself: RandoM1: A Patch Generator/Librarian for the Korg M1." *Electronic Musician* 5 (Aug. 1989): 48–56.

An LDW BASIC program; for the Atari ST.

5772. ———. "Dr. T's Fingers for the Atari ST." *Electronic Musician* 5 (May 1989): 90–91.

Review of the composition/performance software.

5773. ———. "Drumbox, the CZ/ST Connection." *Electronic Musician* 4 (Feb. 1988): 32–43.

Program listing in ST BASIC that generates, plays, and sequences random rhythmic patterns on a CZ synthesizer.

5774. ———. "The MIDI Music Box: More Cheap Thrills for the Atari ST." *Electronic Musician* 5 (Mar. 1989): 58–67.

An algorithmic composition program in LDW BASIC and assembly language.

5775. "Softsynth for the Atari ST." *Canadian Musician* 9 (Oct. 1987): 29.

5776. Tapper, Larry. "Guide to Atari Music Software." *Atari Explorer* 8 (July–Aug. 1988): 34–37.

A list of music software.

5777. Tedsen, Fred. "16-bit Atari Music." *Compute!* 5 (Mar. 1983): 214–20.

Subroutines to improve the Atari's tuning and extend its range.

5778. Thomas, Tony. "Atari Music: Hybrid Arts 'EZ Score' Plus." *Music, Computers & Software* 3 (Oct. 1988): 76–77.

Review of the music notation program.

5779.   Trask, Simon. "Steinberg Pro 24: Software for Atari ST Computers."
Music Technology 1 (Nov. 1986): 60–63.
Review of the multitrack MIDI recording system.

5780.   ——. "Steinberg ProCreator: Software for Yamaha DX/TX and Atari
ST." *Music Technology* 1 (Jan. 1987): 60–62.
Review of the random patch generator.

5781.   Vail, Mark. "Keyboard Report: Dr. T's PVG, Programmable Variations Generator & Master Editor." *Keyboard* 14 (July 1988): 174–75,
178.

5782.   Vinella, Peter. "In Brief: Beam Team TRANSfORM Software."
Music Technology 1 (Jan. 1987): 16.
Pre-release review of librarian software.

5783.   ——. "Review: Hybrid Arts EZ-Track." *Electronic Musician* 3 (Jan.
1987): 67–69.
Sequencing software.

5784.   Waschka, Rodney, and Tózé Ferreira. "Rapid Event Deployment in a
MIDI Environment." *Interface* 17 (1988): 211–22.
Abstract in *Proceedings of the 14th International Computer Music
Conference, Cologne, September 20–25, 1988,* ed. Christoph Lischka
and Johannes Fritsch. Cologne: Feedback-Studio-Verlag; San Fran-
cisco, Calif.: Dist. by Computer Music Association, 1988: 398.
Describes granular synthesis on an Atari 1040stf interfaced via
MIDI to synthesizers.

5785.   Waugh, Ian. "In Brief: Steinberg Cosmo." *Music Technology* 1 (June
1987): 30.
Review of voice editing software for the Casio CZ.

5786.   Wehinger, Rainer. "Computer-Experimente." *Musica* 42 (1988):
37–43.
A BASIC program to create music on an Atari with an expander
via MIDI.

5787.   Williamson, Charles. "Reviews: Dr. T's KCS Level II with MPE for
the Atari ST." *Electronic Musician* 4 (Sept. 1988): 84–91.

5788.   Witt, Richard. "The Simplest Atari Notation Program You'll Ever
See." *Electronic Musician* 5 (Feb. 1989): 98–103.
Description and program listing of Transcribe, in ST BASIC.

MICROCOMPUTERS — COMMODORE

5789. Aikin, Jim. "Keyboard Report: Moog Song Producer, Dr. T's Keyboard Controlled Sequencer & MusicData MIDI Sequencer for the Commodore 64." *Keyboard* 11 (Sept. 1985): 82–91.

5790. Anderton, Craig. "Personal Computers Become Personal Composers. Part I, Basics of the Commodore-64." *Record* 3 (July 1984): 46–47.

5791. ———. "Personal Computers Become Personal Composers. Part II, Music Software for the Commodore 64." *Record* 3 (Aug. 1984): 50.

An overview of Music Construction Set, Music Writer 64, Synthy-64, and MusiCalc.

5792. ———. "Review: Syntech Studio I." *Electronic Musician* 2 (Feb. 1986): 67–68.

A sequencer program.

5793. Bagley, James. "Mozart Magic." *Compute!* 8 (Oct. 1986): 89–91.

Based on a musical game devised by Mozart, this program composes minuets in his style.

5794. Baird, Jock. "Software City: CZ Meets C-64: Six Inexpensive Librarians and Editors That Can Turn Your Casio into a Powerhouse." *Musician* n97 (Nov. 1986): 52–56, 100.

5795. Bateman, Selby. "Commodore's 64 and 128: Marvelous Music Machines." *Compute!'s Gazette* 5 (Aug. 1987): 18–21.

A general description of the music capabilities of the Commodore 64/128.

5796. Brooks, David R. "The Best of Music Products." *Commodore Microcomputers* 7 (Nov.–Dec. 1986): 132.

Lists Keyboard Controlled Sequencer, Casio CZ-101, Sampler-64, and Advanced Music System as the best music products of 1986.

5797. ———. "Making Music with MIDI: By Combining a Commodore with MIDI Technology, Almost Anyone Can Produce Professional-sounding Music." *Run: The Commodore 64/128 User's Guide* 4 (July 1987): 38–42.

5798. ———. "Software Reviews: Dr. T's C128 Keyboard Controlled Sequencer." *Commodore Magazine* 8 (Nov. 1987): 38, 127.

5799. ———. "Software Reviews: The Advanced Music System." *Commodore Magazine* 8 (Feb. 1987): 44–46.

Music composition and editing software.

5800. Butterfield, Jim. "Commodore 64 Music: Happy Birthday." *Compute!* 6 (Oct. 1984): 177–78.

A BASIC program that plays "Happy Birthday."

5801. Campbell, Alan Gary. "Questions and Answers." *Electronic Musician* 3 (Oct. 1987): 44–45, 105–6.

Answers to questions about the Commodore 64, DIN sync converters and the SP-12.

5802. ———. "Triangle Audio C-64 DX/TX and CZ Patch Librarians." *Electronic Musician* 4 (Jan. 1988): 81.

Review of DX/TX Librarian and CZ Librarian.

5803. Campbell, Tom, and Larry McClain. "MusiCalc: MusiCalc Can Make the Commodore 64 Play Sweetly but not without a Lot of Effort on Your Part." *Popular Computing* 4 (Nov. 1984): 158–62.

Review of music composition software.

5804. Chandler, James C. "ES1 Librarian for Ensoniq ESQ-1 and C-64." *Electronic Musician* 4 (Jan. 1988): 79.

Review.

5805. ———. "JiffyDOS/64 for the Commodore 64 and SX-64." *Electronic Musician* 4 (Jan. 1988): 81–82.

Review.

5806. ———. "Keyfrets: Keyboard to Guitar Voicing Translator." *Electronic Musician* 4 (Aug. 1988): 74–81.

A program for the Commodore 64 to make a keyboard sound like a guitar.

5807. ———. "Review: Moog Song Producer." *Electronic Musician* 2 (Mar. 1986): 65–67.

MIDI sequencer software.

5808. ———. "X-LIB Patch Librarian for Yamaha DX/TX Synths and the Commodore 64." *Electronic Musician* 4 (Mar. 1988): 91.

5809. Cross, Hubert. "Sound Manager." *Compute!'s Gazette* 6 (Jan. 1988): 62–70.

A program for installing sound in other programs.

5810. Daniel, Walter K. "Review: Dr. T's CZ Patch Librarian." *Electronic Musician* 2 (July 1986): 74–75.

5811. ———. "Software: Alternate Scales on the Commodore 64: A Tuning Demonstration Program." *Electronic Musician* 3 (Oct. 1987): 38–43.

A BASIC program that produces equal temperament, Pythagorean tuning, or one version of just intonation.

5812. Davies, Rick. "Sonus Sequencer and MIDI Data Editor: Software for Commodore 64." *Music Technology* 1 (Apr. 1987): 68–70.

Review of Super Sequencer 64, MIDI Processor, and MIDI Tech.

5813. Dowty, Tim. "Random Patch Roundup." *Electronic Musician* 3 (Aug. 1987): 56–61, 79.

Description and listing of a random patch generator program in BASIC; for the Commodore 64 and Casio CZ-101 or 1000 synthesizer.

5814. ———. "Software: CZ Patch Librarian." *Electronic Musician* 3 (Feb. 1987): 38–43.

A patch librarian program to move patch data from the Casio CZ-101 to the Commodore 64.

5815. ———. "Software: Using the EM Interface: A MIDI Echo/Delay." *Electronic Musician* 2 (Aug. 1986): 29–32.

A program in BASIC for the C-64 for experimenting with MIDI echo.

5816. "Dr. T's Algorithmic Composer." *Keyboards, Computers & Software* 1 (Dec. 1986): 60–61.

Review of computer aided composition software; for the Commodore 64/128.

5817. Erikson, Chris. "Do-It-Yourself: The EM DX/TX Patch Librarian." *Electronic Musician* 5 (Apr. 1989): 76–81.

Patch librarian program; for the Commodore 64.

5818. Freiberger, Paul. "Learning to Play Music on the C-64." *InfoWorld* 5 (Nov. 14, 1983): 32–33.

Description of MusiCalc 1.

5819. Greenwald, Ted. "Keyboard Report: Algorithmic Composer and KCS 128." *Keyboard* 12 (Oct. 1986): 142–48, 162.

5820.   Guerra, Bob. "64 and 128 Reviews: Super Sequencer 128." *Commodore Magazine* 9 (May 1988): 34.

Review of sequencing software.

5821.   Hanlon, Caroline D. "Buyer's Guide to Music Composition and Programming Software." *Compute!'s Gazette* 6 (Aug. 1988): 45, 53–56.

Very short descriptions of thirty-three music software packages.

5822.   Henry, Thomas. "Practical Circuitry: The Commodore 64 RS-232 Interface." *Electronic Musician* 2 (July 1986): 66–70.

5823.   Herrington, Peggy. "Putting Baby to Sleep with a Commodore 64." *Family Computing* 2 (Sept. 1984): 108–9.

Program listing of Brahms' Lullaby that plays repeatedly until manually stopped.

5824.   Iovine, John. "Building a MIDI Interface Device for the Commodore 64 and 128." *Commodore Magazine* 10 (Mar. 1989): 48–49, 94–95.

5825.   ———. "Sound Digitizer II." *Commodore Magazine* 9 (Nov. 1988): 52–54, 104.

Directions for making an audio digitizer for the Commodore. Includes listings for the Commodore 128.

5826.   Jenkins, Mark. "Control Zone at Frankfurt: Steinberg Pro 16 Software." *Melody Maker* 61 (Feb. 15, 1986): XIV sup.

Review of the Yamaha Steinberg Pro 16 software sequencer for the Commodore 64.

5827.   Johnson, Jim. "KCS Applications." *Keyboards, Computers & Software* 1 (Aug. 1986): 10, 75.

The author describes his use of the Commodore 64 in live performance.

5828.   ———. "Micro Arts Products Sampler-64." *Keyboards, Computers & Software* 1 (Dec. 1986): 51–52.

Review of sound sampling peripheral that includes software, microphone, and monitor adapter cable.

5829.   ———. "MIDI: MIDIPrint: A MIDI Data Display Program." *Electronic Musician* 2 (Sept. 1986): 46–49.

5830.   Kerkhoff, Jim. "Random MIDI." *Electronic Musician* 3 (Dec. 1987): 20–23.

A COMAL (COMmon Algorithmic Language) program listing that generates random pitches and velocities and then converts them into appropriate MIDI Note-on and Note-off commands.

5831. Leonard, Steve. "Computers for Keyboardists: What Do You Say to a Naked Interface Card?" *Keyboard* 12 (May 1986): 98.

Sample program to talk with a MIDI interface card.

5832. Lewis, Bill. "A New York Band Turns to Computers: Dueling Commodores." *Keyboards, Computers & Software* 1 (Feb. 1986): 19–20.

The band Tangerine added two Commodore 64s when their keyboardist left.

5833. ———. "Valhala Sound Library." *Keyboards, Computers & Software* 2 (Feb. 1987): 71, 74.

Review of sound library and patch librarian software for the Commodore 64/128 and Yamaha DX synthesizers.

5834. Lisowski, James A. "Hear the Scales." *Electronic Musician* 3 (Oct. 1987): 42.

A BASIC program to generate scales in equal temperament, Pythagorean tuning, or just intonation.

5835. Mace, Scott. "Sophisticated Synthesizers Target Personal Computers." *InfoWorld* 6 (Feb. 6, 1984): 59–60.

Description of a six-voice synthesizer that interfaces with a Commodore 64.

5836. Malone, Don. "Do-It-Yourself: MIDI Sample and Hold." *Electronic Musician* 4 (Oct. 1988): 86–89.

An algorithmic composition/performance program; for the Commodore 64.

5837. ———. "Dr. Sound for the 64." *Compute!* 8 (Sept. 1986): 89–93.

An algorithmic note sequencer program.

5838. Mansfield, Richard. "Synthy 64." *Compute!* 5 (Oct. 1983): 152–54.

Review of composition software.

5839. Many, Chris. "Auricle II: The Film Composer's Time Processor." *Music Technology* 1 (Apr. 1987): 24–26.

5840. Massey, Howard. *The Compact Guide to MIDI Software for the Commodore 64/128.* London; New York: Amsco Publications, 1988. 72 p.

5841. Monaghan, Dan. "Synthesis." *Compute!* 9 (May 1987): 62–68.

A discussion and listing of a program that turns the Commodore 64 into a music synthesizer.

5842. Moore, Herb. "The Anatomy of a Note." *Classroom Computer Learning* 6 (Jan. 1986): 70–72.

A short discussion on envelopes and a demonstration program.

5843.   Mulvaney, Paul G. "Automatic Irish Jigs on a Commodore-64." *Keyboard* 13 (Mar. 1987): 90–91, 148.

5844.   Nelson, Philip I. "128 Sound and Music. Part 2." *Compute!'s Gazette* 7 (Sept. 1985): 113–16.

How to use the FILTER, SOUND, and PLAY commands in BASIC.

5845.   ———. "Exploring the SID Chip." *Compute!'s Gazette* 5 (Aug. 1987): 22–24, 84.

An overview of the Sound Interface Device (SID) chip.

5846.   ———. "Sound and Music on the Commodore 128. Part 1." *Compute!'s Gazette* 7 (Aug. 1985): 76–78.

How to use the VOL, TEMPO, and ENVELOPE statements in BASIC.

5847.   Petersen, Marty. "Review: Synthesound 64." *InfoWorld* 6 (Apr. 9, 1984): 44–45.

Music-generating software.

5848.   Picard, Ronald V. "64 Sound Tester." *Compute!* 5 (Nov. 1983): 187.

A program to experiment with the sound system of the Commodore 64.

5849.   Pierce, Chuck. "Juno 106/DX21 Random Patch Generator." *Electronic Musician* 4 (Mar. 1988): 38–42.

A BASIC program listing for the Roland Juno 106 or the Yamaha DX21 and the Commodore 64.

5850.   ———. "Reader Tips: Commodore MIDI File Editor." *Keyboard* 14 (Sept. 1988): 20–22, 154.

A MIDI file editor without step editing.

5851.   Russell, Benjamin. "Computers and Music: Music Software for the Commodore 64." *Canadian Musician* 8 (Aug. 1986): 82, 85.

Review of MIDI 4/Plus, Studio I, and Keyboard Controlled Sequencer.

5852.   ———. "Product Report: Dr. T's Sequencer for Commodore 128." *Canadian Musician* 8 (Dec. 1986): 32–33.

Review of a version of Keyboard Controlled Sequencer for the Commodore 128.

5853.   Schulack, Barbara. "Songs in the Key of C-128: Entering Music Is an Exercise in Harmony with Music Editor." *Run: The Commodore 64/128 User's Guide* 5 (Oct. 1988): 49–53.

Program listing of Music Editor, software to facilitate entering music for use by the PLAY statement.

5854. Smith, Steven. "Applications: Sonus Super Sequencer for the C-64 and 128." *Electronic Musician* 3 (Mar. 1987): 100–103.

5855. "Sonus Develops Music Software." *Music Trades* 134 (Sept. 1986): 83–84.

An introduction to Super Sequencer 128, a multi-functional, professional MIDI recording system and librarian; for the Commodore 128.

5856. Speerschneider, Roger. "Dynamusic." *Compute!'s Gazette* 5 (Aug. 1987): 62–63, 90–92.

A set of programs that play music while another program is running.

5857. Sterling, Mark. "Hardware: Commodore, a Work Horse Gets Some Respect." *Keyboards, Computers & Software* 1 (Aug. 1986): 37–39.

5858. Stockford, James. "CZ-Rider." *Whole Earth Review* no. 49 (Winter 1985): 111.

Very brief review of a patch editor/librarian; for the Casio CZ-101 or CZ-1000 and Roland MIDI interface.

5859. Stockford, James. "Dr. T's MIDI Sequencer Program." *Whole Earth Review* no. 49 (Winter 1985): 110.

Very brief review.

5860. Tarabella, Leonello, and Graziano Bertini. "Un sistema di sintesi di elevate prestazioni controllato da personal computer." [A System of Synthesis of Raised Performances Controlled by a Personal Computer] In *Musica e tecnologia: industria e cultura per lo sviluppo del mezzogiorno: VI Colloquio di Informatica Musicale, Napoli 16–19 ottobre 1985*, ed. Carlo Acreman, Immacolata Ortosecco, and Fausto Razzi. Milan: Edizioni Unicopli, 1987: 330–35.

5861. Tarr, Greg. "Basically Music: A Complete Compositional Tool for the 64." *Compute!'s Gazette* 6 (Mar. 1988): 73–81.

A BASIC program for control of the Commodore 64's sound chip.

5862. West, Joe. "A Keyboard for MusiCalc . . . The Colortone Keyboard." *Whole Earth Review* no. 45 (Mar. 1985): 99.

Very brief review.

5863. Williamson, Charles. "Review: Dr. T's Echo Plus." *Electronic Musician* 2 (Apr. 1986): 67–68, 70.

5864. ———. "Review: Dr. T's Keyboard Controlled Sequencer (Version 2)." *Electronic Musician* 2 (Feb. 1986): 60–61.

A sequencer program.

5865.   Zuckerman, Faye. "'Musicalc' Playing Hit Song; Software Chart Analysis." *Billboard* 96 (June 23, 1984): 30.

Development of the music composition program Musicalc I.

MICROCOMPUTERS—IBM AND COMPATIBLES

5866. Ager, Klaus. "Professionelle Musiknotation mit Hilfe eines Personal-Computers." In *Die Musikerziehung in Zeitalter der Elektronik: 20. DACH-Tagung, Golling, Salzburg, April–Mai 1988: Tagungsbericht,* ed. Brigitte Peschl. Vienna: VWGÖ, 1989: 83–87.

   Describes the SCORE program.

5867. Aikin, Jim. "Keyboard Report: Cakewalk, Sequencer for the IBM PC." *Keyboard* 13 (Dec. 1987): 144–47.

5868. ———. "Keyboard Report: Roland MPS, Sequencing/Notation Software." *Keyboard* 12 (Apr. 1986): 124–29, 146.

5869. ———. "Keyboard Report: SampleVision S900, Editor for the IBM." *Keyboard* 14 (Aug. 1988): 124–30.

5870. ———. "Keyboard Report: Score, Notation Software." *Keyboard* 14 (July 1988): 156–66.

5871. Baird, Jock. "The Secret Life of a Business Computer: Ten MIDI Sequencer Programs That'll Definitely Liven up Your IBM-PC." *Musician* n110 (Dec. 1987): 42–50, 54–56.

5872. ———. "Software City." *Musician* n92 (June 1986): 44.

   Brief reviews of Sidekick and Voice Manager from Bäcchus, and the Octave Plateau Patch Master; for the IBM PC.

5873. ———. "Software City: Ensoniq's Vision." *Musician* n101 (Mar. 1987): 56.

   Describes a visual editing software program; for the Ensoniq Mirage and the IBM PC.

5874. ———. "Software City: Roland MPS." *Musician* n88 (Feb. 1986): 107–8.

   Review; MIDI software program.

5875. Banes, Vince. "Audio-Frequency Analyzer: Build IBM PC Accessories to Analyze Your Stereo." *Byte* 10 (Jan. 1985): 223–50.

How to interface a DAC, VCO, and ADC to the IBM PC using a general-purpose I/O device.

5876. Bassett, Rick. "MusicPrinter Plus Offers WYSIWYG Music Notation, MIDI Playback." *PC Magazine* 8 (Mar. 28, 1989): 414.

A short description of the software.

5877. ——, and Jonathan Matzkin. "A MIDI Musical Offering." *PC Magazine* 7 (Nov. 29, 1988): 229–72.

An evaluation of eleven MIDI music software programs.

5878. Bermant, Charles. "Computing Is Just a Song." *Personal Computing* 11 (Oct. 1987): 182–83.

John Kay, of the musical group Steppenwolf, describes his use of a Compaq Deskpro 286 and a Zenith Z-183 laptop to play computerized bass in live performance.

5879. Blezinger, Stephan. "High-tech im Blasinstrumentenbau-EDV-Einsatz bei der Bohrungsmessung." *Tibia* 14,1 (1989): 349–50.

5880. Chaigne, A., and F. Troxler. "SONATE: An Analysis/Synthesis System of Musical Sounds Based on Perceptual Data." In *Proceedings of the 14th International Computer Music Conference, Cologne, September 20–25, 1988,* ed. Christoph Lischka and Johannes Fritsch. Cologne: Feedback-Studio-Verlag; San Francisco, Calif.: Dist. by Computer Music Association, 1988: 399–402. (Feedback Papers; 33)

5881. Charbeneau, Travis. "MS-DOS Music: Voytera's 'Sideman 81Z.'" *Music, Computers & Software* 3 (Oct. 1988): 78–79.

Review of the patch editor/librarian; for the Yamaha TX81Z and IBM compatibles.

5882. ——. "System: The IBM." *Music, Computers & Software* 3 (Aug. 1988): 49–51.

An overview of MIDI sequencers available for IBM compatibles.

5883. Collie, Ashley. "Notes: The System Takes Music and Computers on the Road." *Canadian Musician* 7 (Oct. 1985): 12.

Describes a two member band called The System (Rob Farnham and Grant Cummings) which uses an IBM PC with additional equipment.

5884. Conger, Jim. "Applications: MIDI Programming in C. Part Three, Patch Librarian Basics." *Electronic Musician* 5 (Nov. 1989): 24–27.

5885. ——. "Applications: MIDI Programming in C. Part Two, MIDI Data Debugger." *Electronic Musician* 5 (Oct. 1989): 72–74.

5886. ——. "Do-It-Yourself: MIDI Programming in C. Part 1, MIDI Input and Output." *Electronic Musician* 5 (Sept. 1989): 30–34.

5887. De Furia, Steve. "Software for Musicians: MidiSave, A Generic MIDI Data Storage Program." *Keyboard* 14 (July 1988): 134–38.

5888. DiNucci, Darcy. "Tune Trivia." *PC World* 3 (June 1985): 129–33.
Describes the music game Tune Trivia.

5889. Doerschuk, Bob. "Bob James Takes on the Traditionalists with His High-Tech Treatment of Scarlatti." *Keyboard* 14 (Apr. 1988): 66–72.
How an IBM PC and the sequencer program Texture is used to record piano works by Scarlatti.

5890. Doyle, Frank. "Bacchus: TX81Z Graphic Editing System for IBM PCs/Compatibles." *Music, Computers & Software* 2 (Dec. 1987): 64–65, 77.
Review; for the Yamaha TX81Z frequency modulation synthesizer.

5891. ——. "KCSoftware: Octave Plateau Sequencer-Plus." *Keyboards, Computers & Software* 1 (Oct. 1986): 60–62.
MIDI sequencing software; for the IBM PC.

5892. ——. "Voytera's Sequencer Plus Mark III." *Music, Computers & Software* 2 (Oct. 1987): 79–80.
Review of the MIDI sequencer.

5893. Edwards, Gary A. "M.E.S.A. Critique." *Computer Shopper* 9 (Jan. 1989): 295, 555–56.
Review of M.E.S.A. (Music Editor, Scorer, and Arranger).

5894. Einhorn, Richard. "Review: Texture Version 2." *Electronic Musician* 2 (May 1986): 74–78.
A MIDI sequencer.

5895. Freff. "Freff's DOS Diatribe." *Electronic Musician* 2 (May 1986): 42.

5896. ——. "Keyboard Report: Yamaha C1 & C1/20 Music Computers." *Keyboard* 15 (Feb. 1989): 152–55.

5897. ——. "Making Music with the Well-Synchronized PC." *PC Magazine* 2 (Dec. 1983): 338–50.
An article emphasizing the influence of MIDI.

5898. Gilby, Ian. "Sequencer Plus Mk I, II, and III." *Electronic Musician* 4 (Mar. 1988): 92–98.
Reprinted from *Sound-on-Sound*.
Review.

5899. Goldstein, Burt. "First Take: Bacchus TX802 Graphic Editing System for the IBM PC." *Electronic Musician* 4 (Aug. 1988): 82–83.

5900. ———. "Reader Tips: Enhancing Your IBM Sequencer with Macros." *Keyboard* 14 (Jan. 1988): 18–19.

5901. ———, and Freff. "Keyboard Clinic #15: More Power for the IBM PC." *Keyboard* 14 (Oct. 1988): 58–65, 157–61.

5902. Gray, Stephen B. "SongWright IV: Prints and Plays Music." *Computer Shopper* 9 (Jan. 1989): 108–9.
Review; music processing system.

5903. Greenwald, Ted. "Keyboard Report: IBM Sequencers, 48 Track PC II & Forte." *Keyboard* 13 (Aug. 1987): 122–31, 147.

5904. ———. "Keyboard Report: Sight & Sound MIDI Ensemble Software." *Keyboard* 12 (Feb. 1986): 128–35.
MIDI sequencing software.

5905. ———. "Keyboard Report: Texture 2.0, Sequencer for the IBM PC." *Keyboard* 12 (Oct. 1986): 138–41, 160.

5906. Grupp, Paul. "The 48 Track PC II." *Music, Computers & Software* 2 (Aug. 1987): 65–68.
Review of the MIDI sequencer; for IBM-compatible computers.

5907. ———. "Bering Data Systems: Lighthouse MIDI Sequencer for the IBM PC." *Music, Computers & Software* 2 (Aug. 1987): 76–77.
Review.

5908. ———. "Compatibles: Inside a Trio of Musical Clones." *Music, Computers & Software* 2 (June 1987): 66–67.
Overviews of IBM-compatible systems integrated with MIDI controllers and software from Professional Music Systems, the Teknecom Group, and the Personal Computer Store.

5909. ———. "IBM: The Musician's Choice?" *Music, Computers & Software* 2 (May 1987): 34–38, 51–52.

5910. ———. "A New Kind of Music Box: The IBM Personal System/2 Model 30." *Music, Computers & Software* 2 (Oct. 1987): 38–44.
An overview of the IBM PS/2 and the IBM Music Feature Card.

5911. ———. "Review: OP-4001 IBM PC MIDI Interface." *Electronic Musician* 2 (June 1986): 78–79.

5912. Hayworth, Bill. "Music and Micros, Software Reviews." *Instrumentalist* 39 (Oct. 1984): 92–96.
Review of Marching Band Computer Show Design Software.

5913. Hofstetter, Fred T. *IBM Music Feature: A Primer.* Milford, Conn.: International Business Machines Corp., 1987. 42 p.

5914. "The IBM PC Music Feature." *Computer Buyer's Guide and Handbook* 5 (May–June 1987): 37.

5915. Isaacson, Matt. "Twelve Tone Systems Cakewalk Sequencer." *Music Technology* 2 (Nov. 1987): 75–79.

Review; sequencing software.

5916. Kubicky, Jay. "A MIDI Project: A MIDI Interface with Software for the IBM PC." *Byte* 11 (June 1986): 199–208.

5917. Langdell, James. "Music: The PC's New Frontier." *PC Magazine* 5 (Apr. 29, 1986): 187–201.

Evaluations of Sequencer Plus, Personal Composer, MIDI Ensemble, and Music Processing System.

5918. ——. "Singing in the RAM." *PC Magazine* 3 (Aug. 7, 1984): 57.

A description of a BASIC program that simulates polyphonic sounds on the IBM PC.

5919. Latimer, Joey. "Yamaha C1 Music Computer." *Compute!* 10 (Dec. 1988): 74–76.

Review.

5920. Leytze, David. "Keyboard Report: Music Feature, for the IBM PC." *Keyboard* 13 (Oct. 1987): 128–33.

Full-length option card with eight-voice multi-timbral polyphony and MIDI interfacing.

5921. Mahin, Bruce P. "Software Review." *Instrumentalist* 43 (Dec. 1988): 9.

Review of Sideman DTX, a voice editor and librarian for the Yamaha DX/TX/DX-7II; for the IBM.

5922. Maki, Jim. "System: The Yamaha C1 Computer." *Music, Computers & Software* 3 (Dec. 1988): 48–51.

Review of the portable MIDI-capable IBM-compatible computer.

5923. Many, Chris. "48 Track PC II." *Music Technology* 1 (July 1987): 38–41.

Review of the IBM-based MIDI sequencer.

5924. ——. "Ad Lib Personal Computer Music System." *Music Technology* 2 (Feb. 1988): 58–59.

Review of the IBM-based music system, which includes sequencing software.

5925. ——. "IBM Music Feature: Yamaha Playrec Sequencer." *Music Technology* 2 (Oct. 1987): 48–51.

Review of the IBM Music Feature, and PlayRec, a sequencing package.

5926. ——. "Oberon Music Editor." *Music Technology* 2 (Nov. 1987): 40–42.

Review of music scoring and editing software.

5927. ——. "Passport Designs Score: Music Notation Software for the IBM PC." *Music Technology* 2 (May 1988): 77–80.

Review.

5928. ——. "Roland MESA: Music Editor, Scorer, and Arranger." *Music Technology* 2 (Aug. 1987): 79–83.

Review of the software package.

5929. Marans, Michael. "Keyboard Report: LTA Forte 2.2, IBM Sequencer." *Keyboard* 15 (Oct. 1989): 140–42.

MIDI sequencer software; for IBM PC/ST/AT and compatibles, PS/2, Yamaha C1.

5930. ——. "Keyboard Report: Voyetra Sequencer Plus Mark III IBM Sequencer Software." *Keyboard* 15 (Jan. 1989): 134, 138, 145–46.

5931. Matzkin, Jonathan. "Ad Lib Music-Composing Package Turns Your Computer into an 11-Voice Orchestra." *PC Magazine* 6 (Nov. 24, 1987): 52–53.

A short description of the Ad Lib Personal Computer Music System.

5932. ——. "Bank Street Music Writer Sparks the Creativity of Budding Composers." *PC Magazine* 7 (Nov. 29, 1988): 486.

Announcement of a composition software and add-in card.

5933. ——. "CMS Kit Combines MIDI Adapter with Powerful Sequencing Software." *PC Magazine* 7 (Nov. 29, 1988): 482.

Describes the CMS401 circuit board.

5934. ——. "Creative Music System Offers an Inexpensive Way to Develop Your Musical Talents." *PC Magazine* 7 (Nov. 29, 1988): 484.

Describes a non-MIDI compatible twelve-voice synthesizer on a half-card and a variety of supporting software.

5935. ——. "The Entertainer: Familiar Tunes for Your Basic Routines." *PC Magazine* 8 (Mar. 28, 1989): 412.

Describes a library of little songs and sound effects written in BASIC that can be played through a PC's speaker.

5936. ——. "Getting Started with MIDI: Everything You Need for $219." *PC Magazine* 7 (Sept. 13, 1988): 446.

Describes the MIDI Starter System.

5937. ——. "Make Your Own Melodies: Systems for Amateurs and Virtuosos." *PC Magazine* 7 (Jan. 26, 1988): 420, 418, 416.

A discussion of the Ad Lib Personal Computer Music System and the Music Magic Synthesizer.

5938. ———. "Making Beautiful Music with IBM's Music Feature Card." *PC Magazine* 7 (Sept. 13, 1988): 446.

5939. ———. "Pop-Up Music to Perk up Your Spreadsheets." *PC Magazine* 7 (Nov. 29, 1988): 484.

Describes Pop-Tunes, jukebox software.

5940. ———. "Roland's Desktop Studio Brings the Sound of Music to Your PC." *PC Magazine* 7 (Sept. 13, 1988): 448.

A circuit board.

5941. Mefford, Michael J. "A DOS Music Generator." *PC Magazine* 6 (Apr. 28, 1987): 297–309.

Use of the assembly language PLAY commands.

5942. Meyer, Chris. "Traveling Light." *Music Technology* 1 (Apr. 1987): 42–43.

A description of Todd Rundgren's concert equipment, including an IBM clone.

5943. "MIDI Meets DOS in a Laptop." *Byte* 13 (Nov. 1988): 67.

A short description of the Yamaha C1 laptop computer.

5944. Miller, Dennis. "Reviews: LTA Productions Forte II." *Electronic Musician* 5 (Dec. 1989): 120–25.

Sequencing software.

5945. Mitard, Francis P. "Turn Your PC into a Steinway." *PC Magazine* 7 (Nov. 29, 1988): 484.

Description of Pianoman, software that simulates a piano keyboard on any computer keyboard.

5946. Mocsny, Daniel. "Ad Lib's Personal Computer Music System (PCMS) for IBM-Formats." *Music, Computers & Software* 3 (Apr. 1988): 68.

Review.

5947. ———. "MS-DOS Music: Dominant Functions 'Tiff 1.11.'" *Music, Computers & Software* 3 (Aug. 1988): 58–60.

Review of the MIDI sequencer; for IBM compatibles.

5948. ———. "MS-DOS Music: LTA Productions 'Forte II.'" *Music, Computers & Software* 3 (June 1988): 70–71.

Review of the MIDI sequencer; for IBM compatibles.

5949. Moore, J. B. "Computers: The Big Blue Music Machine." *Electronic Musician* 2 (May 1986): 40–43.

5950. Neiman, Marcus L. "Software Review." *Instrumentalist* 42 (May 1988): 67.

Review of Music Editor, Scorer, and Arranger; for the IBM.

5951. ——. "Software Reviews." *Instrumentalist* 42 (Apr. 1988): 78.

Review of MUSICOM J1 Jazz Course; for the IBM.

5952. Nottoli, Giorgio, and Lindoro Del Duca. "MSYS 7: MIDI Control System." In *Proceedings of the International Computer Music Conference 1986, Royal Conservatory, The Hague, Netherlands, October 20–24, 1986,* ed. Paul Berg. San Francisco, Calif.: Computer Music Association, 1986: 71–72.

A brief description of a system based on an IBM PC or compatible for control of up to eight synthesizers via MIDI.

5953. Osteen, Gary. "Synchronized Recording with Virtual MIDI Tracks." *Electronic Musician* 4 (Feb. 1988): 62–69.

The author describes his use of the sequencing software, Texture, to record music.

5954. Owens, Robert J. "Keller Designs Sequencers for IBM PCs." *Computer Music Journal* 13,3 (Fall 1989): 99–101.

Software review.

5955. Payne, Russell G. "A Microcomputer Based Analysis/Resynthesis Scheme for Processing Sampled Sounds Using FM." In *Proceedings of the 1987 International Computer Music Conference: University of Illinois at Urbana-Champaign, Urbana, Illinois, USA, August 23–26, 1987,* comp. James Beauchamp. San Francisco, Calif.: Computer Music Association, 1987: 282–89.

5956. Pennycook, Bruce W. "PRAESC10–11: Amnesia toward Dynamic Tapeless Performance." In *Proceedings of the 14th International Computer Music Conference, Cologne, September 20–25, 1988,* ed. Christoph Lischka and Johannes Fritsch. Cologne: Feedback-Studio-Verlag; San Francisco, Calif.: Dist. by Computer Music Association, 1988: 383–91. (Feedback Papers; 33)

Presentation of the MIDI-LIVE software system.

5957. Peters, Constantine. "MS-DOS Music: Temporal Acuity 'Music Printer Plus.'" *Music, Computers & Software* 3 (Nov. 1988): 62–64.

Review of the music notation program.

5958. ——. "Music Quest MQX-32 MIDI Interface Card." *Music, Computers & Software* 3 (Dec. 1988): 58–63.

Review of the MPU-401 compatible MIDI interface card; for IBM compatibles.

5959. ——. "Speeding up Your Computer. Part 1." *Music, Computers & Software* 3 (Dec. 1988): 41–43.

Discusses the use of RAM disks as a method of enhancing system performance in IBM compatibles.

5960. Poole, Lon. "Programming Sound in BASIC." *PC World* 1 (July 1983): 176–84.

Chapter 14 of the author's *Using Your IBM Personal Computer.* Indianapolis, Ind.: H. W. Sams, 1983. 326 p.

5961. Proffitt, K. K. "Reviews: Texture 3.5 for the IBM PC." *Electronic Musician* 5 (Nov. 1989): 114–19.

Sequencing software.

5962. ———. "Snap Software GP-8 Companion for the IBM PC." *Electronic Musician* 4 (Dec. 1988): 101–2.

Review of the patch librarian/editor; for the Roland GP-8 guitar effects processor and the IBM PC.

5963. Rich, Jason R. "Computers: Send in the Clones!" *Electronic Musician* 3 (Jan. 1987): 39–42.

5964. Riggs, Robert L. "On Line." *Instrumentalist* 41 (June 1987): 72–73.

Software review of Personal Composer, music writing program; for the IBM.

5965. Rona, Jeff. "Computers On-Line: Reality or Miffed?" *Keyboard* 15 (Apr. 1989): 108.

A preview of IBM's MIDI Interfacing Feature For Emulation of Devices, a combination of hardware and software that allows the PC to run any Macintosh, Mac II, Atari, Amiga, NeXT, or IBM MIDI software.

5966. Rosch, Winn L. "Musical Interludes with the PC." *PC Magazine* 5 (Oct. 14, 1986): 265–81.

Describes MUSICOM, music instruction software, and the Tecmar Music Synthesis System board.

5967. ———. "Tecmar Arranging PC Compositions: Ohio Firm Developing Advanced Music Synthesizer for PC Family." *PC Magazine* 3 (Dec. 25, 1984): 41.

A preview of an expansion card for the IBM PC, XT, or AT, and the software that controls it.

5968. Rose, Philip F. H. "CD-ROM and Roll: Getting Audio from Your Data Drive." *PC Magazine* 7 (Sept. 13, 1988): 444.

Two programs, CD-Play and CD-Audiofile, turn a CD-ROM drive into an audio compact disk player.

5969. Rothstein, Joseph B. "Grandmaster MusicEase Notation Software." *Computer Music Journal* 13,2 (Summer 1989): 94–95.

Software review.

5970. ——. "MusicEase Notation Software for IBM PCs." *Computer Music Journal* 13,3 (Fall 1989): 105–6.
Software review.

5971. ——. "Twelve Tone Systems Cakewalk Sequencer Software." *Computer Music Journal* 13,2 (Summer 1989): 96–98.
Software review.

5972. ——. "Yamaha C1 Music Computer." *Computer Music Journal* 13,4 (Winter 1989): 93–95.
Review.

5973. Rychner, Lorenz. "Bacchus TX802 Graphic Editing System: An Editor/Librarian for the IBM PC and Compatibles." *Music Technology* 2 (May 1988): 70.
Review of the editor/librarian software; for the IBM PC and Yamaha TX802 or DX7II.

5974. Sagman, Stephen. "Windows-based MIDI System Lets PC Musicians Jam." *PC Week* 4 (Dec. 15, 1987): 82.
Review of Cheetah-MIDI Music System and Opus Music software.

5975. Savicky, Randy. "Sights and Sounds." *Jazz Times* (Sept. 1987): 10.
Notes on the release of the IBM Music Feature.

5976. Scholz, Carter. "AdLib Music Synthesizer." *Electronic Musician* 4 (May 1988): 83–84.
Review of the half-slot plug-in card.

5977. ——. "Dominant Functions Tiff Sequencing Software." *Electronic Musician* 4 (June 1988): 100.
Review of a MIDI sequencer.

5978. ——. "First Take: Capsule Comments: 48 Track PC Version 3.0." *Electronic Musician* 4 (Nov. 1988): 86–88.

5979. ——. "First Take: Capsule Comments: PC Desktop Music Studio." *Electronic Musician* 5 (Jan. 1989): 94–95.

5980. ——. "First Take: Magnetic Music Pyramid Voice Editor/Librarian for the DX/TX." *Electronic Musician* 4 (Sept. 1988): 72–73.

5981. ——. "First Take: Music Quest MIDI Starter System." *Electronic Musician* 4 (July 1988): 132.

5982. ——. "Keyboard Report: Escort, MIDI Transcription for Passport Score Notation Software." *Keyboard* 15 (Nov. 1989): 120–22.

5983. ———. "Keyboard Report: GFmusic, IBM Sequencer." *Keyboard* 15 (Dec. 1989): 145–47.

5984. ———. "Keyboard Report: MusicBox, Algorithmic Freeware for the IBM." *Keyboard* 15 (July 1989): 133, 154.

5985. ———. "Keyboard Report: Sound Globs, Algorithmic Composition for the IBM-PC." *Keyboard* 15 (June 1989): 135–37.

5986. ———. "The Musical Computer: Big Blue Does MIDI: A Survey." *Electronic Musician* 4 (Apr. 1988): 46–55.

A general overview of the use of the IBM PC and clones for musical applications.

5987. ———. "Review: Passport Designs Score, An IBM PC Music Notation Program." *Electronic Musician* 4 (Sept. 1988): 76–83.

5988. ———. "Review: The MusiCard from Music Magic." *Electronic Musician* 3 (Dec. 1987): 86–93.

Review of MusiCard, a plug-in synthesis board with software.

5989. ———. "Reviews: FDSoft—Harmonic Analysis and Resynthesis for the IBM." *Electronic Musician* 4 (Dec. 1988): 114–19.

5990. ———. "Reviews: FWAP! and TrackGenie for IBM PC and Compatibles." *Electronic Musician* 5 (Mar. 1989): 84–87.

5991. ———. "Reviews: Jim Miller's Personal Composer V.2.0." *Electronic Musician* 4 (Sept. 1988): 92–97.

5992. ———. "Reviews: SampleVision 1.1." *Electronic Musician* 5 (Apr. 1989): 96–99.

Review of the sample editing software; for the IBM PC/XT/AT, compatibles, and Yamaha C1.

5993. ———. "Six Power Sequencers for the IBM." *Electronic Musician* 5 (Jan. 1989): 57–71, 117.

A discussion of Cakewalk, 48 Track PC, Sequencer Plus, Personal Composer, Texture, and Forte II.

5994. ———. "SPXFILE: An SPX90 Librarian." *Electronic Musician* 4 (June 1988): 44–49.

A program in Turbo Pascal that solves the problem of MIDI out with the Yamaha SPX90 digital multi-effects unit.

5995. Selman, Tom, and David Lourik. "Computers On-Line: The Yamaha C1 & Apple System Blues." *Keyboard* 14 (Nov. 1988): 140.

5996. "Sight & Sound Introduces 'MIDI Ensemble' Software." *Music Trades* 134 (Jan. 1986): 117.

5997. Sirota, Warren. "PCjr Strikes a Chord: Learn about PCjr's Exceptional Music Capabilities." *PC World* 2 (July 1984): 204–9.

Includes a discussion on producing three-voice chords.

5998. ———. "Three-part Harmony: How to Program Three-voice Music on the PCjr." *PC World* 2 (Aug. 1984): 208–14.

5999. Slepian, Don. "Review: 'Vision' for the Mirage." *Electronic Musician* 3 (May 1987): 78–85.

Review of Vision Visual Editing System, a visual sample editor; for the Ensoniq Mirage and IBM PC and clones.

6000. Stockford, James. "Personal Composer." *Whole Earth Review* no. 49 (Winter 1985): 111.

Very brief review.

6001. ———. "Sequencer Plus." *Whole Earth Review* no. 49 (Winter 1985): 111.

Very brief review.

6002. Stone, Michael. "Bacchus: TX81Z Graphic Editing System for IBM PCs/Compatibles." *Music Technology* 2 (Sept. 1987): 44–46.

Review.

6003. ———. "Dominant Functions Tiff Sequencer." *Music Technology* 2 (Feb. 1988): 70–71.

Review of IBM sequencing software.

6004. ———. "Software Roundup: Low-Cost IBM PC Sequencers." *Music Technology* 2 (Mar. 1988): 81–83.

Review of Forte I and Sequencer Plus MkI.

6005. Swearingen, Donald. "MIDI Programming: Processing the MPU–401 Track Data Stream." *Byte* 11 (June 1986): 211–24.

6006. ———. "A MIDI Recorder: Store and Play Back Keyboard Music with Your IBM PC." *Byte* 10 (Fall 1985): 127–38.

MIDI software program in FORTH.

6007. Tamm, Allan C. "Computers: IBM PC Display Systems for the Musician." *Electronic Musician* 2 (July 1986): 52–56.

6008. Thomas, Tony. "Computers: The Little Computer That Could: Yamaha's CX5M." *Electronic Musician* 2 (Aug. 1986): 22–27.

6009. Trivette, Donald B. "IBM Personal Computing: Music for Amadeus." *Compute!* 7 (Jan. 1985): 138–40.

A basic discussion on using the IBM to make music.

6010. Tully, Tim. "Good Vibrations: The PC Joins the Band." *PC Computing* 2 (Feb. 1989): 172–81.

Describes how personal computers are being used for the creation of music.

6011. ———. "PlayRec for the IBM Music Feature." *Electronic Musician* 3 (Dec. 1987): 83–84.

Review of sequencing software; for the IBM Music Feature.

6012. Vail, Mark. "Keyboard Report: Editor/Librarians for Roland D-110 & IBM PC." *Keyboard* 15 (Nov. 1989): 124–38.

Reviews of Big Noise D-10/20/110 Editor/Librarian, D-10/20/110 Master Editor/Librarian, Lilley Freelance D-10/110 Editor/Librarian, and Platinum Series D-110 Editor.

6013. "Voyetra Adds New Software Packages." *Music Trades* 136 (Oct. 1988): 93–94.

6014. "Yamaha to Introduce First PC Designed Specifically for Music Applications." *Canadian Musician* 10 (Oct. 1988): 75.

6015. "Yamaha Unveils Dedicated Music Computer." *Music Trades* 136 (Aug. 1988): 40–42.

Describes the Yamaha C-1, IBM compatible computer.

6016. Zachmann, William F. "Music Is the Best." *PC Magazine* 8 (Mar. 28, 1989): 83–84.

How MIDI can open doors for a range of new applications for computers.

MICROCOMPUTERS — MACINTOSH

6017. Aikin, Jim. "Keyboard Report: Sound Designer Editing Software for the Prophet 2000." *Keyboard* 12 (Apr. 1986): 110–12.

6018. ———. "Keyboard Report: Turbosynth, Sample Synthesizer for the Mac." *Keyboard* 14 (Oct. 1988): 139–43, 155–56.
Software-based modular synthesis and sample processor.

6019. Aker, Sharon Zardetto. "Quick Clicks: Jam Session." *MacUser* 4 (July 1988): 113–15.
Review.

6020. ———. "Software: Of Mice & Music: Two Macintosh Programs That Can Expand Your Repertoire." *A +* 3 (Oct. 1985): 132–38.
Reviews of ConcertWare and Professional Composer.

6021. Amaral, John. "Software City." *Musician* n81 (July 1985): 96, 112.
A discussion of Professional Composer.

6022. Anderton, Craig. "Digital Music Service's TX81Z Pro." *Electronic Musician* 4 (Feb. 1988): 113.
Review of editor/librarian; for the Yamaha TX81Z.

6023. ———. "Editing on the Macintosh." *Electronic Musician* 4 (Apr. 1988): 102.
Short review of MPX820 Editor/Librarian.

6024. ———. "First Take: MacDrums by Coda Music Software." *Electronic Musician* 4 (Feb. 1988): 112–13.
Review of drum machine software.

6025. ———. "Primera Software Different Drummer V1.1 for the Macintosh." *Electronic Musician* 5 (Sept. 1989): 81.

6026. ———. "Review: Master Tracks Pro for the Mac." *Electronic Musician* 3 (Aug. 1987): 68–74.
A multi-track MIDI sequencer.

6027.   ———. "Reviews: Blank Software's Alchemy 1.2." *Electronic Musician* 5 (Feb. 1989): 114–21.

6028.   ———. "Reviews: Opcode Vision for the Macintosh." *Electronic Musician* 5 (Aug. 1989): 76–83.

Sequencing software.

6029.   Austin, Kirk. "Review: Mark of the Unicorn's 'Performer': Beyond Tape Simulations." *Electronic Musician* 2 (Sept. 1986): 68–70.

6030.   ———. "Review: Southworth's Total Music." *Electronic Musician* 2 (Jan. 1986): 60–62, 64–65.

Sequencer and notation software.

6031.   ———. "Review: The Mac/Mirage Interface: Sound Lab Software." *Electronic Musician* 2 (Feb. 1986): 50–52.

A sampling program.

6032.   Barnett, David N. "MIDI Update: Software City." *Musician* n108 (Oct. 1987): 52–55.

Review of the software M and Jam Factory.

6033.   ———. "Musical Interlude: Performer 1.22." *Macworld* 3 (Dec. 1986): 140.

Review of MIDI sequencing software.

6034.   ———. "Play It Again, Mac!: Bring a Whole Music Studio to Your Mac." *MacUser* 1 (Mar. 1986): 74–77, 116.

An overview of Deluxe Music Construction Set.

6035.   ———. "Reviews: A Beautiful Duet." *Macworld* 4 (Mar. 1987): 142–43.

Review of MIDI Mac Sequencer 2.5 and Deluxe Music Construction Set.

6036.   ———. "Software City: New Mac Sequencers from Opcode and Mark of the Unicorn." *Musician* n98 (Dec. 1986): 72–74.

Review of Performer from Mark of the Unicorn and MidiMac Sequencer from Opcode.

6037.   Beamer, Scott. "Wiring Your Mac for Sound." *Macworld* 5 (Apr. 1988): 117–19.

Product announcement of Mac Recorder, a hardware/software sound input package.

6038.   Bell, Bryan. "New Music." *Macworld* 4 (June 1987): 111.

Short review of Macintosh products displayed at NAMM.

6039.   Bell, Jack. "Make Music with Macintosh." *Personal Computing* 9 (May 1985): 178.

Review of MusicWorks.

6040. Bermant, Charles. "Mac and Roll Is Here to Stay." *MacWeek* 2 (Aug. 30, 1988): 14, 16.

Describes the use of the Macintosh by rock musicians.

6041. Bernardo, Mario Sergio. "ConcertWare+ and SongPainter: Two Software Packages for Making Music on the Macintosh." *Byte* 11 (June 1986): 273–76.

6042. Biedny, David. "Roll over Beethoven: Three Innovative Programs Offer Different Ways of Using Your Mac to Write and Generate Music. Each One Commands Its Own Audience." *MacUser* 1 (Oct. 1985): 84–88.

An overview of MusicWorks, ConcertWare, and Professional Composer.

6043. ———. "Six-part Harmony: Is It the Real Thing or Is It Just a Studio Session?" *MacUser* 1 (Dec. 1986): 110–14, 186–90.

An overview of Studio Session.

6044. Birchall, Steve. "Do, Re, Mouse: Music Mouse Gives You Computer-assisted Improvisation and Leaves You Free to Jam." *MacUser* 3 (May 1987): 136–40.

An overview of Music Mouse.

6045. Blevins, R. L. "Alchemy 2.0 Sound File Editor for Apple Macintosh Computers." *Computer Music Journal* 13,4 (Winter 1989): 95–98.

Software review.

6046. Boynton, Lee, and David Cumming. "A Real-Time Acoustic Processing Card for the Mac II." In *Proceedings of the 14th International Computer Music Conference, Cologne, September 20–25, 1988,* ed. Christoph Lischka and Johannes Fritsch. Cologne: Feedback-Studio-Verlag; San Francisco, Calif.: Dist. by Computer Music Association, 1988: 349–56. (Feedback Papers; 33)

6047. Bradbury, James. "Krafty Music Programs." *MacUser* 4 (Oct. 1988): 172.

Describes ExampleKrafter, music typesetting software.

6048. Brandt, Pam. "Women in Computer Music." *MacWeek* 2 (Aug. 16, 1988): 22, 24.

The author comments on the lack of involvement by women in computer music, especially when the user-friendly Macintosh is considered.

6049. Breen, Christopher. "Pick a Pack of MIDI." *MacUser* 4 (Dec. 1988): 41.

Review of MidiPack, sequencer enhancement software.

6050. Brody, Alan. "Composer Glass Collaborates with the Mac." *MacWeek* 2 (July 26, 1988): 6.

Describes the preparation and the performance of Philip Glass' *Music in Twelve Parts,* which uses six Macintoshes and synchronized animation.

6051. Burgess, Jim. "Apple Hypercard." *Music Technology* 2 (Nov. 1987): 20–22.

Review.

6052. ——. "Click Tracks 2.0: Software for Apple Macintosh." *Music Technology* 1 (May 1987): 80–81.

Review of software-based click program for film music composers.

6053. ——. "Computers: Performer: Extremely Versatile Sequencer Program." *Canadian Musician* 8 (June 1986): 69–70.

6054. ——. "Getting More Miles per Mac." *Music Technology* 1 (June 1987): 26–27.

Tips for increasing the speed and efficiency of the Macintosh.

6055. ——. "Intelligent Music Jam Factory: Software for Apple Macintosh." *Music Technology* 1 (Feb. 1987): 36–38.

Review of the music composition software.

6056. ——. "Intelligent Music UpBeat: Software for the Macintosh." *Music Technology* 2 (Aug. 1987): 60–63.

Review of computer-based sequencing and drum pattern programming.

6057. ——. "Intelligent Music 'M': Software for the Apple Macintosh." *Music Technology* 1 (Mar. 1987): 44–46.

Review of the composition software.

6058. ——. "Mark of the Unicorn Performer 2.2." *Music Technology* 2 (Jan. 1988): 68–74.

Review of the sequencing software.

6059. ——. "Master Tracks Pro: Software for Apple Macintosh." *Music Technology* 1 (July 1987): 74–77.

Review of the MIDI sequencing software.

6060. ——. "The New Macintosh." *Music Technology* 1 (May 1987): 15–17.

6061. Butler, Chris, and Bill Lewis. "David van Tieghem." *Music, Computers & Software* 3 (Apr. 1988): 22–29.

Profile/interview with the percussionist, who discusses his use of MIDI and the Macintosh.

6062.   Camp, John. "The College Computing Lab: MACing Music: Powerful Programs for under $500." *Electronic Learning* 6 (Feb. 1987): 39–40.

Reviews of ConcertWare + MIDI, Professional Performer, Professional Composer, and Listen; for the Macintosh.

6063.   Chadabe, Joel, and David Zicarelli. *Jam Factory User's Manual.* Albany, N.Y.: Intelligent Computer Music Systems, 1986.

6064.   ——, and David Zicarelli. *M User's Manual.* Albany, N.Y.: Intelligent Computer Music Systems, 1987.

6065.   ——, and David Zicarelli. *M: The Interactive Composing and Performing System.* Albany, N.Y.: Intelligent Computer Music System, 1987.

With disk and template.

6066.   Clouser, Charlie. "Vision 1.01: Advanced MIDI Sequencer." *Macworld* 6 (Oct. 1989): 185–88.

Review.

6067.   Coale, Kristi. "I Want My M3TV." *MacUser* 4 (Dec. 1988): 40.

Review of *The Open Door,* a music video from Apple on the Macintosh, MIDI, and music.

6068.   "Coda Introduces MusicProse Software." *Music Trades* 137 (Sept. 1989): 102–4.

Product announcement.

6069.   "Coda Software Shows New Low-End Program, Revamps Marketing." *Music Trades* 137 (July 1989): 114.

Review of MusicProse, a music notation program; for the Macintosh.

6070.   Combs, Jim. "Apple Music: Great Wave 'Concertware + MIDI.'" *Music, Computers & Software* 3 (Aug. 1988): 54–55.

Review of the MIDI sequencer/notation program; for the Apple Macintosh.

6071.   ——. "Mac II/SE." *Music, Computers & Software* 2 (June 1987): 39–45.

An overview of the newer additions to the Apple Macintosh line, focusing on musical uses.

6072.   Cummings, Steve. "Deluxe Music Construction Set 2.5: Music Notation and Composition Tool." *Macworld* 6 (Sept. 1989): 235–36.

Review.

6073.   ——. "Different Drummer 1.0: Graphic Rhythm Composer." *Macworld* 6 (Oct. 1989): 197–99.

Review.

6074. ———. "Keyboard Report: Mark of the Unicorn Performer, Sequencer for the Macintosh." *Keyboard* 12 (May 1986): 124–28.

6075. ———. "Keyboard Report: Voicing/Librarian Software for DX & TX Instruments." *Keyboard* 12 (Mar. 1986): 102–6, 122.
Review of Midimac Patch Editor and Patch Librarian, DX-Connect, and DX/TX Master.

6076. ———. "Music for Beginners: A Guide to Playing, Recording, and Learning Music on the Mac." *Macworld* 6 (Apr. 1989): 124–29.

6077. ———. "Musical Musings." *Macworld* 5 (May 1988): 182–83.
Review of Jam Session and M.

6078. ———. "Beaverton Digital TX81Z Editor/Librarian." *Music Technology* 2 (Feb. 1988): 67.
Review of voice editing software; for the Yamaha TX81Z and the Macintosh.

6079. Davies, Rick. "Digidesign SoftSynth & Burner: Software for the Apple Macintosh." *Music Technology* 1 (Sept. 1986): 60–62.
Review.

6080. De Furia, Steve. "Software for Musicians: A MIDI Channel-mapping Program to Build on." *Keyboard* 15 (Feb. 1989): 118–20.
Written in Lightspeed Pascal.

6081. ———. "Software for Musicians: Compiling Stand-alone Applications for the Macintosh." *Keyboard* 14 (Sept. 1988): 131.

6082. ———. "Software for Musicians: Designing a Music Spreadsheet from Scratch." *Keyboard* 14 (Feb. 1988): 129–30.

6083. ———. "Software for Musicians: Installing MIDIBASIC as a Code Resource." *Keyboard* 14 (Oct. 1988): 132.

6084. ———. "Software for Musicians: MIDI Program Example: Turning Our Micro-Tuning Librarian into an Editor." *Keyboard* 13 (Dec. 1987): 128.

6085. ———. "Software for Musicians: MIDIBasic & Other Programming Shortcuts." *Keyboard* 13 (Aug. 1987): 104.

6086. ———. "Software for Musicians: More MIDIBASIC for the Mac: Subroutines for Last Month's Micro-Tuning Librarian." *Keyboard* 13 (Nov. 1987): 126.

6087. ———. "Software for Musicians: Over the Wires and thru the Goods." *Keyboard* 14 (Dec. 1988): 120–23.
A program that turns a Macintosh into a MIDI thru data display.

6088. ———. "Software for Musicians: Programming Example: Micro-Tuning Editor/Librarian." *Keyboard* 13 (Oct. 1987): 117.

A MIDIBasic program that requests a Yamaha device to transmit its micro-tuning edit buffer to the Macintosh.

6089. ———. "Software for Musicians: Son of Designing a Program from Scratch." *Keyboard* 14 (Mar. 1988): 129.

6090. ———. "Software for Musicians: The Last Will and Testament of Music Math." *Keyboard* 14 (Apr. 1988): 127.

6091. ———, and Joe Scacciaferro. *MIDI Programming for the Macintosh.* Redwood City, Calif.: M&T Books, 1988. 371 p.

6092. "Digidesign Sound Designer—The Sampling Answer." *Electronic Musician* 3 (Sept. 1987): 74–75, 96.

Visual editing software; for the Macintosh and Korg DSS-1, as well as the Akai S900, Emulator II, Emax, Mirage, Prophet 2000 and 2002.

6093. Donovan, Joe. "Stanley Jordan Hammers On!" *Music, Computers & Software* 3 (Aug. 1988): 34–38.

Profile/interview with the jazz composer/guitarist, who discusses his use of MIDI guitar controllers and the Macintosh.

6094. Duesenberry, John. "Reviews: Hip Software's Harmony Grid." *Electronic Musician* 5 (Oct. 1989): 102–8.

Software to teach harmonic theory and to use for live improvisation.

6095. Elliott, Kevin. "Note Cards: HyperCard Could Become the Ultimate Musical Instrument. Like the Song Says, 'Be It Ever So Humble, There's No Place Like Home.'" *MacUser* 4 (Oct. 1988): 309–24.

Review of HyperCard-based music software and stacks.

6096. "'Finale' Redefines Music Software Performance: New Transcription Program Takes Music Writing into 20th Century & Beyond." *Music Trades* 136 (Oct. 1988): 58–63.

6097. Freed, Adrian. "MacMix: Mixing Music with a Mouse." In *Proceedings of the International Computer Music Conference 1986, Royal Conservatory, The Hague, Netherlands, October 20–24, 1986,* ed. Paul Berg. San Francisco, Calif.: Computer Music Association, 1986: 127–29.

6098. ———. "Recording, Mixing, and Signal Processing on a Personal Computer." In *The Proceedings of the AES 5th International Conference: Music and Digital Technology,* ed. John Strawn. New York, N.Y.: Audio Engineering Society, 1987: 158–62.

6099.   Freff. "Keyboard Report: Opcode Systems Yamaha Editor/Librarians for the Mac." *Keyboard* 15 (Jan. 1989): 128–32.

6100.   ———. "MIDI for the Macintosh: The First Generation of Products." *A +* 4 (Feb. 1986): 116–22.

6101.   ———. "Rhythm 'n' Views: What It Isn't, What It Is." *MacUser* 4 (Sept. 1988): 265–66.
    Introduction to a new column on the Macintosh and music.

6102.   ———. "Software City." *Musician* n87 (Jan. 1986): 86.
    Reviews of Total Music from Southworth Music Systems, and Sound Designer from Digidesign; for the Macintosh.

6103.   Friedman, Steve. "Macnifty Sound Cap/Studio Session." *Keyboards, Computers & Software* 1 (Oct. 1986): 55–56.
    Review of sampling software.

6104.   Froelich, John P. "Floppy Discography: Music Publisher Version 2.0." *Music Educators Journal* 75 (Mar. 1989): 55–57.
    Software review; for the Macintosh.

6105.   Gibson, Robert S. T. "Aural Fixation." *MacUser* 4 (Apr. 1988): 186–94.
    Review of SoundWave, sound digitizing software.

6106.   Glines, Jeffrey. "Mac Toots Its Own Horn." *Macworld* 2 (May 1985): 33.
    Various uses of the Macintosh in composition.

6107.   Goehner, Ken. "A Little Byte Music." *Macworld* 4 (Nov. 1987): 158–59.
    Review of the music composition program Studio Session 1.0.

6108.   Gotcher, Peter. "Keyboard Clinic: Advanced Applications for Sound Designer." *Keyboard* 14 (Feb. 1988): 68–80.
    Sound editing software.

6109.   ———. "Mac the Axe." *Electronic Musician* 2 (Feb. 1986): 18–21.
    Applications to MIDI, transcription, and signal processing; for the Macintosh.

6110.   Greenberg, Gary. "Composing with Performer Objects." In *Proceedings of the 14th International Computer Music Conference, Cologne, September 20–25, 1988,* ed. Christoph Lischka and Johannes Fritsch. Cologne: Feedback-Studio-Verlag; San Francisco, Calif.: Dist. by Computer Music Association, 1988: 142–49. (Feedback Papers; 33)

6111.   Greenfield, Richard P. "Musicians Who Play the Mac." *MacWeek* 3 (Jan. 17, 1989): 34.

6112.   Greenwald, Ted. "Keyboard Report: Jam Factory & M, Automated Improvisation Software." *Keyboard* 13 (Feb. 1987): 141–46, 163.

6113. ———. "Keyboard Report: Master Tracks Pro, Passport Sequencer for the Macintosh." *Keyboard* 13 (July 1987): 142–49, 170.

MIDI sequencing software.

6114. ———. "Keyboard Report: Midimac, Opcode Sequencer for the Mac." *Keyboard* 13 (Mar. 1987): 134–40.

6115. ———. "Keyboard Report: UpBeat, Intelligent Drum Machine Programmer." *Keyboard* 13 (Oct. 1987): 152–56, 161.

Sequencer, visual editor, and automatic variation generator for drum machines and synthesizers.

6116. Hallerman, David. "MacRecorder." *Family & Home-Office Computing* 6 (May 1988): 62.

Review of a sound digitizer.

6117. Heid, Jim. "Getting Started with Digital Sound: From Beeps to Bach, How to Record and Play Back Sound on the Mac." *Macworld* 6 (Nov. 1989): 299–308.

6118. ———. "Getting Started with Music: Scoring and Sequencing, Mastering MIDI, and Outfitting Your Mac to Make Music." *Macworld* 4 (Nov. 1987): 283–98.

6119. ———. "Is It Live, or, Is It Mac?" *Macworld* 3 (Aug. 1986): 124–27.

Describes several sound programs for the Macintosh.

6120. ———. "Making Tracks." *Macworld* 3 (Sept. 1986): 172–76.

Reviews of MegaTrack XL and Professional Performer, MIDI sequencing software.

6121. ———. "Musical Wares." *Macworld* 3 (Feb. 1986): 92–99.

An overview of music software and hardware for the Macintosh.

6122. Heinbuch, Dean. "Review: Beaverton Digital TX81Z Editor/Librarian." *Electronic Musician* 4 (July 1988): 138–39.

Review of Yamaha TX81Z Editor/Librarian; for the Macintosh.

6123. Holden, Stephen. "Writing Music Electronically." *New York Times* 137 (Feb. 23, 1988): C13.

An account of how Andy Goldmark uses a Macintosh with MIDI for song writing.

6124. Holsinger, Erik. "The Digital Audio Workstation." *Macworld* 4 (Oct. 1987): 162–64.

Review of Sound Designer 1.12 and Softsynth 2.0.

6125. ———. "Film Scoring Simplified." *Macworld* 4 (Sept. 1987): 158–60.

Review of Cue: The Film Music System 1.0 and Clicktracks 2.0, software for use in film scoring.

6126. Ito, Russell. "A Hot Trio." *MacUser* 4 (Oct. 1988): 31.

Product announcement of three Max Audio boards, signal-processing cards.

6127. Jeffery, Mark. "Applications: Turbosynth Tips." *Electronic Musician* 5 (Aug. 1989): 23–27.

Advice on using the software-based sample generator for the Macintosh.

6128. Kelly, Kevin. "ConcertWare." *Whole Earth Review* no. 49 (Winter 1985): 111.

Very brief review of music composition software.

6129. Kempton, David. "Southworth's JamBox/4 + ." *Electronic Musician* 3 (Oct. 1987): 86–91.

SMPTE/MIDI interface; for the Macintosh.

6130. Korte, Karl, and Rick Lawn. "Scoring with Computers. Part III." *Jazz Educators Journal* 21 (Spring 1989): 76–79.

An examination of Professional Composer by Mark of the Unicorn.

6131. Krauss, Bill. "Steamshuffle & Winterbreath: Notes from the Underground." *Music, Computers & Software* 3 (Apr. 1988): 36.

Profile/interview with Christopher Janney and Joan Brigham, who discuss their use of a Macintosh to control steam jets and a sound system for their sculpture.

6132. Krutz, Jamie. "Herbie's Tech Talks Mac." *MacWeek* 2 (Aug. 16, 1988): 38.

Joe Manolakakis, Herbie Hancock's technician, describes his use of the Macintosh for music making.

6133. ———. "The Mac's Not Missing a Beat." *MacWeek* 2 (Aug. 16, 1988): 38–41.

Apple Computers demonstrates its commitment to the music markets.

6134. Latimer, Joey. "Jam Session." *Family & Home-Office Computing* 6 (Apr. 1988): 73–74.

Review.

6135. Lavroff, Nicholas. "Playing It by Eye." *Macworld* 2 (Sept. 1985): 109–10.

Review of SongPainter.

6136. ———. "Roll over Mozart." *Macworld* 2 (June 1985): 72–79.

Review of MusicWorks and ConcertWare, music composition software.

6137.　——. "The Software Rock 'n' Roll Band." *Macworld* 2 (Nov. 1985): 114–19.

Historical and biographical information on the three developers of MacroMind, a software company for Macintosh.

6138.　Lehman, Cliff. "Blank Plans CD, Alchemy Upgrade." *MacWeek* 3 (Mar. 7, 1989): 18.

A short description of Alchemy 2.0, Alchemy Apprentice, and Anatomy of an Automobile.

6139.　——. "Musicians Gain Studio-Quality Control." *MacWeek* 3 (Apr. 11, 1989): 14.

Preview of Portrait, a music composition and recording program.

6140.　——. "New Mac Programs Make Beautiful Music." *MacWeek* 3 (Mar. 7, 1989): 18.

Announcement of Practica Musica, Different Drummer, and Toccata.

6141.　——. "ScoreMaster Searches, Plays Music Selections from Leading Libraries." *MacWeek* 3 (June 13, 1989): 18.

Software for searching and listening to excerpts from musical compositions.

6142.　Lehrman, Paul D. "ConcertWare + MIDI; ConcertWare +." *MacUser* 3 (Dec. 1987): 100, 107.

Software reviews.

6143.　——. "First Take: Capsule Comments: HB Music Engraver Scoring Software for the Macintosh." *Electronic Musician* 4 (Oct. 1988): 90–93.

6144.　——. "Itty-Bitty MIDI." *MacUser* 4 (June 1988): 206–11.

Review of the Apple MIDI Interface.

6145.　——. "Multitracking MIDI Master." *MacUser* 3 (Dec. 1987): 180–90.

In-depth review of Master Tracks Pro.

6146.　——. "Music between the Keys: M and Jam Factory Take You to Parts of the Musical Spectrum You Never Knew Existed." *MacUser* 3 (Oct. 1987): 146–55.

An evaluation of Jam Factory and M.

6147.　——. "Music for the Masses: So You Want to Write Your Own MIDI Program? MIDIBasic Is the Way to Go." *MacUser* 3 (Aug. 1987): 126–33.

Review of MIDIBasic, a set of routines in BASIC for developing MIDI commands.

6148. ——. "Quick Clicks: Deluxe Music Construction Set." *MacUser* 4 (June 1988): 110–16.

Review.

6149. ——. "Quick Clicks: UpBeat." *MacUser* 4 (May 1988): 94–100.

Review of UpBeat, drum machine software.

6150. ——. "Review: MIDIBASIC 2.0: Music Power to the People." *Electronic Musician* 3 (Oct. 1987): 80–85.

A set of BASIC library routines for accessing MIDI within BASIC; for the Macintosh.

6151. ——. "Reviews: Coda Finale for the Macintosh." *Electronic Musician* 5 (July 1989): 122–33.

6152. ——. "Reviews: Digidesign Sound Tools." *Electronic Musician* 5 (Nov. 1989): 84–91, 129.

A hard disk, computer-based digital recording system and sample editor.

6153. ——. "Reviews: Passport Designs ClickTracks 2.0." *Electronic Musician* 5 (May 1989): 94–97.

Film-scoring software; for the Macintosh.

6154. ——. "Scroll over Beethoven." *MacUser* 4 (July 1988): 210–24.

A discussion of problems that occur when music notation programs are transferred to other applications such as page layout programs.

6155. ——. "The Write Staff: A New Generation of Desktop Music Publishing Tools Is Bringing Composers and Arrangers New Ways to Score." *MacUser* 4 (Oct. 1988): 164–78.

A detailed survey of music notation software for the Macintosh: Finale, Music Publisher, HB Music Engraver, NoteWriter, Encore, and Nightingale.

6156. Lentczner, Mark, and John Worthington. "The Sound Manager: A Software Architecture for Device Independent Sound." In *Proceedings of the 14th International Computer Music Conference, Cologne, September 20–25, 1988,* ed. Christoph Lischka and Johannes Fritsch. Cologne: Feedback-Studio-Verlag; San Francisco, Calif.: Dist. by Computer Music Association, 1988: 372–77. (Feedback Papers; 33)

A collection of system routines that support sound and music on the Macintosh.

6157. Levine, Michael, and Bob Kinkel. "Review: Q-Sheet." *Electronic Musician* 4 (May 1988): 98–101, 114.

MIDI event-sequencing software.

6158.   Levy, Steven. "MIDI Life Crisis: Can a Columnist Turn a Rock Superhero with a Boost from the Mac?" *Macworld* 3 (Sept. 1986): 27–34.

6159.   ——. "Whose Music Is It, Anyway?: New Mac Software Makes Virtuosos out of the Fumble-Fingered—So Why Learn the Hard Way?" *Macworld* 5 (Aug. 1988): 37–52.
          A discussion of Jam Session, Studio Session, and Music Mouse.

6160.   Lewis, Bill. "Apple Music: Alchemy for the Macintosh." *Music, Computers & Software* 3 (Nov. 1988): 58–59.
          Review of the sample editor/librarian.

6161.   ——. "Apple Music: 'M' from Intelligent Music." *Music, Computers & Software* 3 (Oct. 1988): 72–73.
          Review of the MIDI processing program; for the Apple Macintosh.

6162.   ——. "Intelligent Music's Upbeat." *Music, Computers & Software* 2 (Dec. 1987): 66–71.
          Review of the MIDI sequencing program; for the Macintosh.

6163.   ——. "Jam Factory." *Music, Computers & Software* 2 (May 1987): 60–62.
          MIDI recording/performance software; for the Macintosh.

6164.   ——. "KCSoftware: Deluxe Music Construction Set." *Keyboards, Computers & Software* 1 (Apr. 1986): 56–57.

6165.   ——. "KCSoftware: Opcode MIDIMAC Sequencer." *Keyboards, Computers & Software* 1 (Aug. 1986): 64–66.

6166.   ——. "Kurzweil Music Systems: MIDIScope for the Macintosh." *Music, Computers & Software* 2 (Aug. 1987): 77.
          Review of the freeware MIDI snooping program.

6167.   ——. "Music Mouse." *Keyboards, Computers & Software* 2 (Feb. 1987): 72–73.
          Review of the software-based audio controller.

6168.   ——. "System: The Macintosh." *Music, Computers & Software* 3 (June 1988): 52–57.
          A overview of the Macintosh computer family and their musical uses.

6169.   Lewis, Peter H. "An Instant Musician." *New York Times* 137 (Jan. 12, 1988): C8.
          Review of Jam Session.

6170. Leytze, David. "Keyboard Report: Performer 2.3, Updated MIDI Sequencing Software for the Mac." *Keyboard* 14 (July 1988): 168, 178.

6171. Litterst, George F. "Notating *Fanfare for Churchill Downs* with Finale." *Journal of the International Trumpet Guild* 14 (Sept. 1989): 89.

The author, one of the developers of Finale, relates his experience using the program to notate a piece of music.

6172. Littman, Jonathan. "Another Way to Play Doctor." *MacWeek* 2 (Oct. 4, 1988): 20.

Dr. Robert Markison of the Performing Arts Health Clinic at San Francisco General Hospital uses the Macintosh for hand surgery on musicians or redesigning instruments.

6173. Lowe, Bill, and Robert Currie. "Digidesign's Sound Accelerator: Lessons Lived and Learned." *Computer Music Journal* 13,1 (Spring 1989): 36–46.

Describes a digital signal processing card based on Motorola's 56001 digital signal processing chip; for the Apple Macintosh II and SE.

6174. Lowry, Bradford. "Spotlight on Software: Preview of Alchemy 2.0." *Active Sensing* 1 (Summer 1989): 1, 9.

6175. MacDonald, Gerry. "System: The Mac Plus." *Music, Computers & Software* 3 (Oct. 1988): 61–64.

Discusses the demo creation of jazz arrangements with the Macintosh and Mark of the Unicorn's "Performer."

6176. Machover, Tod, and Joe Chung. "Hyperinstruments: Musically Intelligent and Interactive Performance and Creativity Systems." In *Proceedings, 1989 International Computer Music Conference, November 2–5, the Ohio State University, Columbus, Ohio.* San Francisco, Calif.: Computer Music Association, 1989: 186–90.

6177. "Macintosh Music." *Changing Times* 40 (May 1986): 91.

A very short discussion of Deluxe Music Construction Set, ConcertWare+, and MusicWorks.

6178. Mahin, Bruce P. "On Line: Digidesign Sound Designer." *Instrumentalist* 42 (Dec. 1987): 6.

6179. ———. "On Line: Opcode Midimac Music Sequencer." *Instrumentalist* 42 (Aug. 1987): 72.

Software review.

6180. ———. "Software Review." *Instrumentalist* 43 (Aug. 1988): 58.

Review of Apple HyperCard.

6181. Mansfield, Ernie, and Freff. "Keyboard Report: HB Imaging, HB Music Engraver Scoring Software for the Macintosh." *Keyboard* 14 (Dec. 1988): 134–42.

6182. Many, Chris. "Digidesign's Q-Sheet: Software for the Apple Mac." *Music Technology* 2 (Jan. 1988): 38–42.

Review of software to perform event sequencing for film and video cue lists and MIDI-controlled automation.

6183. ———. "Opcode Cue 2.0: The Film Music System." *Music Technology* 2 (May 1988): 83–85.

Review.

6184. Marans, Michael. "Keyboard Report: Digidesign Sound Tools, Digital Recording/Editing System." *Keyboard* 15 (Sept. 1989): 108–19.

6185. ———. "Keyboard Report: Opcode Systems Proteus Editor/Librarian Software." *Keyboard* 15 (Oct. 1989): 125, 146.

6186. Massey, Howard. *The Compact Guide to MIDI Software for the Macintosh.* London; New York: Amsco Publications, 1988. 64 p.

6187. Matsuoka, Doug. "Yes, There Is Life after MIDI: Get More out of Your Computer." *Keyboard* 14 (Mar. 1988): 34–40.

6188. McNeill, Dan. "Jam Session." *Compute!* 10 (Oct. 1988): 66.

Review.

6189. Meuse, Steve. "Altech: MIDIBASIC Macintosh MIDI Command Library for Microsoft's MSBASIC and Zedcor's ZBASIC Compiler." *Music, Computers & Software* 2 (Oct. 1987): 73, 81.

Review.

6190. Meyer, Chris. "In Brief: DigiDesign SoftSynth Version 2.0." *Music Technology* 1 (Mar. 1987): 23.

Review.

6191. Milano, Dominic. "Keyboard Report: Alchemy—Sample Editing & Networking Mac Software." *Keyboard* 14 (June 1988): 142–44.

6192. ———. "Keyboard Report: Coda Finale, Music Notation & Transcription Software for the Mac." *Keyboard* 15 (Feb. 1989): 142–51, 155, 165–67.

6193. ———. "Keyboard Report: Digidesign SoftSynth Additive Synthesis for the Mac." *Keyboard* 12 (Dec. 1986): 149–52, 158, 169.

6194. ———. "Keyboard Report: DMP7 PRO, Editor/Librarian Mac Software." *Keyboard* 14 (Apr. 1988): 158–59.

Editor/librarian automation enhancement software; for the Yamaha DMP7 mixer.

6195. ———. "Keyboard Report: MidiPaint, Southworth Mac Sequencer Software." *Keyboard* 13 (Oct. 1987): 142–50.

6196. ———. "Keyboard Report: Q-Sheet, Event Sequencer & MIDI Automation Mac Software." *Keyboard* 13 (Nov. 1987): 153–57.
Review of MIDI/SMPTE automation software, MIDI event sequencer.

6197. Moraz, Patrick. "Blues Player." *Melody Maker* 60 (July 20, 1985): 43.
Macintosh-Kurzweil 250 synth interface.

6198. Morse, Ray. "MusicWorks." *Computing Teacher* 12 (May 1985): 38–40.
Review of composition software.

6199. Nemvalts, Kalle. "Sequences That Swing with Performer." *Electronic Musician* 4 (Mar. 1988): 60–69, 110.
A discussion of techniques for optimal quantization using Performer 2.1.

6200. "New Versions of Performer and Composer Software Debut." *Canadian Musician* 10 (June 1988): 27.
Announcement of Professional Composer, version 2.2, and Performer, version 2.3; for the Apple Macintosh.

6201. O'Brien, Walter. "KCS Telecom." *Keyboards, Computers & Software* 1 (Oct. 1986): 12–13, 75.
Telecommunications; for the Macintosh.

6202. O'Donnell, Bob. "The Sound Art of Programming." *Music Technology* 2 (Sept. 1987): 28–33.
Interview with Steve Roach, who uses a Macintosh in his studio.

6203. ———. "Steps in Time." *Music Technology* 2 (Feb. 1988): 18–21.
Interview with Peter Erskine, a drummer who uses a Macintosh in his home studio.

6204. O'Donnell, Craig. "Apple's NAMM Debut." *MacUser* 4 (Apr. 1988): 38.
A short overview of Apple computer products exhibited at the Winter NAMM expo.

6205. ———. "Insights on HyperCard: How to Digitize and Script Sounds in HyperCard Stacks." *Macworld* 5 (June 1988): 219–30.

6206. ———. "New Music High." *Macworld* 5 (Mar. 1988): 107–9.
Product announcement of DMP7 Pro, a full-function editor/librarian/interactive controller; for the Yamaha DMP7.

6207.   ——. "Review: DASCH." *Electronic Musician* 2 (Dec. 1986): 82–89.
Disk Acceleration/Storage Control Hardware; for the Macintosh.

6208.   Oppenheimer, Larry. "Review: Blank Software's Drum File." *Electronic Musician* 3 (Apr. 1987): 88–94.
SP-12 sound/sequence librarian and sample file conversion software; for the Macintosh.

6209.   ——. "Scorpion Systems SYbil." *Electronic Musician* 5 (Dec. 1989): 103–4.
A real-time MIDI data-processing program allowing multiple instruments to be performed with and controlled from a single controller.

6210.   Perrow, Jonathan. "Spectral Innovation Bets on Signal Processing." *MacWeek* 2 (Nov. 15, 1988): 75–78.
Describes the Spectral Innovations MacDSP board, a real-time digital signal processing workstation built into an NuBus card.

6211.   Placek, Robert W., and Leonard V. Ball. "Floppy Discography: Finale, Version 1.1." *Music Educators Journal* 75 (May 1989): 14–17.
Review of composing and publishing software.

6212.   ——, and Leonard V. Ball. "Floppy Discography: Performer: The MIDI Sequencer Software." *Music Educators Journal* 75 (Dec. 1988): 65–68.
Software review; for the Macintosh.

6213.   Pogue, David. "Finale." *Macworld* 6 (Feb. 1989): 222–23.
Review of sequencing, transcription, and notation software.

6214.   Puckette, Miller. "The Patcher." In *Proceedings of the 14th International Computer Music Conference, Cologne, September 20–25, 1988,* ed. Christoph Lischka and Johannes Fritsch. Cologne: Feedback-Studio-Verlag; San Francisco, Calif.: Dist. by Computer Music Association, 1988: 420–29. (Feedback Papers; 33)
Describes Patcher, a graphical environment for the production of real-time computer music on the Macintosh.

6215.   Reveaux, Anthony. "Digital Sound for the Mac." *A +* 4 (May 1986): 106–13.
Describes two sound digitizers: SoundCap and Natural Sound.

6216.   Rich, Robert. "Southworth JamBox 4+ & MidiPaint." *Music Technology* 2 (Dec. 1987): 68–74.
Review.

6217.   Rietmann, Kearney. "Open Window: An Exchange of Macintosh Discoveries." *Macworld* 1 (Nov. 1984): 124–28.
Describes the use of MacPaint to write music scores.

6218. Roads, Curtis. "Integrated Media Systems Digital Dyaxis: A Digital Audio Workstation." *Computer Music Journal* 13,3 (Fall 1989): 107–9.

Sound recording, editing, and mixing system; for the Apple Macintosh.

6219. Roberts, Jeremy. "MCS Applications." *Music, Computers & Software* 3 (Feb. 1988): 8, 16.

Discusses MACRO programs for use with the Macintosh.

6220. Roberts, Jim. "John Colby: Scoring Musical Points with ESPN." *Keyboard* 13 (May 1987): 18.

John Colby, music director for ESPN, uses music technology, including an Apple Macintosh Plus computer to create music for the network.

6221. Rona, Jeff. "Computers On-Line: A New Era in Software." *Keyboard* 14 (Feb. 1988): 138.

A HyperCard program that instructs the machine to play a sampled sound.

6222. ——. "Reviews: Take Your Cue: Film Scoring Software from Opcode." *Electronic Musician* 4 (Oct. 1988): 108–11.

6223. Russell, Benjamin. "Product Review: Alchemy Sample Editing Software." *Canadian Musician* 11 (Feb. 1989): 26.

A sample-editing package from Blank Software; for the Macintosh.

6224. ——. "Product Review: Ear Training Software for the Mac." *Canadian Musician* 10 (June 1988): 26.

6225. ——. "Product Review: Master Tracks Pro Sequencer." *Canadian Musician* 10 (Aug. 1988): 35.

6226. Scholz, Carter. "Keyboard Report: Ear-Training Software for the Macintosh." *Keyboard* 15 (July 1989): 116–18, 152–54.

6227. Scotchel, Robert. "Timbuk 3." *Music, Computers & Software* 3 (Oct. 1988): 28–29.

Profile/interview with members of the rock band, who discuss their use of synthesis equipment and the Macintosh.

6228. Sherman, Stratford P. "Musical Software: Take a Personal Computer, a Couple of Synthesizers, and 'Voila'—Studio-Quality Sound." *Fortune* 112 (Oct. 14, 1985): 145, 148.

How musicians are using software packages such as Total Music to produce studio-quality music.

6230. Simpson, Joel. "Music Writing Programs for the Macintosh. Part 2, The Second Generation." *Down Beat* 56 (June 1989): 53–56.

Review of Music Publisher and Finale.

6231. ———. "Pro Session: Music Writing Programs for the Macintosh. Part 1, The First Generation." *Down Beat* 56 (Apr. 1989): 54–56.

Review of Deluxe Music Construction Set, Concertware + MIDI, and Professional Composer.

6232. Sisk, Lawrence. "On Line: Professional Composer." *Instrumentalist* 42 (Feb. 1988): 14.

Software review.

6233. Stone, Greg. "Software: It Was Love at First Sight with Hayden Software's MusicWorks." *A+* 3 (May 1985): 112–14.

Review of composition and notation software.

6234. Styles, Bob. "KCSoftware: Total Music." *Keyboards, Computers & Software* 1 (Feb. 1986): 56–57.

Review of sequencing and notation software; for MIDI instruments.

6235. Swearingen, Donald. "Master Tracks Pro, MIDI Sequencer." *Byte* 12 (Nov. 1987): 212–14.

Review.

6236. Swigart, Rob. "They're Playing Our Song." *Macworld* 3 (Feb. 1986): 108–12.

Reviews of Professional Composer and Deluxe Music Construction Set.

6237. Tarabella, Leonello. "The Primula Machine." *Computer Music Journal* 11,2 (Summer 1987): 59–64.

6238. Tarte, Bob. "Intelligent Music OvalTune." *Electronic Musician* 5 (Oct. 1989): 82–84.

6239. Tolinski, Brad. "The Cure." *Music, Computers & Software* 2 (Oct. 1987): 31–32.

Profile/interview with members of the rock band, who discuss their use of the Macintosh.

6240. Tolleson, Robin. "Billy Cobham Piecing Together the Picture—Byte-by-Byte." *Down Beat* 55 (Apr. 1988): 58–59.

Billy Cobham describes his use of a Macintosh computer to write his music.

6241. Tully, Tim. "Altech Systems 1 × 3 MIDI Interface and 2 × 6 MIDI Interface for the Macintosh." *Electronic Musician* 4 (Sept. 1988): 73–74.

6242. ———. "Reviews: Turbosynth: Modular Synthesis Sampling Software." *Electronic Musician* 4 (Nov. 1988): 106–9.

6243. ——. "Simpler Samplers: Is It Live, or, Is It MIDI Hex? Only Your Sampler Knows for Sure." *MacUser* 4 (Oct. 1988): 148–62.

In-depth review of four MIDI sampling programs: Alchemy, Softsynth, Sound Designer, and Turbosynth, as well as a history of samplers and a discussion of sampling.

6244. Unger, Brian. "Apple Music: Yamaha 'DMP7 Pro.'" *Music, Computers & Software* 3 (June 1988): 64–65.

Review of control software; for the Yamaha DMP7 MIDI-controlled mixer and the Apple Macintosh.

6245. Vail, Mark. "Keyboard Report: Different Drummer, Macintosh Drum Machine Software." *Keyboard* 15 (Oct. 1989): 133–34.

6246. ——. "Keyboard Report: Road Warrior II, Macintosh II Compatible Computer." *Keyboard* 15 (May 1989): 137–41.

6247. Vosburg, Matthew. "The Hitch-hiker's Guide to the Macintosh." *Music Technology* 1,1 (1986): 42–46.

Interview with Douglas Adams.

6248. Webster, Bruce. "Ovaltune 1.0: Graphics and Music Software." *Macworld* 6 (Aug. 1989): 199.

Review.

6249. Weinberg, Norman. "Electronic Insights: Custom Creating Your Own Drum Sounds." *Modern Drummer* 12 (May 1988): 76–77.

Visual editors for samplers; covers specific use of one editor, Sound Designer, by Digidesign.

6250. Wessel, David; Pierre Lavoie; Lee Boynton; and Yann Orlarey. "MIDI-LISP: A LISP-based Programming Environment for MIDI on the Macintosh." In *The Proceedings of the AES 5th International Conference: Music and Digital Technology,* ed. John Strawn. New York, N.Y.: Audio Engineering Society, 1987: 185–97.

6251. Whitmer, Clair. "Mac Psychedelia Due to Ship Next Month: Intelligent Music to Ship OvalTune." *MacWeek* 2 (Sept. 6, 1988): 4.

Announcement of the release of OvalTune, a random generator of graphic images and melodies.

6252. ——. "More Choices in Music Software." *MacWeek* 2 (Nov. 8, 1988): 12.

Short descriptions of several music software packages.

6253. Widders-Ellis, Andy. "Keyboard Report: Vision, Macintosh Sequencer from Opcode." *Keyboard* 15 (July 1989): 122–30.

MIDI sequencing software.

6254. Williams, Wheat. "Under Construction." *MacUser* 4 (Oct. 1988): 166–67.

Tips on the use of Deluxe Music Construction Set.

6255. Yavelow, Christopher. "A Concert in PostScript." *Macworld* 5 (Jan. 1988): 163–65.

Review of ConcertWare + MIDI, music notation software.

6256. ——. "Digital Sampling on the Apple Macintosh: Uses of Digital Sampling for Music Applications." *Byte* 11 (June 1986): 171–83.

6257. ——. "From Keyboard to Score: An Introduction to Music Processing and Evaluations of Six Packages That Put Your Performances on Paper." *Macworld* 3 (Dec. 1986): 108–17.

Evaluations of MusicWorks, ConcertWare + MIDI, Deluxe Music Construction Set, and Professional Composer.

6258. ——. "Grand Finale." *Macworld* 5 (June 1988): 105–7.

Product announcement of Finale.

6259. ——. "High Score." *Macworld* 3 (Nov. 1986): 81.

Preview of High Score, a music editor/printer.

6260. ——. "Mac Power User = Power Muser. Part 1." *Electronic Musician* 4 (Apr. 1988): 72–79.

A discussion of power desk accessories; for the Macintosh.

6261. ——. "Mac Power User = Power Muser. Part 2, Power Utilities." *Electronic Musician* 4 (May 1988): 56–62.

A discussion of utilities that improve the performance of the Macintosh.

6262. ——. "Mac Power User = Power Muser. Part 3, Advanced Techniques." *Electronic Musician* 4 (June 1988): 53–62.

How to customize program code, use macros to automate longer tasks, and take advantage of HyperCard.

6263. ——. "MIDI and the Apple Macintosh." *Computer Music Journal* 10,3 (Fall 1986): 11–47.

6264. ——. "MIDI Sequencers: Greatest Hits." *Macworld* 6 (Sept. 1989): 194–201.

A comparison of MIDI sequencing software: Performer, Master Tracks Pro, KCS Level II, Vision and Portrait.

6265. ——. "Music Processing: The Next Generation." *Macworld* 5 (July 1988): 102–11.

A discussion of the newest music-notation software.

6266.   ——. "Review: Performer 2.2." *Electronic Musician* 4 (May 1988): 92–97.

A MIDI sequencer.

6267.   ——. "Reviews: Low-Cost MIDI Interface Quartet." *Macworld* 5 (Aug. 1988): 139–41.

Review of the Apple MIDI Interface, MIDIface II, Professional Plus, and Passport MIDI Interface.

6268.   ——. "Reviews: Miller/Black Sample Disks for the Kurzweil 250." *Electronic Musician* 5 (May 1989): 100–101.

6269.   ——. "Top of the Charts: On Stage and in the Studio, the Mac Is Number One with Music Professionals." *Macworld* 4 (Aug. 1987): 138–45.

How music professionals are using the Macintosh for sound design, film music, and performance.

6270.   Yelton, Geary. "The Musical Computer: The State of the Macintosh: A Musical Perspective." *Electronic Musician* 4 (Apr. 1988): 56–63.

A general overview of the use of the Macintosh for musical applications.

6271.   ——. "Opcode's MIDIMAC Patch Librarian." *Electronic Musician* 2 (Mar. 1986): 68–69.

6272.   ——. "Review: Budget MIDI for the Mac." *Electronic Musician* 2 (Aug. 1986): 72–76.

Review of three programs for MIDI software.

6273.   ——. "Review: Mark of the Unicorn's 'Professional Composer.'" *Electronic Musician* 2 (Mar. 1986): 60–64, 67.

6274.   ——. "Review: Opcode's MIDIMAC Sequencer 2.5 for the Mac." *Electronic Musician* 3 (Nov. 1987): 110–14.

6275.   ——. "Review: Softsynth: Additive Synthesis for the Mac." *Electronic Musician* 3 (Feb. 1987): 94–98.

6276.   ——. "Review: SoundCap: A Lowcost Mac Sampler." *Electronic Musician* 2 (May 1986): 70–73.

6277.   Zicarelli, David. "M and Jam Factory." *Computer Music Journal* 11,4 (Winter 1987): 13–29.

Software packages published by Intelligent Music. Uses Apple Macintosh with a MIDI interface.

6278.   ——, and Joel Chadabe. *Jam Factory—MIDI Music Software for the Macintosh.* Albany, N.Y.: Intelligent Computer Music Systems, 1986.
A user's manual.

6279.   Zilber, Jon. "Apple Jam." *MacUser* 4 (Jan. 1988): 52.
Short review of Jam Session.

6280.   ——. "Can We Talk? With MacRecorder, Applications and Hyper-Card Stacks Come Alive with the Digitized Sound of Music—or Speech. Say Good-bye to the Sounds of Silence." *MacUser* 4 (June 1988): 214–28.
Review of MacRecorder.

6281.   ——. "Interactive Cultures: The Mac Brought Art to the Business World. It Also Helps the Art World Get Down to Business." *MacUser* 4 (Oct. 1988): 100–123.
A detailed discussion on how the Macintosh can be used by artists and musicians, covering film scoring, MIDI, sequencing and cueing software, and additional hardware and software.

6282.   ——. "Mac Your Own Kind of Music." *MacUser* 4 (May 1988): 34–35.
An overview of products exhibited at the Macworld Expo in San Francisco.

6283.   ——. "New on the Menu: For a Song." *MacUser* 4 (May 1988): 46.
Product announcement of Music Publisher, notation software.

6284.   ——. "Quick Clicks: Performer; Professional Composer." *MacUser* 4 (Jan. 1988): 94–103.
Reviews.

6285.   ——. "Synch along with Click." *MacUser* 4 (June 1988): 48.
Product announcement of Clicktracks.

MICROCOMPUTERS— OTHER

6286. Flurry, Henry S. "An Introduction to the Creation Station." *Computer Music Journal* 13,2 (Summer 1989): 56–70.

Use of the NeXT computer.

6287. Hunkins, Arthur B. "Player ZX81: A Tune-playing Program for the Sinclair/Timex." *Compute!* 5 (Jan. 1983): 142–43.

Review.

6288. ——. "Sound on the Sinclair/Timex." *Compute!* 5 (Jan. 1983): 68–70.

How to create simple melodies.

6289. ——. "Update on Sinclair/Timex Sound." *Compute!* 5 (Apr. 1983): 164.

A method to extend the sound range down to middle C.

6290. Jaffe, David A. "Overview of the NeXT Music Kit." In *Proceedings, 1989 International Computer Music Conference, November 2–5, the Ohio State University, Columbus, Ohio.* San Francisco, Calif.: Computer Music Association, 1989: 135–38.

6291. ——, and Lee Boynton. "An Overview of the Sound and Music Kits for the NeXT Computer." *Computer Music Journal* 13,2 (Summer 1989): 48–55.

6292. Jenkins, Mark. "Control Zone: Computers: Switching on to BBC Computers." *Melody Maker* 60 (Jan. 19, 1985): 35.

EMR BBC B MIDI interface.

6293. Lansky, Paul. "It's about Time: Some NeXT Perspectives. Part 1." *Perspectives of New Music* 27 (Summer 1989): 270–81.

After a historical tour of the production of computer music, the author reviews the 0.8 beta release of the NeXT music software.

6294. Miller, Erik. "Reviews: The Fantastic Music Machine." *InfoWorld* 5 (Dec. 19, 1983): 63–66.

Music composition software for the Timex computer.

6295.   Miller, James. "Compose Yourself! Now Any VIC-20 Owner Can Write Original Music." *Family Computing* 2 (Apr. 1984): 108–10.
Program listing of Piano Player, a program that reproduces an octave of the piano keyboard using the QWERTY keyboard.

6296.   Mullen, Christopher J. "The Musical Micro." *Music Teacher* 65 (Nov. 1986): 13–15.
Use of the SOUND command on the BBC micro.

6297.   ———. "The Musical Micro." *Music Teacher* 65 (Dec. 1986): 16–20.
More on producing music on the BBC Micro.

6298.   Nee, Eric. "Workstation Watch." *Computer Systems News* n390 (Oct. 31, 1988): 48.
Describes the NeXT general-purpose workstation which includes a digital signal processing chip and software for voice and music.

6299.   Regena, C. "Programming the TI: Mixing Graphics and Music." *Compute!* 7 (Jan. 1985): 141–44.
How to design a program that incorporates both sound and graphics. Includes a program listing to play "Jolly Old St. Nick"; for the Texas Instruments computer.

6300.   ———. "Programming the TI: Playing Music on the TI." *Compute!* 5 (Oct. 1983): 224–28.
Describes the use of the CALL SOUND command to program music on the Texas Instruments computer.

6301.   Selman, Tom, and David Lourik. "Computers On-Line: The NeXT Computer & Music." *Keyboard* 15 (Jan. 1989): 105.

6302.   Sonneborn, Henry. "The Well-Tempered Computer." *Popular Computing* 3 (Dec. 1983): 218–24.
Two BASIC programs that modify the twelve-tone chromatic scale; for the TI-99/4A.

MICROCOMPUTERS—
TANDY

6303. Alford, Roger C. "Fastdance: Three Seconds of Your Favorite Tunes." *80 Micro* n51 (Apr. 1984): 196–201.

Instruction on constructing a tune-generator board.

6304. Alsop, Brian H. "Polyphonic Play—Multi-Voice Music on the Tandy 1000." *PCM: The Personal Computer Magazine for Tandy Computer Users* 4 (Apr. 1987): 20–24.

Includes a GW BASIC program that plays a shortened version of J. S. Bach's Minuet in G.

6305. Augsburg, Cray. "The CoCo Comes to Life with the Sounds of Lyra." *Rainbow* 6 (Dec. 1986): 133.

Review of Lyra, an eight-voice music editor.

6306. ———. "Maxsound: Breaking the Sound Barrier." *Rainbow* 7 (June 1988): 126–29.

Review of Maxsound, software to digitize and manipulate sound.

6307. Banaszak, David. "A Little Tree-trimming Music." *Rainbow* 3 (Dec. 1983): 35–37.

A BASIC program listing for eight Christmas carols.

6308. Barden, Bill Jr. "The Sounds of Science." *PCM: The Personal Computing Magazine for Tandy Computer Users* 3 (Sept. 1985): 10–24.

Ways to make sound on the Tandy 1000 using BASIC. Includes program listing.

6309. Bell, Jack. "Classical Music Mosquito." *Personal Computing* 9 (Feb. 1985): 22.

Description of Robb Murray, a programmer who used a TRS-80 to generate the sound recording of neo-baroque compositions, "Classical Mosquito."

6310. Boots, Greg. "Print that Tune!" *Rainbow* 7 (June 1988): 52–55.

Program listing of Print Tune, software that prints the Play statement of a specified tune.

6311.   Brothers, Hardin. "Next Step: Sounding Off on the 1000." *80 Micro* n96 (Jan. 1988): 82–88.

An exploration of the capabilities of the sound chip in the Tandy 1000.

6312.   ———. "The Next Step: Sounding Off on the 1000: Encore." *80 Micro* n97 (Feb. 1988): 91–104.

Techniques for making the Tandy 1000's sound chip less mechanical sounding.

6313.   Burke, Val. "Playin' the Blues." *Rainbow* 7 (June 1988): 20–25.

Program listing for a twelve-bar performance of a blues progression.

6314.   Davis, Merton. "The Sound of Musikon." *80 Micro* n51 (Apr. 1984): 138–52.

A music composition program.

6315.   Elliot, Sheila. "LoCo CoCo and the 1812." *Rainbow* 3 (June 1984): 67–72.

A BASIC program to play "I've Been Working on the Railroad" while a train appears on the screen.

6316.   Engelhardt, David. "Reviews: Going for a Song." *80 Micro* n79 (Aug. 1986): 118.

Review of TuneSmith, software to compose, edit, and play music.

6317.   Freese, Peter. "Music-80." *80 Micro* n38 (Mar. 1983): 310–24.

Listing and description of a music-generator program for composing, performing, or teaching.

6318.   Frischein, Ben. "Harmony and Me." *80 Micro* n46 (Nov. 1983): 265–69.

A BASIC program to compose, playback, save, or load music.

6319.   Gibson, Don Phillip. "Tandy Tunes: Make Beautiful Music Together with Your Tandy 1000." *80 Micro* n83 (Dec. 1986): 89–93.

Program listing to play an excerpt from the Bach E-flat Trio Sonata.

6320.   Golias, Ruth E. "Saturday at the Bijou—Remembering Intermission Sing-Alongs." *Rainbow* 5 (June 1986): 36–40.

A BASIC program listing.

6321.   Huang, David. "Internal Sound: A Circuit Enabling You to Produce Sound Internally from Your CoCo." *Rainbow* 7 (June 1988): 99–100. Includes schematics.

6322. Huben, Carl. "Young Programmer's Contest: Music Composer." *80 Micro* n37 (Feb. 1983): 104–7.

A program to compose pieces with up to 200 notes.

6323. Keefe, Robert W. "Music Maker." *PCM: The Personal Computer Magazine for Tandy Computer Users* 4 (Jan. 1987): 99–113.

Presentation of the program Music Maker, written in Turbo Pascal; for the Tandy 1000.

6324. Kirley, Dennis. "Melody Maker: Pleasant Diversion and Tune Maker for the 100." *PCM: The Personal Computer Magazine for Tandy Users* 2 (May 1985): 71–72.

Review of Melody Maker, composition software; for the TRS80, Model 100.

6325. Konecky, Lawrence W. "The CoCo Composer." *Rainbow* 3 (Dec. 1983): 131–35.

A BASIC program for writing four-part harmony.

6326. ——. "Tone Row Composing." *Rainbow* 3 (June 1984): 23–25.

A BASIC program to generate twelve-tone matrices.

6327. Ludwick, Gary A. "Reviews: Let There Be Music." *80 Micro* n62 (Mar. 1985): 114–16.

Review of Orchestra-90 Stereo Music Synthesizer.

6328. Lundlum, Bob. "Making Four-part Harmony Easier." *Rainbow* 3 (June 1984): 74–87.

A BASIC program called Music+ loads a machine language music synthesis program and creates a screen editor for the entry, editing, and playing of four-part music.

6329. ——. "Music+: New Commands, No Bugs." *Rainbow* 5 (June 1986): 51–53.

An enhancement to the author's Music+ program in the June 1984 issue.

6330. Martens, Gordon. "The Piano Tutor." *Rainbow* 3 (June 1984): 19–22.

A BASIC program that utilizes the computer keyboard as a piano keyboard.

6331. Matthews, Becky F. "CoCo Goes Country: A Musical View of Nashville." *Rainbow* 7 (June 1988): 36–41.

Program listing of Rockytop, a program that displays the skyline of Nashville as it plays the title tune.

6332.   ——, and David Matthews. "I Want My CoCo TV." *Rainbow* 5 (June 1986): 42–50.

A BASIC listing of the original song "Shadow of the Rings" and accompanying video display.

6333.   McQuillan, Chuck. "CoCo and the Sequencer: Radio Shack/Syntrax." *Electronic Musician* 3 (Mar. 1987): 82–86.

Review of Syntrax 1.00 and 2.00, MIDI sequencers and MIDI interface; for the Tandy Color Computer.

6334.   Myers, Walter B. "The Lyra Lybrary: An Instant Repertoire for Your CoCo MIDI." *Rainbow* 8 (Dec. 1988): 133–34.

Review; an eleven-disk collection of 230 music files.

6335.   Nickel, Harold. "The CoCo Composer." *Rainbow* 6 (June 1987): 114–23.

Program listing of Piano, software that utilizes the computer keyboard as a two manual organ keyboard.

6336.   Plaster, Gip Wayne. "From Scales to Mozart." *Rainbow* 7 (Jan. 1988): 72–73.

Listing of a program that produces nearly three minutes of music.

6337.   Platt, Joseph D. "The Sweet Strains of CoCo: Transposition Refinements for Music +." *Rainbow* 6 (June 1987): 94–95.

Refinement of the program by Bob Lundlum in the June 1984 and June 1986 issues.

6338.   Pollock, Tony, and Gail Pollock. "Bach to Basic." *Rainbow* 3 (Nov. 1983): 152.

A BASIC program listing that plays Bach's Sinfonia.

6339.   ——, and Gail Pollock. "CoCo Classics." *Rainbow* 3 (June 1984): 131–35.

A BASIC program listing that plays "Hornpipe" by Handel, "Sonatina" by Kuhlau, and "Toccata in D minor" by Bach.

6340.   Ramella, Richard. "Bit Parade: Compose Melodies on Your Portable and Integrate Them into Your BASIC Programs . . ." *PCM: The Personal Computer Magazine for Tandy Computer Users* 3 (Dec. 1985): 30–31.

6341.   Ray, James. "Create the Sounds of Music with The Music Studio." *PCM: The Personal Computer Magazine for Tandy Computer Users* 4 (Feb. 1987): 127–28.

Review; for the Tandy 1000, 1200, or 3000.

6342.   Rogers, Robert. "Finish Your Symphony with the Computer Chord Finder." *Rainbow* 3 (June 1984): 179–82.

Generates a chart to show notes in a chord.

6343. Rutter, Marge. "CoCo Dares You to Name that Tune." *Rainbow* 5 (June 1986): 66–83.

A BASIC program listing for a home version of "Name that Song."

6344. Scoffin, Brad. "Two for the Composer." *Rainbow* 3 (June 1984): 57.

Data listings to play "The Entertainer" and "Looking over a Four-Leaf Clover" on the composer program in the December 1983 issue.

6345. Shelton, Garry L. "Color Composer: A Music 'Processor' to Help You Create and Edit Your Own Songs." *Rainbow* 7 (June 1988): 42–49.

Program listing of Song Writer.

6346. Spiller, Jeremy. "Synthesizer Sound-off: Turn the PLAY Command into a Digital Synthesizer." *Rainbow* 7 (June 1988): 102–8.

Program listing of SuperPlay, in BASIC.

6347. Spiller, Martin, and Jeremy Spiller. "CoCo Synthesizer Produces Out-of-This-World Sounds." *Rainbow* 5 (June 1986): 122–37.

A BASIC program, Piano-Synthesizer/Composer, to turn the computer keyboard into a piano keyboard.

6348. Stajduhar, Jerry. "The Music Machine: Make Melodies to Soothe the Savage Hacker." *PCM: The Personal Computer Magazine for Tandy Computer Users* 3 (May 1986): 33–40.

Program listing in BASIC; for the Tandy 1000.

6349. Tandberg, Dan. "CoCo Instant Music." *Rainbow* 5 (June 1986): 62–65.

A specialized text editor to facilitate creating and using strings for the PLAY command.

6350. "Tandy's 1000 Learns to Speak and Listen." *Byte* 13 (Sept. 1988): 158.

Description of the sound capability of the 1000TL and 1000SL.62

6351. Thompson, Ernie. "Blast from the Past: A Jukebox of Ragtime Selections." *Rainbow* 7 (June 1988): 96–98.

Program listing of Jukebox.

6352. Thompson, Matthew. "Steppin' out with My CoCo." *Rainbow* 6 (June 1987): 58–75.

Program listing of Bells and Whistles 2, a four-voice programmable music synthesizer.

6353. Ward, Paul. "CoCo Midi 2: High Tech Creativity." *Rainbow* 7 (Sept. 1987): 133–36.

Review.

6354.   ——. "Syntrax 2.0—CoCo MIDI Package." *Rainbow* 8 (Aug. 1988): 128–32.
Review.

6355.   Woods, Rick. "Deck the Halls." *Rainbow* 6 (Dec. 1986): 42–48.
The author uses Musica II to provide a program listing of the Christmas carol.

MIDI

6356.   Aikin, Jim. "MIDI." *Keyboard* 12 (Jan. 1986): 28–31.
An introduction to MIDI.

6357.   ———. "MIDI Spoken Here: From Modes & Channels to Kilobaud & Status Bytes." *Keyboard* 12 (Jan. 1986): 30–31.

6358.   Albin, David. "But How Do I Get Started?" *Electronic Musician* 2 (Mar. 1986): 18–19.

6359.   ———. "MIDI: Recording Medium of the Future." *Polyphony* 10 (Apr. 1985): 6–7.

6360.   Amaral, John. "Musings on Musical Instrument Digital Interface." *Musician* n75 (Jan. 1985): 70–71.

6361.   Anderson, David P. "Synthesizer Management Based on Note Priorities." In *Proceedings of the 1987 International Computer Music Conference: University of Illinois at Urbana-Champaign, Urbana, Illinois, USA, August 23–26, 1987,* comp. James Beauchamp. San Francisco, Calif.: Computer Music Association, 1987: 230–37.
Describes a system, Synthesizer Manager, that provides computer control of musical synthesizers.

6362.   Anderton, Craig. "Confessions of a MIDIot." *Electronic Musician* 2 (Mar. 1986): 20–21.

6363.   ———. "MIDI and the Guitarist." *Guitar Player* 19 (Jan. 1985): 104.
An examination of what MIDI means to guitar players.

6364.   ———. "MIDI and the Guitarist. Part II." *Guitar Player* 19 (Feb. 1985): 118.
Continuation of previous article.

6365.   ———. *MIDI for Musicians.* New York, N.Y.: Amsco Publications, 1986. 105 p.
Review by Jim Aikin in *Keyboard* 12 (May 1986): 25.
Review by Curtis Roads in *Computer Music Journal* 11,3 (Fall 1987): 52–53.

6366. ———. "The MIDI Protocol." In *The Proceedings of the AES 5th International Conference: Music and Digital Technology,* ed. John Strawn. New York, N.Y.: Audio Engineering Society, 1987. 109–21

6367. ———. "The MIDI Recording Studio: How to Buy It, How to Set It up, and How to Run It." *Musician* n82 (Aug. 1985): 74–77, 92.

6368. ———. "MIDI: Programming Synthesizer MIDI Parameters." *Electronic Musician* 2 (May 1986): 22–24.

6369. ———. "The MIDIfied Guitarist." *Electronic Musician* 3 (Sept. 1987): 46–57.
Describes the latest MIDI techniques for electronic guitarists from sequencing to MIDI-controlled signal processors.

6370. Austin, Kirk. "Mod: I'm thru with MIDI." *Electronic Musician* 2 (Apr. 1986): 52–53.

6371. Baird, Jock, ed. *Understanding MIDI.* London; New York, N.Y.: Amsco, 1986. 79 p.

6372. Bateman, Selby. "Making Music with MIDI." *Compute!* 8 (Jan. 1986): 24–34.
An introduction to MIDI.

6373. Battles, Brian. "Ad Ventures." *DB, the Sound Engineering Magazine* 22 (May/June 1988): 73–75.
The use of MIDI in radio commercial production.

6374. Benoit, Ellen. "Music's Black Box." *Forbes* 134 (Aug. 13, 1984): 102.
How MIDI is changing the way music is written and recorded.

6375. Bonfoey, Mark. "Ask the Experts: 'How Does One MIDI a Deagan Commander II Vibe.'" *Percussive Notes* 25 (Fall 1986): 50–51.

6376. Boom, Michael. *Music through MIDI: Using MIDI to Create Your Own Electronic Music System.* Redmond, Wash.: Microsoft Press, 1987. 302 p.
Review by Deborah Parisi in *Music Technology* 2 (Nov. 1987): 48.
Review by Bruce P. Mahin in *Instrumentalist* 42 (Feb. 1988): 10.
Review by Tom Mulhern in *Guitar Player* 22 (July 1988): 168.

6377. Brooks, David R. "MIDI Programming. Part I." *Commodore Magazine* 8 (Aug. 1987): 88–90.
An introduction to the MIDI interface.

6378. ———. "MIDI Programming. Part II, Monitoring MIDI Information." *Commodore Magazine* 8 (Sept. 1987): 74–77.

6379. Brooks, Evan. "Software in the Studio." In *The Proceedings of the AES 5th International Conference: Music and Digital Technology,* ed.

John Strawn. New York, N.Y.: Audio Engineering Society, 1987: 141–57.
MIDI applications in the recording studio.

6380. Burger, Jeff. "MIDI Column." *Computer Shopper* 9 (Jan. 1989): 295, 559, 562.
An explanation of MIDI synchronization.

6381. ———. *The Murphy's Law MIDI Book.* Newbury Park, Calif.: Alexander Pub., 1987. 94 p.

6382. Buxton, William. "Masters and Slaves Versus Democracy: MIDI and Local Area Networks." In *The Proceedings of the AES 5th International Conference: Music and Digital Technology,* ed. John Strawn. New York, N.Y.: Audio Engineering Society, 1987: 207–19.

6383. Campbell, Alan Gary. "Build a MIDI Switch." *Electronic Musician* 1 (June 1985): 20–21, 37.

6384. ———. "Making MIDI Work for You." *Electronic Musician* 1 (June 1985): 17–19, 44–46.

6385. Carlucci, Tony. "Brass: MIDI and the Trumpet Player." *Canadian Musician* 9 (Feb. 1987): 51–52.

6386. Casabona, Helen, and Dave Frederick. *Using MIDI.* Cupertino, Calif.: GPI Publications; Sherman Oaks, Calif.: Alfred Pub. Co., 1987. 123 p.
Review by Donald Hodges in *American Music Teacher* 38 (Jan. 1989): 54–56.

6387. Chin, Adam, and Bill Lewis. "MCS Telecom: MCS MIDI Forum." *Music, Computers & Software* 2 (Oct. 1987): 88–89, 98.
Sample question and answer excerpts from the MCS MIDI Forum.

6388. ———, and Bill Lewis. "MCS Telecom: MCS MIDI Forum." *Music, Computers & Software* 2 (Dec. 1987): 81–82.
Sample question and answer excerpts from the MCS MIDI Forum.

6389. ———, and Bill Lewis. "MCS Telecom: MCS MIDI Forum." *Music, Computers & Software* 3 (Feb. 1988): 80–81.
Sample question and answer excerpts from the MCS MIDI Forum.

6390. Civiero, Angelo. "Inside the MIDI Recording Studio." *Canadian Musician* 10 (Oct. 1988): 73.

6391.   Collie, Ashley. "MIDI for All." *Canadian Musician* 10 (June 1988): 50–59.

Covers the impact of MIDI on keyboards, in the recording studio, on software development, in performance, and with guitars.

6392.   ——. "MIDI: MIDI Madness Reigns for Domenic Troiano." *Canadian Musician* 9 (June 1987): 20.

6393.   Combs, Jim. "Computer Music Basics: MIDI Music for Beginners." *Music, Computers & Software* 3 (June 1988): 40–46.

A tutorial on MIDI.

6394.   Conger, Jim. *C Programming for MIDI.* Redwood City, Calif.: M&T Books, 1988. 219 p.
Review by David B. Doty in *Electronic Musician* 4 (Nov. 1988): 118–19.

6395.   ——. *MIDI Sequencing in C.* Redwood City, Calif.: M&T Publishing, 1989. 471 p.

6396.   "Control Zone: Synthi-Pop." *Melody Maker* 59 (Feb. 4, 1984): 24.

MIDI system links with synthesizers.

6397.   Cooper, Jim. "Growing Pains: Inside Report from an Interface Expert." *Keyboard* 12 (Jan. 1986): 35–39.

6398.   ——. "MIDI: MIDI Muting and Mixing for the Masses." *Electronic Musician* 2 (Aug. 1986): 34–35, 65–67.

6399.   ——. "Mind over MIDI: Airdrums, Time Code, and System-Exclusive Formats." *Keyboard* 12 (Sept. 1986): 124–27.

6400.   ——. "Mind over MIDI: Automation Processes." *Keyboard* 14 (Feb. 1988): 135–36.

6401.   ——. "Mind over MIDI: Back to Basics: Modes & Myths." *Keyboard* 13 (Mar. 1987): 116–17.

6402.   ——. "Mind over MIDI: Circuit Checkers, Code Cracking & Continuous Clocks." *Keyboard* 12 (May 1986): 100–104.

6403.   ——. "Mind over MIDI: Clearing the Air Surrounding the MIDI Spec." *Keyboard* 12 (Mar. 1986): 86–87.

6404.   ——. "Mind over MIDI: Diary of a Mad MIDI Scientist." *Keyboard* 12 (June 1986): 136–37.

Mention of the book *MIDI for Musicians* by Craig Anderton; PAN (Performing Artists Network); and an in-depth look at the MIDI Song Position Pointer.

6405. ———. "Mind over MIDI: Happy Trails." *Keyboard* 14 (Sept. 1988): 119.

6406. ———. "Mind over MIDI: Information Sources and System-Exclusive Data Formats." *Keyboard* 12 (Oct. 1986): 110–11, 159.

6407. ———. "Mind over MIDI: Intelligent Data Routing & the One-Button Studio Setup." *Keyboard* 13 (Nov. 1987): 133.

6408. ———. "Mind over MIDI: LANs and MIDI." *Keyboard* 13 (Dec. 1987): 126, 155–56.

6409. ———. "Mind over MIDI: MIDI Delays and System Interrupts." *Keyboard* 12 (Nov. 1986): 128–29.

6410. ———. "Mind over MIDI: MIDI Interfacing for the Rest of the Universe." *Keyboard* 12 (Dec. 1986): 117, 158.

How players of traditional instruments (piano and keyboards, woodwinds, and brass) can play a synthesizer via MIDI.

6411. ———. "Mind over MIDI: MIDI Sequencing & Automation." *Keyboard* 14 (Mar. 1988): 120–24.

6412. ———. "Mind over MIDI: MIDI Time Code. Part 2." *Keyboard* 13 (Oct. 1987): 119, 160.

6413. ———. "Mind over MIDI: MIDI Time Code: The Birth & the Basics." *Keyboard* 13 (Aug. 1987): 101.

6414. ———. "Mind over MIDI: More MIDI Basics: Continuous Controllers Defined." *Keyboard* 13 (May 1987): 106.

6415. ———. "Mind over MIDI: More on MIDI Continuous Controllers." *Keyboard* 13 (July 1987): 132.

6416. ———. "Mind over MIDI: Our Story So Far." *Keyboard* 13 (Feb. 1987): 120, 176.

A short description of MIDI basics.

6417. ———. "Mind over MIDI: Public Day at NAMM: MIDI Data Management." *Keyboard* 14 (June 1988): 126–27, 168.

6418. ———. "Mind over MIDI: Puttin' on the Bits." *Keyboard* 12 (Feb. 1986): 100–101.

An in-depth look at the basic elements of the MIDI Specification 1.0.

6419. ———. "Mind over MIDI: Translating from MIDI to Acoustic Instruments: What's an Engineer to Do?" *Keyboard* 13 (Jan. 1987): 109.

6420. ———. "Mind over MIDI: Using MIDI to Send and Receive SMPTE Time Code." *Keyboard* 12 (July 1986): 130–33.

6421. Crigger, David. *Making MIDI Work by Someone Who Does.* Rev. ed. Newbury Park, Calif.: Alexander Publishing, 1988. 53 p.

6422.   Cummings, Steve, and Dominic Milano. "Computer-to-MIDI Interfaces; How Do I Byte Thee? Let Me Count the Ways." *Keyboard* 12 (Jan. 1986): 41, 46.

6423.   Czeiszperger, Michael S. "Introducing Standard MIDI Files." *Electronic Musician* 5 (Apr. 1989): 49–68.

6424.   Dames, Jean, and Douglas Susu-Mago. "On Line." *Clavier* 24 (Feb. 1985): 28–29.
             Review of MIDI/4, four-channel recording software.

6425.   Daniel, Walter K. "MIDI: Getting the Most out of MIDI thru Boxes." *Electronic Musician* 2 (June 1986): 51–52.

6426.   DaNova, George. "MIDI: The Ins and Outs of Program Change." *Electronic Musician* 3 (July 1987): 44–47.

6427.   De Furia, Steve. "Software for Musicians: Bit-mapped Versus Byte-mapped Data Structures." *Keyboard* 13 (Jan. 1987): 102–6.
             A map of the 4,096 bytes of MIDI data that make up the body of Yamaha DX7 bulk dump system-exclusive messages.

6428.   ——. "Software for Musicians: Eavesdropping on Your MIDI Gear." *Keyboard* 13 (July 1987): 128, 168.
             Handshaking between Roland instruments and a computer via MIDI.

6429.   ——. "Software for Musicians: Parsing MIDI Bytes." *Keyboard* 15 (Apr. 1989): 112–13.

6430.   ——. "Software for Musicians: Real-Time MIDI Data Programming." *Keyboard* 14 (Nov. 1988): 138.

6431.   ——. "Software for Musicians: The Treacherous Trail of the MIDI Programmer." *Keyboard* 12 (Nov. 1986): 127, 129.

6432.   ——. "Software for Musicians: Wading in the MIDI Data Stream." *Keyboard* 15 (May 1989): 112–15.

6433.   ——. "Software for Musicians: Who Was That Masked Byte?" *Keyboard* 13 (Apr. 1987): 120.
             The use of masks in conjunction with bitwise operations in MIDI.

6434.   ——. "Systems & Applications: An On-Stage MIDI System for Cyndi Lauper's *True Colors* Tour." *Keyboard* 13 (Mar. 1987): 120–21.

6435.   ——. "Systems & Applications: Betrayed by MIDI Key Velocity." *Keyboard* 12 (Dec. 1986): 118.

6436.   ——. "Systems & Applications: Enhancing Your Control over the Keyboard through MIDI." *Keyboard* 12 (Sept. 1986): 130.
             How to control a single instrument with two keyboards.

6437.   ——. "Systems & Applications: Gee Whiz! Why Didn't I Think of That?" *Keyboard* 12 (Oct. 1986): 106.

Suggestions to try: connecting a MIDI instrument to itself, and wiring a DIN-to-XLR adapter.

6438.   ——. "Systems & Applications: Reading MIDI Implementation Charts." *Keyboard* 12 (Nov. 1986): 133–34.

6439.   ——, and Joe Scacciaferro. *The MIDI Book: Using MIDI and Related Interfaces*. Rutherford, N.J.: Third Earth Productions: Ferro Technologies; [Milwaukee, Wis.]: Dist. by H. Leonard, 1986. 95 p.
Review by Ted Greenwald in *Keyboard* 12 (Oct. 1986): 33.
Review by Bruce P. Mahin in *Instrumentalist* 41 (June 1987): 6.

6440.   ——, and Joe Scacciaferro. *The MIDI Implementation Book*. Pompton Lakes, N.J.: Third Earth Pub.; Milwaukee, Wis.: Dist. by H. Leonard, 1986. 216 p. (Ferro Music Technology Series//MIDI Reference Books)
Review by Jim Aikin in *Keyboard* 14 (Mar. 1988): 23.
Review by David B. Doty in *Electronic Musician* 4 (Dec. 1988): 124–25.

6441.   ——, and Joe Scacciaferro. *The MIDI Resource Book*. Pompton Lakes, N.J.: Third Earth Pub.: Ferro Technologies, 1987. 148 p. (Ferro Music Technology Series//MIDI Reference Books)
Review by Jim Aikin in *Keyboard* 14 (Mar. 1988): 23.
Review by David B. Doty in *Electronic Musician* 4 (Dec. 1988): 124–25.

6442.   ——, and Joe Scacciaferro. *The MIDI System Exclusive Book*. Pompton Lakes, N.J.: Third Earth Pub.; Milwaukee, Wis.: Dist. by H. Leonard, 1987. 360 p. (Ferro Music Technology Series)
Review by Jim Aikin in *Keyboard* 14 (Mar. 1988): 23.
Review by David B. Doty in *Electronic Musician* 4 (Dec. 1988): 124–25.

6443.   De Smit, Scott. "Home Hardware: MIDI for the Masses." *Music Scene* n364 (Nov.–Dec. 1988): 13.

6444.   Di Perna, Alan. "Beyond Solo: Merging MIDI Traffic." *Musician* n92 (June 1986): 33–34, 46.

6445.   ——. "MIDI Automation." *Musician* n109 (Nov. 1987): 86–91, 110, 126–29.

Use of MIDI-based automated mixing systems.

6446.   ——. "MIDI Law & Order: Using MIDI Mapping to Get Control of Your System." *Musician* n103 (May 1987): 46–48, 59.

6447.   ———. "MIDI Protocol: The Diplomacy of Digital—How Musical Nations of Many Languages Do Business Together." *Musician* n88 (Feb. 1986): 76, 82.

6448.   ———. "MIDI Update: MIDI Weather Bulletin." *Musician* n108 (Oct. 1987): 40–42, 55–56.
              More new MIDI messages, specs, standards, and MIDI Time Code.

6449.   ———. "Tapping into MIDI." *Keyboard* 14 (July 1988): 27.
              Taptronics: MIDI control through tap shoes.

6450.   Doerschuk, Bob. "Disabilities Diminish with MIDI." *Keyboard* 14 (July 1988): 32–33.
              MIDI control for disabled musician.

6451.   ———; Dave Frederick; and Dominic Milano. "The Human Connection: Hosannas & Headaches as Artists Get Midified." *Keyboard* 12 (Jan. 1986): 56–59.
              Steve Porcaro, Mark Mothersbaugh, Alan Howarth, and Jerry Goldsmith relate their experiences with MIDI.

6452.   Donato, Peter. "How MIDI Will Alter Your Life." *Canadian Composer* n211 (May 1986): 24–29.
              French version: La Compositique et vous.

6453.   ———. "Living with MIDI." *Canadian Composer* n210 (Apr. 1986): 30–35.
              French version: Composer avec le MIDI.

6454.   Dowty, Tim. "Build the EM MIDI Interface." *Electronic Musician* 2 (May 1986): 56–61.

6455.   ———. "Mod: The 'Small Tock' MIDI Clock." *Electronic Musician* 2 (Apr. 1986): 54–58.

6456.   Dupler, Steven. "MIDI Standard Celebrates 5 Years: Birthday Bash Warms NAMM Meet." *Billboard* 101 (Jan. 28, 1989): 55.

6457.   Enders, Bernd. "MIDI: Die digitale Brücke zwischen elektronischen und mechanischen Musikinstrumenten: Löst MIDI den Gegensatz zwischen Akustik (Mechanik) und Elektronik?" *Music International* 41 (Jan. 1987): 135–39.
              English version: "MIDI: The Digital Bridge between Electronic and Mechanical Musical Instruments: Does MIDI Resolve the Conflict between the Acoustic (Mechanical) and the Electronic?" *Music International* 41 (Apr. 1987): 323–26.
              French version: "MIDI: pont numerique entre les instruments de musique electroniques et mecaniques: MIDI pourra-t-il résoudre la

contradiction entre l'acoustique (mécanique) et l'électronique?" *Music International* 41 (June 1987): 442–44.

Italian version: "MIDI: il ponte digitale tra gli strumenti elettronici e meccanici: MIDI elimina il contrasts tra l'acustica (meccanica) e l'ettronica?" *Music International* 41 (June 1987): 445–47.

6458. Faris, Charles. "Sound Chip: A Look at MIDI through the Eyes of Some of Today's Top Producers and Performers." *Atari Explorer* 8 (May–June 1988): 90–93.

Short interviews with Mark Droubay, Jeffrey Delman, Bo Tomlyn, Jimmy George, and Hank Donig.

6459. Fast, Larry. "Studio Notes: MIDI in the Studio." *Electronic Musician* 1 (Sept. 1985): 12–13, 42.

6460. Fiore, Jim. "Electronic Insights: MIDI and the Electronic Drummer. Part 1." *Modern Drummer* 10 (Oct. 1986): 46–47.

An introduction to the concept of interfacing electronic percussion devices with sound sources via MIDI.

6461. ——. "Electronic Insights: MIDI and the Electronic Drummer. Part 2." *Modern Drummer* 10 (Nov. 1986): 40–41.

An examination of sound sources that can be used via MIDI and some limitations of MIDI-interfaced systems.

6462. ——. "Electronic Insights: MIDI Effects Devices." *Modern Drummer* 12 (Apr. 1988): 72–73.

6463. ——. "Electronic Insights: MIDI Mode Four, Bass Pedals, and Radioactive Hamsters." *Modern Drummer* 11 (July 1987): 70–72.

6464. ——. "MIDI: An Intro for the Working Percussionist." *Modern Drummer* 10 (Dec. 1986): 42–44.

6465. Fradkin, Leslie, and Elizabeth Rose. "MIDI: The 15 Most Common MIDI Misconceptions." *Electronic Musician* 3 (Feb. 1987): 52–55, 113.

6466. Fraser, Jill. "Scoring." *Music, Computers & Software* 2 (May 1987): 73–74.

6467. Frederick, Dave. "Keyboard Report: MIDI Data Processing Software & Hardware." *Keyboard* 12 (Apr. 1986): 120–23, 136, 146.

Dr. T's Echo Plus for the Commodore, Triangle Audio MIDI Processing Software, Syntech Keyboard Controller, and MIDI Voyce LX4.

6468. Fryer, Terry. "MIDI: Creating Ambience with MIDI-controlled Synthesizers." *Electronic Musician* 2 (May 1986): 25–27.

6469.   Garvin, Mark. "Designing a Music Recorder." *Dr. Dobb's Journal of Software Tools* 12 (May 1987): 22–48.

How to write MIDI software.

6470.   Gotcher, Peter. "Computers for Keyboardists: Groovular and Non-Groovular Clock Resolutions." *Keyboard* 13 (Apr. 1987): 118.

On MIDI time delay.

6471.   Greenwald, Ted. "MIDI Sequencer Software: Ten Leading Programmers Tell Why Computer Magic Won't Solve All Your Musical Problems (Yet)." *Keyboard* 12 (May 1986): 34–45.

6472.   Gualtieri, D. M. "MIDI Output Interface to a Parallel Printer Port." *Computer Music Journal* 10,3 (Fall 1986): 79–82.

6473.   "Hal Leonard Issues 'MIDI' Video." *Music Trades* 137 (Apr. 1989): 116–17.

The video, "Untangling MIDI" is released.

6474.   Hall, W. Vann. "Conquering the MIDI Muddle." *Music Educators Journal* 73 (Dec. 1986): 26–29.

6475.   Hawley, Michael. "MIDI Music Software for UNIX." In *USENIX Association Summer Conference Proceedings, Atlanta, 1986.* El Cerrito, Calif.: USENIX Association, 1986: 1–12.

6476.   Hayworth, Glenn. "MIDI: The Illusion of Music Software." *Canadian Musician* 10 (Aug. 1988): 36.

Aspects to consider in choosing sequencing software.

6477.   Herrold, Edie. "The Audio Angle: MIDI: The Basics." *Hot Wire* 5 (May 1989): 10–11.

6478.   Hirschfeld, Peter. "Editor's Note." *Electronic Musician* 2 (Feb. 1986): 6.

Discusses the problems of MIDI and why they exist.

6479.   Holley, E. A. "MIDI: The MIDI Virtuoso." *Electronic Musician* 3 (June 1987): 76–77.

Suggestions on ways to retain musicality even though using technology.

6480.   Hunter, S. C. Kim; Craig Anderton; E. A. Holley; Alan Gary Campbell; and George Gaboury. "Tips." *Electronic Musician* 3 (May 1987): 72–77.

A collection of hints for using MIDI.

6481.   "Industry Happenings: Standard File Format Developed for MIDI Sequencers." *Modern Drummer* 13 (Mar. 1989): 103.

6482. Isaacson, Matt. "Processing the Data." *Music Technology* 2 (Mar. 1988): 24–27.

How to use MIDI processors to do MIDI merging, MIDI filtering, MIDI mapping, and other types of data manipulation.

6483. Jimenez, Maria. "MIDI Studio." *Music, Computers & Software* 3 (June 1988): 74–75.

A discussion of noise reduction devices.

6484. Johnson, Jim. "Applications." *Music, Computers & Software* 2 (May 1987): 8, 66.

Do-it-yourself programming in BASIC.

6485. ———. "MIDI: Fun with System Exclusives." *Electronic Musician* 3 (Mar. 1987): 87–89.

6486. Knowlton, Joseph. "State of the Art: More on MIDI." *Keyboard Classics* 8 (Jan./Feb. 1988): 42.

How to record at home using a MIDI studio.

6487. ———. "State of the Art: The Midi Studio." *Keyboard Classics* 7 (Nov./Dec. 1987): 43.

6488. Kovach, Mark A. "MCS Recording." *Music, Computers & Software* 3 (Apr. 1988): 12–14.

A discussion of synchronization with MIDI.

6489. Kraul, Doug. "MIDI: MIDI Mergers: Theory, Practice, Applications." *Electronic Musician* 3 (Mar. 1987): 90–96.

6490. LaMarche, Jim. "MIDI: Is It Real, or Is It MIDI?: MIDI . . . Musical Leggos, Let's Build." *Canadian Musician* 11 (Oct. 1989): 33.

Information on assembling MIDI systems.

6491. LaRose, Paul. "High-Tech Guitar: Channels, Voices & MIDI Messages." *Guitar Player* 23 (Jan. 1989): 82–88.

An overview of MIDI fundamentals related to the guitar.

6492. ———. "High-Tech Guitar: Series #8, The Power of MIDI Guitar Control." *Guitar Player* 22 (Oct. 1988): 98–103.

6493. ———. "High-Tech Guitar: Synth & MIDI for Real Guitar Players." *Guitar Player* 22 (June 1988): 38–40, 143.

An in-depth discussion of how MIDI works with synthesizers.

6494. Leonard, Steve. "Computers for Keyboardists: Setting Things Straight with Your Interface Card." *Keyboard* 12 (July 1986): 124.

Corrections to the April and May 1986 columns and answers to readers' questions.

6495. Leopold, Perry. "MIDI by Modem: The Future Is Now." In *The Proceedings of the AES 5th International Conference: Music and Digital Technology,* ed. John Strawn. New York, N.Y.: Audio Engineering Society, 1987: 122–26.

6496. Lewer, Mark. "MIDI: The Serial Nature of MIDI." *Electronic Musician* 2 (July 1986): 58–62.

6497. Leytze, David. "Audio Files." *MacUser* 4 (Oct. 1988): 176–77.
Describes the MIDI file specification.

6498. Litterst, George F. "MIDI Equipment for the Classical Pianist." *Piano Quarterly* 37,n146 (Summer 1989): 44–47.

6499. Loy, D. Gareth. "Musicians Make a Standard: The MIDI Phenomenon." *Computer Music Journal* 9,4 (Winter 1985): 8–26.
Previously **1730.**
Reprinted in *The Music Machine,* ed. Curtis Roads. Cambridge, Mass.: MIT Press, 1989: 181–98.

6500. Mace, Scott. "Electronic Orchestras in Your Living Room: MIDI Could Make 1985 the Biggest Year Yet for Computer Musicians." *InfoWorld* 7 (Mar. 25, 1985): 29–33.
A short overview of MIDI.

6501. Majeski, Brian T. "Editorial: The Human Side of MIDI." *Music Trades* 133 (Oct. 1985): 20.

6502. "Making Sense of the MIDI Implementation Chart." *Music Technology* 1,1 (1986): 94–95.
Covers channels, modes, and note numbers.

6503. Massey, Howard. *The MIDI Home Studio.* New York, N.Y.: Amsco, 1988. 77 p.
Review by Jim Aikin in *Keyboard* 14 (July 1988): 23–24.
Review by David B. Doty in *Electronic Musician* 4 (Aug. 1988): 84–85.

6504. ———. "Synth & MIDI Basics: Defining Tech Terms: Voices & Polyphony." *Keyboard* 15 (Feb. 1989): 128–30.
An explanation of the term "voice.".

6505. McDonald, Jim. "Keyboards: Keyboards and MIDI Used Extensively on New Regime Album." *Canadian Musician* 9 (Aug. 1987): 87.

6506. Meyer, Chris. "Implementing the Sample Dump Standard." *Music Technology* 1 (Dec. 1986): 71–75.
A look at the development of the sample dump standard and its implementation on the Prophet 2000 sampler.

6507. ——. "The Last Word on MIDI Delays." *Music Technology* 1 (June 1987): 32–34.

6508. ——. "Making the Most of the Sample Dump Standard." *Music Technology* 1 (Mar. 1987): 78–82.

6509. ——. "Making the Most of the Sample Dump Standard." *Music Technology* 1 (Apr. 1987): 72–75.
How MIDI's standard for samples can give wavetable synthesizers new sounds from samplers.

6510. ——. "Making the Most of the Sample Dump Standard. Part 3, Several Samplers, a Couple of Problems, and a Truckload of Moral Dilemmas." *Music Technology* 1 (June 1987): 56–58.

6511. ——. "Marrying MIDI and SMPTE." *Music Technology* 1,1 (1986): 89–91.

6512. ——. "MIDI Time Code." *Music Technology* 1 (July 1987): 78–83.

6513. ——. "Modes of Confusion." *Music Technology* 1 (Mar. 1987): 56–60.
A discussion of the various MIDI operating modes.

6514. "MIDI Manufacturers." *Keyboard* 12 (Jan. 1986): 108.

6515. "MIDI Primer: Everything You Need to Know to Profit from the Most Dynamic Musical Technology of the '80s." *Music Trades* 133 (Oct. 1985): 50–67.

6516. "MIDI Spelled out." *Pastoral Music* 13 (Dec.–Jan. 1989): 46.
Sixteen definitions.

6517. Milano, Dominic. "An Armchair Analysis of Electronic Music's Current State-of-the-Art." In *The Proceedings of the AES 5th International Conference: Music and Digital Technology,* ed. John Strawn. New York, N.Y.: Audio Engineering Society, 1987: 5–18.

6518. ——. *Mind over MIDI: A Basic Reference Guide on How MIDI Works and How to Use It.* Milwaukee, Wis.: H. Leonard Books, 1987. 117 p.

6519. ——. "Mind over MIDI: Spec Addendum, Software Channelizing & DX7 ROM Updates." *Keyboard* 11 (Aug. 1985): 68.
Answers to readers' questions.

6520. ——. "Mind over MIDI: Tuning in to Channels & Chaining." *Keyboard* 11 (Sept. 1985): 75.

6521. Mocsny, Daniel. "Virtual Tracking: Synching Sequenced MIDI Instruments to Multi-Track Cassette Records." *Music, Computers & Software* 3 (Apr. 1988): 52–57.

A discussion of synchronization with MIDI.

6522. Moog, Bob. "Ask Mr. Moog: You've Come a Long Way, MIDI." *Keyboard* 15 (Feb. 1989): 117, 168.

A short history of MIDI.

6523. ——. "MIDI: Musical Instrument Digital Interface." *Journal of the Audio Engineering Society* 34 (May 1986): 394–404.

6524. Moore, F. Richard. "The Dysfunctions of MIDI." In *Proceedings of the 1987 International Computer Music Conference: University of Illinois at Urbana-Champaign, Urbana, Illinois, USA, August 23–26, 1987,* comp. James Beauchamp. San Francisco, Calif.: Computer Music Association, 1987: 256–63.

Reprinted in *Computer Music Journal* 21,1 (Spring 1988): 19–28.

6525. Mueller, John E. "Uncovering the MIDI Section." *Rainbow* 6 (June 1987): 36–37.

An introduction to MIDI.

6526. Muhonen, Gary. "Keyboard Clinic #9: Automated Mixing for the Small Studio." *Keyboard* 13 (Nov. 1987): 52–60.

6527. Muir, Chris, and Keith McMillen. "What's Missing in MIDI?" *Guitar Player* 20 (June 1986): 61–62.

6528. Muro, Don. "CAI in Jazz Education: An Overview of MIDI." *Jazz Educators Journal* 20 (Oct./Nov. 1987): 58–61.

6529. "Music, MIDI, and Manufacturers." *Instrumentalist* 41 (June 1987): 67–71.

A directory.

6530. "Musicians Praise MIDI Tools." *MacWeek* 3 (Jan. 31, 1989): 9.

6531. Nathan, Bobby. "MIDI, Digital Sampling Product Unveiled at NAMM." *Billboard* 98 (July 5, 1986): 53–55.

6532. Netsel, Tom. "MIDI Made Simple." *Compute!'s Gazette* 6 (Aug. 1988): 14–20.

The relationship of MIDI to personal computers.

6533. Noxon, James. "Guest Editorial: The Myth of MIDI Delay and the Realities of Human Perception." *Keyboard* 12 (July 1986): 10, 156.

6534. O'Donnell, Bob. "MIDI 101." *Music Technology* 2 (Aug. 1987): 33–37.

A primer on MIDI: why it was developed and the information it can carry.

6535.   ———. "MIDI 102." *Music Technology* 2 (Sept. 1987): 63–66.
         A discussion of the connection between a MIDI keyboard and an
         expander module.

6536.   ———. "MIDI 103." *Music Technology* 2 (Oct. 1987): 58–61.
         An examination of MIDI sequencers and their place in a studio.

6537.   ———. "MIDI 104." *Music Technology* 2 (Nov. 1987): 82–86.
         A dissection of drum machines and their applications in a MIDI
         studio.

6538.   ———. "MIDI 105." *Music Technology* 2 (Dec. 1987): 58–62.
         A look at MIDI-controlled audio processors and MIDI data
         processors.

6539.   ———. "MIDI Standard Proposed." *Macworld* 4 (Nov. 1987): 95–97.
         Describes the file-transfer format.

6540.   Oppenheimer, Larry. "Making Sense out of MIDI." *DB, the Sound
         Engineering Magazine* 20 (Mar./Apr. 1986): 47–51.

6541.   Orlarey, Yann, and Hervé Lequay. "MidiShare: A Real Time Multi-
         Tasks Software Module for MIDI Applications." In *Proceedings, 1989
         International Computer Music Conference, November 2–5, the Ohio
         State University, Columbus, Ohio.* San Francisco, Calif.: Computer
         Music Association, 1989: 234–37.

6542.   Orman, Jack. "Mod: Making MIDI Spec Cables." *Electronic Musician*
         2 (Aug. 1986): 45–46.

6543.   ———. "Opto-mum MIDI." *Electronic Musician* 4 (May 1988): 79–81.
         A discussion of how the opto-isolator/current loop works.

6544.   Otsuka, Akira, and Akihiko Nakajima. *MIDI Basics.* New York,
         N.Y.: Amsco, 1987. 58 p.
         Includes a MIDI signal tracer.
         Review by Marcus Neiman in *Instrumentalist* 42 (Oct. 1987): 10.

6545.   Powell, Roger. "The Challenge of Music Software." *Byte* 11 (June
         1986): 145–50.
         An overview of the current state of computers in music, princi-
         pally the influence of MIDI.

6546.   Powell, Roger. "Editorial: Music and MIDI." *Byte* 11 (June 1986): 6.

6547.   "Q-R-S Introduces Computer." *Music Trades* 133 (May 1985): 109–12.
         New MIDI products.

6548.   Rae, Richard. "AmigaNotes." *Amazing Computing* 1,7 (1986): 61–64.
         An introduction to MIDI.

6549.   ———. "AmigaNotes: Inside MIDI." *Amazing Computing* 2,10 (1987): 51–58.

6550.   Reed, Tony. "Socket to Me." *Melody Maker* 64 (June 18, 1988): 50–51.

Basic knowledge and equipment necessary to assemble a MIDI studio.

6551.   Rona, Jeff. "Does the Future Belong to the MediaLink LAN?" *Keyboard* 15 (Dec. 1989): 54–61.

6552.   ———. *MIDI—The Ins, Outs, and Thrus.* Milwaukee, Wis.: H. Leonard Pub., 1987. 96 p.
Review by Bruce P. Mahin in *Instrumentalist* 42 (Oct. 1987): 10.
Review by Deborah Parisi in *Music Technology* 2 (Nov. 1987): 48.
Review by Robert J. Owens in *Computer Music Journal* 12,4 (Winter 1988): 51.

6553.   Russell, Benjamin. "MIDI for the Masses: Update 1987." *Canadian Musician* 9 (June 1987): 52–61.

Uses of MIDI for composition, recording, and performance.

6554.   ———. "MIDI: Drum Machines vs. Samplers." *Canadian Musician* 9 (Aug. 1987): 37–39.

6555.   ———. "MIDI: Why Oscar Peterson and Others Are into MIDI." *Canadian Musician* 9 (Apr. 1987): 70.

6556.   Rychner, Lorenz. "The Search for Middle C." *Music Technology* 2 (Dec. 1987): 40–41.

Discusses the assignment of note numbers to the keyboard.

6557.   Scacciaferro, Joe. "MCS MIDI." *Music, Computers & Software* 3 (Feb. 1988): 12–14.

A discussion of MIDI delay.

6558.   ———. "MCS MIDI." *Music, Computers & Software* 3 (Apr. 1988): 77–78.

A discussion of the MIDI sample dump and MIDI time code.

6559.   ———. "MIDI Applications." *Music, Computers & Software* 3 (Nov. 1988): 24–25.

A tutorial on basic diagnostics techniques.

6560.   Scholz, Carter. "Build an Eight-in, Eight-out MIDI Patch Bay." *Electronic Musician* 4 (June 1988): 63–65.

6561.   ———. "Mind over MIDI: A MIDI Data Analyzer Program." *Keyboard* 12 (Aug. 1986): 110–12.

A Turbo Pascal program, Peek, to analyze MIDI data; for the Roland MPU-401 MIDI interface.

6562. Schwartz, Rick. "MIDI: MIDI Switch Boxes." *Electronic Musician* 2 (Nov. 1986): 76–82.

6563. "Silver Eagle Releases MIDI Instructional Video." *Music Trades* 136 (Aug. 1988): 92–93.

A short description of the video, *Making the Most of MIDI.*

6564. Sirota, Warren. "Guitar Meets MIDI." *Guitar Player* 20 (June 1986): 44–48, 178.

An in-depth discussion of how MIDI works with guitar synthesizers.

6565. ———. "Implementation Chart: MIDI Specs." *Guitar Player* 20 (June 1986): 59.

How to use and interpret a MIDI implementation chart.

6566. ———. "MIDI Glossary." *Guitar Player* 20 (June 1986): 58.

6567. ———. "MIDI: The Music Interface." *PC World* 3 (Oct. 1985): 208–15.

An in-depth description of MIDI.

6568. ———. "Putting MIDI to Work: Linking Elements." *Guitar Player* 20 (June 1986): 50–58.

6569. Smith, Mark. "Applications: Percussive Control of MIDI Synthesizers." *Electronic Musician* 2 (July 1986): 42–45.

6570. Stephen, Greg. "Computers & Music: Finding the MIDI Holy Grail." *Canadian Musician* 7 (Oct. 1985): 57–58.

6571. Strawn, John. "Editing Time-varying Spectra." *Journal of the Audio Engineering Society* 35 (May 1987): 337–52. Revised version of **3539.**

Presented at the 78th convention of the AES, May 1985; revised Mar. 26, 1986 and Aug. 7, 1986.

6572. Taylor, Joff. "Alternate MIDI Controllers." *Canadian Musician* 11 (Apr. 1989): 37–38.

6573. Tomasso, Ajo. "MIDI: MIDI Machines from Hell." *Canadian Musician* 11 (Dec. 1989): 30.

A discussion of drum machines and MIDI.

6574. Trask, Simon. "MIDI Basics." *Music Technology* 1,1 (1986): 30–31.

A discussion of how the MIDI interface works.

6575. Valenti, Dick. "MIDI by the Numbers." *Electronic Musician* 4 (Feb. 1988): 22–31.

A reference chart of MIDI codes.

6576.   Vangellow, Alex. "MIDI: MIDI Controlled Effects Devices." *Electronic Musician* 3 (Jan. 1987): 33–34.

6577.   Volanski, John J. "Mapping Your Way through MIDI Multi-Tracking." *Electronic Musician* 4 (June 1988): 24–28, 43.
Seven steps for developing a MIDI/multi-track studio.

6578.   Wait, Bradley, ed. *Guitar Synth and MIDI.* Milwaukee, Wis.: H. Leonard Books, 1988. 135 p. (Guitar Player Magazine Basic Library)
A guide to new technology and its musical application for the guitar player. Compiled from *Guitar Player.*

6579.   Weinberg, Norman. "Focus on Performance: A Plain and Simple Introduction to MIDI." *Percussive Notes* 25 (Summer 1987): 64.

6580.   ——. *The Last MIDI Book.* Newbury Park, Calif.: Alexander Pub., 1988. 125 p.
Review by Jim Aikin in *Keyboard* 14 (Sept. 1988): 25.

6581.   Westfall, Lachlan. "The History of MIDI: A Comprehensive Look at the Not So Ancient History of a Still Developing Technology." *Keyboards, Computers & Software* 1 (Oct. 1986): 43–45, 73.

6582.   ——. "I Want My MTC!" *Electronic Musician* 4 (Nov. 1988): 63–67.
Describes MIDI Time Code.

6583.   ——. "KCS MIDI." *Keyboards, Computers & Software* 1 (Feb. 1986): 10, 14.
The use of MIDI software as a creative device.

6584.   ——. "KCS MIDI." *Keyboards, Computers & Software* 1 (Apr. 1986): 10–12.
The basic functions of MIDI and methods of operation.

6585.   ——. "KCS MIDI." *Keyboards, Computers & Software* 1 (June 1986): 17, 27, 76.
An examination of "channel messages," which are used to communicate the bulk of information sent over MIDI.

6586.   ——. "KCS MIDI." *Keyboards, Computers & Software* 1 (Aug. 1986): 14–17, 75.
How to use the MIDI protocol as a compositional aid, as well as for recording and in live performance.

6587.   ——. "KCS MIDI." *Keyboards, Computers & Software* 1 (Oct. 1986): 17–18.
A guide for assembling a computer-based music system with MIDI implementation.

6588. ———. "KCS MIDI." *Keyboards, Computers & Software* 1 (Dec. 1986): 16–17.

Using a MIDI music system to record music on tape, and synchronization of MIDI data streams.

6589. ———. "KCS MIDI." *Keyboards, Computers & Software* 2 (Feb. 1987): 16–18.

A look at misinformation and misconceptions about MIDI.

6590. ———. "The Local Area Network: MIDI's Next Step?" *Electronic Musician* 5 (Nov. 1989): 64–67, 119.

6591. ———. "MCS MIDI." *Music, Computers & Software* 2 (June 1987): 14, 18.

Discusses the development of a MIDI file format standard as proposed by the ANSI X3V1.8M study group.

6592. ———. "MCS MIDI." *Music, Computers & Software* 2 (Aug. 1987): 12–15.

A discussion of a proposed extension to the MIDI standard for synchronization (MIDI time code).

6593. ———. "MIDI." *Music, Computers & Software* 2 (May 1987): 16–17.

Describes extensions to the current 1.0 MIDI specification.

6594. ———. "MIDI Reaches Adolescence." *Electronic Musician* 4 (May 1988): 64–71.

A discussion of MIDI's next stage of development.

6595. ———. "Mind over MIDI: Birth of a Standard for MIDI Files." *Keyboard* 14 (Oct. 1988): 120.

6596. ———. "Mind over MIDI: Dealing with System-exclusive Confusion." *Keyboard* 15 (Feb. 1989): 125.

System-exclusive messages.

6597. ———. "Mind over MIDI: Late Additions to the MIDI Spec." *Keyboard* 15 (Sept. 1989): 104, 136.

6598. ———. "Mind over MIDI: MIDI File Nuts & Bolts." *Keyboard* 14 (Dec. 1988): 119.

6599. ———. "Mind over MIDI: MIDI Files in Action." *Keyboard* 14 (Nov. 1988): 139, 168.

6600. ———. "Mind over MIDI: MIDI Mailbag." *Keyboard* 15 (June 1989): 109.

Answers questions from readers.

6601.   ——. "Mind over MIDI: MIDI Sample Dump Standard." *Keyboard* 15 (July 1989): 110.

6602.   ——. "Mind over MIDI: Much Ado about MIDI Merging." *Keyboard* 15 (Jan. 1989): 111, 146.

6603.   ——. "Mind over MIDI: Struggling with Sys-Ex (Again)." *Keyboard* 15 (Dec. 1989): 115.

6604.   ——. "Mind over MIDI: Sync or Swim with MTC & SPP." *Keyboard* 15 (Mar. 1989): 112.
         MIDI synchronization capabilities and Song Position Pointer.

6605.   ——. "Mind over MIDI: Synching Deeper." *Keyboard* 15 (May 1989): 116–17.

6606.   ——. "Mind over MIDI: The LAN Solution." *Keyboard* 15 (Nov. 1989): 109.
         Development of the MIDI Local Area Network protocol.

6607.   ——. "Mind over MIDI: The MIDI/Computer (R)evolution." *Keyboard* 15 (Aug. 1989): 107, 132.
         New developments to link computers and MIDI.

6608.   Whitmer, Clair. "Warner Combines Digital Audio, MIDI Information." *MacWeek* 2 (July 5, 1988): 10.
         Announcement of the CD + MIDI format.

6609.   Wiffen, Paul. "Making Sense of the MIDI Implementation Chart." *Music Technology* 1 (Sept. 1986): 58.
         Covers the interpretation of performance data, velocity, after-touch, and pitchbend.

6610.   ——. "Making Sense of the MIDI Implementation Chart." *Music Technology* 1 (Oct. 1986): 46–47.
         Covers continuous controllers and switches.

6611.   ——. "Making Sense of the MIDI Implementation Chart." *Music Technology* 1 (Nov. 1986): 46–47.
         Covers what MIDI program change numbers an instrument is capable of sending and receiving.

6612.   ——. "Making Sense of the MIDI Implementation Chart." *Music Technology* 1 (Dec. 1986): 84.
         A look at common and real time system messages.

6613.   ——. "Making Sense of the MIDI Implementation Chart." *Music Technology* 1 (Jan. 1987): 87.
         A look at auxiliary messages available via MIDI.

6614. Wolfe, Harvey. "The Curse of MIDI." *Canadian Musician* 10 (Oct. 1988): 30.

A warning not to sacrifice creativity for MIDI technology.

6615. Wyman, James. "Electromag: It's MIDI Time and Music Will Never Be the Same." *Village Voice* 34 (Mar. 28, 1989): E14–E16.

Describes MIDI and its development.

6616. Yavelow, Christopher. "Music and Microprocessors: MIDI and the State of the Art." In *The Music Machine,* ed. Curtis Roads. Cambridge, Mass.: MIT Press, 1989: 199–234.

"Portions of this article are based on material that originally appeared in the author's article 'Personal Computers and Music: The State of the Art' in *Journal of the Audio Engineering Society* 35,3: 160–93."

6617. Zientara, Marguerite. "Breakthrough Promises to Give Musicians Total Control." *InfoWorld* 6 (Apr. 30, 1984): 23.

A very short introduction to MIDI.

MUSIC INDUSTRY

6618. Albano, Chris. "Using Software to Sell Keyboards." *Music Trades* 137 (June 1989): 97–100.

6619. "Ancott Intros 'SalesEdge' Software." *Music Trades* 136 (Jan. 1988): 130–32.
   A business program for music retailers.

6620. Andresen, Uwe. "Musikcomputer ersetzt Musiker!?: Probleme für den musikalischen Arbeitsmarkt." *Music International* 39 (Okt. 1985): 676–78.

6621. ———. "Orchester aus dem Chip—Musik ohne Musiker?" *Musik International* 38 (Dec. 1984): 815–19.
   English version: "Orchestras from Micro-chips—Music without Musicians." *Music International* 39 (Jan. 1985): 124–28.
   A look at the impact of digital recording and synthesizers on the recording industry.

6622. Beckmen, Tom. "Guest Editorial: Blueprint for Expanding the Hi-Tech Market; Stop Hustling Boxes and Start Offering More Customer Service." *Music Trades* 137 (Feb. 1989): 16, 21.

6623. Berry, Ronald L. "Computers and Pianos: Set up." *Piano Technicians Journal* 31 (Nov. 1988): 22–26.
   How the author has set up his data base to handle his business.

6624. Bessman, Jim. "Computerized Inventory Bows for Smaller Stores." *Billboard* 98 (July 26, 1986): 37.

6625. ———. "Express Music Catalog Making All Locale Stops." *Billboard* 98 (Mar. 22, 1986): 34.
   An electronic shopping service for music sound recordings.

6626. Bethke, Bruce. "Everything You Need to Know to Profitably Sell Computer Music Software." *Music Trades* 132 (June 1984): 72–78, 142–43, 146.

6627. "BIN Unveiling New Database Service: Territorial Rights Reports Set for Debut at Midem." *Billboard* 98 (Jan. 26, 1985): 3.

6628. "CBS Picks up CORD for New Database." *Variety* 314 (Feb. 1, 1984): 127, 130.

6629. "Chasing Rainbows: Korg's Blueprint for Success." *Music Trades* 136 (May 1988): 64–70.

6630. "D-RAM Chip Shortages Force Price Hikes in Music." *Music Trades* 136 (June 1988): 56–58.

6631. DiMauro, Phil. "Digital Synth Consultants Help Artists in Studio with Expertise." *Variety* 328 (Oct. 14, 1987): 219.

   Describes a new breed of studio musician, the programmer, to assist recording artists in using their equipment.

6632. Dupler, Steven. "Unique Recording Opens Two New Rooms; Facility Unveils MIDI City, 'Pre-Programming' Studio." *Billboard* 97 (June 8, 1985): 44.

6633. "Electronic Publishing Is Waiting in Wings of Canadian Catalog." *Variety* 318 (Feb. 6, 1985): 119.

6634. Grygo, Gene. "Listeners May Be Rockin' Around the VAX Tonight." *Digital Review* 6 (Feb. 13, 1989): 3.

   Use of the Macsystems program to maintain data on tracking music hits.

6635. Hertelendy, Paul. "Programming Problems? The Computer Comes to the Rescue." *High Fidelity/Musical America* 36 (June 1986): MA35–MA37.

   Use of the computer in orchestra management, from programming to stage set-ups.

6636. Holunga, Corinna. "Notes: Database Shopping Service Available to Indie Labels." *Canadian Musician* 7 (Dec. 1985): 15.

   Independent record labels can be listed on a music database shopping service called Connections Plus.

6637. Hummler, Richard. "Musicians Okay Synthesizers for 6-Year Freeze on Minimums." *Variety* 327 (July 1, 1987): 141, 146.

   A new contract between theater producers and musicians allows unlimited use of electronic instruments in Broadway shows.

6638. Jones, Peter. "Commentary: Computer Ordering Can Help Dealers: Security, CD Boxes also Require Action." *Billboard* 101 (July 29, 1989): 13.

6639.   Kirk, Elizabeth P. "The Silent Staff Member." *Symphony Magazine* 40 (May/June 1989): 20–25.

How symphony orchestras are using computers to sell tickets, raise funds, and for other day-to-day operations.

6640.   Krepack, Benjamin, and Rod Firestone. *Start Me Up!: The Music Biz Meets the Personal Computer.* Van Nuys, Calif.: Mediac Press, 1986. 167 p.
Review by Steven Dupler in *Billboard* 98 (June 14, 1986): 58.

6641.   Lehrman, Paul D. "Careers: So You Want to Be a Music Software Company?" *Electronic Musician* 2 (Nov. 1986): 66–69, 96–97.

6642.   ———. "Software Fact & Fiction—What You Need to Know to Sell Computer Music: A Review of Product Types, Market Potential, Selling Techniques & Pitfalls." *Music Trades* 134 (Nov. 1986): 44–54.

6643.   Leonard, Steve. "Computers for Keyboardists: Getting Your Soft Wares to Market." *Keyboard* 12 (June 1986): 141.

Steps that software developers must go through to have a product distributed to retail stores.

6644.   Lewis, Bill. "Software: Manage Your Band." *Keyboards, Computers & Software* 1 (June 1986): 28–29.

A discussion of how software can help take care of the business of music.

6645.   "Local 802 Will Go to Arbitration re: Bassey Synthesizer." *Variety* 323 (July 16, 1986): 32.

American Federation of Musicians, Local 802, is going to arbitration over the use of a synthesizer to accompany singer Shirley Bassey.

6646.   Mahin, Bruce P. "Business Uses of Computers." *Instrumentalist* 41 (Feb. 1987): 52–56.

6647.   Majeski, Brian T. "Editorial: MIDI Magic Meets Market Realities." *Music Trades* 136 (Oct. 1988): 17.

Perspectives on the lull in retail sales of MIDI products.

6648.   ———. "Editorial: The Forgotten Customer." *Music Trades* 136 (Apr. 1988): 16.

On the growing number of hobbyists interested in synthesizers and MIDI.

6649.   ———. "Editorial: Who's to Blame for Poor Retail Profits?" *Music Trades* 137 (Feb. 1989): 22.

On the over-distribution of high-tech products.

6650. Mamis, Robert A. "Taking Control." *Inc.* 9 (Feb. 1987): 82–88.
Creating computer systems at Daddy's Junky Music Stores.

6651. Mayfield, Geoff. "Automated Ordering Progresses." *Billboard* 98 (Oct. 25, 1986): 4, 87.

6652. ———. "Labels Move on Automated Trading." *Billboard* 99 (Dec. 5, 1987): 33.
Music distributors use the computer for transactions with retail and wholesale customers.

6653. ———. "NARM Report: Record Dealers Advised to Enter Computer Age." *Billboard* 99 (Mar. 14, 1987): 41, 44.

6654. McDonough, Jack. "An Entertaining Look at New Programming." *Billboard* 96 (Mar. 31, 1984): 29.
How computers streamline the process of creating programming for entertainment.

6655. "Merchandising MIDI." *Music Trades* 135 (Mar. 1987): 46–50.

6656. Moore, Donald J. "Orchestra Management by Microcomputer: An Opportunity and a Challenge." *Symphony Magazine* 36 (Oct./Nov. 1985): 16–23, 67–69.

6657. "New Computer System for Radiothons." *Symphony Magazine* 40 (Jan./Feb. 1989): 67.
The Cincinnati Symphony Orchestra used a specially designed computer software system for its radiothon.

6658. "Passport Forms New Software Distribution Division." *Music Trades* 133 (Oct. 1985): 36, 41.

6659. "'Piano Connection' Network Established." *Piano Technicians Journal* 28 (June 1985): 10.
Announcement of a computerized directory for buying and selling pianos, and a listing of parts and specialized skills.

6660. "Publisher Creates New Song Bank to Encourage Songwriting in Quebec." *Canadian Composer* n202 (July–Aug. 1985): 42.
French version: Une nouvelle banque de chansons pour les auteurs-compositeurs.

6661. "Retailer Roundtable—The Pros & Cons of the MIDI Market." *Music Trades* 136 (Apr. 1988): 64–74.

6662. "Retailer Roundtable—What's Happening with Digital Pianos: Leading Retailers Outline the Market Potential with Digital Pianos." *Music Trades* 135 (Sept. 1987): 59–71.

6663. "Revolutionary Evolution—How Roland Grows." *Music Trades* 135 (Dec. 1987): 76–83.

6664. Ruben, David. "Broadcast News." *PC Computing* 2 (May 1989): 42.
Describes a computerized digital audio system for production use in a radio station.

6665. Shaw, Russell. "Computers' Role Increasing: Lower Costs Make Automation Easier." *Billboard* 101 (Mar. 11, 1989): 35, 39.

6666. Sippel, John. "Automated Print Rack Service in Place; New Carl Fischer Music Arm." *Billboard* 97 (Nov. 30, 1985): 4, 65.

6667. Steinberg, Don. "Voice Mail Is in Harmony with Music-Box Sales." *PC Week* 5 (Sept. 19, 1988): C26.
The San Francisco Music Box Co. has initiated a digital dial-a-tune service for each of the melodies in their music boxes.

6668. Subirana, Emile. "McGill University—Producer or Replacer?" *International Musician* 87 (June 1989): 1, 5.
A discussion of the problems that could be created by the McGill University Master Samples (MUMS), digital samples of acoustic instruments.

6669. Terry, Ken. "New System Can Track Radio with Computers." *Billboard* 101 (Mar. 11, 1989): 1, 86.

6670. "U.K. Software Package Aimed at Music Industry." *Billboard* 96 (Feb. 25, 1984): 69.
An introduction to MusiCalc.

6671. Weissman, Dick. "Music 1999: Examining Technology Issues." *International Musician* 87 (Dec. 1988): 7, 18.

6672. "What's Next! Manufacturers Forecast the Synth Market." *Music Trades* 136 (Apr. 1988): 88–93.

6673. "Who Uses Music Software and, What Do They Want?" *Music Trades* 136 (Feb. 1988): 90–92.
An American Music Conference survey conducted to explore the market for music software products.

6674. "Yamaha DX7 Sets Record; Over 200,000 Sold." *Music Trades* 135 (Mar. 1987): 23–24.

6675. Zuckerman, Faye. "Computer Music Programs Make Instrument Landing." *Billboard* 96 (June 9, 1984): CES–11, CES–34.
Marketing of music software packages.

MUSIC PRINTING
AND TRANSCRIPTION

6676. Assayag, Gerard. "Computer Printing, Storage, and Transfer of Musical Scores." In *Proceedings of the 1987 International Computer Music Conference: University of Illinois at Urbana-Champaign, Urbana, Illinois, USA, August 23–26, 1987,* comp. James Beauchamp. San Francisco, Calif.: Computer Music Association, 1987: 298–301.

6677. ———, and Dan Timis. "A ToolBox for Music Notation." In *Proceedings of the International Computer Music Conference 1986, Royal Conservatory, The Hague, Netherlands, October 20–24, 1986,* ed. Paul Berg. San Francisco, Calif.: Computer Music Association, 1986: 173–78.

6678. Barnett, David N. "Keeping Score." *Music, Computers & Software* 2 (June 1987): 55–58.

A general description of music notation software.

6679. Bianchi, E. "Descrizione di partiture eseguibili su Macintosh 512K mediante reti di Petri." [Description of Feasible Scores on a 512K Macintosh through Petri Nets] Tesi di Laurea in Scienze dell'Informazione, A.A., Università degli Studi, Milano, 1986.

6680. Brancaleoni, M. "Un sistema elettronico per la tipografia musicale." [An Electronic System for Musical Typography] Tesi di Laurea in Scienze dell'Informazione, A.A., Università degli Studi, Milano, 1987.

6681. Byrd, Donald. "User Interfaces in Music-Notation Systems." In *Proceedings of the International Computer Music Conference 1986, Royal Conservatory, The Hague, Netherlands, October 20–24, 1986,* ed. Paul Berg. San Francisco, Calif.: Computer Music Association, 1986: 145–51.

6682. Carter, N. P.; R. A. Bacon; and T. Messenger. "The Acquisition, Representation, and Reconstruction of Printed Music by Computer: A Review." *Computers and the Humanities* 22 (1988): 117–36.

Covers music data entry by automatic pattern recognition, directly connected keyboard, sound track analysis, and other methods; music representational languages including DARMS, MUS-TRAN, and ALMA; and hardware for computer printing of sheet music.

6683. Chafe, Chris; Bernard Mont-Reynaud; and Loren Rush. "Toward an Intelligent Editor of Digital Audio: Recognition of Musical Constructs." *Computer Music Journal* 6,1 (Spring 1982): 30–41.
Previously **1827.**
Reprinted in *The Music Machine,* ed. Curtis Roads. Cambridge, Mass.: MIT Press, 1989: 537–48.

6684. Charnassé, Hélène. "L'ordinateur au service de la musique ancienne." *Diapason* 259 (Mar. 1981): 30–31.
Use of the computer for the transcription of German tablature.

6685. ——. "La transcription automatique des tablatures: un aspect de la recherche méthodologique." In *Report of the Twelfth Congress, Berkeley, 1977, International Musicological Society,* ed. Daniel Heartz and Bonnie Wade. Kassel: Bärenreiter, 1981: 330–36.

6686. Chowning, John M., Loren Rush, Bernard Mont-Reynaud, Chris Chafe, Andrew W. Scholss, and Julius O. Smith. *Intelligent Systems for the Analysis of Digitized Acoustic Signals, Final Report.* Stanford, Calif.: Dept. of Music, Stanford University, 1984. 43 p. (Department of Music Technical Report STAN-M-15)

6687. Clarke, A. T.; B. M. Brown; and M. P. Thorne. "Using a Micro to Automate Data Acquisition in Music Publishing." In *Supercomputers: Technology and Applications: Fourteenth Euromicro Symposium on Microprocessing and Microprogramming (EUROMICRO '88), Zurich, August 29–September 1, 1988,* ed. Stephen Winter and Harald Schumny. Amsterdam; New York, N.Y.: North-Holland, 1988: 549–53. Also in *Microprocessing and Microprogramming* 24 (1988): 549–54.
Use of an IBM PC to automatically recognize the printed music notation on a sheet of music via a scanner.

6688. "Computer Music." *Strad* 96 (Sept. 1985): 314–15.
Announcement of the Oxford Music Processor (OMP), developed by Richard Vendome.

6689. Cook, Diane Joyce. "Orpheus: A Music Notation Program." In *Proceedings of the 1987 International Computer Music Conference: University of Illinois at Urbana-Champaign, Urbana, Illinois, USA, August 23–26, 1987,* comp. James Beauchamp. San Francisco, Calif.: Computer Music Association, 1987: 302–10.

6690. ——. "Orpheus: A Music Notation Program." M.S. thesis, University of Illinois, Dept. of Computer Science, 1987.

6691. Cummings, Steve. "Desktop Music Scores: With Personal Computers You Can Make a Noteworthy Entry into Music Publishing." *Publish!* 2 (Jan.–Feb. 1987): 66–69.

6692. Dannenberg, Roger B. "Music Representation Issues: A Position Paper." In *Proceedings, 1989 International Computer Music Conference, November 2–5, the Ohio State University, Columbus, Ohio.* San Francisco, Calif.: Computer Music Association, 1989: 73–75.

6693. ———. "A Structure for Representing, Displaying, and Editing Music." In *Proceedings of the International Computer Music Conference 1986, Royal Conservatory, The Hague, Netherlands, October 20–24, 1986,* ed. Paul Berg. San Francisco, Calif.: Computer Music Association, 1986: 153–60.

6694. Diener, Glendon R. "Nutation: Structural Organization Versus Graphical Generality in a Common Music Notation Program." In *Proceedings, 1989 International Computer Music Conference, November 2–5, the Ohio State University, Columbus, Ohio.* San Francisco, Calif.: Computer Music Association, 1989: 86–89.
Also issued as: Technical Report STAN-M-59. Stanford, Calif.: Center for Computer Research in Music and Acoustics, Department of Music, Stanford University, 1989. 4 p.

For the NeXT computer.

6695. Dydo, J. Stephen. "Data Structures in *The Note Processor.*" In *Proceedings of the 1987 International Computer Music Conference: University of Illinois at Urbana-Champaign, Urbana, Illinois, USA, August 23–26, 1987,* comp. James Beauchamp. San Francisco, Calif.: Computer Music Association, 1987: 311–16.

6696. Faradji, Thierry. "Huit logiciels d'edition musicale au banc d'essai: ecrivez vous-même votre musique." *Diapason-Harmonie* n346 (Fev. 1989): 53–57.

Review of eight notation programs.

6697. Ford, Clifford. "Computers and Copying: A Love/Hate Relationship." *Canadian Composer* n236 (Dec. 1988): 26–27.
French version: L'Édition électroniq: le débat continue.

Rebuttal to Elma Miller's "Can the New Computer Programs Deliver Scores Composers Can Live With?" in Sept. 1988 issue.

6698. Foster, Scott; W. Andrew Schloss; and A. Joseph Rockmore. "Toward an Intelligent Editor of Digital Audio: Signal Processing Methods." *Computer Music Journal* 6,1 (Spring 1982): 42–51.
Previously **1857.**
Reprinted in *The Music Machine,* ed. Curtis Roads. Cambridge, Mass.: MIT Press, 1989: 549–58.

6699. Fowler, Michael. "Music Printing by Computer." *Musical Times* 129 (July 1988): 335–38.

6700.   Free, John. "Towards an Extensible Data Structure for the Representation of Music on Computers." In *Proceedings of the 1987 International Computer Music Conference: University of Illinois at Urbana-Champaign, Urbana, Illinois, USA, August 23–26, 1987*, comp. James Beauchamp. San Francisco, Calif.: Computer Music Association, 1987: 317–24.

6701.   Gourlay, John S. "A Language for Music Printing." *Communications of the ACM* 29 (May 1986): 388–401.

6702.   Hamel, Keith A. "A Design for Music Editing and Printing Software Based on Notational Syntax." *Perspectives of New Music* 27 (Winter 1989): 70–83.

6703.   ———. "Issues in the Design of Music Notation Systems." In *Proceedings of the 1987 International Computer Music Conference: University of Illinois at Urbana-Champaign, Urbana, Illinois, USA, August 23–26, 1987*, comp. James Beauchamp. San Francisco, Calif.: Computer Music Association, 1987: 325–32.

6704.   Hempel, Christoph. "Notendruck mit dem Computer: Technische Grundlagen und Anwendungsbeispiele." *Musik und Bildung* 21 (Juni 1989): 309–19.

6705.   Holab, William. "Settling the Score on Composer Software." *Symphony Magazine* 40 (May/June 1989): 26–31.
             An overview of music notation programs.

6706.   Hultberg, Warren E. "Transcribing Tablature." In *Report of the Twelfth Congress, Berkeley, 1977, International Musicological Society*, ed. Daniel Heartz and Bonnie Wade. Kassel: Bärenreiter, 1981: 336–39.

6707.   Massazza, S. "Tecniche per l'impaginazione e la stampa di partiture musicali mediante elaboratore elettronico." [Technique for the Pagination and the Printing of Musical Scores through Electronic Computers] Tesi di Laurea in Fisica, A.A., Università degli Studi, Milano, 1984.

6708.   Miller, Elma. "Can the New Computer Programs Deliver Scores Composers Can Live With?" *Canadian Composer* n233 (Sept. 1988): 14–19, 44.
             French version: Avantages et inconvénients de la copie par ordinateur.

6709.   Müller, Giovanni, and Raffaello Giulietti. "High Quality Music Notation: Interactive Editing and Input by Piano Keyboard." In *Proceedings of the 1987 International Computer Music Conference: University of Illinois at Urbana-Champaign, Urbana, Illinois, USA, August 23–26, 1987*, comp. James Beauchamp. San Francisco, Calif.: Computer Music Association, 1987: 333–40.

6710. "New Notation Setter." *Musik International* 37 (Nov. 1983): 692.

6711. Niihara, Takami, and Seiji Inokuchi. "Transcription of Sung Song." In *ICASSP 86 Proceedings: April 7, 8, 9, 10, 11, 1986, Keio Plaza Inter-continental Hotel, Tokyo, Japan.* Piscataway, N.J.: IEEE, 1986: 1277–80.

6712. Piszczalski, Martin. "A Computational Model of Music Transcription." Ph.D. diss., University of Michigan, 1986. 309 p.

6713. Prusinkiewicz, Przemyslaw. "Score Generation with L-systems." In *Proceedings of the International Computer Music Conference 1986, Royal Conservatory, The Hague, Netherlands, October 20–24, 1986,* ed. Paul Berg. San Francisco, Calif.: Computer Music Association, 1986: 455–57.

6714. Roads, Curtis. "A Note on Music Printing by Computer." *Computer Music Journal* 5,3 (Fall 1981): 57–59.
Previously **1940.**
Reprinted in *The Music Machine,* ed. Curtis Roads. Cambridge, Mass.: MIT Press, 1989: 239–41.

6715. Scholz, Carter. "Notation Software Ahead: Proceed with Caution." *Keyboard* 15 (Apr. 1989): 58–80, 105, 125.
Review of many music printing programs for microcomputers.

6716. Stickney, Kimball P. "Computer Tools for Engraving-Quality Music Notation." In *The Proceedings of the AES 5th International Conference: Music and Digital Technology,* ed. John Strawn. New York, N.Y.: Audio Engineering Society, 1987: 129–40.

6717. Yavelow, Christopher. "A Report of the Workshop for Music Notation by Computer." *Computer Music Journal* 11,2 (Summer 1987): 65–70.

MUSICAL INSTRUMENTS

6718.   Adrien, Jean Marie; René Causse; and Eric Ducasse. "Dynamic Modeling of Stringed and Wind Instruments, Sound Synthesis by Physical Models." In *Proceedings of the 14th International Computer Music Conference, Cologne, September 20–25, 1988*, ed. Christoph Lischka and Johannes Fritsch. Cologne: Feedback-Studio-Verlag; San Francisco, Calif.: Dist. by Computer Music Association, 1988: 265–76. (Feedback Papers; 33)

6719.   ———; René Causse; and Xavier Rodet. "Sound Synthesis by Physical Models, Application to Strings." In *Proceedings of the 1987 International Computer Music Conference: University of Illinois at Urbana-Champaign, Urbana, Illinois, USA, August 23–26, 1987*, comp. James Beauchamp. San Francisco, Calif.: Computer Music Association, 1987: 264–69.

6720.   Andresen, Uwe. "Digitaltechnik im Instrumentenbau—auch musikalisch immer ein Fortschritt?" *Musik International* 37 (Juli 1983): 468–73.

6721.   Berry, R. W. "Experiments in Computer Controlled Acoustic Modelling (A Step Backwards??)." In *Proceedings of the 14th International Computer Music Conference, Cologne, September 20–25, 1988*, ed. Christoph Lischka and Johannes Fritsch. Cologne: Feedback-Studio-Verlag; San Francisco, Calif.: Dist. by Computer Music Association, 1988: 333–48. (Feedback Papers; 33)

Description of a series of experiments in the electronic modelling of a variety of acoustic instruments and an affordable computer systems used to construct these.

6722.   Berry, Ronald L. "President's Message: The Future of Pianos." *Piano Technicians Journal* 32 (Mar. 1989): 6.

An appeal to look to the future of MIDI-compatible pianos.

6723.   Bolles, Mark Emery. "A Computer Stringing Program." *Folk Harp Journal* n43 (Dec. 1983): 47–49.

6724.   ———. "Harpmaker's Notebook #4: C.A.H.D." *Folk Harp Journal* n56 (Spring 1987): 29–32.

Computer Assisted Harp Design.

6725.   ———. "Harpmaker's Notebook #5: C.A.H.D. Part Two." *Folk Harp Journal* n57 (Summer 1987): 47–54.

Computer Assisted Harp Design.

6726.   Chafe, Chris. *Bowed String Synthesis and Its Control from a Physical Model.* Stanford, Calif.: Dept. of Music, Stanford University, 1985. (Dept. of Music Technical Report STAN-M-32)

Updated by STAN-M-48.

6727.   ———. "Simulating Performance on a Bowed Instrument." In *Current Directions in Computer Music,* ed. Max V. Mathews and John R. Pierce. Cambridge, Mass.: MIT Press, 1989: 185–98.

Also issued as: Technical Report STAN-M-48. Stanford, Calif.: Center for Computer Research in Music and Acoustics, Department of Music, Stanford University, 1988. (Updates STAN-M-32).

6728.   Chowning, John M.; John M. Grey; James A. Moorer; and Loren Rush. *Instrumental Timbre and Related Acoustical Phenomena in the Perception of Music, Final Report.* Stanford, Calif.: Dept. of Music, Stanford University, 1982. (Department of Music Technical Report STAN-M-11)

6729.   ———; John M. Grey; Loren Rush; James A. Moorer; and Leland Smith. *Simulation of Music Instrument Tones in Reverberant Environments, Final Report.* Stanford, Calif.: Dept. of Music, Stanford University, 1978. (Department of Music Technical Report STAN-M-8)

6730.   Cook, Perry R. *Implementation of Single Reed Instruments with Arbitrary Bore Shapes Using Digital Waveguide Filters.* Stanford, Calif.: Stanford University, Dept. of Music, 1988. 7 p. (Stanford University Department of Music Technical Report STAN-M-50)

6731.   Croft, Simon. "The Perfect Repeat." *Music Technology* 1 (Feb. 1987): 88–90.

Description of the Bösendorfer 290SE, a computer-based playback piano.

6732.   Culotta, Paul. "A Mathematical/Computerizable Approach for the String Layout in the Design of a New Harp." *Folk Harp Journal* n49 (June 1985): 25–28.

6733.   Di Perna, Alan. "The Grand Side of Electronics." *Keyboards, Computers & Software* 1 (Apr. 1986): 48–51.

A look at the sampled sounds of a grand piano on Technics, Ensoniq, Korg, Roland, and Yamaha synthesizers.

6734.   Doerschuk, Bob. "MIDI Retrofits & Factory Models: The World's Most Expressive Keyboard Just Got More Expressive." *Keyboard* 14 (Aug. 1988): 45, 58.

MIDI controlled pianos.

6735.   Dorner, Jane. "Violin Program." *Strad* 98 (July 1986): 183–84.
A report on the latest research by acousticians on stringed instruments.

6736.   Dupler, Steven. "New Hybrid Instrument Scores; One-of-a-Kind Devonsal." *Billboard* 96 (Oct. 6, 1984): 39.
Modified Lyricon that utilizes both digital and analog techniques.

6737.   Falcao, Mario, and David Dunn. "The Camac Hydraulic Harp: A Revolutionary Concept in Harp Design from France." *American Harp Journal* 11 (Summer 1987): 3–7.
Computer control of pedal changes.

6738.   Garnett, Guy E. "Modeling Piano Sound Using Waveguide Digital Filtering Techniques." In *Proceedings of the 1987 International Computer Music Conference: University of Illinois at Urbana-Champaign, Urbana, Illinois, USA, August 23–26, 1987*, comp. James Beauchamp. San Francisco, Calif.: Computer Music Association, 1987: 89–95.

6739.   Hamer, Mick. "Don't Shoot the Computer, It's Doing Its Best!" *New Scientist* 112 (Nov. 20, 1986): 26.
Description of the Bösendorfer computerized piano.

6740.   Harihara, Mohan, and K. Radhakrishna Rao. "Mridangam Simulation." In *Proceedings of the International Computer Music Conference 1986, Royal Conservatory, The Hague, Netherlands, October 20–24, 1986*, ed. Paul Berg. San Francisco, Calif.: Computer Music Association, 1986: 215–17.

6741.   Jimmerson, Herb. "Digital Sampling: Just Strummin' Along." *Keyboard* 15 (Oct. 1989): 110–11.
How to sample and perform acoustic guitar strums.

6742.   "Kaman Harnesses MIDI for Acoustic Guitar." *Music Trades* 134 (July 1986): 97.

6743.   "Kimball & Bösendorfer Announce Computer-based Live Performance Reproducer." *Music Trades* 133 (Nov. 1985): 28–30.

6744.   Kitching, L. K. "From Small Beginnings." In *Proceedings of the 1987 International Computer Music Conference: University of Illinois at Urbana-Champaign, Urbana, Illinois, USA, August 23–26, 1987*, comp. James Beauchamp. San Francisco, Calif.: Computer Music Association, 1987: 270–73.
Use of the Bradford Musical Instrument Simulator to develop starting transients of organ tones.

6745.   Knowlton, Joseph. "State of the Art: Miracle on 57th Street: The Bösendorfer 290 SE." *Keyboard Classics* 8 (Mar./Apr. 1988): 10–12.

A Bösendorfer piano is monitored by optical scanners to record a performance. The performer may then listen to his or her performance repeated by the instrument. Recordings by famous pianists have been archived.

6746. ———. "State of the Art: What's New in Pianos?" *Keyboard Classics* 7 (Jan./Feb. 1987): 43.

An examination of electronic, MIDI-compatible, digital, and performance reproduction system pianos.

6747. "Lowrey Opens New Market with Unique Computer Tie-in." *Music Trades* 133 (Nov. 1985): 46.

A brief review of the Lowrey GX-1 electronic keyboard organ.

6748. Marks, Joseph, and John Polito. "Modeling Piano Tones." In *Proceedings of the International Computer Music Conference 1986, Royal Conservatory, The Hague, Netherlands, October 20–24, 1986,* ed. Paul Berg. San Francisco, Calif.: Computer Music Association, 1986: 263–67.

6749. Massey, Howard; Alex Noyes; and Daniel Shklair. "Sounds Natural. Part 1, Brass Instruments—The Trumpet." *Music Technology* 1 (July 1987): 47–51.
Excerpt from *A Synthesist's Guide to Acoustic Instruments.*

Description of ways that a trumpet produces sound and how to synthesize and sample it.

6750. ———; Alex Noyes; and Daniel Shklair. "Sounds Natural. Part 2, Fender Rhodes." *Music Technology* 2 (Aug. 1987): 68–74.
Excerpt from *A Synthesist's Guide to Acoustic Instruments.*

Ways in which the Fender Rhodes can be synthesized and sampled.

6751. ———; Alex Noyes; and Daniel Shklair. "Sounds Natural. Part 3, The Snare." *Music Technology* 2 (Sept. 1987): 52–61.
Excerpt from *A Synthesist's Guide to Acoustic Instruments.*

Notes on synthesizing and sampling the snare drum.

6752. Moog, Bob. "Ask Mr. Moog: The More Things Change, the More They Change." *Keyboard* 14 (Oct. 1988): 122, 156–57.

Digitally controlled player pianos.

6753. Nakamura, Isao, and Iwaoka Soichiro. "Piano Tone Synthesis Using Digital Filters by Computer Simulation." In *ICASSP 86 Proceedings: April 7, 8, 9, 10, 11, 1986, Keio Plaza Inter-continental Hotel, Tokyo, Japan.* Piscataway, N.J.: IEEE, 1986: 1293–96.

6754. Rivas, David; Steve Watkins; and Paul M. Chau. "VLSI for a Physical Model of Musical Instrument Oscillations." In *Proceedings, 1989*

International Computer Music Conference, November 2–5, the Ohio State University, Columbus, Ohio. San Francisco, Calif.: Computer Music Association, 1989: 253–56.

6755.   Rolle, Günter. "Naturinstrument und künstliche Intelligenz: MIDI im, am und um das Klavier herum—teuflische Elektronik?" *Neue Musikzeitung* 37 (Feb.–Mär. 1988): 49–52.

Discussion of the Yamaha MIDI grand piano.

6756.   "Saville Brings MIDI to Church Market." *Music Trades* 135 (Oct. 1987): 87–88.

MIDI is being offered by the Saville Organ Company on its entire line of church organs.

6757.   Schulz, Reinhard. "Neue Klavierkultur: Midi-Vorführung in Bayreuth." *Neue Musikzeitung* 37 (Feb.–Mär. 1988): 52.

6758.   Serra, Xavier. "A Computer Model for Bar Percussion Instruments." In *Proceedings of the International Computer Music Conference 1986, Royal Conservatory, The Hague, Netherlands, October 20–24, 1986,* ed. Paul Berg. San Francisco, Calif.: Computer Music Association, 1986: 257–62.

6759.   Smith, Julius O. "Efficient Simulation of the Reed-Bore and Bow-String Mechanisms." In *Proceedings of the International Computer Music Conference 1986, Royal Conservatory, The Hague, Netherlands, October 20–24, 1986,* ed. Paul Berg. San Francisco, Calif.: Computer Music Association, 1986: 275–80.

6760.   Weinreich, Gabriel, and René Caussé. "Digital and Analog Bows: Hybrid Mechanical-Electrical Systems." In *ICASSP 86 Proceedings: April 7, 8, 9, 10, 11, 1986, Keio Plaza Inter-continental Hotel, Tokyo, Japan.* Piscataway, N.J.: IEEE, 1986: 1297–99.

6761.   "Yamaha Unveils Disklavier Piano with Onboard Computer." *Music Trades* 136 (Dec. 1988): 96.

A brief description of the Yamaha MX100A Disklavier, an upright piano with an onboard computer that records performances.

MUSICOLOGICAL AND ANALYTIC APPLICATIONS

6762. Alphonce, Bo H. "The State of Research in Music Theory—Computer Applications: Analysis and Modeling." *Music Theory Spectrum* 11 (Spring 1989): 49–59.

6763. Balaban, Mira. "CSM: A Computer Basis for a General, Formal Study of Western Tonal Music." In *Proceedings of the First Annual Artificial Intelligence & Advanced Computer Technology Conference/EAST.* Wheaton, Ill.: Tower Conference Management Co., 1987: 197–213.

6764. ———. "The TTS Language for Music Description." *International Journal of Man-Machine Studies* 28 (1988): 505–23.

A discussion of Twelve Tone Strings.

6765. Barbieri, Patrizio, and Lindoro Del Duca. "Renaissance and Baroque Microtonal Music Research in Computer Real Time Performance." In *Proceedings of the International Computer Music Conference 1986, Royal Conservatory, The Hague, Netherlands, October 20–24, 1986,* ed. Paul Berg. San Francisco, Calif.: Computer Music Association, 1986: 51.

6766. Bauer-Mengelberg, Stefan. "Current Advances in Computer Methods." In *Report of the Twelfth Congress, Berkeley, 1977, International Musicological Society,* ed. Daniel Heartz and Bonnie Wade. Kassel: Bärenreiter, 1981: 319–52.

6767. ———. "Forum." *In Theory Only* 10 (Aug. 1987): 79–85.

Reply by David Kowalski on p. 86–89. In regard to "An Algorithm and a Computer Program for the Construction of Self-deriving Arrays" by David Kowalski, item **6811.**

6768. Baxter, Deborah E. "Women's Voice Classifications in Selected Operas of Jules Massenet: Computer Analyzation and Anecdotal Study." D.M.A. diss., University of Missouri, Kansas City, 1989. 308 p.

6769.   Behrens, Stefan. "Computer-aided Organ Documentation." *Diapason* 80 (Sept. 1989): 9.

Workshop on computer-aided organ documentation at the Institute for Applied Computer Sciences of the Technical University in Berlin.

6770.   Bengtsson, Ingmar. "Men je fårstår int' me på däm da prickar!: om att uppteckna folkmusik." [But I Can't Understand Those Dots!: The Recording of Folk Music] In *Folkmusikboken,* ed. Jan Ling; Gunnar Ternhag; and Märta Ramsten. Stockholm: Prisma, 1980: 297–312. In Danish.

6771.   Bevil, Jack Marshall. "Centonization and Concordance in the American Southern Uplands Folksong Melody: A Study of the Musical Generative and Transmittive Processes of an Oral Tradition." Ph.D. diss., University of North Texas, 1984. 449 p.

6772.   Böker-Heil, Norbert. "Computer-Simulation eines musikalischen Verstehensprozeses." In *Report of the Twelfth Congress, Berkeley, 1977, International Musicological Society,* ed. Daniel Heartz and Bonnie Wade. Kassel: Bärenreiter, 1981: 324–30.

6773.   Brinkman, Alexander R. "A Binomial Representation of Pitch for Computer Processing of Musical Data." *Music Theory Spectrum* 8 (1986): 44–57.

An earlier version of this paper was presented at the annual conference of the Society for Music Theory held at the University of Southern California, Los Angeles, October 1981.

6774.   ———. "Representing Musical Scores for Computer Analysis." *Journal of Music Theory* 30 (Fall 1986): 225–75.

An earlier version of this paper was read at the annual conference of the Society for Music Theory in Nov. 1983. Material from the paper was also presented at the 1983 ICMC (ESM) and 1984 ICMC (IRCAM).

6775.   Camilleri, Lelio. "The Current State of Computer Assisted Research in Musicology in Italy." *Acta Musicologica* 58 (1986): 356–60.

6776.   ———. "A Software Tool for Music Analysis." *Interface* 16 (1987): 23–38.

6777.   Charnassé, Hélène. "Les Bases de données en musicologie." *Fontes Artis Musicae* 31 (1984): 153–59.

6778.   ———, and Bernard Stépien. "Automatic Transcription of Sixteenth Century Musical Notations." *Computers and the Humanities* 20 (1986): 179–90.

6779.   Chave, George B. "A Computer-assisted Analysis of Tonal Relationships in the Third Movement of Roger Sessions' *Second Symphony. Sapphire.*" Ph.D. diss., Washington University, 1988. 164 p.

6780. Ciardi, Fabio Cifariello. "Applicazioni dell'elaboratore nell'analisi dei livelli di tensione intervallare delle strutture microtonali." [Applications of the Computer in Analyses of Levels of Interval Tension in Microtonal Structure] In *Musica e tecnologia: industria e cultura per lo sviluppo del mezzogiorno: VI Colloquio di Informatica Musicale, Napoli 16–19 ottobre 1985,* ed. Carlo Acreman; Immacolata Ortosecco; and Fausto Razzi. Milan: Edizioni Unicopli, 1987: 474–87.

6781. ———. "The Organization of Microtonal Sets in Computer Music." In *Proceedings of the International Computer Music Conference 1986, Royal Conservatory, The Hague, Netherlands, October 20–24, 1986,* ed. Paul Berg. San Francisco, Calif.: Computer Music Association, 1986: A-17–A-20.

6782. Clements, Peter J. "A System for the Complete Enharmonic Encoding of Musical Pitches and Intervals." In *Proceedings of the International Computer Music Conference 1986, Royal Conservatory, The Hague, Netherlands, October 20–24, 1986,* ed. Paul Berg. San Francisco, Calif.: Computer Music Association, 1986: 459–61.

6783. Crawford, David. "Surveying Renaissance Liturgical Materials: Methodology and the Computer." *Studia Musicologica* 30 (1988): 345–54.

6784. D'Ambrosio, P.; A. Guercio; and G. Tortora. "A Grammatical Description of Music Theory." In *Musica e tecnologia: industria e cultura per lo sviluppo del mezzogiorno: VI Colloquio di Informatica Musicale, Napoli 16–19 ottobre 1985,* ed. Carlo Acreman; Immacolata Ortosecco; and Fausto Razzi. Milan: Edizioni Unicopli, 1987: 379–83.

6785. Detlovs, V. K., and A. Z. Klotin'sh. "Statisticheskie issledovaniíā ladovoĭ funkt͡sional'nosti v latyshskikh narodnykh pesiī͡akh." [Statistical Research in Harmonic Functions in Latvian Folksongs] In *Kolichestvennye metody v muzykal'noĭ fol'kloristike i muzykoznanii: sbornik stateĭ,* ed. Ė. E. Alekseev; E. D. Andreeva; M. G. Boroda; and A. S. Tangian. Moscow: Sov. kompozitor, 1988: 18–35. In Russian.

6786. Drummond, Philip J. "Developing Standards for Musicological Data Bases." *Fontes Artis Musicae* 31 (1984): 172–76.

6787. Erickson, Raymond, and Anthony B. Wolff. "The DARMS Project: Implementation of an Artificial Language for the Representation of Music." In *Computers in Language Research 2,* ed. Walter A. Sedelow and Sally Yeates Sedelow. Berlin; New York, N.Y.: Mouton, 1983: 171–219.

6788. Finarelli, L., and Goffredo Haus. "Informatica e musicologia: un sistema per il recupero di fondi musicali." [Informatics and Musicology: A System for the Reconstruction of Musical Sources] In *Atti del 7 Colloquio di Informatica Musicale.* Rome: AIMI/CDIM/SIM, 1988: 106–12.

6789.   Foxley, Eric. "Database of Computer Readable Folk Music." *Folk Music Journal* 5 (1987): 361–62.

A database of British folk dance tunes is established as a project in the Computer Science Dept. at the University of Nottingham.

6790.   Freed, Adrian. "New Media for Musicological Research and Education—The Country Blues in HyperMedia." In *Proceedings, 1989 International Computer Music Conference, November 2–5, the Ohio State University, Columbus, Ohio.* San Francisco, Calif.: Computer Music Association, 1989: 109–12.

6791.   Garnett, Guy E. "Meta-issues in Music Representation." In *Proceedings, 1989 International Computer Music Conference, November 2–5, the Ohio State University, Columbus, Ohio.* San Francisco, Calif.: Computer Music Association, 1989: 117–18.

6792.   Gasparjan, Emma. "Analitiko-informacionno-poiskovaja sistema obrabotki narodnoj pesni." [An Analytical Information Retrieval System for Processing Folk Songs] M.S. diss., Technical Cybernetics and Information Theory: Akademii Nauk Erevan, 1981. 19 p.
In Russian.

6793.   Hall, Thomas. "Computer Implementation of Stemmatics in the Preparation of Critical Editions of Renaissance Music." In *Report of the Twelfth Congress, Berkeley, 1977, International Musicological Society,* ed. Daniel Heartz and Bonnie Wade. Kassel: Bärenreiter, 1981: 320–24.

6794.   Halperin, David. "Distributional Structure in Troubadour Music." *Orbis Musicae* 7 (1979–80): 15–26.

6795.   Harris, Craig R. "Computer Programs for Set-Theoretic and Serial Analysis of Contemporary Music Composition; 'In Such an Hour': I. Down the Rabbit Hole for Orchestra and Computer Generated Tape. II. Pool of Tears for Orchestra." Ph.D. diss., Eastman School of Music, University of Rochester, 1985. 225 p.

6796.   ——, and Alexander R. Brinkman. "An Integrated Software System for Set-Theoretic and Serial Analysis of Contemporary Music." *Journal of Computer-based Instruction* 16 (Spring 1989): 59–70.

6797.   ——, and Alexander R. Brinkman. "A Unified Set of Software Tools for Computer-assisted Set-Theoretic and Serial Analysis of Contemporary Music." In *Proceedings of the International Computer Music Conference 1986, Royal Conservatory, The Hague, Netherlands, October 20–24, 1986,* ed. Paul Berg. San Francisco, Calif.: Computer Music Association, 1986: 331–36.

6798.   Hewlett, Walter B., and Eleanor Selfridge-Field, ed. *Computing in Musicology: A Directory of Research.* Menlo Park, Calif.: Center for Computer Assisted Research in the Humanities, 1989. 170 p.

6799. ———, and Eleanor Selfridge-Field, ed. *Directory of Computer Assisted Research in Musicology, 1986.* Menlo Park, Calif.: Center for Computer Assisted Research in the Humanities, 1986. 86 p.
Review by Richard Koprowski in *Notes* 43 (Mar. 1987): 564–65.
Review by Helmut Schaffrath in *Yearbook for Traditional Music* 19 (1987): 120–21.

6800. ———, and Eleanor Selfridge-Field, ed. *Directory of Computer Assisted Research in Musicology, 1987.* Menlo Park, Calif.: Center for Computer Assisted Research in the Humanities, 1987. 151 p.
Review by Ann Basart in *Cum Notis Variorum* n120 (Mar. 1988): 14.
Review by Jeanette M. Drone and Mark A. Crook in *Fontes Artis Musicae* 36 (1989): 64.

6801. ———, and Eleanor Selfridge-Field, ed. *Directory of Computer Assisted Research in Musicology, 1988.* Menlo Park, Calif.: Center for Computer Assisted Research in the Humanities, 1988. 155 p.
Review by Ann Basart in *Cum Notis Variorum* n127 (Nov. 1988): 20, 24.

6802. Hilfiger, John J. "A Comparison of Some Aspects of Style in the Band and Orchestra Music of Vincent Persichetti." Ph.D. diss., University of Iowa, 1985. 112

6803. Hill, George R., and Murray Gould. *A Thematic Locator for Mozart's Works as Listed in Koechel's Chronologisch-Thematisches Verzeichnis—Sixth Edition.* Hackensack, N.J.: J. Boonin, 1970. 76 p.

6804. Hultberg, Warren E. "Data Bases for the Study of Relationships among Spanish Music Sources of the 16th–17th Centuries." *Fontes Artis Musicae* 31 (1984): 162–67.

6805. Huron, David. "Characterizing Musical Textures." In *Proceedings, 1989 International Computer Music Conference, November 2–5, the Ohio State University, Columbus, Ohio.* San Francisco, Calif.: Computer Music Association, 1989: 131–34.
Describes a project to derive an analytic model for characterizing musical textures.

6806. ———. "Error Categories, Detection, and Reduction in a Musical Database." *Computers and the Humanities* 22 (1988): 253–64.
An examination of four methods of error detection: manual proofreading, double-entry, programmed syntactic checking, and programmed heuristics.

6807. Kassler, Michael. "Transferring a Tonality Theory to a Computer." In *Report of the Twelfth Congress, Berkeley, 1977, International Musicological Society,* ed. Daniel Heartz and Bonnie Wade. Kassel: Bärenreiter, 1981: 339–47.

6808. Kippen, James. "An Ethnomusicological Approach to the Analysis of Musical Cognition." *Music Perception* 5 (Winter 1987): 173–95.

Use of the computer in research to identify cognitive patterns involved in the creation, performance, and appreciation of the tabla of North India.

6809. ———, and Bernard Bel. "The Identification and Modelling of a Percussion 'Language', and the Emergence of Musical Concepts in a Machine-Learning Environment." *Computers and the Humanities* 23 (1989): 199–214.

Describes the Bol Processor, a computer program used to analyze tabla drumming of North India.

6810. Kotok, Judith. "The Madrigals of Scipione Lacorcia." M.M. diss., University of Lowell, 1981. 266 p.

6811. Kowalski, David L. "An Algorithm and a Computer Program for the Construction of Self-deriving Arrays." *In Theory Only* 9 (Jan 1987): 27–49.

6812. ———. "The Array as a Compositional Unit: A Study of Derivational Counterpoint as a Means of Creating Hierarchical Structures in Twelve-Tone Music; Clarinet Quartet." Ph.D. diss., Princeton University, 1985. 534 p.

6813. Koza, Julia E. "Music and References of Music in 'Godey's Lady's Book,' 1830–1877." Ph.D. diss., University of Minnesota, 1988. 1185 p.

6814. Lande, Tor Sverre. "Musikkanalyse med datamaskin I." [Music Analysis with Computers I] In *Nordisk musik och musikveterskap under 1970-talet: en rapport från 8:e Nordiska musikforskar-kongressen, Ljungskile folkhögskola, 25–30 juni 1979,* ed. Anders Carlsson and Jan Ling. Göteborg: Musikvetenskapliga institutionen, Götesborgs universitet, 1980: 92–102.
In Norwegian.

6815. Laske, Otto E. "Introduction to Cognitive Musicology." *Computer Music Journal* 12,1 (Spring 1988): 43–57.

6816. Leppig, Manfred. "Musikuntersuchungen im Rechenautomaten." *Musica* 41 (1987): 140–50.

6817. Lincoln, Harry B. "A Description of the Database in Italian Secular Polyphony Held at SUNY-Binghamton, New York." *Fontes Artis Musicae* 31 (1984): 159–62.

6818. Ling, Jan. "Elektronmusiken är också ett forskningsområde för musikvetenskapen." [Electronic Music Is Also a Research Area for Musicology] *Nutida Musik* 29,1 (1985–86): 23–25.
In Swedish.

6819. Maxwell, Harry J. "An Artificial Intelligence Approach to Computer-implemented Analysis of Harmony in Tonal Music." Ph.D. diss., Indiana University, 1984. 307 p.

6820. Metz, Paul. "Randomness and Correlation in Music: A New Approach to Melodic Analysis." Ph.D. diss., University of Cincinnati, 1983. 180 p.

6821. Morehen, John. "Computer-assisted Musical Analysis: A Question of Validity." In *Proceedings of the International Computer Music Conference 1986, Royal Conservatory, The Hague, Netherlands, October 20–24, 1986,* ed. Paul Berg. San Francisco, Calif.: Computer Music Association, 1986: 337–39.

6822. ———. "Thematic Cataloging by Computer." *Fontes Artis Musicae* 31 (1984): 32–38.

6823. Morse, Ray. "Use of Microcomputer Graphics to Aid in the Analysis of Music." D.M.A. diss., University of Oregon, 1985. 205 p.

6824. Nakamura, Yasuaki, and Seiji Inokuchi. "Music Information Processing System and Its Application to Comparative Musicology." In *IJCAI-79: Proceedings of the Sixth International Joint Conference on Artificial Intelligence, Tokyo, August 20–23, 1979.* [S.l.]: IJCAI, 1979: 633–35.

6825. Noble, Jeremy. "Archival Research." In *Musicology in the 1980s: Methods, Goals, Opportunities,* ed. D. Kern Holoman and Claude V. Palisca. New York, N.Y.: Da Capo Press, 1982: 31–37.
  A call to organize unused research into a common computer data bank so it is not lost.

6826. Oliveira, Alda de Jesus. "A Frequency Count of Music Elements in Bahian Folk Songs Using Computer and Hand Analysis: Suggestions for Applications in Music Education." Ph.D. diss., University of Texas, Austin, 1986. 321 p.

6827. Osborn, F. E. Ann. "A Computer-aided Methodology for the Analysis and Classification of British-Canadian Children's Traditional Singing Games." Ph.D. diss., Ohio State University, 1986. 357 p.

6828. Papum, M. P. "Aktual'nye problemy muzykal'noĭ akustiki (Po materialam Seminara 'Akusticheskie sredy,' 1975–1984)." [Current Problems of Musical Acoustics (Based on the Materials of a Seminar: "Acoustical Environment," 1975–1984)] In *Kolichestvennye metody v muzykal'noĭ fol'kloristike i muzykoznanii: sbornik stateĭ,* ed. É. E. Alekseev; E. D. Andreeva; M. G. Boroda; and A. S. Tangĩan. Moscow: Sov. kompozitor, 1988: 254–58.
  In Russian.

6829. ———. "Metodologicheskie problemy kompyoterizatsii muzykal'nogo ĩazyka." [Methodological Problems of Computerizing Musical Language] In *Kolichestvennye metody v muzykal'noĭ fol'kloristike i*

muzykoznanii: sbornik stateĭ, ed. È. E. Alekseev; E. D. Andreeva; M. G. Boroda; and A. S. Tangīan. Moscow: Sov. kompozitor, 1988: 121–54.
In Russian.

6830. Pope, Stephen T. "Considerations in the Design of a Music Representation Language." In *Proceedings, 1989 International Computer Music Conference, November 2–5, the Ohio State University, Columbus, Ohio.* San Francisco, Calif.: Computer Music Association, 1989: 246–48.

6831. Popovic, Igor. "The Analytical Object: Computer-based Representation of Musical Scores and Analyses." *Computers in Music Research* 1 (Fall 1989): 103–16.

6832. Powell, Kathlyn; John Fowler; and Jorge Strunz. *The Scale-Chord Synopticon.* Woodland Hills, Calif.: Synopticon Pub., 1987. 626 p.
Review by Steve Oppenheimer in *Electronic Musician* 5 (May 1987): 92–93.
A computer-generated book of tables that identifies, classifies, and cross-references all the 274 unique, five- to nine-note scales possible in the twelve-tone system and the 336 distinct chord types that can be derived from them.

6833. Prather, Ronald E., and R. Stephen Elliott. "SML: A Structured Musical Language." *Computers and the Humanities* 22 (1988): 137–51.
Describes a music encoding system.

6834. Prószéky, Gábor. "Szempontok a magyar népzenei anyag számítógépes feldolgozásához." [Some Aspects of Computerizing Hungarian Folk Music Material] *Zenetudomanyi dolgozatok* (1983): 13–48.
In Hungarian.

6835. Rahn, John. "On Some Computational Models of Music Theory." *Computer Music Journal* 4,2 (Summer 1980): 66–72.
Previously **2460.**
Reprinted in *The Music Machine,* ed. Curtis Roads. Cambridge, Mass.: MIT Press, 1989: 663–69.

6836. ———. "Toward a Theory of Chord Progression." *In Theory Only* 11 (May 1989): 1–10.
Describes the similarity function ATMEMB.

6837. Riuĭtel, I., and K. Khaugas. "Metod raspoznavaniīa melodicheskikh tipov i opredeleniīa tipologicheskikh grupp." [A Method of Recognizing Melodic Types: Determining Typological Groups] In *Kolichestvennye metody v muzykal'noĭ fol'kloristike i muzykoznanii: sbornik stateĭ,* ed. È. E. Alekseev; E. D. Andreeva; M. G. Boroda; and A. S. Tangīan. Moscow: Sov. kompozitor, 1988: 116–20.
In Russian.

6838. Roeder, John. "A Declarative Model of Atonal Analysis." *Music Perception* 6 (Fall 1988): 21–34.

6839. Rösing, Helmut, and Joachim Schlichte. "Die Serie A/II des Internationalen Quellenlexikons der Musik." *Fontes Artis Musicae* 31 (1984): 167–72.

6840. ———, and Joachim Schlichte. "Nachtrag zu die Serie A/II des Internationalen Quellenlexikons der Musik." *Fontes Artis Musicae* 32 (1985): 117–18.

6841. Rothgeb, John. "Simulating Musical Skills by Digital Computer." In *Proceedings of the ACM National Conference.* New York, N.Y.: ACM, 1979: 121–25.
Revised version in *Computer Music Journal* 4,2 (Summer 1980): 36–40.
Reprinted in *The Music Machine,* ed. Curtis Roads. Cambridge, Mass: MIT Press, 1989: 657–61.

6842. Rubin, Emanuel L. "The English Glee from William Hayes to William Horsley." Ph.D. diss., University of Pittsburgh, 1986.

6843. Schafer, Wolf-Dieter. "Entwurf einer quantitativen Instrumentationsanalyse. Ein Beitrag zur Methodik von Instrumentationsuntersuchungen, dargestellt an Beispielen aus der Wiener Klassik und der Spätromantik." Ph.D. diss., Ruhruniversität, Bochum, 1982.
Also published: Frankfurt am Main: Lang, 1982. 422 p.

6844. Schaffrath, Helmut. "Computer-Wozu?" *Musica* 41 (1987): 135–39.
Musicological and research uses of the computer.

6845. Schenck-Hamlin, Donna, and George Milliken. "A Multi-Discriminate Analysis of Elizabethan Keyboard Variations." *Interface* 17 (1988): 193–210.
Use of the programs DISCRIM and STEPDISC to discriminate musical style.

6846. Schneider, Albrecht, and Uwe Seifert. "Zu einigen Ansäzen und Verfahren in neueren musiktheoretischen Konzepten." *Acta Musicologica* 58 (1986): 305–38.

6847. Smoliar, Stephen W. "Current Advances in Computer Methods: Remarks." In *Report of the Twelfth Congress, Berkeley, 1977, International Musicological Society,* ed. Daniel Heartz and Bonnie Wade. Kassel: Bärenreiter, 1981: 347–52.

6848. Sochinski, James R. "Instrumental Doubling and Usage in Wind-Band Literature." Ph.D. diss., University of Miami, 1980. 143 p.

6849.   Solomon, Larry. "The List of Chords, Their Properties and Use in Analysis." *Interface* 11 (Nov. 1982): 61–107.

6850.   Sørensen, Olve. "Musikkanalyse med datamaskin II." [Music Analysis with Computer II] In *Nordisk musik och musikveterskap under 1970-talet: en rapport från 8:e Nordiska musikforskar-kongressen, Ljungskile folkhögskola, 25–30 juni 1979,* ed. Anders Carlsson and Jan Ling. Göteborg: Musikvetenskapliga institutionen, Götesborgs universitet, 1980: 177–92.
In Norwegian.

6851.   Suleĭmanov, R. A. "Ob odnom podkhode k statisticheskomu analizu zvukorîada narodnoĭ pesni." [On One Approach to Statistical Analysis of Scales in Folk Songs] In *Kolichestvennye metody v muzykal'noĭ fol'kloristike i muzykoznanii: sbornik stateĭ,* ed. Ė. E. Alekseev; E. D. Andreeva; M. G. Boroda; and A. S. Tangîan. Moscow: Sov. kompozitor, 1988: 116–20.
In Russian.

6852.   ――――, and S. A. Chel'diev. "Muzykal'naîa trassirovka Vypolnîaemykh Programm." [Musical Tracings of Programs in Progress] In *Kolichestvennye metody v muzykal'noĭ fol'kloristike i muzykoznanii: sbornik stateĭ,* ed. Ė. E. Alekseev; E. D. Andreeva; M. G. Boroda; and A. S. Tangîan. Moscow: Sov. kompozitor, 1988: 254–58.
In Russian.

6853.   Tangîan, A. S. "Muzykal'noe ispolnitel'stvo i muzykal'nyĭ analiz." [Musical Performance and Musical Analysis] In *Kolichestvennye metody v muzykal'noi fol'kloristike i muzykoznanii: sbornik stateĭ,* ed. Ė. E. Alekseev; E. D. Andreeva; M. G. Boroda; and A. S. Tangîan. Moscow: Sov. kompozitor, 1988: 187–217.
In Russian.

6854.   ――――. "Raspoznavanie akkordov, interval'nyĭ slukh i muzykal'naîa teoriîa." [Recognizing Chords, Interval Hearing, and Musical Theory] In *Kolichestvennye metody v muzykal'noi fol'kloristike i muzykozna-nii: sbornik stateĭ,* ed. Ė. E. Alekseev; E. D. Andreeva; M. G. Boroda; and A. S. Tangîan. Moscow: Sov. kompozitor, 1988: 155–86.
In Russian.

6855.   Trowbridge, Lynn M. "Style Change in the Fifteenth-Century Chanson: A Comparative Study of Compositional Detail." *Journal of Musicology* 4 (1985–86): 146–70.

6856.   Williams, J. K. "A Method for the Computer-aided Analysis of Jazz Melody in the Small Dimensions." *Jazz Studies* 3 (1985): 41–70.

6857.   Winenger, Dwight. "The Nature of Change and Schoenbergian Harmony." *Ex Tempore* 4 (Spring–Summer 1987–88): 58–67.

Describes a computer program called PRO-EVA written in Microsoft Basic designed for the TRS-80 Color Computer, based on a mathematical technique for analyzing harmonic progression and succession (using principles found in Schoenberg's "Structural Functions of Harmony").

6858. Zimmerman, Franklin B. *Henry Purcell 1659–1695: Melodic and Intervallic Indexes to His Complete Works.* Philadelphia, Pa.: Smith-Edwards-Dunlap, 1975. 133 p.

PROGRAMMING
LANGUAGES AND
SOFTWARE SYSTEMS

6859. Amblard, Paul. "Music Synthesis Description with the Data Flow Language Lustre." In *Design Tools for the 90's: Fifteenth Euromicro Symposium on Microprocessing and Microprogramming (EUROMICRO 89), Cologne, September 4–8, 1989*, ed. Lorenzo Mezzalire and Stephen Winter. Amsterdam; New York, N.Y.: North-Holland, 1989: 551–56.

6860. Ames, Charles. "The ASHTON Score-Transcription Utility." *Interface* 14 (1985): 165–83.

A utility for transcribing conventionally notated musical scores into a numeric format required by digital sound-synthesis packages.

6861. Ban, A. "MUSICIAN—A Music Processing and Synthesis System." M.Sc. thesis, Technion-Israel Institute of Technology, 1985.

6862. ——, and J. A. Makowsky. "Musician—A Music Processing and Synthesis System." In *Proceedings of the International Computer Music Conference 1986, Royal Conservatory, The Hague, Netherlands, October 20–24, 1986*, ed. Paul Berg. San Francisco, Calif.: Computer Music Association, 1986: A-21–A-25.

6863. Blythe, David; John Kitamura; David Galloway; and Martin Snelgrove. "Virtual Patch-Cords for the Katosizer." In *Proceedings of the International Computer Music Conference 1986, Royal Conservatory, The Hague, Netherlands, October 20–24, 1986*, ed. Paul Berg. San Francisco, Calif.: Computer Music Association, 1986: 359–63.

6864. Böcker, Heinz-Dieter, and Andreas Mahling. "What's in a Note?" In *Proceedings of the 14th International Computer Music Conference, Cologne, September 20–25, 1988*, ed. Christoph Lischka and Johannes Fritsch. Cologne: Feedback-Studio-Verlag; San Francisco, Calif.:

Dist. by Computer Music Association, 1988: 166–74. (Feedback Papers; 33)

Describes AMUSED, a knowledge-based editor of musical scores.

6865. Boynton, Lee; Jacques Duthen; Yves Potard; and Xavier Rodet. "Adding a Graphical User Interface to FORMES." In *Proceedings of the International Computer Music Conference 1986, Royal Conservatory, The Hague, Netherlands, October 20–24, 1986,* ed. Paul Berg. San Francisco, Calif.: Computer Music Association, 1986: 105–8.

6866. ———; Pierre Lavoie; Yann Orlarey; Camilo Rueda; and David Wessel. "MIDI-LISP: A LISP-based Music Programming Environment for the Macintosh." In *Proceedings of the International Computer Music Conference 1986, Royal Conservatory, The Hague, Netherlands, October 20–24, 1986,* ed. Paul Berg. San Francisco, Calif.: Computer Music Association, 1986: 183–86.

6867. Brinkman, Alexander R. "Data Structures for a Note-List Preprocessor." *Computers in Music Research* 1 (Fall 1989): 75–101.

6868. Camurri, Antonio. "Un linguaggio per la descrizione e la esecuzione di processi musicali basato sulle reti di Petri." [A Language for the Description and the Execution of Musical Processes Based on Petri Nets] Doctoral thesis, Dept. of Communication, Computer, and System Sciences, University of Genoa, Italy, 1984.

6869. Chemillier, Marc. "Toward a Theory of Formal Musical Languages." In *Proceedings of the 14th International Computer Music Conference, Cologne, September 20–25, 1988,* ed. Christoph Lischka and Johannes Fritsch. Cologne: Feedback-Studio-Verlag; San Francisco, Calif.: Dist. by Computer Music Association, 1988: 175–83. (Feedback Papers; 33)

A proposal for an extension of the traditional theory of formal languages.

6870. Cointe, Pierre; Jean-Pierre Briot; and Bernard Serpette. "The Formes System: A Musical Application of Object-oriented Concurrent Programming." In *Object-oriented Concurrent Programming,* ed. Akinori Yonezawa and Mario Tokoru. Cambridge, Mass.: MIT Press, 1987: 221–58. (MIT Press Series in Computer Systems)

6871. ———, and Xavier Rodet. *Formes: A New Object-Language for a Hierarchy of Events.* Paris: IRCAM, 1983.

6872. ———, and Xavier Rodet. "FORMES: An Object & Time Oriented System for Music Composition and Synthesis." In *Conference Record of the 1984 ACM Symposium on LISP and Functional Programming: Papers Presented at the Symposium, Austin, Texas, August 6–8, 1984.*

New York, N.Y.: Association for Computing Machinery, 1984: 85–95.

A presentation of the structure and implementation of the object-oriented programming environment called FORMES.

6873. ——, and Xavier Rodet. "FORMES: un langage-objet gérant des processus hiérarchisés." In *Quatrième Congrès reconnaissance des formes et intelligence artificielle, 25–27 janvier 1984.* Paris: INRIA AFCET, 1984: 291–311.

6874. Dannenberg, Roger B. "Arctic: A Functional Language for Real-Time Control." In *Conference Record of the 1984 ACM Symposium on LISP and Functional Programming: Papers Presented at the Symposium, Austin, Texas, August 6–8, 1984.* New York, N.Y.: Association for Computing Machinery, 1984: 96–103.

6875. ——. "Arctic: Functional Programming for Real-Time Systems." In *Proceedings of the Nineteenth Hawaii International Conference on System Sciences, 1986. Volume 2, Software,* ed. Bruce D. Shriver. North Hollywood, Calif.: Western Periodicals Co., 1986: 216–26.

6876. ——. "The Canon Score Language." *Computer Music Journal* 13,1 (Spring 1989): 47–56.

6877. ——. "The CMU MIDI Toolkit." In *Proceedings of the International Computer Music Conference 1986, Royal Conservatory, The Hague, Netherlands, October 20–24, 1986,* ed. Paul Berg. San Francisco, Calif.: Computer Music Association, 1986: 53–56.

6878. ——; Paul McAvinney; and Dean Rubine. "Arctic: A Functional Language for Real-Time Systems." *Computer Music Journal* 10,4 (Winter 1986): 67–78.

6879. De Furia, Steve. "Software for Musicians: Correcting Code Formats and Addressing Reader Questions." *Keyboard* 12 (Sept. 1986): 120.

6880. ——. "Software for Musicians: Getting Your Program Structures under Control." *Keyboard* 12 (July 1986): 128–29.

6881. ——. "Software for Musicians: Language and Software Design." *Keyboard* 12 (Apr. 1986): 106–9.

Background on how to design software that can solve musical problems.

6882. ——. "Software for Musicians: Operations and Statements." *Keyboard* 12 (May 1986): 108, 117.

Continues a look into the basic features of programming languages.

6883. ———. "Software for Musicians: References & Resources for C & Pascal Programmers." *Keyboard* 13 (Sept. 1987): 131.

6884. ———. "Software for Musicians: Relational & Logic Operators." *Keyboard* 12 (June 1986): 128–29.

6885. ———. "Software for Musicians: Selection Structures Can Give a Program Freedom of Choice." *Keyboard* 12 (Aug. 1986): 106–8.

6886. Degazio, Bruno. "The Development of Context Sensitivity in the Midiforth Computer Music System." In *Proceedings of the 14th International Computer Music Conference, Cologne, September 20–25, 1988,* ed. Christoph Lischka and Johannes Fritsch. Cologne: Feedback-Studio-Verlag; San Francisco, Calif.: Dist. by Computer Music Association, 1988: 403–11. (Feedback Papers; 33)

6887. Desain, Peter. "Graphical Programming in Computer Music: A Proposal." In *Proceedings of the International Computer Music Conference 1986, Royal Conservatory, The Hague, Netherlands, October 20–24, 1986,* ed. Paul Berg. San Francisco, Calif.: Computer Music Association, 1986: 161–66.

6888. ———, and Henkjan Honing. "LOCO: A Composition Microworld in Logo." *Computer Music Journal* 12,3 (Fall 1988): 30–42.

6889. ———, and Henkjan Honing. "LOCO: Composition Microworlds in LOGO." In *Proceedings of the International Computer Music Conference 1986, Royal Conservatory, The Hague, Netherlands, October 20–24, 1986,* ed. Paul Berg. San Francisco, Calif.: Computer Music Association, 1986: 109–18.

6890. Diener, Glendon R. "TTrees: A Tool for the Compositional Environment." *Computer Music Journal* 13,2 (Summer 1989): 77–85.

6891. ———. *TTREES: An Active Data Structure for Computer Music.* Stanford, Calif.: Stanford University, Dept. of Music, 1988. 5 p. (Department of Music Technical Report STAN-M-53)

6892. ———. "TTrees: An Active Data Structure for Computer Music." In *Proceedings of the 14th International Computer Music Conference, Cologne, September 20–25, 1988,* ed. Christoph Lischka and Johannes Fritsch. Cologne: Feedback-Studio-Verlag; San Francisco, Calif.: Dist. by Computer Music Association, 1988: 184–88. (Feedback Papers; 33)

6893. Duthen, Jacques, and Yves Potard. "Le Loup, an Object-oriented Extension of Le Lisp for an Integrated Computer Music Environment." In *Proceedings of the 1987 International Computer Music Conference: University of Illinois at Urbana-Champaign, Urbana, Illinois, USA, August 23–26, 1987,* comp. James Beauchamp. San Francisco, Calif.: Computer Music Association, 1987: 151–58.

6894. Dyer, Lounette M. "MUSE: An Integrated Software Environment for Computer Music Applications." In *Proceedings of the International Computer Music Conference 1986, Royal Conservatory, The Hague, Netherlands, October 20–24, 1986*, ed. Paul Berg. San Francisco, Calif.: Computer Music Association, 1986: 167–72.

6895. ———. "Position Paper for Music Representation Panel." In *Proceedings, 1989 International Computer Music Conference, November 2–5, the Ohio State University, Columbus, Ohio*. San Francisco, Calif.: Computer Music Association, 1989: 98–100.

6896. Ebcioğlu, Kemal. "An Efficient Logic Programming Language and Its Application to Music." In *Logic Programming: Proceedings of the Fourth International Conference*, ed. Jean-Louis Lassez. Cambridge, Mass.: MIT Press, 1987: 513–32.

6897. Eigenfeldt, Arne. "ConTour: A Real-Time MIDI System Based on Gestural Input." In *Proceedings, 1989 International Computer Music Conference, November 2–5, the Ohio State University, Columbus, Ohio*. San Francisco, Calif.: Computer Music Association, 1989: 101–4.

6898. Evans, Brian. "Enhancing Scientific Animations with Sonic Maps." In *Proceedings, 1989 International Computer Music Conference, November 2–5, the Ohio State University, Columbus, Ohio*. San Francisco, Calif.: Computer Music Association, 1989: 105–8.

A proposal for an integration of music and visual material.

6899. Free, John; Paul Vytas; and William Buxton. "What Ever Happened to SSSP?" In *Proceedings of the International Computer Music Conference 1986, Royal Conservatory, The Hague, Netherlands, October 20–24, 1986*, ed. Paul Berg. San Francisco, Calif.: Computer Music Association, 1986: 17–20.

6900. Gross, Robert W. *The IRCAM Soundfile System*. Paris: IRCAM, 1986.

6901. Hussey, Leigh Ann. "Music Notation in ASCII." *Electronic Musician* 3 (Nov. 1987): 76–78.

How to send music notation via modem using standard ASCII characters.

6902. Johnson, Jim. "Computing." *Music, Computers & Software* 3 (Nov. 1988): 18–21.

A tutorial on computer languages.

6903. Jones, Kevin. "Real-Time Stochastic Composition and Performance with AMPLE." In *Proceedings of the International Computer Music*

Conference 1986, Royal Conservatory, The Hague, Netherlands, October 20–24, 1986, ed. Paul Berg. San Francisco, Calif.: Computer Music Association, 1986: 309–11.

6904. Jordan, Chris. "Random Access to the Time Domain in the AMPLE Language." In *Proceedings of the International Computer Music Conference 1986, Royal Conservatory, The Hague, Netherlands, October 20–24, 1986*, ed. Paul Berg. San Francisco, Calif.: Computer Music Association, 1986: A-33–A-35.

6905. Laurson, Mikael, and Jacques Duthen. "Patchwork: A Graphic Language in PREFORM." In *Proceedings, 1989 International Computer Music Conference, November 2–5, the Ohio State University, Columbus, Ohio*. San Francisco, Calif.: Computer Music Association, 1989: 172–75.

6906. Mahin, Bruce P. "Programming Pascal." *Instrumentalist* 42 (May 1988): 56–60.

6907. ———. "Programming Pascal. Part II." *Instrumentalist* 42 (July 1988): 36–41.

6908. ———. "Programming Pascal. Part III." *Instrumentalist* 43 (Feb. 1989): 84–88.

6909. Misek, Steven M., and Dana C. Massie. "Multitasking Operating System Design for Electronic Music." In *The Proceedings of the AES 5th International Conference: Music and Digital Technology*, ed. John Strawn. New York, N.Y.: Audio Engineering Society, 1987: 37–41.

6910. Moore, F. Richard. *Introduction to Music Synthesis Using CMUSIC*. San Diego, Calif.: Computer Audio Research Laboratory, University of California, San Diego, 1983.

6911. Polansky, Larry; David Rosenboom; and Phil Burk. "HMSL: Overview (Version 3.1) and Notes on Intelligent Instrument Design." In *Proceedings of the 1987 International Computer Music Conference: University of Illinois at Urbana-Champaign, Urbana, Illinois, USA, August 23–26, 1987*, comp. James Beauchamp. San Francisco, Calif.: Computer Music Association, 1987: 220–27.

6912. Pope, Stephen T. "The Development of an Intelligent Composer's Assistant: Interactive Graphics Tools and Knowledge Representation for Music, or, Thoughts about Music Input Languages: Several Generations of MILs and Orchestra/Score Editors." In *Proceedings of the International Computer Music Conference 1986, Royal Conservatory, The Hague, Netherlands, October 20–24, 1986*, ed. Paul Berg. San Francisco, Calif.: Computer Music Association, 1986: 131–44.

6913. ———. "Machine Tongues XI: Object-oriented Software Design." *Computer Music Journal* 13,2 (Summer 1989): 9–22.

6914. ———. "A Smalltalk-80-based Music Toolkit." In *Proceedings of the 1987 International Computer Music Conference: University of Illinois at Urbana-Champaign, Urbana, Illinois, USA, August 23–26, 1987,* comp. James Beauchamp. San Francisco, Calif.: Computer Music Association, 1987: 166–73.
A discussion of HyperScore ToolKit.

6915. Reichbach, Jonathan. "SoundWorks: A Distributed System for Manipulating Digital Sounds." Masters thesis, Computer Science Dept., University of California, Santa Barbara, 1989.
Allows users to create and manipulate sounds using an object-oriented approach.

6916. Rodet, Xavier, and Pierre Cointe. "FORMES: Composition and Scheduling of Processes." *Computer Music Journal* 8,3 (Fall 1984): 32–50.
Previously **3499.**
French version: *FORMES: Composition et ordonnancement de processus.* Paris: IRCAM, 1985. 22 p. (Rapports IRCAM; 85/36)
Reprinted in *The Music Machine,* ed. Curtis Roads. Cambridge, Mass.: MIT Press, 1989: 405–23.

6917. Roos, Peter. "Techno: Csound—Getting Personal." *Ear* 13 (Sept. 1988): 9.
A short description of the software package, Csound.

6918. Scaletti, Carla. "The Kyma/Platypus Computer Music Workstation." *Computer Music Journal* 13,2 (Summer 1989): 23–38.

6919. Schmidt, Brian L. "A Natural Language System for Music." In *Proceedings of the International Computer Music Conference 1986, Royal Conservatory, The Hague, Netherlands, October 20–24, 1986,* ed. Paul Berg. San Francisco, Calif.: Computer Music Association, 1986: 119–25.

6920. ———. "A Natural Language System for Music." *Computer Music Journal* 11,2 (Summer 1987): 25–34.

6921. Serpette, Bernard. "Contextes, processus, objets, séquenceurs: FORMES." Thèse de 3ème cycle, LITP-Université Paris IV, 30 Oct. 1984.
LITP Research Report; no. 85-5.

6922. Steinbeck, Wolfram. "ANTOC: Ein neues Verfahren der Aufzeichung von Melodien durch den Computer." In *Bericht über den Internation-*

alen Musikwissenschaftlichen Kongress, Berlin, 1974, ed. Hellmut Kühn and Peter Nitsche. Kassel: Bärenreiter, 1980: 546–53.

A code (*Alpha-Numerischer-Ton-*Code) for the computer processing of melodies.

6923. Vercoe, Barry. *CSOUND: A Manual for the Audio Processing System and Supporting Programs.* Cambridge, Mass.: MIT Media Lab, 1986.

6924. Wallraff, Dean. *DMX-1000 Programming Manual.* Boston: Digital Music Systems, 1979.

PSYCHOLOGY AND PSYCHOACOUSTICS

6925. Ashley, Richard D. "Modeling Music Listening: General Considerations." *Contemporary Music Review* 4 (1989): 295–310.

6926. Balzano, Gerald J. "Command Performances, Performance Commands." *Contemporary Music Review* 4 (1989): 437–46.

A review of some major concerns in the study of music cognition.

6927. ———. "What Are Musical Pitch and Timbre?" *Music Perception* 3 (Spring 1986): 297–314.

6928. Baumann, Dorothea. "Veränderungen der Hörens im elektronischen Zeitalter." In *Die Musikerziehung in Zeitalter der Elektronik: 20. DACH-Tagung, Golling, Salzburg, April–Mai 1988: Tagungsbericht,* ed. Brigitte Peschl. Vienna: VWGÖ, 1989: 17–37.

6929. ———. "Veränderungen des Hörens im elektronischen Zeitalter." *Musikerziehung* 42 (Apr. 1989): 155–61.

6930. Bharucha, Jamshed J. "Music Cognition and Perceptual Facilitation: A Connectionist Framework." *Music Perception* 5 (Fall 1987): 1–30.

6931. ———, and Katherine L. Olney. "Tonal Cognition, Artificial Intelligence, and Neural Nets." *Contemporary Music Review* 4 (1989): 341–56.

6932. ———, and Peter M. Todd. "Modeling the Perception of Tonal Structures with Neural Nets." *Computer Music Journal* 13,4 (Winter 1989): 44–53.

6933. Camurri, Antonio; Goffredo Haus; and Renato Zaccaria. "Describing and Performing Musical Processes." In *Human Movement Understanding,* ed. P. Morasso and V. Tagliasco. New York, N.Y.: North-Holland Publ., 1986: 335–56. (Advances in Psychology; 33)

Also published as: "Describing and Performing Musical Processes by Means of Petri Nets." *Interface* 15 (1986): 1–23.

An appendix to the *Interface* publication, which includes an analysis of the first part of Fugue 23 from J. S. Bach's *Well Tempered Clavier,* book 1.

6934. Charbonneau, Gérard R. "Timbre and the Perceptual Effects of Three Types of Data Reduction." *Computer Music Journal* 5,2 (Summer 1981): 10–19.
Previously **2632.**
Reprinted in *The Music Machine,* ed. Curtis Roads. Cambridge, Mass.: MIT Press, 1989: 521–30.

6935. Chowning, John M., and Christopher Sheeline. *Auditory Distance Perception under Natural Sounding Conditions, Final Report.* Stanford, Calif.: Dept. of Music, Stanford University, 1982. (Department of Music Technical Report STAN-M-12)

6936. Chung, Joe. "An Agency for the Perception of Musical Beats." M.S. thesis, Massachusetts Institute of Technology, 1989.

6937. Clynes, Manfred. "What Can a Musician Learn about Music Performance from Newly Discovered Microstructure Principles (PM and PAS)." In *Action and Perception in Rhythm and Music: Papers Given at a Symposium in the Third International Conference on Event Perception and Action,* ed. Alf Gabrielsson. Stockholm, Sweden: Royal Swedish Academy of Music, 1987: 201–33.

6938. Cramer, Cheryl L. "Musical Paraphrase: A Computer-based Cognitive Model Derived from Stephen Foster Songs." Ph.D. diss., University of Pittsburgh, 1986. 216 p.

6939. Desain, Peter, and Henkjan Honing. "The Quantization of Musical Time: A Connectionist Approach." *Computer Music Journal* 13,3 (Fall 1989): 56–66.

6940. Deutsch, Diana. "Music Perception." *Musical Quarterly* 66 (Apr. 1980): 165–79.
Adaptation of a paper given at the ninety-seventh meeting of the Acoustical Society of America, Cambridge, Mass., June 1979.

6941. Dolson, Mark. "Machine Tongues XII: Neural Networks." *Computer Music Journal* 13,3 (Fall 1989): 28–40.

6942. Faivre, Irene A. "A Theory of Skill Development in the Absolute Judgment of Tones." Ph.D. diss., University of Colorado, Boulder, 1986. 184 p.

6943. Freed, Daniel J., and William L. Martens. "Deriving Psychophysical Relations for Timbre." In *Proceedings of the International Computer Music Conference 1986, Royal Conservatory, The Hague, Netherlands, October 20–24, 1986,* ed. Paul Berg. San Francisco, Calif.: Computer Music Association, 1986: 393–405.

6944. Freeman, Isabel A. "Rhythmic Beat Perception in a Down's Syndrome Population: A Computerized Measure of Beat Accuracy and Beat Interval Response." Ed.D. diss., University of North Carolina, Greensboro, 1986. 181 p.

6945. Friberg, Anders; Johan Sundberg; and Lars Frydén. "How to Terminate a Phrase. An Analysis-by-Synthesis Experiment on a Perceptual Aspect of Music Performance." In *Action and Perception in Rhythm and Music: Papers Given at a Symposium in the Third International Conference on Event Perception and Action,* ed. Alf Gabrielsson. Stockholm, Sweden: Royal Swedish Academy of Music, 1987: 49–55.

6946. Gabrielsson, Alf. "Once Again: The Theme from Mozart's Piano Sonata in A Major (K. 331)." In *Action and Perception in Rhythm and Music: Papers Given at a Symposium in the Third International Conference on Event Perception and Action,* ed. Alf Gabrielsson. Stockholm, Sweden: Royal Swedish Academy of Music, 1987: 81–103.

6947. Gjerdingen, Robert O. "Using Connectionist Models to Explore Complex Musical Patterns." *Computer Music Journal* 13,3 (Fall 1989): 67–75.

6948. Goldman, Sheryl A. "The Relationship of Acoustics to Musical Preference." M.M. diss., Duquesne University, 1985. 301 p.

6949. Gordon, John W. "The Perceptual Attack Time of Musical Tones." *Journal of the Acoustical Society of America* 82 (July 1987): 88–105.

6950. ——. *The Role of Psychoacoustics in Computer Music.* Stanford, Calif.: Stanford University, Dept. of Music, 1987. 20 p. (Department of Music Technical Report STAN-M-38)

6951. Gregory, Dianne, and Wendy L. Sims. "Music Preference Analysis with Computers." *Journal of Music Therapy* 24 (Winter 1987): 203–12.

6952. Grey, John M., and John W. Gordon. "Perceptual Effects of Spectral Modifications on Musical Timbres." *Journal of the Acoustical Society of America* 63 (May 1978): 1493–1500.

6953. Hair, Harriet I. "Microcomputer Tests of Aural and Visual Directional Patterns." *Psychology of Music* 10,2 (1982): 26–31.

6954. Hunter, Leslie L. "Computer-assisted Assessment of Melodic and Rhythmic Discrimination Skills." *Journal of Music Therapy* 26 (Summer 1989): 79–87.

Use of the software program, Toney Listens to Music, to assess mentally retarded children and adolescents.

6955.   Jones, David Evan. "Compositional Control of Phonetic/Nonphonetic Perception." *Perspectives of New Music* 25 (Winter 1987/Summer 1987): 138–55.

6956.   Kendall, Roger A. "The Role of Transients in Listener Categorization of Musical Instruments: An Investigation Using Digitally Recorded and Edited Musical Phrases." Ph.D. diss., University of Connecticut, 1984. 271 p.
Review by Gayla C. Turk in *Council for Research in Music Education Bulletin* n89 (Fall 1986): 64–68.

6957.   Laden, Bernice, and Douglas H. Keefe. "The Representation of Pitch in a Neural Net Model of Chord Classification." *Computer Music Journal* 13,4 (Winter 1989): 12–26.

6958.   Laske, Otto E. "Toward a Computational Theory of Musical Listening." In *Reason, Emotion, and Music,* ed. Leo Apostel; H. Sabbe; and F. Vandamme. Ghent: Communication & Cognition, 1986: 363–92.

6959.   Lischka, Christoph. "Connectionist Models of Musical Thinking." In *Proceedings of the 1987 International Computer Music Conference: University of Illinois at Urbana-Champaign, Urbana, Illinois, USA, August 23–26, 1987,* comp. James Beauchamp. San Francisco, Calif.: Computer Music Association, 1987: 190–96.

6960.   Lo, David Yee-On. "Techniques of Timbral Interpolation." In *Proceedings of the International Computer Music Conference 1986, Royal Conservatory, The Hague, Netherlands, October 20–24, 1986,* ed. Paul Berg. San Francisco, Calif.: Computer Music Association, 1986: 241–47.

6961.   ——. "Towards a Theory of Timbre." Ph.D. diss., Dept. of Hearing and Speech, Stanford University, 1987. 239 p.
Also issued as: Technical Report STAN-M-42. Stanford, Calif.: Center for Research in Music and Acoustics, Music Department, Stanford University, 1987.

6962.   Longuet-Higgins, H. Christopher. "Perception of Melodies." *Nature* 263 (1976): 646–53.
Previously **2669.**
Reprinted in H. Christopher Longuet-Higgins, *Mental Processes: Studies in Cognitive Science.* Cambridge, Mass.: MIT Press, 1987: 105–29.

6963.   ——. "The Perception of Music." *Interdisciplinary Science Reviews* 3 (June 1978): 148–56.
Previously **2670.**
Reprinted as "The Grammar of Music" in H. Christopher Longuet-Higgins, *Mental Processes: Studies in Cognitive Science.* Cambridge, Mass.: MIT Press, 1987: 130–49.

6964. ———. "The Perception of Music." *Proceedings of the Royal Society of London* Series B 205 (1979): 307–22.
Reprinted in H. Christopher Longuet-Higgins, *Mental Processes: Studies in Cognitive Science.* Cambridge, Mass.: MIT Press, 1987: 169–87.

6965. Loy, D. Gareth. "Preface to the Special Issue on Parallel Distributed Processing and Neural Networks." *Computer Music Journal* 13,3 (Fall 1989): 24–27.

6966. Martens, William L. "Principal Components Analysis and Resynthesis of Spectral Cues to Perceived Direction." In *Proceedings of the 1987 International Computer Music Conference: University of Illinois at Urbana-Champaign, Urbana, Illinois, USA, August 23–26, 1987,* comp. James Beauchamp. San Francisco, Calif.: Computer Music Association, 1987: 274–81.

6967. Mathews, Max V., and John R. Pierce. *The Acquisition of Musical Percepts with a New Scale.* Stanford, Calif.: Stanford University, Dept. of Music, 1987. 16 p. (Department of Music Technical Report STAN-M-40)

6968. McAdams, Stephen E. *L'Image auditive: une metaphore pour la recherche musicale et psychologique sur l'organisation auditive.* Paris: IRCAM, 1985. 26 p. (Rapports de recherche; no 37)
French version of item **2678.**

6969. ———. "Spectral Fusion and the Creation of Auditory Images." In *Music, Mind, and Brain,* ed. Manfred Clynes. New York, N.Y.: Plenum Press, 1982: 279–98.

6970. ———. "Spectral Fusion, Spectral Parsing and the Formation of Auditory Images." Ph.D. diss., Dept. of Hearing and Speech, Stanford University, 1984.
Also issued as: Technical Report STAN-M-22. Stanford, Calif.: Center for Research in Music and Acoustics, Music Department, Stanford University, 1984.

6971. McArthur, Victoria H. "An Application of Instructional Task Analysis and Biomechanical Motion Analysis to Elementary Cognitive and Psychomotor Piano Learning and Performance." Ph.D. diss., Florida State University, 1987. 672 p.

6972. Miller, Robert. "An Introduction to Multidimensional Scaling for the Study of Musical Perception." *Bulletin of the Council for Research in Music Education* n102 (Fall 1989): 60–73.

6973. Parncutt, Richard. *Harmony: A Psychoacoustical Approach.* Berlin; New York, N.Y.: Springer-Verlag, 1989. 206 p.
Uses the computer for psychacoustical experiments.

6974. Pierce, John R. "Residues and Summation Tones: What Do *We* Hear." In *Current Directions in Computer Music,* ed. Max V. Mathews and John R. Pierce. Cambridge, Mass.: MIT Press, 1989: 175–84.

6975. Polansky, Larry. "Morphological Metrics: An Introduction to a Theory of Formal Distances." In *Proceedings of the 1987 International Computer Music Conference: University of Illinois at Urbana-Champaign, Urbana, Illinois, USA, August 23–26, 1987,* comp. James Beauchamp. San Francisco, Calif.: Computer Music Association, 1987: 197–205.

6976. Riotte, André. "Models and Metaphors: Formalizations of Music." *Contemporary Music Review* 4 (1989): 373–80.

6977. Rosenthal, David. "A Model of the Process of Listening to Simple Rhythms." In *Proceedings of the 14th International Computer Music Conference, Cologne, September 20–25, 1988,* ed. Christoph Lischka and Johannes Fritsch. Cologne: Feedback-Studio-Verlag; San Francisco, Calif.: Dist. by Computer Music Association, 1988: 189–97. (Feedback Papers; 33)

6978. ———. "A Model of the Process of Listening to Simple Rhythms." *Music Perception* 6 (1989): 315–28.

6979. Sandell, Gregory J. "Perception of Concurrent Timbres and Implications for Orchestration." In *Proceedings, 1989 International Computer Music Conference, November 2–5, the Ohio State University, Columbus, Ohio.* San Francisco, Calif.: Computer Music Association, 1989: 268–72.

6980. Sano, Hajime, and B. Keith Jenkins. "A Neural Network Model for Pitch Perception." *Computer Music Journal* 13,3 (Fall 1989): 41–48.

6981. Sayegh, Samir I. "An Artificial Intelligence Approach to String Instrument Fingering." M.S.E.E. thesis, Purdue University, 1988.

6982. ———. "Fingering for String Instruments with the Optimum Path Paradigm." *Computer Music Journal* 13,3 (Fall 1989): 76–84.

6983. ———, and Manoel F. Tenorio. "Inverse Viterbi Algorithm as Learning Procedure and Application to Optimization in the String Instrument Fingering Problem." In *IEEE International Conference on Neural Networks: Sheraton Harbor Island, San Diego, California, July 24–27, 1988.* San Diego, Calif.: IEEE, 1988: II-491–II-497.

6984. Scarborough, Don L.; Ben O. Miller; and Jacqueline A. Jones. "Connectionist Models for Tonal Analysis." *Computer Music Journal* 13,3 (Fall 1989): 49–55.

6985. Schnebly-Black, Julia. "Effects of Two Music Labeling Systems on Cognitive Processing: A Comparison of MOD 12 and Diatonic Terminology." Ph.D. diss., University of Washington, 1984. 199 p.

6986. Shaffer, L. H., and N. P. Todd. "The Interpretive Component in Musical Performance." In *Action and Perception in Rhythm and Music: Papers Given at a Symposium in the Third International Conference on Event Perception and Action,* ed. Alf Gabrielsson. Stockholm, Sweden: Royal Swedish Academy of Music, 1987: 139–52.

6987. Sheeline, Christopher. "An Investigation of the Effects of Direct and Reverberant Signal Interactions on Auditory Distance Perception." Ph.D. diss., Dept. of Hearing and Speech, Stanford University, 1982. 81 p.
Also issued as: Technical Report STAN-M-13. Stanford, Calif.: Center for Research in Music and Acoustics, Music Department, Stanford University, 1982.

6988. Sirota, Warren. "Electronic Guitar: Psychoacoustics and Synthesized Sound." *Guitar Player* 23 (May 1989): 125.

6989. Slawson, Wayne. "Sound-Color Dynamics." *Perspectives of New Music* 25 (Winter 1987/Summer 1987): 156–81.

6990. Sundberg, Johan. *Research Aspects on Singing; Autoperception, Computer Synthesis, Emotion, Health, Voice Source.* Stockholm: Royal Swedish Academy of Music, 1981. 110 p. (Publications issued by the Royal Swedish Academy of Music; 33)
Review by Rolf Leanderson in *Svensk tidskrift för musikforskning* 67 (1985): 143–45.

6991. Tanguiane, Andranick S. "An Algorithm for Recognition of Chords." In *Proceedings of the 14th International Computer Music Conference, Cologne, September 20–25, 1988,* ed. Christoph Lischka and Johannes Fritsch. Cologne: Feedback-Studio-Verlag; San Francisco, Calif.: Dist. by Computer Music Association, 1988: 199–210. (Feedback Papers; 33)

6992. Tenney, James, and Larry Polansky. "Temporal Gestalt Perception in Music." *Journal of Music Theory* 24 (Fall 1980): 205–41.

6993. Todd, Neil. "A Computational Model of Rubato." *Contemporary Music Review* 3 (1989): 69–88.

6994. ——. "A Model of Expressive Timing in Tonal Music." *Music Perception* 3 (Fall 1985): 33–57.

6995. ——. "Towards a Cognitive Theory of Expression: The Performance and Perception of Rubato." *Contemporary Music Review* 4 (1989): 405–16.

6996. Vercoe, Barry, and David Cumming. "Connection Machine Tracking of Polyphonic Audio." In *Proceedings of the 14th International Computer Music Conference, Cologne, September 20–25, 1988,* ed. Christoph Lischka, and Johannes Fritsch. Cologne: Feedback-Studio-Verlag; San Francisco, Calif.: Dist. by Computer Music Association, 1988: 211–18. (Feedback Papers; 33)

6997. Vos, Piet G., and Stephen Handel. "Playing Triplets: Fact and Preferences." In *Action and Perception in Rhythm and Music: Papers Given at a Symposium in the Third International Conference on Event Perception and Action,* ed. Alf Gabrielsson. Stockholm, Sweden: Royal Swedish Academy of Music, 1987: 35–47.

6998. Wilde, Martin D.; William L. Martens; and James M. Hillenbrand. "Externalization Mediates Changes in the Perceived Roughness of Sound Signals with Jittered Fundamental Frequency." In *Proceedings of the International Computer Music Conference 1986, Royal Conservatory, The Hague, Netherlands, October 20–24, 1986,* ed. Paul Berg. San Francisco, Calif.: Computer Music Association, 1986: 219–25.

REFERENCE, RESEARCH, AND MUSIC LIBRARY APPLICATIONS

6999. Aigner, Thomas, and Andreas Aigner. "Musikerbriefe im Computer." *Österreichische Musikzeitschrift* 41 (1986): 641–45.

Forty thousand letters by musicians in the Wiener Stadt- und Landesbibliothek have been converted to machine-readable form.

7000. Aikin, Jim. "Electronic Music Glossary. Part 1." *Keyboard* 13 (Feb. 1987): 77–80.

A–M.

7001. ———. "Electronic Music Glossary. Part 2." *Keyboard* 13 (Mar. 1987): 93–95.

N–Z.

7002. Alphonce, Bo H. "Computer Applications in Music Research: A Retrospective." *Computers in Music Research* 1 (Fall 1989): 1–74.

7003. Anderton, Craig. *The Electronic Musician's Dictionary.* New York, N.Y.: Amsco Publications, 1988. 119 p.
Review by Tom Mulhern in *Guitar Player* 22 (Nov. 1988): 155.
Review by David B. Doty in *Electronic Musician* 5 (Apr. 1989): 100–102.
Review by Ann Basart in *Cum Notis Variorum* n132 (May 1989): 22.

7004. Basart, Ann P. "Finding Subjects in GLADIS." *Cum Notis Variorum* n117 (Nov. 1987): 7–9.

7005. ———. "A Quick Guide to GLADIS, the Online UCB Library Catalog." *Cum Notis Variorum* n117 (June 1987): 7.

7006. ———. "Using the GLADIS and MELVYL Online Catalogs." *Cum Notis Variorum* n124 (July 1988): 9–10.

7007. Becker, Glenn. "Micro Music Manager Catalogs Classical Record Collections." *PC Magazine* 8 (Mar. 28, 1989): 412.
Review of Micro Music Manager, Opus 2 for the IBM PC.

7008. Bernardini, Nicola. "Subject Index of *Computer Music Journal,* Volumes 1–9, 1977–1985." *Computer Music Journal* 10,2 (Summer 1986): 51–55.

7009. "Bibliographie der Publikationen zu Elektronischer und Computer-Musik." *Österreichische Musikzeitschrift* 39 (1984): 467–70.

7010. Bower, Susan. "Music in the MELVYL Catalog." *Cum Notis Variorum* n127 (Nov. 1988): 15–18.

7011. Bowles, Garrett H. "The Future of Music Databases." *Fontes Musicae Artis* 34 (1987): 61–66.
Summaries in French and German.

7012. Braun, William. "Find It Fast with a Music Library Data Base." *Music Educators Journal* 73 (Mar. 1987): 52–54.

7013. Campbell, Alan Gary. "Sources." *Electronic Musician* 4 (Feb. 1988): 107–11, 138.
A bibliography for musicians beginning in the field of computer music.

7014. Coakley, W. D. *The Electronic Music Dictionary.* Lantana, Fla.: W.D. Coakley, 1988. 92 p.

7015. Condat, Jean-Bernard. "DIALOG: l'information musicologique immédiate." Mémoire de D.e.a., Université de Lyon 2, Dépt. de Musicologie, 1987. 83 leaves

7016. Coral, Lenore; Ivy Anderson; Keiko Cho; Jeff Rehbach; and Gail Sonneman. "Automation Requirements for Music Information." *Notes* 43 (Sept. 1986): 14–18.

7017. Davis, Deta S. *Computer Applications in Music: A Bibliography.* Madison, Wis.: A-R Editions, 1988. 537 p.
Reviews by Ann Basart in *Cum Notis Variorum* n126 (Oct. 1988): 17–18; *Fontes Artis Musicae* 36 (1989): 65–66.
Review by W. J. Waters in *Choice* (Feb. 1989).
Review in *Academic Library Book Review* 4 (Feb. 1989): 5–6.
Review by W. Holden in *Computer Music Journal* 13,1 (Spring 1989): 60.
Review by William Alves in *Journal SEAMUS* 4 (Apr. 1989): 10–11.
Review by Robert Moog in *Journal of the Audio Engineering Society* 37 (July/Aug. 1989): 645.
Review by Bo Alphonce in *Computers in Music Research* 1 (Fall 1989): 133–59. Includes a chronological index.

7018.   Dingley, Bob. "Choral Music Library Computer Filer for IBM & Compatible PC Version." *Choral Journal* 27 (May 1987): 33–38.

7019.   Drone, Jeanette M. "HyperBach: A Portable, Hypermedia Music Reference System." *OCLC Newsletter* 173 (May–June 1988): 11–12.

7020.   Duggan, Mary Kay. "Teaching Online Reference for Music Librarians." *Fontes Artis Musicae* 34 (1987): 44–53.
Summaries in French and German.

7021.   Elliott, Patricia. "The Beethoven Bibliography Project." *Beethoven Newsletter* 2 (Winter 1987): 56–57.

The Center for Beethoven Studies together with the Research Libraries Group is developing a special database for a Beethoven bibliography on RLIN.

7022.   Enders, Bernd. *Lexikon Musik-Elektronik*. Munich: W. Goldmann; Mainz: B. Schott, 1985. 281 p.
Review by Rainer Wehinger in *Musik und Bildung* 18 (Juli–Aug. 1986): 723.

7023.   ——. *Lexikon Musikelektronik*. New ed. Leipzig: Deutscher Verlag für Musik, 1988. 283 p.
Review by André Ruschkowski in *Musik und Gesellschaft* 38 (Nov. 1988): 607–8.

7024.   Feldstein, Sandy. *Roland Drum Machine Rhythm Dictionary*. Sherman Oaks, Calif.: Alfred Pub., 1985. 120 p.
Review by Rich Holly in *Percussive Notes* 24 (Oct. 1985): 76–77.

7025.   ——. *Roland Drum Machine Rhythm Dictionary*. Completely rev. Van Nuys, Calif.: Alfred Pub., 1987. 103 p.

7026.   "Focus on Electronics: Basic Electronic Terminology." *Modern Drummer* 13 (Feb. 1989): 34–35.
A glossary.

7027.   Garland, Catherine. "PREMARC: Retrospective Conversion at the Library of Congress." *Fontes Artis Musicae* 34 (1987): 132–38.
Summaries in French and German.

7028.   Gies, Stefan. "Glossar-Computer." *Musik und Bildung* 21 (Juni 1989): 339–40.

7029.   "Glossary of Electronic Music Terms." *Compute!* 9 (May 1987): 22–26.

7030.   Gooch, Bryan N. S. "Catalogues and Computers, Or, Bibliography and the Best." *Fontes Artis Musicae* 31 (1984): 38–41.

7031. Heck, Thomas F. "The Relevance of the 'Arts & Humanities' Data Base to Musicological Research." *Fontes Artis Musicae* 28 (1981): 81–87.

7032. Herman, David. "The Computer and the Church Musician IV: A Choral Library." *American Organist* 19 (Feb. 1985): 59–60.

7033. Horn, Marianne. "Computer-based Music Information in Danish Libraries." *Fontes Artis Musicae* 35 (1988): 62–64.
        Summary in German.

7034. Keller, Michael A., and Carol A. Lawrence. "Music Literature Indexes in Review." *Notes* 34 (Mar. 1980): 575–600.
        Review of RILM Abstracts (on-line), and the Arts and Humanities Citation, Music Therapy, Music Psychology, and Recording Industry Indexes.

7035. Kozinn, Allan. "Setting up a Super Catalog." *High Fidelity/Musical America* 34 (Feb. 1984): 41–45.
        The author describes how he organized his collection of seven thousand recordings using dBASEII.

7036. Krueger, Wolfgang. "Online-Bibliographieren in der zukünftigen musikbibliotekarischen Ausbildung in Deutschland." *Fontes Artis Musicae* 34 (1987): 53–61.
        Summaries in English and French.

7037. Lehman, Robert A. "Preparation and Management of a Descriptive Inventory for a Collection of Flutes." *Journal of the American Musical Instrument Society* 12 (1986): 137–48.

7038. Lister, Craig. *The Musical Microcomputer: A Resource Guide.* New York, N.Y.: Garland Pub., 1988. 172 p.

7039. Masters, Ian G. "Hit List: When You Never Get Rid of a Record, Knowing What You Have and Being Able to Find It Aren't Easy." *Stereo Review* 53 (Jan. 1988): 89–92.

7040. McCullaugh, Jim. "Film/TV Info Service into Music Coverage." *Billboard* 98 (Mar. 15, 1986): 57.
        Describes a computer-based information service on music videos.

7041. Morris, Robert. "Jazz Computer." *Mississippi Rag* 14 (Dec. 1986): 8.
        The author describes his use of an IBM clone to catalog his record collection.

7042. Olowacz, Paul V. "For Record Collectors: How to Keep Track of Your Stacks of Wax." *PC Magazine* 7 (Sept. 13, 1988): 444.
        Describes For Record Collectors, a database system for cataloging sound recordings; for the IBM PC.

7043.   Plesske, Hans-Martin. "Einige Bemerkungen zum EDV-Projekt: Bibliographieherstellung der Deutschen Bücherei." *Fontes Artis Musicae* 29 (Jan.–Juni 1982): 51–54.
Summaries in English and French.
The Deutsche Bücherei adds music to their computer processing of data.

7044.   Redfern, Brian. "Dinosaurs to Crush Flies: Computer Catalogues, Classification, and Other Barriers to Library Use." *Brio* 21 (Spring/Summer 1984): 4–8.

7045.   Rona, Jeff. "Soft-Speak Computer Terms." *Keyboard* 14 (Apr. 1988): 130.
A glossary of computer terms.

7046.   Rubenstein, William B. "Data Management of Musical Information." Ph.D. diss., University of California, Berkeley, 1987. 230 p.

7047.   Schaffrath, Helmut. "Datenbanksystem zur Dokumentations von Musik auf Tonträgern." In *Dokumentationsprobleme heutiger Volksmusikforschung: Protokoll der Arbeitstagung der Kommission für Lied-, Tanz- und Musikforschung in der Deutschen Gesellschaft für Volkskunde e.V. 6.–9. September 1984*, ed. Jürgen Dittmar. Bern: P. Lang, 1987: 183–99. (Studien zur Volksliedforschung; Bd. 2)

7048.   ———. "Der Umgang mit Information über Musik: Am Beispiel einer Datenbank ethnomusikologischer Schallplatten der Universität Essen." *Musikpädagogische Forschung* 6 (1985): 253–63.

7049.   Schultz, Lois. "Designing an Expert System to Assign Dewey Classification Numbers to Scores." In *National Online Meeting Proceedings—1989, New York, May 9–11, 1989*, comp. Carol Nixon and Lauree Padgett. Medford, N.J.: Learned Information, 1989: 393–97.

7050.   Scott, John C. "A Computer-based Bibliography of Selected Solo Clarinet Teaching Repertory." D.Mus. diss., Indiana University, 1981. 249 p.

7051.   Skerritt, Doug. "Choral Library Computer Filer." *Choral Journal* 27 (Sept. 1986): 21–27.
For Commodore and Apple computers.

7052.   Skinner, Robert. "Microcomputers in the Music Library." *Notes* 45 (Sept. 1988): 7–14.

7053.   Smiraglia, Richard R., and A. Ralph Papakhian. "Music in the OCLC Online Union Catalog: A Review." *Notes* 38 (Dec. 1981): 257–74.

7054.   "Some Jargon Revealed." *MacWeek* 2 (Aug. 16, 1988): 41.

7055. Stoessel, Klaus. "Computereinsatz in der Musikkatalogisierung im Deutschen Rundfunkarchiv." *Fontes Artis Musicae* 27 (July–Dec. 1980): 178–83.
Summaries in English and French.
The use of computer to catalog music in the Deutsches Rundfunkarchiv.

7056. Wadhams, Wayne. *Dictionary of Music Production and Engineering Terminology.* New York, N.Y.: Schirmer; London: Collier Mac-Millan, 1988. 257 p.
Review by Ann Basart in *Cum Notis Variorum* n121 (Apr. 1988): 17–18.

7057. Warrick, James. "Computerize Your Music Library." *Electronic Music Educator* 1 (Sept. 1988): 7–10.

7058. Waters, William J. *Music and the Personal Computer: An Annotated Bibliography.* New York, N.Y.: Greenwood Press, 1989. 175 p. (Music reference collection; no. 22)

7059. White, J. Perry. "The Church Musician in the Computer Age." *Journal of Church Music* 26 (Jan. 1984): 18–20.
Use of the computer to keep and maintain files.

7060. Zakrzewska-Nikiporczyk, Barbara. "Z Problemów Dokumentacji Muzycznej." [Some Problems of Music Documentation] *Przegląd Biblioteczny* 48 (1980): 57–69.
In Polish; includes summary in English.

SOUND GENERATION FOR MUSIC — HARDWARE

7061. Aaron, Brad. "Forat Electronics MSM 2000." *Electronic Musician* 3 (Dec. 1987): 81–82.
Review of the MSM 2000 Modular System Memory; for the Yamaha DX7.

7062. Aikin, Jim. "How to Buy a Synthesizer." *Guitar Player* 20 (June 1986): 63–69.

7063. ———. "Keyboard Report: Akai S1000, Rack-mount Sampler." *Keyboard* 14 (Dec. 1988): 126–32.

7064. ———. "Keyboard Report: Alesis MMT-8, MIDI Sequencer." *Keyboard* 14 (Apr. 1988): 133–35.

7065. ———. "Keyboard Report: ART DR1 Digital Reverb." *Keyboard* 12 (Sept. 1986): 145.

7066. ———. "Keyboard Report: Casio CZ-1, AZ-1, and SK-1." *Keyboard* 12 (Oct. 1986): 118–25.

7067. ———. "Keyboard Report: Casio CZ-5000 Synthesizer." *Keyboard* 11 (Sept. 1985): 80–81.

7068. ———. "Keyboard Report: Casio FZ-1, Sampling Synthesizer." *Keyboard* 13 (Sept. 1987): 136–42, 155.

7069. ———. "Keyboard Report: Casio VZ-1 Synthesizer." *Keyboard* 14 (Oct. 1988): 149–55.

7070. ———. "Keyboard Report: Dynacord ADS, 16-bit Stereo Sampler." *Keyboard* 15 (Oct. 1989): 136–38.

7071. ———. "Keyboard Report: E-mu Emax II, 16-bit Sampler." *Keyboard* 15 (Dec. 1989): 148–52.

7072. ———. "Keyboard Report: E-mu Proteus, Rack-mount Sample Playback Synthesizer." *Keyboard* 15 (Aug. 1989): 116–18.

7073. ——. "Keyboard Report: E-mu SP-12 Sampling Drum Machine." *Keyboard* 12 (Jan. 1986): 121–24.

7074. ——. "Keyboard Report: Ensoniq EPS Sampling Keyboard." *Keyboard* 14 (Mar. 1988): 132–34.

7075. ——. "Keyboard Report: Ensoniq ESQ-1 Synthesizer." *Keyboard* 12 (Sept. 1986): 134–35.

7076. ——. "Keyboard Report: Ensoniq SQ-80 Synthesizer/Sequencer." *Keyboard* 14 (Feb. 1988): 149–50.

7077. ——. "Keyboard Report: Feel Factory, MIDI Rhythm Processor." *Keyboard* 15 (July 1989): 134–38.

Programmable MIDI timing processor.

7078. ——. "Keyboard Report: Frontal Lobe, Sequencer Expander & Disk Drive for the Korg M1." *Keyboard* 15 (Aug. 1989): 128–29.

7079. ——. "Keyboard Report: Home Keyboards in the Age of MIDI." *Keyboard* 12 (June 1986): 142–49.

Review of Technics SX-K450, Yamaha PSR-70, and Casio CT-6500.

7080. ——. "Keyboard Report: Kawai K3 Synthesizer." *Keyboard* 12 (Sept. 1986): 132–33.

7081. ——. "Keyboard Report: Korg DRV-2000, Digital Effects Processor." *Keyboard* 13 (Aug. 1987): 132, 147.

7082. ——. "Keyboard Report: Korg M1, Sample-playing Synthesizer." *Keyboard* 14 (Aug. 1988): 132–41, 161–63.

7083. ——. "Keyboard Report: Lexicon LXP-1, Preset/Programmable Audio Processor." *Keyboard* 14 (Sept. 1988): 132–33.

Digital reverb and audio effects processor.

7084. ——. "Keyboard Report: Lexicon LXP-5, Effects Processor." *Keyboard* 15 (Nov. 1989): 140–42.

Stereo multi-effects processor.

7085. ——. "Keyboard Report: Marion Systems Akai S900, 16-bit Upgrade Board." *Keyboard* 15 (Apr. 1989): 114–15, 125.

Upgrade board for the Akai S900 or S950 sampler.

7086. ——. "Keyboard Report: Mentor, MIDI Event Processor." *Keyboard* 14 (June 1988): 146–49.

7087. ——. "Keyboard Report: MIDI DJ, Hardware Sequencer." *Keyboard* 14 (Jan. 1988): 136, 150.

7088. ———. "Keyboard Report: MIDI Step Pedalboard." *Keyboard* 13 (Aug. 1987): 118–20.

7089. ———. "Keyboard Report: Midiverb II & Microverb, Digital Reverbs from Alesis." *Keyboard* 13 (Aug. 1987): 134, 147.

7090. ———. "Keyboard Report: Oberheim Matrix-12 Synthesizer." *Keyboard* 11 (July 1985): 88.

7091. ———. "Keyboard Report: Oberheim Systemizer, Navigator & Cyclone, MIDI Data Processors." *Keyboard* 15 (May 1989): 128–34.

7092. ———. "Keyboard Report: Prophet VS Analog/Digital Synthesizer." *Keyboard* 12 (Aug. 1986): 126–28.

7093. ———. "Keyboard Report: Roland R-8, Drum Machine." *Keyboard* 15 (Apr. 1989): 120–22.

7094. ———. "Keyboard Report: Roland U-110, Rack-mount Sample Player." *Keyboard* 15 (June 1989): 138–41.

7095. ———. "Keyboard Report: Sequential Multi-Trak Synthesizer/Sequencer & Tom Drum Machines." *Keyboard* 11 (Aug. 1985): 76–78.

7096. ———. "Keyboard Report: Studio 440, Sequential Sampler/Sequencer/ Drum Machine." *Keyboard* 13 (Apr. 1987): 122–26, 138.

7097. ———. "Keyboard Report: Sycologic M16 MIDI Matrix Switcher." *Keyboard* 12 (Aug. 1986): 130.

7098. ———. "Keyboard Report: TC 2290, Delay Line/Sampler/Effects Processor from T.C. Electronic." *Keyboard* 13 (July 1987): 160–64.

7099. ———. "Keyboard Report: TX81Z, Yamaha Rack Synth." *Keyboard* 13 (Apr. 1987): 132–36.

7100. ———. "Keyboard Report: Updates—Steinberg Pro-24 2.1, Emax HD & TX802." *Keyboard* 13 (Nov. 1987): 148–51.
Review of the Yamaha TX802, E-mu Emax HD, and Steinberg Pro-24.

7101. ———. "Keyboard Report: Yamaha MDF1, MIDI Data Disk Drive." *Keyboard* 13 (June 1987): 143.

7102. ———. "Keyboard Report: Yamaha REV7 & Roland SRV-2000 Digital Reverbs & Lexicon PCM 70 Digital Effects Processor." *Keyboard* 12 (Feb. 1986): 122–27, 149.

7103. ———. "Mechanical, Analog, Digital: Sequencer History in a Nutshell." *Keyboard* 13 (June 1987): 46–47.

7104. ———. "Samplers: The Real Low-down Nitty-gritty (and We Do Mean Gritty)." *Keyboard* 15 (Mar. 1989): 22–23.

7105. ———. "Sequencer Basics: A Guide for the Mystified." *Keyboard* 13 (June 1987): 36–45.

7106. ———. "The Tangled Thread: Sampler Features & Terminology Explained." *Keyboard* 15 (Mar. 1989): 29–48.
Includes charts.

7107. ———, and Mark Vail. "Keyboard Report: Ensoniq VFX, Synthesizer." *Keyboard* 15 (Aug. 1989): 120–25.

7108. "Akai Unveils First Roger Linn Product." *Music Trades* 135 (June 1987): 122–23.
A drum sampler/sequencer.

7109. "Akai Unveils S900 Professional Digital Sampler." *Music Trades* 134 (Nov. 1986): 72–74.

7110. "Akai Unveils X-7000 Sampler." *Music Trades* 135 (Sept. 1987): 96–97.

7111. "Akai Wows Industry with New Sampling Keyboards." *Music Trades* 134 (Aug. 1986): 80–81.
A summary of the Akai X-7000 six-voice digital sampling keyboard.

7112. Allouis, Jean-François. "Syter et le temps réel." *Revue musicale* n394–97 (1986): 64–71.
Excerpts from an interview with François Delalande.

7113. Amaral, John. "New: The Resynator." *Musician, Player & Listener* n27 (Sept.–Oct. 1980): 102, 106.
Review of the Resynator, an analog/digital hybrid synthesizer that can be directly controlled by a signal source, e.g., guitar, microphone, amplified instrument, etc.

7114. Amato, Mia. "NED Synclavier Seminar Offers Sound Solutions." *Billboard* 98 (July 12, 1986): 60–61.

7115. ———. "Synthesizer's Language, Storage Eyed." *Billboard* 98 (July 12, 1986): 60.
Describes problems with SCRIPT, its language software, and memory storage.

7116. "Anatek Introduces Pocket Products MIDI Accessories." *Music Trades* 137 (Feb. 1989): 42–44.
Pocket Merge, Pocket Pedal, Pocket Filter, and Pocket Sequencer.

7117. Anderson, A. Donald. "A Computer for Tin Pan Alley: The Synclavier Puts a Small Company into the Big Leagues of the Music Industry." *New York Times* 137 (July 3, 1988): sec. 3, 11.

7118. Anderton, Craig. "25 Hot MIDI Products for under $500." *Electronic Musician* 4 (Jan. 1988): 52–57.

7119. ———. "Analysis: DAW: Wave of the Future?" *Electronic Musician* 4 (Jan. 1988): 20, 26–28.
A discussion of the digital audio workstation.

7120. ———. "Applications: Fix It in the Mix—with a Sampling Keyboard." *Electronic Musician* 2 (Dec. 1986): 36–37.

7121. ———. "Applications: Guitar-to-MIDI for Almost Cheap: The IVL Pitchrider 4000." *Electronic Musician* 2 (May 1986): 28–29.

7122. ———. "Applications: The Well-Tempered DDL." *Electronic Musician* 2 (Feb. 1986): 24–25.

7123. ———. "Applications: Using the Alesis HR-16 as an Expander Module." *Electronic Musician* 4 (Nov. 1988): 70–75.

7124. ———. "Applications: Using Your Sequencer as a MIDI System Analyzer." *Electronic Musician* 4 (Dec. 1988): 28–34.

7125. ———. "The Art of Freeze-dried Sound: Surveying Digital Sampling Devices." *Record* 3 (June 1984): 52.

7126. ———. "Build a Vocoder: Versatile Signal Processing for Keyboards and Drum Machines." *Keyboard* 11 (May 1985): 18–23.

7127. ———. *The Complete Guide to the Alesis HR-16 and MMT-8.* New York, N.Y.: Amsco Publications, 1989: 181 p.

7128. ———. "Create Your Own Music. Part I, Soul of a Drum Machine." *Electronic Musician* 4 (Oct. 1988): 34–46.

7129. ———. "Ensoniq's 2nd Generation Debuts: New Instruments Combine Features, Cost-effectiveness." *Electronic Musician* 4 (Jan. 1988): 28–30.
Brief review of the Ensoniq Performance Sampler (EPA) and SQ-80 cross wave synthesizer.

7130. ———. "First Take: Capsule Comments: Anatek Pocket MIDI Accessories." *Electronic Musician* 5 (May 1989): 88–89.

7131. ———. "First Take: Capsule Comments: Boss ME-5 Guitar Multiple Effects." *Electronic Musician* 5 (Mar. 1989): 72–74.
Review of the onstage signal processing box.

7132. ——. "Get the Most Out of Your Vocoder: 10 Hookups that Bring Keyboards to Life." *Keyboard* 11 (May 1985): 19.
Includes soundsheet.

7133. ——. "Guitars: Electronic Guitarist: State of the Synth." *Electronic Musician* 2 (Dec. 1986): 64–65.

7134. ——. "MIDI Goes Modular: Reshaping the Nature of Musical Instruments." *Record* 4 (Mar. 1985): 55.
Why musical instruments are being broken down into modular components.

7135. ——. "Music Workstations: Can One Instrument Do It All?" *Electronic Musician* 4 (Nov. 1988): 50–61.

7136. ——. "Review: Akai ME10D MIDI Delay." *Electronic Musician* 2 (Feb. 1986): 57–58.
Special effects data processor.

7137. ——. "Review: Alesis MIDIVERB and MIDIFEX." *Electronic Musician* 2 (Nov. 1986): 92–94.

7138. ——. "Review: GK-1 and GM-70 Guitar-to-MIDI System." *Electronic Musician* 3 (June 1987): 91–95.
Review of the Roland GK-1 synthesizer driver and the GM-1 guitar-to-MIDI converter.

7139. ——. "Review: Roland MKS-70." *Electronic Musician* 3 (Nov. 1987): 101–04.
Review of the Roland MKS-70, 2U rack-mount, MIDI capable, analog/digital hybrid synthesizer.

7140. ——. "Review: Suzuki XG-lm MIDI Guitar Controller." *Electronic Musician* 4 (Jan. 1988): 88–91.

7141. ——. "Review: Yamaha TX802 FM Tone Generator." *Electronic Musician* 3 (Dec. 1987): 94–99.

7142. ——. "Reviews: Beetle Quantar MIDI Guitar." *Electronic Musician* 4 (Oct. 1988): 98–101.

7143. ——. "Reviews: Dynacord ADS Sampler." *Electronic Musician* 5 (Nov. 1989): 100–107.

7144. ——. "Reviews: Lexicon MRC MIDI Remote Controller." *Electronic Musician* 5 (July 1989): 134–37.

7145. ——. "Reviews: Marion Systems MS-9C 16-bit Retrofit for the Akai S900." *Electronic Musician* 5 (Jan. 1989): 106–7.

7146.   ———. "Reviews: Roland W-30 Workstation." *Electronic Musician* 5 (Sept. 1989): 92–97.

Sampling-based workstation.

7147.   ———. "Roland GP-8 Guitar Effects Processor." *Electronic Musician* 4 (Feb. 1988): 116–17.

Review.

7148.   ———. "What's in a Sequencer?" *Electronic Musician* 4 (Aug. 1988): 18–33.

A guide for choosing the right sequencer.

7149.   ———. "Yamaha's G10 MIDI Guitar: Does It Really Work?" *Electronic Musician* 4 (Dec. 1988): 50–56.

7150.   Andreas, Michael. "Akai EWI and EVI Wind Controllers and EWV–2000 Sound Module." *Music Technology* 2 (Dec. 1987): 63–67.

Review.

7151.   ———. "Yamaha WX7: MIDI Wind Controller." *Music Technology* 2 (Mar. 1988): 50–53.

Review.

7152.   Andrews, John; Jim Burgess; Paul Atkinson; and Russ Walker. "Focus on Pro Keyboards: The Hottest Gear from the Hottest Companies. Part I." *Canadian Musician* 8 (Feb. 1986): 52–55.

A look at products from Roland, Yamaha, Emulator, Kurzweil, Casio, Akai, and Sequential/Prophet.

7153.   Anger, Darol. "Alternate Controllers: Fiddlin' Around with MIDI." *Keyboard* 15 (May 1989): 94–95.

MIDI control with the VC-225 violin controller from Zeta Music Systems.

7154.   Appleton, Jon H. *21st-Century Musical Instruments: Hardware and Software.* Brooklyn, N.Y.: Institute for Studies in American Music, Conservatory of Music, Brooklyn College, 1989. 30 p. (I.S.A.M. Monographs; no. 29)

7155.   Armington, Nick, and Lars Lofas. "The Power of Wind: Pioneers Nyle Steiner and Sal Gallina." *Music Technology* 2 (Dec. 1987): 75–78.

A discussion of the development and direction of wind controllers.

7156.   Aronoff, Kenny. "Rock Perspectives: Combining Your Drumkit with a Drum Machine." *Modern Drummer* 13 (July 1989): 44–45.

7157.   Austin, Kirk. "Mobile MIDI for Stage and Video." *Electronic Musician* 2 (Mar. 1986): 22–24.

Hand-held keyboard controllers.

7158. Baird, Jock. "Casio's About-Phase: The New CZ-5000 Will Turn Some Professional Heads." *Musician* n84 (Oct. 1985): 98.
Review of the Casio CZ-5000 keyboard.

7159. ——. "Developments: New Adventures in Sampling." *Musician* n106 (Aug. 1987): 52.
Review of the E-mu Emulator III, a 16-bit sampler.

7160. ——. "Developments: New Sampling Assaults Launched." *Musician* n110 (Dec. 1987): 52–54.
Review of the Prophet 3000 and the Yamaha TX16W samplers.

7161. ——. "Developments: Sequential's Sequencer/Sampling Gamble." *Musician* n97 (Nov. 1986): 64–66.
Review of Sequential's Studio 440 sampler.

7162. ——. "Notes from the MIDI Corner: Hands on the Casio VZ-1 Synth and the Kawai Q-80 Sequencer." *Musician* n130 (Aug. 1989): 94, 111.

7163. ——. "School Daze: A Second Look at the Ensoniq EPS." *Musician* n124 (Feb. 1989): 42–44.
Brief review.

7164. Barbaud, Pierre; Frank Brown; and R. Lengagne. "The Biniou Machine." Abstract in *Proceedings of the International Computer Music Conference 1986, Royal Conservatory, The Hague, Netherlands, October 20–24, 1986,* ed. Paul Berg. San Francisco, Calif.: Computer Music Association, 1986: 61.

7165. Barbour, Eric. "Mods: Sequential DrumTraks Mods." *Electronic Musician* 2 (Sept. 1986): 58–60.

7166. Barrière, Jean-Baptiste; Adrian Freed; Pierre-François Baisnée; and Marie-Dominique Baudot. "A Digital Signal Multiprocessor and Its Musical Application." In *Proceedings, 1989 International Computer Music Conference, November 2–5, the Ohio State University, Columbus, Ohio.* San Francisco, Calif.: Computer Music Association, 1989: 17–20.

7167. Bateman, Jeff. "Fairlight." *Music Scene* n351 (Sept.–Oct. 1986): 15–17.
Comments by some users of the Fairlight.

7168. Bates, John. *The Synthesizer.* Oxford: Oxford University Press, Music Dept., 1988. 48 p.
An elementary approach to the synthesizer, its history, and current digital technology.

7169. Bell, Bryan. "Santana's MIDI Guitar Composition System." *Electronic Musician* 2 (Apr. 1986): 32–35.

7170.   Bergren, Peter. "The Fairlight Computer Music Instrument, Series III: A Primer." *Music Technology* 2 (Nov. 1987): 26–31.

7171.   ———. "The Fairlight Computer Music Instrument, Series III: The Primer Continued." *Music Technology* 2 (Dec. 1987): 34–39.
         A look at software, applications, and additions to the system.

7172.   Betteridge, James. "Control Zone at Frankfurt: Smooth Operator." *Melody Maker* 61 (Feb. 15, 1986): XV sup.
         Review of the Yamaha VS-100 sampler.

7173.   ———. "Control Zone News: Splendiferous Synth." *Melody Maker* 61 (May 17, 1986): 37.
         Review of the Roland JX-10 synthesizer.

7174.   Betts, James. "Review: The Pitchrider 7000 Mark II Guitar-to-MIDI Interface." *Electronic Musician* 3 (Oct. 1987): 92–94.

7175.   Black, Matt. "Control Zone: Keyboards: A Question of Control." *Melody Maker* 60 (Oct. 26, 1985): 42–43.
         Concerns MIDI controllers: Akai ME20A, ME10D, and ME15F.

7176.   "Blackbox Thriller." *Melody Maker* 60 (July 20, 1985): 43.
         Describes the OSC Advanced Sound Generator.

7177.   Boie, Bob; Max V. Mathews; and W. Andrew Schloss. "The Radio Drum as a Synthesizer Controller." In *Proceedings, 1989 International Computer Music Conference, November 2–5, the Ohio State University, Columbus, Ohio.* San Francisco, Calif.: Computer Music Association, 1989: 42–45.

7178.   "Bontempi Introduces New Sampled Wave Technology." *Music Trades* 135 (June 1987): 130–32.
         Brief review of the Bontempi AZ 8000 and AZ 9000.

7179.   "Bontempi Sales Surge with New Digital Sampling Keyboards." *Music Trades* 135 (July 1987): 110–11.
         Brief review of the Bontempi AZ 8000 and AZ 9000.

7180.   Bralower, Jimmy. "Ahead of the Beat!" *Music, Computers & Software* 3 (Feb. 1988): 46–53.
         A history and tutorial on drum machines.

7181.   Brandt, Richard. "A Chip That May Break All Sorts of Sound Barriers." *Business Week* (Oct. 24, 1988): 80.
         Motorola's digital signal processing (DSP) chip.

7182.   Burger, Jeff. "Buying Your First Sequencer." *Electronic Musician* 3 (July 1987): 48–56.

7183. ——. "Percussion: The Acoustic Drummer's Guide to Electronic Drums." *Electronic Musician* 3 (Apr. 1987): 28–34.

7184. ——. "Review: Oberheim Prommer." *Electronic Musician* 3 (Apr. 1987): 81–86.

Review of the Oberheim Prommer, a PROM burner, sampler, MIDI storage and retrieval system.

7185. Burgess, Jim. "Casio FZ1: Sampling Keyboard." *Music Technology* 1 (June 1987): 78–83.

Review.

7186. ——. "Grey Matter Response E! for the DX7, Version 2.0." *Music Technology* 2 (Sept. 1987): 88–89.

Review of a circuit board enhancement.

7187. Butler, Chris. "Data Glove." *Music, Computers & Software* 3 (June 1988): 29.

A discussion of the work on the DATAGlove computer input device developed by Tom Zimmerman.

7188. Buxton, William. "Guest Editorial: Why Not Design Synthesizers a Pro Can Tour with?" *Keyboard* 11 (July 1985): 10.

7189. Cadoz, Claude; Anastasie Luciani; and Jean-Loup Florens. "Responsive Input Devices and Sound Synthesis by Simulation of Instrumental Mechanisms: The Cordis System." *Computer Music Journal* 8,3 (Fall 1984): 60–73.
Previously **2966**.
Reprinted in *The Music Machine*, ed. Curtis Roads. Cambridge, Mass.: MIT Press, 1989: 495–508.

7190. Campbell, Alan Gary. "Alesis Midiverb II; Alesis MPX MIDI Patch Transmitter." *Electronic Musician* 3 (July 1987): 24, 106.

Reviews of a digital reverb unit and MIDI program change transmitter.

7191. ——. "First Take: Capsule Comments: 360 Systems Professional MIDI Bass." *Electronic Musician* 5 (June 1989): 86–88.

7192. ——. "First Take: Casio MG-500 & MG-510 MIDI Guitars." *Electronic Musician* 4 (Jan. 1988): 78–79.

Review.

7193. ——. "Grey Matter Response E! Revision 2." *Electronic Musician* 3 (July 1987): 20–21.

Review of an expansion board for the Yamaha DX7.

7194. ——. "Korg 707 Synthesizer." *Electronic Musician* 5 (Jan. 1989): 96.

Review.

7195.   ——. "Meico MIDI Commander and Patch Commander Programmable Footswitches." *Electronic Musician* 5 (Oct. 1989): 84–85.

7196.   ——. "Mods: CZ Mods." *Electronic Musician* 2 (Aug. 1986): 51–62.
Modifications for the Casio CZ-101 and CZ-1000.

7197.   ——. "New Life for Old Gear: The MIDI Retrofit Story." *Electronic Musician* 5 (Sept. 1989): 36–44, 50–52.
A list of available MIDI retrofits, alphabetically by manufacturer, with comments on features and difficulty of installation.

7198.   ——. "Review: Blacet Research Instantmod for the CZ-101." *Electronic Musician* 4 (July 1988): 140–41.
A modulation-control retrofit for the Casio CZ-101/1000.

7199.   ——. "Review: E! Board for the DX7." *Electronic Musician* 2 (May 1986): 66–68.

7200.   ——. "Review: Elka and FFD MIDI Bass Pedals." *Electronic Musician* 3 (Sept. 1987): 88–93.
Reviews of the Elka PM-13 and Fast Forward Designs MIDI Step, MIDI bass-pedal controllers.

7201.   ——. "Review: Korg DS-8 FM Synthesizer." *Electronic Musician* 4 (Jan. 1988): 94–96, 100–101.

7202.   ——. "Review: Korg DW-8000 MIDI Synthesizer." *Electronic Musician* 2 (Feb. 1986): 53–55.

7203.   ——. "Review: Kurzweil K1000 Keyboard." *Electronic Musician* 4 (Apr. 1988): 110–15, 122.

7204.   ——. "Review: Kurzweil K150 Rack-mount MIDI Sound Module." *Electronic Musician* 3 (Jan. 1987): 77–79.

7205.   ——. "Review: Sampled Grands from Roland, Yamaha, and Korg." *Electronic Musician* 4 (June 1988): 108–13.
Reviews of the Roland RD-300, Yamaha PF85, and Korg SGX-1D digital pianos.

7206.   ——. "Review: Siel DK70 MIDI Synthesizer." *Electronic Musician* 3 (Mar. 1987): 104–6.

7207.   ——. "Review: Wersi M88 and Unique DBM MIDI Keyboard Controllers." *Electronic Musician* 3 (Jan. 1987): 70–74.

7208.   ——. "Reviews: ADA and ART MIDI Programmable Graphic EQs." *Electronic Musician* 4 (Nov. 1988): 102–5.
Review of the ADA MQ-1 and ART IEQ MIDI programmable graphic equalizers.

7209.   ——. "Reviews: The Peavey Ultraverb: Programmable and Afford-able." *Electronic Musician* 5 (Feb. 1989): 124–25.

7210.   Campbell, Tony. "Control Zone: Testing, Testing: Roland R5 Drum Machine." *Melody Maker* 65 (Aug. 26, 1989): 53.

7211.   Cano, Howard W. "Circuit: Build the Alpha Digital Drum." *Electronic Musician* 3 (Feb. 1987): 66–70.

7212.   ——. "SAM: A Simple Sound Sampler." *Electronic Musician* 3 (Nov. 1987): 80–90.

         How to construct a sampler.

7213.   Carlucci, Tony. "Brass: MIDI Controllers for Brass Players." *Canadian Musician* 9 (Dec. 1987): 72.

         See **7428**.

7214.   Carnelli, Steve. "Three Favorite GR-700 Patches." *Guitar Player* 20 (June 1986): 74, 77.

         Patches for the Roland GR-700.

7215.   Carr, Robert. "MD Special Report: The Drum Computer: Friend or Foe?" *Modern Drummer* 6 (Feb./Mar. 1982): 18, 96–97, 100.

         A look at the Linn LM-1.

7216.   Cash, Laurel. "Digital Workstations: The Future is Now." *Billboard* 99 (Oct. 24, 1987): 76–77.

7217.   "Charvel Adds GTM6 Guitar-to-Midi Converter." *Music Trades* 134 (Apr. 1986): 68–69.

7218.   Ciani, Suzanne. "Sampling." *Music, Computers & Software* 2 (Aug. 1987): 38–41.

         The author discusses her experiences with various sampling synthesizers.

7219.   Cioff, Billy. "Creem Showcase: Yamaha Computer Assisted Music System." *Creem* 17 (July 1985): 57.

7220.   Clay, Roger. "Keyboards in the Information Age." *Creem* 16 (June 1984): 60–64.

         A profile of different makes of synthesizers.

7221.   Cogan, Jeff. "Demonstration Performance by John McEnary." *Soundboard* 12 (1985–86): 381.

         A demonstration of the Roland guitar synthesizer.

7222.   Colbert, Paul. "Control Zone: Review Moog: In the Moog." *Melody Maker* 59 (Feb. 4, 1984): 29.

         Review of Memory Moog and Sequencer.

7223. Collinge, Douglas J. "The Oculus Ranae." In *Proceedings of the International Computer Music Conference 1986, Royal Conservatory, The Hague, Netherlands, October 20–24, 1986*, ed. Paul Berg. San Francisco, Calif.: Computer Music Association, 1986: A-1–A-4.

A circuit for interfacing a television camera to a computer.

7224. Comerford, P. J. "The Bradford Musical Instrument Simulator." In *Proceedings of the International Computer Music Conference 1986, Royal Conservatory, The Hague, Netherlands, October 20–24, 1986*, ed. Paul Berg. San Francisco, Calif.: Computer Music Association, 1986: 301–3.

7225. Comerford, P. J. "Further Development of the Bradford Musical Instrument Simulator." *IEE Proceedings. Part A, Physical Science, Measurement and Instrumentation, Management and Education, Reviews* 134 (Dec. 1987): 799–806.

7226. Comerford, P. J., and Barry M. Eaglestone. "Bradford Musical Instrument Simulator and Workstation." In *Supercomputers: Technology and Applications: Fourteenth Euromicro Symposium on Microprocessing and Microprogramming (EUROMICRO '88), Zurich, August 29–September 1, 1988*, ed. Stephen Winter and Harald Schumny. Amsterdam; New York, N.Y.: North-Holland, 1988: 555–61.

7227. "Computer Music Systems." *Keyboards, Computers & Software* 2 (Feb. 1987): 35–43.

Suggestions of five self-contained MIDI systems in a variety of prices.

7228. Cone, Bill. "Oberheim DPX-1." *Music, Computers & Software* 2 (May 1987): 57–60.

A 12-bit linear sound sample reader.

7229. "Control Zone: More from the British Music Fair." *Melody Maker* 60 (Aug. 24, 1985): 44.

Describes the Korg DW8000 and SQD-1.

7230. "Control Zone: New Casio Keyboards." *Melody Maker* 62 (Jan. 3, 1987): 38.

7231. "Control Zone News: The Age of the Yamaha." *Melody Maker* 59 (Feb. 4, 1984): 30–31.

Yamaha CX5 with built-in DX9 synth and QX1 sequencer.

7232. "Control Zone: Review Keyboards: Face to Face." *Melody Maker* 59 (Feb. 4, 1984): 28.

Roland MD-8 MIDI-DCB Interface, and MM-4 MIDI Through Box.

7233. Cooper, Colin. "The MIDI Converter." *Classical Guitar* 6 (Aug. 1987): 38–39.

A discussion of the Shadow GTM-6, a guitar-to-MIDI converter.

7234. Cooper, Jim. "Modifications & Maintenance: Got the Down in the Memory Dump Blues?" *Keyboard* 11 (Aug. 1985): 70.

7235. ———. "Modifications & Maintenance: Plug-in Digital Storage (or, Who Shall I Take to the EPROM?)." *Keyboard* 11 (May 1985): 60.

Erasable Programmable Read-Only Memory.

7236. Costa, J. C. "Turn up the Drummer." *Musician, Player & Listener* n35 (Aug. 1981): 100–106.

Review of the state-of-the-art drum machines.

7237. Crombie, David. *The New Complete Synthesizer: A Comprehensive Guide to the World of Electronic Music.* New York, N.Y.: Omnibus Press, 1986. 112 p.

7238. "Currents: Vocalizing." *High Fidelity* 38 (Dec. 1988): 12.

A report on the Vocalizer 1000 voice controller.

7239. Dale, Chris. "Control Zone: Box of Tricks." *Melody Maker* 65 (May 20, 1989): 53.

Review of the Yamaha TQ5 synth box.

7240. ———. "Control Zone: Testing, Testing: Ensoniq VFX Synthesizer." *Melody Maker* 65 (Aug. 5, 1989): 46.

7241. ———. "Control Zone: Testing, Testing: Kawai K4 & K4R." *Melody Maker* 65 (Oct. 21, 1989): 52.

7242. ———. "Control Zone: Testing, Testing: Yamaha SY77 Synthesizer." *Melody Maker* 65 (Nov. 18, 1989): 53.

7243. ———. "High Flyer." *Melody Maker* 64 (Mar. 5, 1988): 58–59.

Review of the Korg 707 synthesizer.

7244. ———. "Samply Lovely." *Melody Maker* 65 (June 3, 1989): 46.

Review of the Roland W30 sampling workstation.

7245. DaNova, George. "Korg DRV 2000 Digital Reverb." *Electronic Musician* 4 (Jan. 1988): 80.

Review.

7246. Darcey, Glen. "Artisyn SX01 MIDISax." *Music Technology* 2 (Feb. 1988): 80–81.

Review of a wind controller.

7247. ———. "IVL Pitchrider 4000 MkII: Pitch-to-MIDI Converter." *Music Technology* 2 (Jan. 1988): 52–54.

Review.

7248. ———. "Lync Systems LN4: Remote MIDI Keyboard Controller." *Music Technology* 2 (May 1988): 40–41.

Review.

7249. Davies, Rick. "E-mu Forge Ahead." *Music Technology* 1,1 (1986): 10.

A report on developments at E-mu Systems.

7250. ———. "In Brief: 360 Systems MIDI Patcher." *Music Technology* 1,1 (1986): 36.

Review.

7251. ———. "In Brief: 360 Systems MIDIMerge +." *Music Technology* 1 (June 1987): 28.

Review of a data processor that combines, filters, and alters MIDI data.

7252. ———. "In Brief: Fast Forward Designs MIDI Step, MIDI Bass Pedal/Foot Controller." *Music Technology* 1 (Apr. 1987): 20–21.

7253. ———. "In Brief: JL Cooper MSB Plus." *Music Technology* 1 (Dec. 1986): 18.

Review of a MIDI processor.

7254. ———. "In Brief: Kawai K5 Synthesizer." *Music Technology* 1 (May 1987): 20.

Review.

7255. ———. "In Brief: Kawai R50 Drum Machine." *Music Technology* 1 (June 1987): 31.

Review.

7256. ———. "In Brief: Palmtree Instruments Airdrums." *Music Technology* 1 (Dec. 1986): 15.

Review.

7257. ———. "In Brief: Peavey RMC 4512: Remote MIDI Controller." *Music Technology* 2 (Nov. 1987): 66.

Review of a foot-operated MIDI controller.

7258. ———. "In Brief: Sequential Prophet 3000." *Music Technology* 2 (Sept. 1987): 43.

Review of a 16-bit stereo sampler.

7259. ———. "In Brief: Sequential Studio 440." *Music Technology* 1 (Jan. 1987): 18.

Review of a 12-bit sampling sequencer/drum machine.

7260. ——. "In Brief: Toa D-5.5 Electronic Music Mixer." *Music Technology* 1 (Sept. 1986): 30.
Review.

7261. ——. "In Brief: Unisynth XGI and XGIM Electronic Guitars." *Music Technology* 2 (Nov. 1987): 68.
Review.

7262. ——. "Kawai K3, Digital Wave Memory Synthesizer." *Music Technology* 1 (Dec. 1986): 24–26.
Review.

7263. ——. "Korg DRV2000: Programmable MIDI Reverb." *Music Technology* 1 (Apr. 1987): 60–63.
Review.

7264. ——. "Photon MIDI Converter." *Music Technology* 1 (Apr. 1987): 38–40.
Review.

7265. ——. "Roland MKS70, Super JX Synthesizer Expander." *Music Technology* 1 (May 1987): 60–63.
Review.

7266. ——. "Simmons SPM8:2, Programmable MIDI Mixer." *Music Technology* 1 (Mar. 1987): 72–74.
Review.

7267. ——. "A Switch in Time." *Music Technology* 2 (Jan. 1988): 59–61.
An overview of MIDI switchers and discussion of specific models.

7268. ——. "Yamaha DX7IID & DX7IIFD, FM Digital Synthesizers." *Music Technology* 1 (Apr. 1987): 78–81.
Review.

7269. ——. "Yamaha REX50: Digital Signal Processor." *Music Technology* 2 (Oct. 1987): 76–77.
Review.

7270. ——. "Yamaha TX81Z FM Synth & MDF1 MIDI Data Filer." *Music Technology* 1 (July 1987): 64–66.
Review.

7271. ——, and Paul White. "Stepp DG1 Electronic Guitar." *Music Technology* 1 (Jan. 1987): 83–86.
Review.

7272. Davis, Mark. "Applications: Ghost in the Machine. Part 1." *Electronic Musician* 5 (May 1989): 70–73.
How to utilize test routines in Yamaha, Kawai, Korg, and Ensoniq instruments to diagnose problems.

7273.   ——. "Applications: Ghost in the Machine. Part 2." *Electronic Musician* 5 (July 1989): 37–42.

How to utilize test routines in Roland and Oberheim equipment to diagnose problems.

7274.   Dawson, Carlo. "Control Zone: Bank Balance." *Melody Maker* 65 (Mar. 25, 1989): 51.

Review of the Casio MT240 mini-keyboard.

7275.   De Furia, Steve. "Systems & Applications: The MIDI Delay Processor: Not Just Another Echo Device." *Keyboard* 13 (Nov. 1987): 134.

7276.   ——. "Systems: Planning an Integrated Setup: You Don't Always Need What You Want." *Keyboard* 12 (Jan. 1986): 84–94.

7277.   "Der Synthesizer: Aufbau und Entwicklung." *Musik International* 37 (Okt. 1983): 606–14.

Reviews of various synthesizers.

7278.   Deutsch, Herbert A. "Retrospective." *Music, Computers & Software* 3 (Dec. 1988): 14–16.

A discussion of the MiniMoog synthesizer.

7279.   Di Perna, Alan. "As the Mod Wheel Turns: Two New Synths from Ensoniq and Kawai Heat Things up." *Musician* n129 (July 1989): 98–100, 104–5.

Reviews of the Ensoniq VFX and the Kawai K4.

7280.   ——. "Developments: Tales from Finishing School: Gwendolyn Gets Rhythm." *Musician* n122 (Dec. 1988): 54–56, 60.

Review of several kinds of hardware.

7281.   ——. "Ending the War between the Synths: The Xpander Reconciles Modular with Performance." *Musician* n69 (July 1984): 82, 90.

7282.   ——. "The Great Guitar Synth Wait." *Musician* n76 (Feb. 1985): 100–102, 119.

7283.   ——. "The Hybrids: Samploid Synths: Real-World Samples in ROM Fortify the D-50, the SQ-80 and 1000 Series." *Musician* n115 (May 1988): 30–36, 129–30.

Review of the Roland D-50, Ensoniq SQ-80, and the Kurzweil 1000 series synthesizers.

7284.   ——. "KCScope: Casio CZ-5000." *Keyboards, Computers & Software* 1 (Feb. 1986): 52–53.

Review of the Casio CZ-5000 polyphonic synthesizer.

7285.   ——. "KCScope: Ensoniq Digital Multi-Sampler." *Keyboards, Computers & Software* 1 (Apr. 1986): 52–54.

7286.   ——. "Over the Bounding Waveforms: Roland's Digital Ship Comes In." *Musician* n105 (July 1987): 66, 134.
Review of the Roland S-10 and S-50 sampling keyboards, and D-50 digital synth.

7287.   ——. "Roland Juno 2." *Keyboards, Computers & Software* 1 (June 1986): 64–66.
Review.

7288.   "Different Drum Uses Computer, Radio Waves." *Byte* 14 (Mar. 1989): 14–18.
Describes Max Mathews' Radio Drum.

7289.   "Digital Pianos: Understanding What You're Hearing." *Keyboard* 14 (Aug. 1988): 93.

7290.   Dosa, Michael. "Mod: MXR Drum Computer External Sound Module." *Electronic Musician* 2 (Sept. 1986): 56–57.

7291.   Dowty, Tim. "Do-It-Yourself: The Electronic Musician MIDI Channelizer." *Electronic Musician* 5 (May 1989): 80–83.

7292.   ——. "The EM MIDI Channel Filter." *Electronic Musician* 4 (Oct. 1988): 48–55.
How to build a MIDI channel filter.

7293.   Doyle, Frank. "TC 2290 Dynamic Digital Delay & Effects Control Processor." *Music, Computers & Software* 2 (Oct. 1987): 70, 74–79.
Review of the MIDI-controlled digital effects processor.

7294.   Dupler, Steven. "Digital Sampler Prices." *Billboard* 98 (Aug. 2, 1986): 74.

7295.   ——. "Fairlight Is Hopeful About Digital Sampler Growth." *Billboard* 98 (Nov. 15, 1986): 48.

7296.   Eckel, Gerhard; Xavier Rodet; and Yves Potard. "A Sun-Mercury Music Workstation." In *Proceedings of the 1987 International Computer Music Conference: University of Illinois at Urbana–Champaign, Urbana, Illinois, USA, August 23–26, 1987,* comp. James Beauchamp. San Francisco, Calif.: Computer Music Association, 1987: 159–65.

7297.   Eiche, Jon F. *What's a Synthesizer?: Simple Answers to Common Questions about the New Musical Technology.* Milwaukee, Wis.: H. Leonard Books, 1987. 61 p.
Review by Ted Greenwald in *Keyboard* 13 (Dec. 1987): 18.
Review in *Music Trades* 135 (Dec. 1987): 100, 102.

7298.   "The EIII On-Board 16-Track Sequencer." *Keyboard* 14 (July 1988): 151–52.

7299.   Ellis, David. "Ensoniq Digital Piano." *Music Technology* 1 (Nov. 1986): 87–89.
Review.

7300.   ———. "Yamaha FB01, FM Sound Generator." *Music Technology* 1 (Nov. 1986): 22–23.
Review.

7301.   Else, Vanessa. "First Take: Capsule Comments: Technics SX-PR200 Digital Ensemble." *Electronic Musician* 5 (July 1989): 104–7.

7302.   "Ensoniq Unveils New Synth, Diversifies with Hearing Aids." *Music Trades* 137 (July 1989): 49.
Brief review of the Ensoniq VFX80 dynamic component synthesizer.

7303.   "Ensoniq's Miraculous Orchestra in a Chip." *Music Trades* 133 (Jan. 1985): 102–6.
An introduction of the Ensoniq Mirage keyboard.

7304.   Eshleman, Jim. "Hardware: Kurzweil K1000 Keyboard." *Music, Computers & Software* 3 (June 1988): 72–73.
Review of the sampling synthesizer.

7305.   ———. "Musical Instrument: Alesis HR-16 Drum Machine." *Music, Computers & Software* 3 (Aug. 1988): 63–64.
Review.

7306.   Esse, Christopher J. "Currents: Not for Listeners Only." *High Fidelity* 38 (Aug. 1988): 13.
Mention of the latest wind controllers available from Yamaha, Akai, and Casio.

7307.   Ferguson, Jim, and Tom Mulhern. "Technology Showcase: The Latest in Amps, Effects & Synthesizer Gear." *Guitar Player* 22 (May 1988): 48–57, 156–57.

7308.   Fiore, Jim. "Meet Zelda: An Altered Octapad." *Electronic Musician* 4 (May 1988): 33–38.
A MIDI-based drum system designed by the author with volume control and other features.

7309.   ———. "Review: ART DR1 Performance MIDI Reverb." *Electronic Musician* 3 (Jan. 1987): 85–88.
A MIDI compatible digital reverb.

7310.   ———. "Review: Kawai R-100 Drum Machine." *Electronic Musician* 3 (Aug. 1987): 76–78.

7311. ——. "Review: Simmons MTM, TMI, and SDE." *Electronic Musician* 3 (June 1987): 88–90, 102.

Reviews of two drum pad-to-MIDI trigger devices and a six-voice FM synthesizer/expander.

7312. ——. "Shop Talk: Building A MIDI THRU Box." *Modern Drummer* 13 (Mar. 1989): 58–59.

7313. Fischer, Charles R. "MIDI Mods for Your Minimoog." *Electronic Musician* 5 (Sept. 1989): 55–56.

7314. ——. "Mod: Secrets of Memory Expansion." *Electronic Musician* 3 (July 1987): 82–88.

How to expand the memory of older synthesizers at very little cost.

7315. ——, and Alan Gary Campbell. "Applications: Using the Dinosaur with a MIDI-to-CV Converter." *Electronic Musician* 5 (Sept. 1989): 70–73.

A list of common analog synthesizers that can be used with MIDI-to-CV converters.

7316. Fishell, Steve. "Steel Trap: Synth Interface for Steel Guitar." *Guitar Player* 20 (June 1986): 94–96.

7317. Fisher, Chuck. "MCS Applications." *Music, Computers & Software* 3 (Apr. 1988): 8, 16.

A discussion of MIDI event processors.

7318. ——. "Musical Instrument: Oberheim Matrix 1000." *Music, Computers & Software* 3 (Dec. 1988): 64.

Review of the rack mounted digitally controlled analog synthesizer.

7319. ——, and Patrick Longeneker. "Yamaha SPX90." *Keyboards, Computers & Software* 1 (Aug. 1986): 59–60.

Review of a multi-effects processor.

7320. Fluharty, Tim. "Circuit: Sync and Sequence with the Casio SK-1 Sampler." *Electronic Musician* 3 (Apr. 1988): 62–68.

A warranty-voiding circuit to add to the Casio SK-1 for an external trigger to step up the unit's sequencer.

7321. Foister, Dave. "Electronic Instruments, II." *Composer* n81 (Spring 1984): 4–6.

A short survey which includes digital synthesizers, computer instruments, sequencers, and drum machines.

7322. Frederick, Dave. "Keyboard Controllers Don't Make a Sound (But They Sure Feel Good)." *Keyboard* 12 (Jan. 1986): 49–51.

7323. ——. "Keyboard Report: Airdrums; Rhythm Stick; Music Mouse: Make Mine MIDI, but Hold the Keys." *Keyboard* 13 (Jan. 1987): 131–35, 144.

MIDI controllers.

7324. ——. "Keyboard Report: Akai S900 Rack-mount Sampler." *Keyboard* 12 (Sept. 1986): 136–39.

7325. ——. "Keyboard Report: Beetle QR-1 RAM Disk & PR-7 Programmer." *Keyboard* 12 (Nov. 1986): 152, 158–59.

7326. ——. "Keyboard Report: Casio RZ-1, Sampling Drum Machine." *Keyboard* 12 (May 1986): 110.

7327. ——. "Keyboard Report: DEP-5, Digital Effects Processor from Roland." *Keyboard* 13 (Jan. 1987): 136–38, 142.

A programmable stereo multi-effects processor.

7328. ——. "Keyboard Report: Emax, Digital Sampling Keyboard from E-Mu Systems." *Keyboard* 13 (Jan. 1987): 118–28, 144.

7329. ——. "Keyboard Report: Ensoniq SDP-1 Sampled Piano." *Keyboard* 12 (Sept. 1986): 142.

7330. ——. "Keyboard Report: Forte Music MIDI Mod for Pianos." *Keyboard* 12 (Feb. 1986): 108–111.

Internal modification for acoustic, electric grand, and electronic pianos.

7331. ——. "Keyboard Report: Korg DSS-1 Sampling Synthesizer." *Keyboard* 12 (Nov. 1986): 141–42.

7332. ——. "Keyboard Report: Korg DVP-1, Digital Voice Processor." *Keyboard* 12 (May 1986): 120.

MIDI-controlled polyphonic voice processor and vocal synthesizer.

7333. ——. "Keyboard Report: Kurzweil Midiboard & 150 Expander." *Keyboard* 12 (Dec. 1986): 130–34, 160–63.

7334. ——. "Keyboard Report: Lync LN-1 & Oberheim Xk Keyboard Controllers." *Keyboard* 12 (July 1986): 135–39, 156–60.

7335. ——. "Keyboard Report: Mastering the Ability to Express Yourself." *Keyboard* 12 (Mar. 1986): 96–97.

Review of Expression Plus, a programmable rack-mount audio mixer and CV controller.

7336. ——. "Keyboard Report: MIDI Merge Devices." *Keyboard* 12 (May 1986): 118, 144.

Harmony Systems SynHance M1X Plus, Kamlet MIDI Merger, and J. L. Cooper Electronics MIDI Blender.

7337. ——. "Keyboard Report: Oberheim Matrix-6 Synthesizer." *Keyboard* 12 (Mar. 1986): 93.

7338. ——. "Keyboard Report: Roland MC-500 Sequencer." *Keyboard* 12 (Nov. 1986): 144–50.

7339. ——. "Keyboard Report: S-10, Digital Sampling Keyboard from Roland." *Keyboard* 13 (Feb. 1987): 157–63.

7340. ——. "Keyboard Report: Technics Digital Pianos." *Keyboard* 12 (Aug. 1986): 121–22.

   Review of Technics sx-PX5, sx-PX7, and sx-PX9.

7341. ——. "Keyboard Report: The Axxess Unlimited Mapper." *Keyboard* 12 (June 1986): 156–59.

   Review of the Axxess Mapper, a MIDI data control and reassignment device.

7342. ——. "Keyboard Report: Unique Synthesizer Module & Keyboard Controller." *Keyboard* 12 (Dec. 1986): 142–46.

   Review of the DBE analog/digital hybrid programmable synthesizer module and DBM keyboard controller.

7343. ——. "Keyboard Report: X7000 Sampling Keyboard from Akai." *Keyboard* 13 (Feb. 1987): 149–50.

7344. ——. "Keyboard Report: Yamaha FB-01 Sound Module." *Keyboard* 12 (Oct. 1986): 150.

7345. ——. "Keyboard Report: Yamaha SPX90, Digital Effects Processor." *Keyboard* 12 (May 1986): 122, 142.

7346. Freff. "How I Learned to Stop Worrying and Love the Yamaha DX Series: FM Digital Synthesis Makes Its First Big Splash." *Musician* n61 (Nov. 1983): 92–96.

7347. ——. "Keyboard Report: Akai EWI1000 & EWV2000, MIDI Wind Controller & Synth Module." *Keyboard* 15 (Mar. 1989): 114–21, 141.

7348. ——. "Keyboard Report: Akai MPC60, MIDI Production Workstation." *Keyboard* 14 (Nov. 1988): 158–66.

7349. ——. "Keyboard Report: Kahler Human Clock, Rhythm Synchronizer." *Keyboard* 13 (May 1987): 134–39.

   An intelligent trigger-to-MIDI-clock converter.

7350. ——. "Review: JL Cooper MIDI Wind Driver." *Electronic Musician* 2 (Apr. 1986): 65–66.

   Review of the Lyricon.

7351. ——. "Review: Roland MKS-20 Digital Piano Module." *Electronic Musician* 2 (Sept. 1986): 64–66.

7352.   Friedman, Dean. *The Complete Guide to Synthesizers, Sequencers &*
          Drum Machines. New York, N.Y.: Amsco Publications, 1985. 111 p.

7353.   Friend, Marty. "KCS Sampling." *Keyboards, Computers & Software* 1
          (Oct. 1986): 69–70.
          Aspects to consider before purchasing a digital sampling device.

7354.   ———. "MCS Sampling." *Music, Computers & Software* 2 (June 1987):
          80–81.
          Discusses the uses of sampling synthesizers.

7355.   ———. "Sampling Samplers: From the Beginning to the Future."
          Keyboards, Computers & Software 1 (Aug. 1986): 47–52.
          Short reviews of several popular sampling keyboards. Includes a
          comparison chart.

7356.   Fryer, Terry. "Digital Sampling: It's a Sampler and a Drum Machine."
          Keyboard 13 (Jan. 1987): 101, 106.

7357.   Fukuda, Yasuhika. *Yamaha DX7 Digital Synthesizer.* London:
          Amsco, 1985. 139 p.
          Translated from Japanese.

7358.   Gershin, Scott. "Iota Systems MIDI-Fader." *Music Technology* 2
          (Sept. 1987): 16–18.
          Review.

7359.   "Gibson/Roland Guitar Synth." *Melody Maker* 60 (Nov. 16, 1985): 35.

7360.   Gilanze, M. *The Musicglove.* Cambridge, Mass.: Massachusetts Insti-
          tute of Technology, 1989. (Media Laboratory Internal Memo)

7361.   Gilchrist, Trevor. "Korg DDD1, Digital Drum Machine." *Music*
          Technology 1 (Nov. 1986): 76–79.
          Review.

7362.   ———. "Yamaha RX5, Programmable Digital Drum Machine." *Music*
          Technology 1 (May 1987): 31–34.
          Review.

7363.   Goldstein, Dan. "Casio SK2100, Portable Sampling Keyboard." *Music*
          Technology 1 (May 1987): 83–85.
          Review.

7364.   ———. "In Brief: Boss Dr Pads." *Music Technology* 1 (Oct. 1986): 24.
          Review.

7365.   ———. "In Brief: Korg DRV1000 Digital Reverb." *Music Technology*
          1 (Feb. 1987): 16.
          Review.

7366.   ——. "In Brief: Yamaha DMP7 Digital Mixer." *Music Technology* 1 (Feb. 1987): 17.
Review.

7367.   ——. "In Brief: Yamaha TX802: FM Synthesizer Module." *Music Technology* 2 (Sept. 1987): 36.
Review.

7368.   ——. "Roland RD1000, Digital Piano." *Music Technology* 1 (Sept. 1986): 54–56.
Review.

7369.   ——. "RSF SD140: Sampling Drum Machine." *Music Technology* 2 (Nov. 1987): 51–53.
Review.

7370.   Goodyer, Tim. "Eighth Wonder." *Music Technology* 1 (May 1987): 54–55.
Review of the Roland Jupiter 8, an analog synthesizer.

7371.   ——. "In Brief: Akai EWI & EVI." *Music Technology* 2 (Oct. 1987): 16.
Review of wind controllers.

7372.   ——. "Korg DVP1, Digital Voice Processor." *Music Technology* 1,1 (1986): 56–58.
Review.

7373.   Gore, Joe, and Tom Mulhern. "The Multi-Effects Processor: Can One Box Really Do It All?" *Guitar Player* 23 (June 1989): 24–46, 138–39.
Includes reviews of over fifteen models.

7374.   Gotcher, Peter. "Computers for Keyboardists: Mass Storage Media." *Keyboard* 13 (Feb. 1987): 126–28.
Use of hard disks for mass storage.

7375.   ——. "Digital Sampling: Hard Disks for Samplers." *Keyboard* 14 (June 1988): 136, 171.

7376.   ——. "Digital Sampling: Sampling Spec Wars Revisited." *Keyboard* 13 (Dec. 1987): 134.
Advice to listen to the sound as a criterion in selecting a sampler.

7377.   Greenwald, Ted. "Accessories: Routing & Processing from A to Z." *Keyboard* 12 (Jan. 1986): 53–55, 140.
An introduction to MIDI processing accessory hardware.

7378.   ——. "Keyboard Report: E! Enhancement from Grey Matter for the DX7." *Keyboard* 12 (Apr. 1986): 116–19.
An internal enhancement board for the Yamaha DX7.

7379. ——. "Keyboard Report: E!, Expansion Board for the DX7." *Keyboard* 13 (May 1987): 122–24.

An internal enhancement board for the Yamaha DX7.

7380. ——. "Keyboard Report: Kat MIDI Percussion Controller." *Keyboard* 13 (June 1987): 138–40.

A mallet controller.

7381. ——. "Keyboard Report: Kawai K5, Additive Synthesizer." *Keyboard* 13 (Oct. 1987): 120–27.

7382. ——. "Keyboard Report: Korg DS-8, Digital FM Synthesizer." *Keyboard* 13 (July 1987): 150–54.

7383. ——. "Keyboard Report: Korg DW-8000 Synthesizer." *Keyboard* 12 (Mar. 1986): 94–95.

7384. ——. "Keyboard Report: Midiverb and Midifex, Digital Effects Processors." *Keyboard* 12 (Dec. 1986): 136–41.

7385. ——. "Keyboard Report: Nady Wireless Link MIDI Transmitter." *Keyboard* 12 (Apr. 1986): 115, 136.

7386. ——. "Keyboard Report: Oberheim DPX-1, Rack-mount Sample Player." *Keyboard* 13 (July 1987): 157–59, 169–70.

7387. ——. "Keyboard Report: Roland D-50, Digital Synthesizer." *Keyboard* 13 (Sept. 1987): 144–46, 150.

7388. ——. "Keyboard Report: Wind Controllers, IVL Pitchrider 400 & Yamaha WX7." *Keyboard* 14 (Mar. 1988): 136–43, 154.

A pitch-to-MIDI converter and reed-style MIDI wind controller.

7389. ——. "Keyboard Report: Yamaha DX100 Synthesizer." *Keyboard* 12 (July 1986): 134–35.

7390. ——. "Samplers Laid Bare: How We Set-up Our Lab Tests & What We Learned." *Keyboard* 15 (Mar. 1989): 50–65, 138–40.

Includes results of tests on specific samplers.

7391. ——. "The Synclavier Phenomenon." *Keyboard* 12 (Apr. 1986): 48–55.

7392. "Group Centre to Unveil Stepp Guitar." *Music Trades* 135 (Jan. 1987): 58.

Brief review of the Stepp DG-1, digital guitar synthesizer.

7393. Grupp, Paul. "Reviews: Scholz R & D MIDI Octopus." *Electronic Musician* 5 (Sept. 1989): 98–101.

7394.   ——. "Roland's MC-500 Sequencer." *Music, Computers & Software* 2 (Dec. 1987): 71–73.

Review of the MIDI sequencer.

7395.   "Guitar Gear '88: New Tools of the Trade." *Guitar Player* 21 (Dec. 1987): 58–88.

An overview of the latest developments in guitars, basses, signal processors, and accessories.

7396.   "Gulbransen Debuts Crystal Combo I." *Music Trades* 136 (Sept. 1988): 96–97.

A short description of a single digital unit that installs on an acoustic piano.

7397.   Hailstone, Erik, and Clark Salisbury. "Magic Boxes: Small Boxes/Big Sounds." *Music, Computers & Software* 3 (Aug. 1988): 40–43.

A discussion of signal processing devices.

7398.   Haken, Lippold. "A Digital Music Synthesizer." M.S. diss., University of Illinois at Urbana-Champaign, 1984.

7399.   Hallas, Aaron. "In Brief: Roland S220 Sampler." *Music Technology* 2 (Nov. 1987): 18.

Review.

7400.   ——. "Stepp DGX: MIDI Guitar Controller." *Music Technology* 2 (Dec. 1987): 50–51.

Review.

7401.   "Hammond's New Organs Create Sound Completely by Software." *Music Trades* 136 (June 1988): 108–10.

An introduction to Hammond's CX-2000 and SX-2000.

7402.   Hara, Craig. "The Akai EVI and EWI: A Personal Approach." *Electronic Musician* 4 (Oct. 1988): 56–66.

7403.   Heermans, Andy. "Harmony Systems SynHance MTS-1 MIDI Tape Synchronizer." *Music, Computers & Software* 2 (Aug. 1987): 81–82.

Review of the MIDI-to-multitrack tape synchronizer.

7404.   Heinbuch, Dean. "Review: Roland MPU-101." *Electronic Musician* 3 (Feb. 1987): 86–92.

Four-channel MIDI-to-CV/gate converter.

7405.   Henry, Thomas. "The Connection: A 4-voice, MIDI-to-Analog Synthesizer Interface." *Electronic Musician* 5 (July 1989): 84–101.

Schematics to build an interface that connects analog synthesizers to MIDI keyboards and sequencers.

7406. ——. "The MIDI-to-Trigger Converter." *Electronic Musician* 5 (June 1989): 58–70.

A project to build or buy that provides a link between analog, trigger-based electronic music devices and MIDI.

7407. ——. "Practical Circuitry: Fun with UARTs." *Electronic Musician* 2 (Jan. 1986): 42–46.

A discussion of Universal Asynchronous Receiver/Transmitters.

7408. ——. "Practical Circuitry: The RS-232 Drummer." *Electronic Musician* 2 (Feb. 1986): 38–42.

7409. Hirschfeld, Peter. "Reviews: Lexicon CP-1 Stereo Processor." *Electronic Musician* 5 (June 1989): 98–105.

A digital ambience generator and video decoder.

7410. Hodas, Bob. "Reviews: Wendel jr.: The Sample Playback Machine." *Electronic Musician* 5 (June 1989): 90–93.

7411. Holdsworth, Allan; Lee Ritenour; and Tom Mulhern. "SynthAxe." *Guitar Player* 20 (June 1986): 109–12.

Two artists, Allan Holdsworth and Lee Ritenour, describe their experiences with the SynthAxe, as told to Tom Mulhern.

7412. Holland, Anthony G. "Sampling and Composition with the Kurzweil 250: Today's Aesthetic Choices." In *Proceedings of the International Computer Music Conference 1986, Royal Conservatory, The Hague, Netherlands, October 20–24, 1986*, ed. Paul Berg. San Francisco, Calif.: Computer Music Association, 1986: 299–300.

7413. Holley, E. A. "MIDI: Maximum MIDI for Minimum Money." *Electronic Musician* 3 (Apr. 1987): 59–60.

Advice on setting up an inexpensive MIDI studio.

7414. Horn, Delton T. *Digital Electronic Music Synthesizers*. 2d ed. Blue Ridge Summit, Pa.: Tab Books, 1988. 259 p.

Review by Charles Fischer in *Electronic Musician* (Dec. 1988): 96–100.

7415. "How Silicon Chips Revolutionized Electronic Pianos." *Music Trades* 135 (Sept. 1987): 72–74.

7416. Hubbard, Patrick. "Review: Fostex 4050 Synchronizer." *Electronic Musician* 2 (June 1986): 80–84.

7417. Hurtig, Brent. "Keyboard Report: Garfield Electronics Time Commander." *Keyboard* 14 (Aug. 1988): 143–53.

A programmable live synchronization box.

7418. ——. "Keyboard Report: JL Cooper Mixmate, 8-Channel Automated Mixing System." *Keyboard* 14 (Sept. 1988): 134–39.

7419. "Ibanez Develops MIDI Guitar System." *Music Trades* 134 (Jan. 1986): 102.

A MIDI guitar controller.

7420. Isaacson, Matt. "360 Systems Pro MIDI Bass." *Music Technology* 2 (Feb. 1988): 14–16.

Review of a dedicated bass sound sampler.

7421. ———. "Axxess Mapper 2.0: MIDI Processor." *Music Technology* 2 (May 1988): 18–21.

Review.

7422. ———. "Garfield Electronics Time Commander." *Music Technology* 2 (Oct. 1987): 83–86.

Review of a sync box.

7423. ———. "In Brief: Boss MPD4, MIDI Drum Pad." *Music Technology* 2 (Dec. 1987): 26.

Review.

7424. ———. "Korg DRM1: Digital Rhythm Machine." *Music Technology* 2 (Jan. 1988): 18–21.

Review.

7425. ———. "Roland PM16: Pad-to-MIDI Converter." *Music Technology* 2 (Jan. 1988): 84–86.

Review of a programmable drum pad converter.

7426. ———, and Chris Meyer. "Kahler Human Clock." *Music Technology* 1 (May 1987): 72–75.

Review.

7427. ———, and Chris Meyer. "We Can't Go on Beating Like This. Part 6." *Music Technology* 2 (Sept. 1987): 20–24.

Review of Palmtree's Airtriggers and Airdrums, and PKI's Gun Drums.

7428. Janis, Peter. "Feedback: You Missed the Point on the EVI/EWI." *Canadian Musician* 10 (Feb. 1988): 8.

A letter to the editor regarding item **7213**. An explanation of how the EVI/EWI works in order to show how misleading the article is.

7429. Jehuda, J. "AMOS—A Real-Time Polyphonic Sound Processor." M.Sc. thesis, Technion-Israel Institute of Technology, 1985.

7430. Jenkins, Chris. "Control Zone: Testing, Testing: Cheetah Master Series 7P Keyboard." *Melody Maker* 65 (Oct. 7, 1989): 53.

7431. ——. "Sampling Expandability: Akai S9V2.0 & ASK90." *Music Technology* 2 (Oct. 1987): 28–30.

Review of the Akai S9V2.0 is an upgrade for the Akai S900 sampler; the ASK90 is an interface board for the Akai S900.

7432. ——. "Testing, Testing: Cheetah MQ8 Sequencer." *Melody Maker* 65 (Sept. 16, 1989): 52.

7433. Jenkins, Mark. "Control Zone after Frankfurt: Roland Butter up the Trade." *Melody Maker* 60 (Feb. 23, 1985): 34–35.

Roland products for 1985.

7434. ——. "Control Zone at Frankfurt: It's a Mirage." *Melody Maker* 61 (Feb. 15, 1986): XIV sup.

Review of the Mirage digital multi-sampler.

7435. ——. "Control Zone at Frankfurt: The Max Factor." *Melody Maker* 60 (Feb. 9, 1985): 46.

Review of the SCI MAX synthesizer.

7436. ——. "Control Zone at Frankfurt: TR Triumphs." *Melody Maker* 60 (Feb. 9, 1985): 48.

Review of the Roland TR707 digital drum.

7437. ——. "Control Zone News: ROM at the TOP." *Melody Maker* 61 (May 3, 1986): 45.

Review of Skyslip ROM/RAM cartridges; for Yamaha DX synthesizers.

7438. ——. "Control Zone Review: Equipment: Blowing Your Mind." *Melody Maker* 59 (Aug. 11, 1984): 35.

Review of the Simmons SDS EPB drum sampler.

7439. ——. "Control Zone Review: Equipment: Casio's New Baby." *Melody Maker* 59 (Aug. 25, 1984): 37.

Review of the Casio MT 400V keyboard.

7440. ——. "Control Zone Review: Equipment: Deadly Synth." *Melody Maker* 59 (June 9, 1984): 38.

Review of SynthAxe.

7441. ——. "Control Zone Review: Equipment: Re-Flex Action." *Melody Maker* 59 (Aug. 25, 1984): 36.

Review of Simmons SDS7 and Oberheim Xpander drum machines.

7442. ——. "Control Zone Review: Guitars: Roland's No Rat." *Melody Maker* 59 (June 9, 1984): 41.

Review of the Roland GR-700/G707 guitar synth.

7443. ———. "Control Zone: Amplifiers." *Melody Maker* 60 (Sept. 21, 1985): 44.

Review of the Prophet 2000 sampler.

7444. ———. "Control Zone: Casio Tones: Casio CZ-3000." *Melody Maker* 61 (Mar. 8, 1986): 35.

Review of the Casio CZ-3000 keyboard.

7445. ———. "Control Zone: Computers." *Melody Maker* 60 (Jan. 19, 1985): 32.

Review of the digital keyboard recorder, Roland MSQ700.

7446. ———. "Control Zone: Computers—Go Johnny Go." *Melody Maker* 60 (May 4, 1985): 42–43.

Interview with Johnny Fingers; Greengate DS3.

7447. ———. "Control Zone: Gear of the Year Awards: Computer Peripherals." *Melody Maker* 60 (Dec. 21–28, 1985): 58.

Reviews of Syntron Digidrum 2; Greengate DS-3 Eprom Blower.

7448. ———. "Control Zone: It's a Mirage." *Melody Maker* 61 (Dec. 6, 1986): 36.

Review of the Ensoniq Mirage MK II.

7449. ———. "Control Zone: Keyboards Preview." *Melody Maker* 61 (Nov. 29, 1986): 36.

Review of the Roland S10 sampler.

7450. ———. "Control Zone: Keyboards: Out Come the Shrieks." *Melody Maker* 60 (Mar. 30, 1985): 36–37.

Review of Korg DW6000.

7451. ———. "Control Zone: Keyboards: Schwanzkopf AF1." *Melody Maker* 60 (Mar. 30, 1985): 37.

Describes the digital sampling synthesizer.

7452. ———. "Control Zone: Keyboards: Siel of Approval." *Melody Maker* 60 (Mar. 30, 1985): 38.

Review of Siel DK 80.

7453. ———. "Control Zone: Keyboards: Tricky DX." *Melody Maker* 60 (Mar. 30, 1985): 35.

Review of Yamaha DX5.

7454. ———. "Control Zone: MIDI Mania." *Melody Maker* 61 (Mar. 29, 1986): 36.

Review of the Roland TR505, TR727, and Pad-8 Octapad.

7455.   ——. "Control Zone: Percussion: This Year's Model, Casio RZ-1."
        Melody Maker 61 (Mar. 29, 1986): 35.
        Review of the Casio RZ-1 drum machine.

7456.   ——. "Control Zone: Review Keyboards." *Melody Maker* 59 (Mar.
        31, 1984): 33–37.
        Review of seven digital synthesizers.

7457.   ——. "Control Zone: Review Keyboards: Surf Boardin'." *Melody
        Maker* 59 (Apr. 21, 1984): 36.
        Review of the PPG System.

7458.   ——. "Control Zone: Review of the Year." *Melody Maker* 61 (Dec.
        20–27, 1986): 60–62.
        Review of the Akai S900 sampler, Roland MC500 MIDI unit,
        Stepp DG-1 guitar synthesizer, and Steinberg Pro-24 software.

7459.   ——. "Control Zone: Vesta Kozo MDI-1 Box and DIG-420 Sam-
        pler." *Melody Maker* 61 (June 14, 1986): 45.
        Review of the Vesta Kozo MDI-1 MIDI box MIDI-to-CV inter-
        face and the DIG-420 DDL/Sampler.

7460.   ——. "Control Zone: Wave Machine." *Melody Maker* 61 (Nov. 29,
        1986): 36.
        Review of the Kawai K3 synthesizer.

7461.   ——. "Control Zone: X and the Single Sampler." *Melody Maker* 61
        (Nov. 29, 1986): 37.
        Review of the Akai X7000 sampler.

7462.   ——. "EK of a Synth!" *Melody Maker* 61 (Dec. 6, 1986): 37.
        Review of the Elka EK44 synthesizer.

7463.   ——. "Keyboards: All Hands on DX!" *Melody Maker* 61 (Jan. 25,
        1986): 34.
        Review of the Yamaha DX-100/DX-27.

7464.   ——. "The X Factor." *Melody Maker* 60 (Jan. 19, 1985): 33.
        Review of the XRI Micon MIDI Interface.

7465.   Jimenez, Maria. "Song Construction." *Music, Computers & Software* 3
        (Aug. 1988): 72–73.
        A discussion of automated mixers.

7466.   Johnson, Jim. "Applications: The Korg M1: Drum Machine of the
        Gods?" *Electronic Musician* 5 (Dec. 1989): 81–83.

7467.   ——. "Computing." *Music, Computers & Software* 3 (Aug. 1988):
        18–20.
        A tutorial on CPUs.

7468. ——. "Computing." *Music, Computers & Software* 3 (Dec. 1988): 18–20.

A discussion of disk drives.

7469. ——. "Ensoniq ESQ-1 Digital Synth/Sequencer." *Keyboards, Computers & Software* 1 (Oct. 1986): 50–55.

Review.

7470. ——. "Harmony Systems Voice Vault." *Keyboards, Computers & Software* 1 (Dec. 1986): 52–56.

Review of a memory expansion and voice organization system for the Yamaha DX7.

7471. ——. "Review: Alesis HR-16 Drum Machine." *Electronic Musician* 4 (May 1988): 86–91.

7472. ——. "Review: Digitech's DSP-128 Digital Effects Signal Processor." *Electronic Musician* 4 (Aug. 1988): 86–89.

7473. ——. "Review: E-mu SP-1200 Sampling Drum Machine." *Electronic Musician* 4 (Jan. 1988): 92–93, 104.

7474. ——. "Review: Garfield Electronics' Time Commander." *Electronic Musician* 3 (Dec. 1987): 101–3.

Review of a real time synchronizer.

7475. ——. "Review: Kahler's Human Clock." *Electronic Musician* 3 (June 1987): 84–87.

Review of a machine-to-live playing MIDI synchronizer.

7476. ——. "Review: SynHance M1X and M1X+ MIDI Mixers." *Electronic Musician* 2 (Aug. 1986): 78.

Review of MIDI data processors.

7477. ——. "Reviews: AKG Acoustics ADR 68K Digital Reverb and Effects Processor." *Electronic Musician* 4 (Nov. 1988): 112–17.

7478. Kahrs, Mark. "Notes on Very-Large-Scale Integration and the Design of Real-Time Digital Sound Processors." *Computer Music Journal* 5,2 (Summer 1981): 20–28.
Previously **3111**.
Reprinted in *The Music Machine,* ed. Curtis Roads. Cambridge, Mass.: MIT Press, 1989: 623–31.

7479. Kaplan, S. Jerrold. "Developing a Commercial Digital Sound Synthesizer." *Computer Music Journal* 5,3 (Fall 1981): 62–73.
Previously **3113**.
Reprinted in *The Music Machine,* ed. Curtis Roads. Cambridge, Mass.: MIT Press, 1989: 611–22.

7480.   Karr, David. "Review: Akai MPX820 MIDI-controlled 8 × 2 Mixer."
             Electronic Musician 4 (Apr. 1988): 94–103.

7481.   "KAT Introduces MIDI Controller for Drummers." *Music Trades* 137
             (Apr. 1989): 119–20.
             Brief review of drumKAT.

7482.   Kauffman, Jim. "Coping with Information Overload." *Music, Com-
             puters & Software* 3 (June 1988): 49–51.
             A buyers guide to choosing MIDI equipment.

7483.   "Kawai Offers New Improved K1 Synth." *Music Trades* 137 (July
             1989): 126.
             Brief review of the Kawai K1II.

7484.   "Kawai Offers New MIDI Sequencer." *Music Trades* 137 (Jan. 1989):
             156–58.
             A brief introduction to Kawai's Q-80 sequencer.

7485.   Keane, David, and Peter Gross. "The MIDI Baton." In *Proceedings,
             1989 International Computer Music Conference, November 2–5, the
             Ohio State University, Columbus, Ohio.* San Francisco, Calif.: Com-
             puter Music Association, 1989: 151–54.

7486.   Keislar, Douglas. *History and Principles of Microtonal Keyboard
             Design.* Stanford, Calif.: Stanford University, Dept. of Music, 1988. 10
             p.
             Also issued as: Technical Report STAN-M-45. Stanford, Calif.: Cen-
             ter for Computer Research in Music and Acoustics, Department of
             Music, Stanford University, 1988.

7487.   ———. "History and Principles of Microtonal Keyboards." *Computer
             Music Journal* 11,1 (Spring 1987): 18–28.

7488.   Kettelkamp, Larry. "A Look at the Latest in Electronic Keyboards."
             Clavier 27 (Feb. 1988): 39–43.

7489.   "Keyboards: Big Brother." *Melody Maker* 60 (Apr. 6, 1985): 38.
             Review of the Casio CZ-1000 keyboard.

7490.   "Keyboards: Casio FZ-1 16 Bit Sampler." *Canadian Musician* 9 (June
             1987): 65–66.

7491.   "Keyboards: Roland D-50 Linear Synthesizer." *Canadian Musician* 9
             (June 1987): 66.

7492.   "Keyboards: Yamaha Introduces Second Generation of DX7 Synthe-
             sizers." *Canadian Musician* 9 (Apr. 1987): 61.
             DX7IID and DX7IIFD synthesizers.

7493.   "Keys to Your Heart." *Melody Maker* 60 (July 20, 1985): 42.
Oberheim Matrix 12 keyboard.

7494.   Knowlton, Joseph. "State of the Art." *Keyboard Classics* 6 (May/June 1986): 35.
Discusses the current state of electronic/digital keyboards.

7495.   ———. "State of the Art: Digital Sampling Keyboards." *Keyboard Classics* 7 (June/July 1987): 41.

7496.   ———. "State of the Art: Reverberation." *Keyboard Classics* 6 (Sept./Oct. 1986): 42.
A history of the artificial production of reverberation and a description of digital reverb units.

7497.   ———. "State of the Art: Samplers." *Keyboard Classics* 7 (Sept./Oct. 1987): 39.

7498.   ———. "State of the Art: The Synclavier." *Keyboard Classics* 7 (May/June 1987): 47.

7499.   ———. "State of the Art: Understanding the Sequencer." *Keyboard Classics* 6 (July/Aug. 1986): 41.

7500.   Kohn, Lory. "Reviews: Roland R-8 Human Rhythm Composer." *Electronic Musician* 5 (May 1989): 102–8.

7501.   Kokodyniak, M. "Interconnection of MIDI Devices through a LAN." M.A.Sc. diss., University of Toronto, 1987?

7502.   "Korg Adds Two Sampling Grands." *Music Trades* 134 (Oct. 1986): 99.
Brief review of the Korg SG-1 and SG-1D, sampling grands.

7503.   "Korg Introduces Q1 MIDI Workstation." *Music Trades* 136 (June 1988): 124.

7504.   "Korg Offers the SQ-8 8-Track MIDI Sequencer." *Music Trades* 135 (Apr. 1987): 91–92.

7505.   "Korg Unveils SQD-8 MIDI Sequencer." *Music Trades* 136 (Feb. 1988): 116.

7506.   Kovach, Mark A. "KCScope: ART DR-1." *Keyboards, Computers & Software* 1 (June 1986): 59–60.
Review of a digital reverb unit.

7507.   ———. "Korg DVP-1 Digital Voice Processor." *Keyboards, Computers & Software* 1 (Aug. 1986): 60–63.
Review.

7508.   Kramer, Gregory; Bob Moog; and Alan Peevers. "The Hybrid: A Music Performance System." In *Proceedings, 1989 International Computer Music Conference, November 2–5, the Ohio State University, Columbus, Ohio.* San Francisco, Calif.: Computer Music Association, 1989: 155–59.

7509.   Kumin, Daniel. "First Take: Capsule Comments: Ensoniq/Bose Acoustic Wave Piano." *Electronic Musician* 5 (Oct. 1989): 80–82.

7510.   ——. "Korg P3 Piano Module." *Electronic Musician* 5 (Mar. 1989): 74–80.

7511.   ——. "Korg Symphony Module." *Electronic Musician* 5 (Mar. 1989): 80–82.

7512.   "Kurzweil 250 Duels with World's Largest Pipe Organ." *Music Trades* 136 (Oct. 1988): 42–44.
              A playoff between a Kurzweil 250 and the John Wanamaker Organ.

7513.   Lambert, Mel. "Dream Machines: Exploring High-End Audio Workstations." *Electronic Musician* 5 (June 1989): 34–48, 72–73.

7514.   LaRose, Paul. "Product Profiles: Yamaha G10 Guitar Synthesizer Controller System." *Guitar Player* 23 (July 1989): 147–50.
              Review of the Yamaha G10 MIDI guitar controller.

7515.   Lehrman, Paul D. "Review: Palmtree Instruments' Airdrums." *Electronic Musician* 4 (June 1988): 102–7.

7516.   ——. "Review: Roland VP-70 Voice Processor." *Electronic Musician* 4 (Feb. 1988): 124–29.
              Review of a pitch-to-MIDI converter, and MIDI-controllable harmony synthesizer/vocoder.

7517.   Lent, Chris, ed. *Rockschool 2: Electronics, Keyboards, and Vocals.* New York, N.Y.: Simon & Schuster, 1987. 191 p.

7518.   Levin, Geoff. "Barcus Berry Electronics Model 402 & 802 Sonic Processors." *Music Technology* 1 (Mar. 1987): 34–35.
              Review.

7519.   Levine, Michael. "Applications: Secrets of the Emulator II." *Electronic Musician* 2 (Dec. 1986): 40–41.

7520.   ——. "Review: The Zeta Electric Violin, Effects Preamp and MIDI Controller." *Electronic Musician* 3 (Sept. 1987): 101–3.
              Review of a violin-type MIDI controller.

7521. Lewis, Bill. "ART Pro Verb." *Music, Computers & Software* 2 (June 1987): 64–65.

Review of the MIDI-controlled digital effects processor.

7522. ——. "Casio CZ-1; Casio AZ-1." *Keyboards, Computers & Software* 2 (Feb. 1987): 65–68.

Review.

7523. ——. "Casio FZ-1; MB-10; FL1-FL8." *Music, Computers & Software* 2 (Dec. 1987): 60–62, 66.

Reviews of the sampling keyboard, its memory upgrade, and sound libraries.

7524. ——. "E! Grey Matter Response." *Keyboards, Computers & Software* 1 (Oct. 1986): 56–58.

Review of a circuit card for internal memory and operating system expansion for the Yamaha DX7.

7525. ——. "Hardware: Hard Disks: Mega-Storage of Mega-Bytes." *Keyboards, Computers & Software* 1 (Dec. 1986): 42–44.

A tutorial on the operation and maintenance of hard disk drives.

7526. ——. "Hardware: WorldPort 2400 Modem." *Music, Computers & Software* 3 (Aug. 1988): 68.

Review.

7527. ——. "A Human Drum Machine: Brocktron-X." *Keyboards, Computers & Software* 1 (Aug. 1986): 20.

Describes the Brocktron-X Drum Suit, a portable, electronic, MIDIed drum system controlled by sensors attached to clothing and shoes.

7528. ——. "Kahler Human Clock." *Music, Computers & Software* 2 (Aug. 1987): 79–81.

Review of the audio-to-MIDI clock converter.

7529. ——. "KCScope: Wersi MK-1 Digital Keyboard." *Keyboards, Computers & Software* 1 (Oct. 1986): 48–50.

Review.

7530. ——. "MCS Computing." *Music, Computers & Software* 3 (Apr. 1988): 73–74.

A tutorial on floppy disk drives.

7531. ——. "MCScope Hardware." *Music, Computers & Software* 3 (Feb. 1988): 74.

Review of the Korg DSM-1 rack-mount digital synthesizer.

7532.   ———. "MCScope Hardware." *Music, Computers & Software* 3 (Apr. 1988): 64–65.

Review of the Ensoniq SQ-80 digital synthesizer.

7533.   ———. "MCScope Hardware." *Music, Computers & Software* 3 (Apr. 1988): 70.

Review of the Yamaha DMP7 MIDI-controlled mixer.

7534.   ———. "MIDI DJ." *Music, Computers & Software* 2 (Oct. 1987): 67–68.

Review of the MIDI-to-disk recorder/sequencer.

7535.   ———. "MIDI Mixers." *Music, Computers & Software* 2 (June 1987): 51–52.

A comparison of MIDI-controlled mixers from Akai, Simmons, and Yamaha.

7536.   ———. "MIDIVERB." *Keyboards, Computers & Software* 1 (June 1986): 59–60.

Review of a digital reverb unit.

7537.   ———. "Musical Hardware: Grey Matter Response E!" *Music, Computers & Software* 3 (Oct. 1988): 58–59.

Review of the upgrade system for the Yamaha DX7II.

7538.   ———. "Musical Instrument: Ensoniq EPS Sampler." *Music, Computers & Software* 3 (Nov. 1988): 66–69.

Review.

7539.   ———. "Prophet 2000 Digital Sampling Keyboard/Sound Designer 2000 Software." *Keyboards, Computers & Software* 1 (June 1986): 60–64.

Review.

7540.   ———. "Simmons SPM 8:2." *Music, Computers & Software* 2 (Aug. 1987): 73–74, 79.

Review of the eight-channel MIDI-programmable mixer.

7541.   ———. "Starting Up." *Music, Computers & Software* 2 (Dec. 1987): 45–51.

A tutorial and buyer's guide to MIDI equipment.

7542.   ———. "Voyce LX9 MIDI Controller; Hardware MIDI Data Controller for All MIDI Devices." *Music, Computers & Software* 3 (Feb. 1988): 79.

Review.

7543.   ———. "Yamaha RX5 Digital Rhythm Programmer." *Music, Computers & Software* 2 (June 1987): 62–63.

Review of the digital drum machine/MIDI sequencer.

7544.   ——, and Lisa Pratt. "Brock Seiler: Playing the Body Electric, Brockton-X Pushes the MIDI Beat." *Music, Computers & Software* 3 (Dec. 1988): 34.

Profile/interview with the rock bandleader, who discusses his use of a MIDI sample-triggering system incorporated into a suit/costume.

7545.   Leytze, David. "Keyboard Report: Digitech DSP 128 Multi-Effects Processor." *Keyboard* 14 (May 1988): 132.

7546.   ——. "Keyboard Report: JL Cooper MSB Plus MIDI Switcher & Processor." *Keyboard* 13 (Nov. 1987): 144, 161.

7547.   ——, and Ted Greenwald. "Keyboard Report: Korg DDD-5, Drum Machine." *Keyboard* 13 (Sept. 1987): 148–50.

7548.   Lieberman, Henry. "Casio CZ-1 Digital Synthesizer: A User's Report." *Computer Music Journal* 11,1 (Spring 1987): 86–88.

7549.   Lipson, Stefan B. "Massive Memory." *Music Technology* 2 (Feb. 1988): 64–65.

An overview on the use of hard disks in music.

7550.   Lisowski, James A. "Optical Disk Drum Machine." *Polyphony* 10 (Apr. 1985): 22–24.

7551.   ——. "Review: From Ha! to SK-1: Casio's Sampling Keyboard." *Electronic Musician* 2 (Oct. 1986): 70–71.

Review of a digital sampling keyboard.

7552.   Lord, Nigel. "Hits from the Stick." *Music Technology* 1 (Oct. 1986): 48–50.

Review of the Dynacord Rhythm Stick MIDI controller.

7553.   ——. "Simmons SDS1000 Electronic Drum Kit." *Music Technology* 1,1 (1986): 50–54.

Review.

7554.   "Lowrey to Handle MIDI Component Line." *Music Trades* 136 (Jan. 1988): 104–6.

Brief review of DSEs, digital sound expanders, and DMC-5, MIDI controller keyboard.

7555.   Loy, D. Gareth. "Designing a Computer Music Workstation from Musical Imperatives." In *Proceedings of the International Computer Music Conference 1986, Royal Conservatory, The Hague, Netherlands, October 20–24, 1986,* ed. Paul Berg. San Francisco, Calif.: Computer Music Association, 1986: 375–80.

7556.   Machover, Tod, and Joe Chung. *Hyperinstruments.* Cambridge, Mass.: Massachusetts Institute of Technology, 1988. (Media Laboratory Internal Memo)

7557.   Manilou, Mihai. "In Brief: Roland GP8, Guitar Effects Processor." *Music Technology* 2 (Jan. 1988): 23.
Review.

7558.   Many, Chris. "Beetle PR7 Programmer and QR1 RAM Disk." *Music Technology* 1 (Feb. 1987): 82–83.
Review.

7559.   ———. "Grey Matter Response E! Board for the DX7II." *Music Technology* 2 (May 1988): 60–62.
Review.

7560.   ———. "In Brief: DX-MAX Expansion Board." *Music Technology* 1 (Mar. 1987): 27.
Review of an expansion board for the DX7.

7561.   ———. "In Brief: JL Cooper MAGI." *Music Technology* 2 (Oct. 1987): 22.
Review of a remote console automation with an Atari or Macintosh interface.

7562.   ———. "JL Cooper MidiMation." *Music Technology* 1 (Feb. 1987): 60–61.
Review of MIDI Mute, a MIDI-controlled muting device for recording, live and keyboard mixers, and SAM, SMPTE Automation Manager.

7563.   ———. "Kurzweil 1000: Digital Sample Player & Wavetable Synthesizer." *Music Technology* 2 (Feb. 1988): 92–94.
Review.

7564.   Marans, Michael. "The Ears Have It: Surprising Results of Blind Listening Tests." *Keyboard* 15 (Mar. 1989): 24–27, 137, 140.
Tests on samplers.

7565.   ———. "Keyboard Report: Anatek Pocket Products." *Keyboard* 15 (Aug. 1989): 127, 133.
A MIDI merger, a MIDI data filter, an analog footpedal/footswitch-to-MIDI converter, and a sequencer by Anatek Microcircuits.

7566.   ———. "Keyboard Report: Dynacord ADS, Audio Specification Tests." *Keyboard* 15 (Nov. 1989): 145, 156.

7567. ——. "Keyboard Report: Kawai PH50, Pop Keyboard." *Keyboard* 15 (Apr. 1989): 124.

7568. ——. "Keyboard Report: Kawai Q-80 MIDI Sequencer." *Keyboard* 15 (Jan. 1989): 120–21.

7569. ——. "Keyboard Report: Roland W-30, Music Workstation." *Keyboard* 15 (Oct. 1989): 126–31.
A sampling keyboard with built-in sequencer and ROM sounds.

7570. ——. "Keyboard Report: Yamaha EM Series Modules." *Keyboard* 15 (Feb. 1989): 157–59.

7571. ——. "Keyboard Report: Yamaha V50, Digital Synthesizer." *Keyboard* 15 (June 1989): 122–24.

7572. Massey, Howard. *The Complete DX7*. New York, N.Y.: Amsco, 1986. 277 p.
Includes 3 sound discs.
Review by Ted Greenwald in *Keyboard* 12 (Oct. 1986): 33, 37.

7573. ——. "Decisions, Decisions." *Music Technology* 1 (July 1987): 14–16.
The author gives his opinion on upgrading the Yamaha DX7.

7574. ——. "Ensoniq SQ80: Cross Wave Synthesizer." *Music Technology* 2 (Feb. 1988): 42–44.
Review.

7575. ——. "Reviews: Yamaha V50 Digital Workstation." *Electronic Musician* 5 (July 1989): 112–21.
Review of Yamaha's FM synthesizer.

7576. ——. "Synth & MIDI Basics: Introducing the Casio CZ." *Keyboard* 14 (July 1988): 141–42.

7577. ——. "Synth & MIDI Basics: The Difference between a Piano and Cousin Egbert." *Keyboard* 14 (Feb. 1988): 141–42.
Envelope generators.

7578. ——. "Synth & MIDI Basics: What's the Difference between a Sampler & a Synth?" *Keyboard* 13 (Nov. 1987): 125, 161.

7579. ——. "Synth & MIDI Basics: Why Your Synth Doesn't Have Knobs." *Keyboard* 14 (Mar. 1988): 130.

7580. ——. "Yamaha QX3 Sequencer." *Music Technology* 2 (Oct. 1987): 62–65.
Review.

7581. ———. "Yamaha RX7: Drum Machine." *Music Technology* 2 (Feb. 1988): 26–28.

Review.

7582. ———. "Yamaha TX802, FM Synthesizer." *Music Technology* 2 (Nov. 1987): 90–95.

Review.

7583. Mathews, Max V. *Pickups for the Vibrations of Violin and Guitar Strings Using Piezoelectric Bimorphic Bender Elements.* Stanford, Calif.: Stanford University, Dept. of Music, 1988. 5 p.

Also issued as: Technical Report STAN-M-54. Stanford, Calif.: Center for Computer Research in Music and Acoustics, Department of Music, Stanford University, 1988.

7584. Mattingly, Rick. "Electronic Review: Yamaha RX5 Digital Rhythm Programmer." *Modern Drummer* 11 (Dec. 1987): 122–27.

7585. Mauchley, J. William, and Albert J. Charpentier. "Practical Considerations in the Design of Music Using VLSI." In *The Proceedings of the AES 5th International Conference: Music and Digital Technology,* ed. John Strawn. New York, N.Y.: Audio Engineering Society, 1987: 28–36.

7586. McConnell, Brian. "Woodwinds: Introduction to Wind Synthesizers." *Canadian Musician* 11 (Apr. 1989): 35.

7587. McCormick, Bart. "Modifying the DD-2 (or, a Great Digital Delay for Cheap)." *Electronic Musician* 3 (Dec. 1987): 75–76.

A modification for the Boss DD-2.

7588. McKamey, Neil. "Review: Alesis MMT-8 Sequencer." *Electronic Musician* 4 (Aug. 1988): 90–97.

7589. McKenzie, Kevan. "Product Report: Casio RZ-1 Digital Sampling Rhythm Composer." *Canadian Musician* 8 (Dec. 1986): 32.

7590. McLaughlin, John; Al Di Meola; Frank Zappa; Jim Ferguson; and Dan Forte. "Synclavier." *Guitar Player* 20 (June 1986): 122–27, 155.

Three artists, John McLaughlin, Al Di Meola, and Frank Zappa, describe their experiences with the Synclavier, as told to Jim Ferguson and Dan Forte.

7591. Means, Ben, and Jean Means. "PPG Hard Disk Unit." *Music, Computers & Software* 2 (Oct. 1987): 68–70.

Review of the direct-to-hard disk digital sampler.

7592. ———, and Jean Means. "Sampling Revisited: The 16-bit Invasion." *Music, Computers & Software* 2 (Dec. 1987): 40–44, 79.

Overviews of 16-bit sampling synthesizers from E-mu, Sequential Circuits, Casio, Forat, Kurzweil, and others.

7593. Meiere, Keith. "Roland TR-707: Drum Machine or Sequencer?" *Electronic Musician* 4 (July 1988): 108–11.

7594. Messick, Paul, and John Battle. "Keyboard Construction Project: Build a MIDI Input for Your Casio SK-1." *Keyboard* 13 (Aug. 1987): 34–40.

7595. Messina, Tony. "Percussion: MIDI Drums: Percussion Steps into the Future." *Keyboards, Computers & Software* 1 (Aug. 1986): 43–46.

7596. Meuse, Steve. "Ensoniq: Five New ROM Cartridges for the ESQ-1 and ESQ-M." *Music, Computers & Software* 3 (Feb. 1988): 77, 79.
Review.

7597. Meyer, Chris. "Ensoniq Performance Sampler." *Music Technology* 2 (Mar. 1988): 58–61.
Review of the Ensoniq EPS.

7598. ———. "Keytek CTS-2000 Crosstable Sampled Synthesizer." *Music Technology* 2 (Nov. 1987): 32–35.
Review.

7599. ———. "Oberheim Prommer." *Music Technology* 1 (Mar. 1987): 80–81.
Review of a EPROM burning and reading unit.

7600. ———. "Yamaha TX16W: Digital Wave Filtering Sampler." *Music Technology* 2 (May 1988): 42–48.
Review.

7601. ———, and Bob O'Donnell. "Regeneration." *Music Technology* 1 (July 1987): 54–59.
Review of updates for the Oberheim DPX1, Sequential Prophet 2000, 2002, 2002 +, and Roland S50 samplers.

7602. "MIDI Guitar: How Far Will It Go?" *Music Trades* 135 (Apr. 1987): 70–72.

7603. Milano, Dominic. "Keyboard Report: Emax SE Synth Functions Update." *Keyboard* 14 (May 1988): 134, 142.
A disc update for the Emax SE.

7604. ———. "Keyboard Report: Emulator Three, 16-bit Sampler & Production Facility." *Keyboard* 14 (July 1988): 150–55, 185.

7605. ———. "Keyboard Report: Garfield Doctor Click 2 Sync Interface." *Keyboard* 11 (July 1985): 101.

7606. ———. "Keyboard Report: Kawai 250 & 150 Digital Pianos." *Keyboard* 13 (Mar. 1987): 131, 148.

7607.   ——. "Keyboard Report: Kawai K1 & K1m Multi-Timbral Wave-table Synth & Module." *Keyboard* 14 (June 1988): 151–52.

7608.   ——. "Keyboard Report: Kawai M8000, MIDI Keyboard Controller." *Keyboard* 13 (Nov. 1987): 136–41.

7609.   ——. "Keyboard Report: Korg DW-6000 Polyphonic Synthesizer." *Keyboard* 11 (May 1985): 80–81.

7610.   ——. "Keyboard Report: MDB Window Recorder 16-bit Sampler." *Keyboard* 12 (June 1986): 154–55.

7611.   ——. "Keyboard Report: MIDI Switchers by Cooper, Kamlet & Zaphod." *Keyboard* 12 (Feb. 1986): 120–21.
         J.L. Cooper MIDI Switch Box MSB-1, Kamlet MIDI Patcher, and Zaphod MIDI Switcher.

7612.   ——. "Keyboard Report: PPG Wave Synthesizer—2.2 to 2.3 Update." *Keyboard* 11 (May 1985): 82.

7613.   ——. "Keyboard Report: ProVerb, Digital Reverb from ART." *Keyboard* 13 (Mar. 1987): 132, 148.

7614.   ——. "Keyboard Report: Quantec QRS/L, Mono-in, Stereo-out Room Simulator." *Keyboard* 11 (Aug. 1985): 91.

7615.   ——. "Keyboard Report: Roland JX-8P Polyphonic Synthesizer." *Keyboard* 11 (May 1985): 78–79.

7616.   ——. "Keyboard Report: Roland S-50 Sampler Version 2.0." *Keyboard* 13 (Dec. 1987): 136–43.

7617.   ——. "Keyboard Report: Yamaha DX7IIFD Digital FM Synthesizer." *Keyboard* 13 (May 1987): 116–18, 124.

7618.   ——. "Keyboard Report: Yamaha QX5, MIDI Sequence Recorder." *Keyboard* 13 (Mar. 1987): 122–28.

7619.   ——. "Synth & MIDI Basics: Internal Memory Basics: What It Is & What It Ain't." *Keyboard* 13 (May 1987): 108.

7620.   ——. "Synth & MIDI Basics: Memories Are Made of This." *Keyboard* 13 (Apr. 1987): 116.
         Describes internal memory and cartridges of digital synthesizers.

7621.   ——. "Yamaha X-Days: DX7 Mark II Unveiled in Tokyo." *Keyboard* 13 (Feb. 1987): 26–28.
         New Yamaha products, including new models of the DX7.

7622.   ——; Kyle Kevorkian; and Mark Vail. "American Synthesizer Builders." *Keyboard* 14 (May 1988): 42–43, 45–54.

7623. Mocsny, Daniel. "System: Roland PC Desk Top Music Studio." *Music, Computers & Software* 3 (Nov. 1988): 51–53.

An overview of the Roland MT-32 Multi-Timbre Sound Module and MPU-401 MIDI interface; for IBM compatibles.

7624. Moncrief, Doug. "MIDI Studio." *Music, Computers & Software* 3 (Nov. 1988): 73–74.

A tutorial on assembling a MIDI studio.

7625. Moog, Bob. "Ask Mr. Moog: An Industrial Design Student's MIDI Controller." *Keyboard* 15 (Jan. 1989): 106–9.

An overview of a performance controller designed by Stephen O'Hearn.

7626. ———. "On Synthesizers: Digital Sampling Keyboards. Part I, A Brief History of Tape and Optical Sampling." *Keyboard* 11 (Sept. 1985): 76, 91.

7627. ———. "Position and Force Sensors and Their Application to Keyboards and Related Control Devices." In *The Proceedings of the AES 5th International Conference: Music and Digital Technology,* ed. John Strawn. New York, N.Y.: Audio Engineering Society, 1987: 173–81.

7628. Moore, F. Richard. "Applications for an Integrated Computer Music Workstation." In *Proceedings of the International Computer Music Conference 1986, Royal Conservatory, The Hague, Netherlands, October 20–24, 1986,* ed. Paul Berg. San Francisco, Calif.: Computer Music Association, 1986: 381–86.

7629. ———. "What Is a Computer Music Workstation?" In *The Proceedings of the AES 5th International Conference: Music and Digital Technology,* ed. John Strawn. New York, N.Y.: Audio Engineering Society, 1987: 45–57.

7630. Moore, Scott McGregor. "Review: Ibanez SDR1000 Stereo Digital Reverb." *Electronic Musician* 3 (July 1987): 112–18.

7631. Moorer, James A. "The Lucasfilm Audio Signal Processor." *Computer Music Journal* 6,3 (Fall 1982): 22–32.

Previously **3184.**

Reprinted in *The Music Machine,* ed. Curtis Roads. Cambridge, Mass.: MIT Press, 1989: 599–609.

7632. ———. "Synthesizers I Have Known and Loved." *Computer Music Journal* 5,1 (Spring 1981): 4–12.

Previously **3187.**

Reprinted in *The Music Machine,* ed. Curtis Roads. Cambridge, Mass.: MIT Press, 1989: 589–97.

7633. Moorhead, Jan Paul. "Review: The Kawai Keyboard System." *Electronic Musician* 3 (Jan. 1987): 80–84.

7634. Morgan, Christopher. "The Kurzweil 250 Digital Synthesizer." *Byte* 11 (June 1986): 279–88.

7635. Morgan, Scott. "Mod: Casio CZ-101 Memory Expander." *Electronic Musician* 2 (July 1986): 64–65, 92.

7636. Morris, Don, and Tom Mulhern. "The Ibanez MC1 MIDI Controller." *Guitar Player* 20 (June 1986): 78–80.

7637. Mulhern, Tom. "British High-Tech: SynthAxe & Bond." *Guitar Player* 19 (Mar. 1985): 29–35.
Review of the SynthAxe guitar synthesizer.

7638. ———. "Controllers: An Overview." *Guitar Player* 20 (June 1986): 82–86.

7639. ———. "The Guitar Synthesizer: History & Development." *Guitar Player* 20 (June 1986): 16–17, 21–23, 178.

7640. ———. "Roland's GR-700 & GR-77B: An Introduction." *Guitar Player* 20 (June 1986): 70–73.

7641. ———. "Yamaha FX500." *Guitar Player* 23 (Nov. 1989): 136–41.
Review of the Yamaha FX500 multi-effects processor.

7642. Mulvaney, Elisa Welch. "Zeta VR-204 RetroPak and VC-225 Controller." *Frets* 11 (June 1989): 19, 66.
Review of a violin MIDI controller.

7643. Muro, Don. "The Contemporary Musician and the Electronic Medium: A Survey of Equipment. Part Twelve." *International Musician* 83 (Jan. 1985): 1, 30.

7644. ———. "The Contemporary Musician and the Electronic Medium: High Cost Digital Synthesizers. Part Eleven."
International Musician 83 (July 1984): 1, 15.

7645. ———. "The Contemporary Musician and the Electronic Medium: New Synthesizers. Part Fifteen." *International Musician* 86 (July 1987): 1, 14.
An overview of new developments in hardware, including drum machines and synthesizers.

7646. ———. "Digital Synthesizers and Live Performance." *Jazz Educators Journal* 16 (Feb./Mar. 1984): 15–17.

7647. Murray, Alex. "Control Zone: Sample Minds!" *Melody Maker* 62 (June 20, 1987.): 43.
Inexpensive hardware and sampling software.

7648. Nathan, Bobby. "In the Studio: Staying One Sample Ahead of Technological Change." *Keyboard* 13 (Feb. 1987): 122.

How to deal with technologically improved samplers.

7649. "New Digital Synth Is Portable, Low-priced; Computer Separate." *Variety* 315 (June 20, 1984): 59.

Describes the Kurzweil 250.

7650. "New Digital Synthesizer from Kawai Offers Top Sound, Affordable Price." *Music Traces* 136 (June 1988): 144, 146.

Describes the Kawai K1 and K1m.

7651. "New DX Products Broaden Yamaha Synth Line." *Music Trades* 133 (July 1985): 95–96.

Brief review of the Yamaha DX-21 and DX-5.

7652. Nichols, Geoff. "Reviews: Skin Deep." *Melody Maker* 61 (Aug. 2, 1986): 53.

Review of the Simmons SDS1000 drum synthesizer.

7653. Nieberle, Rupert C., and Paul Modler. "An Open Multiprocessing Architecture for Realtime Music Performance." In *Proceedings of the 14th International Computer Music Conference, Cologne, September 20–25, 1988,* ed. Christoph Lischka and Johannes Fritsch. Cologne: Feedback-Studio-Verlag; San Francisco, Calif.: Dist. by Computer Music Association, 1988: 258–64. (Feedback Papers; 33)

Presentation of a hardware design of a multiprocessor architecture for real-time audio signal processing.

7654. Nord, Kevin. "Review: The Fairlight Voicetracker." *Electronic Musician* 3 (Apr. 1987): 95–97.

Voice/wind instrument-to-MIDI monophonic converter.

7655. Nunn, Peter. "Keyboards: Product Review: The EPS Sampler by Ensoniq." *Canadian Musician* 10 (Dec. 1988): 16.

7656. O'Donnell, Bob. "Alesis HR-16:B." *Electronic Musician* 5 (Nov. 1989): 82.

Review of the Alesis HR-16:B drum machine.

7657. ———. "In Brief: Alesis HR16 Drum Machine & MMT8 MIDI Recorder." *Music Technology* 2 (Sept. 1987): 34–35.

Review.

7658. ———. "In Brief: Ensoniq SQ80 Cross Wave Synthesizer and EPS Performance Sampler." *Music Technology* 2 (Jan. 1988): 24–25.

Review.

7659. ——. "In Brief: Kawai K1 and K1M Digital Multi-Timbral Synthesizers." *Music Technology* 2 (Mar. 1988): 15.

Review.

7660. ——. "In Brief: Technos Acxel Resynthesizer." *Music Technology* 2 (Mar. 1988): 22–23.

Review.

7661. ——. "J. L. Cooper FaderMaster." *Electronic Musician* 5 (Nov. 1989): 75–76.

Review of the MIDI remote control.

7662. ——. "Kawai K5 and K5M: Multi-Dimensional Synthesizers." *Music Technology* 2 (Aug. 1987): 75–78.

Review.

7663. ——. "Korg DDD5: Dynamic Digital Drum Machine." *Music Technology* 1 (June 1987): 37–39.

Review.

7664. ——. "Korg M3R." *Electronic Musician* 5 (Dec. 1989): 108.

A reduced version of the Korg M1.

7665. ——. "Korg SQ8: Eight-Track MIDI Sequencer." *Music Technology* 1 (June 1987): 84–86.

7666. ——. "Programmable Crunch: A Survey of Guitar Multi-Effects Processors." *Electronic Musician* 5 (Oct. 1989): 36–45.

7667. ——. "Reviews: E-mu Proteus." *Electronic Musician* 5 (Oct. 1989): 92–95.

Review of a MIDI expander.

7668. ——. "Reviews: Ensoniq VFX Synthesizer." *Electronic Musician* 5 (Sept. 1989): 86–91.

Review of a wavetable synthesizer.

7669. ——. "Roland VP70 Voice Processor." *Music Technology* 2 (Nov. 1987): 70–74.

Review.

7670. ——. "Synhance MTS1: MIDI Synchronization Unit." *Music Technology* 1 (July 1987): 30–33.

7671. O'Donnell, Craig. "Review: Roland DDR-30 and Pad-8 Controller." *Electronic Musician* 2 (July 1986): 78–82.

7672. O'Donnell, Rich. "Feature: Electronics in Percussion—Listening to a Different Drummer." *Percussive Notes* 26 (Spring 1988): 13–15.

Discusses the pros and cons of drum machines and details of several specific machines.

7673. Oppenheimer, Larry. "Review: The E-mu SP-12." *Electronic Musician* 2 (July 1986): 84–90.

Review of a 12-bit sampling drum computer.

7674. Oppenheimer, Steve. "First Take: Capsule Comments: Kawai K1II Wavetable Synthesizer." *Electronic Musician* 5 (Sept. 1989): 80–81.

7675. ———. "Lexicon LXP-5 Effects Processing Module." *Electronic Musician* 5 (Nov. 1989): 78.

7676. Packham, Blair. "Product Review: Akai MPC60, A Great 'All-in-One' Unit." *Canadian Musician* 10 (Dec. 1988): 28.

7677. Paretti, Rob. "Keyboards: Product Review: Casio FZ-1." *Canadian Musician* 9 (Aug. 1987): 87.

Review of a synthesizer.

7678. Parisi, Deborah. "Elka MK88: Master Keyboard Controller." *Music Technology* 2 (Mar. 1988): 16–18.

Review.

7679. ———. "In Brief: Kawai M8000 MIDI Controller Keyboard." *Music Technology* 2 (Oct. 1987): 20.

Review.

7680. "Peavey Expands Effects Pedal Line." *Music Trades* 135 (Nov. 1987): 78.

Brief review of the SRP-16, digital reverb, and DEP-16, stereo effects processor.

7681. "Peavey Introduces DEP 3.2S Digital Sampling Processor." *Music Trades* 136 (Mar. 1988): 89.

7682. "Peavey Shows New Software-based Synth." *Music Trades* 137 (Feb. 1989): 113.

Introduction of the Peavey DPM-3.

7683. "Peavey Takes Aim at MIDI Market." *Music Trades* 135 (July 1987): 95–96.

Products unveiled at the tenth dealer pre-show.

7684. "Peavey Unveils Unprecedented MIDI Programmable Mixer." *Music Trades* 135 (Sept. 1987): 88.

Brief review of the Peavey PKM 8128.

7685. Pennycook, Bruce W.; Jeffrey Kulick; and Dave Dove. "Music Workstations: Real-Time Subsystem Design." In *The Proceedings of the AES 5th International Conference: Music and Digital Technology,* ed. John Strawn. New York, N.Y.: Audio Engineering Society, 1987: 58–73.

7686. Perkis, Tim. "Just Intonation on Yamaha's New FM Synths." *Electronic Musician* 4 (July 1988): 98–107.

7687. Petersen, George. "Lexicon LXP-1 Multi-Effect Processing Module." *Electronic Musician* 4 (Oct. 1988): 93–96.
Review.

7688. ———. "P.K.I. Gun-Drums." *Electronic Musician* 4 (June 1988): 99–100.
Review of hand-held drum machines.

7689. Pitonzo, Joseph D. "Buying Your First Synthesizer." *Pastoral Music* 12 (Aug.–Sept. 1988): 35.

7690. Pogan, Charles. "Casio CZ-101." *Electronic Musician* 1 (Sept. 1985): 30–31.
Describes the polyphonic synthesizer.

7691. ———. "Review: Sequential Circuits 610 MIDI Six-trak." *Polyphony* 10 (Apr. 1985): 32–33.
Review of a polyphonic keyboard.

7692. Pohlman, Ken C. "Signals: Chips Ahoy." *Stereo Review* 54 (May 1989): 22.
A discussion of various chips used in a variety of computing hardware.

7693. Ponting, Tim. "Simmons Silicon Mallet." *Music Technology* 2 (Feb. 1988): 99–101.
Review of a xylophone MIDI controller.

7694. Porter, David. "Techno: Casio's PG-380: Fresh Chops from a New Axe." *Ear* 13 (Oct. 1988): 9.
Describes a guitar controller.

7695. Powell, Steven. "The ABCs of Synthesizers." *Music Educators Journal* 74 (Dec. 1987): 27–31.

7696. Powers, Tracy. "Control Zone: Me & My Shadow." *Melody Maker* 64 (Feb. 13, 1988): 36.
Review of the Shadow SH075 guitar-to-MIDI converter.

7697. ———. "Mad on Add-ons?" *Melody Maker* 65 (Feb. 18, 1989): 44.
Review of two add-ons for the DX7.

7698. "Product News: Rack-mountable Digital Sampling from Sequential." *Canadian Musician* 8 (June 1986): 76.
Review of the Prophet 2002.

7699. "Quark Energy." *Melody Maker* 60 (May 18, 1985): 36.
Quark MIDI-Links, MIDI switching unit.

7700. Radier, J. C.; Charles Deforeit; and D. Provost. "A User Friendly Synthesizer by Means of a Touch Input Wide LCD Graphic Display." In *Proceedings of the International Computer Music Conference 1986, Royal Conservatory, The Hague, Netherlands, October 20–24, 1986,* ed. Paul Berg. San Francisco, Calif.: Computer Music Association, 1986: 99–100.

7701. Ramo, John. "New Products." *Jazz Times* (Aug. 1985): 21.
Describes the Simmons SDS9 drum machine and the Roland JX-8P keyboard synthesizer.

7702. Reed, Tony. "Control Zone: Small Wonders." *Melody Maker* 64 (Jan. 9, 1988): 36–37.
Review of various samplers.

7703. ———. "Control Zone: Straight 8." *Melody Maker* 65 (Apr. 29, 1989): 44.
Review of the Yamaha RX8 drum machine.

7704. "Reviews: Cosmo Small Piece!" *Melody Maker* 61 (Aug. 2, 1986): 51.
Review of the Casio CZ-1 synthesizer and AZ-1 remote keyboard.

7705. Rich, Robert. "Reviews: Peavey MIDI Effects Automation System." *Electronic Musician* 5 (Oct. 1989): 86–91.

7706. ———. "Tuning Facilities in the Ensoniq EPS Sampling Keyboard." *Computer Music Journal* 13,1 (Spring 1989): 68–69.
Review.

7707. Roads, Curtis. "Dynachord DRP-20 Reverberator and Effects Processor." *Computer Music Journal* 13,1 (Spring 1989): 69–70.
Review of a two-channel reverberation and effects processor that incorporates a proprietary 32-bit floating-point signal processing chip, the DSP338396.

7708. ———. "The Eventide Ultra-Harmonizer H3000." *Computer Music Journal* 13,2 (Summer 1989): 89–90.
Review of MIDI-controlled reverberator and effects device.

7709. "Roland Adds New Juno Synthesizers." *Music Trades* 134 (May 1986): 90–92.
Brief review of the Roland alpha Juno-1 and alpha Juno-2.

7710. "Roland Adds VLSI Chip to Keyboard Samplers." *Music Trades* 34 (Dec. 1986): 96, 98.
A discussion of the Roland S-50 and S-10 samplers.

7711. "Roland Expands Computer Music Horizons." *Music Trades* 131 (Dec. 1983): 92–94.
Brief review of the Roland MIDI processing unit, MPU-401.

7712. "Roland Shows W-30, Urges Better Retail Marketing Efforts." *Music Trades* 137 (Feb. 1989): 120–21.
Introduction of the Roland W-30, a synthesizer workstation.

7713. "Roland's Guitar Processor Features Eight Programmable Effects." *Music Trades* 135 (Oct. 1987): 91.
A discussion of the Roland GP-8.

7714. "Roland's JX-8P Serves as MIDI Controller, Sound Module." *Music Trades* 133 (June 1985): 124, 127.
Brief review of the Roland JX-8P, a six-voice polyphonic synthesizer.

7715. "Roland's VP-70 Lets Vocalists Use MIDI." *Music Trades* 135 (May 1987): 127.
Brief review of the Roland VP-70, a MIDI voice processor.

7716. Rolle, Günter. "Wenn Mensch und Computer gemeinsam hören—der kleine Alleskönner: 'Stimmungs' bericht über eine neues Stimmgerät." *Neue Musikzeitung* 38 (Apr.–Mai 1989): 52.
A discussion of the TLA Tuning Set CTS-4.

7717. Rona, Jeff. "Arranging Series: Wind Synthesis: Programming Technique with or without the Keyboard." *Keyboard* 13 (July 1987): 47–57.

7718. Rosenthal, David. "Review: The Casio FZ-1 Digital Sampling Synthesizer." *Electronic Musician* 3 (Sept. 1987): 78–80.

7719. Rossum, Dave. "Digital Musical Instrument Design: The Art of Compromise." In *The Proceedings of the AES 5th International Conference: Music and Digital Technology*, ed. John Strawn. New York, N.Y.: Audio Engineering Society, 1987: 21–27.

7720. Rothstein, Joseph B. "Ambience Effects System." *Computer Music Journal* 10,3 (Fall 1986): 114.
Review of the AES-357 audio processor by Marshall Electronic.

7721. ———. "Bass Trap for Sound Studios." *Computer Music Journal* 10,3 (Fall 1986): 111.
Review of Tube Trap, a portable basstrap, by Acoustic Sciences Corp.

7722. ———. "Lexicon Digital Effects Processor." *Computer Music Journal* 10,3 (Fall 1986): 112.
Review of the PCM-70, which incorporates MIDI control.

7723.   ———. "REV-7 Digital Reverberator from Yamaha." *Computer Music Journal* 10,3 (Fall 1986): 110–11.
Review.

7724.   Rowland, Nicholas. "Roland TR626 Rhythm Composer." *Music Technology* 2 (Dec. 1987): 18–21.
Review of a drum machine.

7725.   ———. "Simmons MTX9: Percussion Voice Expander." *Music Technology* 2 (Aug. 1987): 56–58.
Review.

7726.   ———. "Simmons SDE: Percussion Voice Expander." *Music Technology* 1 (Jan. 1987): 64–66.
Review.

7727.   ———. "Simmons SDX: Electronic Percussion System." *Music Technology* 2 (May 1988): 88–93.
Review.

7728.   Rubbazzer, Maurizio; Maurizio Santoiemma; and Gianantonio Patella. "Some Advances in the Development of a New Architecture for a Digital Sound Synthesizer." In *Proceedings of the International Computer Music Conference 1986, Royal Conservatory, The Hague, Netherlands, October 20–24, 1986,* ed. Paul Berg. San Francisco, Calif.: Computer Music Association, 1986: 353–58.

7729.   ———; Maurizio Santoiemma; and Gianantonio Patella. "Una nuova architettura per un sintetizzatore digitale di suoni." [A New Architecture for a Digital Sound Synthesizer] In *Musica e tecnologia: industria e cultura per lo sviluppo del mezzogiorno: VI Colloquio di Informatica Musicale, Napoli 16–19 ottobre 1985,* ed. Carlo Acreman; Immacolata Ortosecco; and Fausto Razzi. Milan: Edizioni Unicopli, 1987: 301–3.

7730.   Rubine, Dean, and Paul McAvinney. "The VideoHarp." In *Proceedings of the 14th International Computer Music Conference, Cologne, September 20–25, 1988,* ed. Christoph Lischka and Johannes Fritsch. Cologne: Feedback-Studio-Verlag; San Francisco, Calif.: Dist. by Computer Music Association, 1988: 49–55. (Feedback Papers; 33)
An optical-scanning musical instrument controller.

7731.   Rudes, Jordan. "KCScope: Casio SK-1." *Keyboards, Computers & Software* 1 (Aug. 1986): 58–59.
Review of a low-cost sampling keyboard.

7732.   ———. "Lexicon PCM-70 Digital Effects Processor." *Keyboards, Computers & Software* 1 (Feb. 1986): 54–55.
Review.

7733.   ——. "Oberheim Matrix-6." *Keyboards, Computers & Software* 1 (Apr. 1986): 54–55.

Review of the six-voice analog synthesizer.

7734.   Russell, Benjamin. "Product Report: Alesis MIDIVERB." *Canadian Musician* 8 (Aug. 1986): 31.

7735.   ——. "Product Report: Casio CZ-1 Synthesizer." *Canadian Musician* 9 (Feb. 1987): 24.

7736.   ——. "Product Report: Ensoniq ESQ-1 Synthesizer." *Canadian Musician* 9 (Feb. 1987): 24–25.

7737.   ——. "Product Report: Korg DDD-1 Drum Machine." *Canadian Musician* 9 (Feb. 1987): 25.

7738.   ——. "Product Report: Korg DW-8000, EX-8000, MEX-8000." *Canadian Musician* 8 (June 1986): 33.

7739.   ——. "Product Report: Roland TR-505 Digital Drum Machine." *Canadian Musician* 8 (Aug. 1986): 32.

7740.   ——. "Product Report: Yamaha Digital Multi-Effects: Rev 7 and SPX90." *Canadian Musician* 8 (Aug. 1986): 31–32.

7741.   ——. "Product Review: Ibanez MIDI Guitar and IMC1 (MIDI Guitar System)." *Canadian Musician* 9 (Apr. 1987): 71.

Review of the Ibanez IMG2010 guitar and IMC1.

7742.   Rychner, Lorenz. "Recasting the Mold: Korg DSM1 & E-Mu SP1200." *Music Technology* 2 (Jan. 1988): 75–78.

Review of the Korg DSM1, digital sampling synthesizer module, and E-mu SP1200, sampling drum machine.

7743.   Ryckebusch, Jules. "A 64-Patch CZ RAM Cartridge for $15." *Electronic Musician* 4 (July 1988): 127–30.

Directions on how to add sixty-four patches to a CZ-series synthesizer.

7744.   Sagman, Stephen. "Industry Trends." *Electronic Musician* 2 (Mar. 1986): 15.

Review of general trends of electronic musical instrument manufacturers.

7745.   Sandler, Mark. "High Complexity Resonator Structures for Formant Synthesis of Musical Instruments." In *Design Tools for the 90's: Fifteenth Euromicro Symposium on Microprocessing and Micropro- gramming (EUROMICRO 89), Cologne, September 4–8, 1989*, ed. Lorenzo Mezzalire and Stephen Winter. Amsterdam; New York, N.Y.: North-Holland, 1989: 557–62.

7746. Savicky, Randy. "Sights and Sounds." *Jazz Times* (Aug. 1988): 24. Describes the Vocalizer 1000 by Breakaway Music Systems.

7747. Saydlowski, Bob. "Electronic Review: Dynacord P-20 Digital MIDI Drumkit." *Modern Drummer* 12 (Jan. 1988): 126–27.

7748. ———. "Electronic Review: E-mu Systems SP-1200 Sampling Percussion System." *Modern Drummer* 12 (May 1988): 108–9.

7749. ———. "Electronic Review: Pearl SC-40 Syncussion-X." *Modern Drummer* 11 (Oct. 1987): 128–29.

7750. ———. "Product Close-up: Casio RZ-1 Digital Sampling Rhythm Composer." *Modern Drummer* 10 (July 1986): 98.

7751. ———. "Product Close-up: MPC and Instant Replay." *Modern Drummer* 8 (Feb. 1984): 42–43.
Review of MPC, Music Percussion Computer, and Instant Replay, a two-second sampler.

7752. Scacciaferro, Joe. "MCS MIDI." *Music, Computers & Software* 2 (Dec. 1987): 12–13.
A tutorial on evaluating MIDI capabilities of various equipment.

7753. Schmidt, Paul. "The Casio DH-100 Digital Horn." *Electronic Musician* 5 (Jan. 1989): 101, 117.
Review.

7754. Schneider, Albrecht. "Sample and Hold: Das Instrument aus dem Chip." *Musikhandel* 36 (Apr. 1985): 150–54.
An overview of trends in synthesizers.

7755. Schneider, Henry. "Computers: Have You Tried This?" *Electronic Musician* 2 (June 1986): 46.
Random patches for parameter control synthesizers.

7756. Scholz, Carter. "Reference Sheet for the DX7 E! Expansion Board." *Electronic Musician* 4 (July 1988): 116.

7757. Schroeder, Michael. "Computers You Control with a Wave of Your Hand." *Business Week* (Feb. 20, 1989): 142.
Describes Paul McAvinney's Videoharp and Sensor Frame.

7758. Selfe, Ned. "Review: Digitech/IVL Steel Guitar-to-MIDI Interface." *Electronic Musician* 3 (Sept. 1987): 82–87.
Review of Steelrider.

7759. Sharp, Mike, and Bill Burns. "Reviews: Roland GR-50 Guitar Synthesizer System." *Electronic Musician* 5 (Oct. 1989): 96–101.

7760. Shea, Mike. "Get Rhythm: The Boss DR-110 Rhythm Machine." *Record* 3 (July 1984): 52.

Review.

7761. Shelef, Itai; Uri Shimony; and Itai Nehoran. "A Modular Real-Time Digital Processor of Audio Signals." In *Proceedings of the International Computer Music Conference 1986, Royal Conservatory, The Hague, Netherlands, October 20–24, 1986*, ed. Paul Berg. San Francisco, Calif.: Computer Music Association, 1986: 101–3.

7762. Shelstad, Kirby. "Alternate Controllers: Kat MIDI Percussion: Let's Play Fast." *Keyboard* 15 (Mar. 1989): 109–10.

Techniques for using the Kat MIDI Percussion Controller.

7763. Shrieve, Michael, and David Beal. "Alternate Controllers: Drums Across the MIDI Stream: Pad Percussion Tips." *Keyboard* 15 (June 1989): 116–17.

7764. ——, and David Beal. "Alternate Controllers: Exploring MIDI Percussion. Part II." *Keyboard* 15 (July 1989): 102–3, 152.

7765. Sirota, Warren. "Product Profiles: Photon Guitar Synth Controller." *Guitar Player* 22 (Dec. 1988): 140–41.

7766. ——. "Roland GR-50 Guitar Synthesizer." *Guitar Player* 23 (July 1989): 152, 172.

7767. Smith, Bennett K., and Paul Chervin. "Boris: An Application of the Fujitsu MB8764 DSP Chip." In *Proceedings of the International Computer Music Conference 1986, Royal Conservatory, The Hague, Netherlands, October 20–24, 1986*, ed. Paul Berg. San Francisco, Calif.: Computer Music Association, 1986: 365–68.

7768. Smith, David G. "The Digital Workstation: The Emulator III." *Active Sensing* 1 (Summer 1989): 5.

Review.

7769. Smith, Mark. "A Basic Checklist of MIDI Guitars." *Down Beat* 53 (Nov. 1986): 64–65.

7770. Sofer, Daniel. "The Music Processor: Sequencers Mature, Bringing Across-the-Board Liberation." *Musician* n75 (Jan. 1985): 68–70, 88–89.

7771. "Son of DX7 Debuts at Winter NAMM." *Music Trades* 135 (Feb. 1987): 91–93.

A brief introduction to the Yamaha DX7II synthesizers.

7772. Sterling, Mark. "Chips: EPROM Blower: The Answer My Friend Is Blowin' in the . . ." *Keyboards, Computers & Software* 1 (Dec. 1986): 37–38.

Discusses the use of commercial EPROM programmers to expand/replace sound samples in sampling synthesizers.

7773. ———. "Guitar Controllers II: The Second Generation." *Music, Computers & Software* 2 (Aug. 1987): 54–57, 64.

A discussion of new advances in guitar MIDI controllers.

7774. Strom, Pauline Anna. "Review: Yamaha QX1." *Electronic Musician* 1 (Sept. 1985): 21, 42.

Review of an eight-track MIDI sequencer.

7775. Summers, Andy; Steve Morse; Robert Fripp; and Jan Obrecht. "Roland GR." *Guitar Player* 20 (June 1986): 113–21, 155.

Three artists, Andy Summers, Steve Morse, and Robert Fripp, describe their experiences with the Roland GR, as told to Jan Obrecht.

7776. "Synclavier: Past, Present, and Future." *Music Technology* 1,1 (1986): 82–84.

7777. Tamm, Allan C. "Yamaha TX7 MIDI Expander." *Electronic Musician* 1 (Sept. 1985): 27–29.

FM tone generator.

7778. "Technics Adds Three PCM Keyboards." *Music Trades* 133 (Sept. 1985): 82, 87.

Brief review of models SX-K300, SX-K350, and SX-K450.

7779. "Test: Der Yamaha TX802 FM-Expander: Das FM-MIDI-Orchester ganz in Schwarz." *Musik International* 42 (Jan.–Feb. 1988): 82–86.

7780. "Test: Für Feinschmecker: Digital Sampling Synthesizer Hohner HS-1." *Musik International* 42 (Jan.–Feb. 1988): 87–89.

7781. "Test: Hohner KS 49 MIDI—klein aber fein!" *Musik International* 42 (Jan.–Feb. 1988): 90–92.

7782. Thomas, Tony. "Review: Yamaha FB-01 Sound Module." *Electronic Musician* 2 (Nov. 1986): 90–91.

Review of an eight-voice, velocity and aftertouch sensitive multi-timbral MIDI expander module.

7783. ———. "Review: Yamaha's DX21 Synthesizer." *Electronic Musician* 2 (Jan. 1986): 50–51.

7784. ———. "Tripping the Light Fantastic: The Fiber Optic Link." *Music, Computers & Software* 3 (Apr. 1988): 51, 57.

Discusses the use of optic fiber as a replacement for copper wire.

7785. Tolinski, Brad. "Digital Music Services' FB Pro/Yamaha FB-01/Yamaha MIDI Data Filer I." *Music, Computers & Software* 2 (Aug. 1987): 71–73.

Reviews of the FB-01 sound module, an editor/librarian for the FB-01 and the Macintosh, and a MIDI data storage device.

7786. ———. "Korg DS-8." *Music, Computers & Software* 2 (Aug. 1987): 68–71.

Review of the digital synthesizer.

7787. ———. "Sequential's STUDIO 440 Version 2.0: The Final Revision." *Music, Computers & Software* 2 (Dec. 1987): 73–76.

Review of the sampling synthesizer/MIDI sequencer.

7788. Trask, Simon. "Akai X7000 Sampling Keyboard." *Music Technology* 1 (Jan. 1987): 12–14.

Review.

7789. ———. "Alesis MMT8 Sequencer." *Music Technology* 2 (Mar. 1988): 86–88.

Review.

7790. ———. "ART DR1, Programmable Digital Reverb." *Music Technology* 1 (May 1987): 42–47.

Review.

7791. ———. "Casio MG: MIDI Guitar." *Music Technology* 2 (Dec. 1987): 55–57.

Review.

7792. ———. "In Brief: Akai MX73 MIDI Master Keyboard." *Music Technology* 1 (Oct. 1986): 18.

Review.

7793. ———. "In Brief: Casio AZ1 Remote Keyboard." *Music Technology* 1 (Feb. 1987): 18.

Review.

7794. ———. "In Brief: Casio CZ1 Polyphonic Synthesizer." *Music Technology* 1 (Oct. 1986): 22.

Review.

7795. ———. "In Brief: Oberheim Matrix 6R Expander." *Music Technology* 1 (Sept. 1986): 28.

Review of a polyphonic synthesizer.

7796. ———. "In Brief: Yamaha DX7II Synthesizers." *Music Technology* 1 (Mar. 1987): 24–25.

Review.

7797. ———. "Kawai R50 Digital Drum Machine." *Music Technology* 2 (Sept. 1987): 68–70.

Review.

7798. ——. "Korg 707 FM Synthesizer." *Music Technology* 2 (May 1988): 100–101.
Review.

7799. ——. "Korg DS8: Digital FM Synthesizer." *Music Technology* 1 (July 1987): 24–28.
Review.

7800. ——. "Korg SG1 Digital Piano." *Music Technology* 1 (Mar. 1987): 88–89.
Review.

7801. ——. "Roland D50: Linear Arithmetic Synthesizer." *Music Technology* 1 (July 1987): 84–89.
Review.

7802. ——. "Roland D50: Linear Arithmetic Synthesizer. Part 1." *Music Technology* 1 (June 1987): 24–25.
Review.

7803. ——. "Roland MKB200: MIDI Controller Keyboard." *Music Technology* 1 (Apr. 1987): 46–47.
Review.

7804. ——. "Roland MT32: Multitimbral Synth Expander." *Music Technology* 2 (Oct. 1987): 24–26.
Review.

7805. ——. "Roland RD300: SAS Electronic Piano." *Music Technology* 1 (Feb. 1987): 50–51.
Review.

7806. ——. "Taking Notes." *Music Technology* 1 (Oct. 1986): 82–83.
Review of the Akai ME30P patchbay and ME25S note separator.

7807. ——. "Unique DBM, MIDI Master Keyboard." *Music Technology* 1 (Nov. 1986): 24–26.
Review.

7808. ——. "Wersi MK1 Polyphonic Synthesizer." *Music Technology* 1 (Dec. 1986): 36–38.
Review.

7809. ——. "Yamaha MCS2, MIDI Control Station." *Music Technology* 1 (Oct. 1986): 54–55.
Review.

7810. ——. "Yamaha QX5: Digital Multitrack Sequencer." *Music Technology* 1 (Jan. 1987): 36–38.
Review.

7811. ———, and Dan Goldstein. "Future Shock." *Music Technology* 1 (Sept. 1986): 42–46.

Review of the Series III Fairlight and the PPG Realizer.

7812. ———, and Paul Wiffen. "Roland Sampling Keyboards." *Music Technology* 1 (Dec. 1986): 86–92.

Review of the Roland S10 and S50.

7813. Tully, Tim. "Applications: Choosing the Right Sampler." *Electronic Musician* 2 (Dec. 1986): 26–34.

7814. ———. "Applications: Korg's DSS-1: Schizophrenia as Art." *Electronic Musician* 3 (Sept. 1987): 66–73.

Review of the Korg DSS-1 digital sampling synthesizer.

7815. ———. "Korg DSM-1." *Electronic Musician* 4 (Feb. 1988): 116.

Review of the Korg DSM-1 digital sampling synthesizer module.

7816. ———. "Review: Akai EWI1000/EVI1000 and EWV2000." *Electronic Musician* 4 (Feb. 1988): 118–23.

Review of The Akai Electronic Woodwind Instrument (EWI1000), Electronic Valve Instrument (EVI1000), and EWV2000 synthesizer.

7817. ———. "Review: The Yamaha WX7 Wind MIDI Controller." *Electronic Musician* 4 (May 1988): 102–7.

7818. ———. "Reviews: E-mu Systems Emax SE HD." *Electronic Musician* 4 (Oct. 1988): 102–7.

Review of a sampler.

7819. ———. "Reviews: Forte Music's Mentor MIDI Master Controller." *Electronic Musician* 5 (Mar. 1989): 88–95.

7820. ———. "Reviews: Synthophone: The MIDI Sax from Softwind Instruments." *Electronic Musician* 4 (Dec. 1988): 106–11.

7821. ———. "Reviews: The H3000S Ultra Harmonizer from Eventide." *Electronic Musician* 5 (Jan. 1989): 102–5.

Review of the 16-bit, stereo multiple effects generator.

7822. ———. "Yamaha REV5 Digital Reverberator." *Electronic Musician* 4 (Jan. 1988): 82–83.

7823. Twigg, Geoff. "Guitar Synthesis: The Next Big Thing?" *Music Technology* 1,1 (1986): 80–81.

7824. Unger, Brian. "Musical Hardware: Digital Music Corp. MX-8." *Music, Computers & Software* 3 (Nov. 1988): 65.

Review of the programmable MIDI patch-bay device.

7825. "Unisynth MIDI Guitars . . . at $299, a Hit at NAMM." *Music Trades* 135 (Oct. 1987): 83–84.

Describes the Unisynth XG-1m MIDI guitar.

7826. "V50 Tops New Yamaha Synth Line." *Music Trades* 137 (Feb. 1989): 115–17.

7827. Vail, Mark. "Keyboard Report: Casio VZ-8M, Rack-mount Synthesizer." *Keyboard* 15 (Nov. 1989): 112–19.

7828. ———. "Keyboard Report: Consumer Keyboards: Funstations in Focus." *Keyboard* 14 (Nov. 1988): 149–52, 171.

Review of the Yamaha DSR-2000, Casio HT-6000, and Technics SX-K700.

7829. ———. "Keyboard Report: Grey Matter Response E!, Enhancement for the Yamaha DX7II/DX7S." *Keyboard* 14 (May 1988): 138–42.

7830. ———. "Keyboard Report: KMX MIDI Central & 360 Systems MIDI Patcher." *Keyboard* 14 (Dec. 1988): 158–63, 167–68.

7831. ———. "Keyboard Report: Korg 707, Digital FM Synthesizer." *Keyboard* 14 (June 1988): 154–55, 171.

7832. ———. "Keyboard Report: Kurzweil 1000 Series, Sample Playing Keyboard and Rack-mount Modules." *Keyboard* 14 (Apr. 1988): 136–41.

7833. ———. "Keyboard Report: MIDI Mitigator RFC-1, Foot Controller." *Keyboard* 15 (Apr. 1989): 127, 130.

Multi-switch MIDI foot controller.

7834. ———. "Keyboard Report: MidiDisk, Sys-ex Data Recorder." *Keyboard* 14 (Sept. 1988): 145–46.

Rack-mount MIDI system-exclusive data filing system.

7835. ———. "Keyboard Report: Pitch-to-MIDI Converters, Digigram MIDIMic & Vicnair Chromatic Translator Module." *Keyboard* 14 (Dec. 1988): 149–57, 167.

7836. ———. "Keyboard Report: Roland D-20 Digital Synthesizer." *Keyboard* 14 (Oct. 1988): 134–37.

7837. ———. "Keyboard Report: Roland HP-5000S & MT-100, Digital Piano & Sequencer/Tone Module." *Keyboard* 15 (June 1989): 126–28, 146–47.

7838. ———. "Keyboard Report: SP-1, Spatial Sound Processor." *Keyboard* 15 (July 1989): 141–44.

7839.   ———. "Keyboard Report: Yamaha TX16W 12-bit Sampler." *Keyboard* 14 (June 1988): 138–41, 170–71.

7840.   ———. "Keyboard Report: Yamaha TX1P, Rack-mount Piano Module." *Keyboard* 14 (July 1988): 170–72.
          Digital piano module.

7841.   Van Patten, Paul. "Electronic Review: Yamaha RX-8 Digital Rhythm Programmer." *Modern Drummer* 13 (Sept. 1989): 54–57.

7842.   Vangellow, Alex. "KCScope: Axxess Mapper." *Keyboards, Computers & Software* 1 (Dec. 1986): 50–51.
          Review of a MIDI mapping device that can redefine MIDI codes to perform new tasks.

7843.   ———. "KCScope: Yamaha Studio 100 System." *Keyboards, Computers & Software* 2 (Feb. 1987): 63–65.
          Review of a a MIDI studio setup in one package, including synthesizer, sequencer, drum computer, cassette, and powered speakers.

7844.   ———. "Korg DSS-1." *Keyboards, Computers & Software* 1 (Dec. 1986): 57–58.
          Review of a digital, multi-sampling synthesizer.

7845.   ———. "Roland JX10." *Music, Computers & Software* 2 (May 1987): 56–57.

7846.   "Vom Synthesizer zum Musik-Computer: Analog und Digital: Wer die Wahl hat, kauft am besten beides." *Musikhandel* 35 (Apr. 1984): 128–29.

7847.   Walker, Russ; Jim Burgess; Benjamin Russell; and Paul Atkinson. "Focus on Pro Keyboards: The Hottest Gear from the Hottest Companies. Part II." *Canadian Musician* 8 (Apr. 1986): 47–52.
          A look at products from Korg, PPG Synthesizers, Ensoniq Mirage, Oberheim, Synclavier, Chroma Polaris, Kawai, and Technics.

7848.   Warrick, James. "An Armchair Shopper's Guide to Synthesizers." *Clavier* 26,8 (Oct. 1987): 30–31.
          A comparison chart.

7849.   ———. "A Survey of Synthesizers and Drum Machines. Part II." *Jazz Educators Journal* 19 (Feb./Mar. 1987): 23–25.

7850.   ———, and Robert L. Tjarks. "An Armchair Shopper's Guide to Synthesizers." *Instrumentalist* 42 (Feb. 1988): 31–36.

7851.   Weinberg, Norman. "The Akai S950 Sampler." *Modern Drummer* 13 (June 1989): 42–44.

7852.   ———. "Electronic Review: R8 Human Rhythm Composer." *Modern Drummer* 13 (Aug. 1989): 58–60.
Review of the Roland R8 drum machine.

7853.   ———. "Electronic Review: Yamaha D8 Electronic Kit." *Modern Drummer* 13 (Apr. 1989): 44–46.

7854.   ———. "Focus on Electronics: Electronic Setups." *Modern Drummer* 13 (Feb. 1989): 28–33.
Drum machine set-ups.

7855.   ———. "The Machine Shop: Drum Machine Reference Chart." *Modern Drummer* 13 (Feb. 1989): 52–57.

7856.   Weiss, Daniel. "360 Systems MIDI Patcher." *Electronic Musician* 5 (July 1989): 107–9.

7857.   Wells, Richard; T. Lavitz; Jock Baird; Larry Fast; and Fay Lovsky. "Studios of the (Not Yet) Rich and (Almost) Famous." *Electronic Musician* 5 (Feb. 1989): 68–83.
Musicians describe their working studios.

7858.   "Wendel: The Amazing Drum Machine." *InfoWorld* 6 (Apr. 30, 1984): 24.
Describes a prototype drum machine.

7859.   Westfall, Lachlan. "Casio's New Drum Machine—The CZ-101?" *Electronic Musician* 3 (June 1987): 78–79.
How to use the Casio CZ-101 as a drum machine.

7860.   White, Paul. "Alesis MIDIverb." *Music Technology* 1,1 (1986): 76–78.
Review.

7861.   ———. "Alesis MIDIverb II: Preset Digital Reverb Unit." *Music Technology* 1 (May 1987): 64–65.

7862.   ———. "In Brief: ADA Pitchtraq." *Music Technology* 1 (Jan. 1987): 23.
Review of a programmable pitch-shifter.

7863.   ———. "In Brief: Alesis Microverb." *Music Technology* 1 (Feb. 1987): 22.
Review of a digital reverb unit.

7864.   ———. "In Brief: Ibanez SRD 1000 Digital Reverb." *Music Technology* 1 (Sept. 1986): 26.
Review.

7865.   ———. "Roland DEP3: Digital Effects Processor." *Music Technology* 1 (July 1987): 94–95.
          Review.

7866.   ———. "Roland DEP5 Multi-Effects Unit." *Music Technology* 1 (Nov. 1986): 50–53.
          Review.

7867.   ———. "Roland GM70: Guitar-to-MIDI Converter." *Music Technology* 1 (Apr. 1987): 28–31.
          Review.

7868.   ———. "Sound Effects." *Music Technology* 1 (Sept. 1986): 84–85.
          Review of the Alesis MIDIfex digital reverb unit.

7869.   ———. "Yamaha SPX90 Digital Multi-Effects Processor." *Music Technology* 1,1 (1986): 59–62.
          Review.

7870.   Widders-Ellis, Andy. "Alternate Controllers: The Chapman Stick Meets MIDI: Some Practical Applications." *Keyboard* 15 (Feb. 1989): 126–27, 168.

7871.   ———. "Keyboard Report: 360 Systems, Audio Matrix 16." *Keyboard* 15 (Apr. 1989): 116–17.
          Programmable, MIDI-controlled 16 × 16 audio patch bay.

7872.   ———. "Keyboard Report: Alesis HR-16 MIDI Drum Machine." *Keyboard* 15 (Jan. 1989): 124–27.

7873.   ———. "Keyboard Report: Korg A3, Multi-Effects Processor." *Keyboard* 15 (Sept. 1989): 120–21, 128, 136.

7874.   ———. "Keyboard Report: UltraVerb, MultiVerb, QuadraVerb, SPX900, DSR 1000 & DSP-128 Plus, Multi-Effects Processors." *Keyboard* 15 (May 1989): 118–21, 145–47.

7875.   ———. "Keyboard Report: Yamaha FX500, Multi-Effects Device." *Keyboard* 15 (Sept. 1989): 122–25.

7876.   ———. "Multi-Effects Buyer's Guide: Compare the Specs on 24 Top Processors." *Keyboard* 15 (Dec. 1989): 33–40, 158–61, 172.

7877.   Wiffen, Paul. "Akai S900 MIDI Digital Sampler." *Music Technology* 1,1 (1986): 64–67.
          Review.

7878.   ———. "Alternate Controllers: The Vital Difference between Mono and Monophonic." *Keyboard* 14 (Nov. 1988): 131, 168–69.
          Use of monophonic instruments with MIDI control.

7879. ———. "E-mu Systems Emax: Polyphonic Sampling Keyboard." *Music Technology* 1 (Jan. 1987): 90–93.
Review.

7880. ———. "Elka Professional Synthesizers." *Music Technology* 1 (Oct. 1986): 40–44.
Review of Elka EK44/EM44 and EK22/EM22.

7881. ———. "Ensoniq ESQ1: Digital Synthesizer/Sequencer." *Music Technology* 1 (Sept. 1986): 32–35.
Review.

7882. ———. "The Euro-Synth Industry." *Keyboard* 14 (July 1988): 34–56.
Synthesizers from Europe.

7883. ———. "In Brief: Dynacord ADD-One Advanced Digital Drums." *Music Technology* 1 (Nov. 1986): 20.
Review.

7884. ———. "In Brief: E-mu Emax Sampling Keyboard." *Music Technology* 1 (Sept. 1986): 92–93.
Review.

7885. ———. "In Brief: PPG Hard Disk Unit." *Music Technology* 1 (Oct. 1986): 26.
Review of a sampler/recorder.

7886. ———. "In Brief: Roland MC500 Sequencer." *Music Technology* 1,1 (1986): 32.
Review.

7887. ———. "In Brief: Technics PX Series Digital Pianos." *Music Technology* 1,1 (1986): 34.
Review.

7888. ———. "Kawai R100: Digital Drum Machine." *Music Technology* 1 (Jan. 1987): 24–26.
Review.

7889. ———. "Korg DSS-1, Polyphonic Sampling Synthesizer." *Music Technology* 1 (Oct. 1986): 76–81.
Review.

7890. ———. "Lexicon Model 480L Digital Effects System." *Music Technology* 1 (Sept. 1986): 16–18.
Review.

7891. ———. "Oberheim DPX1: Eight-voice Sample Replay Unit." *Music Technology* 1 (Feb. 1987): 12–14.
Review.

7892. ———. "Sequential Prophet VS." *Music Technology* 1,1 (1986): 26–28.
Review of a digital synthesizer.

7893. ———. "Sequential Studio 440: Sampling Drum Machine/Sequencer."
Music Technology 1 (Mar. 1987): 50–55.
Review.

7894. ———, and Mark Vail. "The Hot New Options in Digital & Sampled
Pianos: Closing in on Perfection." *Keyboard* 14 (Aug. 1988): 90–102,
160–61.

7895. Williams, Mark. "MG Maestro." *Melody Maker* 63 (Aug. 1, 1987):
XV.
Review of the Casio MG500/510 MIDI guitars.

7896. Worley, Jeff; Patrick Longeneker; and Chuck Fisher. "At Home:
Building a MIDI Studio, or, How to Digitize Your Living Room."
Keyboards, Computers & Software 1 (Dec. 1986): 47–49.
Points to consider when establishing a home studio.

7897. Wright, Jim. "Basics: Guitar Synthesis: What You Need to Know."
Electronic Musician 2 (Apr. 1986): 19–28, 31.

7898. ———. "Review: Korg SDD-2000 Sampling Digital Delay." *Electronic
Musician* 2 (Feb. 1986): 62–66.

7899. Yale, Rob. "Keyboards: The Fairlight Series III." *Canadian Musician*
8 (Oct. 1986): 59–60.

7900. "Yamaha Adds Entry-Level DX Synthesizers." *Music Trades* 134
(Apr. 1986): 66.
Brief review of the Yamaha DX100 and DX27.

7901. "Yamaha DX7S to Retail for under $1,500." *Music Trades* 135 (Sept.
1987): 99.

7902. "Yamaha Unveils DS55 Affordable Synthesizer." *Music Trades* 137
(June 1989): 160–61.
Brief review of the Yamaha DS55 synthesizer.

7903. "Yamaha Unveils Home Music Computer." *Music Trades* 131 (Dec.
1983): 52.
Yamaha introduces the MSX, a personal home computer music
system, in Japan.

7904. Yannes, Bob, and Tom Metcalf. "Mod: Stereo Mirage—The Sequel."
Electronic Musician 3 (June 1987): 34–38.
How to retrofit an Ensoniq Mirage for stereo output.

7905. Yelton, Geary. "Chroma-Polaris." *Electronic Musician* 1 (June 1985): 32–33, 38.

Review of the software-based, analog/digital hybrid synthesizer.

7906. ——. "Gambatte! MidiStar Pro Wireless MIDI System." *Electronic Musician* 5 (June 1989): 88–89.

7907. Zander, Helmut. "The APS 1000 Series of Digital Audio Processors." In *Proceedings of the International Computer Music Conference 1986, Royal Conservatory, The Hague, Netherlands, October 20–24, 1986,* ed. Paul Berg. San Francisco, Calif.: Computer Music Association, 1986: 427–29.

7908. Zimmermann, Kevin. "Digital Samplers: Workhorses in the Studio." *Variety* 334 (Feb. 15, 1989): 102, 105.

SOUND GENERATION
FOR MUSIC —
PERFORMANCE
PRACTICES

7909. Aikin, Jim. "The Fine Art of Programming Synthesizers." *Keyboard* 11 (June 1985): 16–17.

7910. ——. "First Steps in Sequencing: How to Get Real Music Out of a Little Plastic Box." *Keyboard* 14 (June 1988): 94–103.

7911. ——. "Keyboard Clinic #3: Programming the Oberheim Xpander." *Keyboard* 12 (May 1986): 54–60, 147.

7912. ——. "Keyboard Clinic #21: Secrets of Synthesizer Programming: Make the Invisible Connections." *Keyboard* 15 (Oct. 1989): 58–64.

7913. ——. "Sequencers: Are We Making Music Yet?" *Keyboard* 13 (June 1987): 32–35.

7914. Altekruse, Mark, and Tom Mulhern. "History & Basics: First Steps: Getting over the Jitters." *Guitar Player* 20 (June 1986): 38–42.

A walk-through of the first steps in using a guitar synthesizer.

7915. Anderton, Craig. "Applications: Better Samples through Digital Limiting." *Electronic Musician* 5 (Dec. 1989): 84–86.

7916. ——. "Applications: Re-creating Classic Drum Machine Sounds." *Electronic Musician* 5 (Sept. 1989): 66–69.

How to create analog drum sounds using a sampler.

7917. ——. "Applications: TX81Z Tips for the MIDI Guitarist." *Electronic Musician* 4 (Oct. 1988): 30–32.

7918. ——. "Automated FX Systems for Guitarists." *Electronic Musician* 5 (Oct. 1989): 46–60.

Suggestions on how to use MIDI tools to switch effects, change levels, and work pedals.

7919. ———. "High-Tech Guitar No. 6: Sampling for the Working Guitarist." *Guitar Player* 22 (Aug. 1989): 42–44.

Ways samplers can be used with a non-MIDI guitar.

7920. ———. "High-Tech Guitar: MIDI in the Real World: Save Time, and Avoid Headaches, When Recording with a Guitar Synth." *Guitar Player* 23 (Sept. 1989): 100–106.

The author relates his experiences using a MIDI guitar to record a CD.

7921. ———. "Reel Application: How to Get It All in Sync: Synchronicity Made Simple: A Guide to Clock Pulses, MIDI Synching, and SMPTE Time Code." *Musician* n85 (Nov. 1985): 86–90, 74–75.

7922. ———. "Sampling Takes Hold: Bringing a Hot Technique to the Masses." *Record* 4 (May 1985): 46.

An overview of the E-mu Emulator II.

7923. ———. "Software: Making Quantization Work for You." *Electronic Musician* 3 (July 1987): 72–74.

7924. Appleton, Jon H. "The Computer and Live Musical Performance." In *Proceedings of the International Computer Music Conference 1986, Royal Conservatory, The Hague, Netherlands, October 20–24, 1986,* ed. Paul Berg. San Francisco, Calif.: Computer Music Association, 1986: 321–26.

7925. "Application Tips: Get the Most out of Your Sequencer—New Dimensions for 11 Major Devices." *Keyboard* 13 (June 1987): 74–104.

7926. Arnell, Billy. "MCS Applications." *Music, Computers & Software* 2 (Oct. 1987): 10, 97.

Discusses the special effects available on the Yamaha DX7 and RX11, and the Casio CZ 101/1000.

7927. Baker, J. R. "Bach, Beethoven, Brahms & Bytes." *Music, Computers & Software* 3 (Apr. 1988): 43–46.

Discusses arranging notated music for MIDI sequencers.

7928. Bettine, Michael. "Rock Perspectives: The Art of Drum Computing." *Modern Drummer* 8 (Dec. 1984): 106–7.

7929. Bloch, Phil, and Scott Plunkett. "Powerful Percussion with FM Synthesis." *Electronic Musician* 4 (May 1988): 20–26.

How to program percussion sounds using FM synthesis.

7930.   Brooks, Clive. "The Machine Shop: Outside 4/4." *Modern Drummer* 12 (Aug. 1988): 88–89.

Drum machine programming.

7931.   ———. "The Machine Shop: Programming Shuffles." *Modern Drummer* 12 (Feb. 1988): 60–61.

Drum machine programming.

7932.   Campbell, Alan Gary. "Applications: CZ Secrets." *Electronic Musician* 2 (Mar. 1986): 38–43.

Casio CZ-101.

7933.   Chapman, Jay. "The DX Explained." *Music Technology* 1 (Sept. 1986): 36–40.

7934.   ———. "The DX Explained." *Music Technology* 1 (Oct. 1986): 84–89.

Suggestions on user-programming by editing existing factory voices.

7935.   ———. "The DX Explained." *Music Technology* 1 (Nov. 1986): 36–39.

How to use sub-algorithms as a part of DX programming.

7936.   ———. "The DX Explained." *Music Technology* 1 (Dec. 1986): 80–83.

An exploration of touch-sensitivity in the Yamaha DX models.

7937.   ———, and Paul Wiffen. "The DX Explained." *Music Technology* 1,1 (1986): 70–73.

7938.   "Control Zone: Tips: 10 Ways to Liven up a Dull Sequencer." *Melody Maker* 64 (Jan. 16, 1988): 37.

7939.   Corso, Chris; Jules Ryckebusch; Daniel Shear; and Shiv Naimpally. "Getting the Most from Your Drum Machine." *Electronic Musician* 4 (May 1988): 28–31.

7940.   Cox, Steven. "Applications: Getting the Most out of the Akai S900." *Electronic Musician* 2 (Dec. 1986): 42–46.

7941.   Crigger, David. *How to Make Your Drum Machine Sound Like a Drummer with the Korg DDD-5.* Newbury Park, Calif.: Alexander Publishing, 1987. 186 p.

7942.   ———. *How to Make Your Drum Machine Sound Like a Drummer with the Roland TR-707.* Newbury Park, Calif.: Alexander Pub., 1987. 141 p.

7943.   ———. *How to Make Your Drum Machine Sound Like a Drummer: For All Makes and Models.* Newbury Park, Calif.: Alexander Pub., 1987. 123 p.

7944.   ———. *The MIDI Drummer: By a Drummer for a Drummer.* Newbury Park, Calif.: Alexander Pub., 1987. 59 p.

7945.   Davies, Rick. "Getting the Most from Mono Mode. Part 6, MIDI Guitar Controllers." *Music Technology* 1 (Jan. 1987): 88–89.

7946.   ———. "Getting the Most from Mono Mode. Part 7, More Guitar Controllers." *Music Technology* 1 (Feb. 1987): 72–74.

7947.   Davis, Steve. "Drum Set Forum: Increasing Time Awareness with a Drum Machine." *Percussive Notes* 25 (Fall 1986): 40.

7948.   De Furia, Steve. *Power Play DX!: Keyboard, Pitch Bend & Control Techniques for the Yamaha DX7II.* Milwaukee, Wis.: Ferro Technologies/H. Leonard Books, 1988. 160 p. + cassette
Review by David B. Doty in *Electronic Musician* 5 (Sept. 1989): 102.

7949.   ———. "Systems & Applications: Creative Applications: After-Touch and Pitch-bending." *Keyboard* 12 (Feb. 1986): 105.

7950.   ———. "Systems & Applications: Getting the Most from MIDI Delays." *Keyboard* 13 (Dec. 1987): 132.

7951.   ———. "Systems & Applications: Making the Walls Move with MIDI." *Keyboard* 12 (July 1986): 120.
The second of two patches for the Lexicon PCM-70 digital effects processor.

7952.   ———. "Systems & Applications: MIDI-controlled Digital Effects. Part 1." *Keyboard* 12 (June 1986): 138, 170.
The first of two patches for the Lexicon PCM-70 digital effects processor.

7953.   ———. "Systems & Applications: More Distortion Techniques for Synths." *Keyboard* 14 (Sept. 1988): 127.

7954.   ———. "Systems & Applications: Special Pitch-bending Techniques." *Keyboard* 14 (Feb. 1988): 144–46.
Pitch-bending on some Yamaha synthesizers.

7955.   Doyle, Frank. "Sequencing: Inside Sequencing: The Multi Sides of Digital Multi-Tracking." *Keyboards, Computers & Software* 1 (Oct. 1986): 37–38.

7956.   Edwards, David W. "The Feel Formula." *Electronic Musician* 4 (Mar. 1988): 70–71.
A discussion on how to correlate clock pulses to time.

7957.   Elliott, Kevin, and Clark Salisbury. "Keyboard Clinic #18: Power Layering Memory Savers, Looping Tools & More on the Ensoniq EPS." *Keyboard* 15 (May 1989): 32–41, 145.

7958. Enders, Bernd. *Die Klangwelt des Musiksynthesizers: Die Einführung in die Funktions- und Wirkungsweise eines Modulsynthesizers.* Munich: Franzis, 1985. 174 p. (Franzis Unterhaltungs-Elektronik)
Review by Rainer Wehinger in *Musik und Bildung* 18 (Juli–Aug. 1986): 723.

7959. Fiore, Jim. "The Casio FZ-1: A Drum Machine by Any Other Name . . . ?" *Electronic Musician* 4 (May 1988): 36.
How to use the Casio FZ-1 keyboard as a drum machine.

7960. ———. "MIDI Corner: Playing Drum Machines with Drumsticks." *Modern Drummer* 12 (Oct. 1988): 42–44.

7961. Fisher, Chuck, and Patrick Longeneker. "Effects: An Effects Primer: Understanding the Ghosts in the Machine." *Keyboards, Computers & Software* 1 (Oct. 1986): 34–36.

7962. Freeman, Peter. "Bill Bruford: Art-Rock Percussionist Punks up Jazz." *Music, Computers & Software* 2 (Aug. 1987): 31–33.
Profile/interview with the rock/jazz percussionist, who discusses his use of electronic percussion.

7963. ———. "D-Train: Fueling the Grooves with Techno Rhythm & Blues." *Music, Computers & Software* 2 (Aug. 1987): 34–36.
Profile/interview with keyboardist/arranger Hubert Eaves, who discusses his synthesis equipment.

7964. Freff. "Get More Sizzle from Your Multi-FX: Workin' on the Signal Chain Gang." *Keyboard* 15 (Nov. 1989): 58–66.
A general overview and specific applications of multi-effects processors.

7965. ———. "Getting Creative with Sequencers: 44 Twisted Ways to Tie Knots in Your Music." *Keyboard* 13 (June 1987): 66–72.

7966. Friend, Marty. "Sampling." *Music, Computers & Software* 2 (May 1987): 67–68.

7967. Gans, David. "Rhythmic Self-Determination: Better Songwriting through Drum Machines." *Record* 3 (July 1984): 50–51.

7968. Gartman, Mark Bennett. *The Easy CZ Book.* Butler, N.J.: Micro-W Distributing, 1986. 231 p.
Review by Alan Gary Campbell in *Electronic Musician* 3 (Dec. 1987): 80.
Instructions for synthesizing 350 instrumental sounds and sound effects with Casio CZ-101.

7969. Gieseler, Achim. "Einsatz von Sequenzerprogrammen in der Rock- und Popmusik." *Musik und Bildung* 21 (Juni 1989): 320–23.

7970. Goodwin, Simon. "The Machine Shop: Living with the Machine." *Modern Drummer* 10 (Nov. 1986): 56, 62.

Use of a drum machine for home practice.

7971. Gotcher, Peter. "Computers for Keyboardists: Now You See It, Now You Don't: Optical Data Storage." *Keyboard* 13 (Mar. 1987): 106–8.

7972. ———. "Digital Sampling: Eking a Lot out of a Little: Alternate Data Formats Explained." *Keyboard* 14 (Mar. 1988): 117, 125.

7973. ———. "Digital Sampling: Sample Swapping." *Keyboard* 14 (May 1988): 112.

How to retain samples when upgrading samplers.

7974. Hatchard, Mike. "Playing the Synthesizer." *Crescendo International* 24 (Dec. 1987): 33–34.

How to use a pitch-bend wheel. Includes exercises.

7975. ———. "Playing the Synthesizer: Harmonic Encoding." *Crescendo International* 25 (Jan. 1988): 33–34.

How to voice chords when playing complex tones on the synthesizer.

7976. ———. "Playing the Synthesizer: Programming: A Few Observations." *Crescendo International* 25 (Feb. 1988): 32.

Recommendations on using an Apple Macintosh or Atari ST to program instruments. Knobs with single functions are gone, making manual adjustments very difficult on digital synthesizers.

7977. Hotop, Jack, and Jim Aikin. "Keyboard Clinic #16: Velocity & Pressure Cross-Fades, Effects & Sequencer Tricks, Output Routings & Modulation on the Korg M1." *Keyboard* 14 (Dec. 1988): 52–62.

7978. Howell, Steve. "Getting the Most from Mono Mode. Part 8, Ensoniq ESQ1 Synthesizer/Sequencer." *Music Technology* 1 (July 1987): 34–36.

7979. Hurley, Mark. "The Machine Shop: Soloing with the Machine." *Modern Drummer* 12 (Mar. 1988): 66–67.

Drum machine programming.

7980. Hurtig, Brent. *Synthesizer Basics.* Rev. ed. Milwaukee, Wis.: H. Leonard Books, 1988. 129 p. (Keyboard Magazine Basic Library)

7981. Isaacson, Matt. "We Can't Go on Beating Like This." *Music Technology* 1 (July 1987): 68–73.

How to program electronic drums using electronic drum pads and sticks.

7982. ———. "We Can't Go on Beating Like This. Part 7." *Music Technology* 2 (Oct. 1987): 52–57.

An investigation of sensing devices placed on analog drums or other items that cause electronic triggering.

7983. ———, and Chris Meyer. "We Can't Go on Beating Like This." *Music Technology* 1 (May 1987): 66–69.

How to make a drum machine behave more like the percussion instruments it is simulating.

7984. ———, and Chris Meyer. "We Can't Go on Beating Like This." *Music Technology* 1 (June 1987): 18–23.

A look at trigger-to-MIDI converters and their use for triggering drum samples and/or sounds.

7985. ———, and Chris Meyer. "We Can't Go on Beating Like This. Part 5." *Music Technology* 2 (Aug. 1987): 42–47.

A look at alternatives to conventional drum pads.

7986. Johnson, Bashiri. "KCS Applications." *Keyboards, Computers & Software* 1 (June 1986): 10, 77.

The author, a percussionist, describes how to program rhythms on the Yamaha RX-11.

7987. Johnson, Jim. "Applications: Secrets of the Yamaha FB-01." *Electronic Musician* 5 (Jan. 1989): 26–30.

How to use system exclusive codes of the Yamaha FB-01 sound module.

7988. ———. "Sequencing for Live Performance." *Electronic Musician* 4 (Mar. 1988): 72–76.

A discussion of ways to minimize problems with MIDI equipment in live performance.

7989. Kaczynski, Richard. "MIDI Applications." *Music, Computers & Software* 3 (Oct. 1988): 24–25.

Discusses setting up a MIDI system for use in live performance.

7990. Kempton, David. "Synthesis: Optimizing S900 Sample Rates." *Electronic Musician* 3 (Nov. 1987): 26–30.

Advice on finding the right sampling rate for the Akai S900.

7991. Kennedy, Terry. "The Experienced Sequencer: 12 Tips for the Roland MC-500 and the Yamaha QX5." *Electronic Musician* 4 (June 1988): 92–97.

7992. Knowlton, Joseph. "State of the Art: Effects and Signal Processors." *Keyboard Classics* 6 (Nov./Dec. 1986): 39.

Discussion of the techniques of flanging and digital delay, and the use of pitch transposers and digital effects processors.

7993. Kotrubenko, Viktor. *Tajemství syntezátorů.* [The Secret of Synthesizers] Prague: Supraphon, 1988. 147 p.

Review by Václav Syrový in *Hudebni Veda* 25 (1988): 369–71.

7994. Kovarsky, Jerry, and Jim Aikin. "Keyboard Clinic #2: How to Program the CZ-101." *Keyboard* 12 (Mar. 1986): 40–43.

7995. LaCroix, James K. "MIDI Applications." *Music, Computers & Software* 3 (June 1988): 24–25.

Dicusses the use of the Akai S-900 sampling synthesizer.

7996. Levinger, Lowell. "Applications: The Performing DX7." *Electronic Musician* 3 (Mar. 1987): 97–99, 106.

7997. Lewis, Bill. "Alone in the Spotlight: A Workingman's Guide to MIDI." *Music, Computers & Software* 2 (Oct. 1987): 62–65, 82–85.

A discussion of the possibilities on solo performance with the aid of MIDI.

7998. Marans, Michael. "Keyboard Clinic #17: Emax to the Max." *Keyboard* 15 (Feb. 1989): 42–49, 56–57.

7999. Massey, Howard. "Keyboard Clinic #7: Tricks, Traps, and Undocumented Features of the DX7 II." *Keyboard* 13 (Sept. 1987): 42–56.

8000. Mater, Bob. "Electronic Insights: Threshold of a Drum." *Modern Drummer* 12 (June 1988): 38.

Dynamic problems of triggering the Akai S900 using the ASK90 from an acoustic drum.

8001. Mattingly, Rick. "The Machine Shop: Tricking Your Drum Machine." *Modern Drummer* 12 (Apr. 1988): 46.

Drum machine programming.

8002. Means, Ben, and Jean Means. "Yes: A 'Big Generator' Revitalizes Symphonic Rockers." *Music, Computers & Software* 2 (Aug. 1987): 22–30.

Profile/interview with members of the rock band, who discuss their use of synthesizers.

8003. Meyer, Chris, and Bill Aspromonte. "The Art of Looping. Part One." *Music Technology* 2 (Sept. 1987): 80–86.

8004. ——, and Matt Isaacson. "We Can't Go on Beating Like This." *Music Technology* 1 (Apr. 1987): 64–67.

A discussion on drum machine programming.

8005. Milano, Dominic. *Synthesizer Programming.* Milwaukee, Wis.: H. Leonard Books, 1987. 111 p. (Keyboard Synthesizer Library)

8006. Millar, William. "Applications: Handling MPU-401 Interrupts with Turbo Pascal." *Electronic Musician* 5 (May 1989): 74–79.

Tips on writing custom routines for an IBM/Roland MPU-401 combination.

8007.   Moog, Bob. "On Synthesizers: Unexplored Resources of the Casio CZ-101." *Keyboard* 12 (Apr. 1986): 94.

8008.   Moore, Greg. "The Machine Shop: Go with the Flow." *Modern Drummer* 13 (Dec. 1989): 84.

    Drum machine programming.

8009.   Muro, Don. "Sonic Options: Some Basics of Synthesizer Performance." *Music Educators Journal* 74 (Dec. 1987): 44–45, 60.

8010.   ——. "Synthesizers in Performance: Esoteric Ways of Controlling the Pitch." *Keyboard* 11 (Aug. 1985): 66.

8011.   Oppenheimer, Larry. "Processors: Digital Signal Processors in Live Performance." *Electronic Musician* 3 (Jan. 1987): 24–32.

8012.   Penner, Les. "Software: Programming the MPU-401 MIDI Interface." *Electronic Musician* 3 (July 1987): 77–80.

    How to program the split-keyboard function.

8013.   Persing, Eric. "Keyboard Clinic #10: Mixing & Matching Structures & Partials—Unleash the Personal Dimensions of the Roland D–50." *Keyboard* 13 (Dec. 1987): 34–48.

8014.   ——. "Keyboard Clinic #4: Programming the Roland JX-8P & JX–10." *Keyboard* 12 (Oct. 1986): 56–64.

8015.   Richardson, Ric. "Applications: The Fairlight 'MIDI Slave': Champaign Sounds on a Beer Budget." *Electronic Musician* 4 (Oct. 1988): 68–72.

    Preparation for working with the Fairlight Series III and description of how to take advantage of its most salient features.

8016.   Rona, Jeff. "Keyboard Clinic #14: Sample Rates, Looping Shortcuts, Output Assignments & Power Sounds on the Akai S900." *Keyboard* 14 (Sept. 1988): 46–56.

    How to use a sampler, including a frequency table for figuring sampling bandwidths and a tip on improving signal-to-noise ratio.

8017.   Sani, Nicola, and Serena Tamburini. *Programmare i sintetizzatori Yamaha DX7.* [Programming the Yamaha DX7 Synthesizers] Padua: F. Muzzio, 1987. 158 p. (Gli strumenti della musica; 21)

8018.   Sanko, Anton. "MCS Applications." *Music, Computers & Software* 2 (Aug. 1987): 10, 17.

    The synthesist discusses his work with singer Suzanne Vega.

8019. Scacciaferro, Joe. *The Essential Guide to Practical Applications, Casio FZ-1 & FZ-10M : Digital Sampling Synthesizer.* Milwaukee, Wis.: H. Leonard Books, 1988. 143 p.
Review by Patrick Houlihan in *Electronic Musician* 4 (Aug. 1988): 85.

8020. ———. "Sound Design." *Music, Computers & Software* 3 (Dec. 1988): 72–74.
A tutorial on keyboard performance techniques to emulate the sound of a guitar.

8021. Schlesinger, Andrew. *An Insider's Guide to Casio CZ Synthesizers: The Most Complete Hands-on Approach to Programming All CZ Synths.* Los Angeles, Calif.: Alfred Pub., 1988. 95 p.
Review by Jim Aikin in *Keyboard* 14 (Sept. 1988): 25.

8022. Smith, David G. "Beyond Notes: Percussion/Sequence Calls." *Electronic Musician* 4 (Aug. 1988): 36–39.
A discussion of using sequencers to trigger sound events.

8023. Spitzenberger, Harold. "Keyboard Clinic #20: Seamless Loops, Call/ Set Tricks, Envelope Effects & Optional Software on the Casio FZ-1." *Keyboard* 15 (July 1989): 50–64.

8024. Stratton, Kevin. "Synthesis: The Continually Expanding Universe: Tips to Tame the DX7II." *Electronic Musician* 3 (Nov. 1987): 38–45.

8025. *Synthesizer Technique.* Rev. ed. Milwaukee, Wis.: H. Leonard Books, 1987. 129 p. (The Keyboard Synthesizer Library)

8026. Thompson, Bill. "Mastering the Yamaha TX81Z." *Electronic Musician* 4 (Jan. 1988): 64–66, 73–77.

8027. Tobenfeld, Emile. "Humanize Your Sequenced Music." *Electronic Musician* 5 (May 1989): 48–54.
How to make sequenced music more interesting.

8028. Tolinski, Brad. "Roger Waters: Radio KAOS: The Wall Comes Tumbling Down." *Music, Computers & Software* 2 (Oct. 1987): 22–25, 29.
Profile/interview with the rock computer/guitarist, who discusses his use of synthesizers.

8029. ———. "Sampling Roundtable." *Music, Computers & Software* 2 (Dec. 1987): 34–39.
A collective interview with rock performers Eleanor, Jimmy Bralower, Roma Baran, and the Residents, who discuss their use of sampling synthesizers.

8030. Tucker, Mike. "Sample Your House and Other Fun Emax Tricks." *Electronic Musician* 5 (June 1989): 50–55.

8031.   ——. "Stretching the Samples on an Akai S612." *Electronic Musician* 4 (July 1988): 118–20.

8032.   Vilardi, Frank, and Steve Tarshis. *Electronic Drums: Everything You Need to Know about Electronic Drum Kits and Drum Computers.* New York, N.Y.: Amsco, 1985. 85 p. + sound disc

8033.   Volanski, John J. "Applications: MIDI/CV Conversion with the Vesta Fire MDI-1." *Electronic Musician* 4 (Nov. 1988): 37–40.

How to use an analog synthesizer with a MIDI sequencer or keyboard.

8034.   Wehrman, Bob. "Keyboard Clinic #5: Programming the Ensoniq Mirage." *Keyboard* 12 (Nov. 1986): 88–94, 157.

Use of visual editing.

8035.   ——, and Mark Vail. "Keyboard Clinic #13: Get More Sounds and MIDI Applications from the Ensoniq ESQ-1." *Keyboard* 14 (July 1988): 74–81.

8036.   Weinberg, Norman. "The Machine Shop: New Sounds for Your Old Machines." *Modern Drummer* 11 (Dec. 1987): 44–46.

Use of a sampling synthesizer with a drum machine.

8037.   Westfall, Lachlan. "MCS MIDI." *Music, Computers & Software* 2 (Oct. 1987): 12–13, 96.

Discusses the applications of MIDI to stage lighting and other device control function.

8038.   Wiffen, Paul. "Alternate Controllers: Keyboards Are for Wimps." *Keyboard* 14 (Oct. 1988): 117.

Control of synthesizers by non-keyboard controllers via MIDI.

8039.   ——. "Getting the Most from Mono Mode. Part 1, The CZ Series." *Music Technology* 1,1 (1986): 38–41.

8040.   ——. "Getting the Most from Mono Mode. Part 2, Prophet 2000/2002." *Music Technology* 1 (Sept. 1986): 68–70.

8041.   ——. "Getting the Most of Mono Mode. Part 3, Akai S900." *Music Technology* 1 (Oct. 1986): 72–74.

8042.   ——. "Keyboard Clinic #8: Looping, Mapping, and Secrets of Mono Mode on the Prophet 2000/2002." *Keyboard* 13 (Oct. 1987): 52–62.

8043.   ——. "Making the Most of Mono Mode. Part 4, Yamaha SPX90." *Music Technology* 1 (Nov. 1986): 91–92.

8044.   ——. "Making the Most of Mono Mode. Part 5, Sequential Tom." *Music Technology* 1 (Dec. 1986): 60–62.

Drum machines and MIDI.

8045. ———. "Making the Most of Sequencers. Part 1, Real Time Recording." *Music Technology* 1 (Oct. 1986): 38–39.

8046. ———. "Making the Most of Sequencers. Part 2, Step Time Programming." *Music Technology* 1 (Nov. 1986): 80–83.

8047. ———. "Making the Most of Sequencers. Part 3, Transferring Sequences." *Music Technology* 1 (Dec. 1986): 50–53.

Step-by-step directions on transferring data from one sequencer to another.

8048. ———. "Toward More Creative Sampling. Part 1, Multi-Sampling, the Answer or the Problem?" *Music Technology* 1,1 (1986): 68–69.

8049. ———. "Toward More Creative Sampling. Part 3, Looping the Loop." *Music Technology* 1 (Oct. 1986): 51–53.

8050. ———. "Toward More Creative Sampling. Part 4, New Sounds from Old." *Music Technology* 1 (Nov. 1986): 34–35.

How to use a sampler to synthesize completely new sounds.

8051. Yale, Rob. "Computers: The Fairlight Series III in Action." *Canadian Musician* 8 (Dec. 1986): 62–63.

8052. ———. "Keyboards: Performing Sampled Sounds." *Canadian Musician* 9 (Feb. 1987): 46.

8053. Zantay, Rob. *The Complete Synthesist: Synthesizer Technique and Theory.* Woodstock, N.Y.: Homespun Tapes, 1985. 44 p. + 6 cassettes

Review by Jon Balleras in *Down Beat* 53 (July 1986): 60.

8054. Zummo, Vinnie. "Sound Design." *Music, Computers & Software* 3 (Oct. 1988): 85–86.

Discusses uses of sampling synthesizers.

SOUND GENERATION
FOR MUSIC—
SOFTWARE

8055. Abbott, Curtis. "The 4CED Program." *Computer Music Journal* 5,1 (Spring 1981): 13–33.
Previously **3313.**
Reprinted in *The Music Machine,* ed. Curtis Roads. Cambridge, Mass.: MIT Press, 1989: 311–31.

8056. Adams, Parker. "Reviews: Roland Super-MRC Software for the MC-Series Sequencers." *Electronic Musician* 5 (Feb. 1989): 126–28.

8057. Aikin, Jim. "Keyboard Report: FB-01 Editor/Librarian Software." *Keyboard* 13 (Oct. 1987): 135–38.
Five programs to customize the Yamaha FB-01DX.

8058. Amaral, John. "Software City." *Musician* n80 (June 1985): 90.
A potpourri of software products.

8059. Anderson, David P., and Ron Kuivila. "Continuous Abstractions for Discrete Event Languages." *Computer Music Journal* 13,3 (Fall 1989): 11–23.

8060. Anderton, Craig. "CZ Orchestra and CZ Rainbow." *Electronic Musician* 5 (Dec. 1989): 109.
Patch libraries.

8061. ———. "Synthware DX/TX Voice Packs 1, 2, and 3." *Electronic Musician* 5 (July 1989): 111.

8062. ———. "Yamaha G10 ROM Update 1.2." *Electronic Musician* 5 (Nov. 1989): 82.
Review of the latest ROM update to the Yamaha G10 guitar synthesizer.

8063. Banger, Colin, and Bruce W. Pennycook. "Gcomp: Graphic Control of Mixing and Processing." *Computer Music Journal* 7,4 (Winter

1983): 33–39.

Previously **3342.**

Reprinted in *The Music Machine,* ed. Curtis Roads. Cambridge, Mass.: MIT Press, 1989: 277–83.

8064. Campbell, Alan Gary. "Korg DS-8/707 Program ROM Cards: DSCU-400; PSU-100, NY Synthesis; DSC-01, Bo Tomlyn; DSC-04, Charles Guerin." *Electronic Musician* 5 (Jan. 1989): 97–98.

Review of patch cards.

8065. Camurri, Antonio; Renato Zaccaria; Goffredo Haus; and G. Jacomini. "Il sistema MAP per il controllo del CMI Fairlight." [The MAP System for the Control of the CMI Fairlight] In *Musica e tecnologia: industria e cultura per lo sviluppo del mezzogiorno: VI Colloquio di Informatica Musicale, Napoli 16–19 ottobre 1985,* ed. Carlo Acreman; Immacolata Ortosecco; and Fausto Razzi. Milan: Edizioni Unicopli, 1987: 209–25.

8066. Dannenberg, Roger B., and Christopher Lee Fraley. "Fugue: Composition and Sound Synthesis with Lazy Evaluation and Behavioral Abstraction." In *Proceedings, 1989 International Computer Music Conference, November 2–5, the Ohio State University, Columbus, Ohio.* San Francisco, Calif.: Computer Music Association, 1989: 76–79.

8067. De Furia, Steve. "Software for Musicians: Getting Input from the User." *Keyboard* 15 (Aug. 1989): 114–15.

Three different ways of entering a transposition interval value.

8068. ———. "Software for Musicians: Handy Equations for Converting Time Values." *Keyboard* 14 (Jan. 1988): 117.

8069. ———. "Software for Musicians: More on Getting User Input." *Keyboard* 15 (Sept. 1989): 106–7.

Possible ways of handling multi-parameter input routines.

8070. ———. "Software for Musicians: Program Your Own." *Keyboard* 12 (Feb. 1986): 92.

The first in a series of columns to teach the fundamentals of designing and creating computer programs to enhance music skills.

8071. ———. "Software for Musicians: Shake Hands with Sys-Ex." *Keyboard* 13 (May 1987): 107.

8072. ———. "Software for Musicians: The Bytes that Almost Got Away . . ." *Keyboard* 15 (July 1989): 114–15.

Parsing routines and messages.

8073.   ——. "Software for Musicians: The Sys-Ex Family Tree." *Keyboard* 13 (Mar. 1987): 110–11.

System-exclusive messages; for the Yamaha DX-series synthesizers.

8074.   ——. "Systems & Applications: Pushing the Envelope." *Keyboard* 12 (Apr. 1986): 98.

An examination of the envelope generator in Casio CZ instruments.

8075.   ——. "Systems & Applications: Pushing the Envelope. Part II." *Keyboard* 12 (May 1986): 94, 142.

Envelope experiments for the Yamaha DX.

8076.   Dewdney, A. K. "Computer Recreations: The Sound of Computing is Music to the Ears of Some." *Scientific American* 256 (Apr. 1987): 14–21.

Describes two programs: SOLFEGGIO, to create melodies, and CANON, to generate two-part harmony.

8077.   Favreau, Emmanuel; M. Fingerhut; O. Koechlin; Patrick Potacsek; Miller Puckette; and Robert Rowe. "Software Developments for the 4X Real-Time System." In *Proceedings of the International Computer Music Conference 1986, Royal Conservatory, The Hague, Netherlands, October 20–24, 1986,* ed. Paul Berg. San Francisco, Calif.: Computer Music Association, 1986: 369–73.

8078.   Frederick, Dave. "In Review—Sounds: K-Muse Samples for Ensoniq Mirage." *Keyboard* 12 (July 1986): 23–24.

Review of Sound Composer Series.

8079.   ——. "In Review—Sounds: ROM Cartridge Voice for Yamaha DX7." *Keyboard* 12 (July 1986): 24.

Review of a four-bank DX7 ROM cartridge from Sound Connection.

8080.   Freff. "Keyboard Report: Roland MC-500mkII Sequencer & Super-MRC Software." *Keyboard* 14 (Dec. 1988): 146.

8081.   Greenwald, Ted. "In Review—Sounds: Synthware RX5 Drum Patches." *Keyboard* 14 (Mar. 1988): 24.

Data cassette for the Yamaha RX5 drum machine.

8082.   ——. "Software: Tape Deck, Performer, Score Paper—The Computer Does It All." *Keyboard* 12 (Jan. 1986): 66–80, 96–107.

Covers the computer as sequencer, patch voicing and librarian programs, transcription, scoring and notation, etc.

8083. Jenkins, Mark. "Control Zone: Computers." *Melody Maker* 60 (Oct. 12, 1985): 36.

Acorn Soft's "Creative Sound for the BBC"; Passport Music Systems; Jellinghaus Musik-Systems; Syntron Digidrum; Roland MPS.

8084. ———. "Control Zone: New Keys: Keyboard News." *Melody Maker* 61 (Dec. 6, 1986): 37.

Short reviews of software for the Yamaha DX synthesizers.

8085. "Keyboard Cooperative Debuts: Library of Programs." *Billboard* 96 (Feb. 25, 1984): 59.

A library of programs for most programmable music devices.

8086. LaRose, Paul. "G10 Editor/Librarian Music Software." *Guitar Player* 23 (July 1989): 151–52.

Software for the Yamaha G10 MIDI guitar controller.

8087. Leonard, Steve. "Computers for Keyboardists: Computers: How They Do What They Do for Keyboard Players." *Keyboard* 12 (Feb. 1986): 98.

Understanding the basic concepts of program operations.

8088. Leytze, David. "In Review—Sounds: Synthware Sounds for the DX7II." *Keyboard* 14 (Mar. 1988): 24.

Sounds available in various formats.

8089. Loy, D. Gareth. "Notes on the Implementation of MUSBOX: A Compiler for the Systems Concepts Digital Synthesizer." *Computer Music Journal* 5,1 (Spring 1981): 34–50.
Previously **3450.**
Reprinted in *The Music Machine,* ed. Curtis Roads. Cambridge, Mass.: MIT Press, 1989: 333–49.

8090. Milano, Dominic. "Synth & MIDI Basics: Librarians and Stranger Breeds of Memory." *Keyboard* 13 (July 1987): 137.

8091. Moore, F. Richard. "The CMUSIC Sound Synthesis Program." In *The CARL Startup Kit.* La Jolla, Calif.: UCSD Center for Music Experiment, 1985.

8092. Nencini, Giovanni; Pietro Grossi; Graziano Bertini; C. Camilleri; and Leonello Tarabella. "TELETAU: A Computer Music Permanent Service." In *Proceedings of the International Computer Music Conference 1986, Royal Conservatory, The Hague, Netherlands, October 20–24, 1986,* ed. Paul Berg. San Francisco, Calif.: Computer Music Association, 1986: 451–53.

8093.   Nottoli, Giorgio. "MSYS7: sistema di controllo MIDI." [MSYS7: A System for MIDI Control] In *Musica e tecnologia: industria e cultura per lo sviluppo del mezzogiorno: VI Colloquio di Informatica Musicale, Napoli 16–19 ottobre 1985,* ed. Carlo Acreman; Immacolata Ortosecco; and Fausto Razzi. Milan: Edizioni Unicopli, 1987: 226–31.

8094.   Oppenheimer, Steve. "Synthetic Productions MASTERAM-64." *Electronic Musician* 5 (Sept. 1989): 81.
        Review of MASTERAM-64 RAM patch cards for the Kawai K1.

8095.   Peterson, Jeff. "Cesium Sound Programs for the Roland D–50." *Electronic Musician* 5 (Feb. 1989): 112–13.
        Review.

8096.   Rahn, John. "Computer Music: A View from Seattle." *Computer Music Journal* 12,3 (Fall 1988): 15–29.

8097.   Rothstein, Joseph B. "Products of Interest: Pro Sonus Studio Reference Disk and Sample Library Compact Disks." *Computer Music Journal* 13,4 (Winter 1989): 92–93.

8098.   Santoiemma, Maurizio. "A Theoretical Approach to Computational Modules for Sound Synthesis." *Interface* 13 (1984): 115–32.
        Revised and updated version of **3508**.

8099.   Schmidt, Brian L. "Natural Language Interfaces and Their Application to Music Systems." In *The Proceedings of the AES 5th International Conference: Music and Digital Technology,* ed. John Strawn. New York, N.Y.: Audio Engineering Society, 1987: 198–206.

8100.   Scholz, Carter. "Do-It-Yourself Software: Any MIDI Keyboard Can Play in Just Intonation with Computerized Pitch-Bending." *Keyboard* 12 (Feb. 1986): 49–52, 142–43.

8101.   ——. "Review: Soundprocess Software for the Mirage." *Electronic Musician* 4 (Aug. 1988): 98–101.

8102.   Schottstaedt, Bill. *PLA—A Tutorial and Reference Manual.* Stanford, Calif.: Stanford University, Dept. of Music, 1984. 140 p. (Department of Music Technical Report STAN-M-24)

8103.   ——. "Pla: A Composer's Idea of a Language." *Computer Music Journal* 7,1 (Spring 1983): 11–20.
        Previously **3518**.
        Reprinted in *The Music Machine,* ed. Curtis Roads. Cambridge, Mass.: MIT Press, 1989: 285–94.

8104.   Shannon, William, and Dave Frederick. "Tired of Imitation Rhodes Patches?: Generate & Graph Exotic New DX7 Sounds with This Random Program in BASIC." *Keyboard* 12 (July 1986): 72–74, 162.

8105. Sundberg, Johan; Anders Friberg; and Lars Frydén. "Rules for Automated Performance of Ensemble Music." *Contemporary Music Review* 3 (1989): 89–109.

Presentation of a computer program that contains a rule system which automatically converts music scores to musical performance.

8106. Taylor, Graham. "Screen Test: Digital Music Systems DMS-1." *Melody Maker* 61 (Jan. 25, 1986): 35.

Review of music software for the Yamaha CX-5.

8107. Tocchetti, Gino. "MUSIC 6: un preprocessore al linguaggio per la sintesi musicale MUSIC 5." [MUSIC 6: A Preprocessor for the MUSIC 5 Language] In *Musica e tecnologia: industria e cultura per lo sviluppo del mezzogiorno: VI Colloquio di Informatica Musicale, Napoli 16–19 ottobre 1985,* ed. Carlo Acreman; Immacolata Ortosecco; and Fausto Razzi. Milan: Edizioni Unicopli, 1987: 232–47.

8108. Tully, Tim. "Studio Series Patch ROMS for the Roland D-50." *Electronic Musician* 4 (Sept. 1988): 75.

Review of Valhala Music patch cards.

8109. Vail, Mark. "Sounds and Editor/Librarian Software: A Keyboard Survey." *Keyboard* 15 (Jan. 1989): 78–94, 101.

A list of sound and editor/librarian software, organized by synthesizer. Also includes a directory of publishers.

8110. Walker, William Franklin. "Kiwi: A Parallel System for Software Sound Synthesis." In *Proceedings, 1989 International Computer Music Conference, November 2–5, the Ohio State University, Columbus, Ohio.* San Francisco, Calif.: Computer Music Association, 1989: 328–31.

8111. Walsh, Kevin. "Taking Aim at the Music Colossus: The Companies behind the Software." *Music, Computers & Software* 2 (Dec. 1987): 53–56, 80.

An overview of various MIDI programs.

8112. Williams, Wheat. "First Take: Capsule Comments: TuneUp Microtuning Library for the TX81Z/DX11 and DX7II/TX802." *Electronic Musician* 5 (Apr. 1989): 84–87.

SOUND GENERATION FOR MUSIC — SYNTHESIS TECHNIQUES

8113.   Aikin, Jim. "CD Sound Libraries: Sample Lovers Take Note." *Keyboard* 14 (Feb. 1988): 21.

8114.   ———. "In Review—Voice Cartridges: Musicdata DX7 Programs by Suzanne Ciani, Clark Spangler, David Boruff." *Keyboard* 11 (July 1985: 28.

8115.   Anderton, Craig. "Applications: 'Sampanalog' Synthesis." *Electronic Musician* 2 (May 1986): 37–38.

   Digitally sampling analog synthesizers.

8116.   ———. *The Digital Delay Handbook.* New York, N.Y.: Amsco, 1985. 133 p.
   Review by David B. Doty in *Electronic Musician* 2 (June 1986): 76.

   A source of information on echo, feedback, resonance, etc.

8117.   ———. "A Field Guide to Sampling." *Electronic Musician* 5 (Feb. 1989): 39–54.

8118.   ———. "Inside L/A Synthesis." *Electronic Musician* 4 (May 1988): 40–55.

   Describes linear arithmetic synthesis, the instruments that use it (Roland D-50 and MT-32), the software, and trends.

8119.   ———. "Prosonus CD Sound Library; Ear Works CD Percussion Sound Library." *Electronic Musician* 4 (May 1988): 82–83.
   Includes sample disks.

   Review.

8120.   ———. "Secrets of Dynamic Sequences." *Electronic Musician* 5 (May 1989): 40–45.

8121. Ashley, Richard D. "A Knowledge-based Approach to Assistance in Timbral Design." In *Proceedings of the International Computer Music Conference 1986, Royal Conservatory, The Hague, Netherlands, October 20–24, 1986,* ed. Paul Berg. San Francisco, Calif.: Computer Music Association, 1986: 11–16.

8122. Austin, Kirk. "Software: Pick of the Disks." *Electronic Musician* 2 (June 1986): 44, 84.

Sampling disks; for the Ensoniq Mirage.

8123. Bartlett, Bruce. "Recording Techniques: Sampling, Sequencing, and MIDI." *DB, the Sound Engineering Magazine* 20 (Nov./Dec. 1986): 4–14.

An in-depth description of sampling and sequencing.

8124. Batel, Günther, and Dieter Salbert. *Synthesizermusik und Live-Elektronik: geschichtliche, technologische, kompositorische und pädagogische Aspekte der elektronischen Musik.* Wolfenbüttel: Möseler, 1985. 106 p.
Review by Bernd Enders in *Musik und Bildung* 19 (Feb. 1987): 147–48.

8125. Bennett, Gerald, and Xavier Rodet. "Synthesis of the Singing Voice." In *Current Directions in Computer Music,* ed. Max V. Mathews and John R. Pierce. Cambridge, Mass.: MIT Press, 1989: 19–44.

8126. Borgonovo, Aldo, and Goffredo Haus. "Sound Synthesis by Means of Two-Variable Functions: Experimental Criteria and Results." *Computer Music Journal* 10,3 (Fall 1986): 57–71.

8127. Borin, G.; Giovanni De Poli; and A. Sarti. "A Modular Approach to Excitator-Resonator Interaction in Physical Model Interaction." In *Proceedings, 1989 International Computer Music Conference, November 2–5, the Ohio State University, Columbus, Ohio.* San Francisco, Calif.: Computer Music Association, 1989: 46–50.

8128. Bosetto, A., and Eugenio Guarino. "Un sistema di sintesi basato sull'uso di 'semicustom' sviluppati in Iselqui." [A System of Synthesis Based on the Use of 'Semicustom' Developed in Iselqui] In *Musica e tecnologia: industria e cultura per lo sviluppo del mezzogiorno: VI Colloquio di Informatica Musicale, Napoli 16–19 ottobre 1985,* ed. Carlo Acreman; Immacolata Ortosecco; and Fausto Razzi. Milan: Edizioni Unicopli, 1987: 304–14.

8129. Bowler, Ian W.; Peter D. Manning; Alan Purvis; and Nick J. Bailey. "A Transputer-based Additive Synthesis Implementation." In *Proceedings, 1989 International Computer Music Conference, November 2–5, the Ohio State University, Columbus, Ohio.* San Francisco, Calif.: Computer Music Association, 1989: 58–61.

8130.   Boyer, Frédéric, and Richard Kronland-Martinet. "Granular Resynthesis and Transformation of Sounds through Wavelet Transform Analysis." In *Proceedings, 1989 International Computer Music Conference, November 2–5, the Ohio State University, Columbus, Ohio.* San Francisco, Calif.: Computer Music Association, 1989: 51–54.

8131.   Brown, Frank. "Synthèse rapide de sons musicaux par ordinateur." Ph.D. diss., Univ. du Maine, Le Mans, 1980. 134 p.

8132.   Burger, Jeff. "Balloons, Jelly, and Climaxing Cougars." *Keyboard* 12 (Oct. 1986): 18, 30.

   Frank Serafine describes his use of sampling for the movie Poltergeist II.

8133.   Buxton, William; Sanand Patel; William Reeves; and Ronald Baecker. "Objed and the Design of Timbral Resources." *Computer Music Journal* 6,2 (Summer 1982): 32–44.
   Previously **3611.**
   Reprinted in *The Music Machine,* ed. Curtis Roads. Cambridge, Mass.: MIT Press, 1989: 263–75.

8134.   Calderaro, Tom, and Paul Wiffen. "Real Stereo Samples from a Monaural Sampler." *Keyboard* 13 (Apr. 1987): 98–104.

8135.   Carr, Robert. "Basics: Electronic Tone Synthesis." *Electronic Musician* 2 (Nov. 1986): 52–53, 56–59.

   Covers additive synthesis, subtractive synthesis, digital sampling, and FM synthesis.

8136.   Cavaliere, Sergio; Gianpaolo Evangelista; Immacolata Ortosecco; and Aldo Piccialli. "Una tecnica di sintesi per modulazione di fase: sviluppi." [A Technique of Synthesis for Phase Modulation: Developments] In *Musica e tecnologia: industria e cultura per lo sviluppo del mezzogiorno: VI Colloquio di Informatica Musicale, Napoli 16–19 ottobre 1985,* ed. Carlo Acreman; Immacolata Ortosecco; and Fausto Razzi. Milan: Edizioni Unicopli, 1987: 186–94.

8137.   ——; Gianpaolo Evangelista; and Aldo Piccialli. "Synthesis by Phase Modulation and Its Implementation in Hardware." *Computer Music Journal* 12,1 (Spring 1988): 29–42.

8138.   ——, and Aldo Piccialli. "Phase Modulation with Interpolated Time Functions: Synthesis by Formants." In *Proceedings of the International Computer Music Conference 1986, Royal Conservatory, The Hague, Netherlands, October 20–24, 1986,* ed. Paul Berg. San Francisco, Calif.: Computer Music Association, 1986: 293–97.

8139.   Cavanaugh, Bill. "MCS Sound Design." *Music, Computers & Software* 3 (Apr. 1988): 79–80.

   A discussion of timbre layering using MIDI.

8140. Chowning, John M. "Frequency Modulation Synthesis of the Singing Voice." In *Current Directions in Computer Music,* ed. Max V. Mathews and John R. Pierce. Cambridge, Mass.: MIT Press, 1989: 57–63.

8141. ———, and David Bristow. *FM Theory and Applications.* Tokyo: Yamaha Music Foundation, 1986. 192 p.
Review by Marc Locascio in *Computer Music Journal* 11,4 (Winter 1987): 48–49.
Review by Geary Yelton in *Electronic Musician* 4 (Feb. 1988): 114–16.

8142. Clarke, John Michael; Peter D. Manning; Ron Berry; and Alan Purvis. "VOCEL: New Implementations of the FOF Synthesis Method." In *Proceedings of the 14th International Computer Music Conference, Cologne, September 20–25, 1988,* ed. Christoph Lischka and Johannes Fritsch. Cologne: Feedback-Studio-Verlag; San Francisco, Calif.: Dist. by Computer Music Association, 1988: 357–71. (Feedback Papers; 33)

A method for making FOF (Fonction d'Onde Formantique) synthesis available within Music 11.

8143. "Control Zone: Sample That: Timbre Sampling Tapes." *Melody Maker* 61 (Mar. 29, 1986): 35.

Timbre-sampling tapes that provide samples of many different instruments for samplers.

8144. Cook, Perry R. "Synthesis of the Singing Voice Using a Physically Parameterized Model of the Human Vocal Tract." In *Proceedings, 1989 International Computer Music Conference, November 2–5, the Ohio State University, Columbus, Ohio.* San Francisco, Calif.: Computer Music Association, 1989: 69–72.
Also issued as: Technical Report STAN-M-57. Stanford, Calif.: Center for Research in Music and Acoustics, Music Department, Stanford University, 1989. 4 p.

8145. Damiano, Bob. "The Plucked String Revisited." *Electronic Musician* 3 (Dec. 1987): 24–30.

A program in BASIC and Assembler based on the Karplus-Strong algorithm that creates the plucked string wave; for the Apple II or Commodore 64.

8146. Daniel, Walter K. "Synthesis: Sampling Time-varying Waveforms." *Electronic Musician* 3 (Nov. 1987): 32–35.

8147. Dashow, James. "New Approaches to Digital Sound Synthesis and Transformation." *Computer Music Journal* 10,4 (Winter 1986): 56–66.

8148. De Furia, Steve. *The Secrets of Analog and Digital Synthesis.* Rutherford, N.J.: Third Earth Productions: Ferro Productions, 1986. 130 p. + videocassette

Review by Jon Balleras in *Down Beat* 54 (May 1987): 53.
Review by Bruce P. Mahin in *Instrumentalist* 41 (June 1987): 8.

8149. ——, and Joe Scacciaferro. *The Sampling Book.* Milwaukee, Wis.: H. Leonard, 1987. 150 p.
Review by David B. Doty in *Electronic Musician* 4 (July 1988): 135–36.
Review by Tom Mulhern in *Guitar Player* 22 (July 1988): 170.
Review by Jim Aikin in *Keyboard* 14 (July 1988): 24.

8150. De Poli, Giovanni. "A Tutorial on Digital Sound Synthesis Techniques." *Computer Music Journal* 7,4 (Winter 1983): 8–26.
Previously **3640.**
Reprinted in *The Music Machine,* ed. Curtis Roads. Cambridge, Mass.: MIT Press, 1989: 429–47.

8151. Del Duca, Lindoro. *Musica digitale: sintesi, analisi e filtraggio digitale nella musica elettronica.* [Digital Music: Synthesis, Analysis, and Digital Filtering of Electronic Music] Padova: F. Muzzio, 1987. 261 p. (Strumenti della musica; 15)
Review by Rodolfo N. Giassone in *Computer Music Journal* 13,3 (Fall 1989): 95–96.

8152. ——. "Sintesi del suono con risuonatori digitali." [Synthesis of Sounds with Digital Resonators] In *Musica e tecnologia: industria e cultura per lo sviluppo del mezzogiorno: VI Colloquio di Informatica Musicale, Napoli 16–19 ottobre 1985,* ed. Carlo Acreman; Immacolata Ortosecco; and Fausto Razzi. Milan: Edizioni Unicopli, 1987: 177–85.

8153. Di Perna, Alan. "Additive Synths: Sine of the Times." *Musician* n115 (May 1988): 38–40, 130.

How the Kurzweil 150 Fourier Synthesizer, the Kawai K5, and Digidesign Softsynth program create sounds using additive synthesis.

8154. "Digital Sampling—The Pros & Cons of the Latest in Musical Technology." *Music Trades* 133 (June 1985): 68–74.

8155. Dolson, Mark. "Fourier-Transform-based Timbral Manipulations." In *Current Directions in Computer Music,* ed. Max V. Mathews and John R. Pierce. Cambridge, Mass.: MIT Press, 1989: 105–12.

8156. Downes, Pat. "Motion Sensing in Music and Dance Performance." In *The Proceedings of the AES 5th International Conference: Music and Digital Technology,* ed. John Strawn. New York, N.Y.: Audio Engineering Society, 1987. 165–72

8157. Ehle, Robert C. "Synthesizing the Symphony Orchestra II." *American Music Teacher* 34 (Jan. 1985): 42–43.

A brief description of various sound synthesis methods that include the use of microprocessors.

8158. Eshleman, Jim. "Song Construction." *Music, Computers & Software* 3 (Dec. 1988): 70–71.

A tutorial on sequencers.

8159. Federer, Bob. "Synthesizers: Introduction to Digital Synthesis." *Canadian Musician* 6 (Mar./Apr. 1984): 66.

A short description of additive synthesis and FM synthesis.

8160. Ferrucci, Frank. "KCS Sampling." *Keyboards, Computers & Software* 1 (Feb. 1986): 60–61.

A basic discussion of sampling technology and what to expect from samplers.

8161. Fisher, Chuck. "MIDI Studio." *Music, Computers & Software* 3 (June 1988): 76–78.

A tutorial on uses of envelope generators.

8162. Friend, Marty. "KCS Sampling." *Keyboards, Computers & Software* 1 (Apr. 1986): 60–61.

Methods of sampling techniques.

8163. ——. "KCS Sampling." *Keyboards, Computers & Software* 1 (Aug. 1986): 70–71.

Basic rules of sampling and outline of some limitations.

8164. ——. "KCS Sampling." *Keyboards, Computers & Software* 1 (Dec. 1986): 68–69.

Suggestions on ways to create new samples.

8165. Fryer, Terry. "Digital Sampling: A Good Reason to Dust off that Calculator." *Keyboard* 12 (Mar. 1986): 82–83.

How to calculate a sampling rate.

8166. ——. "Digital Sampling: Better Samples through Equalization." *Keyboard* 12 (Sept. 1986): 123.

8167. ——. "Digital Sampling: How to Control Aliasing by Filtering and Half-Speed-Mastering Your Samples." *Keyboard* 12 (Apr. 1986): 102.

8168. ——. "Digital Sampling: Make Your Samples Work Together." *Keyboard* 13 (Sept. 1987): 132.

8169. ——. "Digital Sampling: More Distortion Solutions." *Keyboard* 12 (May 1986): 106–7.

8170. ——. "Digital Sampling: Realistically Sampling Multi-Register Acoustic Instruments." *Keyboard* 12 (Oct. 1986): 104.

8171. ——. "Digital Sampling: Sampling Basics, Setting Levels & Truncating." *Keyboard* 13 (July 1987): 134.

8172.   ———. "Digital Sampling: Sampling Resolution Bit by Bit." *Keyboard* 12 (Feb. 1986): 99, 148.

8173.   ———. "Digital Sampling: Share the Wealth and the Memory through Multisampling." *Keyboard* 12 (July 1986): 126, 154.

8174.   ———. "Digital Sampling: Stop, Look & Listen before You Sample." *Keyboard* 12 (June 1986): 135.

8175.   ———. "Digital Sampling: Transposing Samples: Not for the Squeamish." *Keyboard* 12 (Aug. 1986): 119.

8176.   ———. "Digital Sampling: What to Do When Your Samples Exceed the Dynamic Range of Your Sampler." *Keyboard* 13 (Aug. 1987): 103.

8177.   ———. "Sampling Jargon Illustrated." *Keyboard* 14 (June 1988): 66–73.
         With soundsheet.

8178.   ———, and Dominic Milano. "Secrets of Syncing: Ten Ways to Get Locked up (without Committing a Crime)." *Keyboard* 12 (June 1986): 94–104.

8179.   Garnett, Guy E. *Designing Digital Instruments with Hierarchical Waveguide Networks.* Stanford, Calif.: Stanford University, Dept. of Music, 1988. 7 p. (Department of Music Technical Report STAN-M-49)

8180.   Goodman, Paul. "The User and the MIDIM System." *Interface* 15 (1986): 163–84.
         Describes a practical workshop for users of the MIDIM8X system, report on some concert activities, and comments on a few compositions composed using the MIDIM system.

8181.   Gotcher, Peter. "Basics: Making Waves: Visual Editing Basics." *Electronic Musician* 2 (July 1986): 32–35, 93.

8182.   ———. "Digital Sampling: Overcoming the Fear of Sampling." *Keyboard* 14 (Sept. 1988): 126, 155.

8183.   ———. "Digital Sampling: Sampling Drums & Percussion." *Keyboard* 14 (Nov. 1988): 137.

8184.   ———. "Digital Sampling: Sampling Spec Wars." *Keyboard* 13 (Nov. 1987): 128.
         An overview of sampling specifications.

8185.   ———. "Digital Sampling: Stereo Sampling: Friend or Foe?" *Keyboard* 14 (Apr. 1988): 126.

8186.   ——. "Digital Sampling: The Ups & Downs of Pitch-shifting Techniques." *Keyboard* 14 (Jan. 1988): 118–20.

8187.   Hart, Dave. "For the Advanced User: Sample Editing." *Active Sensing* 1 (Summer 1989): 6, 10.

8188.   Heckert, Paul. "Digital Sampling: Getting Down to Brass Attacks." *Keyboard* 15 (May 1989): 109.

8189.   ——. "Digital Sampling: Playing Realistic Snare Drum Parts." *Keyboard* 15 (Apr. 1989): 106–7.

8190.   ——. "Digital Sampling: Using Envelopes to Customize String Samples." *Keyboard* 15 (Feb. 1989): 110–11.

8191.   Hilts, Philip. "Bulldozers, Bassoons, and Silicon Chips." *Science 80* 1 (Jan.–Feb. 1980): 77–79.
          Announcement of J. Chowning's discovery of FM synthesis.

8192.   Humphrey, Scott. "Computers: The Spoons and Triumph Syncing to Multi Track with SMPTE." *Canadian Musician* 9 (Feb. 1987): 53–54.

8193.   Ishii, Rokuya; Hiroshi Katsumoto; and Yoshinori Kihara. "A Signal Source in a Digital Musical Synthesizer." In *ICASSP 86 Proceedings: April 7, 8, 9, 10, 11, 1986, Keio Plaza Inter-continental Hotel, Tokyo, Japan.* Piscataway, N.J.: IEEE, 1986: 1273–76.

8194.   Jaffe, David A., and Julius O. Smith. "Extensions of the Karplus-Strong Plucked-String Algorithm." *Computer Music Journal* 7,2 (Summer 1983): 56–69.
          Previously **3672.**
          Reprinted in *The Music Machine,* ed. Curtis Roads. Cambridge, Mass.: MIT Press, 1989: 481–94.

8195.   Janssen, Jos, and Heinerich Kaegi. "MIDIM—Duplication of a Central–Javanese Sound Concept." *Interface* 15 (1986): 185–229.

8196.   Jentzsch, Wilfried. "Mit neuen Technologien Träume verwirklichen: Der Computer als Mittel kompositorischer Arbeit. Teil I, Die Klangfarbe." *Neue Musikzeitung* 35 (Dez. 1986): 32.

8197.   Jimmerson, Herb. "Digital Sampling: Hip Horn Hits." *Keyboard* 15 (Dec. 1989): 109–10.

8198.   ——. "Digital Sampling: Oohs, Aahs & Hhaahhs." *Keyboard* 15 (Nov. 1989): 106.
          Ways to create vocal sounds and sequenced effects.

8199.   ——. "Digital Sampling: Sampled Percussion. Part I." *Keyboard* 15 (July 1989): 107–9.

8200.   ———. "Digital Sampling: Sampled Percussion. Part II." *Keyboard* 15 (Aug. 1989): 112–13.

8201.   ———. "Digital Sampling: Sampling Analog Bass." *Keyboard* 15 (June 1989): 101–2.

8202.   Johnson, Jim. "Software: Humanizing Sequences." *Electronic Musician* 3 (Feb. 1987): 32–33.

8203.   Jones, Douglas L., and Thomas W. Parks. "Generation and Combination of Grains for Music Synthesis." *Computer Music Journal* 12,2 (Summer 1988): 27–34.

8204.   Kaegi, Heinerich; Jos Janssen; and Paul Goodman. "MIDIM Sound-Duplications and Their Applications." In *Proceedings of the International Computer Music Conference 1986, Royal Conservatory, The Hague, Netherlands, October 20–24, 1986,* ed. Paul Berg. San Francisco, Calif.: Computer Music Association, 1986: 249–55.

8205.   Kaegi, Werner. "Controlling the VOSIM Sound Synthesis System." *Interface* 15 (1986): 71–82.

8206.   ———. "The MIDIM Language and Its VOSIM Interpretation." *Interface* 15 (1986): 83–161.

8207.   Kaiser, Henry. "The Basics of Sampling." *Guitar Player* 20 (June 1986): 104–6.

8208.   Karplus, Kevin, and Alex Strong. "Digital Synthesis of Plucked-String and Drum Timbres." *Computer Music Journal* 7,2 (Summer 1983): 43–55.
Previously **3678.**
Reprinted in *The Music Machine,* ed. Curtis Roads. Cambridge, Mass.: MIT Press, 1989: 467–79.

8209.   Kerscher, Jeff. "MIDI: Software Sequencing Tips." *Electronic Musician* 3 (Feb. 1987): 45–46.

8210.   Kleckowski, Piotr. "Group Additive Synthesis." *Computer Music Journal* 13,1 (Spring 1989): 12–20.

8211.   Kuipers, Pieter. "CANON: A System for the Description of Musical Patterns." *Interface* 15 (1986): 257–70.
Describes CANON, an extension to the MIDIM language formulated by Werner Kaegi.

8212.   LaCerra, Steve. "MIDI Corner: Syncing Drum Machines to Tape." *Modern Drummer* 13 (Mar. 1989): 64.

8213.   Lansky, Paul. "Linear Prediction: The Hard, but Interesting Way to Do Things." In *The Proceedings of the AES 5th International Conference: Music and Digital Technology,* ed. John Strawn. New York, N.Y.: Audio Engineering Society, 1987: 77–82.

8214.   ——, and Kenneth Steiglitz. "Synthesis of Timbral Families by Warped Linear Prediction." *Computer Music Journal* 5,3 (Fall 1981): 45–49.

Previously **3682**.

Reprinted in *The Music Machine*, ed. Curtis Roads. Cambridge, Mass.: MIT Press, 1989: 531–35.

8215.   Laske, Otto E. "Computermusik und musikalische Informatik." *Neuland* 2 (1981–82): 209–13.

Describes three kinds of music synthesis by computer: synthesis of scores, synthesis of sounds, and synthesis of musical knowledge.

8216.   Lee, J. Robert. "Digital Sound Synthesis Algorithms: A Tutorial Introduction and Comparison of Methods." Ph.D. diss., University of California, San Diego, 1988. 252 p.

8217.   Lent, Keith. "An Efficient Method for Pitch Shifting Digitally Sampled Sounds." *Computer Music Journal* 13,4 (Winter 1989): 65–71.

8218.   Lorrain, Denis. "Situation de la synthèse sonore par ordinateur." *Canadian University Music Review* 3 (1982): 170–202.

8219.   Lowengard, J. Henry. "Techno: Methods for Multiples." *Ear* 14 (Sept. 1989): 24–25.

The author describes quick and easy digital processing methods to create ensemble sounds.

8220.   Lowy, Kenn. "Ensoniq EPS Signature Series." *Electronic Musician* 5 (Nov. 1989): 81–82.

Three disks with samples from various musicians.

8221.   Lupone, Michelangelo. "System Fly." In *Musica e tecnologia: industria e cultura per lo sviluppo del mezzogiorno: VI Colloquio di Informatica Musicale, Napoli 16–19 ottobre 1985,* ed. Carlo Acreman; Immacolata Ortosecco; and Fausto Razzi. Milan: Edizioni Unicopli, 1987: 315–22.

8222.   Mann, Ed. "Electronic Insights: Percussive Sound Sources and Synthesis." *Modern Drummer* 11 (Dec. 1987): 68–69.

8223.   Marks, Miles A. "Resource Allocation in an Additive Synthesis System for Audio Waveform Generation." In *Proceedings of the 14th International Computer Music Conference, Cologne, September 20–25, 1988,* ed. Christoph Lischka and Johannes Fritsch. Cologne: Feedback-Studio-Verlag; San Francisco, Calif.: Dist. by Computer Music Association, 1988: 378–82. (Feedback Papers; 33)

8224.   Massey, Howard. "Sampling in Stereo." *Music Technology* 1 (May 1987): 22–23.

8225.   ——. "Synth & MIDI Basics: Analog vs. Digital." *Keyboard* 13 (Dec. 1987): 123–25.

An introduction to subtractive synthesis.

8226. ———. "Synth & MIDI Basics: Beginner's Guide to FM Synthesis." *Keyboard* 14 (Apr. 1988): 117, 152.

8227. ———. "Synth & MIDI Basics: Digital FM." *Keyboard* 14 (May 1988): 122–25.

8228. ———. "Synth & MIDI Basics: More Than Just a Pretty Phase." *Keyboard* 14 (Oct. 1988): 128.
Phase distortion synthesis.

8229. ———. "Synth & MIDI Basics: Using Algorithms in Digital FM." *Keyboard* 14 (June 1988): 122–25.

8230. Meyer, Chris. "All about Additive. Part Two." *Music Technology* 2 (May 1988): 26–31.
Conclusion of the discussion on additive synthesis and a survey of equipment that has that capability.

8231. ———. "A Deeper Wave Than This." *Music Technology* 2 (Aug. 1987): 23–26.
An explanation of wavetable synthesis, how it works, and how it is implemented.

8232. ———, and Scott Peer. "Every Little Bit." *Music Technology* 2 (Feb. 1988): 82–86.
A discussion of sampling quality.

8233. Milano, Dominic. "Top Studio Programmers: Tell How They Make Those Million Dollar Sounds." *Keyboard* 11 (June 1985): 38–45.
Interviews with Michael Boddicker, Suzanne Ciani, Ed Walsh, and Alan Howarth.

8234. Moog, Bob. "Ask Mr. Moog: Granular Synthesis Explained." *Keyboard* 14 (Dec. 1988): 117–18, 144.

8235. ———. "Ask Mr. Moog: More on Resynthesis Macros." *Keyboard* 14 (Aug. 1988): 117–18.

8236. ———. "Ask Mr. Moog: Musical Applications on Resynthesis." *Keyboard* 14 (June 1988): 134–35.

8237. ———. "Ask Mr. Moog: Playing a Sampler Expressively." *Keyboard* 14 (Mar. 1988): 119.

8238. ———. "Ask Mr. Moog: Resynthesis through Linear Predictive Coding." *Keyboard* 14 (Nov. 1988): 132–33.

8239. ———. "Ask Mr. Moog: Resynthesis. Part 1: Taking Sounds Apart." *Keyboard* 14 (May 1988): 117–18.

8240.   ——. "Digital Music Synthesis: The Many Different Shapes of the Waveform." *Byte* 11 (June 1986): 155–68.

A review of various synthesis techniques with trends for the future.

8241.   ——. "On Synthesizers: Sampling Instruments. Part 4, More Listening Tests for Digital Samplers." *Keyboard* 12 (Feb. 1986): 94.

Tests for hearing distortion components, one at a time.

8242.   Mulhern, Tom. "Basic Synthesis: Building Sounds from the Ground up." *Guitar Player* 20 (June 1986): 24–37.

Covers varieties of subtractive and additive synthesis.

8243.   Oppenheimer, Larry. "Basics: Sing a Song of Reverb. Part 1." *Electronic Musician* 2 (Feb. 1986): 26–29, 58.

Digitally processed reverberation.

8244.   Petrarca, Stefano. "Descrizione di un metodo di sintesi non lineare e non stazionario." [Description of a Non-Linear and Non-Stationary Method of Synthesis] In *Musica e tecnologia: industria e cultura per lo sviluppo del mezzogiorno: VI Colloquio di Informatica Musicale, Napoli 16–19 ottobre 1985*, ed. Carlo Acreman; Immacolata Ortosecco; and Fausto Razzi. Milan: Edizioni Unicopli, 1987: 139–43.

8245.   Petzold, Charles. "Riding the Wave of Sound Synthesis: The Origins of FM Synthesis." *PC Magazine* 7 (Nov. 29, 1988): 232–33.

A short historical survey of sound synthesis techniques.

8246.   Reynolds, Sam. "Synthesis." *ITA Journal* 15 (Summer 1987): 40–43.

A general article on how sounds are synthesized.

8247.   Risset, Jean-Claude. "Additive Synthesis of Inharmonic Tones." In *Current Directions in Computer Music,* ed. Max V. Mathews and John R. Pierce. Cambridge, Mass.: MIT Press, 1989: 159–63.

8248.   ——. "Musical Sound Models for Digital Synthesis." In *ICASSP 86 Proceedings: April 7, 8, 9, 10, 11, 1986, Keio Plaza Inter-continental Hotel, Tokyo, Japan.* Piscataway, N.J.: IEEE, 1986: 1269–71.

8249.   ——. "Paradoxical Sounds." In *Current Directions in Computer Music,* ed. Max V. Mathews and John R. Pierce. Cambridge, Mass.: MIT Press, 1989: 149–58.

8250.   Roads, Curtis. "Granular Synthesis of Sound: Past Research and Future Prospects." In *Musica e tecnologia: industria e cultura per lo sviluppo del mezzogiorno: VI Colloquio di Informatica Musicale, Napoli 16–19 ottobre 1985*, ed. Carlo Acreman; Immacolata Ortosecco; and Fausto Razzi. Milan: Edizioni Unicopli, 1987: 195–208.

8251.   ——. "Introduction to Granular Synthesis." *Computer Music Journal* 12,2 (Summer 1988): 11–13.

8252.   Rodet, Xavier; P. Depalle; and G. Poirot. "Diphone Sound Synthesis Based on Spectral Envelopes and Harmonic/Noise Excitation Functions." In *Proceedings of the 14th International Computer Music Conference, Cologne, September 20–25, 1988,* ed. Christoph Lischka and Johannes Fritsch. Cologne: Feedback-Studio-Verlag; San Francisco, Calif.: Dist. by Computer Music Association, 1988: 313–21. (Feedback Papers; 33)

8253.   ——; Yves Potard; and Jean-Baptiste Barrière. "The CHANT Project: From the Synthesis of the Singing Voice to Synthesis in General." *Computer Music Journal* 8,3 (Fall 1984): 15–31.
Previously **3730.**
Reprinted in *The Music Machine,* ed. Curtis Roads. Cambridge, Mass.: MIT Press, 1989: 449–65.

8254.   ——; Yves Potard; and Jean-Baptiste Barrière. *CHANT: de synthèse de la voix chantée à la synthèse en general.* Paris: IRCAM, 1985. 21 p. (Rapports de recherche; no 35)
French version of **8253.**

8255.   "Roland Intro's New S/AS Technology." *Music Trades* 134 (Feb. 1986): 102–4.
Describes Structured/Adaptive Synthesis.

8256.   Rubbazzer, Maurizio, and G. Capuzzo. "Sistema di conversione analogico digitale a 16 bit per audio professionale." [A System of Analog/Digital Conversion to 16-Bit through Professional Sound] In *Musica e tecnologia: industria e cultura per lo sviluppo del mezzogiorno: VI Colloquio di Informatica Musicale, Napoli 16–19 ottobre 1985,* ed. Carlo Acreman; Immacolata Ortosecco; and Fausto Razzi. Milan: Edizioni Unicopli, 1987: 323–29.

8257.   Rudolph, Mark. "On the Use of Cepstral Representation in Synthesis from Reduced Performance Information." In *Proceedings, 1989 International Computer Music Conference, November 2–5, the Ohio State University, Columbus, Ohio.* San Francisco, Calif.: Computer Music Association, 1989: 264–67.

8258.   Russell, Benjamin. "SampleWare Sound Disks Quality OK to Great." *Canadian Musician* 10 (Feb. 1988): 34.
Nineteen disks of sampled sounds from SampleWare.

8259.   Rychner, Lorenz. "Inside Envelopes." *Music Technology* 2 (Feb. 1988): 37–39.
An in-depth look at types of envelopes and how to program them.

8260.   ——. "Shaping the Wave." *Music Technology* 2 (Jan. 1988): 46–50.
An overview of subtractive/analog synthesis and how to use it in
programming digital synthesizers.

8261.   Salisbury, Clark. "Applications: Envelope Intimacy and the Art of
Shaping Sound." *Electronic Musician* 3 (June 1987): 80–83.

8262.   Seeger, Chris Arley. "MCS Sound Design." *Music, Computers &
Software* 2 (Dec. 1987): 85–86.
A discussion of sampling techniques.

8263.   Serafine, Frank. "KCS Applications." *Keyboards, Computers & Software* 1 (Feb. 1986): 8, 16.
The author describes his use of equipment to create sound effects
for motion pictures.

8264.   Serra, Xavier. *An Environment for the Analysis, Transformation, and
Resynthesis of Music Sounds.* Stanford, Calif.: Stanford University,
Dept. of Music, 1988. 10 p. (Department of Music Technical Report
STAN-M-52)

8265.   ——. "A System for Sound Analysis/Transformation/Synthesis Based
on a Deterministic Plus Stochastic Decomposition." Ph.D. diss.,
Stanford University, 1989. 147 p.
Also issued as: Technical Report STAN-M-58. Stanford, Calif.: Cen-
ter for Research in Music and Acoustics, Music Department, Stanford
University, 1989.

8266.   ——, and Julius O. Smith. "Spectral Modeling Synthesis." In *Proceedings, 1989 International Computer Music Conference, November
2–5, the Ohio State University, Columbus, Ohio.* San Francisco, Calif.:
Computer Music Association, 1989: 281–83.

8267.   Shimony, Uri; Noam Elroy; and Ehud Hamami. "LZW Compression
of Musical Files." In *Proceedings, 1989 International Computer Music
Conference, November 2–5, the Ohio State University, Columbus,
Ohio.* San Francisco, Calif.: Computer Music Association, 1989:
285–88.

8268.   Silverstein, Steven. "Sampling Heaven and Hell." *Ear* 14 (May 1989):
16–17.
Describes the basics of sampling.

8269.   Smith, Julius O. *Music Applications of Digital Waveguides.* Stanford,
Calif.: Stanford University, Dept. of Music, 1987. 10 p. (Department
of Music Technical Report STAN-M-39)
A compendium containing **3831,** the author's "Elimination of
Limit Cycles and Overflow Oscillations in Time-varying Lattice
and Ladder Digital Filters," and "Efficient Simulation of the

Reed-bore and Bow-string Mechanisms," a general chapter on Waveguide Digital Filters, and copies of presentation viewgraphs.

8270.   ———. "PARSHL: An Analysis/Synthesis Program for Non-Harmonic Sounds Based on a Sinusoidal Representation." In *Proceedings of the 1987 International Computer Music Conference: University of Illinois at Urbana-Champaign, Urbana, Illinois, USA, August 23–26, 1987,* comp. James Beauchamp. San Francisco, Calif.: Computer Music Association, 1987: 290–97.
Also issued as: Technical Report STAN-M-43. Stanford, Calif.: Center for Research in Music and Acoustics, Music Department, Stanford University, 1987.

8271.   Spitzenberger, Harold. "Back to Basics: Sampling." *Active Sensing* 1 (Summer 1989): 4.

8272.   Stapleton, John C. "Karhunen-Loeve Based Additive Synthesis of Musical Tones." Ph.D. diss., Purdue University, 1985. 182 p.

8273.   Stewart, Dave. "Rock Keyboards: Factory Samples Are a Disease: Originality Is the Cure." *Keyboard* 12 (Aug. 1986): 97.

8274.   Strawn, John. "Approximation and Syntatic Analysis of Amplitude and Frequency Functions for Digital Sound Synthesis." *Computer Music Journal* 4,3 (Fall 1980): 3–24.
Previously **3746.**
Also in *Proceedings of the 1980 International Computer Music Conference,* comp. Hubert S. Howe. San Francisco, Calif.: Computer Music Association, 1982: 116–37.
Reprinted in *The Music Machine,* ed. Curtis Roads. Cambridge, Mass.: MIT Press, 1989: 671–92.

8275.   Sundberg, Johan. "Computer Synthesis of Music Performance." In *Generative Processes in Music: The Psychology of Performance, Improvisation, and Composition,* ed. John A. Sloboda. Oxford: Clarendon Press, 1988: 52–69.
Describes a project to analyze music performance by synthesizing it with a digital computer.

8276.   ———. "Synthesis of Singing." In *Musica e tecnologia: industria e cultura per lo sviluppo del mezzogiorno: VI Colloquio di Informatica Musicale, Napoli 16–19 ottobre 1985,* ed. Carlo Acreman; Immacolata Ortosecco; and Fausto Razzi. Milan: Edizioni Unicopli, 1987: 145–62.

8277.   ———. "Synthesis of Singing by Rule." In *Current Directions in Computer Music,* ed. Max V. Mathews and John R. Pierce. Cambridge, Mass.: MIT Press, 1989: 45–55.

8278.   Tempelaars, Stan. "Linear Digital Oscillators." *Interface* 11 (Nov. 1982): 109–30.

8279. Tisato, Graziano. "Sintesi dei suoni vocali e del canto in modulazione di frequenza." [Synthesis of Vocal Sounds and Singing with Frequency Modulation] In *Musica e tecnologia: industria e cultura per lo sviluppo del mezzogiorno: VI Colloquio di Informatica Musicale, Napoli 16–19 ottobre 1985,* ed. Carlo Acreman; Immacolata Ortosecco; and Fausto Razzi. Milan: Edizioni Unicopli, 1987: 163–76.

8280. Truax, Barry. "Real-Time Granular Synthesis with a Digital Signal Processor." *Computer Music Journal* 12,2 (Summer 1988): 14–26.

8281. Vangellow, Alex. "Sound Design." *Music, Computers & Software* 3 (Nov. 1988): 71–72.

Discusses subtleties of natural sounds and techniques to achieve similar results with synthesizers.

8282. Viard, Richard. "Applications: FM Synthesis: 6-Op to 4-Op Program Translation." *Electronic Musician* 5 (Nov. 1989): 30–34.

A method for translating some of the existing library of six-operator sounds to a four-operator synthesizer.

8283. Wawrzynek, John C. "VLSI Concurrent Computation for Music Synthesis." Ph.D. diss., California Institute of Technology, 1987. 164 p.
Dept. of Computer Science Report no. 5247.

8284. ———. "VLSI Models of Sound Synthesis." In *Current Directions in Computer Music,* ed. Max V. Mathews and John R. Pierce. Cambridge, Mass.: MIT Press, 1989: 113–48.

8285. ———, and Carver Mead. "A VLSI Architecture for Sound Synthesis." In *VLSI Signal Processing: A Bit-Serial Approach,* ed. Peter Denyer and David Renshaw. Wokingham, Eng.: Addison-Wesley, 1985: 277–97.

8286. Weitekamp, Joe. "Understanding Technology: Digital Signals in an Analog World." *Active Sensing* 1 (Summer 1989): 4–5.

A short description of the difference between digital (incremental) and analog (continuous) signals.

8287. Wessel, David; David Bristow; and Zack Settel. "Control of Phrasing and Articulation in Synthesis." In *Proceedings of the 1987 International Computer Music Conference: University of Illinois at Urbana-Champaign, Urbana, Illinois, USA, August 23–26, 1987,* comp. James Beauchamp. San Francisco, Calif.: Computer Music Association, 1987: 108–16.

8288. Wiffen, Paul. "An Introduction to Sampling. Part 1." *Music Technology* 1,1 (1986): 63.

8289.   ———. "An Introduction to Sampling. Part 2, The Mechanics of Sampling." *Music Technology* 1 (Sept. 1986): 64–67.

8290.   ———. "Toward More Creative Sampling. Part II, Aliasing, and How to Avoid It." *Music Technology* 1 (Sept. 1986): 88.

8291.   Yelton, Geary. "McGill University Master Samples." *Electronic Musician* 4 (June 1988): 98.

Review.

8292.   ———. "Review: Sampling Alternatives: The Sound Ideas Sampler Library." *Electronic Musician* 4 (Feb. 1988): 84–87.

Review of the six-CD set of instrumental sounds and sound effects.

SOUND GENERATION WITH REAL-TIME APPLICATIONS

8293.   Allik, Kristi; Shane Dunne; and Robert Mulder. "ArcoNet: A Pro-
         posal for a Standard Network for Communication and Control in
         Real-Time Performance." In *Proceedings of the International Com-
         puter Music Conference 1986, Royal Conservatory, The Hague, Neth-
         erlands, October 20–24, 1986,* ed. Paul Berg. San Francisco, Calif.:
         Computer Music Association, 1986: 413–21.

8294.   ——, and Robert Mulder. "The Interactive Arts System: Introduction
         to a Real Time Performance Tool." In *Proceedings, 1989 International
         Computer Music Conference, November 2–5, the Ohio State University,
         Columbus, Ohio.* San Francisco, Calif.: Computer Music Association,
         1989: 1–4.

8295.   Anderson, David P., and Ron Kuivila. "A Model of Real-Time
         Computation for Computer Music." In *Proceedings of the International
         Computer Music Conference 1986, Royal Conservatory, The Hague,
         Netherlands, October 20–24, 1986,* ed. Paul Berg. San Francisco,
         Calif.: Computer Music Association, 1986: 35–41.

8296.   Baird, Bridget; Donald Blevins; and Noel Zahler. "The Artificially
         Intelligent Computer Performer on the Macintosh II and a Pattern
         Matching Algorithm for Real-Time Interactive Performance." In
         *Proceedings, 1989 International Computer Music Conference, Novem-
         ber 2–5, the Ohio State University, Columbus, Ohio.* San Francisco,
         Calif.: Computer Music Association, 1989: 13–16.

8297.   Basinée, Pierre-François; Jean-Baptiste Barrière; O. Koechlin; and
         Robert Rowe. "Real-Time Interaction between Musicians and Com-
         puter: Live Performance Utilisations of the 4X Musical Workstation."
         In *Proceedings of the International Computer Music Conference 1986,
         Royal Conservatory, The Hague, Netherlands, October 20–24, 1986,*
         ed. Paul Berg. San Francisco, Calif.: Computer Music Association,
         1986: 237–39.

8298. Beyls, Peter. "Introducing Oscar." In *Proceedings of the 14th International Computer Music Conference, Cologne, September 20–25, 1988,* ed. Christoph Lischka and Johannes Fritsch. Cologne: Feedback-Studio-Verlag; San Francisco, Calif.: Dist. by Computer Music Association, 1988: 219–30. (Feedback Papers; 33)

Oscar (OSCillator ARtist) is the name of a computer program that simulates a live musician.

8299. Boesch, Rainer, and Daniel Weiss. "An Inexpensive Composer Work Station Featuring High Quality Real Time Sound Synthesis." In *Proceedings of the International Computer Music Conference 1986, Royal Conservatory, The Hague, Netherlands, October 20–24, 1986,* ed. Paul Berg. San Francisco, Calif.: Computer Music Association, 1986: 63–64.

8300. Bokkel, Aad te. "De Erratiese Synkretiseur = The Errant Syncretizer." In *Proceedings of the International Computer Music Conference 1986, Royal Conservatory, The Hague, Netherlands, October 20–24, 1986,* ed. Paul Berg. San Francisco, Calif.: Computer Music Association, 1986: 179–82.

8301. Cadoz, Claude. "Instrumental Gesture and Musical Composition." In *Proceedings of the 14th International Computer Music Conference, Cologne, September 20–25, 1988,* ed. Christoph Lischka and Johannes Fritsch. Cologne: Feedback-Studio-Verlag; San Francisco, Calif.: Dist. by Computer Music Association, 1988: 1–12. (Feedback Papers; 33)

8302. Chabot, Xavier. "Performance with Electronics: Gesture Interfaces and Software Toolkit." In *Proceedings, 1989 International Computer Music Conference, November 2–5, the Ohio State University, Columbus, Ohio.* San Francisco, Calif.: Computer Music Association, 1989: 65–68.

8303. ———; Roger B. Dannenberg; and Georges Bloch. "A Workstation in Live Performance: Composed Improvisation." In *Proceedings of the International Computer Music Conference 1986, Royal Conservatory, The Hague, Netherlands, October 20–24, 1986,* ed. Paul Berg. San Francisco, Calif.: Computer Music Association, 1986: 57–59.

8304. Collinge, Douglas J., and S. M. Parkinson. "The Oculus Ranae." In *Proceedings of the 14th International Computer Music Conference, Cologne, September 20–25, 1988,* ed. Christoph Lischka and Johannes Fritsch. Cologne: Feedback-Studio-Verlag; San Francisco, Calif.: Dist. by Computer Music Association, 1988: 15–19. (Feedback Papers; 33)

8305. Dannenberg, Roger B. "A Real Time Scheduler/Dispatcher." In *Proceedings of the 14th International Computer Music Conference,*

Cologne, September 20–25, 1988, ed. Christoph Lischka and Johannes Fritsch. Cologne: Feedback-Studio-Verlag; San Francisco, Calif.: Dist. by Computer Music Association, 1988: 239–42. (Feedback Papers; 33)

8306.   ——. "Real-Time Scheduling and Computer Accompaniment." In *Current Directions in Computer Music,* ed. Max V. Mathews and John R. Pierce. Cambridge, Mass.: MIT Press, 1989: 225–61.

8307.   ——, and Bernard Mont-Reynaud. "Following an Improvisation in Real Time." In *Proceedings of the 1987 International Computer Music Conference: University of Illinois at Urbana-Champaign, Urbana, Illinois, USA, August 23–26, 1987,* comp. James Beauchamp. San Francisco, Calif.: Computer Music Association, 1987: 241–48.

Techniques for the design of a computer system that recognizes, follows, and then finds a matching chord progression to jazz improvisations.

8308.   ——, and Hirofumi Mukaino. "New Techniques for Enhanced Quality of Computer Accompaniment." In *Proceedings of the 14th International Computer Music Conference, Cologne, September 20–25, 1988,* ed. Christoph Lischka and Johannes Fritsch. Cologne: Feedback-Studio-Verlag; San Francisco, Calif.: Dist. by Computer Music Association, 1988: 243–49. (Feedback Papers; 33)

8309.   Dupler, Steven. "Very Vivid Bows Interactive Vid Computer Device." *Billboard* 98 (Dec. 27, 1986): 74.

A MIDI-interfaced computer instrument derives input from body movements of stage artists.

8310.   Eaglestone, Barry M. "A Database Environment for Musician-Machine Interaction Experimentation." In *Proceedings of the 14th International Computer Music Conference, Cologne, September 20–25, 1988,* ed. Christoph Lischka and Johannes Fritsch. Cologne: Feedback-Studio-Verlag; San Francisco, Calif.: Dist. by Computer Music Association, 1988: 20–27. (Feedback Papers; 33)

8311.   Florens, Jean-Loup; Aime Razafindrakoto; Anastasie Luciani; and Claude Cadoz. "Optimized Real Time Simulation of Objects for Musical Synthesis and Animated Image Synthesis." In *Proceedings of the International Computer Music Conference 1986, Royal Conservatory, The Hague, Netherlands, October 20–24, 1986,* ed. Paul Berg. San Francisco, Calif.: Computer Music Association, 1986: 65–70.

8312.   François, Jean-Charles; Xavier Chabot; and John Silber. "MIDI Synthesizers in Performance: Realtime Dynamic Timbre Production." In *Proceedings of the 1987 International Computer Music Conference: University of Illinois at Urbana-Champaign, Urbana, Illinois, USA, August 23–26, 1987,* comp. James Beauchamp. San Francisco, Calif.: Computer Music Association, 1987: 238–40.

8313.   Gibet, Sylvie, and Jean-Loup Florens. "Instrumental Gesture Modeling by Identification with Time-varying Mechanical Models." In *Proceedings of the 14th International Computer Music Conference, Cologne, September 20–25, 1988,* ed. Christoph Lischka and Johannes Fritsch. Cologne: Feedback-Studio-Verlag; San Francisco, Calif.: Dist. by Computer Music Association, 1988: 28–40. (Feedback Papers; 33)

8314.   Greenhough, Michael. "A Microcomputer System for the Real-Time Exploration of Musical Structures." In *Proceedings of the International Computer Music Conference 1986, Royal Conservatory, The Hague, Netherlands, October 20–24, 1986,* ed. Paul Berg. San Francisco, Calif.: Computer Music Association, 1986: 91–93.

8315.   Hirata, Keiji, and Tatsuya Aoyahi. "Music Server." In *Proceedings, 1989 International Computer Music Conference, November 2–5, the Ohio State University, Columbus, Ohio.* San Francisco, Calif.: Computer Music Association, 1989: 123–26.

8316.   Holm, Frode. "CESAM, a Concept Engine for Synthesis of Audio and Music." Cand. Scient. thesis, Institute of Informatics, University of Oslo, 1986.

8317.   ———. "Frequency Scheduling: Realtime Scheduling in Multiprocessing Systems." In *Proceedings, 1989 International Computer Music Conference, November 2–5, the Ohio State University, Columbus, Ohio.* San Francisco, Calif.: Computer Music Association, 1989: 127–30.

8318.   Keislar, Douglas. "Software for Real-Time Microtonal Control." In *Proceedings of the International Computer Music Conference 1986, Royal Conservatory, The Hague, Netherlands, October 20–24, 1986,* ed. Paul Berg. San Francisco, Calif.: Computer Music Association, 1986: 83–85.

8319.   Kuivila, Ron, and David P. Anderson. "Timing Accuracy and Response Time in Interactive Systems." In *Proceedings of the International Computer Music Conference 1986, Royal Conservatory, The Hague, Netherlands, October 20–24, 1986,* ed. Paul Berg. San Francisco, Calif.: Computer Music Association, 1986: 327–29.

8320.   Lent, Keith; Russell F. Pinkston; and Peter Silsbee. "Accelerando: A Real-Time, General Purpose Computer Music System." *Computer Music Journal* 13,4 (Winter 1989): 54–64.

8321.   ———, and Peter Silsbee. "A Real Time Computer Music Synthesis System Based on the Motorola 56001." In *Proceedings, 1989 International Computer Music Conference, November 2–5, the Ohio State University, Columbus, Ohio.* San Francisco, Calif.: Computer Music Association, 1989: 176–79.

8322.   LoCascio, Marc. "Audio Time Companion for Studio and Performance Synchronization." In *Proceedings of the 1987 International Computer Music Conference: University of Illinois at Urbana-Champaign, Urbana, Illinois, USA, August 23–26, 1987,* comp. James Beauchamp. San Francisco, Calif.: Computer Music Association, 1987: 249–55.

8323.   Longton, Michael. "Self-Proliferating Musical Objects." In *Proceedings of the International Computer Music Conference 1986, Royal Conservatory, The Hague, Netherlands, October 20–24, 1986,* ed. Paul Berg. San Francisco, Calif.: Computer Music Association, 1986: A-5–A-6.

8324.   Manen, Vloris van, and Stichting Klankschap. "Ringo: A Percussive Installation." In *Proceedings of the International Computer Music Conference 1986, Royal Conservatory, The Hague, Netherlands, October 20–24, 1986,* ed. Paul Berg. San Francisco, Calif.: Computer Music Association, 1986: 193–95.

8325.   Mathews, Max V. "The Conductor Program and Mechanical Baton." In *Current Directions in Computer Music,* ed. Max V. Mathews and John R. Pierce. Cambridge, Mass.: MIT Press, 1989: 263–81.
         Also issued as: Technical Report STAN-M-47. Stanford, Calif.: Center for Research in Music and Acoustics, Music Department, Stanford University, 1988. 19 p.

8326.   "Max von Robot's First Diskette Concerto in X Flat." *Economist* 303 (Apr. 25, 1987): 79–80.
         Describes Barry Vercoe's program "The Synthetic Performer," for accompanying live soloists.

8327.   Medovich, Mark J. "Demodulated Vector Quantization (DVQ), and Real Time Music Synthesis via DVQ Codebooks." In *Proceedings, 1989 International Computer Music Conference, November 2–5, the Ohio State University, Columbus, Ohio.* San Francisco, Calif.: Computer Music Association, 1989: 203–6.

8328.   Morrill, Dexter. "Loudspeakers and Performers: Some Problems and Proposals." *Computer Music Journal* 5,4 (Winter 1981): 25–29. Previously **3799.**
         Reprinted in *On the Wires of Our Nerves,* ed. Robin Julian Heifetz. Lewisburg: Bucknell University Press, 1989: 163–70.

8329.   ———, and Perry R. Cook. "Hardware, Software, and Compositional Tools for a Real Time Improvised Solo Trumpet Work." In *Proceedings, 1989 International Computer Music Conference, November 2–5, the Ohio State University, Columbus, Ohio.* San Francisco, Calif.: Computer Music Association, 1989: 211–14.

Also issued as: Technical Report STAN-M-56. Stanford, Calif.: Center for Research in Music and Acoustics, Music Department, Stanford University, 1989. 4 p.

8330.   Nottoli, Giorgio, and Francesco Galante. "Soft Machine: A Real Time Fully Programmable Computer Music System." In *Proceedings of the International Computer Music Conference 1986, Royal Conservatory, The Hague, Netherlands, October 20–24, 1986*, ed. Paul Berg. San Francisco, Calif.: Computer Music Association, 1986: 73–74.

8331.   Pinkston, Russell F. "The Accelerando Project." In *Proceedings, 1989 International Computer Music Conference, November 2–5, the Ohio State University, Columbus, Ohio*. San Francisco, Calif.: Computer Music Association, 1989: 242–45.

An inexpensive real time computer music system designed to facilitate both teaching and composition.

8332.   Prevot, Philippe. "Tele-Detection and Large Dimension Gestual Control." In *Proceedings of the International Computer Music Conference 1986, Royal Conservatory, The Hague, Netherlands, October 20–24, 1986*, ed. Paul Berg. San Francisco, Calif.: Computer Music Association, 1986: 95–97.

8333.   Puckette, Miller. "Interprocess Communication and Timing in Real-Time Computer Music Performance." In *Proceedings of the International Computer Music Conference 1986, Royal Conservatory, The Hague, Netherlands, October 20–24, 1986*, ed. Paul Berg. San Francisco, Calif.: Computer Music Association, 1986: 43–46.

8334.   Robinson, Charlie Q. "Real Time Synthesis of Bowed String Timbres." In *Proceedings of the 1987 International Computer Music Conference: University of Illinois at Urbana-Champaign, Urbana, Illinois, USA, August 23–26, 1987*, comp. James Beauchamp. San Francisco, Calif.: Computer Music Association, 1987: 125–29.

8335.   Serra, Marie-Hélène; Dean Rubine; and Roger B. Dannenberg. "The Analysis and Resynthesis of Tones via Spectral Interpolation." In *Proceedings of the 14th International Computer Music Conference, Cologne, September 20–25, 1988*, ed. Christoph Lischka and Johannes Fritsch. Cologne: Feedback-Studio-Verlag; San Francisco, Calif.: Dist. by Computer Music Association, 1988: 323–32. (Feedback Papers; 33)

8336.   Shortess, George K. "Interactive Sound Installations Using Microcomputers." *Leonardo* 20,2 (1987): 149–53.

8337.   Sinkevičiûtė, Birutè, and Saulis Sondeckis. "On the Identification of Violin Strokes in a Real-Time System." In *Proceedings of the International Computer Music Conference 1986, Royal Conservatory, The*

Hague, Netherlands, October 20–24, 1986, ed. Paul Berg. San Francisco, Calif.: Computer Music Association, 1986: 187–91.

8338. Snell, John M. "General-Purpose Hi-Fidelity Affordable Real-Time Computer Music System." In *Proceedings of the 1987 International Computer Music Conference: University of Illinois at Urbana-Champaign, Urbana, Illinois, USA, August 23–26, 1987,* comp. James Beauchamp. San Francisco, Calif.: Computer Music Association, 1987: 130–37.

8339. Starkier, Michel, and Philippe Prevot. "Real-Time Gestural Control." In *Proceedings of the International Computer Music Conference 1986, Royal Conservatory, The Hague, Netherlands, October 20–24, 1986,* ed. Paul Berg. San Francisco, Calif.: Computer Music Association, 1986: 423–26.

8340. Truax, Barry. "Real-Time Granular Synthesis with the DMX-1000." In *Proceedings of the International Computer Music Conference 1986, Royal Conservatory, The Hague, Netherlands, October 20–24, 1986,* ed. Paul Berg. San Francisco, Calif.: Computer Music Association, 1986: 231–35.

8341. ———. "Real-Time Granulation of Sampled Sound with the DMX-1000." In *Proceedings of the 1987 International Computer Music Conference: University of Illinois at Urbana-Champaign, Urbana, Illinois, USA, August 23–26, 1987,* comp. James Beauchamp. San Francisco, Calif.: Computer Music Association, 1987: 130–37.

SPATIAL SIMULATION
AND ROOM
ACOUSTICS

8342. Bagella, Mauro; E. Cocco; P. Marrama; and Stefano Petrarca. "Un sistema per la spazializzazione del suono." [A System for the Spatialization of Sound] In *Musica e tecnologia: industria e cultura per lo sviluppo del mezzogiorno: VI Colloquio di Informatica Musicale, Napoli 16–19 ottobre 1985,* ed. Carlo Acreman; Immacolata Ortosecco; and Fausto Razzi. Milan: Edizioni Unicopli, 1987: 288–94.

8343. Begault, Durand R. "Control of Auditory Distance." Ph.D. diss., University of California, San Diego, 1987. 161 p.

8344. Bernardini, Nicola, and Peter Otto. "TRAILS: An Interactive System for Sound Location." In *Proceedings, 1989 International Computer Music Conference, November 2–5, the Ohio State University, Columbus, Ohio.* San Francisco, Calif.: Computer Music Association, 1989: 29–33.

8345. Borish, Jeffrey. "Electronic Simulation of Auditorium Acoustics." Ph.D. diss., Dept. of Electrical Engineering, Stanford University, 1984. 140 p.
Also issued as: Technical Report STAN-M-18. Stanford, Calif.: Center for Research in Music and Acoustics, Music Department, Stanford University, 1984.

A model is developed for simulating hall acoustics with two phases: synthesis (using an extension of the image model which includes complex geometrics) and analysis of actual hall acoustics.

8346. Cook, Perry R. *Reverberation Cancellation in Musical Signals Using Adaptive Filters.* Stanford, Calif.: Stanford University, Dept. of Music, 1988. 43 p. (Stanford University Department of Music Technical Report STAN-M-51)

8347. Galante, Francesco. "A.A.S.: Acoustic Ambience Simulator System." In *Proceedings of the International Computer Music Conference 1986,*

Royal Conservatory, The Hague, Netherlands, October 20–24, 1986, ed. Paul Berg. San Francisco, Calif.: Computer Music Association, 1986: 281–84.

8348.   Kendall, Gary S.; William L. Martens; and Shawn L. Decker. "Spatial Reverberation: Discussion and Demonstration." In *Current Directions in Computer Music,* ed. Max V. Mathews and John R. Pierce. Cambridge, Mass.: MIT Press, 1989: 65–87.

8349.   ——; William L. Martens; Daniel J. Freed; M. Derek Ludwig; and Richard W. Karstens. "Spatial Processing Software at Northwestern Computer Music." In *Proceedings of the International Computer Music Conference 1986, Royal Conservatory, The Hague, Netherlands, October 20–24, 1986,* ed. Paul Berg. San Francisco, Calif.: Computer Music Association, 1986: 285–92.

8350.   Küpper, Leo. "Musikprojektion im elektroakustischen Raum." *Österreichische Musikzeitschrift* 41 (1986): 293–301.

8351.   ——. "Space Perception in the Computer Age." In *Proceedings of the International Computer Music Conference 1986, Royal Conservatory, The Hague, Netherlands, October 20–24, 1986,* ed. Paul Berg. San Francisco, Calif.: Computer Music Association, 1986: 47–50.

8352.   Martel, Alain. "The SS-1 Sound Spatializer: A Real-Time MIDI Spatialization Processor." In *Proceedings of the International Computer Music Conference 1986, Royal Conservatory, The Hague, Netherlands, October 20–24, 1986,* ed. Paul Berg. San Francisco, Calif.: Computer Music Association, 1986: 305–7.

8353.   Moore, F. Richard. "A General Model for Spatial Processing of Sounds." *Computer Music Journal* 7,3 (Fall 1983): 6–15.
Previously **3823.**
Reprinted in *The Music Machine,* ed. Curtis Roads. Cambridge, Mass.: MIT Press, 1989: 559–68.

8354.   ——. "Spatialization of Sounds over Loudspeakers." In *Current Directions in Computer Music,* ed. Max V. Mathews and John R. Pierce. Cambridge, Mass.: MIT Press, 1989: 89–103.

8355.   Scott, Douglas. "A Processor for Locating Stationary and Moving Sound Sources in a Simulated Acoustical Environment." In *Proceedings, 1989 International Computer Music Conference, November 2–5, the Ohio State University, Columbus, Ohio.* San Francisco, Calif.: Computer Music Association, 1989: 277–80.

8356.   Stautner, John, and Miller Puckette. "Designing Multi-Channel Reverberators." *Computer Music Journal* 6,1 (Spring 1982): 52–65.
Previously **3833.**

Reprinted in *The Music Machine,* ed. Curtis Roads. Cambridge, Mass.: MIT Press, 1989: 569–82.

8357. White, Paul. "Space, the Final Frontier?" *Music Technology* 1 (Feb. 1987): 24–26.

SPEECH

8358. Berkel, Pierre van. "Notes by a Film-Maker." *Interface* 15 (1986): 231–56.

Covers some aspects of speech synthesis that are realized with the help of the MIDIM/VOSIM system.

8359. Carlson, Rolf; Anders Friberg; Lars Frydén; Björn Granström; and Johan Sundberg. "Speech and Music Performance: Parallels and Contrasts." *Contemporary Music Review* 4 (1989): 391–404.

STUDIOS

8360. Barrière, Jean-Baptiste. "Musical Production at IRCAM in 1986–87: A Studio Report." In *Proceedings of the 1987 International Computer Music Conference: University of Illinois at Urbana-Champaign, Urbana, Illinois, USA, August 23–26, 1987,* comp. James Beauchamp. San Francisco, Calif.: Computer Music Association, 1987: 57–64.

8361. Beauchamp, James. "The Computer Music Project at the University of Illinois at Urbana-Champaign: 1989." In *Proceedings, 1989 International Computer Music Conference, November 2–5, the Ohio State University, Columbus, Ohio.* San Francisco, Calif.: Computer Music Association, 1989: 21–24.

8362. Bennett, Gerald; Rainer Boesch; Antonio Greco; and Bruno Spoerri. "Studio Report: The Swiss Center for Computer Music." In *Proceedings of the International Computer Music Conference 1986, Royal Conservatory, The Hague, Netherlands, October 20–24, 1986,* ed. Paul Berg. San Francisco, Calif.: Computer Music Association, 1986: 197–98.

8363. Bernardini, Nicola, and Peter Otto. "Studio Report: Tempo Reale." In *Proceedings, 1989 International Computer Music Conference, November 2–5, the Ohio State University, Columbus, Ohio.* San Francisco, Calif.: Computer Music Association, 1989: 25–28.

8364. Biggelaar, Johan C. M. den. "Hogeschool voor de Kunsten Utrecht Studio Report: Centrum voor Muziek en Informatica (Center for Music and Information Technology)." In *Proceedings of the International Computer Music Conference 1986, Royal Conservatory, The Hague, Netherlands, October 20–24, 1986,* ed. Paul Berg. San Francisco, Calif.: Computer Music Association, 1986: 313–16.

8365. Cappiello, Carmelo. "Informatica musicale e pedagogia." [Musical Informatics and Pedagogy] In *Musica e tecnologia: industria e cultura per lo sviluppo del mezzogiorno: VI Colloquio di Informatica Musicale, Napoli 16–19 ottobre 1985,* ed. Carlo Acreman; Immacolata Ortosecco; and Fausto Razzi. Milan: Edizioni Unicopli, 1987: 275–84.
Studio report of the CEMAMU.

8366. Century, Michael. "The Banff Centre Media Arts Program: Studio Report and Artistic Retrospective." In *Proceedings, 1989 International Computer Music Conference, November 2–5, the Ohio State University, Columbus, Ohio.* San Francisco, Calif.: Computer Music Association, 1989: 62–64.

8367. Chafe, Chris; Julius O. Smith; and Patte Wood. "Current Work at CCRMA: An Overview." In *Proceedings of the International Computer Music Conference 1986, Royal Conservatory, The Hague, Netherlands, October 20–24, 1986,* ed. Paul Berg. San Francisco, Calif.: Computer Music Association, 1986: 431–34.

8368. Colleoni, Mario Corti. "Andante con moto." In *I profili del suono: scritti sulla musica electroacustica e la computer music,* ed. Serena Tamburini and Mauro Bagella. Salerno: Musica Verticale-Galzerano, 1987: 119–23.

8369. Colyer, Cornelia. "Studio Report: Centre d'Etudes de Mathematique et Automatique Musicales." In *Proceedings of the International Computer Music Conference 1986, Royal Conservatory, The Hague, Netherlands, October 20–24, 1986,* ed. Paul Berg. San Francisco, Calif.: Computer Music Association, 1986: 317–19.

8370. "Composing by Computer: A Little Byte Music." *Economist* 298 (Mar. 29, 1986): 80–81.

Developments by Pierre Boulez at IRCAM.

8371. Dodge, Charles, and Curtis R. Bahn. "Studio Report for the Center for Computer Music at Brooklyn College." In *Proceedings, 1989 International Computer Music Conference, November 2–5, the Ohio State University, Columbus, Ohio.* San Francisco, Calif.: Computer Music Association, 1989: 90–93.

8372. Dolnick, Edward. "Inventing the Future." *New York Times Magazine* 136 (Aug. 23, 1987): 30–33, 41, 59.

Developments in newspapers, movies, television, and music at M.I.T.

8373. "An Education at Berklee: Music Technology." *Keyboards, Computers & Software* 1 (Feb. 1986): 19.

Installation of a lab designed for teaching synthesizer technology at the Berklee College of Music.

8374. Frisius, Rudolf. "Avantgardistische Vormachtstellung: Zehn Jahre IRCAM in Paris." *Neue Musikzeitung* 36 (Aug.–Sept. 1987): 41.

8375. Gariepy, Louise. "The Electro-acoustics Unit of the Faculty of Music of the University of Montreal." In *Proceedings of the International Computer Music Conference 1986, Royal Conservatory, The Hague,*

Netherlands, October 20–24, 1986, ed. Paul Berg. San Francisco, Calif.: Computer Music Association, 1986: 203–5.

8376. Gordon, David. "More Power to the Plant." *Music Technology* 1 (Feb. 1987): 58–59.

A brief overview of Record Plant's Studio L, a comprehensive computer music studio for audio-visual work.

8377. Graham, Ann. "KCS Scoring." *Keyboards, Computers & Software* 1 (Dec. 1986): 74–75.

An inside look at the Droid Works.

8378. Halász, Péter. "Utolérni Európát: Beszélgetés az MTA Zenetudományi Intézet Kísérleti Zenetudományi Stúdiójának munkatársaival." [To Catch up with Europe: Discussion with the Members of the Experimental Music Studio of the Institute of the Hungarian Academy of Sciences] *Muzsika* 32 (May 1989): 8–12.

8379. Harnden, Eric; Ron Massaro; and Gary Gibian. "The Development of a Computer Music Facility at the American University." In *Proceedings of the 1987 International Computer Music Conference: University of Illinois at Urbana-Champaign, Urbana, Illinois, USA, August 23–26, 1987,* comp. James Beauchamp. San Francisco, Calif.: Computer Music Association, 1987: 65–72.

8380. Haus, Goffredo. "Music Processing at L.I.M." In *Supercomputers: Technology and Applications: Fourteenth Euromicro Symposium on Microprocessing and Microprogramming (EUROMICRO '88), Zurich, August 29–September 1, 1988,* ed. Stephen Winter and Harald Schumny. Amsterdam; New York, N.Y.: North-Holland, 1988: 435–41.

8381. Jameux, Dominique. "L'intelligence des sons." *Diapason-Harmonie* n317 (June 1986): 42–44.

Describes the Media Lab at MIT.

8382. Junglieb, Stanley. "Stanford's Computer Music Lab: Where Today's Research Becomes Tomorrow's Pushbutton Magic." *Keyboard* 13 (Dec. 1987): 58–65, 156, 160.

8383. Kahrs, Mark; Thomas J. Killian; and Max V. Mathews. "Computer Music Research at Bell Labs, 1986." In *Proceedings of the International Computer Music Conference 1986, Royal Conservatory, The Hague, Netherlands, October 20–24, 1986,* ed. Paul Berg. San Francisco, Calif.: Computer Music Association, 1986: 199–201.

8384. Kendall, Robert A. "Center for Electronic Music Lets You Try Before You Buy." *PC Computing* 2 (Apr. 1989): 52.

8385. Kuchera-Morin, JoAnn, and Dan Timis. "The Computer Music Studio at the University of California, Santa Barbara: A Studio Report." In

Proceedings of the 1987 International Computer Music Conference: University of Illinois at Urbana-Champaign, Urbana, Illinois, USA, August 23–26, 1987, comp. James Beauchamp. San Francisco, Calif.: Computer Music Association, 1987: 80–83.

8386.   ———, and Dan Timis. "Recent Developments at the Center for Computer Music Composition." In *Proceedings, 1989 International Computer Music Conference, November 2–5, the Ohio State University, Columbus, Ohio*. San Francisco, Calif.: Computer Music Association, 1989: 160–63.

8387.   Mailliard, Bénédict. "A la recherche du studio musical." *Revue musicale* n394–97 (1986): 51–63.

A report on the studio numérique 123. Paper originally given at Conférence aux Journées d'Etudes du Festival du Son 1981.

8388.   Mancini, Joseph, and Paul Freiberger. "European Computer Music Research Challenges American Efforts." *Popular Computing* 4 (Apr. 1985): 22.

An overview of developments at IRCAM, GRM, CEMAMu, and the Computer Music Studio at the Royal Dutch Conservatory in The Hague.

8389.   Naglar, Joseph C. "CEM Outreach." *Active Sensing* 1 (Summer 1989): 10.

A description of the Center for Electronic Music outreach programs, including BIOMUSE, a system for disabled people to create music using attached electrodes.

8390.   Núñez, Adolfo. "The Computer and Electronic Music Studio at the CDMC, Madrid." In *Proceedings, 1989 International Computer Music Conference, November 2–5, the Ohio State University, Columbus, Ohio*. San Francisco, Calif.: Computer Music Association, 1989: 223–25.

8391.   Pennycook, Bruce W. "Computer Applications in Music at McGill University." In *Proceedings, 1989 International Computer Music Conference, November 2–5, the Ohio State University, Columbus, Ohio*. San Francisco, Calif.: Computer Music Association, 1989: 238–41.

8392.   Reynolds, Roger. "Musical Production and Related Issues at CARL." In *Proceedings of the International Computer Music Conference 1986, Royal Conservatory, The Hague, Netherlands, October 20–24, 1986*, ed. Paul Berg. San Francisco, Calif.: Computer Music Association, 1986: 387–91.

8393.   Rich, Henry. "Electromag: CEM-ocracy." *Village Voice* 34 (Mar. 28, 1989): E15.

Describes the Center for Electronic Music and the services it provides.

8394.   Rothstein, Joseph B. "Studios: Yamaha Communication Center, New York." *Computer Music Journal* 12,4 (Winter 1988): 46.
         Studio review.

8395.   Saba, Andrea. "Innovazione tecnologica e nuovo ruolo dello IASM nella politica di sviluppo del mezzogiorno." [Technological Innovations and the New Role of the IASM in the Development of Southern Italy] In *Musica e tecnologia: industria e cultura per lo sviluppo del mezzogiorno: VI Colloquio di Informatica Musicale, Napoli 16–19 ottobre 1985*, ed. Carlo Acreman; Immacolata Ortosecco; and Fausto Razzi. Milan: Edizioni Unicopli, 1987: 46–51.

8396.   Sani, Nicola. "L'attività in corso di sviluppo presso la Società di Informatica Musicale di Roma." [Activity in the Course of Development at the Società di Informatica Musicale di Roma] In *Musica e tecnologia: industria e cultura per lo sviluppo del mezzogiorno: VI Colloquio di Informatica Musicale, Napoli 16–19 ottobre 1985*, ed. Carlo Acreman; Immacolata Ortosecco; and Fausto Razzi. Milan: Edizioni Unicopli, 1987: 285–87.

8397.   ———. "Musica Verticale: considerazioni sui primi dieci anni di attivita." [Musica Verticale: Thoughts on the First Ten Years of Activity] In *I profili del suono: scritti sulla musica electroacustica e la computer music,* ed. Serena Tamburini and Mauro Bagella. Salerno: Musica Verticale-Galzerano, 1987: 125–29.

8398.   Serra, Xavier, and Patte Wood. *OVERVIEW, Center for Computer Research in Music and Acoustics (Recent Work)*. Stanford, Calif.: Stanford University, Dept. of Music, 1988. (Department of Music Technical Report STAN-M-44)

8399.   Shuttleworth, Justin, and Michael Greenhough. "Music Processing by Transputer Networks at the Electronic Music Studio in Cardiff." In *Proceedings, 1989 International Computer Music Conference, November 2–5, the Ohio State University, Columbus, Ohio.* San Francisco, Calif.: Computer Music Association, 1989: 289–92.

8400.   Siegel, Wayne. "DIEM Studio Report." In *Proceedings, 1989 International Computer Music Conference, November 2–5, the Ohio State University, Columbus, Ohio.* San Francisco, Calif.: Computer Music Association, 1989: 293–95.

8401.   Terenzi, Fiorella. "The Computer Audio Research Laboratory at the Center for Music Experiment and Related Research." In *Supercomputers: Technology and Applications: Fourteenth Euromicro Symposium on Microprocessing and Microprogramming (EUROMICRO '88), Zurich, August 29–September 1, 1988,* ed. Stephen Winter and Harald Schumny.. Amsterdam; New York, N.Y.: North-Holland, 1988: 443–46.

8402.   "University's Sound Technology: San Jose State." *Keyboards, Computers & Software* 1 (Apr. 1986): 14.

  Describes course offerings in music technology at San Jose State University in California.

8403.   Wessel, David; Richard Felciano; and Adrian Freed. "The Center for New Music and Audio Technologies." In *Proceedings, 1989 International Computer Music Conference, November 2–5, the Ohio State University, Columbus, Ohio.* San Francisco, Calif.: Computer Music Association, 1989: 336–39.

8404.   Wexler, Richard. *The Department of Music Computer Guide.* College Park, Md.: Dept. of Music, University of Maryland, 1988. 25 p.

8405.   Yavelow, Christopher. "Berklee School of Music." *Macworld* 4 (June 1987): 109–11.

  An overview of the music LAN at the Berklee College of Music.

8406.   Zahler, Noel. "Studio Report: The Impact of Computer Music on the Small Liberal Arts College in the United States." In *Proceedings of the International Computer Music Conference 1986, Royal Conservatory, The Hague, Netherlands, October 20–24, 1986,* ed. Paul Berg. San Francisco, Calif.: Computer Music Association, 1986: 207–9.

  Studio report for Connecticut College.

TRADE SHOWS

8407. "1989 Winter NAMM's Greatest Hits." *Electronic Musician* 5 (May 1989): 18–26.

8408. "Aktuelles: Sphärenklänge aus Frankreich." *Musik International* 41 (Oct. 1987): 597.

8409. Anderton, Craig. "Digital Workstations Highlight AES '87: New Product Blitz." *Electronic Musician* 4 (Jan. 1988): 20–25.

8410. ——. "On Location: Musicom 84, Holland." *Polyphony* 10 (Apr. 1985): 16–18.

8411. ——. "On Location: Summer 1985 NAMM." *Electronic Musician* 1 (Sept. 1985): 9, 31–33.
A brief description of new products.

8412. ——. "Special Report: The 1988 Summer NAMM Show." *Electronic Musician* 4 (Sept. 1988): 16–24.

8413. ——. "Special Report: Winter '88 NAMM Show." *Electronic Musician* 4 (Apr. 1988): 13–17.

8414. ——. "What's New: AES Report: Tweaking the Human Interface." *Electronic Musician* 5 (Mar. 1989): 14–19, 96–97.
How the terms *user interface* and *ergonomics* were the descriptions given to new products at the AES show.

8415. ——, and George Petersen. "What's New: New Gear: Winter 1989 NAMM Show. Part 1." *Electronic Musician* 5 (Apr. 1989): 10–14.

8416. Baird, Jock. "Developments: A Hero Takes a Fall." *Musician* n91 (May 1986): 28–29.
The end of Linn Electronics, and new NAMM products.

8417. ——. "Developments: Synching Up, Software Revisions & Other A.E.S. Surprises." *Musician* n85 (Nov. 1985): 96–98.
An overview of products displayed at the A.E.S. show in New York, N.Y., October 1985.

8418. ———. "Heat Wave in Anaheim: The Best of N.A.M.M." *Musician* n66 (Apr. 1984): 84–86.

A review of new products displayed at NAMM.

8419. ———. "The Neo-Analog Revival Hits NAMM: New Muscle from the Guitar/Analog Camp Surprises the Keyboard-Digital Contingent." *Musician* n114 (Apr. 1988): 34–44, 97–98.

An overview of the trends at the NAMM show.

8420. ———. "P & O Paradigm & the Works-in-a-Box Syndrome." *Musician* n108 (Oct. 1987): 48.

New products at the NAMM show aimed toward home use.

8421. ———. "Software City." *Musician* n91 (May 1986): 76–78.

A report on the winter NAMM show.

8422. ———. "What's New in Guitars and Other NAMM Action." *Musician* n107 (Sept. 1987): 58–65, 114.

8423. ———, and Alan Di Perna. "Sneak Previews Goes to NAMM." *Musician* n126 (Apr. 1989): 51–59, 94.

8424. Collie, Ashley. "NAMM Showcases Latest MIDI Gear." *Canadian Musician* 9 (Oct. 1987): 27.

8425. "Control Zone: Fair Do Two: BMF Part II." *Melody Maker* 65 (Aug. 19, 1989): 44.

Covers computer software demonstrated at the British Music Fair.

8426. "Control Zone: Fair Do: BMF. Part 1." *Melody Maker* 65 (Aug. 12, 1989): 44–46.

A report on the British Music Fair.

8427. "Control Zone: Frankfurt Preview." *Melody Maker* 64 (Mar. 5, 1988): 48–57.

A preview of products to be shown at the Frankfurt Music Fair.

8428. "Control Zone: XX Spex: Yamaha X-perience Shows." *Melody Maker* 61 (May 17, 1986): 37.

A review of Yamaha "X-Perience" shows in Glasgow and London during Apr. 1986.

8429. Cooper, Jim. "Mind over MIDI: April Showers Bring on the Crazies." *Keyboard* 13 (Apr. 1987): 119.

Off-the-track demos at the NAMM show in Anaheim.

8430. ———. "Mind over MIDI: Is There Life after the NAMM Show?" *Keyboard* 12 (Apr. 1986): 100–101.

Comments about the NAMM show.

8431. ———. "Mind over MIDI: New Products on the Trailing Edge." *Keyboard* 14 (Apr. 1988): 122.

New products at the NAMM show.

8432. Di Perna, Alan. "Developments: A NAMM Sneak Preview." *Musician* n124 (Feb. 1989): 41–45.

8433. ———. "MIDI Update: The Big Algorithm Hits NAMM." *Musician* n108 (Oct. 1987): 44–50.

8434. ———. "Stalking the Wild MIDI Machines." *Musician* n131 (Sept. 1989): 90–91, 88.

The author relates his findings of MIDI equipment at the NAMM show.

8435. Doherty, W. Charles. "Evolution at NAMM Expo '84." *Down Beat* 51 (Sept. 1984): 48.

8436. Ferguson, Jim; Tom Mulhern; and Jon Sievert. "Anaheim NAMM '89: Guitar Gear Devours Southern California!" *Guitar Player* 23 (May 1989): 67–81, 143.

8437. Frederick, Dave. "Keyboards & Hot Racks: NAMM Trade Show '86, Summer of the Sampler." *Keyboard* 12 (Sept. 1986): 36–48.

8438. Freff. "Rhythm 'n' Views: What a Difference a Year Makes." *MacUser* 4 (Dec. 1988): 223–28.

Comments on how computer retailers present their products and software at NAMM.

8439. Goldstein, Dan. "Messe Magic." *Music Technology* 1 (Apr. 1987): 48–54.

A report on the Frankfurt Music Fair.

8440. ———; Rick Davies; and Paul White. "Biggest Is Best." *Music Technology* 1 (Mar. 1987): 12–21.

An overview of the 1987 NAMM Expo.

8441. ———; Bob O'Donnell; Rick Davies; and Paul White. "Show Stoppers." *Music Technology* 2 (Aug. 1987): 49–55.

A report on the summer NAMM show.

8442. Greenwald, Ted. "NAMM Music Expo '87. Part 1, Synthesizers, Samplers, Pianos, Home Keyboards, Software." *Keyboard* 13 (Oct. 1987): 38–50, 160–61.

8443. ———. "NAMM Music Expo '87: Better Sounding through Electronics. Part 2, Controllers, Sequencers, Sound Reinforcement, Processors, Drum Machines." *Keyboard* 13 (Nov. 1987): 36–50, 142, 147, 158–60.

8444. ———. "NAMM. Part 1." *Keyboard* 13 (Apr. 1987): 52–62.
Winter NAMM '87 products.

8445. ———. "NAMM. Part 2." *Keyboard* 13 (May 1987): 38–48, 140.

8446. Hanson, Mark, and Phil Hood. "Soft Sell: The Changing Face of the Music Business." *Frets* 10 (Oct. 1988): 28–33, 56.
A report on the NAMM International Music and Sound Expo in Atlanta.

8447. Hirschfeld, Peter. "CES Report: Winter Consumer Electronics Show: Digital Technology Seduces the Masses." *Electronic Musician* 4 (Apr. 1988): 19–20.

8448. Holzman, Adam. "Pro Session: Creative Synthesizer Technique II—in MIDI Wonderland." *Down Beat* 56 (Feb. 1989): 59–60.
A keyboard and MIDI Show at Cal State University, Northridge, a trade show open to the public.

8449. "Hot Gear, Big Show, Windy City." *Guitar Player* 23 (Oct. 1989): 52–65, 152.
A review of the NAMM show in Chicago.

8450. Hughes, Chuck. "New from NAMM." *Musician, Player & Listener* n20 (Sept.–Oct. 1979): 70–71.

8451. "Japan Showing Out." *Music Technology* 2 (Feb. 1988): 23–25.
A review of the Tokyo Music Fair.

8452. Jenkins, Mark. "British Music Fair: Making Music 85." *Melody Maker* 60 (Aug. 3, 1985): 41–52.

8453. ———. "British Music Fair: World Champion!: Previews." *Melody Maker* 61 (Aug. 2, 1986): 43–49.
A preview of equipment to be shown at the British Music Fair.

8454. ———. "Control Zone after Frankfurt: New Products." *Melody Maker* 60 (Feb. 23, 1985): 36.
An overview of various new products.

8455. ———. "Control Zone Frankfurt Report: Big Softies." *Melody Maker* 62 (Feb. 28, 1987): 47.
An introduction to software products for microcomputers.

8456. ———. "Control Zone: Casio's Frankfurter: Casio at Frankfurt." *Melody Maker* 61 (Jan. 4, 1986): 37.
A preview of Casio products to be shown at the Frankfurt Music Festival.

8457.   ——. "Control Zone: Computer Update." *Melody Maker* 60 (Jan. 19, 1985): 33.

A preview of the Frankfurt Music Fair.

8458.   ——. "New Keys." *Melody Maker* 61 (Jan. 25, 1986): 35.

A preview of the keyboards to be shown at the Frankfurt Music Festival.

8459.   Marans, Michael. "Ready for the '90s: NAMM Wraps up a Tumultuous Decade with a Subdued Summer Show." *Keyboard* 15 (Sept. 1989): 34–38.

8460.   ——. "Surf's Up at Anaheim NAMM: New Music Hardware, Software & Beach Togs." *Keyboard* 15 (Apr. 1989): 82–97.

8461.   "Melody Maker 1987 British Music Fair Pull-out." *Melody Maker* 63 (Aug. 1, 1987): I–XVI.

A preview of the British Music Fair that includes an exhibitor list and a floor plan.

8462.   Milano, Dominic. "Music Expo '85: Everything's Coming up Software." *Keyboard* 11 (Sept. 1985): 30–34.

8463.   ——, and Dave Frederick. "Keyboards, Samplers, MIDI Software: Digital Firestorm at NAMM!" *Keyboard* 12 (Apr. 1986): 64–76.

8464.   Mulhern, Tom. "NAMM Expo '85: MIDI Meets Guitar." *Guitar Player* 19 (Sept. 1985): 20–29, 128.

A discussion of how MIDI is affecting guitar manufacture and reviews of several new guitar models.

8465.   "Musikmesse in Frankfurt: Grosse Vielfalt bei Schlaginstrumenten." *Musikhandel* 37 (Apr. 1986): 136–38.

8466.   Nathan, Bobby. "Cutting-Edge Technology Unveiled at NAMM." *Billboard* 99 (Aug. 1, 1987): 52.

A discussion of developments in computer music software, signal processing, and other areas at the NAMM meeting, Chicago, 27–30 June 1987.

8467.   ——. "NAMM Meet Displays Plethora of Technological Innovations." *Billboard* 99 (July 25, 1987): 49.

A discussion of technical highlights in the area of digital sampling at the NAMM meeting, Chicago, 27–30 June 1987.

8468.   ——. "Winter NAMM '86: 'MIDI Thruway' Runs through Anaheim." *Billboard* 98 (Feb. 8, 1986): 53.

New products on the market.

8469. "New Gear from the Summer Music Expo." *Electronic Musician* 5 (Sept. 1989): 17–26.

A report on products shown at the summer NAMM.

8470. O'Donnell, Bob. "Digital Days & Digital Nights: The AES Report." *Music Technology* 2 (Dec. 1987): 46–49.

A report on the products displayed at the AES convention in New York City.

8471. ———; Rick Davies; Deborah Parisi; Amy Ziffer; and Michael McFall. "Theme and Variations: The NAMM Report." *Music Technology* 2 (Mar. 1988): 32–39.

8472. Reed, Tony. "Control Zone." *Melody Maker* 63 (Aug. 22, 1987): 45.

Completion of the author's diary from six days at the British Music Fair.

8473. ———. "Control Zone: Diary of a Madman." *Melody Maker* 63 (Aug. 15, 1987): 36–37.

An introduction to products displayed at the British Music Fair.

8474. ———. "Control Zone: Frankfurt Preview." *Melody Maker* 65 (Jan. 28, 1989): 40–41.

8475. ———. "Control Zone: NAMM 2." *Melody Maker* 64 (Feb. 6, 1988): 36–37.

8476. ———. "Control Zone: NAMM 88: The Untold Story." *Melody Maker* 64 (Jan. 30, 1988): 36–37.

8477. ———. "Soft Hits." *Melody Maker* 64 (Oct. 1, 1988): 54.

A report on products from the Personal Computer Show.

8478. Rolle, Günter. "Tastentendenzen: Aufblähen oder Abspeken—auf der Frankfurter Messe waren Verschiebungen beim Klavierbau zu beobachten." *Neue Musikzeitung* 37 (Apr.–Mai 1988): 7–8.

8479. Savicky, Randy. "Sights and Sounds." *Jazz Times* (Feb. 1989): 26.

A report on the Winter NAMM Show.

8480. Schneider, Albrecht. "Miditation: Wann bekommt auch die Tuba ein Interface?" *Musikhandel* 37 (Apr. 1986): 133–36.

An overview of products displayed at the Frankfurt Music Fair.

8481. ———. "Musik und Elektronik: Workstations, Sampler, Software, und was sonst noch in Frankfurt zu sehen war." *Musikhandel* 40 (Mai 1989): 184–87.

An overview of products displayed at the Frankfurt Music Fair.

8482.   Trask, Simon, and Tim Goodyer. "Trading Places: Frankfurt Musik-messe 1988." *Music Technology* 2 (May 1988): 14–16.

8483.   Tully, Tim. "MIDI for the Masses at CES." *Electronic Musician* 4 (Apr. 1988): 20.
    An overview of new equipment that uses MIDI technology.

8484.   Vail, Mark. "NAMM." *Keyboard* 14 (Apr. 1988): 34–46.

8485.   ——. "Summer NAMM '88: The Tech Well Runs Dry?" *Keyboard* 14 (Oct. 1988): 74–88.

8486.   Waldingen, Karl-Georg. "Mikrochips und Mahagony; Eindrücke vom 'Welt-Musikmarkt 1985' auf der Frankfurter Messe." *Musik und Bildung* 17 (Mai 1985): 372–74.

8487.   "What's New: The Greatest Hits of the 1988 Summer NAMM Show." *Electronic Musician* 4 (Oct. 1988): 21–29.

8488.   Wiffen, Paul; Paul White; and Chris Meyer. "Perspectives on Chicago." *Music Technology* 1 (Sept. 1986): 80–83.
    A report on the NAMM show.

GENERAL

8489. Åhlén, Carl-Gunnar. "Argentinsk elektronmusik—ett liv i Kåppsäck." [Argentinian Electronic Music: A Life in Kappsack] *Nutida Musik* 27,1 (1984–85): 45–46. In Swedish.

An overview of the contribution of Argentinian musician, Francisco Kröpfl.

8490. Aikin, Jim. "Exotic New Chords and Melodies for All Tunable Synthesizers: Discover 19-Tone Equal Temperament." *Keyboard* 14 (Mar. 1988): 74–80.

8491. ——. "Plug in Here: The ABC's of Techno-Music Literacy." *Keyboard* 14 (June 1988): 34–56.

8492. Allgeier, Jeffrey H. "Cabaret Voltaire." *Music, Computers & Software* 3 (Apr. 1988): 30.

Profile/interview with members of the rock band, who discuss their use of synthesis equipment.

8493. ——. "MCS Scoring." *Music, Computers & Software* 3 (Apr. 1988): 75–76.

A discussion of the techniques used in scoring the film *The Source of Power.*

8494. ——. "Red Flag: Computer Dance Music Propelled by Jet Engine Samples!" *Music, Computers & Software* 3 (Dec. 1988): 28–29.

Profile/interview with members of the rock band, who discuss their use of sequencers and sampling synthesizers.

8495. ——. "Scoring." *Music, Computers & Software* 3 (Dec. 1988): 78–80.

A discussion of the techniques used in scoring the television program "In Care of: Families and Their Elders."

8496. ——. "Yanni." *Music, Computers & Software* 3 (June 1988): 26.

Profile/interview of the New Age keyboardist.

8497. Alvaro, Susan. "Guest Editorial: What Is Musical Property? The Ethics of Sampling." *Keyboard* 12 (Oct. 1986): 10, 157.

8498. Anderton, Craig. "20 Great Achievements in Twenty Years of Musical Electronics 1968–1988." *Electronic Musician* 4 (July 1988): 28–97.

8499. ———. "Frankie Goes to Hollywood: Frank Serafine's Movie MIDI Studio, Where Sonic Worlds Collide." *Musician* n82 (Aug. 1985): 62–66, 90.

8500. ———. "Interview: Jan Hammer's Electronic Cottage." *Electronic Musician* 3 (Mar. 1987): 50–59.

Jan Hammer describes his equipment and inspiration.

8501. Andresen, Uwe. "Ein Symphonieorchester aus dem Computer? Anmerkungen zum Stand und zur Entwicklung der Musikcomputer." *Orchester* 33 (Mar. 1985): 233–37.

8502. Baird, Jock. "Roger Linn, the Missing Link: Musicians & Computers Meet in the Mind of a Modest Revolutionary." *Musician* n82 (Aug. 1985): 86–90, 95.

Biographical sketch of Roger Linn, developer of the drum machine.

8503. Balaban, Mira. "The Cross Fertilization Relationship between Music and AI (Based on Experience with the CSM Project)." *Interface* 18 (1989): 89–115.

8504. ———. "A Music-Workstation Based on Multiple Hierarchical Views of Music." In *Proceedings of the 14th International Computer Music Conference, Cologne, September 20–25, 1988,* ed. Christoph Lischka and Johannes Fritsch. Cologne: Feedback-Studio-Verlag; San Francisco, Calif.: Dist. by Computer Music Association, 1988: 56–65. (Feedback Papers; 33)

8505. Barilla, John. "Life in the Electronic Cottage." *DB, the Sound Engineering Magazine* 22 (May/June 1988): 31–32.

How the computer revolution and MIDI have affected musicians.

8506. Barlow, Clarence. "Two Essays on Theory." *Computer Music Journal* 11,1 (Spring 1987): 44–60.

8507. Barry, Rick. "The Fear of Displacement: Artists Must View Computers as Tools." *MacWeek* 2 (Nov. 1, 1988): 24.

Encourages musicians to use computers instead of avoiding the technology.

8508. Bartardi, M. "Translitterazione di testi letterari in partiture musicali: strumenti di sintesi." [Transliteration of Literary Texts in Musical Scores:Instruments of Synthesis] Tesi di Laurea in Scienze dell'Informazione, A.A., Università degli Studi, Milano, 1987.

8509. Bateman, Jeff. "Sampling—Sin or Musical Godsend?" *Music Scene* n363 (Sept.–Oct. 1988): 14–15.

8510. Bernardini, Nicola. "Computer Music: The State of the Nation." In *Proceedings of the International Computer Music Conference 1986, Royal Conservatory, The Hague, Netherlands, October 20–24, 1986,* ed. Paul Berg. San Francisco, Calif.: Computer Music Association, 1986: A-13–A-15.

8511. Bernstein, Bob. "Commentary: Sampling Challenges Copyright Theories." *Billboard* 99 (Dec. 19, 1987): 9, 77.

8512. Berry, Ronald L. "Computers and Pianos: How Can a Piano Technician Use a Computer." *Piano Technicians Journal* 31 (May 1988): 27–28.

An analysis of why a piano technician would want to use a computer.

8513. Beyer, Hermann. "Erfahrungen mit einem neuen elektronischen Metronom." *Neuland* 1 (Nov. 1980): 96–101.

Describes the construction and operation of a computer metronome.

8514. Bianchini, Laura. "Musica con l'elaboratore: alcune considerazioni." [Computer Music: Some Considerations] In *I profili del suono: scritti sulla musica electroacustica e la computer music,* ed. Serena Tamburini and Mauro Bagella. Salerno: Musica Verticale-Galzerano, 1987: 51–56.

8515. Bisel, Larry D. "Seeking a Perceptual Preference among Pythagorean Tuning, Just Intonation, One-Quarter Comma Meantone Tuning, and Equal Temperament (Computer)." Ph.D. diss., University of Michigan, 1987. 248 p.

8516. Botusharov, Liuben; Plamen Dzhurov; Ivan Slavov; Zhivko Paskalev; and George Dimkov. "Nauchno-Tekhnicheskata Revoliutsiia i Muzikata." [The Scientific-Technical Revolution and Music] *Bulgarska Muzika* 37,4 (Apr. 1986): 15–25.
In Bulgarian.

8517. Briefel, Ron. "Computers, Music, and Art." *Music Technology* 1 (Jan. 1987): 52–54.

Interview with Morton Subotnick.

8518. Brotbeck, Roman. "Zürich: Konzertreihe mit Computermusik." *Dissonanz* 11 (Feb. 1987): 20–21.

Different ways the computer is used for the performance of music.

8519. Bubenik, Anton. "Bloss keine Angst vor den Tricks der Chips: Über Berührungsprobleme beim Umgang mit einem neuen 'Werkzeug.'" *Neue Musikzeitung* 37 (Aug.–Sept. 1988): 37.

8520.   Burgess, Jim. "Computers: Dave Oppenheim/Opcode Systems." *Canadian Musician* 8 (Oct. 1986): 66.

A short interview with Dave Oppenheim of Opcode Systems.

8521.   Butler, Chris. "Michael Waisvisz: The 'Hands' Are Quicker Than the Hands." *Music, Computers & Software* 2 (Oct. 1987): 33–34.

Profile/interview with the composer, who discusses his development and use of a new, hand-operated MIDI controller.

8522.   ——. "Running Bytes: Putting It on the Line: Texas MIDI." *Keyboards, Computers & Software* 1 (Aug. 1986): 19.

A brief description of KCB Systems in Denton, Tex., a full-service MIDI company.

8523.   ——. "Sound to Pictures: Suzanne Ciani." *Keyboards, Computers & Software* 1 (Aug. 1986): 19–20.

A short description of Suzanne Ciani's non-commercial music.

8524.   Buxton, William. "A (Highly) Selective View of Canadian Electroacoustic Music." *Musicanada* n57 (June 1986): 5–6.
French version: L'Électroacoustique: un aperçu subjectif.

8525.   Campbell, Alan Gary. "Just and Mean Tone Tuning for Electronic Keyboards." *Electronic Musician* 2 (Nov. 1986): 46–48.

8526.   ——. "Service Clinic: Dare to Be Serviced." *Electronic Musician* 3 (Apr. 1987): 72–76.

Anecdotes on service provided for synthesizers in various unusual situations.

8527.   ——. "Service Clinic: Preventive Maintenance, Shipping, and Storage." *Electronic Musician* 2 (July 1986): 26–31.

8528.   Camurri, Antonio. "Temporal Logic Issues in Music Knowledge Representation." In *Design Tools for the 90's: Fifteenth Euromicro Symposium on Microprocessing and Microprogramming (EUROMICRO 89), Cologne, September 4–8, 1989,* ed. Lorenzo Mezzalire and Stephen Winter. Amsterdam; New York, N.Y.: North-Holland, 1989: 541–46.

8529.   Canale, Larry. "Us Festival." *Microcomputing* 6 (Nov. 1982): 98–101.

Describes the Us Festival, Sept. 3–5 in San Bernadino, Calif., sponsored by Steven Wozniak, which juxtaposed rock music and computer technology.

8530.   "Capotasto." *Classical Guitar* 6 (Apr. 1988): 53.
Anonymous musings on the computer and music.

8531.   Carlos, Wendy. "Guest Editorial: The Psychology of Copy Protection (DAT's All, Folks)." *Keyboard* 14 (Jan. 1988): 12–15.

8532. ———. "Tuning: At the Crossroads." *Computer Music Journal* 11,1 (Spring 1987): 29–43.
With soundsheet.

8533. Ceccato, Silvio; Gastone Zotto; and Giuseppe Porzionato. *Dalla cibernetica all'arte musicale.* [From Cybernetics to Musical Art] Padova: G. Zanibon, 1980. 55 p.
Review by Nicola Sani in *Nuova rivista musicae italiana* 16 (July–Sept. 1982): 487–88.

8534. Chaley, Chris. "Software: What and Where to Buy." *Canadian Musician* 10 (Feb. 1988): 30.
Software purchasing guidelines on how to deal with salespeople and what to look for in software.

8535. Charbeneau, Travis. "Music's Electronic Future." *Futurist* 21 (Sept.– Oct. 1987): 35–37.
How MIDI and personal computers have given some musicians more freedom, while putting others out of business.

8536. Chin, Adam. "MCS Telecom." *Music, Computers & Software* 2 (June 1987): 12–13.
Discusses the preparation of scripts for automated telecommunications.

8537. Clark, Thomas. "Coasts: On the Creative Edge with Composer Larry Austin." *Computer Music Journal* 13,1 (Spring 1989): 21–35.
Interview with Larry Austin.

8538. Clarke, A. T.; B. M. Brown; and M. P. Thorne. "Coping with Some Really Rotten Problems in Automatic Music Recognition." In *Design Tools for the 90's: Fifteenth Euromicro Symposium on Microprocessing and Microprogramming (EUROMICRO 89), Cologne, September 4–8, 1989,* ed. Lorenzo Mezzalire and Stephen Winter. Amsterdam; New York, N.Y.: North-Holland, 1989: 547–50.

8539. "CMC Issues Source Book for Computer Musicians." *Music Trades* 135 (Dec. 1987): 96–98.
Computer Musicians Cooperative issues a new publication, *Computer Musicians Source Book.*

8540. Comer, Brooke. "Computers in the Studio: How Hard Drives Changed Four Engineer's Lives." *Music, Computers & Software* 2 (Oct. 1987): 50–58.
Profiles/interviews with four recording engineers and producers.

8541. Cornyn, Stan. "CD-I and the Media." In *The Proceedings of the AES 5th International Conference: Music and Digital Technology,* ed. John Strawn. New York, N.Y.: Audio Engineering Society, 1987: 233–44.

8542.   "Craig Frost: A Midwest Silver Bullet Gives Digital a Shot." *Keyboards, Computers & Software* 2 (Feb. 1987): 30–31.

Profile/interview with the rock keyboardist, who discusses his synthesis equipment.

8543.   Crippa, P. "Translitterazione di testi letterari in partiture musicali: strumenti di analisi." [Transliteration of Literary Texts in Musical Scores: Instruments of Analysis] Tesi di Laurea in Scienze dell'Informazione, A.A., Università degli Studi, Milano, 1987.

8544.   Czeiszperger, Michael S. "Basics: Music, Art, and Technology." *Electronic Musician* 3 (May 1987): 18–20.

How high-level computers are being used in an academic context to merge several art forms, including music, at once.

8545.   ——. "A Multiple Workstation Environment for Joint Computer Music/Computer Graphics Production." In *Proceedings of the 14th International Computer Music Conference, Cologne, September 20–25, 1988,* ed. Christoph Lischka and Johannes Fritsch. Cologne: Feedback-Studio-Verlag; San Francisco, Calif.: Dist. by Computer Music Association, 1988: 66–81. (Feedback Papers; 33)

8546.   Daragan, D. "Prodolzhenie Temy." [Continuation of Themes] *Sovetskaia Muzyka* n3 (Mar. 1986): 71–72.

In Russian.

8547.   "Datorer—Hjälpmedel eller fetisch?" [Computers—Assistance or Fetish?] *Nutida Musik* 29,1 (1985–86): 18–22.

In Swedish.

Bill Brunson and Hans Lunell converse with composers Paer Lindgren and Bo Rydberg.

8548.   "Datorn är inget mål—den är ett medel för ljudkonst." [The Computer Is not a Goal—Rather It Is a Medium for the Art of Sound Production] *Nutida Musik* 29,2 (1985–86): 44–46.

In Swedish.

8549.   Davidson, Corey. "Paramount's Electronic Cottage." *DB, the Sound Engineering Magazine* 22 (May/June 1988): 13.

Interview with Frank Serafine.

8550.   Davies, Rick. "College Days." *Music Technology* 1 (Feb. 1987): 80–81.

Interview with Lee Berk and Don Puluse of the Berklee College of Music.

8551.   ——. "Just Another Day in MIDI Hell." *Music Technology* 2 (Aug. 1987): 16–21.

Interview with Danny Elfman.

8552. ———. "Mark Isham." *Music Technology* 1,1 (1986): 86–88.

Interview with Mark Isham, who discusses his playing and programming.

8553. ———. "MIDI and All that Jazz." *Music Technology* 1 (Oct. 1986): 64–70.

Interviews with David Torn and Kurt Wortman, who use MIDI technology in jazz improvisation.

8554. ———. "Western Music, Eastern Sounds." *Music Technology* 1 (Apr. 1987): 12–18.

Interview with Ravi Shankar and Frank Serafine on their musical collaborations.

8555. DeSmit, Scott. "Home Hardware: Building the Perfect Beat." *Music Scene* n360 (Mar.–Apr. 1988): 18–19.

Song writing with computer and synthesizer.

8556. Deutsch, Herbert A. "Harald Bode." *Music, Computers & Software* 3 (Apr. 1988): 37–38.

Profile of the electronic music pioneer.

8557. ———. "Raymond Scott: The Original Master Cylinder on the New Frontier." *Music, Computers & Software* 3 (Feb. 1988): 37.

Profile of the electronic music pioneer.

8558. ———. "Retrospective." *Music, Computers & Software* 3 (June 1988): 16–17.

Profile of Thaddeus Cahill and his teleharmonium.

8559. ———. "Retrospective." *Music, Computers & Software* 3 (Aug. 1988): 16–17.

Profile of the theremin and Clara Rockmore.

8560. ———. "Retrospective." *Music, Computers & Software* 3 (Oct. 1988): 16–17.

A discussion of Otto Luening's and Vladimir Ussachevsky's first concert of tape music.

8561. ———. "Retrospective." *Music, Computers & Software* 3 (Nov. 1988): 14–16.

A discussion of the Cologne Electronic Music Studio and the Columbia-Princeton Electronic Music Studio and the RCA Mark II Synthesizer.

8562. Di Giugno, Giuseppe; Domenico Corradetti; Alvise Vidolin; Giorgio Nottoli; Roberto De Simone; Luigi Pestalozza; Pasquale Santoli;

Fulvio Basso; Giuseppe Savarese; Eugenio Corti; Carlo Turco; Vittorio Silvestrini; Paolo Strolin; Filippo Canavese; Jean Pierre Armand; and Virginio Sala. "Tavola rotonda: Opinioni a confronto sul progetto 'Suono e Immagine' del Iasm." [Round Table: Opinions in Comparison with the Project 'Sound and Images' of IASM] In *Musica e tecnologia: industria e cultura per lo sviluppo del mezzogiorno: VI Colloquio di Informatica Musicale, Napoli 16–19 ottobre 1985*, ed. Carlo Acreman; Immacolata Ortosecco; and Fausto Razzi. Milan: Edizioni Unicopli, 1987: 62–108.

8563.   Di Perna, Alan. "Carrie Hamilton: Don't Call Her an Actress." *Music, Computers & Software* 3 (Dec. 1988): 30.

Profile/interview with the singer/actress, who discusses her use of synthesis equipment.

8564.   ———. "John Dentino and the Fabulous Fibs." *Music, Computers & Software* 3 (Aug. 1988): 32–33.

Profile/interview with the rock keyboardist, who discusses his use of synthesis equipment.

8565.   ———. "Orchestral Manoeuvres in the Dark." *Keyboards, Computers & Software* 1 (Feb. 1986): 22–25, 58.

Members of the band OMD describe their use of computer technology to produce music.

8566.   ———. "Primitive Modern: Technology Unlocks New Means of Making Old Rhythms." *Musician* n125 (Mar. 1989): 32–34, 41, 80, 97.

A look at artificial intelligence applied to rhythm.

8567.   ———. "Wally Badarou: An International Musician Creates a Very Global Music." *Keyboards, Computers & Software* 1 (June 1986): 35–36.

Mr. Badarou describes his studios in Nassau and Paris.

8568.   ———. "Zappa: Megabytes at Barking Pumpkin." *Keyboards, Computers & Software* 1 (Apr. 1986): 22–25.

Describes Frank Zappa's use of computer technology with a studio based on the Synclavier.

8569.   Diliberto, John. "Conversations with John Cage." *Electronic Musician* 4 (Mar. 1988): 78–89.

Interview.

8570.   ———. "Seduced by Samplers." *Music Technology* 2 (Mar. 1988): 54–57.

Interview with Steve Reich.

8571.   Doati, Roberto; Gianantonio Patella; and Daniele Torresan. "La materia è sorda." [Matter Is Death] In *Musica e tecnologia: industria e* *cultura per lo sviluppo del mezzogiorno: VI Colloquio di Informatica Musicale, Napoli 16–19 ottobre 1985,* ed. Carlo Acreman; Immacolata Ortosecco; and Fausto Razzi. Milan: Edizioni Unicopli, 1987: 463–73.

8572. Dodge, Charles, and Thomas A. Jerse. *Computer Music, Synthesis, Composition, and Performance.* New York, N.Y.: Schirmer, 1985. 383 p.

Review by Mark Zuckerman in *Perspectives of New Music* 24 (Spring/ Summer 1986): 423–26.

Review by Alan West in *Computer Music Journal* 10,4 (Winter 1986): 92.

Review by William R. Mathews in *College Music Symposium* 27 (1987): 196–97.

Review by Lars-Gunnar Bodin in *Svensk Tidskrift för Musikforskning* 69 (Jan. 1987): 168–71.

Review by Susan T. Sommer in *Notes* 43 (Sept. 1986): 53.

Review by Stan Tempelaars in *Interface* 17 (1988): 63–64.

Review by Alistair MacDonald in *Brio* 25 (Spring/Summer 1988): 37–38.

8573. Donato, Peter. "A Basic Digital Primer for Analog Composers." *Canadian Composer* n197 (Jan. 1985): 10–15.

French version: Comment vaincre la peur des machines à composer.

8574. ———. "Looking for New Sounds." *Canadian Composer* n200 (Apr. 1985): 4–7, 42–43.

French version: La Barrière du son.

Impressions of three composers (Lauri Conger, John Lang, and Nil Parent) on new electronic and computer sounds.

8575. Donovan, Joe. "The Arts Take High-Tech—Seriously." *Music, Computers & Software* 3 (Nov. 1988): 33–38.

Profile/interview with members of the vocal quartet, who discuss their use of signal processors and sampling synthesizers.

8576. ———. "Tangerine Dream." *Music, Computers & Software* 3 (Nov. 1988): 26–32.

Profile/interview with members of the German rock band, who discuss their performing synthesis equipment.

8577. Doty, David B. "Guest Editorial: Intonation: When Technology Becomes a Barrier to Expression." *Keyboard* 12 (Nov. 1986): 14, 129.

8578. Drake, Adèle, and Jim Grant. "Music Gives Disability a Byte." *New Scientist* 113 (Jan. 22, 1987): 37–39.

Describes how the Charlton Park School in London is using MIDI technology to enable disabled children to create music.

8579. Duisberg, Robert. "On the Role of Affect in Artificial Intelligence and Music." *Perspectives of New Music* 23 (Fall–Winter 1984): 6–35.

8580. Dupler, Steven. "Digital Sampling: Is It Theft?" *Billboard* 98 (Aug. 2, 1986): 1, 74.

8581. ———. "'Music' Maker Scores at Age 17." *Billboard* 96 (June 9, 1984): 36.

Profile of Will Harvey, creator of the composition program Music Construction Set.

8582. Einhorn, Richard. "Techno: Sync or Swim: Scoring in the Studio." *Ear* 14 (July–Aug. 1989): 16–17.

The author describes his experiences using the computer for film music.

8583. Faber, Randall. "Computer Applications in Music: A Quick Lesson in Basic Technology and Terminology." *American Music Teacher* 37 (June/July 1988): 22–23, 54.

8584. Fiore, Jim. "Electronic Insights: Protecting Your Gear from AC Power Monsters." *Modern Drummer* 12 (Feb. 1988): 58–59.

8585. Firnkees, Niko. "Münchens Computer-Diva zeigt Staralüren: Die Hydraulik der Bayerischen Staatsoper hat Probleme mit dem MAN–Rechner." *Neue Musikzeitung* 35 (Juni-Juli 1986): 10.

8586. Fisher, Chuck. "MIDI Applications." *Music, Computers & Software* 3 (Dec. 1988): 24–25.

Discusses the use of sequencers as metronomes in practicing instrumental technique.

8587. Fisher, Lawrence M. "Tandy Is Preparing to Sell Erasable CD." *New York Times* 137 (Apr. 22, 1988): D4.

8588. Flohil, Richard. "The Taming of the Beasts on Our Desks." *Canadian Composer* n227 (Jan.–Feb. 1988): 2–3.
French version: L'équipe de rédaction se modernise enfin.

The switch to desktop publishing of *Canadian Composer*.

8589. Ford, Ric. "Court Awards Refund to User: Bugs Prompt User to Sue Unicorn." *MacWeek* 2 (Oct. 18, 1988): 64.

David Hollender won a small claims court case against Mark of the Unicorn because of the excessive number of bugs in the Professional Composer music software.

8590. Fraser, Jill. "KCS Scoring." *Keyboards, Computers & Software* 1 (June 1986): 70–73.

How the soundtrack for a Porsche commercial was put together using the Oberheim DSX sequencer.

8591. ———. "KCS Scoring." *Keyboards, Computers & Software* 1 (Aug. 1986): 72–73.

Special problems to consider when creating the scores for musicals.

8592.   ——. "MCS Scoring." *Music, Computers & Software* 2 (Aug. 1987): 86–87.

A discussion of movie theater sound reinforcement equipment and the VHS hi-fi standard.

8593.   Freedberger, Peter. "MIDI Mall." *Village Voice* 34 (Sept. 26, 1989): E15.

Describes the Yamaha Communication Center in New York City.

8594.   Friberg, Anders; Lars Frydén; Lars-Gunnar Bodin; and Johan Sundberg. "Rules for Computer Controlled Performance of Contemporary Keyboard Music." *Speech Transmission Laboratory Quarterly Progress and Status Report* 4 (1987): 79–85.

8595.   Friend, Marty. "KCS Sampling." *Keyboards, Computers & Software* 2 (Feb. 1987): 84–85.

Options to consider when establishing a sampling studio.

8596.   Fryer, Terry. "Digital Sampling: The Legality of Sampling from Unauthorized Sources." *Keyboard* 12 (Dec. 1986): 120.

8597.   Fuchs, Mathias. "Zufall un Regelmässigkeit in elektronischer Musik." M.A. diss., Technische Universität Wien, 1981. 52 p.

Includes a history of computer music.

8598.   Fujinaga, Ichiro. "Optical Music Recognition Using Projections." Masters thesis, McGill University, 1988.

8599.   ——; Bo H. Alphonce; and Bruce W. Pennycook. "Issues in the Design of an Optical Music Recognition System." In *Proceedings, 1989 International Computer Music Conference, November 2–5, the Ohio State University, Columbus, Ohio.* San Francisco, Calif.: Computer Music Association, 1989: 113–16.

8600.   ——; Bo H. Alphonce; Bruce W. Pennycook; and Natalie Boisvert. "Optical Recognition of Musical Notation by Computer." *Computers in Music Research* 1 (Fall 1989): 161–64.

8601.   Gesuè, Francesco. "Apertura dei lavori." [Opening of the Works] In *Musica e tecnologia: industria e cultura per lo sviluppo del mezzogiorno: VI Colloquio di Informatica Musicale, Napoli 16–19 ottobre 1985*, ed. Carlo Acreman; Immacolata Ortosecco; and Fausto Razzi. Milan: Edizioni Unicopli, 1987: 37–39.

8602.   Gilchrist, Trevor. "Keep in Time with the Times." *Music Technology* 1 (Feb. 1987): 42–43.

An introduction to technology for reluctant drummers.

8603.   Goebèl, Johannes. "Man-Machine Interaction." In *Proceedings of the 14th International Computer Music Conference, Cologne, September 20–25, 1988*, ed. Christoph Lischka and Johannes Fritsch. Cologne:

Feedback-Studio-Verlag; San Francisco, Calif.: Dist. by Computer Music Association, 1988: 41–48. (Feedback Papers; 33)
Parallel texts in English and German.

8604.   Goethals, Luc. "Computers voor Musici?" [Computers for Musicians?] *Adem* 24 (Apr.–Juni 1988): 75–79.
In Dutch; summaries in English and French.

Explores five applications of the computer in music: composition, music printing, music education, research, and administration.

8605.   Goldstein, Dan. "Technology's Champion." *Music Technology* 1,1 (1986): 18–24.

Interview with Peter Gabriel.

8606.   Goodyer, Tim. "Dawn of a New Age." *Music Technology* 1 (Jan. 1987): 28–34.

Interview with members of OMD that includes a discussion of their use of music technology to create their music.

8607.   Greenwald, Ted. "An Apple for the Teacher: Computer Music in Universities." *Keyboard* 13 (Jan. 1987): 40, 86–87.

Computer music programs at Cal Arts, MIT, CCRMA, Brooklyn College, and Mills College.

8608.   Grossi, Pietro. *Musica senza musicisti: scritti 1966/1986* [Music without Musicians: Writings 1966/1986], ed. Lelio Camilleri; Francesco Carreras; and Albert Mayr. Firenze: CNUCE/C.N.R., 1987. 110 p.

A collection of previously published articles.

8609.   Grula, Richard J. "David Sylvian: Keeping the Pop World at a Distance." *Music, Computers & Software* 3 (Aug. 1988): 30–32.

Profile/interview with the rock composer/guitarist.

8610.   Guarino, Eugenio. "Elettronica musicale e musica elettronica." [Musical Electronics and Electronic Music] In *I profili del suono: scritti sulla musica electroacustica e la computer music,* ed. Serena Tamburini and Mauro Bagella. Salerno: Musica Verticale-Galzerano, 1987: 133–36.

8611.   Hall, Ian Kendrick. "Music and the Personal Computer." *Guitar Review* n57 (Spring 1984): 10–13.

Interview with Hubert S. Howe.

8612.   Hammond, Ray. "Peter Gabriel—Behind the Mask." *Keyboards, Computers & Software* 1 (Aug. 1986): 22–26, 55.

Interview.

8613.   Harris, Craig R. "A Composer's Computer Music System: Practical Considerations." *Computer Music Journal* 11,3 (Fall 1987): 36–43.

Describes workstations.

8614. ——. "The Missing Link." In *Proceedings of the 1987 International Computer Music Conference: University of Illinois at Urbana-Champaign, Urbana, Illinois, USA, August 23–26, 1987,* comp. James Beauchamp. San Francisco, Calif.: Computer Music Association, 1987: 73–79.

8615. ——, and Stephen T. Pope. *Computer Music Association Source Book: Activities and Resources in Computer Music.* San Francisco, Calif.: Computer Music Association, 1987: 245 p.
Review by Ann Basart in *Cum Notis Variorum* n126 (Oct. 1988): 17–18; and *Fontes Artis Musicae* 36 (1989): 65.

8616. Harrison, Jonty. "Denis Smalley, EMAS and (Electroacoustic) Music." *Musical Times* 130 (Sept. 1989): 528–31.

8617. Harrison, Tom. "MIDI Hasn't Killed the Guitar: Ten Fingers, Six Strings, One Heart." *Canadian Musician* 8 (June 1986): 54–55.

8618. Hassig, Richard. "The Technical Forum: Computer for the Sightless Technician." *Piano Technicians Journal* 28 (May 1985): 17.

8619. Haus, Goffredo. *Elementi di informatica musicale.* Milan: Gruppo Editoriale Jackson, 1984. 226 p.
Review by Marco Stroppa in *Computer Music Journal* 10,1 (Spring 1986): 100–102.

8620. ——. "Ruolo ed obiettivi dell'Associazione di Informatica Musicale Italiana." [The Role and Objectives of the Associazione di Informatica Musicale Italiana] In *Musica e tecnologia: industria e cultura per lo sviluppo del mezzogiorno: VI Colloquio di Informatica Musicale, Napoli 16–19 ottobre 1985,* ed. Carlo Acreman; Immacolata Ortosecco; and Fausto Razzi. Milan: Edizioni Unicopli, 1987: 42–45.

8621. Hawkes, Greg. "Scoring." *Music, Computers & Software* 3 (Oct. 1988): 83–84.
A discussion of techniques used in scoring the film "Anna."

8622. Henderson, Ian. *Computer Assistance for the Setting of Historic Tunings and Temperaments.* Brockport, N.Y.: I. Henderson, 1986. 17 p.

8623. Herrington, Peggy. "Suzanne Ciani: Making Music that Sells." *Amiga World* 3 (July–Aug. 1987): 53.

8624. Hill, Ralph David. "Just Intonation on a Home Built Digital Synthesizer-Computer." *Interval* 4 (Fall 1983): 15–22.

8625. "Historic Recordings on Computer." *Music Trades* 135 (Jan. 1987): 114.
The Q-R-S piano roll library has been transferred to floppy disks for performance on musical instruments via MIDI.

8626. Hofstetter, Fred T. *Computer Literacy for Musicians.* Englewood Cliffs, N.J.: Prentice Hall, 1988. 351 p.

Review by Charles G. Boody in *Computers in Music Research* 1 (Fall 1989): 123–31.

8627. Holland, Bill, and Steven Dupler. "Experts Doubt Legality of Sampling." *Billboard* 98 (Aug. 9, 1986): 4, 84.

8628. Holland, Penny. *Looking at Computer Sounds and Music.* New York, N.Y.: F. Watts, 1986. 32 p.

An introduction to how computers make music and synthesize sounds and speech, with related projects.

8629. Höller, York. "Zur gegenwärtigen Situation der elektronischen Musik." *Österreichische Musikzeitschrift* 39 (1984): 452–58.

8630. Holub, Allen. "The Ultimate Metronome: Writing Interrupt Service Routines in C." *Dr. Dobb's Journal of Software Tools* 12 (Sept. 1987): 106–21, 82–96.

8631. Hong, A. "Mach 5: A Development Environment for Timbral Hyper-instrument Controllers." B.S. thesis, Massachusetts Institute of Technology, 1989.

8632. Hood, Phil. "1999: Musical Trends of the Coming Decade." *Frets* 11 (Mar. 1989): 25–31.

A forecast of musical trends that includes heavy reliance on the computer.

8633. Hord, Christopher. "Zappa Embraces 'Music Information Systems.'" *Information Week* n128 (Aug. 3, 1987): 19.

Frank Zappa gives his viewpoint on the technological developments in music.

8634. Hospers, Al. "Guest Editorial: Copy-Protection and Theft." *Keyboard* 13 (Aug. 1987): 10, 146–47.

8635. Hunt, Newton J. "The Computerized Technician: Things I Do with a Computer." *Piano Technicians Journal* 29 (May 1986): 21–22, 24.

8636. Hurtig, Brent, ed. *Synthesizers and Computers.* Rev. ed. Milwaukee, Wis.: H. Leonard Books, 1987. 128 p. (Keyboard Magazine Basic Library)

8637. Jenkins, Mark. "Control Zone: Electric Dreams." *Melody Maker* 59 (Oct. 13, 1984): 34.

Studio and stage use of computers by the group Tangerine Dream.

8638. ———. "Control Zone: Keyboards: Foxxing Clever." *Melody Maker* 60 (Oct. 26, 1985): 41.

Interview with John Foxx.

8639. ——. "Control Zone: Review of 1984." *Melody Maker* 60 (Jan. 5, 1985): 35–37.

The author reviews the keyboards, use of the silicon chip, and the computer in the year 1984.

8640. ——. "Michael Oldfield's Vision: A One Man Orchestra." *Music, Computers & Software* 3 (June 1988): 34–39.

Profile/interview with the rock composer/synthesist.

8641. Jimenez, Maria. "MCS Telecom." *Music, Computers & Software* 3 (Apr. 1988): 81–82.

A discussion of telecommunications with European contacts and gives sample question and answer excerpts from the MCS MIDI Forum.

8642. Jones, Peter, and Steven Dupler. "U.K. Producer Asks Action on Digital Sampling Issue." *Billboard* 99 (Oct. 24, 1987): 3, 107.

8643. Joppig, Gunther. "Die Gralsglocken läuten elektroakustische: Wie steht es um die Zukunft der klassischen Musikinstrumente?" *Neue Musikzeitung* 38 (Feb.–Mär. 1989): 49.

8644. Kahn, Douglas. "It's Intelligent: Minsky and Artificial Intelligence." *Ear* 13 (Sept. 1988): 10–11.

Interview with Marvin Minsky.

8645. Katayose, Haruhiro, and Seiji Inokuchi. "The Kansei Music System." *Computer Music Journal* 13,4 (Winter 1989): 72–77.

8646. ——; H. Kato; M. Imai; and Seiji Inokuchi. "An Approach to an Artificial Music Expert." In *Proceedings, 1989 International Computer Music Conference, November 2–5, the Ohio State University, Columbus, Ohio.* San Francisco, Calif.: Computer Music Association, 1989: 139–46.

Discusses the creation of a "computer musician" that can listen, read, play, and print music.

8647. ——; K. Takami; T. Fukuoka; and Seiji Inokuchi. "Music Interpreter in the Kansei Music System." In *Proceedings, 1989 International Computer Music Conference, November 2–5, the Ohio State University, Columbus, Ohio.* San Francisco, Calif.: Computer Music Association, 1989: 147–50.

8648. Kauffman, Jim. "The Interactive Compact Disk: The Age of Elastic Media." *Music, Computers & Software* 3 (Aug. 1988): 44–47.

A discussion of CD-ROM and CD-I.

8649. Keane, David. "The Birth of Electronic Music in Canada." *Studies in Music from the University of Western Ontario* 9 (1984): 55–78.

A history of the development of electroacoustic music in Canada.

8650.   Kerner, Rochele. "Those Legal Sampling Blues." *Music, Computers & Software* 3 (Dec. 1988): 45–47.

A discussion of the issues of sampling as it applies to copyright.

8651.   Kopyc, D. "Fantastic Electronic Sounds from Runs, Skips, and Twirls." B.S. thesis, Massachusetts Institute of Technology, 1989.

8652.   Kovach, Mark A. "KCS Applications." *Keyboards, Computers & Software* 1 (Oct. 1986): 10, 63–64.

An explanation of the SMPTE time code.

8653.   ——. "KCS Applications." *Keyboards, Computers & Software* 1 (Dec. 1986): 8, 63–64.

Methods for solving multitrack tape recorder synching problems.

8654.   Krout, Robert E. "Evaluating Software for Music Therapy Applications." *Journal of Music Therapy* 24 (Winter 1987): 213–23.

8655.   ——, and Mark Mason. "Using Computer and Electronic Music Resources in Clinical Music Therapy with Behaviorally Disordered Students, 12 to 18 Years Old." *Music Therapy Perspectives* 5 (1988): 114–18.

8656.   Kusek, David. "Guest Editorial: Copying Software Is a Crime and a Shame." *Music Trades* 137 (Jan. 1989): 24.

8657.   Kvifta, Tellef. *Instruments and the Electronic Age: Toward a Terminology for a Unified Description of Playing Technique.* [Oslo, Norway?]: Solum Forlag; Atlantic Highlands, N.J.: Distributed throughout North America by Humanities Press International, 1989. 198 p.

Includes two chapters that cover digital synthesizers and computer music.

8658.   Lander, David. "Raymond Kurzweil: Revolutionary Tradition." *Audio* 73 (Jan. 1989): 62–69.

8659.   Lansky, Paul. "The Sound of Software: Computer-made Music." *Perspectives in Computing* 5 (Fall–Winter 1985): 34–42. Includes soundsheet.

An historical overview of computer music, methods of synthesis, and future direction.

8660.   LaRose, Paul. "High-Tech Guitar: What's in It for You." *Guitar Player* 22 (Feb. 1988): 66–67.

Inaugural appearance of a new series of articles that focuses on explaining rapidly changing technology.

8661.   Larson, Gary. "How East Met West." *Music Technology* 1 (Oct. 1986): 28–29.

How computer music has moved from the provenance of the elite to being available to almost anyone.

8662.   Laske, Otto E. "Computermusik und musikalische Informatik." *Neuland Ansätze zur Musik der Gegenwart* 2 (1981–82): 209–13.

8663.   Latimer, Joey. "Making Money, Making Music." *Family & Home–Office Computing* 6 (July 1988): 46–48.

Kayte and Jack Goga, Mark Freedman, and Brian Vigo describe their studios.

8664.   Lehrman, Paul D. "Musical Protection." *MacUser* 4 (Jan. 1988): 44.

The pros and cons of copy protection for music programs.

8665.   ———. "Profile: Michael Waisvisz Hands It to Himself." *Keyboard* 12 (Aug. 1986): 21–22.

A discussion of the development of Michael Waisvisz's MIDI-controller called the Hands.

8666.   Leibs, Albert S. "Music & the Microchip: Instruments Get User Friendly: Today's Technology Could Bring out the Mozart in You." *Information Week* n128 (Aug. 3, 1987): 18–21.

Describes the current uses of technology in music.

8667.   Leonard, Steve. "Computers for Keyboardists: Back It Up or Pack It Up." *Keyboard* 12 (Jan. 1986): 117.

Advice to make back-up copies of diskettes.

8668.   Levitt, David. "Pushing the Sound Envelope." *Dr. Dobb's Journal of Software Tools* 12 (May 1987): 16–19.

A short history of computers in music and developments in MIDI, sampling, transient-oriented synthesis methods, and composing software.

8669.   Lewis, Bill. "Chris Currell: Few Good Boys Do Bad." *Music, Computers & Software* 3 (Feb. 1988): 36, 72.

Profile/interview with the rock keyboardist, who discusses his use of the Synthaxe and other synthesizer equipment.

8670.   ———. "Chuck Fisher: Computerization Takes a Musician beyond Physical Limitations." *Keyboards, Computers & Software* 1 (Apr. 1986): 18–19.

A disabled musician uses computer technology to continue making music.

8671.   ———. "Golden MIDI Software: MIDI Data Files of Top 40 Songs." *Music, Computers & Software* 3 (Apr. 1988): 69.

Review.

8672.   ———. "MCS Computing." *Music, Computers & Software* 3 (Feb. 1988): 89–90.

A tutorial on computer terms such as binary and byte.

8673.   ——. "Pete Bardens: . . . and the Music Goes 'Round and 'Round."
          Music, Computers & Software 3 (Feb. 1988): 32.
          Profile/interview with the New Age keyboardist, who discusses his
          use of synthesis equipment.

8674.   Lipson, Stefan B. "Getting On Line." *Music Technology* 2 (Mar.
          1988): 74–75.
          A discussion of on-line computer services.

8675.   Lischka, Christoph, and Hans-Werner Güsgen. "MvSC—A Con-
          straint-based Approach to Musical Knowledge Representation." In
          *Proceedings of the International Computer Music Conference 1986,
          Royal Conservatory, The Hague, Netherlands, October 20–24, 1986,*
          ed. Paul Berg. San Francisco, Calif.: Computer Music Association,
          1986: 227–29.

8676.   Logemann, George W. "Experiments with a Gestural Controller." In
          *Proceedings, 1989 International Computer Music Conference, Novem-
          ber 2–5, the Ohio State University, Columbus, Ohio.* San Francisco,
          Calif.: Computer Music Association, 1989: 184–85.

8677.   Lohner, Henning. "Von der Technik zur Aesthetik: ein Gespräch mit
          dem Elektroakustiker Robert Moog." *NZ, Neue Zeitschrift für Musik*
          147 (Juli–Aug. 1986): 49–53.
          Interview with Bob Moog.

8678.   Looney, Kevin. "Guest Editorial: Artificial Intelligence & Other
          Buzzwords." *Keyboard* 14 (Feb. 1988): 12, 168.

8679.   "Lutheran Home Installs Computerized Program on Carillon." *Jour-
          nal of Church Music* 26 (Sept. 1984): 46.

8680.   Machlitt, Manfred, and Georg Katzer. "Technik kontra Geige? Ein
          Gespräch zur Situation der elektroakustischen Musik." *Musik und
          Gesellschaft* 39 (Apr. 1989): 172–79.
          A conversation between Manfred Machlitt and Georg Katzer.

8681.   Mahoney, J. V. "Automatic Analysis of Musical Score Images." B.S.
          thesis, Dept. of Computer Science and Engineering, Massachusetts
          Institute of Technology, 1982.

8682.   Mailliard, Bénédict. "*Germinal*: Une Experience." *Revue musicale*
          n394–97 (1986): 238–41.
          A project formed in Mar.–Apr. 1984 to provide for production of
          short musical works.

8683.   Maloney, Kevin. "Saxophonist, Composer, and Orchestra Create
          Landmark in Musical History: John Sampen Plays the Yamaha WX7 in
          London." *Saxophone Journal* 13 (Spring 1988): 8–10.

8684. Mansfield, Richard. "Music in the Computer Age." *Compute!* 7 (Jan. 1985): 30–39.

A general article on the influence of the computer on music.

8685. Marten, Neville. "Steppin' Out." *Music Technology* 1 (May 1987): 48–53.

Interview with Steven Randall, inventor of the Stepp DG-1 guitar controller.

8686. Martin, Gottfried. "Zur Situation der Computermusik." *Österreichische Musikzeitschrift* 39 (1984): 433–34.

On the state of computer music in Europe.

8687. Mathews, Max V., and John R. Pierce. "The Computer as a Musical Instrument." *Scientific American* 256 (Feb. 1987): 126–33.
Also issued as: Technical Report STAN-M-37. Stanford, Calif.: Center for Research in Music and Acoustics, Music Department, Stanford University, 1987.

8688. ———, and John R. Pierce, eds. *Current Directions in Computer Music.* Cambridge, Mass.: MIT Press, 1989. 432 p. (System Development Foundation Benchmark Series)
Contains items: 4726, 4735, 4737, 4758, 4759, 4799, 4824, 6727, 6974, 8125, 8140, 8155, 8247, 8249, 8277, 8284, 8306, 8325, 8348, 8354.

8689. ———; John R. Pierce; Alyson Reeves; and Linda A. Roberts. "Theoretical and Experimental Explorations of the Bohlen-Pierce Scale." *Journal of the Acoustical Society of America* 84 (Oct. 1988): 1214–22.

A description of a musical scale based on the 3:5:7:9 tetrachord.

8690. Matsushima, Toshiaki; T. Harada; I. Sonomoto; K. Kanamori; A. Uesugi; Y. Nimura; Shuji Hashimoto; and Sadamu Ohteru. "Automated Recognition System for Musical Score—the Vision System of WABOT-2." *Bulletin of Science and Engineering Research Laboratory, Waseda University* 112 (Sept. 1985): 25–52.

8691. ———; Sadamu Ohteru; and Shuji Hashimoto. "An Integrated Music Information Processing System: PSB-er." In *Proceedings, 1989 International Computer Music Conference, November 2–5, the Ohio State University, Columbus, Ohio.* San Francisco, Calif.: Computer Music Association, 1989: 191–98.

A report on the development of a system that can input and output via musical performance, printed score, and braille music.

8692. ———; I. Sonomoto; T. Harada; K. Kanamori; and Sadamu Ohteru. "Automated High Speed Recognition of Printed Music (Wabot-2 Vision System)." In *Proceedings of '85 International Conference on*

Advanced Robotics: 9, 10 September 1985. Tokyo: Japan Industrial Robot Association, 1985: 477–82.

A report on the vision system of an intelligent robot that can play an electric piano while reading printed music.

8693.   McGuiness, Timothy. "Box of Magic." *Electronic Musician* 3 (Dec. 1987): 42–46.

Describes the author's experiences in mainland China when he demonstrated a Kurzweil 250 sampling keyboard, Macintosh, and MIDI.

8694.   McNeil, Michael. "An Analysis Tool for Contemporary and Historical Tunings." *Diapaison* 78 (Feb. 1987): 14–16.

A listing of a BASIC program to analyze and create tunings.

8695.   Means, Ben, and Jean Means. "Clark Spangler." *Music, Computers & Software* 3 (June 1988): 32–33.
Profile/interview with the synthesist.

8696.   ——, and Jean Means. "Craig Chaquico: Lost in Intermodal Space with Starship." *Music, Computers & Software* 2 (Dec. 1987): 30–33.

Profile/interview with the rock guitarist, who discusses his use of synthesis equipment and guitar effect devices.

8697.   ——, and Jean Means. "Oingo Boingo: Animatin' Rhythms." *Music, Computers & Software* 2 (June 1987): 34–37.

Profile/interview with Danny Elfman and Steve Bartek, who discuss their synthesis equipment and film scoring techniques.

8698.   "Medical Tests Put to Music." *Wall Street Journal* 209 (June 17, 1987): 29.

A Moog synthesizer and specialized computer programs are used to decipher graphs created by an automated urine analyzer and play music based on the results.

8699.   Mendelssohn, John. "Eleganza: Music the New Old Fashioned Way." *Creem* 19 (Sept. 1987): 26.

An exposition on music performed by pre-programmed computers vs. human performers.

8700.   Mentiūkov, A., and A. Ustinov. "Muzyka i NTR: Nekotorye Problemy." [Music and the Scientific-Technical Revolution: Some Problems] *Sovetskaiā Muzyka* n3 (Mar. 1986): 68–71.
In Russian.

8701.   Merkin, Robby. "MCS Scoring." *Music, Computers & Software* 2 (Dec. 1987): 87–89.

Discusses the scoring of the film *Little Shop of Horrors.*

8702.   ——. "MCS Scoring." *Music, Computers & Software* 3 (Feb. 1988): 87–88.

A discussion of the techniques used in scoring the film *The Little Mermaid.*

8703.   ——. "Scoring." *Music, Computers & Software* 3 (June 1988): 79–80.

A discussion of techniques used in scoring the television pilot "Act II."

8704.   Meyer, Chris. "I Want Your Samples." *Music Technology* 1 (Oct. 1986): 58–60.

A look at what musicians will do with samplers after the factory disks have been exhausted, and the implications of sampling on the music business.

8705.   Michaels, Stephan, and Melinda Newman. "Turtles' Flo & Eddie Sue De La Soul over Sampling." *Billboard* 101 (Aug. 26, 1989): 10–41.

A report on sampling litigation.

8706.   Midge, Nikita. "Guest Editorial: Stop Progress Now!" *Keyboard* 14 (July 1988): 12.

A demand for quality engineering rather than new products.

8707.   Milano, Dominic. "Wendy Carlos: Defying Conventions, Discovering New Worlds." *Keyboard* 12 (Nov. 1986): 50–86.
Includes soundsheet.

8708.   ——; Jim Aikin; and Ted Greenwald. "The Pros Tell How Sequencers Changed Their Lives (or Didn't)." *Keyboard* 13 (June 1987): 50–62.

Interviews with Jan Hammer, Mark Isham, Jeff Lorber, Eddie Jobson, Wendy Carlos, and Morton Subotnick.

8709.   Miller, Ed. "Backstage at B'way's *Phantom,* a Maze of Hi-Tech Showmanship." *Variety* 335 (May 17, 1989): 76.

How the computer is used in the production of Andrew Lloyd Webber's *Phantom of the Opera.*

8710.   Mills, David. "Electromag: Acoustic Blues: A Fundamentalist in Electronic Babylon." *Village Voice* 33 (Nov. 22, 1988): 15–16, 19.

The author muses on the use of his computer for making music.

8711.   Mockensturm, Dan, and Jim Ferguson. "DeMeola's Programmer." *Guitar Player* 20 (June 1986): 125, 178.

Interview with Dan Mockensturm, Al DiMeola's programmer.

8712.   Mont-Reynaud, Bernard. "Problem-solving Strategies in a Music Transcription System." In *IJCAI 85: Proceedings of the Ninth International Joint Conference on Artificial Intelligence, August 18–23, 1985.* Los Altos, Calif.: M. Kaufmann, 1985: 916–18.

8713.   "Moog! A Candid Conversation with Bob Moog, the Man Who Started the Synthesizer Revolution." *Music Trades* 136 (Apr. 1988): 76–87.

8714.   Moog, Bob. "Ask Mr. Moog: Ground Loops: What Goes Around, Hums Around." *Keyboard* 15 (June 1989): 110–11, 146.
         More on hum.

8715.   ———. "Ask Mr. Moog: Hum, Hum, and More Hum." *Keyboard* 15 (May 1989): 110–11.
         Sources of and solutions to hum.

8716.   ———. "So You Want to Design Electronic Musical Instruments." *Keyboard* 14 (Feb. 1988): 128, 136.
         Advice on how to prepare for a career in electronic musical instrument design.

8717.   Moorhead, Jan Paul. "Personal Sound—Pulse Music." *DB, the Sound Engineering Magazine* 21 (Mar./Apr. 1987): 22–24.
         The author describes his MIDI studio.

8718.   Morita, H.; Sadamu Ohteru; and Shuji Hashimoto. "Computer Music System which Follows a Human Conductor." In *Proceedings, 1989 International Computer Music Conference, November 2–5, the Ohio State University, Columbus, Ohio.* San Francisco, Calif.: Computer Music Association, 1989: 207–10.

8719.   Müllmann, Bernd. "Kreativität aus dem Chip? Kasseler Musiktage 1987 zur documenta." *Orchester* 35 (Dec. 1987): 1301–3.

8720.   Muro, Don. "Organists Plug in: Praise the Lord & Pass the MIDI Cables." *Keyboard* 13 (Dec. 1987): 21.
         On the use of synthesizers by church musicians.

8721.   Murphy, Elliott. "Jerry Harrison and the Talking Heads." *Keyboards, Computers & Software* 1 (Oct. 1986): 22–29, 78.
         Jerry Harrison describes his use of music technology to create his band's sounds.

8722.   Naglar, Joseph C., and Mathew H. Lee. "Use of Microcomputers in the Music Therapy Process of a Postviral Encephalitic Musician." *Medical Problems of Performing Artists* 2 (June 1987): 72–74.

8723.   Nathan, Bobby. "Computerized Studios: It's the Way of the World." *Billboard* 99 (Oct. 24, 1987): 79.
         Various uses of the computer in recording studios.

8724.   Neiman, Marcus L. "If You Can't Find It—Write It." *Instrumentalist* 42 (Sept. 1987): 80–82.

8725. Nencini, Giovanni; Pietro Grossi; Leonello Tarabella; and Graziano Bertini. "Studi sulla telematica musicale." [Studies on Musical Telematics] In *Musica e tecnologia: industria e cultura per lo sviluppo del mezzogiorno: VI Colloquio di Informatica Musicale, Napoli 16–19 ottobre 1985,* ed. Carlo Acreman; Immacolata Ortosecco; and Fausto Razzi. Milan: Edizioni Unicopli, 1987: 295–99.

8726. Netsel, Tom. "Computers: The Powerful New Music Machines." *Compute!* 10 (Mar. 1988): 6–11.

A general article that covers MIDI and popular music, the workstations at Dartmouth College, and Lorne Strider, a programmer who programs classical works to play through a Commodore's three voices.

8727. Netzle, Klaus. "Der Musiker und der Musik-Computer." *Orchester* 35 (July–Aug. 1987): 757–59.

8728. Neubert, David. "In Search of the Missing Link: Music, Technology & the Double Bass." *International Society of Bassists* 15 (Fall 1988): 44–46.

A suggestion to embrace the current technology and use it creatively.

8729. "A New Kind of Resident Artist." *Ovation* 7 (May 1986): 8.

A robot performs music at the Tsukuba Expo '85 in Japan.

8730. Newman, Melinda. "NMS Panel: Legally, There Are No 'Free' Samples." *Billboard* 101 (Aug. 12, 1989): 24.

A report on panel discussion on sampling versus plagiarism at the New Music Seminar.

8731. Newquist, Harvey P. "Networking." *Music Technology* 2 (Mar. 1988): 78–80.

An overview of LANs.

8732. ———. "Real Music through Artificial Intelligence." *Music Technology* 2 (Feb. 1988): 60–62.

A report on the session "AI in Music" at an artificial intelligence conference in Atlantic City, N.J., 30 October 1987.

8733. O'Brien, Walter. "KCS Telecom." *Keyboards, Computers & Software* 1 (Aug. 1986): 12, 18.

An in-depth look at the PAN Network, a network designed for musicians.

8734. ———. "KCS Telecom." *Keyboards, Computers & Software* 2 (Feb. 1987): 12, 82–83.

A look at the music SIG of CompuServe.

8735.   Ogden, Warren. "Letters: Copy Protection." *Keyboard* 13 (Nov. 1987): 10.

A reply to item **8634,** Al Hospers' "Guest Editorial: Copy-Protection and Theft."

8736.   Oppenheimer, Larry. "Serafine FX: MIDI in the Movies." *DB, the Sound Engineering Magazine* 20 (Mar./Apr. 1986): 43–46.

Frank Serafine describes how he uses MIDI and SMPTE to create movie music.

8737.   Oswald, John. "Guest Editorial: Neither a Borrower nor a Sampler Prosecute." *Keyboard* 14 (Mar. 1988): 12–14.

Reprinted as: "Ethics and the Wonderful New World of Sampling" and "Le pour et le contre de l'échantillonage" in *Canadian Composer* n232 (July–Aug. 1988): 18–23.

8738.   Parisi, Deborah. "A Love of Sound." *Music Technology* 2 (May 1988): 36–39.

Interviews with Reek Havok, Kiki Ebsen, Ken Hirsch, and Larry Williams, professional programmers for music groups.

8739.   Phillips, Chuck. "Digital Sampling: The Battle over Borrowed Beats." *Cash Box* 52 (May 27, 1989): 5, 16.

8740.   Pohlman, Ken C. "Technical Overview of the CD-I Format." In *The Proceedings of the AES 5th International Conference: Music and Digital Technology,* ed. John Strawn. New York, N.Y.: Audio Engineering Society, 1987: 223–32.

8741.   Polansky, Larry. "Interview with David Rosenboom." *Computer Music Journal* 7,4 (Winter 1983): 40–44.

Previously **4414.**

Reprinted in *The Music Machine,* ed. Curtis Roads. Cambridge, Mass.: MIT Press, 1989: 45–49.

8742.   ———. "Paratactical Tuning: An Agenda for the Use of Computers in Experimental Intonation." *Computer Music Journal* 11,1 (Spring 1987): 61–68.

8743.   Politelli, Patrizia. "Disarmonia della sfera." [Disharmony of the Sphere] In *Musica e tecnologia: industria e cultura per lo sviluppo del mezzogiorno: VI Colloquio di Informatica Musicale, Napoli 16–19 ottobre 1985,* ed. Carlo Acreman; Immacolata Ortosecco; and Fausto Razzi. Milan: Edizioni Unicopli, 1987: 449–54.

8744.   Porter, Martin. "16-bit Seduction of Roger Powell." *PC Magazine* 3 (Apr. 3, 1984): 156–60.

A look at Roger Powell's dual career as rock musician and computer hacker.

8745.   ——. "Roger Powell: A Musician Seduced into Computer Programming." *Keyboards, Computers & Software* 1 (Feb. 1986): 26–27.

A biographical sketch of Roger Powell.

8746.   Potter, Tully. "Computer Help." *Strad* 99 (Aug. 1988): 599.

A computer system has been developed to monitor the voting at the City of London Carl Flesch International Violin Competition.

8747.   Powell, Steven. "Using Synthesizers in Choral Performance." *Choral Journal* 29 (May 1989): 21–23.

The author recommends substituting synthesizers in choral performance when appropriate acoustic instruments are unavailable.

8748.   Quayle, Mac. "MCS Telecom." *Music, Computers & Software* 2 (Aug. 1987): 88, 93.

A discussion of the MCS Forum on CompuServe and the PAN network.

8749.   Raczinski, Jean-Michel, and Gerard Marino. "A Real Time Synthesis Unit." In *Proceedings of the 14th International Computer Music Conference, Cologne, September 20–25, 1988,* ed. Christoph Lischka and Johannes Fritsch. Cologne: Feedback-Studio-Verlag; San Francisco, Calif.: Dist. by Computer Music Association, 1988: 90–100. (Feedback Papers; 33)

A discussion of the UPIC workstation developed at CEMAMu.

8750.   Rampazzi, Teresa. "La computer music: in questi giorni." [Computer Music: In These Days] In *I profili del suono: scritti sulla musica electroacustica e la computer music,* ed. Serena Tamburini and Mauro Bagella. Salerno: Musica Verticale-Galzerano, 1987: 41–44.

8751.   Razzi, Fausto; Francesco Guerra; Jean-Claude Risset; Luigi Pestalozza; Curtis Roads; and Johan Sundberg. "Musica e scienza: un rapporto conflittuale?: tavola rotonda." [Music and Science: A Conflicting Report?: Round Table] In *Musica e tecnologia: industria e cultura per lo sviluppo del mezzogiorno: VI Colloquio di Informatica Musicale, Napoli 16–19 ottobre 1985,* ed. Carlo Acreman; Immacolata Ortosecco; and Fausto Razzi. Milan: Edizioni Unicopli, 1987: 497–515.

8752.   Reetze, Jan. *Musikcomputer—Computermusik: Gegenwart und Zukunft eines neuen Mediums.* Stuttgart: J.B. Metzler, 1987. 176 p.

Review by Horst-Peter Hesse in *Neue Zeitschrift für Musik* 150 (Jan. 1989): 53–54.

8753.   Regh, Joseph. "Computer-supported Judging of Instruments and Bows." *Journal of the Violin Society of America* 7,4 (1986): 74–87.

Use of computers in the judging process during the Sixth International VSA Competition in Ottawa in 1984.

8754.   Rich, Robert. "Applications: Just Intonation for MIDI Synthesizers."
        Electronic Musician 2 (Nov. 1986): 42–44.

8755.   ——. "Why Just Intonation?" *Music Technology* 2 (Sept. 1987):
        72–73.

8756.   Riggs, Michael. "Brave New (Digital) World." *High Fidelity* 38 (Apr.
        1988): 6.
        Comments on technological developments at the CES and digital
        audio cable broadcasts of music.

8757.   Rimmer, Steve. "Computers and Music. Part 1." *Canadian Musician* 6
        (Nov./Dec. 1984): 42–46.
        A general article covering how computers make music, microcom-
        puters, and MIDI.

8758.   ——. "Computers and Music. Part 2." *Canadian Musician* 7 (Mar.
        1985): 38–45.
        An examination of specific computers and software.

8759.   Risset, Jean-Claude. "Computer Music Experiments 1964- . . ." *Com-
        puter Music Journal* 9,1 (Spring 1985): 11–18.
        Previously **4440.**
        Reprinted in *The Music Machine,* ed. Curtis Roads. Cambridge,
        Mass.: MIT Press, 1989: 67–74.

8760.   ——. "Musica, calcolatore, ricerca." [Music, Computers, Research]
        In *I profili del suono: scritti sulla musica electroacustica e la computer
        music,* ed. Serena Tamburini and Mauro Bagella. Salerno: Musica
        Verticale-Galzerano, 1987: 11–20.

8761.   ——. "Musik und Computer." *Österreichische Musikzeitschrift* 39
        (1984): 442–46.
        A survey which includes the use of the computer for composition,
        the processes of synthesis, and psychoacoustics.

8762.   Roads, Curtis. "Active Music Representations." In *Proceedings, 1989
        International Computer Music Conference, November 2–5, the Ohio
        State University, Columbus, Ohio.* San Francisco, Calif.: Computer
        Music Association, 1989: 257–59.

8763.   ——. "A Conversation with James A. Moorer." *Computer Music
        Journal* 6,4 (Winter 1982): 10–21.
        Previously **4459.**
        Reprinted in *The Music Machine,* ed. Curtis Roads. Cambridge,
        Mass.: MIT Press, 1989: 13–24.

8764.   ——. "Interview with Dexter Morrill." *Computer Music Journal* 11,3
        (Fall 1987): 11–16.

8765.　——. "Interview with Max Mathews." *Computer Music Journal* 4,4 (Winter 1980): 15–22.
Previously **4463.**
Reprinted in *The Music Machine,* ed. Curtis Roads. Cambridge, Mass.: MIT Press, 1989: 5–12.

8766.　——. "Interview with Morton Subotnick." *Computer Music Journal* 12,1 (Spring 1988): 9–18.
Includes soundsheet.

8767.　——. "Interview with Paul Lansky." *Computer Music Journal* 7,3 (Fall 1983): 16–24.
Previously **4464.**
Reprinted in *The Music Machine,* ed. Curtis Roads. Cambridge, Mass.: MIT Press, 1989: 35–43.

8768.　——, ed. *The Music Machine: Selected Readings from 'Computer Music Journal.'* Cambridge, Mass.: MIT Press, 1989. 725 p.
Contains items: 4623, 4653, 4670, 4674, 4696, 4704, 4719, 4722, 4727, 4734, 4769, 4786, 4791, 4801, 4805, 4807, 4813, 4820, 4840, 4841, 5281, 5431, 6499, 6616, 6683, 6698, 6714, 6835, 6841, 6916, 6934, 7189, 7478, 7479, 7631, 7632, 8055, 8063, 8089, 8103, 8133, 8150, 8194, 8208, 8214, 8253, 8274, 8353, 8356, 8741, 8759, 8763, 8765, 8767.

8769.　——. "The Tsukuba Musical Robot." *Computer Music Journal* 10,2 (Summer 1986): 39–43.
A performing robot, WABOT-2, can read and perform music as well as converse with audience.

8770.　Rodet, Xavier, and Gerhard Eckel. "Dynamic Patches: Implementation and Control in the SUN-Mercury Workstation." In *Proceedings of the 14th International Computer Music Conference, Cologne, September 20–25, 1988,* ed. Christoph Lischka and Johannes Fritsch. Cologne: Feedback-Studio-Verlag; San Francisco, Calif.: Dist. by Computer Music Association, 1988: 82–89. (Feedback Papers; 33)

8771.　Roeder, John, and Keith A. Hamel. "A General-Purpose Object-oriented System for Musical Graphics." In *Proceedings, 1989 International Computer Music Conference, November 2–5, the Ohio State University, Columbus, Ohio.* San Francisco, Calif.: Computer Music Association, 1989: 260–63.

8772.　"Roland's Seminar Explores Latest Music Technology." *Music Trades* 133 (June 1985): 55–56.
Brief review of the Roland Electronic Music Seminar.

8773.　Rolnick, Neil B. "A Performance Literature for Computer Music: Some Problems from Personal Experience." In *Proceedings of the International Computer Music Conference 1986, Royal Conservatory,*

The Hague, Netherlands, October 20–24, 1986, ed. Paul Berg. San Francisco, Calif.: Computer Music Association, 1986: 29–34.

The author relates his experiences of transferring his computer compositions to a new system.

8774. Romero, M. "Objects to Interpret Real-Time Performances in a Hyperinstrument Contest." B.S. thesis, Massachusetts Institute of Technology, 1989.

8775. Rona, Jeff. "Computer Concepts." *Keyboard* 14 (June 1988): 82–92, 165.

8776. ———. "Computers On-Line: It's a Hard Life. Part 1, Survival with Floppies." *Keyboard* 14 (Oct. 1988): 131.

Practical advice regarding disk usage.

8777. ———. "Computers On-Line: It's a Hard Life. Part 2, The Crash of '88." *Keyboard* 14 (Dec. 1988): 125.

Advice and anecdote on backing-up hard disks.

8778. ———. "Computers On-Line: Safe Sectors: Living with Viruses." *Keyboard* 15 (Mar. 1989): 104–6.

8779. ———. "Computers On-Line: Tapping into the Universe." *Keyboard* 15 (Aug. 1989): 108–9.

Using modems to access information through commercial services and Bulletin Board Systems.

8780. ———. "Computers On-Line: Twelve Well-Known Computer Lies Exposed." *Keyboard* 14 (May 1988): 127–28.

8781. Rosenbluth, Jean. "Island Suit Tests Digital Sampling." *Billboard* 99 (Nov. 28, 1987): 3, 93.

8782. Rosenthal, David. "Live Keyboards with Cyndi Lauper." *Electronic Musician* 3 (July 1987): 35–41.

The author describes the setup that he used for Cyndi Lauper's 1986–87 world tour.

8783. Rowe, R. *Cypher.* Cambridge, Mass.: Massachusetts Institute of Technology, 1989. (Media Laboratory Internal Memo)

8784. Rubin, Emanuel L. "Data Processing in Arts Administration: Problems and Applications." *Proceedings of the National Association of Schools of Music* n71 (1983): 79–95.

8785. Rudes, Jordan, and Brad Rolinski. "Kitaro: New Age Mystic Reconciles His Rhythm & Blues." *Music, Computers & Software* 2 (May 1987): 29–30.

Background on Kitaro and his choice of musical instruments.

8786. Ruschkowski, André. "Musik und Computer." *Musik und Gesellschaft* 39 (Apr. 1989): 169–71.

A general overview of the uses of the computer in music.

8787. Russell, Benjamin. "The Digital Revolution." *Canadian Musician* 11 (Apr. 1989): 72–75, 79–80.

8788. Salmon, Paul, and Jonathan Newmark. "Clinical Applications of MIDI Technology." *Medical Problems of Performing Artists* 4 (Mar. 1989): 25–31.

8789. Salvatore, Gianfranco. "Videoclips (per un metalinguaggio audiovisuale)." [Videoclips (for an Audiovisual Metalanguage)] In *Musica e tecnologia: industria e cultura per lo sviluppo del mezzogiorno: VI Colloquio di Informatica Musicale, Napoli 16–19 ottobre 1985,* ed. Carlo Acreman; Immacolata Ortosecco; and Fausto Razzi. Milan: Edizioni Unicopli, 1987: 455–59.

8790. Savel, Jay. "MIDI Meets Metal: Def Leppard Goes High-Tech." *Electronic Musician* 4 (Mar. 1988): 52–58.

A narrative about Rich Allen, drummer for Def Leppard, who used MIDI technology to continue his career after a serious car accident.

8791. Savicky, Randy. "Sights and Sounds." *Jazz Times* (Oct. 1987): 12.

A discussion of the influence of technology on the evolution of music performance.

8792. Savouret, Alain, and Gilles Racot. "Sur Germinal." *Revue musicale* n394–97 (1986): 243–47.

Comments by composers who have participated in the Germinal project.

8793. Schmidt, Brian L. "Designing Sound Tracks for Coin-Op Games or Computer Music for under $65.00." In *Proceedings, 1989 International Computer Music Conference, November 2–5, the Ohio State University, Columbus, Ohio.* San Francisco, Calif.: Computer Music Association, 1989: 273–76.

8794. Schrodt, Philip A. "Meet You at the Fair; High-Tech Meets an Old Tradition at the US Festival." *Byte* 8 (Jan. 1983): 186–94.

Describes the Us (United in Song) Festival, sponsored by Steve Wozniak. Includes fairlike exhibits on computers and music.

8795. Scott, Jordan. "So: Plotting for Success." *Music, Computers & Software* 3 (Aug. 1988): 26.

Profile/interview with members of the rock band.

8796. Seeger, Chris Arley. "MCS Sound Design." *Music, Computers & Software* 3 (Feb. 1988): 82–84.

A discussion of the synthesis equipment used by Suzanne Ciani in her live performances.

8797. "Sequencers: Further Reading & Listening." *Keyboard* 13 (June 1987): 126.

8798. Sherrill, John. "Hardware: Electricity." *Keyboards, Computers & Software* 1 (June 1986): 23–26.

A look at problems of and solutions to power surges with electronic gear.

8799. Shimony, Uri; Shlomo Markel; and Josef Tal. "Icon Notation for Electroacoustic and Computer Music." In *Proceedings of the 14th International Computer Music Conference, Cologne, September 20–25, 1988,* ed. Christoph Lischka and Johannes Fritsch. Cologne: Feedback-Studio-Verlag; San Francisco, Calif.: Dist. by Computer Music Association, 1988: 430–36. (Feedback Papers; 33)

8800. "Silicon Minstrels: These Computers Ain't Just Whistling Dixie." *Scientific American* 259 (Sept. 1988): 131.

Bellcore sponsors a phone line for computer music recitals.

8801. Sims, Ezra. "Yet Another 72-Noter." *Computer Music Journal* 12,4 (Winter 1988): 28–45.

8802. Sippel, John. "AFM Enters Computer Age: CMI Player Joins L.A. Local." *Billboard* 97 (June 22, 1985): 6.

The first card-carrying member who plays a musical computer is admitted to the American Federation of Musicians.

8803. Slawson, Wayne. *Sound Color.* Berkeley: University of California Press, 1985. 266 p.

Review by Lar-Gunnar Bodin in *Svensk Tidskrift för Musikforskning* 69 (1987): 168–71.

8804. Sloan, Carl. "Letters to the Editor: A Simplified Method of Beat-Rate Calculation." *Diapaison* 78 (June 1987): 2.

A response to item **8694.** Reply by Michael McNeil.

8805. Sloan, Donald. "Precis of the Standard Music Description Language." In *Proceedings, 1989 International Computer Music Conference, November 2–5, the Ohio State University, Columbus, Ohio.* San Francisco, Calif.: Computer Music Association, 1989: 296–302.

8806. Smeijsters, Henk. "Moet de Musicus Worden Omgeschoold tot Informaticus? Technologie: Diabolus in Musica of Gradus ad parnassum?" [Does the Musicus Have to Be Transformed to the Informaticus?

Technology: Diabolus in Musica of Gradus ad parnassum?] *Mens en Melodie* 42 (Feb. 1987): 52–59.
In Dutch.

8807. "Sound and Light Spectacle in Houston." *Computer Music Journal* 10,3 (Fall 1986): 7.

Celebration of the one hundred fiftieth anniversary of the city of Houston with computer music, computer-controlled projections, lasers, and fireworks.

8808. Spagnardi, Ronald. "Editor's Overview: Facing the Future." *Modern Drummer* 9 (Feb. 1985): 2.

Drum machines can be accepted as friends or rejected.

8809. Stein, Alexander. "Aus Gesten und Bewegungen entsteht Musik: Zu den Kasseler Musiktagen '87 und der Tagung 'Neue Musik in der Kirche.'" *Neue Musikzeitung* 36 (Dez. 1987): 47.

Concert review.

8810. Steinberg, Daniel, and Time Learmont. "The Multimedia File System." In *Proceedings, 1989 International Computer Music Conference, November 2–5, the Ohio State University, Columbus, Ohio.* San Francisco, Calif.: Computer Music Association, 1989: 307–11.

8811. Stephen, Bill. "Debbie Gibson: MIDI-Pop Turns One Person's Dream into a Reality." *Music, Computers & Software* 3 (Dec. 1988): 37–40.

Profile/interview with the pop composer/singer, who discusses her use of MIDI and synthesis equipment both on stage and in the recording studio.

8812. ———. "Greg Hawkes." *Keyboards, Computers & Software* 1 (June 1986): 30–33, 78.

The keyboardist of the group Cars' uses MIDI, computers, sampling, and a variety of his own techniques.

8813. Stephen, Greg. "Computers & Music: The Computer Musician and Quantum Mechanics." *Canadian Musician* 7 (Dec. 1985): 62–64.

A physics lesson in computer music that borders on metaphysics.

8814. ———. "Computers: Bruce Mitchell: MIDI Pioneer." *Canadian Musician* 8 (Feb. 1986): 58–61.

A look at Bruce Mitchell's contribution to computer music.

8815. Sterling, Mark, and Brad Tolinski. "Tomita: Pyramid Power and Classic Architecture." *Keyboards, Computers & Software* 1 (Dec. 1986): 26, 39.

Interview with Isao Tomita.

8816. Straessle, Carla. "The Pianist Comes to Terms with the Computer: The Challenge of a New Way of Composing." *Canadian Composer* n207 (Jan. 1986): 11–15, 37.

French version: Anton Kuerti, ou le concertiste engagé: le défi de la composition électronique.

    Profile of A. Kuerti. Mentions use of the computer for composition.

8817.   Strolin, Paolo. "Ricerca scientifica, diffusione tecnologica e fruizione della cultura." [Scientific Research, Technological Distribution, and Fruition of the Culture] In *Musica e tecnologia: industria e cultura per lo sviluppo del mezzogiorno: VI Colloquio di Informatica Musicale, Napoli 16–19 ottobre 1985,* ed. Carlo Acreman; Immacolata Ortosecco; and Fausto Razzi. Milan: Edizioni Unicopli, 1987: 40–41.

8818.   Szwarcman, Dorota. "'Trzecia fala' w Muzyce." ['Third Wave' in Music] *Ruch Muzyczny* 32,5 (28 Lutego 1988): 20–21.

In Polish.

8819.   Tamburini, Serena, and Mauro Bagella, eds. *I profili del suono: scritti sulla musica electroacustica e la computer music.* [Profiles of Sound: Writings on Electroacoustic and Computer Music] Salerno: Musica Verticale-Galzerano, 1987. 239 p.

Contains items: 4590, 4630, 4664, 4752, 4790, 4802, 4809, 4815, 4822, 4833, 4834, 4839, 8368, 8397, 8514, 8610, 8750, 8760, 8854.

Review by Claude Dubois in *Computer Music Journal* 12, 3 (Fall 1988): 69.

8820.   Tedde, Giorgio. "Per una teoria scientifica della musica: saggio sulla fenomenologia della comunicazione musicale." [Towards a Scientific Theory of Music: Essay on the Phenomenology of Musical Communication] In *Musica e tecnologia: industria e cultura per lo sviluppo del mezzogiorno: VI Colloquio di Informatica Musicale, Napoli 16–19 ottobre 1985,* ed. Carlo Acreman; Immacolata Ortosecco; and Fausto Razzi. Milan: Edizioni Unicopli, 1987: 337–78.

8821.   ———. "Phenomenology of Musical Communication." In *Proceedings of the International Computer Music Conference 1986, Royal Conservatory, The Hague, Netherlands, October 20–24, 1986,* ed. Paul Berg. San Francisco, Calif.: Computer Music Association, 1986: A-7–A-12.

    An investigation of musical structure problems.

8822.   Terpstra, Siemen. "The Modular Keyboard: Novel Tuning for MIDI Synthesizers." *Interval* 5 (Spring 1986): 1, 11–13.

8823.   Terry, Ken. "Digital Sampling, Master Mixing Pose New Copyright Challenges." *Variety* 327 (July 22, 1987): 75.

8824.   Tharper, Ian. "The System." *Keyboards, Computers & Software* 1 (Feb. 1986): 27–28.

    Describes the band, The System, and its use of computers and technology in its music.

8825. Thies, Wolfgang. "Notationsmöglichkeiten für elektronische Musik." *Interface* 14 (1985): 185–235.
Summary in English.
Discusses of the possibilities of notating electronic music.

8826. Thompson, W. F.; Anders Friberg; Lars Frydén; and Johan Sundberg. "Evaluating Rules for the Synthetic Performance of Melodies." *Speech Transmission Laboratory Quarterly Progress and Status Report* 2–3 (1986): 27–44.
Revised version to appear in *Psychology of Music.*

8827. Thorington, Helen. "It's Alive: Tod Machover's Hyperinstrument." *Ear* 13 (Sept. 1988): 10–11.
Describes Tod Machover's work at MIT's Media Lab.

8828. Tingen, Paul. "Hands across the Keyboard." *Music Technology* 1 (Mar. 1987): 36–41.
Interviews with Peter Hammill and Paul Ridout.

8829. ———. "Modes of Operation." *Music Technology* 1 (Oct. 1986): 12–16.
Interview with members of Depeche Mode.

8830. ———. "Stranger in a Strange World." *Music Technology* 1 (July 1987): 100–102.
Interview with Ryuichi Sakamoto, who relies heavily on a NEC computer, Yamaha DX7, and Yamaha SPX90.

8831. ———. "Would Your Mother Recognize You on the Radio?" *Music Technology* 1 (Feb. 1987): 44–47.
Interview with John Porter, an R&B guitar player who uses a Yamaha CX5 computer and a LinnDrum.

8832. Toft, Bob. "Kit Watkins: A Self-contained Musician with a Studio to Match." *Keyboards, Computers & Software* 1 (Apr. 1986): 26–29.
Interview.

8833. Tolinski, Brad. "Arif Mardin: Producing Results with an Eye on the Future and an Ear to the Ground." *Keyboards, Computers & Software* 2 (Feb. 1987): 32–33.
Interview with the producer, who discusses his use of MIDI in the recording studio.

8834. ———. "The B-52s: From Farfisas to Fairlights." *Keyboards, Computers & Software* 1 (Dec. 1986): 30–31.
Profile/interview with the rock band, discussing their synthesizers.

8835. ———. "Carlos Alomar." *Music, Computers & Software* 2 (June 1987): 32–33.
Profile/interview with the rock guitarist, who discusses his use of MIDI guitar controllers and sampling synthesizers.

8836. ———. "The Cars: American Pop Icons Go Door to Door." *Music, Computers & Software* 2 (Dec. 1987): 22–29.

Profile/interviews with members of the rock band, who discuss their use of synthesis equipment.

8837. ———. "Le Cirque du Soleil: The Flying Synthesizer Brothers." *Music, Computers & Software* 3 (Feb. 1988): 33.

Profile/interview with the musicians in the Cirque du Soleil pit band.

8838. ———. "Howard Jones One to One." *Keyboards, Computers & Software* 1 (Dec. 1986): 22–25.

Interview with the songwriter/keyboardist, who discusses his stage equipment.

8839. ———. "Human League: A 'Crash' Course in Synth Pop." *Music, Computers & Software* 2 (May 1987): 22–25.

Interview with Phil Oakey.

8840. ———. "Joe Jackson's Will Power." *Music, Computers & Software* 2 (June 1987): 22–25, 29.

Profile/interview with the rock composer/performer, who discusses his mixed electronic/orchestral arrangements.

8841. ———. "Joe Zawinul: Weather Report's Finest and His Stormy Solo Career." *Keyboards, Computers & Software* 1 (Aug. 1986): 31–32, 34.

A description of Joe Zawinul's use of music technology in his music.

8842. ———. "Richard Scher: When Arthur Baker Needs a Keyboard Gun for Hire He Calls the Man with the Killer Hooks." *Keyboards, Computers & Software* 1 (June 1986): 34–35.

Synthesist Richard Scher uses a conservative approach with a Yamaha DX7.

8843. ———. "Stewart Copeland: Computers Liberate the Rhythmatist." *Keyboards, Computers & Software* 2 (Feb. 1987): 22–29, 34.

Interview with the drummer/composer in which he discusses film scoring.

8844. ———. "Telecommunications: Let Your Telephone Do the Sampling." *Keyboards, Computers & Software* 1 (Apr. 1986): 30–33.

Three on–line networks with musical information.

8845. ———. "Vince Clark: From Depeche Mode to Yaz to Erasure, a Technical Pioneer Cuts a Definitive Style." *Keyboards, Computers & Software* 1 (Aug. 1986): 32–34.

8846. Tomlyn, Bo. "Guest Editorial: Bootleg Synthesizer Programs Hurt Everybody." *Keyboard* 12 (Sept. 1986): 11, 154.

8847. ———, and Steve Leonard. *Electronic Musician's Dictionary: A Glossary of the Specialized Terms Relating to the Music and Sound Technology of Today.* Milwaukee, Wis.: H. Leonard Books, 1988. 77 p. Review by David B. Doty in *Electronic Musician* 5 (Apr. 1989): 100–102.

8848. Trask, Simon. "Fairlight's Father." *Music Technology* 1 (May 1987): 38–41.

Interview with Kim Ryrie, cofounder of the Fairlight.

8849. ———. "Fairlight's Father." *Music Technology* 1 (June 1987): 52–55.

Completion of the interview with Kim Ryrie.

8850. Turco, Carlo. "Il progetto 'Suono e immagine': motivazioni ed obiettivi." [The Project 'Sound and Images': Motivations and Objectives] In *Musica e tecnologia: industria e cultura per lo sviluppo del mezzogiorno: VI Colloquio di Informatica Musicale, Napoli 16–19 ottobre 1985,* ed. Carlo Acreman; Immacolata Ortosecco; and Fausto Razzi. Milan: Edizioni Unicopli, 1987: 52–59.

8851. Uslan, Mark; Lindsay Russell; and Carl Weiner. "A 'Musical Pathway' for Spatially Disoriented Blind Residents of a Skilled Nursing Facility." *Journal of Visual Impairment and Blindness* 82 (Jan. 1988): 21–24.

8852. Van Horn, Rick. "Electronic Percussion on Stage." *Modern Drummer* 6 (May 1982): 32–33.

The author describes how he utilizes a pair of Synare 3 synthesizers.

8853. Varon, Nelson. "How to Avoid Getting Burned by Computer Music Products." *Music Trades* 132 (Aug. 1984): 54–57.

A checklist for sorting through hype in computer advertising.

8854. Vidolin, Alvise. "Ambienti Esecutivi." [Executive Environments] In *I profili del suono: scritti sulla musica electroacustica e la computer music,* ed. Serena Tamburini and Mauro Bagella. Salerno: Musica Verticale-Galzerano, 1987: 159–63.

8855. "What's New in the Music Industry?" *Instrumentalist* 42 (Feb. 1988): 38–52.

Covers digital instruments and microcomputer applications, as well as use of computers to manufacture instruments.

8856. Wheeler, Harvey. "Letters: Synthesizers Are Not . . ." *American Organist* 21 (Nov. 1987): 16.

A follow-up to the Nov. 1986 article.

8857. ———. "Synthesizers in Worship." *American Organist* 20 (Nov. 1986): 68–69.

8858. White, Paul. "Techtalk." *Music Technology* 1 (Oct. 1986): 32–34.
Interview with Keith Barr, the developer of the Alesis MIDIverb and MIDIfex.

8859. Wiesand, Andreas Johannes. "Zukunftsvision: Datenbücher oder Datenbanken; Gedanken anlässlich einiger Neuerscheinungen zur Kulturpolitik und Musikförderung." *Neue Musikzeitung* 34 (Dez. 1985): 1, 50.

8860. Wiffen, Paul. "Creation, Recreation, or Imitation?: The Uses and Abuses of Sampling." *Music Technology* 1,1 (1986): 16.

8861. ———. "Guest Editorial: User-Friendliness—Boon or Bane?" *Keyboard* 13 (Sept. 1987): 12.
Questions if, after the description "user friendly," anyone has asked if the equipment sounds or works any better.

8862. Wilkinson, Scott R. *Tuning In: Microtonality in Electronic Music.* Milwaukee, Wis.: H. Leonard Books, 1988. 120 p.
A basic guide to alternate scales, temperaments, and microtuning using synthesizers and computers.

8863. Williams, Mike. "The Life of a Music Software Author." *Electronic Music Educator* 1 (Sept. 1988): 20, 18.

8864. Williams, Wheat. "Exploring East Indian Microtonality." *Electronic Musician* 5 (Mar. 1989): 44–54.
How to tune a synthesizer capable of user-definable tunings to East Indian tonalities.

8865. Winkler, Wolfgang. "Ars Electronica 79–84: Computermusik." *Österreichische Musikzeitschrift* 39 (1984): 465–66.
Short review of various developments in the use of the computer in music.

8866. Woodard, Josef. "I Was a Computer Idiot!: Kicking and Screaming, a Guitarist Enters the Digital Age." *Musician* n82 (Aug. 1985): 84, 90.
A personal narrative on the author's experiences with computers.

8867. Yakal, Kathy. "The Computerized Musician: Compute! Interviews Wendy Carlos and Frank Zappa." *Compute!* 8 (Jan. 1986): 36–46.

8868. Yavelow, Christopher. "The Musical Future of Computers & Software." *Music, Computers & Software* 2 (May 1987): 43–50, 75.
A panel discussion that looks to the future of computer music.

8869. Young, Gayle, and Larry Lake. "Electronic Music: New Kid on the Block." *Music Magazine* 9 (Sept./Oct. 1986): 6–12.

A history of electronic and computer music.

8870. Young, Jeffrey S. "Peerless Itzhak Perlman." *Macworld* 2 (June 1985): 160–63.

Interview with Itzhak Perlman on the current state of technology and music.

8871. Zakrzewska-Nikiporczyk, Barbara. "Kilka słów o muzyce komputerowej w Stanach Zjednoczonych." [A Few Words about Computer Music in the United States] *Ruch Muzyczny* 32,11 (22 Maja 1988): 24. In Polish.

8872. Zimmermann, Kevin. "Sampling a Boon in Synchronizing, Editing Sound on Film." *Variety* 334 (Feb. 15, 1989): 102.

8873. Zummo, Vinnie. "Scoring." *Music, Computers & Software* 3 (Aug. 1988): 77–78.

The author discusses his experiences using MIDI sequencers in commercial jingle sessions.

SUBJECT INDEX

N

O

Z

AUTHOR-TITLE INDEX

B

Becker, Frank
Bleibt der Mensch als Musiker auf der Strecke? Diskussionsbeitrag über den Einsatz von Computern in der U-Musik, **4589**

Becker, Glenn
Micro Music Manager Catalogs Classical Record Collections, **7007**

Beckman, Jesper
Længe leve mangfoldigheden: Systemes Personnels et Informatique Musicale Ircam d. 11–13/10 1986, International Computer Music Conference 1986, Royal Conservatory, The Hague 20–24/10 1986, **5174**

Beckmen, Tom
Guest Editorial: Blueprint for Expanding the Hi-Tech Market; Stop Hustling Boxes and Start Offering More Customer Service, **6622**

Beecher, Mike
Control Zone: Review Computers—Things to Come, **5306**

Begault, Durand R.
Control of Auditory Distance, **8343**

Beggio, Bernardino
Performance strumentale e supporto magnetico: alcune esperienze di esecuzione, **4790**

Behrens, Stefan
Computer-aided Organ Documentation, **6769**

Bel, Bernard
The Identification and Modelling of a Percussion 'Language,' and the Emergence of Musical Concepts in a Machine-Learning Environment, **6809**

Belian, Barry
The Atari Musician, **5695**

Belkin, Alan
Orchestration, Perception, and Musical Time: A Composer's View, **4660**

Bell, Bryan
New Music, **6038**
Santana's MIDI Guitar Composition System, **7169**

Bell, Jack
Classical Music Mosquito, **6309**
Make Music with Macintosh, **6039**

Bellini, S.
Un sistema per l'analizi/sintesi di testi musicali, **4661**

Bengtsson, Ingmar
Men je fårstår int' me på däm da prickar!: om att uppteckna folkmusik, **6770**

Benneth, Gerald
Enkelhed og kompleksitet i elektro-akustisk musik: et indlæg ved ICEM konferencen 26/9 1985 i Stockholm, **5175**

Bennett, Gerald
Studio Report: The Swiss Center for Computer Music, **8362**
Synthesis of the Singing Voice Current Directions in Computer Music, **8125**

Benoit, Ellen
Music's Black Box, **6374**

Bentley, Andrew
The Composers' Desktop Project, **5692**

Brothers, Hardin
  Next Step: Sounding Off on the 1000, **6311**
  The Next Step: Sounding Off on the 1000: Encore, **6312**
Brown, B. M.
  Coping with Some Really Rotten Problems in Automatic Music Recognition, **8538**
  Using a Micro to Automate Data Acquisition in Music Publishing, **6687**
Brown, Daphne
  Advantage to Music Teachers! **4874**
Brown, Frank
  The Biniou Machine, **7164**
  La musique par ordinateur, **4667**
  Synthèse rapide de sons musicaux par ordinateur, **8131**
Brown, Judith C.
  Musical Information from a Narrowed Autocorrelation Function, **5246**
Brown, Michael
  Music Mouse, **5488**
Bruhn, Gothard
  Mit der Technik sinnvoll umgehen lernen: Zur Verwendung elektronischer
    Musikinstrumente im Musikunterricht, **4875**
Brün, Herbert
  Composer's Input Outputs Music, **4593**
  Guest Editorial: Volume, the Tyranny of the Beat, Mating Video with Audio &
    Improvisation vs. Originality, **4594**
Bubenik, Anton
  Bloss keine Angst vor den Tricks der Chips: Über Berührungsprobleme beim
    Umgang mit einem neuen 'Werkzeug,' **8519**
  Sättigungsgrenzen, Innovationen, Fossilien: Ein- und Ausblicke auf Vielfalt und
    Einfallt unserer Medienlandschaft. Teil II, **5312**
Bumgarner, Marlene Anne
  Education/Fun Learning: Bank Street Music Writer, **5313**
Burbat, Wolf
  Jazz arrangieren und komponieren am Computer, **4668**
Burch, Fern
  Bach by Computer: Making Music on the Atari 800, **4876**
Burger, Jeff
  Balloons, Jelly, and Climaxing Cougars, **8132**
  Buying Your First Sequencer, **7182**
  MIDI Column, **6380**
  The Murphy's Law MIDI Book, **6381**
  Percussion: The Acoustic Drummer's Guide to Electronic Drums, **7183**
  Review: Mimetics' SoundScape Pro MIDI Studio, **5489**
  Review: Oberheim Prommer, **7184**
  Review: Syntech's Studio II, **5586**
Burgess, Jim
  Apple Hypercard, **6051**
  Casio FZ1: Sampling Keyboard, **7185**
  Click Tracks 2.0: Software for Apple Macintosh, **6052**
  The Computer Music Revolution, **5314**
  Computers: Dave Oppenheim/Opcode Systems, **8520**
  Computers: Performer: Extremely Versatile Sequencer Program, **6053**

Husarik, Stephen
  John Cage and Lejaren Hiller: *HPSCHD,* 1969, **4811**
Hussey, Leigh Ann
  Music Notation in ASCII, **6901**

I

Iannuccelli, E.
  Computer and Music Software in an Educative-Formative Role in Italy, **4888**
Ibanez Develops MIDI Guitar System, 7419
The IBM PC Music Feature, 5914
Idea Bank: Computers in the Classroom, 4977
Imai, M.
  An Approach to an Artificial Music Expert, **8646**
Industry Happenings: Standard File Format Developed for MIDI Sequencers, 6481
Ingber, Phil
  The Apple District: The Apple as Musician: New Software Packages Are Music to
    the Ear, **4978**
Inokuchi, Seiji
  An Approach to an Artificial Music Expert, **8646**
  The Kansei Music System, **8645**
  Music Information Processing System and Its Application to Comparative
    Musicology, **6824**
  Music Interpreter in the Kansei Music System, **8647**
  Transcription of Sung Song, **6711**
Intelligent Music Adds Six Software Programs, 5350
Iovine, John
  Building a MIDI Interface Device for the Commodore 64 and 128, **5824**
  Sound Digitizer II, **5825**
Isaacson, Matt
  360 Systems Pro MIDI Bass, **7420**
  Axxess Mapper 2.0: MIDI Processor, **7421**
  Garfield Electronics Time Commander, **7422**
  In Brief: Boss MPD4, MIDI Drum Pad, **7423**
  Kahler Human Clock, **7426**
  Korg DRM1: Digital Rhythm Machine, **7424**
  Processing the Data, **6482**
  Roland PM16: Pad-to-MIDI Converter, **7425**
  Twelve Tone Systems Cakewalk Sequencer, **5915**
  We Can't Go on Beating Like This, **7981**
  We Can't Go on Beating Like This, **7983**
  We Can't Go on Beating Like This, **7984**
  We Can't Go on Beating Like This, **8004**
  We Can't Go on Beating Like This. Part 5, **7985**
  We Can't Go on Beating Like This. Part 6, **7427**
  We Can't Go on Beating Like This. Part 7, **7982**
Isaak, Troy J.
  Micros and Music: Lesson Plans, a Directory of Software for Achieving Educational
    Objectives and Procedures for Evaluating Software, **4979**

The Atari ST Power User. Pt. I, The Hardware, **5736**
Atari ST Public Domain Patch Editors and Librarians, **5737**
Caged Artist's ESQ-apade: Editor/Librarian Program for the Ensoniq ESQ Synthesizers and the Atari ST, **5738**
Chord: An Algorithmic Composing Program in Atari ST BASIC, **5739**
Computing, **5353**
Computing, **6902**
Computing, **7467**
Computing, **7468**
Dr. T's Keyboard Controlled Sequencer for the Atari ST, **5740**
Ensoniq ESQ-1 Digital Synth/Sequencer, **7469**
Harmony Systems Voice Vault, **7470**
KCS Applications, **4718**
KCS Applications, **5827**
Micro Arts Products Sampler-64, **5828**
MIDI: Fun with System Exclusives, **6485**
MIDI: MIDIPrint: A MIDI Data Display Program, **5829**
Music Service Software's Data Dumpstor ST, **5741**
Review: Alesis HR-16 Drum Machine, **7471**
Review: Digitech's DSP-128 Digital Effects Signal Processor, **7472**
Review: E-mu SP-1200 Sampling Drum Machine, **7473**
Review: Garfield Electronics' Time Commander, **7474**
Review: Kahler's Human Clock, **7475**
Review: SynHance M1X and M1X+ MIDI Mixers, **7476**
Reviews: AKG Acoustics ADR 68K Digital Reverb and Effects Processor, **7477**
Sequencing for Live Performance, **7988**
Software: Humanizing Sequences, **8202**
The ST Power User. Pt. II, The Software, **5742**

Jones, David Evan
Compositional Control of Phonetic/Nonphonetic Perception, **6955**

Jones, David L.
Getting Started: Designing and Programming a CAI Music Lesson, **5089**
Floppy Discography: Uniform Manager Program, **5610**

Jones, Douglas L.
Generation and Combination of Grains for Music Synthesis, **8203**

Jones, Henry L.
Economic Affairs: Are You Tired of Playing Games? **5354**

Jones, Jacqueline A.
Connectionist Models for Tonal Analysis, **6984**

Jones, Kevin
Compositional Applications of Stochastic Processes, **4719**
Exploring Music with the BBC Micro and Electron, **5355**
Generative Models in Computer-assisted Musical Composition, **4720**
Real-Time Stochastic Composition and Performance with AMPLE, **6903**

Jones, Peter
Commentary: Computer Ordering Can Help Dealers: Security, CD Boxes also Require Action, **6638**
U.K. Producer Asks Action on Digital Sampling Issue, **8642**

Jones, Tim
An Exclusive Preview: Music Mouse, **5511**

Lande, Tor Sverre
  Musikkanalyse med datamaskin I, **6814**
Lander, David
  Raymond Kurzweil: Revolutionary Tradition, **8658**
Langdell, James
  Music: The PC's New Frontier, **5917**
  Singing in the RAM, **5918**
Langston, Peter S.
  (201) 644-2332: Eedie & Eddie on the Wire: An Experiment in Music Generation
    USENIX Association Summer Conference Proceedings, Atlanta, 1986, **4817**
  Six Techniques for Algorithmic Composition, **4724**
  Six Techniques for Algorithmic Music Composition (Extended Abstract), **4725**
Languepin, Olivier
  Les Micro-ordinateurs, **5365**
Lansky, Paul
  Compositional Applications of Linear Predictive Coding, **4726**
  It's about Time: Some NeXT Perspectives. Part 1, **6293**
  Linear Prediction: The Hard, but Interesting Way to Do Things, **8213**
  Report on the 1985 International Computer Music Conference, **5191**
  The Sound of Software: Computer-made Music, **8659**
  Synthesis of Timbral Families by Warped Linear Prediction, **8214**
Laroche, Jean
  A New Analysis/Synthesis System of Musical Signals Using Prony's Method:
    Application to Heavily Damped Percussive Sounds, **5268**
  The Use of Prony's Method for the Analysis of Musical Sounds: Application to
    Percussive Sounds, **5269**
LaRose, Paul
  G10 Editor/Librarian Music Software, **8086**
  High-Tech Guitar: Channels, Voices & MIDI Messages, **6491**
  High-Tech Guitar: Series #8, The Power of MIDI Guitar Control, **6492**
  High-Tech Guitar: Synth & MIDI for Real Guitar Players, **6493**
  High-Tech Guitar: What's in It for You, **8660**
  Product Profiles: Yamaha G10 Guitar Synthesizer Controller System, **7514**
  Synthesizers and Smiles in Broward County Schools, **5020**
Larson, Brendan
  Amazing Review: AudioMaster, **5516**
Larson, Gary
  How East Met West, **8661**
Laske, Otto E.
  Comments on the First Workshop on A.I. and Music: 1988 AAAI Conference, St.
    Paul, Minnesota, **5199**
  Composition Theory: An Enrichment of Music Theory, **4728**
  Composition Theory in Koenig's *Project One* and *Project Two*, **4727**
  Computermusik und musikalische Informatik, **8215**
  Computermusik und musikalische Informatik, **8662**
  Introduction to Cognitive Musicology, **6815**
  Toward a Computational Theory of Musical Listening Reason, Emotion, and
    Music, **6958**

Mathews, Becky F.
CoCo Goes Country: A Musical View of Nashville, **6331**

Mathews, Max V.
The Acquisition of Musical Percepts with a New Scale, **6967**
The Bohlen-Pierce Scale, **4737**
The Computer as a Musical Instrument, **8687**
Computer Music Research at Bell Labs, 1986, **8383**
The Conductor Program and Mechanical Baton, **8325**
Current Directions in Computer Music, **8688**
Pickups for the Vibrations of Violin and Guitar Strings Using Piezoelectric
   Bimorphic Bender Elements, **7583**
The Radio Drum as a Synthesizer Controller, **7177**
Theoretical and Experimental Explorations of the Bohlen-Pierce Scale, **8689**

Matsuoka, Doug
Yes, There Is Life after MIDI: Get More out of Your Computer, **6187**

Matsushima, Toshiaki
An Integrated Music Information Processing System: PSB-er, **8691**
Automated High Speed Recognition of Printed Music (Wabot-2 Vision System)
   Proceedings of '85 International Conference on Advanced Robotics: 9, 10
   September 1985, **8692**
Automated Recognition System for Musical Score—the Vision System of
   WABOT-2, **8690**

Matthews, Becky
I Want My CoCo TV, **6332**

Matthews, David
I Want My CoCo TV, **6332**

Mattingly, Rick
Electronic Review: Yamaha RX5 Digital Rhythm Programmer, **7584**
The Machine Shop: Tricking Your Drum Machine, **8001**

Matzkin, Jonathan
Ad Lib Music-composing Package Turns Your Computer into an 11-Voice
   Orchestra, **5931**
Bank Street Music Writer Sparks the Creativity of Budding Composers, **5932**
CMS Kit Combines MIDI Adapter with Powerful Sequencing Software, **5933**
Creative Music System Offers an Inexpensive Way to Develop Your Musical
   Talents, **5934**
The Entertainer: Familiar Tunes for Your Basic Routines, **5935**
Getting Started with MIDI: Everything You Need for $219, **5936**
Make Your Own Melodies: Systems for Amateurs and Virtuosos, **5937**
Making Beautiful Music with IBM's Music Feature Card, **5938**
A MIDI Musical Offering, **5877**
Pop-Up Music to Perk up Your Spreadsheets, **5939**
Roland's Desktop Studio Brings the Sound of Music to Your PC, **5940**

Mauchley, J. William
Practical Considerations in the Design of Music Using VLSI, **7585**

Maxwell, Harry J.
An Artificial Intelligence Approach to Computer-implemented Analysis of Harmony
   in Tonal Music, **6819**

Mayfield, Geoff
Automated Ordering Progresses, **6651**

W